Fundamentals of
Data Structures in Pascal

COMPUTER SOFTWARE ENGINEERING SERIES

Fundamentals of Data Structures in Pascal

Third Edition

Ellis Horowitz

University of Southern California

Sartaj Sahni

University of Minnesota

COMPUTER SCIENCE PRESS

An imprint of W. H. Freeman and Company

New York

Library of Congress Cataloging-in-Publication Data

Horowitz, Ellis.
    Fundamentals of data structures in Pascal/Ellis Horowitz, Sartaj
Sahni. — 3d ed.
    p. cm. — (Computer software engineering series)
    Includes bibliographical references.
    ISBN 0-7167-8217-0
    1. Data structures (Computer science) 2. Pascal (Computer program
language) I. Sahni, Sartaj. II. Title. III. Series.
QA76.9.D35H67   1990
005.7′3 — dc20   89-27669
                                                              CIP

Fundamentals of Data Structures in Pascal is the result of the combined
efforts of the authors. Their names have been listed in alphabetical order
with no implication that one is senior and the other junior.

Printed in the United States of America

Computer Science Press

An imprint of W. H. Freeman and Company
41 Madison Avenue, New York, NY 10010
20 Beaumont Street, Oxford   OX1 2NQ, England

1 2 3 4 5 6 7 8 9 0   RRD   9 9 8 7 6 5 4 3 2 1 0

CONTENTS

PREFACE TO
THE THIRD EDITION

Over the past decade the field of data structures has not stood still, but has matured significantly. New and useful data structures have been devised and new forms of complexity measures have been introduced. In this new edition we attempt to keep up with these developments.

The most significant change we have made to the book is the new chapter 10, Advanced Data Structures. The focus of this chapter is to cover the important data structures that were developed during the 1980s. We begin with a discussion of priority queues, structures that permit insertion and removing the maximum and/or minimum element. Special forms are discussed including the min-max heap and the deap, both of which are forms of double ended priority queues. Next, we discuss a data structure that supports the combining of priority queues, leftist trees. These also have min and max forms. A Fibonacci heap is introduced as a data structure that supports all leftist tree operations. We introduce binomial trees, of which Fibonacci heaps are a special case.

A more thorough treatment of 2-3 trees now can be found in Chapter 10. In addition, we have included a section on 2-3-4 trees. The 2-3-4 tree has some advantages over the 2-3 tree, thereby supporting its presentation in this chapter. Red-black trees are a binary tree representation of a 2-3-4 tree. All of these data structures are important special cases of the B-tree. They are emphasized here because the insertion and deletion algorithms that maintain the tree's balance are substantially simpler than for AVL trees, while the $O(\log n)$ bounds are maintained. Moreover, by understanding these structures it should be considerably easier to understand the more general, yet also more complicated B-tree in Chapter 11, Files.

Another issue treated more thoroughly in this edition is amortized complexity. Most of the algorithms have their best, worst, and occasionally their average computing time analyzed. Amortized complexity considers how efficiently a sequence of operations is carried out. This form of complexity measure was popularized by R. Tarjan and in many cases it is a more accurate measure of a data structure's performance than the more traditional ones.

AVL, 2-3, 2-3-4, and red-black trees permit the operations insert, delete, and find to be performed in time $O(\log n)$ in the worst case. If one considers amortized complexity, the bound for any of these operations becomes higher. In Chapter 10, we show how, by using priority queues, one can maintain an $O(\log n)$ amortized complexity over a sequence of operations and at the same time have a simpler structure, than the AVL, 2-3, and 2-3-4 trees. However, if one also wants to be able to search for a given element, then the splay tree should be used as it has an amortized complexity of $O(\log n)$. A splay tree is a binary search tree, where after each insert, delete, or find, a rotation is performed.

A digital search tree is a data structure that uses the bit representation of an identifier to determine its place in the structure. It is a special case of the trie, which is discussed more extensively in Chapter 11, Files.

In Chapter 9 we preserved the discussion of symbol tables and hashing. We have updated the hashing material with a discussion of dynamic hashing. This method extends the traditional method with the ability to handle files that grow unpredictably large, without having to recompile or reset the size of a table.

In this new edition we have tried to minimize the movement of topics and we have succeeded especially in the earlier chapters. Instructors will find most of the familiar topics in the same places. Significant changes were made from our original Chapter 9, entitled Symbol Tables. Several data structures contained there were moved to Chapter 10, Advanced Data Structures, namely Huffman trees, optimal binary search trees, and AVL trees.

USING THIS TEXT FOR A COURSE

For the instructor who intends to use this book and is teaching on a semester basis we present the following two possibilities, a medium pace and a rigorous pace. The medium pace is recommended when the course is for beginning computer science majors, possibly their second or third course of the curriculum. Most people, including the authors, have taught according to the medium pace. The outline below corresponds to the curriculum recommended by the ACM, in particular course C2, (Curriculum '78, CACM 3/79, and CACM 8/85).

SEMESTER SCHEDULE - MEDIUM PACE

Week	Subject	Reading Assignment
1	Intro. to Algorithms and Data Organization	Chapter 1
2	Arrays	Chapter 2
3	Stacks and Queues	Chapter 3
		First program due
4	Linked Lists (singly and doubly linked)	Chapter 4
5	Linked Lists (generalized lists)	
6	Linked Lists (strings)	Second program due
7	Trees (basic facts, binary trees)	Chapter 5
8	Trees (game, search, heap)	
9	Mid Term	
10	Graphs (basic facts, representations)	Chapter 6
11	Graphs (shortest paths, spanning trees, topological sorting)	Third program due
12	Internal Sorting (insertion, quick, and merge)	Chapter 7
13	Internal Sorting (heap, radix, practical considerations)	Fourth program due
14	Hashing	Chapter 9
15	Advanced Tree Structures	Chapter 10
16	File Structures	Chapter 11

We recommend that several programming assignments be given, spaced somewhat evenly throughout the semester. The aim of the first program is primarily to get the students familiar with the computing environment. The second program should emphasize list structures, as discussed in Chapter 4. There are several suggestions for projects at the end of the exercises of Chapter 4. One topic we have chosen to skip is external sorting. This leaves time to cover one of the most important of techniques, hashing. This topic is used in several courses later on in the curriculum, so it is important to cover it this semester. The instructor will likely not have time to cover the material in the Advanced Tree Structures and File Structures chapters. Perhaps one or two topics can be selectively chosen.

The more rigorous pace would be appropriate when the book is used for a first year graduate course, or for an advanced undergraduate course. Our suggested outline follows.

SEMESTER SCHEDULE - RIGOROUS PACE

Week	Subject	Reading Assignment
1	Intro. to Algorithms and Data Organization	Chapter 1
2	Arrays	Chapter 2
3	Stacks and Queues	Chapter 3
		First program due
4	Linked Lists	Chapter 4
5	Trees	Chapter 5
6	Trees continued	Second program due
7	Mid Term	
8	Graphs	Chapter 6
9	Graphs continued	Third program due
10	Internal Sorting	Chapter 7
11	External Sorting	Chapter 8
12	Hashing	Chapter 9
13	Advanced Tree Structures	Chapter 10
		Fourth program due
14	Advanced Tree Structures	Chapter 10
15	File Structures	Chapter 11
16	File Structures	Chapter 11

The programming assignments and midterm exam are paced exactly as in the medium case. However, the lectures proceed at a faster rate. For the rigorous pace, two weeks are allotted for Chapters 10 and 11. Chapter 11 is especially valuable as a foundation for a future course on databases.

Finally we present a curriculum for an advanced Data Structures course. This presupposes that the student has already encountered the basic material, in particular the material on lists, trees, and graphs. Four weeks on advanced data structures and three weeks on file organization gives the instructor enough time to cover all of the relevant topics in depth.

SEMESTER SCHEDULE - ADVANCED DATA STRUCTURES COURSE

Week	Subject	Reading Assignment
1	Review of Basic Material on Algorithms	Chapters 1-2
2	Review of Basic List structures	Chapters 3-4
3	Review of Trees	Chapter 5
4	Review of Graphs	Chapter 6
5	Review of Internal Sorting	Chapter 7

		First program due
6	External Sorting	Chapter 8
7	External Sorting (continued)	
8	Hashing	Chapter 9
		Second program due
9	Advanced Tree Structures (min-max heaps, deaps, leftist trees)	Chapter 10
10	Mid Term	
11	Advanced Tree Structures (Fibonacci heaps, Huffman trees, Optimal binary search trees)	Chapter 10
12	Advanced Tree Structures (AVL trees, 2-3 trees, 2-3-4 trees)	Third program due
13	Advanced Tree Structures (Red-black trees, splay trees, digital trees)	
14	File Structures (file organization, indexing)	Chapter 11
15	File Structures (B-trees, tries)	Fourth program due
16	File Organizations, Differential Files	

For schools on the quarter system, the following two quarter sequence is possible. It assumes prior exposure to algorithm analysis and elementary data structures at the level obtained from an advanced programming course.

QUARTER 1

Week	Subject	Reading Assignment
1	Review of algorithms, arrays, stacks, and queues	Chapters 1-3
2	Linked Lists (stacks, queues, polynomials)	Chapter 4
3	Linked Lists (storage management)	
4	Linked Lists (generalized lists, marking)	
5	Linked Lists (marking, compaction, strings)	First program due
6	Mid Term	
7	Trees (traversal, set representation)	Chapter 5
8	Trees (heaps, search, selection)	
9	Graphs (traversal, components, minimum spanning trees)	Chapter 6 Second program due
10	Graphs (shortest paths, activity networks)	

QUARTER 2

Week	Subject	Reading Assignment
1	Internal Sorting (insertion, quick, bound, O(1) space merging, merge sort)	Chapter 7
2	Sorting (heap, radix, list, table)	
3	External Sorting	Chapter 8
4	Hashing	Chapter 9
5	Mid Term	First program due
6	Advanced Tree Structures (Fibonacci heaps, Huffman trees, Optimal binary search trees)	Chapter 10
7	Advanced Tree Structures (AVL trees, 2-3 trees, 2-3-4 trees)	
8	Advanced Tree Structures (Red-black trees, splay trees, digital trees)	
9	File Structures (file organization, indexing)	Chapter 11
10	File Structures (B-trees, tries)	Second program due

Once again we would like to thank the people who have assisted us in preparing this new edition. Thanks go to Professor Ravi Janardan and the many students in our data structures classes who have assisted in the debugging of this edition. Special thanks go to Barbara and Art Friedman, our first publishers who nurtured the book through its early years. Thanks also to our new publisher, W.H. Freeman for their support and especially to the new computer science editor, Bill Gruener. His enthusiasm really helped the project along.

Ellis Horowitz
Sartaj Sahni
September 1989

CHAPTER 1
INTRODUCTION

1.1 OVERVIEW

The field of *computer science* is so new that one feels obliged to furnish a definition before proceeding with this book. One often quoted definition views computer science as the *study of algorithms*. This study encompasses four distinct areas:

(1) *Machines for executing algorithms.* This area includes everything from the smallest pocket calculator to the largest general purpose digital computer. The goal is to study various forms of machine fabrication and organization so that algorithms can be effectively carried out.

(2) *Languages for describing algorithms.* These languages can be placed on a continuum. At one end are the languages which are closest to the physical machine and at the other end are languages designed for sophisticated problem solving. One often distinguishes between two phases of this area: language design and translation. The first calls for methods for specifying the syntax and semantics of a language. The second requires a means for translation into a more basic set of commands.

(3) *Foundations of algorithms.* Here people ask and try to answer such questions as: "Is a particular task accomplishable by a computing device?," or "What is the minimum number of operations necessary for any algorithm that performs a certain function?" Abstract models of computers are devised so that these properties can be studied.

(4) *Analysis of algorithms.* Whenever an algorithm can be specified it makes sense to wonder about its behavior. This was realized as far back as 1830 by Charles Babbage, the father of computers. An algorithm's behavior pattern or *performance profile* is measured in terms of the computing time and space that are consumed while the algorithm is processing. Questions such as the worst and average time

1

and how often they occur are typical.

We see that in this definition of computer science, "algorithm" is a fundamental notion. Thus, it deserves a precise definition. The dictionary's definition, "any mechanical or recursive computational procedure," is not entirely satisfying since these terms are not basic enough.

Definition: An *algorithm* is a finite set of instructions that, if followed, accomplish a particular task. In addition, every algorithm must satisfy the following criteria:

(1)   *Input.* There are zero or more quantities which are externally supplied.

(2)   *Output.* At least one quantity is produced.

(3)   *Definiteness.* Each instruction must be clear and unambiguous.

(4)   *Finiteness.* If we trace out the instructions of an algorithm, then for all cases the algorithm will terminate after a finite number of steps.

(5)   *Effectiveness.* Every instruction must be sufficiently basic that it can, in principle, be carried out by a person using only pencil and paper. It is not enough that each operation be definite as in (3), but it must also be feasible. □

In formal computer science, one distinguishes between an algorithm and a program. A program does not necessarily satisfy condition (4). One important example of such a program for a computer is its operating system, which never terminates (except for system crashes) but continues in a wait loop until more jobs are entered. In this book we will deal strictly with programs that always terminate. Hence, we will use these terms interchangeably.

An algorithm can be described in many ways. A natural language such as English can be used but we must be very careful that the resulting instructions are definite (condition (3)). An improvement over English is to couple its use with a graphical form of notation such as flowcharts. This form places each processing step in a "box" and uses arrows to indicate the next step. Different shaped boxes stand for different kinds of operations. All this can be seen in Figure 1.1 where a flowchart is given for obtaining a can of Coca-Cola from a vending machine. The point is that algorithms can be devised for many common activities.

Have you studied the flowchart? Then you probably have realized that it isn't an algorithm at all! Which properties does it lack?

Returning to our earlier definition of computer science, we find it extremely unsatisfying as it gives us no insight as to why the computer is revolutionizing our society nor why it has made us re-examine certain basic assumptions about our own role in the universe. While this may be an unrealistic demand on a definition, even from a technical point of view it is unsatisfying. The definition places great emphasis on the concept of algorithm, but never mentions the word "data." If a computer is merely a means to an end, then the means may be an algorithm but the end is the transformation of data. That is why we often hear a computer referred to as a data processing machine. Raw data is input and algorithms are used to transform it into refined data. So, instead of saying that computer science is the study of algorithms, alternatively, we might say that

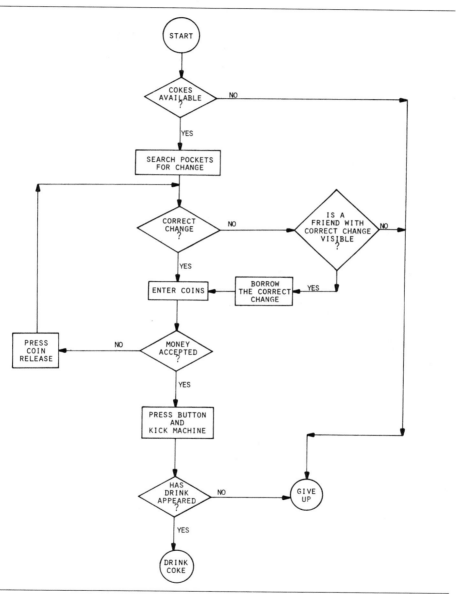

Figure 1.1 Flowchart for obtaining a Coca-Cola

computer science is the *study of data:*

(1)   machines that hold data

(2)   languages for describing data manipulation

(3)   foundations that describe what kinds of refined data can be produced from raw data

(4)   structures for representing data

There is an intimate connection between the structuring of data, and the synthesis of algorithms. In fact, a data structure and an algorithm should be thought of as a unit, neither one making sense without the other. For instance, suppose we have a list of n pairs of names and phone numbers $(a_1, b_1), (a_2, b_2), \ldots, (a_n, b_n)$, and we want to write a program which when given any name, prints that person's phone number. This task is called searching. Just how we would write such an algorithm critically depends upon how the names and phone numbers are stored or structured. One algorithm might just forge ahead and examine names, $a_1, a_2, a_3, \ldots$ etc., until the correct name was found. This might be fine in Oshkosh, but in Los Angeles, with hundreds of thousands of names it would not be practical. If, however, we knew that the data was structured so that the names were in alphabetical order, then we could do much better. We could make up a second list which told us for each letter in the alphabet, where the first name with that letter appeared. For a name beginning with, say, S, we would avoid having to look at names beginning with other letters. So because of this new structure, a very different algorithm is possible. Other ideas for search algorithms become possible when we realize that we can organize the data as we wish. We will discuss many more searching strategies in later chapters.

Therefore, computer science can be defined as the study of data, its representation and transformation by a digital computer. The goal of this book is to explore many different kinds of data objects. For each object, we consider the class of operations to be performed and then the way to represent this object so that these operations may be efficiently carried out. This implies a mastery of two techniques: the ability to devise alternative forms of data representation, and the ability to analyze the algorithm which operates on that structure. The pedagogical style we have chosen is to consider problems which have arisen often in computer applications. For each problem we will specify the data object or objects and what is to be accomplished. After we have decided upon a representation of the objects, we will give a complete algorithm and analyze its computing time. After reading through several of these examples you should be confident enough to try one on your own.

There are several terms we need to define carefully before we proceed. These include data structure, data object, data type and data representation. These four terms have no standard meaning in computer science circles, and they are often used interchangeably.

A *data type* is a term which refers to the kinds of data that variables may "hold" in a programming language. In FORTRAN the data types are INTEGER, REAL, LOGICAL, COMPLEX, and DOUBLE PRECISION. In PL/1 there is the data type

CHARACTER. The fundamental data type of SNOBOL is the character string and in LISP it is the list (or S-expression). Some of the standard data types in Pascal are: integer, real, boolean, char, and array. With every programming language there is a set of built-in data types. This means that the language allows variables to name data of that type and provides a set of operations which meaningfully manipulate these variables. Some data types are easy to provide because they are already built into the computer's machine language instruction set. Integer and real arithmetic are examples of this. Other data types require considerably more effort to implement. In some languages, there are features which allow one to construct combinations of the built-in types. In COBOL and PL/1 this feature is called a STRUCTURE while in PASCAL it is called a RECORD. However, it is not necessary to have such a mechanism.

Data object is a term that refers to a set of elements, say D. For example, the data object *integers* refers to $D = \{0, \pm 1, \pm 2, \ldots\}$. The data object *alphabetic character strings of length at least one* implies $D = \{A, B, \ldots, Z, AA, \ldots\}$. Thus, D may be finite or infinite and if D is very large we may need to devise special ways of representing its elements in our computer.

The notion of a data structure as distinguished from a data object is that we want to describe not only the set of objects, but the way they are related. Saying this another way, we want to describe the set of operations which may legally be applied to elements of the data object. This implies that we must specify the set of operations and show how they work. For integers we would have the arithmetic operations $+, -, *, /$, and perhaps many others such as mod, ceil, floor, greater than, less than, etc. The data object integers plus a description of how $+, -, *, /$, etc. behave constitutes a data structure definition.

To be more precise let's examine a modest example. Suppose we want to define the data structure natural number (abbreviated natno) where natno = $\{0, 1, 2, 3, \ldots\}$ with the three operations being a test for zero, addition, and equality. The notation of Structure 1.1 can be used.

In the declare statement five functions are defined by giving their names, inputs and outputs. ZERO is a constant function which means it takes no input arguments and its result is the natural number zero, written as ZERO. ISZERO is a boolean function whose result is either **true** or **false**. SUCC stands for successor. Using ZERO and SUCC we can define all of the natural numbers as: ZERO, 1 = SUCC(ZERO), 2 = SUCC(SUCC(ZERO)), 3 = SUCC(SUCC(SUCC(ZERO))), ... etc. The rules on line 8 tell us exactly how the addition operation works. For example if we wanted to add two and three we would get the following sequence of expressions:

$$ADD(SUCC(SUCC(ZERO)),SUCC(SUCC(SUCC(ZERO))))$$

which, by line 8 equals

$$SUCC(ADD(SUCC(ZERO),SUCC(SUCC(SUCC(ZERO)))))$$

which, by line 8 equals

---

structure *NATNO*
1 **declare** *ZERO* ( ) → *natno*
2   *ISZERO* (*natno*) → *boolean*
3   *SUCC* (*natno*) → *natno*
4   *ADD* (*natno*, *natno*) → *natno*
5   *EQ* (*natno*, *natno*) → *boolean*
6 **for all** *x*, *y* ε *natno* **let**
7   *ISZERO* (*ZERO*) ::= **true;** *ISZERO* (*SUCC* (*x*)) ::= **false**
8   *ADD* (*ZERO*, *y*) ::=*y*, *ADD* (*SUCC* (*x*), *y*) ::= *SUCC* (*ADD* (*x*, *y*))
9   *EQ* (*x*, *ZERO*) ::= **if** *ISZERO* (*x*) **then true else false**
10   *EQ* (*ZERO*, *SUCC* (*y*)) ::= **false**
11   *EQ* (*SUCC* (*x*), *SUCC* (*y*)) ::= *EQ* (*x*, *y*)
12   **end**
13 **end** *NATNO*

Structure 1.1 Specification of the data structure: natural number

$$SUCC(SUCC(ADD(ZERO),SUCC(SUCC(SUCC(ZERO))))))$$

which, by line 8 equals

$$SUCC(SUCC(SUCC(SUCC(SUCC(ZERO))))))$$

Of course, this is not the way to implement addition. In practice we use bit strings which is a data structure that is usually provided on our computers. But, however the ADD operation is implemented, it must obey these rules. Hopefully, this motivates the following definition.

Definition: A *data structure* is a set of domains D, a designated domain $d \in D$, a set of functions F and a set of axioms A. The triple (D, F, A) denotes the data structure d and it will usually be abbreviated by writing d. □

In the previous example

$$d = \text{natno}, D = \{\text{natno, boolean}\}$$
$$F = \{\text{ZERO, ISZERO, SUCC, ADD}\}$$
$$A = \{\text{lines 7 thru 10 of the structure NATNO}\}$$

The set of axioms describes the semantics of the operations. The form in which we choose to write the axioms is important. Our goal here is to write the axioms in a representation independent way. Then, we discuss ways of implementing the functions using a conventional programming language.

An *implementation* of a data structure d is a mapping from d to a set of other data structures e. First, this mapping specifies how every object of d is to be represented by the objects of e. Second, it requires that every function of d must be written using the functions of the implementing data structures e. Thus, we say that integers are represented by bit strings, boolean is represented by zero and one, and an array is represented by a set of consecutive words in memory.

In current parlance the triple (D, F, A) is referred to as an *abstract data type*. It is called abstract precisely because the axioms do not imply a form of representation. Another way of viewing the implementation of a data structure is that it is the process of refining an abstract data type until all of the operations are expressible in terms of directly executable functions. But at the first stage a data structure should be designed so that we know *what* it does, but not necessarily *how* it will do it. This division of tasks, called specification and implementation, is useful because it helps to control the complexity of the entire process.

1.2 HOW TO CREATE PROGRAMS

Now that you have moved beyond the first course in computer science, you should be capable of developing your programs using something better than the seat-of-the-pants method. This method uses the philosophy: write something down and then try to get it working. Surprisingly, this method is in wide use today, with the result that an average programmer on an average job turns out only between five to ten lines of correct code per day. We hope your productivity will be greater. But to improve requires that you apply some discipline to the process of creating programs. To understand this process better, we consider it as broken up into five phases: requirements, design, analysis, coding, and verification.

(1) *Requirements.* Make sure you understand the information you are given (the input) and what results you are to produce (the output). Try to write down a rigorous description of the input and output which covers all cases.

You are now ready to proceed to the design phase. Designing an algorithm is a task which can be done independent of the programming language you eventually plan to use. In fact, this is desirable because it means you can postpone questions concerning *how* to represent your data and *what* a particular statement looks like and concentrate on the order of processing.

(2) *Design.* You may have several data objects (such as a maze, a polynomial, or a list of names). For each object there will be some basic operations to perform on it (such as print the maze, add two polynomials, or find a name in the list). Assume that these operations already exist in the form of procedures and write an algorithm which solves the problem according to the requirements. Use a notation which is natural to the way you wish to describe the order of processing.

(3) *Analysis.* Can you think of another algorithm? If so, write it down. Next, try to compare these two methods. It may already be possible to tell if one will be more desirable than the other. If you can't distinguish between the two, choose one to work on for now and we will return to the second version later.

(4) *Refinement and coding.* You must now choose representations for your data objects (a maze as a two dimensional array of zeros and ones, a polynomial as a one dimensional array of degree and coefficients, a list of names possibly as an array) and write algorithms for each of the operations on these objects. The order in which you do this may be crucial, because once you choose a representation, the resulting algorithms may be inefficient. Modern pedagogy suggests that all processing which is independent of the data representation be written out first. By postponing the choice of how the data is stored we can try to isolate the operations that depend upon the choice of data representation. You should consider alternatives, note them down, and review them later. Finally you produce a complete version of your first program.

It is often at this point that one realizes that a much better program could have been built. Perhaps you should have chosen the second design alternative or perhaps you have spoken to a friend who has done it better. This happens to industrial programmers as well. If you have been careful about keeping track of your previous work it may not be too difficult to make changes. One of the criteria of a good design is that it can absorb changes relatively easily. It is usually hard to decide whether to sacrifice this first attempt and begin again or just continue to get the first version working. Different situations call for different decisions, but we suggest you eliminate the idea of working on both at the same time. If you do decide to scrap your work and begin again, you can take comfort in the fact that it will probably be easier the second time. In fact you may save as much debugging time later on by doing a new version now. This is a phenomenon which has been observed in practice.

The graph in Figure 1.2 shows the time it took for the same group to build 3 FORTRAN compilers (A, B, and C). For each compiler there is the time they estimated it would take them and the time it actually took. For each subsequent compiler their estimates became closer to the truth, but in every case they underestimated. Unwarranted optimism is a familiar disease in computing. But prior experience is definitely helpful and the time to build the third compiler was less than one fifth that for the first one.

(5) *Verification.* Verification consists of three distinct aspects: program proving, testing, and debugging. Each of these is an art in itself. Before executing your program you should attempt to prove it is correct. Proofs about programs are really no different from any other kind of proof, only the subject matter is different. If a correct proof can be obtained, then one is assured that for all possible combinations of inputs, the program and its specification agree. Testing is the art of creating sample data upon which to run your program. If the program fails to respond correctly then debugging is needed to determine what went wrong and how to correct it. One proof tells us more than any finite amount of testing, but proofs can be hard to obtain. Often, during the proving process errors are discovered in the code. The proof can't be completed until these are eliminated. This is another use of program proving, namely as a methodology for discovering errors. Finally, there may be tools available at your computing center to

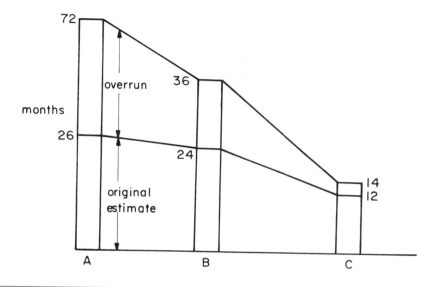

Figure 1.2 History of three FORTRAN compilers

aid in the testing process. One such tool instruments your source code and then tells you for every data set: the number of times a statement was executed; the number of times a branch was taken; and the smallest and largest values of all variables. As a minimal requirement, the test data you construct should force every statement to execute and every condition to assume the value true and false at least once.

One thing you have forgotten to do is to document. But why bother to document until the program is entirely finished and correct? Because for each procedure you made some assumptions about its input and output. If you have written more than a few procedures, then you have already begun to forget what those assumptions were. If you note them down with the code, the problem of getting the procedures to work together will be easier to solve. The larger the software, the more crucial is the need for documentation.

The previous discussion applies to the construction of a single procedure as well as to the writing of a large software system. Let us concentrate for a while on the question of developing a single procedure which solves a specific task. This shifts our emphasis away from the management and integration of the various procedures to the disciplined formulation of a single, reasonably small, and well-defined task. The design process consists essentially of taking a proposed solution and successively refining it until an executable program is obtained. The initial solution may be expressed in English or some form of mathematical notation. At this level the formulation is said to be abstract because it contains no details regarding how the objects will be represented and manipulated in a computer. If possible, the designer attempts to partition the solution into logical subtasks. Each subtask is similarly decomposed until all tasks are expressed within a programming language. This method of design is called the *top-down* approach. Inversely, the designer might choose to solve different parts of the problem directly in his programming language and then combine these pieces into a complete program. This is referred to as the *bottom-up* approach. Experience suggests that the top-down approach should be followed when creating a program. However, in practice it is not necessary to unswervingly follow the method. A look ahead to problems that may arise later is often useful.

Underlying all of these strategies is the assumption that a language exists for adequately describing the processing of data at several abstract levels. For this purpose we use the language Pascal coupled with carefully chosen English narrative. Such a language might be called pseudo-Pascal. Let us examine two examples of top-down program development.

Suppose we devise a program for sorting a set of $n \geq 1$ integers. One of the simplest solutions is given by the following:

From those integers which remain unsorted, find the smallest and place it next in the sorted list.

This statement is sufficient to construct a sorting program. However, several issues are not fully specified such as where and how the integers are initially stored and where the result is to be placed. One solution is to store the values in an array in such a way that the i'th integer is stored in the i'th array position, $a[i]$ $1 \leq i \leq n$. Program 1.1 is a refinement of the solution.

```
for i := 1 to n do
begin
  examine a [i] to a [n] and suppose the smallest integer is at a [j];
  interchange a [i] and a [j];
end;
```

Program 1.1 Selection sort

Note how we have begun to use Pascal pseudo-code. There now remain two clearly defined subtasks: (1) to find the smallest integer and (2) to interchange it with $a[i]$. This latter problem can be solved by the code

$$t := a[i]; a[i] := a[j]; a[j] := t;$$

The first subtask can be solved by assuming the minimum is $a[i]$, checking $a[i]$ with $a[i+1], a[i+2], \ldots$ and whenever a smaller element is found regarding it as the new minimum. Eventually $a[n]$ is compared to the current minimum and we are done. Putting all these observations together we get the procedure *sort* (Program 1.2). *ElementList* is an array of integers.

```
1  procedure sort (var a : ElementList; n : integer);
2  {sort the n integers a[1..n] into nondecreasing order}
3  var i, j, k, t : integer;
4  begin
5    for i := 1 to n do
6    begin
7      j := i;
8      {find smallest integer in a[j..n]}
9      for k := j+1 to n do
10       if a[k] < a[j] then j := k;
11     {interchange}
12     t := a[i]; a[i] := a[j]; a[j] := t;
13   end; {of for i}
14 end; {of sort}
```

Program 1.2 Selection sort

The obvious question to ask at this point is: "does this procedure work correctly?"

Theorem 1.1: Procedure *sort(a,n)* correctly sorts a set of $n \geq 1$ integers; the result remains in $a[1..n]$ such that $a[1] \leq a[2] \leq \ldots \leq a[n]$.
Proof: We first note that for any i, say $i = q$, following the execution of lines 7-12, it is the case that $a[q] \leq a[r]$, $q < r \leq n$. Also observe that when i becomes greater than q, $a[1..q]$ is unchanged. Hence, following the last execution of these lines (i.e., $i = n$), we have $a[1] \leq a[2] \leq \ldots \leq a[n]$. $\square$

We observe at this point that the upper limit of the **for**-loop in line 5 can be changed to $n - 1$ without damaging the correctness of the algorithm.

Let us develop another program. We assume that we have $n \geq 1$ distinct integers which are already sorted and stored in the array $a[1..n]$. Our task is to determine if the integer x is present and if so to return j such that $x = a[j]$; otherwise return $j = 0$. By making use of the fact that the set is sorted we conceive of the following efficient method:

Let $a[mid]$ be the middle element. There are three possibilities. Either $x < a[mid]$ in which case x can only occur as $a[1]$ to $a[mid - 1]$; or $x > a[mid]$ in which case x can only occur as $a[mid + 1]$ to $a[n]$; or $x = a[mid]$ in which case set j to mid and return. Continue in this way by keeping two pointers, *lower* and *upper*, to indicate the range of elements not yet tested.

At this point you might try the method out on some sample numbers. This method is referred to as *binary search.* Note how at each stage the number of elements in the remaining set is decreased by about one half. Note also that at each stage, x is compared with $a[mid]$ and depending on whether $x > a[mid]$, or $x < a[mid]$, or $x = a[mid]$, we do a different thing. To implement this in Pascal we could use the **if-then-else** construct:

$$\textbf{if } x > a[mid] \textbf{ then} \ldots$$
$$\textbf{else if } x < a[mid] \textbf{ then} \ldots$$
$$\textbf{else} \ldots$$

From this construct it isn't readily apparent that we are considering the three cases that can result from the comparison between x and $a[i]$. To make the program more transparent, we introduce a compare function that has value $>$, $<$, or $=$, depending on the outcome of the comparison. This function is given in Program 1.3.

```
function compare(x, y : element) : char;
begin
  if x > y then compare := '>'
        else if x < y then compare := '<'
                    else compare := '='
end; {of compare}
```

Program 1.3 Compare

We can now refine the description of binary search to get a pseudo-Pascal procedure. The result is given in Program 1.4.

Another refinement yields the Pascal procedure of Program 1.5. To prove this program correct we make assertions about the relationship between variables before and after the **while** loop of lines 6-14. As we enter this loop and as long as x is not found the following holds:

$$lower \leq upper \textbf{ and } a[lower] \leq x \leq a[upper] \textbf{ and } SORTED(a, n)$$

Now, if control passes out of the **while** loop past line 14, then we know the condition of line 6 is false, so $lower > upper$. This, combined with the above assertion, implies that x is not present.

```
procedure BinarySearch(var a : ElementList; x : element; var n,j : integer);
{search the sorted array a [1..n ] for x}
initialize lower and upper
while there are more elements do
begin
   let a [mid] be the middle element;
   case compare(x, a [mid]) of
      '>':  set lower to mid+1;
      '<':  set upper to mid −1;
      '=':  found x;
   end; {of case}
end; {of while}
not found;
end; {of BinarySearch}
```

Program 1.4 Algorithm for binary search

```
1   procedure BinarySearch(var a : ElementList; x : element; var n,j : integer);
2   {search the sorted array a [1..n ] for x}
3   var lower, upper, mid : integer; found : boolean;
4   begin
5      lower := 1; upper := n; found := false; j := 0;
6      while (lower <= upper) and (not found) do  {while more elements}
7      begin
8         mid := (lower+upper) div 2;
9         case compare (x, a [mid]) of
10           '>':  lower := mid+1;   {x > a [mid]}
11           '<':  upper := mid −1;   {x < a [mid]}
12           '=':  begin j := mid; found := true; end;  {x = a [mid]}
13        end; {of case}
14     end; {of while}
15  end; {of BinarySearch}
```

Program 1.5 Pascal procedure for binary search

Unfortunately, a complete proof takes us beyond our scope but those who wish to pursue program proving should consult our references at the end of this chapter. An analysis of the computing time for *BinarySearch* is carried out in Section 7.1.

We have tried to emphasize the need to structure a program to make it easier to achieve the goals of readability and correctness. Actually one of the most useful syntactical features for accomplishing this is the procedure. Given a set of instructions which perform a logical operation, perhaps a very complex and long operation, they can be grouped together as a procedure. The procedure name and its parameters are viewed as a new instruction which can be used in other programs. Given the input-output specifications of a procedure, we don't even have to know how the task is accomplished, only that it is available. This view of the procedure implies that it is invoked, executed and returns control to the appropriate place in the calling procedure. What this fails to stress is the fact that procedures may call themselves (direct recursion) before they are done or they may call other procedures which again invoke the calling procedure (indirect recursion). These recursive mechanisms are extremely powerful, but even more importantly, many times they can express an otherwise complex process very clearly. For these reasons we introduce recursion here.

Most students of computer science view recursion as a somewhat mystical technique that is useful only for some very special class of problems (such as computing factorials or Ackermann's function). This is unfortunate because any program that can be written using assignment, the **if-then-else** statement and the **while** statement can also be written using assignment, **if-then-else** and recursion. Of course, this does not say that the resulting program will necessarily be easier to understand. However, there are many instances when this will be the case. When is recursion an appropriate mechanism for algorithm exposition? One instance is when the problem itself is recursively defined. Factorial fits this category, also binomial coefficients where

$$\begin{pmatrix} n \\ m \end{pmatrix} = \frac{n!}{m!(n-m)!}$$

can be recursively computed by the formula

$$\begin{pmatrix} n \\ m \end{pmatrix} = \begin{pmatrix} n-1 \\ m \end{pmatrix} + \begin{pmatrix} n-1 \\ m-1 \end{pmatrix}$$

Another example is reversing a character string, $s = {}^{\backprime}x_1 \ldots x_n{}^{\prime}$. Let us assume that the **type** string has been declared as:

```
type string = record
                 length : integer;  {length of string}
                 c : array[1..100] of char;
               end;
```

and that the following functions have already been defined:

(1) *substring* (*s,i,j*) This yields the string made up of the *i*'th through *j*'th characters in *s*; for appropriately defined *i* and *j*. Thus if $0 < i \leq j \leq s.length$, then the string *s.c* [*i*]. . .*s.c* [*j*] is the desired substring.

(2) *concat*(*s*1,*s*2) This function yields a string of length *s*1.*length* + *s*2.*length* obtained by concatenating *s*1 and *s*2 with *s*1 preceding *s*2.

Using these functions, a recursive function (Program 1.6) to reverse the string *s* is easily obtained.

```
function reverse (s : string) : string;
{reverse the string s}
var n : integer;
begin
  n := s.length;
  if n <= 1
  then reverse := s
  else reverse := concat (reverse (substring (s,2,n)), s.c[1]);
end; {of reverse}
```

Program 1.6 String reversal

If this looks too simple let us develop a more complex recursive procedure. Given a set of $n \geq 1$ elements the problem is to print all possible permutations of this set. For example if the set is {*a,b,c*}, then the set of permutations is {(*a,b,c*), (*a,c,b*), (*b,a,c,*), (*b,c,a*), (*c,a,b*), (*c,b,a*)}. It is easy to see that given *n* elements there are *n*! different permutations. A simple algorithm can be obtained by looking at the the case of four elements (*a,b,c,d*). The answer can be constructed by writing

(1) *a* followed by all permutations of (*b,c,d*)

(2) *b* followed by all permutations of (*a,c,d*)

(3) *c* followed by all permutations of (*a,b,d*)

(4) *d* followed by all permutations of (*a,b,c*)

The expression ''followed by all permutations'' is the clue to recursion. It implies that we can solve the problem for a set with *n* elements if we have an algorithm which works on $n - 1$ elements. These considerations lead to Program 1.7 which is invoked by *perm* (*a*, 1,*n*).

Try this algorithm out on sets of length one, two, and three to ensure that you understand how it works. Then try to do one or more of the exercises at the end of this chapter that ask for recursive procedures.

Another time when recursion is useful is when the data structure that the algorithm is to operate on is recursively defined. We shall see several important examples of such structures, especially lists in Section 4.8 and binary trees in Section 5.2. Another

---

```
procedure perm (a : ElementList; k,n : integer);
{generate all the permutations of a [k..n]}
var t : element;   {type of entries in a}
    i : integer;
begin
  if k = n
  then begin {output permutation}
              for i := 1 to n do
                      write(a [i]);
              writeln;
        end
  else begin
          {a [k..n] has more than one permutation.
          Generate these recursively.}
          for i := k to n do
          begin
            {interchange a [k] and a [i]}
            t := a [k]; a [k] := a [i]; a [i] := t;
            perm (a, k+1, n); {all permutations of a [k +1..n]}
          end;
        end; {of else}
end; {of perm}
```

Program 1.7 Permutation

instance when recursion is invaluable is when we want to describe a backtracking procedure.

1.3 PERFORMANCE ANALYSIS AND MEASUREMENT

One goal of this book is to develop skills for making evaluative judgements about programs. There are many criteria upon which we can judge a program, for instance:

(1)   Does it do what we want it to do?

(2)   Does it work correctly according to the original specifications of the task?

(3)   Is there documentation that describes how to use it and how it works?

(4)   Are **procedures** created in such a way that they perform logical sub-functions?

(5)   Is the code readable?

The above criteria are all vitally important when it comes to writing software, most especially for large systems. Though we will not be discussing how to reach these goals, we will try to achieve them throughout this book with the programs we write. Hopefully this more subtle approach will gradually infect your own program writing habits so that you will automatically strive to achieve these goals.

There are other criteria for judging programs that have a more direct relationship to performance. These have to do with their computing time and storage requirements.

Definition: The *space complexity* of a program is the amount of memory it needs to run to completion. The *time complexity* of a program is the amount of computer time it needs to run to completion. □

Performance evaluation can be loosely divided into two major phases: (1) a priori estimates and (2) a posteriori testing. We refer to these as *performance analysis* and *performance measurement*, respectively.

1.3.1 Performance Analysis

1.3.1.1 Space Complexity

Function *abc* (Program 1.8) computes the expression $a+b+b*c + (a+b-c)/(a+b)+4.0$; function *sum* (Program 1.9) computes the sum $\sum_{i=1}^{n} a[i]$ iteratively, where the $a[i]$'s are real numbers; and function *rsum* (Program 1.10) is a recursive program that computes $\sum_{i=1}^{n} a[i]$.

---

function *abc* (*a*, *b*, *c* : **real**) : **real**;
begin
   abc := $a+b+b*c +(a+b-c)/(a+b)+4.0$;
end; {of *abc*}

Program 1.8 Function to compute $a+b+b*c + (a+b-c)/(a+b)+4.0$

The space needed by each of these programs is seen to be the sum of the following components:

(1)   A fixed part that is independent of the characteristics (e.g., number, size) of the inputs and outputs. This part typically includes the instruction space (i.e., space for the code), space for simple variables and fixed size component variables (also called *aggregate*), space for constants, etc.

---

line	
	function *sum*(*a* : *ElementList* ; *n* : **integer**) : **real**;
1	**var** *s* : **real**; *i* : **integer**;
2	**begin**
3	*s* := 0;
4	**for** *i* := 1 **to** *n* **do**
5	*s* := *s* + *a* [*i*];
6	*sum* := *s*;
7	**end**; {of *sum*}

Program 1.9 Iterative function for sum

---

line	
	function *rsum*(*a* : *ElementList* ; *n* : **integer**) : **real**;
1	**begin**
2	**if** *n*<=0 **then** *rsum* := **0**
3	**else** *rsum* := *rsum* (*a*, *n*−1) + *a* [*n*];
4	**end**; {of *rsum*}

Program 1.10 Recursive function for sum

(2)   A variable part that consists of the space needed by component variables whose size is dependent on the particular problem instance being solved, space needed by referenced variables (to the extent that this depends on instance characteristics), and the recursion stack space (in so far as this space depends on the instance characteristics).

The space requirement $S(P)$, of any program P may therefore be written as $S(P) = c + S_P$(instance characteristics) where c is a constant.

When analyzing the space complexity of a program, we shall concentrate solely on estimating S_P (instance characteristics). For any given problem, we shall need to first determine which instance characteristics to use to measure the space requirements. This is very problem specific and we shall resort to examples to illustrate the various possibilities. Generally speaking, our choices are limited to quantities related to the number and magnitude of the inputs to and outputs from the program. At times, more complex measures of the interrelationships amongst the data items are used.

Example 1.1: For Program 1.8, the problem instance is characterized by the specific values of *a*, *b*, and *c*. Making the assumption that one word is adequate to store the values of each of *a*, *b*, *c*, and *abc*, we see that the space needed by function *abc* is independent of the instance characteristics. Consequently, S_P(instance characteristics) = 0. □

Example 1.2: The problem instances for Program 1.9 are characterized by n, the number of elements to be summed. Since a and n are value formal parameters, space for these must be allocated. The space needed by the variable n is one word as it is of type **integer**. The space needed by a is the space needed by variables of type *ElementList*. This is at least n words as a must be large enough to hold the n elements to be summed. So, we obtain $S_{sum}(n) \geq n$.

Notice that if we change the formal parameter a from value to reference (or **var**), only the address of the actual parameter gets transferred to the function and the space needed by the function is independent of n. In this case, $S_{sum}(n) = 0$.

So, even though the values of the individual components of a do not get changed by *sum*, it is desirable to make a a variable parameter in order to conserve space. As a variable parameter, only enough space to store a memory address is needed. This is typically just one or two words. □

Example 1.3: Let us consider the function *rsum*. As in the case of *sum*, the instances are characterized by n. The recursion stack space includes space for the formal parameters, the local variables, and the return address. Since a is a value formal parameter, the values of all its components get saved on the stack. Assume that the return address requires only one word of memory. Each call to *rsum* requires at least $(n + 3)$ words (including space for the values of n, a, and *rsum* and the return address). More space is required if *ElementList* has been declared as an array $[1..MaxSize]$ where $MaxSize > n$. In this case, each call to *rsum* takes up $(MaxSize + 3)$ space.

Since the depth of recursion is $n+1$, the recursion stack space needed is $(n+1)(MaxSize+3)$ or $(n+1)(n+3)$ depending on whether or not the size of *ElementList* is changed whenever n changes.

Now that we realize the space cost of having a a value formal parameter, we see that *rsum* will fail when n is suitably large. For example, when $n = 1000$, at least $1001*1003 = 1,004,003$ words of memory are needed for the recursion stack space alone.

If we make a a variable parameter, then each call to *rsum* requires only four words of space. The recursion stack space becomes $4(n+1)$ or 4004 words when $n = 1000$. We can solve much larger instances now with a given amount of memory. Of course, we can do much better by not using recursion at all and sticking with the modified version of Program 1.9 in which a is a variable formal parameter. □

1.3.1.2 Time Complexity

The time, $T(P)$, taken by a program P, is the sum of the compile time and the run (or execution) time. The compile time does not depend on the instance characteristics. Also, we may assume that a compiled program will be run several times without recompilation. Consequently, we shall concern ourselves with just the run time of a program. This run time is denoted by t_P (instance characteristics).

Because many of the factors t_P depends on are not known at the time a program is conceived, it is reasonable to attempt to only estimate t_P. If we knew the characteristics of the compiler to be used, we could proceed to determine the number of additions, subtractions, multiplications, divisions, compares, loads, stores, etc. that would be made by the code for P. Having done this, we could present a formula for t_P. Letting n denote the instance characteristics, we might then have an expression for $t_P(n)$ of the form:

$$t_P(n) = c_a ADD(n) + c_s SUB(n) + c_m MUL(n) + c_d DIV(n) + \ldots$$

where c_a, c_s, c_m, c_d, etc., respectively, denote the time needed for an addition, subtraction, multiplication, division, etc., and ADD, SUB, MUL, DIV, etc., are functions whose value is the number of additions, subtractions, multiplications, divisions, etc., that will be performed when the code for P is used on an instance with characteristic n.

Obtaining such an exact formula is in itself an impossible task as the time needed for an addition, subtraction, multiplication, etc., often depends on the actual numbers being added, subtracted, multiplied, etc. In reality then, the true value of $t_P(n)$ for any given n can be obtained only experimentally. The program is typed, compiled, and run on a particular machine. The execution time is physically clocked and $t_P(n)$ obtained. Even with this experimental approach, one could face difficulties. In a multiuser system, the execution time will depend on such factors as system load, the number of other programs running on the computer at the time program P is run, the characteristics of these other programs, etc.

Given the minimal utility of determining the exact number of additions, subtractions, etc., that are needed to solve a problem instance with characteristics given by n, we might as well lump all the operations together (provided that the time required by each is relatively independent of the instance characteristics) and obtain a count for the total number of operations. We can go one step further and count only the number of program steps.

A *program step* is loosely defined as a syntactically or semantically meaningful segment of a program that has an execution time that is independent of the instance characteristics. For example, the entire statement

$$abc := a + b + b * c + (a + b - c) / (a + b) + 4.0;$$

of Program 1.8 could be regarded as a step since its execution time is independent of the instance characteristics (this statement isn't strictly true as the time for a multiply and divide will generally depend on the actual numbers involved in the operation).

The number of steps any program statement is to be assigned depends on the nature of that statement. The following discussion considers the various statement types that can appear in a Pascal program and states the complexity of each in terms of the number of steps:

(1) *Comments.* Comments are nonexecutable statements and have a step count of zero.

(2) *Declarative statements.* This includes all statements of type **const**, **label**, **type**, and **var**. These count as zero steps as these are either nonexecutable or their cost may be lumped into the cost of invoking the procedure/function they are associated with.

(3) *Expressions and assignment statements.* Most expressions have a step count of one. The exceptions are expressions that contain function calls. In this case, we need to determine the cost of invoking the functions. This cost can be large if the functions employ many-element value parameters as the values of all actual parameters need to be assigned to the formal parameters. This is discussed further under procedure and function invocation. When the expression contains functions, the step count is the sum of the step counts assignable to each function invocation.

The assignment statement <variable> := <expr> has a step count equal to that of <expr> unless the size of <variable> is a function of the instance characteristics. In this latter case, the step count is the size of <variable> plus the step count of <expr>. For example, the assignment $a := b$ where a and b are of type *ElementList* has a step count equal to the size of *ElementList*.

(4) *Iteration statements.* This class of statements includes the **for**, **while**, and **until** statements. We shall consider the step counts only for the control part of these statements. These have the form:

> **for** i := <expr> **to** <expr1> **do**
> **for** i := <expr> **downto** <expr1> **do**
> **while** <expr> **do**
> **until** <expr>;

Each execution of the control part of a **while** and **until** statement will be given a step count equal to the number of step counts assignable to <expr>. The step count for each execution of the control part of a **for** statement is one, unless the counts attributable to <expr> and <expr1> are a function of the instance characteristics. In this latter case, the first execution of the control part of the **for** has a step count equal to the sum of the counts for <expr> and <expr1> (note that these expressions are computed only when the loop is started). Remaining executions of the **for** have a step count of one.

(5) *Case statement.* This statement consists of a header followed by one or more sets of condition and statement pairs.

```
case <expr> of
    cond1: <statement1>
    cond2: <statement2>
        .
        .
        .
    else: <statement>
end
```

The cost of the header: **case** <expr> **of** is given a cost equal to that assignable to <expr>. The cost of each following condition-statement pair is the cost of this condition plus that of all preceding conditions plus that of this statement.

(6) *If-then-else statement.* The if-then-else statement consists of three parts:

```
if <expr>
then <statements1>
else <statements2>;
```

Each part is assigned the number of steps corresponding to <expr>, <statements1>, and <statements2>, respectively. Note that if the **else** clause is absent, then no cost is assigned to it.

(7) *Procedure and function invocation.* All invocations of procedures and functions count as one step unless the invocation involves value parameters whose size depends on the instance characteristics. In this latter case, the count is the sum of the sizes of these value parameters. In case the procedure/function being invoked is recursive, then we must also consider the local variables in the procedure or function being invoked. The sizes of local variables that are characteristic dependent need to be added into the step count.

(8) *Begin, end, with, and repeat statements.* Each **with** statement counts as one step. Each **begin**, **end**, and **repeat** statement counts as zero steps.

(9) *Procedure and function statements.* These count as zero steps as their cost has already been assigned to the invoking statements.

(10) *Goto statement.* This has a step count of 1.

With the above assignment of step counts to statements, we can proceed to determine the number of steps needed by a program to solve a particular problem instance. We can go about this in one of two ways. In the first method, we introduce a new variable, *count*, into the program. This is a global variable with initial value 0. Statements to increment *count* by the appropriate amount are introduced into the program. This is done so that each time a statement in the original program is executed, *count* is incremented by the step count of that statement.

Example 1.4: When the statements to increment *count* are introduced into Program 1.9 the result is Program 1.11. The change in the value of *count* by the time this program terminates is the number of steps executed by Program 1.9.

Since we are interested in determining only the change in the value of *count*, Program 1.11 may be simplified to Program 1.12. It should be easy to see that for every initial value of *count*, Program 1.11 and Program 1.12 compute the same final value for *count*. It is easy to see that in the **for** loop the value of *count* will increase by a total of $2n$. If *count* is zero to start with, then it will be $2n+3$ on termination. So, each invocation of *sum* (Program 1.9) executes a total of $2n+3$ steps. □

```
function sum(a : ElementList ; n :integer) :real;
var s : real; i : integer;
begin
  s := 0;
  count := count+1; {count is global}
  for i := 1 to n do
  begin
    count := count+1; {for for}
    s := s +a [i ];
    count := count+1;  {for assignment}
  end;
  count := count+1;  {for last time of for}
  sum := s;
  count := count+1;  {for assignment}
end; { of sum}
```

Program 1.11 Program 1.9 with count statements added

```
function sum(a : ElementList ; n :integer) :real;
var s : real; i : integer;
begin
  for i := 1 to n do
    count := count+2;  {end of for}
  count := count+3;
end; { of sum}
```

Program 1.12 Simplified version of Program 1.11

Example 1.5: When the statements to increment count are introduced into Program 1.10, Program 1.13 is obtained. In this program, we have assumed that the declared size of *ElementList* is m. Note that $m \geq n$. Let $t_{rsum}(n)$ be the increase in the value of *count* when Program 1.13 terminates. We see that $t_{rsum}(0) = 2$. When $n > 0$, *count* increases by $m+1$ plus whatever increase results from the invocation of *rsum* from within the **else** clause. From the definition of t_{rsum}, it follows that this additional increase is $t_{rsum}(n-1)$. So, if the value of *count* is zero initially, its value at the time of termination is $m+1+t_{rsum}(n-1)$, $n > 0$.

```
function rsum(a : ElementList ; n : integer) : real;
begin
    count := count+1;  {for if conditional}
    if n<=0 then begin
                    rsum := 0;
                    count := count+1;  {for assignment}
                end
    else begin
            rsum := rsum (a, n-1) + a [n ];
            count := count+m;  {for assignment, m is the size of ElementList}
        end;
end;  {of rsum}
```

Program 1.13 Program 1.10 with count statements added

When analyzing a recursive program for its step count, we often obtain a recursive formula for the step count (i.e., say $t_{rsum}(n) = m+1+t_{rsum}(n-1)$, $n > 0$ and $t_{rsum}(0)=2$). These recursive formulas are referred to as *recurrence relations*. This recurrence may be solved by repeatedly substituting for t_{rsum} as below:

$$t_{rsum}(n) = m+1+t_{rsum}(n-1)$$
$$= m+1 + m+1 + t_{rsum}(n-2)$$
$$= 2(m+1) + t_{rsum}(n-2)$$
$$\cdot$$
$$\cdot$$
$$\cdot$$
$$= n(m+1) + t_{rsum}(0)$$
$$= n(m+1)+2, \, n \geq 0.$$

So, the step count for procedure *rsum* (Program 1.10) is $n(m+1)+2$. This is significantly larger than that for the iterative version (Program 1.9). If a is made a variable parameter, then the step count becomes $2n+2$. $\square$

Comparing the step count of Program 1.9 to that of Program 1.10 with a changed to a variable parameter, we see that the count for Program 1.10 is less than that for Program 1.9. From this, we cannot conclude that Program 1.9 is slower than Program 1.10. This is so because a step doesn't correspond to a definite time unit. Each step of *rsum* may take more time than every step of *sum*. So, it might well be (and we expect it) that *rsum* is slower than *sum*.

The step count is useful in that it tells us how the run time for a program changes with changes in the instance characteristics. From the step count for *sum*, we see that if *n* is doubled, the run time will also double (approximately); if *n* increases by a factor of 10, we expect the run time to increase by a factor of 10; etc. So, we expect the run time to grow *linearly* in *n*. We say that *sum* is a linear program (the time complexity is linear in the instance characteristic *n*).

Example 1.6: [Matrix addition] Program 1.14 is a program to add two $m \times n$ matrices *a* and *b* together. Introducing the *count* incrementing statements leads to Program 1.15. Program 1.16 is a simplified version of Program 1.15 that computes the same value for *count*. Examining Program 1.16, we see that line 6 is executed *n* times for each value of *i* or a total of *mn* times; line 7 is executed *m* times; and line 9 is executed once. If *count* is zero to begin with, it will be $2mn + 2m + 1$ when Program 1.16 terminates.

From this analysis we see that if $m > n$, then it is better to interchange the two **for** statements in Program 1.14. If this is done, the step count becomes $2mn + 2n + 1$. Note that in this example the instance characteristics are given by *m* and *n*. □

```
line  procedure add (var a, b, c : matrix; m,n :integer);
 1      var i, j : integer;
 2      begin
 3        for i := 1 to m do
 4          for j := 1 to n do
 5            c [i,j] := a [i,j]+b [i,j];
 6      end; {of add}
```

Program 1.14 Matrix addition

The second method to determine the step count of a program is to build a table in which we list the total number of steps contributed by each statement to *count*. This figure is often arrived at by first determining the number of steps per execution of the statement and the total number of times (i.e., frequency) each statement is executed. By combining these two quantities, the total contribution of each statement is obtained. By adding up the contributions of all statements, the step count for the entire program is obtained.

There is an important difference between the step count of a statement and its steps per execution (s/e). The step count does not necessarily reflect the complexity of the statement. For example, the statement

$$x := sum(a,m);$$

has a step count of *m* (assuming that *a* is defined to be a size *m* array) while the total

```
procedure add (var a, b, c : matrix; m,n :integer);
var i, j : integer;
begin
  for i := 1 to m do
  begin
    count := count+1; {for for i}
    for j := 1 to n do
    begin
      count := count+1; {for for j}
      c [i,j] := a [i,j]+b [i,j];
      count := count+1; {for assignment}
    end;
    count := count+1; {for last time of for j}
  end;
  count := count+1; {for last time of for i}
end; {of add}
```

Program 1.15 Matrix addition with counting statements

```
line  procedure add (var a, b, c : matrix; m,n : integer);
1     var i, j : integer;
2     begin
3       for i := 1 to m do
4       begin
5         for j := 1 to n do
6           count := count+2;
7         count := count+2;
8       end;
9       count := count+1;
10    end; {of add}
```

Program 1.16 Simplified program with counting only

change in *count* resulting from the execution of this statement is actually m plus the change resulting from the invocation of *sum* (i.e., $2m+3$). The steps per execution of the above statement is $m+2m+3 = 3m+3$. *The s/e of a statement is the amount by which count changes as a result of the execution of that statement.*

In Table 1.1, the number of steps per execution and the frequency of each of the statements in procedure *sum* (Program 1.9) have been listed. The total number of steps required by the program is determined to be $2n+3$. It is important to note that the frequency of line 4 is $n+1$ and not n. This is so as i has to be incremented to $n+1$ before the **for** loop can terminate.

line	s/e	frequency	total steps
1	0	0	0
2	0	0	0
3	1	1	1
4	1	$n+1$	$n+1$
5	1	n	n
6	1	1	1
7	0	1	0
		Total number of steps	$2n+3$

Table 1.1 Step table for Program 1.9

Table 1.2 gives the step count for procedure *rsum* (Program 1.10). Line 2(a) refers to the **if** conditional of line 2 and line 2(b) refers to the statement in the **then** clause of the **if**. Notice that under the s/e (steps per execution) column, line 3 has been given a count of $m+t_{rsum}(n-1)$. This is the total cost of line 3 each time it is executed. It includes all the steps that get executed as a result of the invocation of *rsum* from line 3. The frequency and total steps columns have been split into two parts: one for the case $n = 0$ and the other for the case $n > 0$. This is necessary as the frequency (and hence total steps) for some statements is different for each of these cases.

line	s/e	frequency		total steps	
		$n = 0$	$n > 0$	$n = 0$	$n > 0$
1	0	0	0	0	0
2(a)	1	1	1	1	1
2(b)	1	1	0	1	0
3	$m+t_{rsum}(n-1)$	0	1	0	$m+t_{rsum}(n-1)$
4	0	1	1	0	0
	Total number of steps			2	$m+1+t_{rsum}(n-1)$

Table 1.2 Step table for Program 1.10

Table 1.3 corresponds to procedure *add* (Program 1.14). Once again, note that the frequency of line 3 is $m+1$ and not m. This is so as i needs to be incremented up to $m+1$ before the loop can terminate. Similarly, the frequency for line 4 is $m(n+1)$. When you have obtained sufficient experience in computing step counts, you may avoid constructing the frequency table and obtain the step count as in the following example.

line	s/e	frequency	total steps
1	0	0	0
2	0	0	0
3	1	$m+1$	$m+1$
4	1	$m(n+1)$	$mn+m$
5	1	mn	mn
6	0	1	0
		Total	$2mn+2m+1$

Table 1.3 Step table for Program 1.14.

Example 1.7: [Fibonnaci numbers] The Fibonacci sequence of numbers starts as

$$0, 1, 1, 2, 3, 5, 8, 13, 21, 34, 55, \ldots$$

Each new term is obtained by taking the sum of the two previous terms. If we call the first term of the sequence F_0 then $F_0 = 0$, $F_1 = 1$ and in general

$$F_n = F_{n-1} + F_{n-2}, n \geq 2$$

The program *fibonacci* (Program 1.17) inputs any non-negative integer n and prints the value F_n.

To analyze the time complexity of this program, we need to consider the two cases: (1) $n = 0$ or 1, and (2) $n > 1$. Line 7 will be regarded as two lines: 7(a), the conditional part, and 7(b), the **then** clause. When $n = 0$ or 1, lines 6, 7(a), 7(b), and 19 get executed once each. Since each line has a s/e of 1, the total step count for this case is 4. When $n > 1$, lines 6, 7(a), 10, and 17 are each executed once. Line 11 gets executed n times while lines 12-16 get executed $n-1$ times each (note that the last time line 11 is executed, i is incremented to $n + 1$ and the loop exited). Line 10 has a s/e of 2 while the remaining lines that get executed have a s/e of 1. The total steps for the case $n > 1$ is therefore $4n + 2$. □

Summary

The time complexity of a program is given by the number of steps taken by the program to compute the function it was written for. The number of steps is itself a function of the instance characteristics. While any specific instance may have several characteristics (e.g., the number of inputs, the number of outputs, the magnitudes of the

```
 1   program fibonacci (input, output);
 2   {compute the Fibonacci number F_n}
 3   type natural = 0 .. maxint;
 4   var fnm1, fnm2, fn, n, i : natural;
 5   begin
 6     readln(n);
 7     if n <= 1 then writeln(n) {F_0 = 0 and F_1 = 1}
 8             else
 9             begin { compute F_n }
10               fnm2 := 0; fnm1 := 1;
11               for i := 2 to n do
12               begin
13                 fn := fnm1+fnm2;
14                 fnm2 := fnm1;
15                 fnm1 := fn;
16               end; {of for}
17               writeln(fn);
18             end; {of else}
19   end. {of fibonacci}
```

Program 1.17 Fibonacci numbers

inputs and outputs, etc.), the number of steps is computed as a function of some subset of these. Usually, we choose those characteristics that are of importance to us. For example, we might wish to know how the computing (or run) time (i.e., time complexity) increases as the number of inputs increase. In this case the number of steps will be computed as a function of the number of inputs alone. For a different program, we might be interested in determining how the computing time increases as the magnitude of one of the inputs increases. In this case the number of steps will be computed as a function of the magnitude of this input alone. Thus, before the step count of a program can be determined, we need to know exactly which characteristics of the problem instance are to be used. These define the variables in the expression for the step count. In the case of *sum*, we chose to measure the time complexity as a function of the number, n, of elements being added. For procedure *add* the choice of characteristics was the number, m, of rows and the number, n, of columns in the matrices being added.

Once the relevant characteristics (n, m, p, q, r, ...) have been selected, we can define what a step is. A step is any computation unit that is independent of the characteristics (n, m, p, q, r, ...). Thus, 10 additions can be one step; 100 multiplications can also be one step; but n additions cannot. Nor can $m/2$ additions, $p+q$ subtractions, etc., be counted as one step.

A systematic way to assign step counts was also discussed. Once this has been done, the time complexity (i.e., the total step count) of a program can be obtained using either of the two methods discussed.

The examples we have looked at so far were sufficiently simple that the time complexities were nice functions of fairly simple characteristics like the number of elements, and the number of rows and columns. For many programs, the time complexity is not dependent solely on the number of inputs or outputs or some other easily specified characteristic. Consider the procedure *BinarySearch* of Chapter 2. This procedure searches $a[1..n]$ for x. A natural parameter with respect to which you might wish to determine the step count is the number, n, of elements to be searched. That is, we would like to know how the computing time changes as we change the number of elements n. The parameter n is inadequate. For the same n, the step count varies with the position of x in a. We can extricate ourselves from the difficulties resulting from situations when the chosen parameters are not adequate to determine the step count uniquely by defining two kinds of steps counts: worst case and average.

The *worst case step count* is the maximum number of steps that can be executed for the given paramenters. The *average step count* is the average number of steps executed on instances with the given parameters.

1.3.1.3 Asymptotic Notation (O, Ω, Θ)

Our motivation to determine step counts is to be able to compare the time complexities of two programs that compute the same function and also to predict the growth in run time as the instance characteristics change.

Determining the exact step count (either worst case or average) of a program can prove to be an exceedingly difficult task. Expending immense effort to determine the step count exactly isn't a very worthwhile endeavor as the notion of a step is itself inexact. (Both the instructions $x := y$ and $x := y + z + (x/y) + (x*y*z-x/z)$ count as one step.) Because of the inexactness of what a step stands for, the exact step count isn't very useful for comparative purposes. An exception to this is when the difference in the step counts of two programs is very large as in $3n+3$ versus $100n+10$. We might feel quite safe in predicting that the program with step count $3n+3$ will run in less time than the one with step count $100n+10$. But even in this case, it isn't necessary to know that the exact step count is $100n+10$. Something like, "it's about $80n$, or $85n$, or $75n$," is adequate to arrive at the same conclusion.

For most situations, it is adequate to be able to make a statement like $c_1 n^2 \le t_P^{WC}(n) \le c_2 n^2$ or $t_Q^{WC}(n,m) = c_1 n + c_2 m$ where c_1 and c_2 are nonnegative constants. This is so because if we have two programs with a complexity of $c_1 n^2 + c_2 n$ and $c_3 n$, respectively, then we know that the one with complexity $c_3 n$ will be faster than the one with complexity $c_1 n^2 + c_2 n$ for sufficiently large values of n. For small values of n, either program could be faster (depending on c_1, c_2, and c_3). If $c_1 = 1, c_2 = 2$, and $c_3 = 100$ then $c_1 n^2 + c_2 n \le c_3 n$ for $n \le 98$ and $c_1 n^2 + c_2 n > c_3 n$ for $n > 98$. If $c_1 = 1, c_2 = 2$, and $c_3 = 1000$, then $c_1 n^2 + c_2 n \le c_3 n$ for $n \le 998$.

No matter what the values of c_1, c_2, and c_3, there will be an n beyond which the program with complexity c_3n will be faster than the one with complexity $c_1n^2 + c_2n$. This value of n will be called the *break even point*. If the break even point is 0 then the program with complexity c_3n is always faster (or at least as fast). The exact break even point cannot be determined analytically. The programs have to be run on a computer in order to determine the break even point. To know that there is a break even point it is adequate to know that one program has complexity $c_1n^2 + c_2n$ and the other c_3n for some constants c_1, c_2, and c_3. There is little advantage in determining the exact values of c_1, c_2, and c_3.

With the previous discussion as motivation, we introduce some terminology that will enable us to make meaningful (but inexact) statements about the time and space complexities of a program. In the remainder of this chapter, the functions f and g are nonnegative functions.

Definition: [Big "oh"] $f(n) = O(g(n))$ (read as "f of n is big oh of g of n") iff (if and only if) there exist positive constants c and n_0 such that $f(n) \leq cg(n)$ for all $n, n \geq n_0$. □

Example 1.8: $3n + 2 = O(n)$ as $3n + 2 \leq 4n$ for all $n \geq 2$. $3n + 3 = O(n)$ as $3n + 3 \leq 4n$ for all $n \geq 3$. $100n + 6 = O(n)$ as $100n + 6 \leq 101n$ for $n \geq 10$. $10n^2 + 4n + 2 = O(n^2)$ as $10n^2 + 4n + 2 \leq 11n^2$ for $n \geq 5$. $1000n^2 + 100n - 6 = O(n^2)$ as $1000n^2 + 100n - 6 \leq 1001n^2$ for $n \geq 100$. $6*2^n + n^2 = O(2^n)$ as $6*2^n + n^2 \leq 7*2^n$ for $n \geq 4$. $3n + 3 = O(n^2)$ as $3n + 3 \leq 3n^2$ for $n \geq 2$. $10n^2 + 4n + 2 = O(n^4)$ as $10n^2 + 4n + 2 \leq 10n^4$ for $n \geq 2$. $3n + 2 \neq O(1)$ as $3n + 2$ is not less than or equal to c for any constant c and all $n, n \geq n_0$. $10n^2 + 4n + 2 \neq O(n)$. □

We write $O(1)$ to mean a computing time which is a constant. $O(n)$ is called linear, $O(n^2)$ is called quadratic, $O(n^3)$ is called cubic, and $O(2^n)$ is called exponential. If an algorithm takes time $O(\log n)$ it is faster, for sufficiently large n, than if it had taken $O(n)$. Similarly, $O(n \log n)$ is better than $O(n^2)$ but not as good as $O(n)$. These seven computing times, $O(1)$, $O(\log n)$, $O(n)$, $O(n \log n)$, $O(n^2)$, $O(n^3)$, and $O(2^n)$ are the ones we will see most often in this book.

As illustrated by the previous example, the statement $f(n) = O(g(n))$ only states that $g(n)$ is an upper bound on the value of $f(n)$ for all $n, n \geq n_0$. It doesn't say anything about how good this bound is. Notice that $n = O(n^2)$, $n = O(n^{2.5})$, $n = O(n^3)$, $n = O(2^n)$, etc. In order for the statement $f(n) = O(g(n))$ to be informative, $g(n)$ should be as small a function of n as one can come up with for which $f(n) = O(g(n))$. So, while we shall often say $3n + 3 = O(n)$, we shall almost never say $3n + 3 = O(n^2)$ even though this latter statement is correct.

From the definition of O, it should be clear that $f(n) = O(g(n))$ is not the same as $O(g(n)) = f(n)$. In fact, it is meaningless to say that $O(g(n)) = f(n)$. The use of the symbol "=" is unfortunate as this symbol commonly denotes the "equals" relation. Some of the confusion that results from the use of this symbol (which is standard terminology) can be avoided by reading the symbol "=" as "is" and not as "equals."

Theorem 1.1 obtains a very useful result concerning the order of $f(n)$ (i.e., the $g(n)$ in $f(n) = O(g(n))$) when $f(n)$ is a polynomial in n.

Theorem 1.1: If $f(n) = a_m n^m + \ldots + a_1 n + a_0$, then $f(n) = O(n^m)$.

Proof: $f(n) \leq \sum_{i=0}^{m} |a_i| n^i$

$$\leq n^m \sum_0^m |a_i| n^{i-m}$$

$$\leq n^m \sum_0^m |a_i|, \text{ for } n \geq 1$$

So, $f(n) = O(n^m)$. □

Definition: [Omega] $f(n) = \Omega(g(n))$ (read as "f of n is omega of g of n") iff there exist positive constants c and n_0 such that $f(n) \geq cg(n)$ for all n, $n \geq n_0$. □

Example 1.9: $3n + 2 = \Omega(n)$ as $3n + 2 \geq 3n$ for $n \geq 1$ (actually the inequality holds for $n \geq 0$ but the definition of Ω requires an $n_0 > 0$). $3n + 3 = \Omega(n)$ as $3n + 3 \geq 3n$ for $n \geq 1$. $100n + 6 = \Omega(n)$ as $100n + 6 \geq 100n$ for $n \geq 1$. $10n^2 + 4n + 2 = \Omega(n^2)$ as $10n^2 + 4n + 2 \geq n^2$ for $n \geq 1$. $6*2^n + n^2 = \Omega(2^n)$ as $6*2^n + n^2 \geq 2^n$ for $n \geq 1$. Observe also that $3n + 3 = \Omega(1)$; $10n^2 + 4n + 2 = \Omega(n)$; $10n^2 + 4n + 2 = \Omega(1)$; $6*2^n + n^2 = \Omega(n^{100})$; $6*2^n + n^2 = \Omega(n^{50.2})$; $6*2^n + n^2 = \Omega(n^2)$; $6*2^n + n^2 = \Omega(n)$; and $6*2^n + n^2 = \Omega(1)$. □

As in the case of the "big oh" notation, there are several functions $g(n)$ for which $f(n) = \Omega(g(n))$. $g(n)$ is only a lower bound on $f(n)$. For the statement $f(n) = \Omega(g(n))$ to be informative, $g(n)$ should be as large a function of n as possible for which the statement $f(n) = \Omega(g(n))$ is true. So, while we shall say that $3n + 3 = \Omega(n)$ and that $6*2^n + n^2 = \Omega(2^n)$, we shall almost never say that $3n + 3 = \Omega(1)$ or that $6*2^n + n^2 = \Omega(1)$ even though both these statements are correct.

Theorem 1.2 is the analogue of Theorem 1.1 for the omega notation.

Theorem 1.2: If $f(n) = a_m n^m + \ldots + a_1 n + a_0$ and $a_m > 0$, then $f(n) = \Omega(n^m)$.

Proof: Left as an exercise. □

Definition: [Theta] $f(n) = \Theta(g(n))$ (read as "f of n is theta of g of n") iff there exist positive constants c_1, c_2, and n_0 such that $c_1 g(n) \leq f(n) \leq c_2 g(n)$ for all n, $n \geq n_0$. □

Example 1.10: $3n + 2 = \Theta(n)$ as $3n + 2 \geq 3n$ for all $n \geq 2$ and $3n + 2 \leq 4n$ for all $n \geq 2$, so c_1 3, $c_2 = 4$, and $n_0 = 2$. $3n + 3 = \Theta(n)$; $10n^2 + 4n + 2 = \Theta(n^2)$; $6*2^n + n^2 = \Theta(2^n)$; and $10*\log n + 4 = \Theta(\log n)$. $3n + 2 \neq \Theta(1)$; $3n + 3 \neq \Theta(n^2)$; $10n^2 + 4n + 2 \neq \Theta(n)$; $10n^2 +$

$4n + 2 \neq \Theta(1)$; $6*2^n + n^2 \neq \Theta(n^2)$; $6*2^n + n^2 \neq \Theta(n^{100})$; and $6*2^n + n^2 \neq \Theta(1)$. $\square$

The theta notation is more precise than both the "big oh" and omega notations. $f(n) = \Theta(g(n))$ iff $g(n)$ is both an upper and lower bound on $f(n)$.

Notice that the coefficients in all of the $g(n)$'s used in the preceding three examples has been 1. This is in accordance with practice. We shall almost never find ourselves saying that $3n + 3 = O(3n)$, or that $10 = O(100)$, or that $10n^2 + 4n + 2 = \Omega(4n^2)$, or that $6*2^n + n^2 = \Omega(6*2^n)$, or that $6*2^n + n^2 = \Theta(4*2^n)$, even though each of these statements is true.

Theorem 1.3: If $f(n) = a_m n^m + \ldots + a_1 n + a_0$ and $a_m > 0$, then $f(n) = \Theta(n^m)$.

Proof: Left as an exercise. $\square$

Let us reexamine the time complexity analyses of the previous section. For procedure *sum* (Program 1.9) we had determined that $t_{sum}(n) = 2n + 3$. So, $t_{sum}(n) = \Theta(n)$. $t_{rsum}(n) = n(m+1) + 2 = \Theta(nm)$ and $t_{add}(m,n) = 2mn + 2n + 1 = \Theta(mn)$.

While we might all see that the O, Ω, and Θ notations have been used correctly in the preceding paragraphs, we are still left with the question: "Of what use are these notations if one has to first determine the step count exactly?" The answer to this question is that the asymptotic complexity (i.e., the complexity in terms of O, Ω, and Θ) can be determined quite easily without determining the exact step count. This is usually done by first determining the asymptotic complexity of each statement (or group of statements) in the program and then adding up these complexities. Tables 1.4 to 1.6 do just this for *sum*, *rsum*, and *add*.

Note that in the table for *add*, lines 4 and 5 have been lumped together even though they have different frequencies. This lumping together of these two lines is possible because their frequencies are of the same order.

line(s)	s/e	frequency	total steps
1,2	0	-	$\Theta(0)$
3	1	1	$\Theta(1)$
4	1	$n+1$	$\Theta(n)$
5	1	n	$\Theta(n)$
6	1	1	$\Theta(1)$
7	0	-	$\Theta(0)$

$$t_{sum}(n) = \Theta(\max_{0 \leq i \leq 7}\{g_i(n)\}) = \Theta(n)$$

Table 1.4 Asymptotic complexity of *sum*

While the analyses of Tables 1.4 through 1.6 are actually carried out in terms of step counts, it is correct to interpret $t_P(n) = \Theta(g(n))$, or $t_P(n) = O(g(n))$, or $t_P(n) = \Omega(g(n))$ as a statement about the computing time of program P. This is so because each

line	s/e	frequency		total steps	
		$n = 0$	$n > 0$	$n = 0$	$n > 0$
1	0	-	-	0	$\Theta(0)$
2(a)	1	1	1	1	$\Theta(1)$
2(b)	1	1	0	1	$\Theta(0)$
3	$m + t_{rsum}(n-1)$	0	1	0	$\Theta(m + t_{rsum}(n-1))$
4	0	-	-	0	$\Theta(0)$
	$t_{rsum}(n) =$			2	$\Theta(m + t_{rsum}(n-1))$

Table 1.5 Asymptotic complexity of *rsum*

line(s)	s/e	frequency	total steps
1,2	0	0	$\Theta(0)$
3	1	$\Theta(m)$	$\Theta(m)$
4,5	1	$\Theta(mn)$	$\Theta(mn)$
6	0	-	$\Theta(0)$
	$t_{add}(m,n) =$		$\Theta(mn)$

Table 1.6 Asymptotic complexity of *add*

step takes only $\Theta(1)$ time to execute.

After you have had some experience using the table method, you will be in a position to arrive at the asymptotic complexity of a program by taking a more global approach. We elaborate on this method in the following examples.

Example 1.11: [*perm*] Consider procedure *perm* (Program 1.7). Assume that a is of size n. When $k = n$, we see that the time taken is $\Theta(n)$. When $k < n$, the **else** clause is entered. At this time, the second **for** loop is entered $n - k + 1$ times. Each iteration of this loop takes $\Theta(n + t_{perm}(k + 1, n))$ time. So, $t_{perm}(k, n) = \Theta((n - k + 1)(n + t_{perm}(k + 1, n)))$ when $k < n$. Since, $t_{perm}(k + 1, n)$, is at least n when $k + 1 \leq n$, we get $t_{perm}(k, n) = \Theta((n - k + 1)t_{perm}(k + 1, n))$ for $k < n$. Using the substitution method, we obtain $t(1,n) = \Theta(n(n!))$, $n \geq 1$. $\square$

Example 1.12: [Binary search] Let us obtain the time complexity of the binary search procedure *BinarySearch* (Program 1.4). The instance characteristic that we shall use is the number n of elements in a. Each iteration of the **while** loop takes $\Theta(1)$ time. We can show that the **while** loop is iterated at most $\lceil \log_2(n+1) \rceil$ times (see the book by S. Sahni cited in the references). Since an asymptotic analysis is being performed, we don't need such an accurate count of the worst case number of iterations. Each iteration except for the last results in a decrease in the size of the segment of a that has to be searched by a factor of about 2. So, this loop is iterated $\Theta(\log n)$ times in the worst case. As each iteration takes $\Theta(1)$ time, the overall worst case complexity of *BinarySearch* is $\Theta(\log n)$. Note that, if a were not a **var** parameter, the complexity of using *BinarySearch* would be more than this as it would take $\Omega(n)$ time just to invoke the procedure. □

Example 1.13: [Magic square] Our final example is a problem from recreational mathematics. A magic square is an $n \times n$ matrix of the integers 1 to n^2 such that the sum of every row, column and diagonal is the same. Figure 1.3 gives an example magic square for the case $n = 5$. In this example, the common sum is 65.

15	8	1	24	17
16	14	7	5	23
22	20	13	6	4
3	21	19	12	10
9	2	25	18	11

Figure 1.3 Example magic square

When n is odd H. Coxeter has given a simple rule for generating a magic square:
Start with 1 in the middle of the top row; then go up and left assigning numbers in increasing order to empty squares; if you fall off the square imagine the same square as tiling the plane and continue; if a square is occupied, move down instead and continue.

The magic square of Figure 1.3 was formed using this rule. Program 1.18 is the Pascal program for creating an $n \times n$ magic square for n odd that results from Coxeter's rule.

```
program magic (input, output);
{create a magic square of size n}
const MaxSize = 50; {maximum square size − 1}
var square : array [0..MaxSize, 0..MaxSize] of integer;
      i, j, k, l : integer; {indices}
      key : integer; {counter}
      n : integer; {square size}
begin
   readln(n);  {input square size}

{check correctness of n}
   if (n > MaxSize+1) or (n < 1)
   then writeln('error..n out of range')
   else
   if n mod 2 = 0 then writeln('error..n is even')

{n is odd; Coxeter's rule can be used}
   else begin
   for i := 0 to n−1 do {initialize square to zero}
     for j := 0 to n−1 do square [i,j] := 0;
   square [0,(n−1) div 2] := 1; {middle of first row}
   {i and j are current position}
   key := 2; i := 0; j := (n−1) div 2;
   while key <= n*n do
   begin
      {move up and left. The next two if statements may
      be replaced by the mod operator if −1 mod n is implemented to have value n−1}
      if i−1 < 0 then k := n−1 else k := i−1;
      if j−1 < 0 then l := n−1 else l := j−1;
      if square [k,l] < > 0
      then i := (i+1) mod n {square occupied, move down}
      else begin {square [k,l] is unoccupied}
             i := k;
             {the mod operator may be used here if −1 mod n = n−1}
             if j−1 < 0 then j := n−1
                        else j := j−1;
          end;
      square [i,j] := key;
      key := key+1;
   end; {of while}

   {output the magic square}
   writeln('magic square of size', n);
```

```
    for i := 0 to n−1 do
    begin
      for j := 0 to n−1 do
        write(square [i,j]);
      writeln;
    end; {of for}
        end; {of n is odd}
end. {of magic}
```

Program 1.18 Magic square

The magic square is represented using a two dimensional array having n rows and n columns. For this application it is convenient to number the rows (and columns) from zero to $n - 1$ rather than from one to n. Thus, when the program "falls off the square," the **mod** operator sets i and/or j back to zero or $n - 1$.

The **while** loop is governed by the variable *key* which is an integer variable initialized to 2 and increased by one each time through the loop. Thus, each statement within the **while** loop will be executed no more than $n^2 - 1$ times, and the computing time for *magic* is $O(n^2)$. Since there are n^2 positions in which the algorithm must place a number, we see that $O(n^2)$ is the best bound an algorithm for the magic square problem can have. □

1.3.1.4 Practical Complexities

We have seen that the time complexity of a program is generally some function of the instance characteristics. This function is very useful in determining how the time requirements vary as the instance characteristics change. The complexity function may also be used to compare two programs P and Q that perform the same task. Assume that program P has complexity $\Theta(n)$ and program Q is of complexity $\Theta(n^2)$. We can assert that program P is faster than program Q for "sufficiently large" n. To see the validity of this assertion, observe that the actual computing time of P is bounded from above by cn for some constant c and for all n, $n \geq n_1$, while that of Q is bounded from below by dn^2 for some constant d and all n, $n \geq n_2$. Since $cn \leq dn^2$ for $n \geq c/d$, program P is faster than program Q whenever $n \geq \max\{n_1, n_2, c/d\}$.

You should always be cautiously aware of the presence of the phrase "sufficiently large" in the assertion of the preceding discussion. When deciding which of the two programs to use, we must know whether the n we are dealing with is, in fact, "sufficiently large." If program P actually runs in $10^6 n$ milliseconds while program Q runs in n^2 milliseconds and if we always have $n \leq 10^6$, then, other factors being equal, program Q is the one to use, other factors being equal.

To get a feel for how the various functions grow with n, you are advised to study Table 1.7 and Figure 1.4 very closely. As is evident from the table and the figure, the function 2^n grows very rapidly with n. In fact, if a program needs 2^n steps for execution, then when $n = 40$, the number of steps needed is approximately $1.1*10^{12}$. On a computer performing 1 billion steps per second, this would require about 18.3 minutes. If $n = 50$, the same program would run for about 13 days on this computer. When $n = 60$, about 310.56 years will be required to execute the program and when $n = 100$, about $4*10^{13}$ years will be needed. So, we may conclude that the utility of programs with exponential complexity is limited to small n (typically $n \leq 40$).

$\log n$	n	$n \log n$	n^2	n^3	2^n
0	1	0	1	1	2
1	2	2	4	8	4
2	4	8	16	64	16
3	8	24	64	512	256
4	16	64	256	4096	65536
5	32	160	1024	32768	4294967296

Table 1.7 Function values

Programs that have a complexity that is a polynomial of high degree are also of limited utility. For example, if a program needs n^{10} steps, then using our 1 billion steps per second computer we will need 10 seconds when $n = 10$; 3,171 years when $n = 100$; and $3.17*10^{13}$ years when $n = 1000$. If the program's complexity had been n^3 steps instead, then we would need 1 second when $n = 1000$; 110.67 minutes when $n = 10,000$; and 11.57 days when $n = 100,000$.

Table 1.8 gives the time needed by a 1 billion instructions per second computer to execute a program of complexity $f(n)$ instructions. You should note that currently only the fastest computers can execute about 1 billion instructions per second. From a practical standpoint, it is evident that for reasonably large n (say $n > 100$), only programs of small complexity (such as n, $n\log n$, n^2, n^3) are feasible. Further, this is the case even if one could build a computer capable of executing 10^{12} instructions per second. In this case, the computing times of Table 1.8 would decrease by a factor of 1000. Now, when $n = 100$ it would take 3.17 years to execute n^{10} instructions, and $4*10^{10}$ years to execute 2^n instructions.

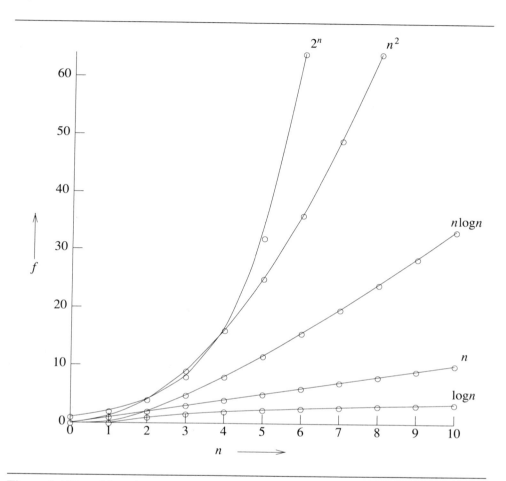

Figure 1.4 Plot of function values

n	$f(n)=n$	$f(n)=\log_2 n$	$f(n)=n^2$	$f(n)=n^3$	$f(n)=n^4$	$f(n)=n^{10}$	$f(n)=2^n$
				Time for $f(n)$ instructions on a 10^9 instr/sec computer			
10	.01μs	.03μs	.1μs	1μs	10μs	10sec	1μs
20	.02μs	.09μs	.4μs	8μs	160μs	2.84hr	1ms
30	.03μs	.15μs	.9μs	27μs	810μs	6.83d	1sec
40	.04μs	.21μs	1.6μs	64μs	2.56ms	121.36d	18.3min
50	.05μs	.28μs	2.5μs	125μs	6.25ms	3.1yr	13d
100	.10μs	.66μs	10μs	1ms	100ms	3171yr	$4*10^{13}$yr
1,000	1.00μs	9.96μs	1ms	1sec	16.67min	$3.17*10^{13}$yr	$32*10^{283}$yr
10,000	10.00μs	130.03μs	100ms	16.67min	115.7d	$3.17*10^{23}$yr	
100,000	100.00μs	1.66ms	10sec	11.57d	3171yr	$3.17*10^{33}$yr	
1,000,000	1.00ms	19.92ms	16.67min	31.71yr	$3.17*10^7$yr	$3.17*10^{43}$yr	

μs = microsecond = 10^{-6} seconds
ms = millisecond = 10^{-3} seconds
sec = seconds
min = minutes
hr = hours
d = days
yr = years

Table 1.8 Times on a 1 billion instruction per second computer

1.3.2 Performance Measurement

Performance measurement is concerned with obtaining the actual space and time requirements of a program. These quantities are dependent on the particular compiler and options used as well as on the specific computer on which the program is run. Unless otherwise stated, all performance values provided in this book are obtained using the Turbo Pascal compiler; the default compiler options are used; and the computer used is an early model IBM-PC.

In keeping with the discussion of the preceding section, we shall not concern ourselves with the space and time needed for compilation. We justify this by the assumption that each program (after it has been fully debugged) will be compiled once and then executed several times. Certainly, the space and time needed for compilation are important during program testing when more time is spent on this task than in actually running the compiled code.

We shall not explicitly consider measuring the run time space requirements of a program. Rather, we shall focus on measuring the computing time of a program. In order to obtain the computing (or run) time of a program, we need a clocking procedure. We assume the existence of a procedure *time* (*hsec*) which returns in the variable *hsec* the current time in hundredths of a second.

Suppose we wish to measure the worst case performance of the sequential search procedure (Program 1.19).

```
line  function seqsearch (a : ElementList ; n,x : integer): integer;
 1     var i : integer;
 2     begin
 3       i := n; a [0] := x;
 4       while a [i] <> x do
 5         i := i −1;
 6       seqsearch := i;
 7     end; {of seqsearch}
```

Program 1.19 Sequential search

Before we can do this, we need to:

(1)   decide on the values of *n* for which the times are to be obtained; and

(2)   determine, for each of the above values of *n*, the data that exhibits the worst case behavior.

The decision on which values of *n* to use is to be based on the amount of timing we wish to perform and also on what we expect to do with the times once they are obtained. Assume that for Program 1.19, our intent is to simply predict how long it will take, in the worst case, to search for *x* given the size *n* of *a*. An asymptotic analysis reveals that this time is $\Theta(n)$. So, we expect a plot of the times to be a straight line. Theoretically, if we know the times for any two values of n, the straight line is determined and we can obtain the time for all other values of n from this line. In practice, we need the times for more than two values of n. This is so for the following reasons:

(1) Asymptotic analysis only tells us the behavior for "sufficiently large" values of n. For smaller values of n the run time may not follow the asymptotic curve. To determine the point beyond which the asymptotic curve is followed, we need to examine the times for several values of n.

(2) Even in the region where the asymptotic behavior is exhibited, the times may not lie exactly on the predicted curve (straight line in the case of Program 1.19) because of the effects of low order terms that are discarded in the asymptotic analysis. For instance, a program with asymptotic complexity $\Theta(n)$ can have an actual complexity that is $c_1 n + c_2 \log n + c_3$, or for that matter any other function of n in which the highest order term is $c_1 n$ for some constant, $c_1, c_1 > 0$.

It is reasonable to expect that the asymptotic behavior of Program 1.19 will begin for some n that is smaller than 100. So, for $n > 100$ we shall obtain the run time for just a few values. A reasonable choice is $n = 200, 300, 400, \ldots, 1000$. There is nothing magical about this choice of values. We can just as well use $n = 500, 1000, 1500, \ldots, 10,000$ or $n = 512, 1024, 2048, \ldots, 2^{15}$. It will cost us more in terms of computer time to use the latter choices and we will probably not get any better information about the run time of Program 1.19 using these choices.

For n in the range [0, 100] we shall carry out a more refined measurement as we aren't quite sure where the asymptotic behavior begins. Of course, if our measurements show that the straight line behavior doesn't begin in this range, we shall have to perform a more detailed measurement in the range [100, 200] and so on, until the onset of this behavior is detected. Times in the range [0, 100] will be obtained in steps of 10 beginning at $n = 0$.

It is easy to see that Program 1.19 exhibits its worst case behavior when x is chosen such that it is not one of the $a[i]$s. For definiteness, we shall set $a[i] = i$, $1 \leq i \leq n$ and $x = 0$.

At this time, we envision using a program such as the one given in Program 1.20 to obtain the worst case times.

The output obtained from this program is summarized in Figure 1.5 The times obtained are too small to be of any use to us. Most of the times are zero indicating that the precision of our clock is inadequate. The nonzero times are just noise and not representative of the actual time taken.

In order to time a short event, it is necessary to repeat it several times and divide the total time for the event by the number of repetitions.

Since our clock has an accuracy of about one-hundredth of a second, we should not attempt to time any single event that takes less than about 1 second. With an event time of at least 1 second, we can expect our observed times to be accurate to 1 percent.

```
program TimeSearch(input,output);
{Program to time Program 1.19}
type ElementList = array [0..1000] of integer;
var z : ElementList;
    i, j, k, h, m, s, f, h 1, m 1, s 1, f1, t 1 : integer;
    n : array [1..20] of integer;

    .
    .
    .

begin {body of TimeSearch}
    for j := 1 to 1000 do {initialize z}
      z [j] := j;
    for j := 1 to 10 do  {values of n}
    begin
      n [j] := 10*(j−1); n [j +10] := 100*j;
    end;
    writeln('n':5,' ','time');
    for j := 1 to 20 do {obtain computing times}
    begin
      time (h); {get time}
      k := seqsearch (z, n [j], 0); {unsuccessful search}
      time (h 1); {get time}
      {time spent in hundredths of a second}
      t 1 := h 1−h;
      writeln(n [j]:5,' ',t 1:5);
    end;
    writeln('Times are in hundredths of a second'};
end. {of TimeSearch}
```

Program 1.20 Program to time Program 1.19

The body of Program 1.20 needs to be changed to that of Program 1.21. In this program, $r[i]$ is the number of times the search is to be repeated when the number of elements in the array is $n[i]$. Notice that rearranging the timing statements as in Programs 1.14 or 1.15 does not produce the desired results. For instance, from the data of Figure 1.5, we expect that with the structure of Program 1.22, the value output for $n = 0$ will still be 0. With the structure of Program 1.23, we expect the program to never exit the **while** loop when $n = 0$ (in reality, the loop will be exited as occasionally the measured time will turn out to be five- or six-hundredths of a second). Yet another alternative is to move the first call to *time* out of the **while** loop of Program 1.23, and change the

n	time	n	time
0	0	100	0
10	6	200	5
20	0	300	6
30	0	400	0
40	0	500	0
50	0	600	0
60	5	700	0
70	0	800	0
80	0	900	6
90	5	1000	5

Times in hundredths of a second

Figure 1.5 Output from Program 1.20

assignment to t within the **while** loop to

$$t := h1 - h;$$

This approach can be expected to yield satisfactory times. This approach cannot be used when the timing procedure available gives us only the time since the last invocation of *time*. Another difficulty is that the measured time includes the time needed to read the clock. For small n, this time may be larger than the time to run *search*. This difficulty can be overcome by determining the time taken by the timing procedure and subtracting this time later. In further discussion, we shall use the explicit repetition factor technique.

The output from the timing program, Program 1.21, is given in Figure 1.6. The times for n in the range [0, 100] are plotted in Figure 1.7. The remaining values have not been plotted as this would lead to severe compression of the range [0, 100]. The linear dependence of the worst case time on n is apparent from this graph.

The graph of Figure 1.7 can be used to predict the run time for other values of n. For example, we expect that when $n = 24$, the worst case search time will be 0.87 hundredths of a second. We can go one step further and get the equation of the straight line. The equation of this line is $t = c + mn$ where m is the slope and c the value for $n = 0$. From the graph, we see that $c = 0.78$. Using the point $n = 60$ and $t = 1.01$, we obtain $m = (t-c)/n = 0.23/60 = 0.00383$. So, the line of Figure 1.7 has the equation $t = 0.78 + 0.00383n$, where t is the time in hundredths of a second. From this, we expect that when $n = 1000$, the worst case search time will be 4.61 hsec and when $n = 500$, it will be 2.675 hsec. Compared with the actual observed times of Figure 1.6, we see that these figures are very accurate!

```
{repetition factors}
const r: array[1..20] of integer =
        (700, 700, 600, 600, 600, 600, 500, 500, 500, 500, 500,
        400, 400, 300, 300, 200, 200, 200, 100, 100);
begin {body of TimeSearch}
   for j := 1 to 1000 do {initialize z}
     z [j] := j;
   for j := 1 to 10 do  {values of n}
   begin
     n [j] := 10*(j−1); n [j +10] := 100*j;
   end;


   writeln('n':5,' ', 't 1',' ','t');
   for j := 1 to 20 do {obtain computing times}
   begin
     time (h); {get time}
     for b := 1 to r [j] do
       k := seqsearch (z, n [j], 0); {unsuccessful search}
     time (h); {get time}
     {time spent in hundredths of a second}
     t 1 := h 1−h;
     t := t 1; t := t/r [j]; {time per search}
     writeln(n [j]:5,' ',t 1:5, t:8:3);
   end;
   writeln('Times are in hundredths of a second'};
end. {of TimeSearch}
```

Program 1.21 Timing program

An alternate approach to obtain a good straight line for the data of Figure 1.6 is to obtain the straight line that is the least squares approximation to the data. The result is $t = 0.77747 + 0.003806n$. When $n = 1000$ and 500, this equation yields $t = 4.583$ and 2.680.

Now, we are probably ready to pat ourselves on the back for a job well done. However, this action is somewhat premature as our experiment is flawed. First, the measured time includes the time taken by the repetition **for** loop. So, the times of Figure 1.6 are excessive. This can be corrected by determining the time for each iteration of this statement. A quick test run indicates that 30,000 executions take only 65 hundredths of a second. So, subtracting the time for the **for** $b := 1$ **to** $r [j]$ **do** statement reduces the reported times by only 0.002. We can ignore this difference as the use of a higher repetition factor could well result in measured times that are lower by about 0.002 hsec per search. Our times are not accurate to a hundredth of a second and it is not very

---

```
t := 0;
for b := 1 to r [ j ] do
begin
    time (h);
    k := seqsearch (a, n [ j ], 0);
    time (h);
    t := t + h 1 − h;
end;
t := t/r [ j ];
```

Program 1.22 Improper timing construct

```
t := 0; i := 0;
while t < DesiredTime do
begin
    time (h);
    k := seqsearch (a, n [ j ], 0);
    time (h 1);
    t := t + h 1 − h;
    i := i +1;
end;
t := t/i;
```

Program 1.23 Another improper timing construct

meaningful to worry about the two-hundredths of a second spent on each repetition.

The second and more serious problem is caused by the fact that *ElementList* has been defined to be an array of size 1000. Consequently, each invocation of *seqsearch* begins by copying the 1000 values of the actual parameter z into the value formal parameter a. The measured times are therefore representative of the actual time to use *seqsearch* only when *ElementList* is of this size! If the size of *ElementList* is changed to 2000 or 10,000, the measured times will change. A substantial part of the time reported in this figure is the time spent copying the 1000 elements of the actual parameter into the formal parameter.

So, what constitutes a meaningful test for Program 1.19? The size of *ElementList* isn't known to us, and yet it is perhaps the most important factor. The realization that the worst case run time of Program 1.19 is a function of both n and s (the size of *ElementList*, i.e., 1001 in the case of Program 1.20) motivates us to obtain the time for the body of Program 1.19 and that for its invocation separately. The former is independent of s and the latter is independent of n. The total time to use Program 1.19 is the sum

n	$t1$	t	n	$t1$	t
0	549	0.784	100	582	1.164
10	571	0.816	200	615	1.537
20	516	0.860	300	763	1.907
30	539	0.898	400	686	2.287
40	555	0.925	500	801	2.670
50	583	0.972	600	610	3.050
60	505	1.010	700	687	3.435
70	522	1.044	800	758	3.790
80	538	1.076	900	826	4.230
90	566	1.132	1000	922	4.610

Times in hundredths of a second

Figure 1.6 Worst case run times for Program 1.19

of these two times.

To obtain the time for the body of Program 1.19, we place the timing loop directly into function *seqsearch* as in Program 1.24. This is preferable to placing the code of *seqsearch* directly into the body of *TimeSearch*. This is because the strategy of Program 1.24 yields times that include the overhead of using parameters.

When Program 1.24 is used in place of Program 1.19, and the timing and repetition statements removed from Program 1.20, the times shown in Figure 1.8 are obtained. The repetition factors used are $r[1..20] = [32000, 12000, 6000, 5000, 4000, 3000, 2500, 2000, 2000, 1500, 1500, 800, 600, 500, 400, 300, 200, 200, 150, 150]$.

The time of 0.002 for each execution of the repetition **for** statement needs to be subtracted from the times of Figure 1.8. This subtraction has a material effect (i.e., at least 10 percent) only on the time for $n = 0$.

To time the invocation of Program 1.19 for different sizes s of *ElementList*, we delete all statements between the **begin** and **end** statements of Program 1.19 and run Program 1.20 for different values of s. The repetition factor needed varies with s. The observed times for various values of s are shown in Figure 1.9. Again, the time for the repetition **for** loop has not been subtracted. This does not materially affect the times shown.

The least squares straight line for the data of Figure 1.8 is $t = 0.008531 + 0.003785n$ and that for Figure 1.9 is $t = 0.018009 + 0.000756s$. Adding these two contributions, we get $t = 0.02654 + 0.000756s + 0.003785n$. We can see how good this equation is in predicting actual run times by using it with $s = 1000$. The equation becomes $t = 0.78254 + 0.003785n$. This is quite close to the least squares line for the data of Program 1.20.

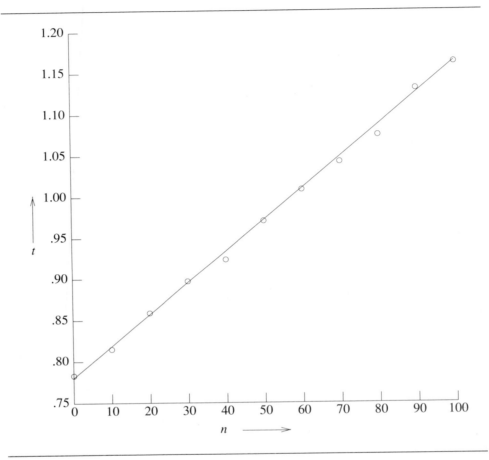

Figure 1.7 Plot of the data in Figure 1.6

Note that we can make the run time of *seqsearch* independent of *s* by making *a* a variable formal parameter.

Summary
    In order to obtain the run time of a program, we need to plan the experiment. The following issues need to be addressed during the planning stage:

(1)   What is the accuracy of the clock? How accurate do our results have to be? Once the desired accuracy is known, we can determine the length of the shortest event that should be timed.

```
function seqsearch (a : ElementList ; n,x : integer): integer;
var i, k : integer;
begin
  time (h); {get time}
  for k := 1 to r [j] do {r [j] is global}
  begin
    i := n; a [0] := x;
    while a [i] <> x do
      i := i −1;
    seqsearch := i;
  end; {of repetition for}
  time (h 1); {get time}
  {time spent in hundredths of a second}
  t 1 := h 1−h;
  t := t 1; t := t/r [j]; {time per search}
  writeln(n [j]:5,' ',t 1:5, t:8:3);
end; {of seqsearch}
```

Program 1.24 Timing the body of *seqsearch*

n	t 1	t	n	t 1	t
0	275	0.009	100	583	0.389
10	560	0.047	200	610	0.762
20	511	0.085	300	687	1.145
30	610	0.122	400	764	1.528
40	643	0.161	500	758	1.895
50	594	0.198	600	686	2.287
60	593	0.237	700	527	2.635
70	544	0.272	800	609	3.045
80	626	0.313	900	511	3.407
90	522	0.348	1000	571	3.807

Times in hundredths of a second

Figure 1.8 Times for body of Program 1.19 using Program 1.24

s	r	time	time/r
10	30,000	769	0.026
20	30,000	999	0.033
30	30,000	1225	0.041
40	20,000	967	0.048
50	12,000	670	0.056
60	12,000	767	0.064
70	10,000	714	0.071
80	10,000	791	0.079
90	10,000	862	0.086
100	10,000	939	0.094
200	5,000	846	0.169
500	2,000	795	0.398
1000	1,000	774	0.774
5000	200	758	3.790
10,000	100	758	7.58

Times in hundredths of a second

Figure 1.9 Time needed to invoke Program 1.19

(2)   For each instance size, a repetition factor needs to be determined. This is to be chosen such that the event time is at least the minimum time that can be clocked with the desired accuracy.

(3)   Are we measuring worst case or average case performance? Suitable test data needs to be generated.

(4)   What is the purpose of the experiment? Are the times being obtained for comparative purposes, or are they to be used to predict actual run times? If the latter is the case, then contributions to the run time from such sources as the repetition loop and data generation need to be subtracted (in case they are included in the measured time). If the former is the case, then these times need not be subtracted (provided they are the same for all programs being compared).

(5)   In case the times are to be used to predict actual run times, then we need to fit a curve through the points. For this, the asymptotic complexity should be known. If the asymptotic complexity is linear, then a least squares straight line can be fit; if it is quadratic, then a parabola is to be used (i.e., $t = a_0 + a_1 n + a_2 n^2$). If the complexity is $\Theta(n \log n)$, then a least squares curve of the form $t = a_0 + a_1 n + a_2 n \log_2 n$ can be fit. When obtaining the least squares approximation, one should discard data corresponding to "small" values of n as the program does not exhibit its asymptotic behavior for these n.

1.3.3 Generating Test Data

Generating a data set that results in the worst case performance of a program isn't always easy. In some cases, it is necessary to use a computer program to generate the worst case data. In other cases, even this is very difficult. In these cases, another approach to estimating worst case performance is taken. For each set of values of the instance characteristics of interest, we generate a suitably large number of random test data. The run times for each of these test data are obtained. The maximum of these times is used as an estimate of the worst case time for this set of values of the instance characteristics.

To measure average case times, it is usually not possible to average over all possible instances of a given characteristic. While it is possible to do this for sequential and binary search, it is not possible for a sort program. If we assume that all keys are distinct, then for any given n, $n!$ different permutations need to be used to obtain the average time.

Obtaining average case data is usually much harder than obtaining worst case data. So, we often adopt the strategy outlined above and simply obtain an estimate of the average time.

Whether we are estimating worst case or average time using random data, the number of instances that we can try is generally much smaller than the total number of such instances. Hence, it is desirable to analyze the algorithm being tested to determine classes of data that should be generated for the experiment. This is a very algorithm specific task and we shall not go into it here.

1.4 ALGORITHM DESIGN METHODS

1.4.1 Introduction

While the design of a good algorithm for any given problem is more an art than a science, there are some design methods that have proved effective in the solution of many problems. These methods are studied in this section. When posed with a problem for computer solution, you can apply these methods and see how good the resulting algorithm is. Generally, it will be necessary to fine tune the resulting algorithm to get acceptable performance. In some cases, this fine tuning will not be possible and you will have to think of some other way to solve the problem.

Many of the examples used in this section are *optimization problems*. In an optimization problem we are given a set of *constraints* and an *optimization function*. Solutions that satisfy the constraints are called *feasible solutions*. A feasible solution for which the optimization function has the best possible value is called an *optimal solution*.

Example 1.14: [Loading problem] A large ship is to be loaded with cargo. The cargo is containerized and each container has the same size. Different containers may have different weight. Let w_i be the weight of the ith container, $1 \le i \le n$. The cargo capacity of the ship is c. We wish to load the ship with the maximum number of containers.

This problem can be formulated as an optimization problem in the following way. Let x_i be a variable whose value can be either 0 or 1. If we set x_i to 0, then container i is not to be loaded. If x_i is 1, then it is to be loaded. We wish to assign values to the x_is that satisfy the constraints:

$$\sum_{i=1}^{n} w_i x_i \leq c$$

and

$$x_i \in \{0,1\}, \quad 1 \leq i \leq n$$

The optimization function is:

$$\sum_{i=1}^{n} x_i$$

Every set of x_is that satisfies the constraints is a feasible solution. Every feasible solution that maximizes $\sum_{i=1}^{n} x_i$ is an optimal solution. □

Example 1.15: [Thirsty baby] In this problem a thirsty baby needs to drink a total of t units of liquids to quench her thirst. There are n different liquids and a_i units of the i'th liquid are available. Each unit of the i'th liquid provides s_i units of satisfaction. The baby's objective is to quench her thirst and derive maximum satisfaction while doing so. Let x_i denote the amount of liquid i the baby elects to drink. The constraints are:

$$\sum_{i=1}^{n} x_i = t$$

and

$$0 \leq x_i \leq a_i$$

The optimization function is:

$$\sum_{i=1}^{n} s_i x_i$$

Every set of x_is that satisfies the constraints is a feasible solution. Every feasible solution that maximizes $\sum_{i=1}^{n} s_i x_i$ is an optimal solution. □

1.4.2 Greedy Method

In the *greedy* method we attempt to construct an optimal solution in stages. At each stage, we make a decision that appears to be the best (under some criterion) at this time. Since this decision cannot be changed at a later stage, the decision should be such that feasibility is assured.

Loading Problem

The terminology is from Example 1.14. The greedy method to load the ship is to first select the container that has least weight, then the one with the next smallest weight, and so on until either all containers have been loaded or there isn't enough capacity for the next one.

Suppose that $n = 8$, $w[1:8] = [100, 200, 50, 90, 150, 50, 20, 80]$, and $c = 400$. Using the greedy algorithm outlined above, the containers are considered for loading in the order 7, 3, 6, 8, 4, 1, 5, 2. Containers 7, 3, 6, 8, 4, and 1 together weigh 390 units. This leaves us with a capacity of 10 units. This is inadequate for any of the remaining containers. In the greedy solution, we have $x[1:8] = [1, 0, 1, 1, 0, 1, 1, 1]$ and $\sum x[i] = 6$.

The optimality of the solution produced by the greedy algorithm above may be established in the following way. Let $x[1:n]$ be the solution produced by the greedy algorithm. Let $y[1:n]$ be any feasible solution. We shall show that $\sum_{i=1}^{n} x[i] \geq \sum_{i=1}^{n} y[i]$. Without loss of generality, we may assume that the containers have been ordered so that $w[i] \leq w[i+1]$, $1 \leq i \leq n$. We shall transform y, in several steps, into x. Each step of the transformation will produce a new y that is feasible and for which $\sum_{i=1}^{n} y[i]$ is no smaller than before the transformation. As a result, $\sum_{i=1}^{n} x[i] \geq \sum_{i=1}^{n} y[i]$ initially.

From the way the greedy algorithm works, it follows that there is a k in the range $[0, n]$ such that $x[i] = 1$, $i \leq k$ and $x[i] = 0$, $i > k$. Find the least integer, j, in the range $[1, n]$ such that $x[j] \neq y[j]$. If no such j exists, then $\sum_{i=1}^{n} x[i] = \sum_{i=1}^{n} y[i]$. If such a j exists, then $j \leq k$ as otherwise y is not a feasible solution. Since, $x[j] \neq y[j]$ and $x[j] = 1$, it follows that $y[j] = 0$. Set $y[j]$ to 1. If the resulting y denotes an infeasible solution, there must be an l in the range $[j+1, n]$ for which $y[l] = 1$. Set $y[l]$ to 0. As $w[j] \leq w[l]$, the resulting y is feasible. Also, the new y has at least as many 1's as the old one.

By repeatedly using this transformation several times, y may be transformed into x. As each transformation produces a new y that has at least as many ones as the previous one, it follows that x has at least as many ones as does the y we started with.

A pseudo Pascal version of the greedy algorithm for the loading problem is given in Program 1.25. Since the sort can be carried out in O($n\log n$) time (see Chapter 7) and the remainder of the algorithm takes O(n) time, its overall time complexity is O($n\log n$).

```
procedure LoadingProblem(var x : answers ; w : weights ;
                            c : capacity ; n : integer);
{Greedy algorithm for the loading problem}
var t: array [1..MaxContainers ]; i: integer;  NotDone: boolean;
begin
    Use a sort procedure to set t [1..n ] so that w [t [i ]] ≤ w [t [i +1]], 1≤i <n.
    i := 1; NotDone := true;
    Set x [1:n] to 0;
    while (i <= n) and NotDone do
        if w [t [i ]] <= c then begin {it fits}
                            x [t [i ]] := 1;
                            c := c −w [t [i ]];
                            i := i +1;
                        end
                    else NotDone := false; {no more fit}
end; {of LoadingProblem}
```

Program 1.25 Pseudo-Pascal code for greedy loading algorithm

0/1 Knapsack Problem

This is a generalization of the loading problem to the case where the profit earned from each container is different. The problem formulation is:

$$\text{maximize} \sum_{i=1}^{n} p [i]x [i]$$

subject to the constraints:

$$\sum_{i=1}^{n} w [i]x [i] \leq c$$

and

$$x [i] \in \{0,1\}, \ 1 \leq i \leq n$$

Several greedy strategies for this problem are possible. We may load our ship by being greedy on profit. The container with the largest p is loaded first (provided enough capacity is available); then the one with next largest p, and so on. This strategy does not guarantee an optimal solution. For instance, consider the case $n = 3$, $w [1:3] = [100, 10, 10]$, $p [1:3] = [20, 15, 15]$, and $c = 105$. When we are greedy on profit, the solution $x [1:3] = [1, 0, 0]$ is obtained. The total profit from this solution is 20. The optimal solution is $[0, 1, 1]$. This solution has profit 30.

An alternative is to be greedy on weight. Load the ship in nondecreasing order of weight. While this yields an optimal solution for the above instance, it does not do so in general. Consider the instance: $n = 2$, $w[1:2] = [10, 20]$, $p[1:2] = [5, 100]$, and $c = 25$. When we are greedy on weight, we obtain the solution $x[1:2] = [1, 0]$. This is inferior to the solution $[0, 1]$.

Yet another possibility is to be greedy on profit density. This is the ratio $p[i]/w[i]$. Load the ship by considering the containers in nonincreasing order of the profit density. This strategy does not guarantee optimal solutions either. To see this, simply consider the instance $n = 3$, $w[1:3] = [20, 15, 15]$, $p[1:3] = [40, 25, 25]$, and $c = 30$.

The moral of this example is that there exist problems for which it is quite easy to formulate greedy algorithms that generate feasible solutions. However, *it is necessary to prove that these algorithms generate an optimal solution.* It will often be the case that what appears to be a promising algorithm actually does not guarantee optimality.

1.4.3 Divide-and-Conquer Method

The *divide-and-conquer* methodology is very similar to the modularization approach to software design. To solve a large problem, we divide it into some number of smaller problems; solve each of these; and combine these solutions to obtain the solution to the original problem. Often, the subproblems generated are simply smaller instances of the original problem and may be solved using the divide-and-conquer strategy recursively.

We have already seen one example of the divide-and-conquer strategy: binary search. To search for x in the sorted array $a[1..n]$, we search for x in the three sub arrays: $a[1..mid-1]$, $a[mid..mid]$, and $a[mid+1..n]$. By comparing the keys of x and $a[mid]$, two of these three searches can be eliminated.

Before looking at further examples, we study how to solve the recurrence equations that most frequently arise when divide-and-conquer algorithms are analyzed. The complexity of many divide-and-conquer algorithms is given by a recurrence of the form:

$$t(n) = \begin{cases} t(1) & n=1 \\ a*t(n/b)+g(n) & n>1 \end{cases} \tag{1.1}$$

where a and b are known constants. We shall assume that $t(1)$ is known and that n is a power of b. It can be shown that

$$t(n) = n^{\log_b a}[t(1) + f(n)]$$

where $f(n) = \sum_{j=1}^{k} h(b^j)$ and $h(n) = g(n)/n^{\log_b a}$.

Figure 1.10 tabulates the asymptotic value of $f(n)$ for various values of $h(n)$. This table allows one to easily obtain the asymptotic value of $t(n)$ for many of the recurrences one encounters when analyzing divide-and-conquer algorithms.

$h(n)$	$f(n)$
$O(n^r), r < 0$	$O(1)$
$\Theta((log n)^i), i \geq 0$	$\Theta(((log n)^{i+1})/(i+1))$
$\Omega(n^r), r > 0$	$\Theta(h(n))$

Figure 1.10 $f(n)$ values for various $h(n)$ values

Let us consider some examples using this table. The recurrence for binary search when n is a power of 2 is:

$$t(n) = \begin{cases} t(1) & n=1 \\ t(n/2)+c & n>1 \end{cases}$$

Comparing with Equation (1.1), we see that $a = 1$, $b = 2$, and $g(n) = c$. So, $log_b(a) = 0$ and $h(n) = g(n)/n^{log_b a} = c = c(log n)^0 = \Theta((log n)^0)$. From Figure 1.10, we obtain: $f(n) = \Theta(log n)$. So, $t(n) = n^{log_b a}(c + \Theta(log n)) = \Theta(log n)$.

As another example, consider the recurrence:

$$t(n) = 7t(n/2) + 18n^2, n \geq 2 \text{ and } n \text{ a power of } 2$$

we obtain: $a = 7$, $b = 2$, and $g(n) = 18n^2$. So, $log_b a = log_2 7 \sim 2.81$ and $h(n) = 18n^2/n^{log_2 7} = 18n^{2-log_2 7} = O(n^r)$ where $r = 2 - log_2 7 < 0$. So, $f(n) = O(1)$. The expression for $t(n)$ is:

$$t(n) = n^{log_2 7}(t(1) + O(1))$$

$$= \Theta(n^{log_2 7})$$

as $t(1)$ is assumed to be a constant.

As another example, consider the recurrence:

$$t(n) = 9t(n/3) + 4n^6, n \geq 3 \text{ and a power of } 3$$

Comparing with Equation (1.1), we obtain $a = 9$, $b = 3$, and $g(n) = 4n^6$. So, $log_b a = 2$ and $h(n) = 4n^6/n^2 = 4n^4 = \Omega(n^4)$. From Figure 1.11, we see that $f(n) = \Theta(h(n)) =$

$\Theta(n^4)$. So,

$$t(n) = n^2(t(1)+\Theta(n^4))$$

$$= \Theta(n^6)$$

as $t(1)$ may be assumed constant.

Suppose that we wish to multiply two positive n digit integers x and y. Doing this using the classical long multiplication method takes $O(n^2)$ time. The divide-and-conquer strategy suggests we split each number into two parts, left and right, with each part containing approximately half the number of digits. For simplicity, we assume that n is a power of 2. With this assumption x and y can each be split into two parts with an equal number of digits. Additionally, these parts can be further split into halves and the halves further split and so on. Let $x_l, x_r, y_l,$ and y_r denote the four parts obtained by this splitting. Then, $x = x_l 10^{n/2} + x_r$ and $y = y_l 10^{n/2} + y_r$. Hence the product xy may be computed as:

$$xy = (x_l 10^{n/2} + x_r)(y_l 10^{n/2} + y_r)$$
$$= x_l y_l 10^n + (x_l y_r + x_r y_l)10^{n/2} + x_r y_r$$

If the products $x_l y_l, x_l y_r, x_r y_l,$ and $x_r y_r$ are computed using the above splitting process recursively and the recursion stopped when the numbers to be multiplied have one digit each, then the complexity of the divide-and-conquer integer product algorithm becomes:

$$t(n) = \begin{cases} k & n=1 \\ 4t(n/2) + cn & n>1 \end{cases}$$

where k is a constant that represents the time to multiply two one digit integers and c is a constant such that cn accounts for the time needed to perform all operations other than the four products of pairs of $n/2$ digit integers. Using the table method we obtain $t(n) = n^2$. This is no better than when the classical multiplication method is used.

If we compute $x_l y_r + x_r y_l$ as $(x_l + x_r)(y_l + y_r) - x_l y_l - x_r y_r$, then the number of $n/2$ digit products to be computed recursively is three instead of four. The number of add/subtracts, however, increases from three to six. The complexity of the resulting divide-and-conquer integer product algorithm is:

$$t(n) = \begin{cases} a & n=1 \\ 3t(n/2) + bn & n>1 \end{cases}$$

where a and b are constants. Using the table method, we obtain $t(n) = O(n^{1.581})$.

Next consider the problem of multiplying two $n \times n$ matrices A and B to get the product matrix C where $C(i,j)$ is given by:

$$C(i,j) = \sum_{k=1}^{n} A(i,k)*B(k,j)$$

for $1 \le i \le n$ and $1 \le j \le n$. Using this equation directly, each $C(i,j)$ can be computed in $O(n)$ time. Hence the n^2 entries of C can be computed in $O(n^3)$ time.

Using the divide-and-conquer strategy, we partition each of the three matrices A, B, and C into four $n/2 \times n/2$ matrices as shown in Figure 1.12 (again, we assume that n is a power of 2). The four submatrices of C are related to the submatrices of A and B by the equations:

$$C_{11} = A_{11}B_{11} + A_{12}B_{21}$$
$$C_{12} = A_{11}B_{12} + A_{12}B_{22}$$
$$C_{21} = A_{21}B_{11} + A_{22}B_{21}$$
$$C_{22} = A_{21}B_{12} + A_{22}B_{22}$$

$$\begin{bmatrix} A_{11} & A_{12} \\ A_{21} & A_{22} \end{bmatrix} \begin{bmatrix} B_{11} & B_{12} \\ B_{21} & B_{22} \end{bmatrix} = \begin{bmatrix} C_{11} & C_{12} \\ C_{21} & C_{22} \end{bmatrix}$$

Figure 1.12 Partitioning into $n/2 \times n/2$ submatrices

If matrix products of the form $A_{ik}B_{kj}$ are computed using the above division strategy recursively until A_{ij} is a $1 \hat{} \times \hat{} 1$ matrix then the complexity, $t(n)$, of the resulting algorithm is given by the recurrence

$$t(n) = \begin{cases} a & n=1 \\ 8t(n/2) + bn^2 & n>1 \end{cases}$$

where a is the time needed to multiply two numbers and b is a constant such that bn^2 is the time needed to perform four matrix additions of size $n/2 \times n/2$. Using the table method, we obtain $t(n) = O(n^3)$. The resulting divide-and-conquer algorithm is actually slower than the classical $O(n^3)$ algorithm by a constant factor because of the overheads involved in the former.

By trading one matrix product with several less expensive matrix additions we can obtain a divide-and-conquer algorithm that is asymptotically superior to the classical algorithm. Suppose the C_{ij}'s are computed using the following sequence of computations

$$P = (A_{11} + A_{22})(B_{11} + B_{22})$$

$$Q = (A_{21} + A_{22})B_{11}$$
$$R = A_{11}(B_{12} - B_{22})$$
$$S = A_{22}(B_{21} - B_{11})$$
$$T = (A_{11} + A_{12})B_{22}$$
$$U = (A_{21} - A_{11})(B_{11} + B_{12})$$
$$V = (A_{12} - A_{22})(B_{21} + B_{22})$$

$$C_{11} = P + S - T + V$$
$$C_{12} = R + T$$
$$C_{21} = Q + S$$
$$C_{22} = P + R - Q + U$$

The total number of matrix products is seven and that of matrix additions is 18. Suppose the matrix products are performed using the above strategy recursively until the matrix size becomes 1×1. The complexity of the divide-and-conquer matrix multiplication algorithm is now given by the recurrence

$$t(n) = \begin{cases} a & n = 1 \\ 7t(n/2) + bn^2 & n > 1 \end{cases}$$

where a and b are constants. The solution to this recurrence is $t(n) = O(n^{\log_2 7}) \sim O(n^{2.81})$.

1.4.4 Dynamic Programming Method

Dynamic programming is an algorithm design method that can be used when the solution to a problem may be viewed as the result of a sequence of decisions. The solution to the 0/1 knapsack problem of Section 1.4.2 may be so viewed. The values of $x[i]$, $1 \le i \le n$ need to be determined. We can first make a decision on $x[1]$, then on $x[2]$, then on $x[3]$, and so on. An optimal decision sequence is one which maximizes $\sum_{=1}^{n} p[i]x[i]$ and also satisfies the constraints $\sum_{i=1}^{n} w[i]x[i] \le c$ and $x[i] \in \{0, 1\}$, $1 \le i \le n$.

For some of the problems that may be viewed in this way, an optimal decision sequence can be constructed making the decisions one at a time and never making an erroneous decision. This is true for all problems solvable by the greedy method. For many problems an optimal decision sequence cannot be constructed in this way. For these problems, a possible strategy is to enumerate all possible decision sequences and determine which is optimal. In dynamic programming, the enumeration effort is drastically reduced by avoiding the enumeration of certain decision sequences that cannot possibly be optimal.

An optimal decision sequence is arrived at by making explicit appeal to the *Principle of optimality*. This states that *an optimal decision sequence has the property that whatever the initial state and decision are, the remaining decisions must constitute an optimal decision sequence with regard to the state that results from the first decision.* Since the principle of optimality does not hold for every problem whose solution may be viewed as the result of a sequence of decisions, dynamic programming is not applicable to all decision problems. The essential difference between the greedy method and dynamic programming is that when the former is used only one decision sequence is generated. In dynamic programming many decision sequences may be generated. However, sequences containing suboptimal subsequences are not generated as these cannot be optimal (if the principle of optimality holds).

We may verify that the principle of optimality holds for the 0/1 knapsack problem. Suppose that $x[i] = y[i]$, $1 \leq i \leq n$ is an optimal solution. Then $y[2], \ldots, y[n]$ must be an optimal solution to the knapsack instance

$$\text{maximize } \sum_{i=2}^{n} p[i]x[i]$$

subject to the constraints:

$$\sum_{i=2}^{n} w[i]x[i] \leq c - w[1]y[1]$$

and

$$x[i] \in \{0,1\}, \ 2 \leq i \leq n$$

If we define a knapsack state to be the remaining capacity, then the sequence $y[2], \ldots, y[n]$ must be optimal with respect to the state, $c - w[1]y[1]$, following the decision on $x[1]$.

For simplicity, assume that the weights w and the capacity c are positive integers. Let $f_j(l)$ be the value of an optimal solution to the knapsack instance

$$\text{maximize } \sum_{i=j+1}^{n} p[i]x[i]$$

subject to the constraints:

$$\sum_{i=j+1}^{n} w[i]x[i] \leq l$$

and

$$x[i] \in \{0,1\}, \; j+1 \le i \le n$$

$f_0(c)$ is the value of an optimal solution to the original n object knapsack instance; $f_n(l)$ is zero for all l, $l \ge 0$; $f_j(0) = 0$, for all j; and $f_j(l) = -\infty$ for all $l < 0$ and all j. From the principle of optimality it follows that

$$f_j(l) = \max\{f_{j+1}(l), \; f_{j+1}(l - w[j+1]) + p[j+1]\}$$

Since f_n is known, the above equation can be used to compute f_{n-1}. Using f_{n-1} and this equation, f_{n-2} can be computed. Continuing in this way, f_0 can be obtained.

As an example of this computation, consider the case $n = 5$, $p[1..5] = [5, 10, 2, 4, 8]$, $w[1..5] = [3, 4, 2, 1, 5]$, and $c = 10$. The functions $f_5, \ldots, f_0$ are given in Figure 1.13. The optimal solution has value $f_0(10) = 22$. The optimal decision sequence can be found by beginning at $f_0(c)$. If $f_0(c) = f_1(c)$, then we can set $x[1] = 0$. If this is not the case, then it must be that $f_1(c - w[1]) = f_0(c) - p[1]$ and we can set $x[1] = 1$. In the example, $f_0(10) = f_1(10)$. So, we set $x[1] = 0$. For $x[2]$, we compare $f_1(10)$ and $f_2(10)$. Since these are not equal, we set $x[2] = 1$. The remaining capacity is $10 - w[2] = 6$. For $x[3]$, we compare $f_2(6)$ and $f_3(6)$. These are equal. So, $x[3] = 0$. Since $f_3(6) \ne f_4(6)$, $x[4] = 1$, and the capacity that remains is $6 - w[4] = 5$. Now, since $f_4(5) \ne f_5(5)$, $x[5] = 1$.

	(1)	(2)	(3)	(4)	(5)	(6)	(7)	(8)	(9)	(10)
f_5	0	0	0	0	0	0	0	0	0	0
f_4	0	0	0	0	8	8	8	8	8	8
f_3	4	4	4	4	8	12	12	12	12	12
f_2	4	4	6	6	8	12	12	14	14	14
f_1	4	4	6	10	14	14	16	16	18	22
f_0	4	4	6	10	14	14	16	19	19	22

Figure 1.13 0/1 knapsack example

The complexity of the dynamic programming solution to the 0/1 knapsack problem is seen to be $O(nc)$.

As another example of the application of dynamic programming, consider the string editing problem. The inputs to this problem are: two strings $A = a_1 \ldots a_n$ and $B = b_1 \ldots b_m$; and three cost functions C, D, and I. $C(i,j)$ is the cost of changing a_i to b_j, $1 \le i \le n$, $1 \le j \le m$; $D(i)$ is the cost of deleting a_i from string A, $1 \le i \le n$; and $I(i)$ is the cost of inserting b_i into string A.

The string A is to be edited using a sequence of *change*, *delete*, and *insert* operations. The result of the editing is string B. The cost of the edit sequence is the sum of the costs of the individual edit operations. Suppose that $n = 3$, $m = 4$, $D = [6, 1, 2]$, $I = [5, 3, 1, 1]$, and C is the matrix:

$$
\begin{array}{cccc}
1 & 2 & 1 & 1 \\
2 & 1 & 2 & 2 \\
3 & 1 & 2 & 4
\end{array}
$$

The edit sequence: delete a_i, $1 \le i \le n$; insert b_i, $1 \le i \le m$ transforms A into B. The cost of this sequence is $\sum_{i=1}^{n} D(i) + \sum_{i=1}^{m} I(i) = 9 + 10 = 19$. Another edit sequence that transforms A to B is: change a_1 to b_1; change a_2 to b_2; delete a_3; insert b_3; insert b_4. The cost of this sequence is $1 + 1 + 2 + 1 + 1 = 6$.

The objective of the string edit problem is to find a least cost edit sequence to transform A to B. The solution may be regarded as a decision sequence in which the first decision is to determine j_1 such that $a_1 \ldots a_{j_1}$ is edited to b_1. The next is to determine $j_2 \ge j_1$ such that $a_1 \ldots a_{j_2}$ is edited to $b_1 b_2$. The remaining decisions are to determine $j_3, \ldots, j_m$. An optimal edit of a substring of A to a single character of B is easy to find. The pair (j_i, i) defines the problem state following decision i. The principle of optimality holds as given a state, the remaining edits must form an optimal edit sequence with respect to this state.

Define $cost(i, j)$ to be the cost of a least cost edit sequence to transform $a_1 \ldots a_i$ to $b_1 \ldots b_j$. $cost(n, m)$ is the cost of an optimal edit sequence to transform A to B. For i or j or both equal to zero we get the following:

$$
\begin{aligned}
cost(0, 0) &= 0 \\
cost(i, 0) &= \sum_{k=1}^{i} D(k), \; 1 \le i \le n \\
cost(0, j) &= \sum_{k=1}^{j} I(k), \; 1 \le j \le m
\end{aligned}
$$

For $i > 0$ and $j > 0$, the following recurrence is obtained:

$$
cost(i, j) = \min\{cost(i-1, j)+D(i), \; cost(i-1, j-1)+C(i,j), \; cost(i, j-1)+I(j)\}
$$

This recurrence can be used to obtain $cost(n, m)$ and also the optimal edit sequence. If we compute the $cost$ terms in increasing order of the sum $i + j$, then the terms on the right hand side of the above recurrence are computed before the term on the left hand side. So, the right hand side terms are known when we are ready to compute the left hand side term. Hence, we shall compute $cost$ in order of its off diagonals. That is, compute $cost(i, j)$ for all i and j such that $i + j = k$ in the order $k = 2, 3, \ldots, n+m$. Program 1.26 gives a procedure that computes $cost$ in this manner. In this procedure $min\,2$, $min\,3$, and $max\,2$ are, respectively, functions that return the smaller of its two parameters, the smallest of its three parameters, and the larger of its two parameters. The complexity of procedure $StringEdit$ is O(mn).

```
procedure StringEdit;
{Compute the global cost matrix cost; cost [i, j] for i = 0
and/or j = 0 is predefined; n, m, D, and I are also global}
var i, j, k : integer;
begin
   for k := 2 to m +n do
      for i := max 2(k −m, 1) to min 2(k −1, n) do
      begin
         j := k −i;
         cost [i, j] := min 3(cost [i −1, j]+D [i], cost [i −1, j −1]+C [i, j], cost [i, j −1]+I [j]);
      end;
end;
```

Program 1.26 Procedure to compute *cost*

The order in which procedure *StringEdit* computes the entries of *cost* is given below for the case $n = 3$ and $m = 4$.

$$
\begin{array}{ccccc}
X & X & X & X & X \\
X & 1 & 2 & 4 & 7 \\
X & 3 & 5 & 8 & 10 \\
X & 6 & 9 & 11 & 12
\end{array}
$$

The X's denote terms in row zero and column zero. These are computed before procedure *StringEdit* is invoked. For our example, the matrix *cost* following the execution of procedure *StringEdit* is:

$$
\begin{array}{ccccc}
0 & 5 & 8 & 9 & 10 \\
6 & 1 & 4 & 5 & 6 \\
7 & 2 & 2 & 3 & 4 \\
9 & 4 & 3 & 4 & 5
\end{array}
$$

Hence the cost of an optimal edit sequence is $cost (3, 4) = 5$. The edit sequence is easily constructed if during the computation of *cost* we remember which of the three terms in the *min* 3 computation provided the minimum value. Ties may be broken arbitrarily. Suppose this information is saved in the array *MinTerm* [1 .. n, 1 .. m]. For our example, this array is:

<pre>
C   I   I   I
D   C   I   I
D   C   C   I
</pre>

where C, D, and I, respectively, denote the change, delete, and insert terms in the $min\,3$ computation. An I in column j denotes the edit operation insert b_j; a D in row i denotes delete a_i; and a C in row i and column j denotes change a_i to b_j. The optimal edit sequence is obtained by following a path from $MinTerm\,[n, m\,]$ back to $MinTerm\,[1, 1]$. If the symbol at the current position is an I, the path moves one position left on this row; if it is a D, the path moves one position up in the current column; and if it is C, then we move one up and one left. For the example, the path to [1, 1] is [3, 4], [3, 3], [2, 2], [1, 1]. The edit operations will actually be performed in the reverse order of this path. The optimal edit sequence is: change a_1 to b_1; change a_2 to b_2; change a_3 to b_3; insert b_4.

We leave the writing of the procedure to generate the optimal edit sequence as an exercise.

1.4.5 Backtracking Method

Backtracking is a systematic way to search for the solution to a problem. We begin by defining a *solution space* for the problem. This must include at least one (optimal) solution to the problem. In the case of the rat in a maze problem, we may define the solution space to consist of all paths from the entrance to the exit. For the case of the 0/1 knapsack problem with n containers, a reasonable choice for the solution space is the set of 2^n 0/1 vectors of size n. When $n = 3$, this is the set {(0,0,0), (0,1,0), (0,0,1), (1,0,0), (0,1,1), (1,0,1), (1,1,0), (1,1,1)}. This set represents all possible ways to assign the values 0 and 1 to $x\,[1:n\,]$.

The next step is to organize the solution space so that it can be searched easily. Figure 1.14 shows a possible organization for a 3×3 maze. Each circle in this figure is called a *node* or *vertex*. Each line that joins two vertices is an *edge*. A *path* between two vertices is a sequence of vertices that begins at the first of these two vertices and ends at the second. Adjacent vertices in the path are connected by an edge. All paths from the vertex labeled (1,1) to the one labeled (3,3) define an element of the solution space for a 3×3 maze. Depending on the placement of obstacles, some of these paths may be infeasible.

A possible organization for the three container 0/1 knapsack solution space is shown in Figure 1.15. All paths from the root (A) to a leaf (H-O) define an element of the solution space. Depending on the values $w\,[1:3]$ and c, some or all of these paths may define infeasible solutions. The path from the root to the leaf labeled H defines the solution $x\,[1:3] = [1,1,1]$.

The solution space is searched beginning at a start node (the entrance node (1,1) in the rat in a maze problem or the root node in the case of the 0/1 knapsack problem). This node is called a *live* node. From this live node, an attempt is made to move to a new node. The node from which we are trying to move is called the $E-node$ (expansion node). If we can move to a new node from the current E-node, then we do so. The new

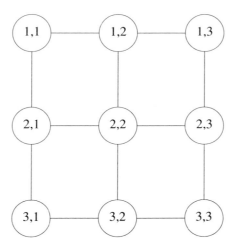

Figure 1.14 Solution space for a 3 × 3 maze

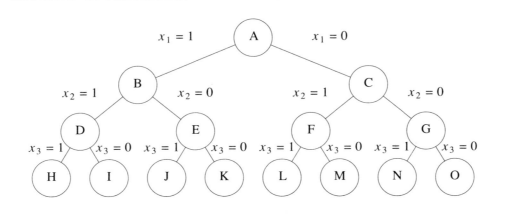

Figure 1.15 Solution space for a 3 container 0/1 knapsack

node becomes a live node and also becomes the new E-node. If we cannot move to a new node, the current E-node dies and we move to the nearest live node that remains. This becomes the new E-node. The search terminates when we have found the answer or when we run out of live nodes to back up to.

Rat In A Maze

Consider the 3×3 rat in a maze instance given by the matrix of Figure 1.16(a). We shall search this maze using the solution space organization of Figure 1.14.

0	0	0		1	1	0		1	1	1
0	1	1		0	1	1		0	1	1
0	0	0		0	0	0		0	0	0
	(a)				(b)				(c)	

Figure 1.16 Mazes

Every path from the entrance of the maze to the exit corresponds to a path from (1,1) to (3,3) in Figure 1.14. However, some of the (1,1) to (3,3) paths in this organization do not correspond to entrance to exit paths in the example maze. The search begins at position (1,1). This is the only live node at this time. It is also the E-node. To avoid going through this position again, we set *maze*[1,1] to 1. From this position, we can move to either (1,2) or (2,1). For the particular instance we are dealing with, both moves are feasible as the maze has a zero at each position. Suppose we choose to move to (1,2). *maze*[1,2] is set to 1 to avoid going through here again. The status of *maze* is as in Figure 1.16(b). At this time we have two live nodes (1,1), and (1,2). (1,2) becomes the E-node. From the current E-node, there are three moves possible in Figure 1.14. Two of these are infeasible as *maze* has a 1 in these positions. The only feasible move is to (1,3). This position is blocked and the *maze* of Figure 1.13(c) obtained. Figure 1.14 indicates two possible moves from (1,3). Neither of these is feasible. So, the E-node (1,3) dies and we back up to the nearest live node which is (1,2). No feasible moves from here remain and this node dies too. The only remaining live node is (1,1). This becomes the E-node again. From here, there is an untried move. This gets us to position (2,1). The live nodes now are (1,1), and (2,1). Continuing in this way, the position (3,3) is reached. At this time, the list of live nodes is (1,1), (2,1), (3,1), (3,2), (3,3). This is also the path to the exit.

0/1 Knapsack

Consider the knapsack instance $n = 3$, $w[1:3] = [20, 15, 15]$, $p[1:3] = [40, 25, 25]$, and $c = 30$. We search the organization of Figure 1.15 beginning at the root. This is the only live node at this time. It is also the E-node. From here, we can move to either B or C. Suppose we move to B. The live nodes now are A and B. B is the current E-node. At node B, the remaining capacity, r, is 10 and the profit earned, p, is 40. From B we can move to either D or E. The move to D is infeasible as the the capacity needed to move there is $w[2] = 15$. The move to E is feasible as no capacity is used in this move. E becomes the new E-node. The live nodes at this time are A, B, and E. At node E, $r = 10$, and $p = 40$. From E, there are two possible moves (i.e., to nodes J and K). The move to node J is infeasible while that to K is not. Node K becomes the new E-node. Since this is a leaf, we have a feasible solution. This solution has $p = 40$. The values of x are determined by the path from the root to K. This path is also the live node sequence at this time, i.e., A, B, E, K. Since we cannot expand K further, this node dies and we back up to E. This cannot be expanded further and it dies too. Next, we back up to B which also dies. A becomes the E-node again. It can be expanded further and node C is reached. At this node, $r = 30$, and $p = 0$. From C, we can move to either F or G. Suppose we move to F. This becomes the new E-node. The live nodes are A, C, and F. At F, $r = 15$, and $p = 25$. From F we can move to either L or M. Suppose a move to L is made. At this node $r = 0$, and $p = 50$. Since L is a leaf and it represents a better feasible solution than the best found so far (i.e., the one at node K), we remember this as the best solution. Node L dies and we back up to node F. Continuing in this way, the entire solution space is searched. The best solution found during the search is the optimal one.

The search for an optimal solution can be speeded by determining whether or not a newly reached node can possibly lead to a solution better than the best found so far. If it cannot, then we might as well kill it. A simple strategy to use is to just see if $(p + ($sum of remaining $p[i]$'s$))$ is bigger than the profit from the best solution found so far. If it isn't, then expanding the current E-node is unnecessary and it is killed. Strategies such as this that are used to kill live nodes are called *bounding functions*. A more effective strategy is discussed in the text by Horowitz and Sahni that is cited in the readings section.

1.4.6 Branch-and-bound Method

Branch-and-bound is another way to systematically search a solution space. It differs from backtracking primarily in the way an E-node is expanded. Each live node becomes an E-node exactly once. At this time, all new nodes that can be reached using a single move are generated. Those of these that cannot possibly lead to a (optimal) feasible solution are killed. The remaining nodes are added to the list of live nodes. From the list of live nodes, one is selected to become the next E-node. This node is extracted from the list of live nodes and expanded. This expansion process is continued until either the answer is found or the list of live nodes becomes empty.

There are three common ways to select the next E-node. These are:

(1) *FIFO (First-in-first-out)*. In this scheme, nodes are extracted from the list of live nodes in the same order as they are put into it. The live node list behaves as a queue.

(2) *LIFO (Last-in-first-out)*. Here the list of live nodes behaves as a stack.

(3) *Least cost or max profit*. In this scheme, a cost or profit is associated with each node. If we are searching for a solution with least cost, then the list of live nodes can be set up as a min heap. If a solution with maximum profit is sought, this list can be set up as a max heap.

Rat in a Maze

Consider the rat in a maze instance of Figure 1.16(a) and the solution space organization of Figure 1.14. In a FIFO branch-and-bound, we begin with (1,1) as the E-node. The list of live nodes is empty and the maze position (1,1) set to 1. (1,1) is expanded and the nodes (1,2) and (2,1) added to the queue (i.e., the list of live nodes). Positions (1,2) and (2,1) are set to 1 in the maze to prevent moving to these positions again. The maze now is as in Figure 1.17(a).

1	1	0	1	1	1	1	1	1
1	1	1	1	1	1	1	1	1
0	0	0	0	0	0	1	0	0
	(a)			(b)			(c)	

Figure 1.17 Rat in a maze example

Node (1,2) is removed from the queue and expanded. Its three neighbors (Figure 1.14) are examined. Only (1,3) represents a feasible move and it is added to the queue. This maze position is set to 1 and the status of *maze* is as in Figure 1.17(b). Node (1,2) is killed. The next E-node is extracted from the queue. It is (2,1). When this is expanded, node (3,1) is added to the queue, *maze* [3,1] is set to 1, and node (2,1) killed. *maze* is as in Figure 1.17(c) and the queue has the nodes (1,3) and (3,1) on it. (1,3) becomes the next E-node. This does not get us to any new nodes. It is killed and (3,1) becomes the new E-node. At this time, the queue is empty. (3,1) gets us to (3,2). This is added to the queue and (3,1) is killed. (3,2) is the next E-node. Expanding this, we reach the exit (3,3) and the search terminates.

A FIFO search of a maze has the desirable property that the path found (if any) is a shortest path from the entrance to the maze. This is not the case for a path found by backtracking.

0/1 Knapsack

We shall carry out a maximum profit branch-and-bound on the knapsack instance $n = 3$, $w[1:3] = [20, 15, 15]$, $p[1:3] = [40, 25, 25]$, and $c = 30$. The search begins at the node A (Figure 1.15). This is the initial E-node and the max heap of live nodes is empty. Expanding this node yields the nodes B and C. Both are feasible and are inserted into the heap. A is killed and B becomes the next E-node as its profit value (40) is larger than that of C. When B is expanded, the nodes D and E are generated. D is infeasible and is killed. E is added to the heap. E becomes the next E-node as its profit value is 40 while that of C is 0. When E is expanded, the nodes J and K are generated. J is infeasible and is killed. K represents a feasible solution. This solution is recorded as the best found so far and K is killed. Only one live node remains. This is node C. It becomes the new E-node. Nodes F and G are generated and inserted into the max heap. F has a profit of 25 and becomes the next E-node. Nodes L and M are generated. Both are killed as they are leaf nodes. The solution corresponding to L is recorded as the best found so far. Finally, G becomes the E-node and the nodes N and O generated. Both are leaves and are killed. Neither represents a solution that is better than the best found so far. So, no solution update takes place. The heap is empty and there is no next E-node. The search terminates with J representing the optimal solution.

As in the case of backtracking, the search for an optimal solution can be speeded by using a bounding function. This function places an upper bound on the maximum profit that can possibly be obtained by expanding a particular node. If a node's bound isn't larger than the profit of the best solution found so far, it may be killed without expansion. Further, nodes may be extracted from the heap in nonincreasing order of the profit bound, rather than by the actual profit for the node.

You are referred to the text by Horowitz and Sahni that is cited in the readings section for further information on the use of bounding functions in the solution of the 0/1 knapsack and other problems.

1.5 REFERENCES AND SELECTED READINGS

For a discussion of programming techniques and how to develop programs, see *The science of programming*, by D. Gries, Springer Verlag, NY, 1981; *A discipline of programming*, by E. W. Dijkstra, Prentice-Hall, Englewood Cliffs, NJ, 1976; and *The elements of programming style*, Second Edition, by B. W. Kernighan and P.J. Plauger, McGraw Hill, NY 1978.

A good discussion of tools and procedures for developing very large software systems appears in the texts *Practical strategies for developing very large software systems*, by E. Horowitz, Addisson-Wesley, 1975, and *Software engineering*, by Ian Sommerville, Third Edition, Addisson-Wesley, Workingham, England, 1989.

For a more detailed discussion of performance analysis and measurement, see *Software development in Pascal*, by S. Sahni, Camelot Publishing Co., Minnesota, 1985.

Additional examples of the design methods given in this chapter appear in later chapters of this book as well as in *Fundamentals of computer algorithms*, by S. Sahni and E. Horowitz, Computer Science Press, Maryland, 1978.

The divide-and-conquer matrix multiplication algorithm is due to Volker Strassen and appears in the paper ''Gaussian elimination is not optimal,'' by V. Strassen, *Numerische Mathematik*, 13, pp. 354-356.

The dynamic programming string editing algorithm is due to Wagner and Fisher. Their paper ''The string to string correction problem,'' by R. Wagner and M. Fischer, *JACM*, 21, 1, 1974, pp 168-173 also contains variants of the problem studied here.

For a discussion of the more abstract formulation of data structures see the text *Data structures with abstract data types and Pascal*, by D. Stubbs and N. Webre, Brooks/Cole Publishing Co., Monterey, California, 1985.

Writing a correct version of binary search is discussed in the papers "Programming pearls: Writing correct programs", by J. Bentley, *CACM*, 26, 1983, pp. 1040-1045 and "Some lessons drawn from the history of the binary search algorithm" by R. Levisse, *The Computer Journal*, 26, 1983, pp. 154-163.

For a general discussion of permutation generation, see the paper "Permutation generation methods", by R. Sedgewick, *Computer Surveys*, 9, 1977, pp. 137-164.

1.6 EXERCISES

1. Look up the word *algorithm* or its older form, *algorism*, in the dictionary.

2. Consider the two statements: (a) Is $n = 2$ the largest value of n for which there exists positive integers x, y, and z such that $x^n + y^n = z^n$ has a solution; (b) Store 5 divided by zero into X and go to statement 10. Both fail to satisfy one of the five criteria of an algorithm. Which criteria do they violate?

3. Describe the flowchart in Figure 1.1. by using a combination of Pascal and English. Can you do this without using the **goto** statement?

4. Discuss how you would actually represent the list of name and telephone number pairs in a real machine. How would you handle people with the same last name?

5. Horner's rule is a means for evaluating a polynomial $A(x) = a_n x^n + a_{n-1} x^{n-1} + \ldots + a_1 x + a_0$ at a point x_0 using a minimum number of multiplications. This rule is:

$$A(x) = (\ldots((a_n x_0 + a_{n-1})x_0 + \ldots + a_1)x_0 + a_0$$

Write a Pascal program to evaluate a polynomial using Horner's rule. Determine how many times each statement is executed.

6. Given n boolean variables $x_1, \ldots, x_n$ we wish to print all possible combinations of truth values they can assume. For instance, if $n = 2$, there are four possibilities: true, true; true, false; false, true; false, false. Write a Pascal program to accomplish this and do a frequency count.

7. Compare the two functions n^2 and $2^n/4$ for various values of n. Determine when the second becomes larger than the first.

8. Write a Pascal program which prints out the integer values of x, y, z in nondecreasing order. What is the computing time of your method?

9. Write a Pascal procedure which searches an array $a[1..n]$ for the element x. If x occurs, then set j to its position in the array else set j to zero. Try writing this without using the **goto** statement.

10. One useful facility we might add to Pascal is the ability to manipulate character strings. Suppose we choose to implement the data **type** string as a **record** as below:

$$\textbf{type } string = \textbf{record}$$
$$length : \textbf{integer}; \quad \{\text{number of characters}\}$$
$$c : \textbf{array}[1..100] \textbf{ of char};$$
$$\textbf{end};$$

(a) Write the functions *concat, substring*, and *reverse* described in Section 1.2.

(b) Write a function *index* (x,y) which searches string x for the first occurrence of string y. If y does not appear in x, then *index* equals zero. Otherwise, *index* is the starting position in x of the first occurrence of y.

Test these functions out using suitable test data.

11. Suppose that strings are represented as in Exercise 11. Write a function *compact* (s) that replaces each sequence of blanks in s by a single blank. Test your function using suitable data.

12. Write a program that accepts as input a string s (see Exercise 11) and determines the frequency of occurrence of each of the distinct characters in s. Test your program using suitable test data.

13. Trace the action of the code:

$$i := 1; j := n$$
$$\textbf{repeat}$$
$$k := (i + j)/2$$
$$\textbf{if } a[k] < = x \textbf{ then } i := k + 1$$
$$\textbf{else } j := k - 1$$
$$\textbf{until } i > j$$

on the elements 2, 4, 6, 8, 10, 12, 14, 16, 18, 20 searching for $x = 1, 3, 13,$ or 21. What is the computing time for this segment in terms of n?

14. Prove by induction:

(a) $\sum_{1 \le i \le n} i = n(n + 1)/2, n \ge 1$

(b) $\sum_{1 \le i \le n} i^2 = n(n + 1)(2n + 1)/6, n \ge 1$

(c) $\sum_{0 \le i \le n} x^i = (x^{n+1} - 1)/(x - 1), x \ne 1, n \ge 0$

15. Determine the frequency counts for all statements in the following two program segments:

```
1 for i := 1 to n do
2   for j := 1 to i do
3     for k := 1 to j do
4       x := x + 1 ;
```

(a)

```
1 i := 1;
2 while i ≤ n do
3 begin
4   x := x + 1 ;
5   i := i + 1 ;
6 end;
```

(b)

16. (a) Introduce statements to increment *count* at all appropriate points in Program 1.27.

```
procedure d (var x : list ; n : integer);
var i : integer;
begin
  i := 1;
  repeat
    x [i ] := x [i ] + 2;
    i := i + 2;
  until (i > n);
  i := 1;
  while i <= (n div 2) do
  begin
    x [i ] := x [i ] + x [i +1];
    i := i + 1;
  end;
end; {of d}
```

Program 1.27

(b) Simplify the resulting program by eliminating statements. The simplified program should compute the same value for *count* as computed by the program of (a).

(c) What is the exact value of *count* when the program terminates? You may assume that the initial value of *count* is 0.

(d) Obtain the step count for Program 1.27 using the frequency method. Clearly show the step count table.

17. Do the Exercise 16 for procedure *transpose* (Program 1.28).

line	**procedure** *transpose*(**var** a : *matrix*; n : **integer**);
1	**var** i, j : **integer**; t : *element*;
2	**begin**
3	**for** $i := 1$ **to** $n-1$ **do**
4	**for** $j := i+1$ **to** n **do**
5	**begin**
6	$t := a[i,j]$; $a[i,j] := a[j,i]$; $a[j,i] := t$;
7	**end**;
8	**end**; {of *transpose*}

Program 1.28

18. Do the Exercise 16 for Program 1.29. This program multiplies two $n \times n$ matrices a and b.

```
procedure mult (var a, b, c : matrix; n : integer);
var i, j, k : integer;
begin
  for i := 1 to n do
    for j := 1 to n do
    begin
      c [i,j] := 0;
      for k := 1 to n do
        c [i,j] := c [i,j] + a [i,k] * b [k,j];
    end;
end; {of mult}
```

Program 1.29

19. (a) Do the Exercise 16 for Program 1.30. This program multiplies two matrices a and b where a is an $m \times n$ matrix and b is an $n \times p$ matrix.

    (b) Under what conditions will it be profitable to interchange the two outermost **for** loops?

20. Show that the following equalities are correct:

    (a) $5n^2 - 6n = \Theta(n^2)$

    (b) $n! = O(n^n)$

```
procedure prod (var a, b, c : matrix; m, n, p : integer);
var i, j, k : integer;
begin
  for i := 1 to m do
    for j := 1 to p do
    begin
      c [i,j] := 0;
      for k := 1 to n do
        c [i,j] := c [i,j] + a [i,k] * b [k,j];
    end;
end; {of prod}
```

Program 1.30

(c) $2n^2 2^n + n\log n = \Theta(n^2 2^n)$

(d) $\sum_{i=0}^{n} i^2 = \Theta(n^3)$

(e) $\sum_{i=0}^{n} i^3 = \Theta(n^4)$

(f) $n^{2^n} + 6*2^n = \Theta(2^{2^n})$

(g) $n^3 + 10^6 n^2 = \Theta(n^3)$

(h) $6n^3/(\log n + 1) = O(n^3)$

(i) $n^{1.001} + n\log n = \Theta(n^{1.001})$

(j) $n^k + \varepsilon + n^k \log n = \Theta(n^k + \varepsilon)$ for all k and ε, $k \geq 0$, and $\varepsilon > 0$

(k) $10n^3 + 15n^4 + 100n^2 2^n = O(100n^2 2^n)$

(l) $33n^3 + 4n^2 = \Omega(n^2)$

(m) $33n^3 + 4n^2 = \Omega(n^3)$

21.   Show that the following equalities are incorrect:

(a) $10n^2 + 9 = O(n)$

(b) $n^2 \log n = \Theta(n^2)$

(c) $n^2/\log n = \Theta(n^2)$

(d) $n^3 2^n + 6n^2 3^n = O(n^3 2^n)$

22. Obtain the average run time of procedure *BinarySearch*. Do this for suitable values of n in the range $[0, 100]$. Your report must include a plan for the experiment as well as the measured times. These times are to be provided both in a table and as a graph.

23. Analyze the computing time of procedure *sort* (Program 1.2).

24. Obtain worst case run times for procedure *sort* (Program 1.2). Do this for suitable values of n in the range $[0, 100]$. Your report must include a plan for the experiment as well as the measured times. These times are to be provided both in a table and as a graph.

25. Consider procedure *add* (Program 1.14).

    (a)   Obtain run times for $n = 1, 10, 20, \ldots, 100$.

    (b)   Plot the times obtained in part (a).

26. Do the previous exercise for matrix multiplication (Program 1.30).

27. List as many rules of style in programming that you can think of that you would be willing to follow yourself.

28. Using the notation introduced at the end of Section 1.1, define the structure Boolean with operators AND, OR, NOT, IMP, and EQV (equivalent) using only the **if-then-else** statement. For example, NOT $(X) :: =$ **if X then false else true**.

29. Give a version of a binary search procedure which initializes *lower* to zero and *upper* to $n + 1$.

30. Take any version of binary search, express it using assignment, **if-then-else**, and **goto**, and then give an equivalent recursive program.

31. Write a recursive procedure for computing the binomial coefficient $\binom{n}{m}$ as defined in Section 1.2, where $\binom{n}{0} = \binom{n}{n} = 1$. Analyze the time and space requirements of your algorithm.

32. Ackermann's function $A(m,n)$ is defined as follows:

$$A(m,n) = \begin{cases} n + 1 & \text{, if } m = 0 \\ A(m-1, 1) & \text{, if } n = 0 \\ A(m-1, A(m,n-1)) & \text{, otherwise} \end{cases}$$

This function is studied because it grows very fast for small values of m and n. Write a recursive procedure for computing this function. Then write a nonrecursive algorithm for computing Ackermann's function.

33. (Towers of Hanoi) There are three towers and sixty four disks of different diameters placed on the first tower. The disks are in order of decreasing diameter as one scans up the tower. Monks were reputedly supposed to move the disks from tower 1 to tower 3 obeying the rules: (a) only one disk can be moved at any time; and (b) no disk can be placed on top of a disk with smaller diameter. Write a recursive procedure which prints the sequence of moves which accomplish this task.

34. Write an equivalent recursive version of program *magic* as given in Section 1.3.

35. The *pigeon hole principle* states that if a function f has n distinct inputs but less than n distinct outputs then there exist two inputs a and b such that $a \neq b$ and $f(a) = f(b)$. Write a program to find the values a and b for which the range values are equal.

36. Given n, a positive integer, determine if n is the sum of all of its divisors; i.e. if n is the sum of all t such that $1 \leq t < n$ and t divides n.

37. Consider the function $F(x)$ defined by

$$\textbf{if } x \text{ is even } \textbf{then } F := x \textbf{ div } 2$$
$$\textbf{else } F := F(F(3x + 1))$$

Prove that $F(x)$ terminates for all integers x. (Hint: Consider integers of the form $(2i + 1)2^k - 1$ and use induction.)

38. If S is a set of n elements, the *powerset* of S is the set of all possible subsets of S. For example, if $S = (a,b,c)$, then *powerset* $(S) = \{(\ ), (a), (b), (c), (a,b), (a,c), (b,c), (a,b,c)\}$. Write a recursive procedure to compute *powerset* (S).

39. Extend the greedy solution of Section 1.2 to the loading of two ships. Does the algorithm generate optimal solutions always?

40. Consider the continuous knapsack problem that is defined as:

$$\text{maximize } \sum_{i=1}^{n} p[i]x[i]$$

subject to the constraints:

$$\sum_{i=1}^{n} w[i]x[i] \leq c$$

and

$$0 \leq x[i] \leq 1, \ 1 \leq i \leq n$$

(a) Show that feasible solutions obtained by being greedy on profit aren't necessarily optimal.

(b) Show that feasible solutions obtained by being greedy on weight aren't necessarily optimal.

(c) Show that feasible solutions obtained by being greedy on the profit density $p[i]/w[i]$ are always optimal.

(d) Write a greedy algorithm using the strategy of (c). Your algorithm should have a worst case time complexity that is $O(n\log n)$. Show that this is so.

41. Use the table method to show that the solution to the divide-and-conquer recurrence for integer multiplication using three products of $n/2$ digit numbers is $O(n^{1.581})$.

42. Devise a problem for which the principle of optimality does not hold.

43. Consider the 0/1 knapsack instance: $n = 6$, $w[1..6] = [2, 2, 5, 3, 4, 1]$, $p[1..6] = [4, 9, 2, 6, 9, 5]$, and $c = 11$. Use the dynamic programming method of the text to obtain an optimal solution. What is the value of this solution? Show all the f_j's you compute using a table similar to that of Figure 1.13.

44. (a) Write a procedure to compute the function values $f_j(l)$ in the dynamic programming solution of the 0/1 knapsack problem. Use a two-dimensional array F such that $F[j, l] = f_j(l)$.

(b) Write a procedure that uses the result of (a) to determine an optimal solution and the value of this solution.

45. Consider a string edit instance for which $n = 3$, $m = 4$, $D = [1, 6, 1]$, $I = [2, 3, 2, 1]$, and C is the matrix:

$$
\begin{array}{cccc}
5 & 4 & 1 & 3 \\
1 & 1 & 2 & 4 \\
2 & 2 & 6 & 4
\end{array}
$$

Compute the *cost* and *MinTerm* arrays for this instance. From these obtain the cost of an optimal edit sequence as well as the sequence itself.

46. Do the preceding exercise for the string edit instance that has $n = 4$, $m = 4$, $D = [2, 1, 6, 1]$, $I = [2, 3, 2, 1]$, and C is the matrix:

$$
\begin{array}{cccc}
1 & 6 & 4 & 1 \\
5 & 4 & 1 & 3 \\
1 & 1 & 2 & 4 \\
2 & 2 & 6 & 4
\end{array}
$$

47. (a) Modify procedure *StringEdit* (Program 1.26) so that it also computes the array *MinTerm*.

    (b) Write a procedure that uses the array *MinTerm* computed in (a) and obtains an optimal edit sequence. What is the complexity of your procedure?

48. Consider the 0/1 knapsack instance: $n = 4$, $w[1:4] = [20, 25, 15, 35]$, $p[1:4] = [40, 49, 25, 60]$, and $c = 62$.

    (a) Draw the solution space organization for 0/1 knapsack instances when $n = 4$.

    (b) Trace the working of a backtracking algorithm on this organization (use the above instance). Clearly label the nodes in the order in which the backtrack algorithm first reaches them. Identify the nodes that do not get reached.

    (c) Do part (b) for the case of a FIFO branch-and-bound.

    (d) Do part (b) for the case of a max profit branch-and-bound.

49. In the n queens problem we wish to find a placement of n queens on an $n \times n$ chessboard such that no two queens attack. Two queens are said to attack iff they are in the same row, column, diagonal, or antidiagonal of the chess board. Hence, we may assume that in any feasible solution, queen i is placed in row i of the chess board. So, we are interested only in determining the column placement of each queen. Let $c[i]$ denote the column that queen i is placed in. If no two queens attack, then $c[1:n]$ is a permutation of $(1, 2, \ldots, n)$. The solution space for the n queens problem can therefore be limited to all permutations of $(1, 2, \ldots, n)$.

    (a) Organize the n queens solution space using an organization similar to that used for the 0/1 knapsack problem.

    (b) Write a backtracking procedure to search this for a feasible placement of the n queens.

50. Show that the path (if any) found by a FIFO search of a maze is a shortest length path. Show that this is not necessarily true for a path found using backtracking.

CHAPTER 2
ARRAYS

2.1 AXIOMATIZATION

It is appropriate that we begin our study of data structures with the array. The array is often the only means for structuring data that is provided in a programming language. Therefore it deserves a significant amount of attention. If one asks a group of programmers to define an array, the most often quoted response is: "a consecutive set of memory locations." This is unfortunate because it clearly reveals a common point of confusion, namely the distinction between a data structure and its representation. It is true that arrays are almost always implemented by using consecutive memory, but not always. Intuitively, an array is a set of pairs, index and value. For each index which is defined there is a value associated with that index. In mathematical terms we call this a *correspondence* or a *mapping*. However, as computer scientists we want to provide a more functional definition by giving the operations which are permitted on this data structure. For arrays this means we are concerned with only two operations, one that retrieves and the other that stores values. This structure can be defined as in Structure 2.1.

The function CREATE produces a new, empty array. RETRIEVE takes as input an array and an index, and either returns the appropriate value or an error. STORE is used to enter new index-value pairs. The second axiom is read as "to retrieve the j'th item where x has already been stored at index i in A is equivalent to checking if i and j are equal and if so, x, or search for the j'th value in the remaining array, A." This axiom was originally given by J. McCarthy. Notice how the axioms are independent of any representation scheme. Also, i and j need not necessarily be integers, but we assume only that an EQUAL function can be devised.

If we restrict the index values to be integers, then assuming a conventional random access memory we can implement STORE and RETRIEVE so that they operate in a constant amount of time. If we interpret the indices to be n-dimensional $(i_1, i_2, \ldots, i_n)$, then

---

structure *ARRAY* (*value*, *index*)
   declare *CREATE* ( ) $\rightarrow$ *array*
         RETRIEVE (*array*,*index*) $\rightarrow$ *value*
         STORE (*array*,*index*,*value*) $\rightarrow$ *array* ;
   for all *A* ε *array*, *i*,*j* ε *index*, *x* ε *value* **let**
     RETRIEVE (*CREATE*,*i*) ::= **error**
     RETRIEVE (*STORE* (*A*,*i*,*x*),*j*) ::= **if** *EQUAL* (*i*,*j*) **then** *x* **else** *RETRIEVE* (*A*,*j*)
   end
end *ARRAY*

Structure 2.1 The array data structure

the previous axioms apply immediately and define *n*-dimensional arrays. In Section 2.4 we will examine how to implement *RETRIEVE* and and *STORE* for multi-dimensional arrays using consecutive memory locations.

2.2 ORDERED LISTS AND POLYNOMIALS

One of the simplest and most commonly found data object is the ordered or linear list. Examples are the days of the week

(MONDAY, TUESDAY, WEDNESDAY, THURSDAY,
FRIDAY, SATURDAY, SUNDAY)

or the values in a card deck

(2, 3, 4, 5, 6, 7, 8, 9, 10, Jack, Queen, King, Ace)

or the floors of a building

(basement, lobby, mezzanine, first, second, third)

or the years the United States fought in World War II

(1941, 1942, 1943, 1944, 1945)

If we consider an ordered list more abstractly, we say that it is either empty, written as ( ), or it can be written as

$(a_1,a_2,a_3,\ldots,a_n)$

where the a_i are atoms from some set S.

There are a variety of operations that are performed on these lists. These operations include:

(1)   Find the length, n, of the list.

(2)   Read the list from left to right (or right to left).

(3)   Retrieve the i'th element, $1 \leq i \leq n$.

(4)   Store a new value into the i'th position, $1 \leq i \leq n$.

(5)   Insert a new element at the position i, $1 \leq i \leq n + 1$ causing elements numbered $i, i + 1, \ldots, n$ to become numbered $i + 1, i + 2, \ldots, n + 1$.

(6)   Delete the element at position i, $1 \leq i \leq n$ causing elements numbered $i + 1, \ldots, n$ to become numbered $i, i + 1, \ldots, n - 1$.

It is not always necessary to be able to perform all of these operations; many times a subset will suffice. In the study of data structures we are interested in ways of representing ordered lists so that these operations can be carried out efficiently.

Perhaps the most common way to represent an ordered list is by an array where we associate the list element a_i with the array index i. This we will refer to as *sequential mapping*, because using the conventional array representation we are storing a_i and $a_{i + 1}$ into consecutive locations i and $i + 1$ of the array. This gives us the ability to retrieve or modify the values of random elements in the list in a constant amount of time, essentially because a computer memory has random access to any word. We can access the list element values in either direction by changing the subscript values in a controlled way. It is only operations (5) and (6) which require real effort. Insertion and deletion using sequential allocation forces us to move some of the remaining elements so that sequential mapping is preserved in its proper form. It is precisely this overhead that leads us to consider nonsequential mappings of ordered lists in Chapter 4.

Let us jump right into a problem requiring ordered lists, which we will solve by using one-dimensional arrays. This problem has become the classical example for motivating the use of list processing techniques, which we will see in later chapters. Therefore, it makes sense to look at the problem and see why arrays offer only a partially adequate solution. The problem calls for building a set of subroutines that allow for the manipulation of symbolic polynomials. By "symbolic," we mean the list of coefficients and exponents that accompany a polynomial; e.g., two such polynomials are

$$A(x) = 3x^2 + 2x + 4 \text{ and } B(x) = x^4 + 10x^3 + 3x^2 + 1$$

For a start, the capabilities we would include are the four basic arithmetic operations: addition, subtraction, multiplication, and division. We will also need input and output routines and some suitable format for preparing polynomials as input. The first step is to consider how to define polynomials as a computer structure. For a mathematician a polynomial is a sum of terms where each term has a form ax^e; x is the variable, a is the coefficient, and e is the exponent. However, this is not an appropriate definition for our purposes. When defining a data object you must decide what functions will be available, what their input is, what their output is, and exactly what it is that they do. A complete specification of the data structure polynomial is given in Structure 2.2.

---

structure *POLYNOMIAL*
   declare *ZERO* ( ) $\rightarrow$ *poly* ; *ISZERO* (*poly*) $\rightarrow$ *Boolean*
         COEF (*poly*,*exp*) $\rightarrow$ *coef* ;
         ATTACH (*poly*,*coef*,*exp*) $\rightarrow$ *poly*
         REM (*poly*,*exp*) $\rightarrow$ *poly*
         SMULT (*poly*,*coef*,*exp*) $\rightarrow$ *poly*
         ADD (*poly*,*poly*) $\rightarrow$ *poly* ; *MULT* (*poly*,*poly*) $\rightarrow$ *poly* ;
   for all *P*,*Q* ε *poly*, *c*,*d* ε *coef* , *e*,*f* ε *exp* **let**
     REM (*ZERO*,*f*) ::= *ZERO*
     REM (*ATTACH* (*P*,*c*,*e*),*f*) ::=
       if $e = f$ **then** *REM* (*P*,*f*) **else** *ATTACH* (*REM* (*P*,*f*),*c*,*e*)
     ISZERO (*ZERO*) ::= **true**
     ISZERO (*ATTACH* (*P*,*c*,*e*)) ::=
       if *COEF* (*P*,*e*) $= -c$ **then** *ISZERO* (*REM* (*P*,*e*)) **else false**
     COEF (*ZERO*,*e*) ::= 0
     COEF (*ATTACH* (*P*,*c*,*e*),*f*) ::=
       if $e = f$ **then** c + *COEF* (*P*,*f*) **else** *COEF* (*P*,*f*)
     SMULT (*ZERO*,*d*,*f*) ::= *ZERO*
     SMULT (*ATTACH* (*P*,*c*,*e*),*d*,*f*) ::=
     ATTACH (*SMULT* (*P*,*d*,*f*), $c*d$,$e + f$)
     ADD (*P*,*ZERO*) ::= *P*
     ADD (*P*,*ATTACH* (*Q*,*d*,*f*)) ::= *ATTACH* (*ADD* (*P*,*Q*),*d*,*f*)
     MULT (*P*,*ZERO*) ::= *ZERO*
     MULT (*P*,*ATTACH* (*Q*,*d*,*f*)) ::= *ADD* (*MULT* (*P*,*Q*),*SMULT* (*P*,*d*,*f*))
   end
end *POLYNOMIAL*

Structure 2.2 Specification of a polynomial

In this specification, every polynomial is either ZERO or constructed by applying *ATTACH* to a polynomial. For example the polynomial $P = 10x - 12x^3 - 10x + 0x^2$ is represented by the string

      ATTACH(ATTACH(ATTACH(ATTACH(ZERO,10,1),−12,3),−10,1),0,2).

Notice the absence of any assumptions about the order of exponents, about nonzero coefficients, etc. These assumptions are decisions of representation. Suppose we wish to remove from P those terms having exponent 1. Then we would write *REM* (*P*,1) and by the axioms the above string would be transformed into

$$ATTACH(REM(ATTACH(ATTACH(ATTACH(ZERO,10,1),-12,3),-10,1),1),0,2)$$

which is transformed into

$$ATTACH\ (REM\ (ATTACH\ (ATTACH\ (ZERO,10,1),-12,3),1),0,2)$$

which becomes

$$ATTACH\ (ATTACH\ (REM\ (ATTACH\ (ZERO,10,1),1),-12,3),0,2)$$

which becomes

$$ATTACH\ (ATTACH\ (REM\ (ZERO,1),-12,3),0,2)$$

which becomes finally

$$ATTACH\ (ATTACH\ (ZERO,\ -12,3),0,2)$$

or

$$-12x^3 + 0x^2.$$

These axioms are valuable in that they describe the meaning of each operation concisely and without implying an implementation. Note how trivial the addition and multiplication operations have become.

Now we can make some representation decisions. A very reasonable first decision is that exponents should be unique and in decreasing order. This considerably simplifies the operations *ISZERO*, *COEF*, and *REM* while *ADD*, *SMULT*, and *MULT* remain unchanged. Now assuming a new function EXP $(poly) \rightarrow exp$, which returns the leading exponent of poly, we can write a version of *ADD* which is expressed more like a program (Program 2.1), but is still representation independent.

The basic loop of this algorithm consists of merging the terms of the two polynomials, depending upon the result of comparing the exponents. The **case** statement determines how the exponents are related and performs the proper action. Since the tests within the **case** statement require two terms, if one polynomial gets exhausted we must exit and the remaining terms of the other can be copied directly into the result. With these insights, suppose we now consider the representation question more carefully.

A general polynomial $A(x)$ can be written as

$$a_n x^n + a_{n-1} x^{n-1} + \ldots + a_1 x + a_0$$

```
{c := a + b where a and b are the input polynomials}
c := ZERO;
while not ISZERO (a) and not ISZERO (b) do
begin
  case compare (EXP (a), EXP (b)) of
    '<': begin
          c := ATTACH (c, COEF (b, EXP (b)), EXP (b));
          b := REM (b, EXP (b));
        end;
    '=': begin
          c := ATTACH (c, COEF (a, EXP (a))+COEF (b, EXP (b)), EXP (a));
          a := REM (a, EXP (a)); b := REM (b, EXP (b));
        end;
    '>': begin
          c := ATTACH (c, COEF (a, EXP (a)), EXP (a));
          a := REM (a, EXP (a));
        end
  end; {of case}
end; {of while}
```

insert any remaining terms of a or b into c

Program 2.1 Initial version of *ADD*

where $a_n \neq 0$ and we say that the degree of A is n. Each $a_i x^i$ is a *term* of the polynomial. If $a_i = 0$ then it is a *zero term*, otherwise it is a *nonzero* term.

One way to represent polynomials in Pascal is to define the data type *poly*:

```
type poly = record
              degree : 0..MaxDegree;
              coef : array[0..MaxDegree] of real;
            end;
```

where *MaxDegree* is a constant representing the largest degree polynomial that is to be represented. Now, if *a* is of type *poly* and $n \leq MaxDegree$, then the polynomial $A(x)$ above would be represented as

$$a.degree = n$$
$$a.coef[i] = a_{n-i}, \ 0 \leq i \leq n$$

Note that $a.coef[i]$ is the coefficient of x^{n-i} and the coefficients are stored in order of decreasing exponents. This representation leads to very simple algorithms for many of the operations you wish to perform on polynomials (addition, subtraction, evaluation, multiplication, etc.). It is, however, quite wasteful in its use of computer memory. For instance, if $a.degree \ll MaxDegree$, (the double "less than" should be read as "is much less than"), then most of the positions in $a.coef[0..MaxDegree]$ are unused. To avoid this waste, we would like to be able to define the data type *poly* using variable sized records as below:

> **type** *poly* = **record**
> > *degree* : 0..*maxint*;
> > *coef* : **array**[0..*degree*] **of real**;
> **end**;

Such a declaration is, of course, not permitted in standard or Turbo Pascal. While such a type definition solves the problem mentioned earlier, it does not yield a desirable representation. To see this, let us consider polynomials that have many zero terms. Such polynomials are called *sparse*. For instance, the polynomial $x^{1000} + 1$ has two nonzero terms and 999 zero terms. Using variable sized records as above, 999 of the entries in *coef* will be zero.

Suppose we take the polynomial $A(x)$ above and keep only its nonzero coefficients. Then we will really have the polynomial

$$b_{m-1}x^{e_{m-1}} + b_{m-2}x^{e_{m-2}} + \ldots + b_0x^{e_0}$$

where each b_i is a nonzero coefficient of A and the exponents e_i are decreasing $e_{m-1} > e_{m-2} > \ldots > e_0 \geq 0$. If all of A's coefficients are nonzero, then $m = n + 1$, $e_i = i$, and $b_i = a_i$ for $0 \leq i \leq n$. Alternatively, only a_n may be nonzero, in which case $m = 1$, $b_0 = a_n$, and $e_0 = n$.

All our polynomials will be represented in a global array called *terms* that is defined as below:

> **type** *term* = **record**
> > *coef* : **real**; {coefficient}
> > *exp* : 0..**maxint**; {exponent}
> **end**;
> **var** *terms* : **array**[1..*MaxTerms*] **of** *term*;

where *MaxTerms* is a constant.

Consider the two polynomials $A(x) = 2x^{1000} + 1$ and $B(x) = x^4 + 10x^3 + 3x^2 + 1$. These could be stored in the array *terms* as shown in Figure 2.1. Note that *af* and *bf* give the location of the first term of A and B, respectively, while *al* and *bl* give the location of the last term of A and B; *free* gives the location of the next free location in the array *terms*. For our example, $af = 1$, $al = 2$, $bf = 3$, $bl = 6$, and $free = 7$.

	af↓	al↓	bf↓			bl↓	free↓
coef	2	1	1	10	3	1	
exp	1000	0	4	3	2	0	
	1	2	3	4	5	6	7

Figure 2.1 Array representation of two polynomials

This representation scheme does not impose any limit on the number of polynomials that can be stored in *terms*. Rather, the total number of nonzero terms in all the polynomials together cannot exceed *MaxTerms*.

Is this representation any better than the one that used records with large array size? Well, it certainly solves our problem when many zero terms are present. $A(x) = 2x^{1000} + 1$ uses only 6 units of space (one for *af*, one for *al*, two for the coefficients, and two for the exponents). However, when all terms are nonzero as in $B(x)$ above, the new scheme uses about twice as much space as the previous one that used variable sized records. Unless we know beforehand that each of our polynomials has very few zero terms in it, the representation using the array *terms* will be preferred.

When the global array *terms* is used, a polynomial $D(x) = 0$ with no nonzero terms will have *df* and *dl* such that $dl = df - 1$. In general, a polynomial E that has n nonzero terms will have *ef* and *el* such that $el = ef + n - 1$.

Let us now write a Pascal procedure to add two polynomials A and B represented as above to obtain the sum $C = A + B$. Procedure *padd* (Program 2.2) adds $A(x)$ and $B(x)$ term by term to produce $C(x)$. The terms of C are entered into the array *terms* starting at the position *free* (procedure *NewTerm*, Program 2.3. In case there isn't enough space in *terms* to accommodate C, an error message is printed and the program terminates.

Let us now analyze the computing time of this algorithm. It is natural to carry out this analysis in terms of the number of nonzero terms in A and B. Let m and n be the number of nonzero terms in A and B, respectively. The assignments of line 5 are made only once and hence contribute $O(1)$ to the overall computing time. If either $n = 0$ or $m = 0$, the **while** loop of line 6 is not executed.

```
 1  procedure padd (af,al,bf,bl : integer; var cf,cl : integer);
 2  {add A (x) and B (x) to get C (x)}
 3  var p,q : integer; c : real;
 4  begin
 5      p := af; q := bf; cf := free;
 6      while (p <= al) and (q <= bl) do
 7        case compare (terms [p ].exp, terms [q ].exp) of
 8          '=': begin
 9                  c := terms [p ].coef + terms [q ].coef;
10                  if c <> 0 then NewTerm (c, terms [p ].exp);
11                  p := p + 1; q := q + 1;
12                end;
13          '<': begin
14                  NewTerm (terms [q ].coef, terms [q ].exp);
15                  q := q + 1;
16                end;
17          '>': begin
18                  NewTerm (terms [p ].coef, terms [p ].exp);
19                  p := p + 1;
20                end;
21        end; {of case and while}
22      {add in remaining terms of A (x)}
23      while p <= al do
24      begin
25        NewTerm (terms [p ].coef, terms [p ].exp);
26        p := p + 1;
27      end;
28      {add in remaining terms of B (x)}
29      while q <= bl do
30      begin
31        NewTerm (terms [q ].coef, terms [q ].exp);
32        q := q + 1;
33      end;
34      cl := free − 1;
35  end; {of padd}
```

Program 2.2 Procedure to add two polynomials

```
procedure NewTerm (c : real; e :integer);
{add a new term to C (x)}
begin
  if free > MaxTerms
  then begin
          writeln('too many terms in polynomials');
          halt; {terminate program}
        end;
    terms [free].coef := c;
    terms [free].exp := e;
   free := free + 1;
end; {of NewTerm}
```

Program 2.3 Procedure to add a new term

In case neither m nor n equals zero, the **while** loop of line 6 is entered. Each iteration of the **while** loop requires O(1) time. At each iteration, either the value of p or q or both increases by 1. Since the iteration terminates when either p or q exceeds al or bl, respectively, the number of iterations is bounded by $m + n - 1$. This worst case is achieved, for instance, when $A (x) = \sum_{i=0}^{n} x^{2i}$ and $B (x) = \sum_{i=0}^{n} x^{2i+1}$. Since none of the exponents are the same in A and B, $terms [p].exp \neq terms [q].exp$. Consequently, on each iteration the value of only one of p or q increases by 1. So, the worst case for the **while** loops of lines 23 and 29 is bounded by O($n + m$), as the first cannot be iterated more than m times and the second more than n. Taking the sum of all of these steps, we obtain O($n + m$) as the asymptotic computing time of this algorithm.

As we create polynomials, $free$ is continually incremented until it tries to exceed $MaxTerms$. When this happens must we quit? We must unless there are some polynomials which are no longer needed. There may be several such polynomials whose space can be reused. We could write a procedure that would compact the remaining polynomials, leaving a large, contiguous free space at one end. But this may require much data movement. Even worse, if we move a polynomial we must change its start and end pointers. This demands a sophisticated compacting routine coupled with a disciplined use of names for polynomials. In Chapter 4, we will see an elegant solution to these problems.

2.3 SPARSE MATRICES

A matrix is a mathematical object that arises in many physical problems. As computer scientists, we are interested in studying ways to represent matrices so that the operations to be performed on them can be carried out efficiently. A general matrix consists of m rows and n columns of numbers as in Figure 2.2.

$$
\begin{array}{c}
\begin{array}{ccc}
\text{col 1} & \text{col 2} & \text{col 3}
\end{array}\\
\begin{array}{c}
\text{row 1}\\
\text{row 2}\\
\text{row 3}\\
\text{row 4}\\
\text{row 5}
\end{array}
\begin{bmatrix}
-27, & 3, & 4\\
6, & 82, & -0.3\\
109, & -64, & 4\\
.12, & 8, & 9\\
3.4, & 36, & 27
\end{bmatrix}\\
\text{(a)}
\end{array}
\qquad
\begin{array}{c}
\begin{array}{cccccc}
\text{col 1} & \text{col 2} & \text{col 3} & \text{col 4} & \text{col 5} & \text{col 6}
\end{array}\\
\begin{bmatrix}
15, & 0, & 0, & 22, & 0, & -15\\
0, & 11, & 3, & 0, & 0, & 0\\
0, & 0, & 0, & -6, & 0, & 0\\
0, & 0, & 0, & 0, & 0, & 0\\
91, & 0, & 0, & 0, & 0, & 0\\
0, & 0, & 28, & 0, & 0, & 0
\end{bmatrix}\\
\text{(b)}
\end{array}
$$

Figure 2.2 Example of two matrices

The first matrix has five rows and three columns, the second six rows and six columns. In general, we write $m \times n$ (read "m by n") to designate a matrix with m rows and n columns. Such a matrix has mn elements. When m is equal to n, we call the matrix *square*.

It is very natural to store a matrix in a two-dimensional array, say $A[1..m, 1..n]$. Then we can work with any element by writing $A[i,j]$; and this element can be found very quickly, as we will see in the next section. Now if we look at the second matrix of Figure 2.2, we see that it has many zero entries. Such a matrix is called *sparse*. There is no precise definition of when a matrix is sparse and when it is not, but it is a concept that we can all recognize intuitively. Above, only eight out of 36 possible elements are nonzero and that is sparse! A sparse matrix requires us to consider an alternate form of representation. This comes about because in practice many of the matrices we want to deal with are large, e.g., 1000×1000, but at the same time they are sparse: say only 1000 out of 1 million possible elements are nonzero. On most computers today it would be impossible to store a full 1000×1000 matrix in the memory at once. Therefore, we seek an alternative representation for sparse matrices. The alternative representation should explicitly store only the nonzero elements.

Each element of a matrix is uniquely characterized by its row and column position, say i,j. We might then store a matrix as a list of 3-tuples of the form

$$(i, j, \text{value})$$

Also it might be helpful to organize this list of 3-tuples in some way, perhaps placing them so that the row numbers are increasing. We can go one step farther and require that all the 3-tuples of any row be stored so that the column indices are increasing. Thus, we might store the second matrix of Figure 2.2 in the array $A[0..t, 1..3]$, where $t = 8$ is the number of nonzero terms (see Figure 2.3). The elements $A[0,1]$ and $A[0,2]$ contain the number of rows and columns of the matrix. $A[0,3]$ contains the number of nonzero terms.

Now what are some of the operations we might want to perform on these matrices? One operation is to compute the transpose matrix. This is where we move the elements so that the element in the i,j position gets put in the j,i position. Another way of saying this is that we are interchanging rows and columns. The elements on the diagonal will remain unchanged, since $i = j$.

	1]	2]	3]			1]	2]	3]
$A[0,$	6,	6,	8		$B[0,$	6,	6,	8
$[1,$	1,	1,	15		$[1,$	1,	1,	15
$[2,$	1,	4,	22		$[2,$	1,	5,	91
$[3,$	1,	6,	−15		$[3,$	2,	2,	11
$[4,$	2,	2,	11		$[4,$	3,	2,	3
$[5,$	2,	3,	3		$[5,$	3,	6,	28
$[6,$	3,	4,	−6		$[6,$	4,	1,	22
$[7,$	5,	1,	91		$[7,$	4,	3,	−6
$[8,$	6,	3,	28		$[8,$	6,	1,	−15
	(a)					(b)		

Figure 2.3 Sparse matrix and its transpose stored as triples

The transpose of the example matrix in Figure 2.3(a) is shown in Figure 2.3(b). Since A is organized by row, our first idea for a transpose algorithm might be

> **for** each row i **do**
> take element (i,j,val) and
> store it in (j,i,val) of the transpose;

The difficulty is in not knowing where to put the element (j,i,val) until all other elements that precede it have been processed. In Figure 2.3, for instance, we have item

(1,1,15),	which becomes	(1,1,15)
(1,4,22),	which becomes	(4,1,22)
(1,6,−15),	which becomes	(6,1,−15)

If we just place them consecutively, then we will need to insert many new triples, forcing us to move elements down very often. We can avoid this data movement by finding the elements in the order we want them, which would be

> **for** all elements in column j **do**
> place element (i,j,val) in position (j,i,val);

This says "find all elements in column 1 and store them into row 1, find all elements in column 2 and store them in row 2, etc." Since the rows are originally in order, this means that we will locate elements in the correct column order as well.

Define the data type *SparseMatrix* as below:

> **type** *SparseMatrix* = **array**[0..*MaxTerms*, 1..3] **of integer**;

where *MaxTerms* is a constant. The procedure *transpose* (Program 2.4) computes the transpose of A. A is initially stored as a sparse matrix in the array a and its transpose is obtained in the array b.

It is not too difficult to see that the procedure is correct. The variable q always gives us the position in b where the next term in the transpose is to be inserted. The terms in b are generated by rows. Since the rows of B are the columns of A, row i of B is obtained by collecting all the nonzero terms in column i of A. This is precisely what is being done in lines 15-21. On the first iteration of the **for** loop of lines 15-21 all terms from column 1 of A are collected, then all terms from column 2, and so on, until eventually, all terms from column n are collected.

How about the computing time of this algorithm? For each iteration of the loop of lines 15-21, the **if** clause of line 17 is tested t times. Since the number of iterations of the loop of lines 15-21 is n, the total time for line 17 becomes nt. The assignments in lines 19 and 20 take place exactly t times as there are only t nonzero terms in the sparse matrix being generated. Lines 10-14 take a constant amount of time. The total time for the algorithm is therefore O(nt). In addition to the space needed for a and b, the algorithm requires only a fixed amount of additional space, i.e., space for the variables m, n, t, q, col, and p.

We now have a matrix transpose algorithm that we believe is correct and that has a computing time of O(nt). This computing time is a little disturbing since we know that in case the matrices had been represented as two dimensional arrays, we could have obtained the transpose of an $n \times m$ matrix in time O(nm). The algorithm for this has the simple form:

```
 1  procedure transpose (a : SparseMatrix; var b : SparseMatrix);
 2  {b is set to be the transpose of a}
 3  var m,n,p,q,t,col : integer;
 4  {m : number of rows in a
 5   n : number of columns in a
 6   t : number of terms in a
 7   q : position of next term in b
 8   p : current term in a}
 9  begin
10    m := a[0,1]; n := a[0,2]; t := a[0,3];
11    b[0,1] := n; b[0,2] := m; b[0,3] := t;
12    if t > 0 then {nonzero matrix}
13    begin
14      q := 1;
15      for col := 1 to n do {transpose by columns}
16        for p := 1 to t do
17          if a [p,2] = col then
18          begin
19            b [q,1] := a [p,2]; b [q,2] := a [p,1];
20            b [q,3] := a [p,3]; q := q + 1;
21          end;
22    end; {of if}
23  end; {of transpose}
```

Program 2.4 Procedure *transpose*

$$\textbf{for } j := 1 \textbf{ to } n \textbf{ do}$$
$$\textbf{for } i := 1 \textbf{ to } m \textbf{ do}$$
$$B [j,i] := A [i,j];$$

The $O(nt)$ time for procedure *transpose* becomes $O(n^2 m)$ when t is of the order of nm. This is worse than the $O(nm)$ time using arrays. Perhaps, in an effort to conserve space, we have traded away too much time. Actually, we can do much better by using a little more storage. We can, in fact, transpose a matrix represented as a sequence of triples in time $O(n + t)$. This algorithm, *FastTranspose* (Program 2.5), proceeds by first determining the number of elements in each column of A. This gives us the number of elements in each row of B. From this information, the starting point in b of each of its rows is easily obtained. We can now move the elements of a one by one into their correct position in b. *MaxCol* is a constant such that the number of columns in A never exceeds *MaxCol*.

```
 1  procedure fasttranspose (a : SparseMatrix; var b : SparseMatrix);
 2  {The transpose of a is placed in b and is found in O(n +t) time where
 3   n is the number of columns and t the number of terms in a}
 4  var s,u : array[1..MaxCol] of integer;
 5    i,j,n,t : integer;
 6  begin
 7    n := a[0,2]; t := a[0,3];
 8    b[0,1] := n; b[0,2] := a[0,1]; b[0,3] := t;
 9    if t > 0 then {nonzero matrix}
10    begin
11      {compute s [i] = number of terms in row i of b}
12      for i := 1 to n do s [i] := 0; {initialize}
13      for i := 1 to t do s [a [i,2]] := s [a [i,2]] + 1;
14      {u [i] = starting position of row i in b}
15      u [1] := 1;
16      for i := 2 to n do u [i] := u [i−1] + s [i−1];
17      for i := 1 to t do {move from a to b}
18      begin
19        j := u [a [i,2]];
20        b [j,1] := a [i,2]; b [j,2] := a [i,1]; b [j,3] := a [i,3];
21        u [a [i,2]] := j + 1;
22      end;
23    end; {of if}
24  end; {of fasttranspose}
```

Program 2.5 Procedure *fasttranspose*

The correctness of procedure *FastTranspose* follows from the preceding discussion and the observation that the starting point of row i, $i > 1$ of B is $u[i-1] + s[i-1]$ where $s[i-1]$ is the number of elements in row $i-1$ of B and $u[i-1]$ is the starting point of row $i-1$. The computation of s and t is carried out in lines 12-16. In lines 17-22 the elements of a are examined one by one starting from the first and successively moving to the t'th element. $u[j]$ is maintained so that it is always the position in b where the next element in row j is to be inserted.

There are four loops in *FastTranspose* which are executed n, t, $n-1$, and t times respectively. Each iteration of the loops takes only a constant amount of time, so the order of magnitude is $O(n + t)$. The computing time of $O(n + t)$ becomes $O(nm)$ when t is of the order of nm. This is the same as when two dimensional arrays were in use. However, the constant factor associated with *FastTranspose* is bigger than that for the array algorithm. When t is sufficiently small compared to its maximum of nm, *FastTranspose* will be faster. Hence in this representation, we save both space and time! This was not true of *transpose* since t will almost always be greater than max$\{n,m\}$ and nt

will therefore always be at least *nm*. The constant factor associated with *transpose* is also bigger than the one in the array algorithm. Finally, you should note that *FastTranspose* requires more space than does *transpose*. The space required by *FastTranspose* can be reduced by utilizing the same space to represent the two arrays *s* and *t*.

If we try the algorithm on the sparse matrix of Figure 2.3, then after execution of the third **for** loop, the values of *s* and *t* are

	[1]	[2]	[3]	[4]	[5]	[6]
$s =$	2	1	2	2	0	1
$u =$	1	3	4	6	8	8

$s[i]$ is the number of entries in row *i* of the transpose. $u[i]$ points to the position in the transpose where the next element of row *i* is to be stored.

Suppose now you are working for a machine manufacturer who is using a computer to do inventory control. Associated with each machine that the company produces, say MACH[1] to MACH[*m*], there is a list of parts that it is comprised of. This information could be represented in a two-dimensional table as in Figure 2.4.

	PART[1]	PART[2]	PART[3]	. . .	PART[*n*]
MACH[1]	0,	5,	2,	. . .,	0
MACH[2]	0,	0,	0,	. . .,	3
MACH[3]	1,	1,	0,	. . .,	8
.	.	.	.		.
.	.	.	.		.
.	.	.	.		.
MACH[*m*]	6,	0,	0,	. . .,	7
		array	MACHPT[*m*,*n*]		

Figure 2.4 Machine parts table

The table will be sparse and all entries will be nonnegative integers; MACHPT[*i*,*j*] is the number of units of PART[*j*] in MACH[*i*]. Each part is itself composed of smaller parts called microparts. This data will also be encoded in a table whose rows are PART[1] to PART[*n*] and whose columns are MICPT[1] to MICPT[*p*]. We want to determine the number of microparts that are necessary to make up each machine.

Observe that the number of MICPT[*j*] making up MACH[*i*] is

$$\text{MACHPT}[i,1] * \text{MICPT}[1,j] + \text{MACHPT}[i,2] * \text{MICPT}[2,j]$$
$$+ \ldots + \text{MACHPT}[i,n] * \text{MICPT}[n,j]$$

where the arrays are named MACHPT[m,n] and MICPT[n,p]. This sum is more conveniently written as

$$\sum_{k=1}^{n} \text{MACHPT}[i,k] * \text{MICPT}[k,j]$$

If we compute these sums for each machine and each micro part then we will have a total of mp values that we might store in a third table MACHSUM[m,p]. Regarding these tables as matrices, this application leads to the general definition of matrix product:

Given A and B where A is $m \times n$ and B is $n \times p$, the product matrix C has dimension $m \times p$. Its i,j element is defined as

$$c_{ij} = \sum_{1 \leq k \leq n} a_{ik}b_{kj}$$

for $1 \leq i \leq m$ and $1 \leq j \leq p$. The product of two sparse matrices may no longer be sparse, for instance,

$$\begin{bmatrix} 1, & 0, & 0 \\ 1, & 0, & 0 \\ 1, & 0, & 0 \end{bmatrix} \begin{bmatrix} 1, & 1, & 1 \\ 0, & 0, & 0 \\ 0, & 0, & 0 \end{bmatrix} = \begin{bmatrix} 1 & 1 & 1 \\ 1 & 1 & 1 \\ 1 & 1 & 1 \end{bmatrix}$$

Consider an algorithm that computes the product of two sparse matrices represented as an ordered list instead of an array. To compute the elements of C row-wise so we can store them in their proper place without moving previously computed elements, we must do the following: fix a row of A and find all elements in column j of B for $j = 1,2,\ldots,p$. Normally, to find all the elements in column j of B we would have to scan all of B. To avoid this, we can first compute the transpose of B which will put all column elements consecutively. Once the elements in row i of A and column j of B have been located, we just do a merge operation similar to the polynomial addition of Section 2.2. An alternative approach is explored in the exercises.

Before we write a matrix multiplication procedure, it will be useful to define a subprocedure as in Program 2.6.

The procedure *mmult* (Program 2.7) multiplies the matrices A and B to obtain the product matrix C using the strategy outlined above. A, B, and C are stored as sparse matrices in the arrays a, b, and c, respectively. Procedure *mmult* makes use of variables i, j, q, r, *col*, and *RowBegin*. The variable r is the row of A that is currently being multiplied with the columns of B. *RowBegin* is the position in a of the first element of row r. *col* is the column of B that is currently being multiplied with row r of A. q is the position of c for the next element generated. i and j are used to examine successively elements of row r and column *col* of A and B, respectively. In addition to all this, line 20 of the algorithm introduces a dummy term into each of a and d. This enables us to handle end

```
procedure StoreSum(var c : SparseMatrix; var q : integer;
                        row, col: integer; var sum: integer);
{If sum ≠ 0, then it along with its row and column position
is stored as the q+1'st entry in c}
begin
  if sum <> 0 then
    if q < MaxTerms then begin
                          q := q + 1;
                          c [q,1] := row;
                          c [q,2] := col;
                          c [q,3] := sum;
                          sum := 0;
                       end
    else begin
            writeln('Number of terms in product exceeds MaxTerms');
            halt; {terminate program}
          end;
end; {of StoreSum}
```

Program 2.6 Storesum

conditions (i.e., computations involving the last row of *A* or last column of *B*) in an elegant way.

```
 1  procedure mmult (a,b : SparseMatrix; var c : SparseMatrix);
 2  {c = a*b; a is m×n and b is n×p}
 3  var i,j,m,n,p,q,r,ta,tb,col,sum,RowBegin : integer;
 4     d : SparseMatrix;
 5  begin
 6    m := a[0,1]; n := a[0,2]; ta := a[0,3];
 7    if n <> b[0,1] then begin
 8                          writeln('Incompatible matrices');
 9                          halt; {terminate program}
10                        end;
11    p := b[0,2]; tb := b[0,3];
12    if (ta >= MaxTerms) or (tb >= MaxTerms) then
13              begin
14                 writeln('Too many terms in a or b');
15                 halt; {terminate program}
16              end;
17    fasttranspose (b,d);
18    i := 1; q := 0; RowBegin := 1; r := a[1,1];
```

```
19     {set boundary conditions}
20     a [ta+1,1] := m + 1; d [tb+1,1] := p + 1;
21     d [tb+1,2] := 0; sum := 0;
22     while i <= ta do {generate row r of c}
23     begin
24       col := d [1,1]; j := 1;
25       while j <= tb + 1 do {multiply row r of a by column col of b}
26       begin
27         if a [i,1] <> r
28         then begin  {end of row r}
29                 StoreSum (c,q,r,col,sum);
30                 i := RowBegin;
31                 {go to next column}
32                 while d [j,1] = col do j := j + 1;
33                 col := d [j,1];
34               end
35         else if d [j,1] <> col
36               then begin {end of column col of b}
37                     StoreSum (c,q,r,col,sum);
38                     {set to multiply row r with next column}
39                     i := RowBegin; col := d [j,1];
40                   end
41               else if a [i,2] < d [j,2]
42                     then i := i + 1 {advance to next term in row}
43                     else if a [i,2] = d [j,2]
44                         then begin {add to sum}
45                             sum := sum + a [i,3] * d [j,3];
46                             i := i + 1;  j := j + 1;
47                           end
48                         else {advance to next term in column col}
49                             j := j + 1;
50       end; {of while j <= tb + 1}
51       while a [i,1] = r do {advance to next row}
52         i := i + 1;
53       RowBegin := i; r := a [i,1];
54     end; {end of while i <= ta}
55     c[0,1] := m; c[0,2] := p; c[0,3] := q;
56 end; {of mmult}
```

Program 2.7 Procedure *mmult*

We leave the correctness proof of this algorithm as an exercise. Let us examine its complexity. In addition to the space needed for *a, b, c,* and some simple variables, space is also needed for the transpose matrix *d*. Algorithm *FastTranspose* also needs some additional space. The exercises explore a strategy for *mmult* which does not explicitly compute d, and the only additional space needed is the same as that required by *Fast-Transpose*. Turning our attention to the computing time of *mmult*, we see that lines 6-21 require only $O(p + tb)$ time. The **while** loop of lines 22-54 is executed at most m times (once for each row of A). In each iteration of the **while** loop of lines 25-50 either the value of i or of j or both increases by 1 or i and *col* are reset. The maximum total increment in j over the whole loop is tb. If d_r is the number of terms in row r of A, then the value of i can increase at most d_r times before i moves to the next row of A. When this happens, i is reset to *RowBegin* in line 30. At the same time *col* is advanced to the next column. Hence, this resetting can take place at most p times (there are only p columns in B). The total maximum increments in i is therefore pd_r. The maximum number of iterations of the **while** loop of lines 25-50 is therefore $p + pd_r + tb$. The time for this loop while multiplying with row r of A is $O(pd_r + tb)$. Lines 51-53 take only $O(d_r)$ time. Hence, the time for the outer **while** loop, lines 22-54, for the iteration with row r of A is $O(pd_r + tb)$. The overall time for this loop is then $O(\Sigma_r(pd_r + tb)) = O(p*ta + m*tb)$.

Once again, we may compare the computing time with the time to multiply matrices when arrays are used. The classical multiplication algorithm is

```
for i := 1 to m do
  for j := 1 to p do
  begin
    sum := 0;
    for k := 1 to n do
      sum := sum + a [i,k] * b [k,j];
    c [i,j] := sum;
  end;
```

The time for this is $O(mnp)$. Since $ta \leq nm$ and $tb \leq np$, the time for *mmult* is at most $O(mnp)$. However, its constant factor is greater than that for matrix multiplication using arrays. In the worst case when $ta = nm$ or $tb = np$, *mmult* will be slower by a constant factor. However, when ta and tb are sufficiently smaller than their maximum values, i.e., A and B are sparse, *mmult* will outperform the above multiplication algorithm for arrays.

The above analysis for *mmult* is nontrivial. It introduces some new concepts in algorithm analysis and you should make sure you understand the analysis.

This representation for sparse matrices permits one to perform operations such as addition, transpose, and multiplication efficiently. There are, however, other considerations that make this representation undesirable in certain applications. Since the number of terms in a sparse matrix is variable, we would like to represent all our sparse matrices in one array (as we did for polynomials in Section 2.2), rather than using a separate array for each matrix. This would enable us to make efficient utilization of space. However, when this is done, we run into difficulties in allocating space from this array to any individual matrix. These difficulties also arise with the polynomial representation of the previous section and will become apparent when we study a similar representation for multiple stacks and queues in Section 3.4.

2.4 REPRESENTATION OF ARRAYS

Even though multidimensional arrays are provided as a standard data object in most high level languages, it is interesting to see how they are represented in memory. Recall that memory may be regarded as one-dimensional with words numbered from 1 to m. So we are concerned with representing n dimensional arrays in a one-dimensional memory. While many representations might seem plausible, we must select one in which the location in memory of an arbitrary array element, say $A[i_1, i_2, \ldots, i_n]$, can be determined efficiently. This is necessary since programs using arrays may, in general, use array elements in a random order. In addition to being able to retrieve array elements easily, it is also necessary to be able to determine the amount of memory space to be reserved for a particular array. Assuming that each array element requires only one word of memory, the number of words needed is the number of elements in the array. If an array is declared $A[l_1..u_1, l_2..u_2, \ldots, l_n..u_n]$, then it is easy to see that the number of elements is

$$\prod_{i=1}^{n} (u_i - l_i + 1)$$

One of the common ways to represent an array is in *row major order*. If we have the declaration

$$A[4..5, 2..4, 1..2, 3..4]$$

then we have a total of $2*3*2*2 = 24$ elements. Using row major order, these elements will be stored as

$$A[4,2,1,3], A[4,2,1,4], A[4,2,2,3], A[4,2,2,4]$$

and continuing

$$A[4,3,1,3], A[4,3,1,4], A[4,3,2,3], A[4,3,2,4]$$

for three more sets of four until we get

$$A[5,4,1,3], A[5,4,1,4], A[5,4,2,3], A[5,4,2,4]$$

We see that the subscript at the right moves the fastest. In fact, if we view the subscripts as numbers, we see that they are, in some sense, increasing:

$$4213, 4214, \ldots, 5423, 5424$$

A synonym for row major order is *lexicographic order*.

From the compiler's point of view, the problem is how to translate from the name $A[i_1, i_2, \ldots, i_n]$ to the correct location in memory. Suppose $A[4,2,1,3]$ is stored at location 100. Then $A[4,2,1,4]$ will be at 101 and $A[5,4,2,4]$ at location 123. These two addresses are easy to guess. In general, we can derive a formula for the address of any element. This formula makes use of only the starting address of the array plus the declared dimensions.

To simplify the discussion we shall assume that the lower bounds on each dimension l_i are 1. The general case when l_i can be any integer is discussed in the exercises. Before obtaining a formula for the case of an n-dimensional array, let us look at the row major representation of one-, two-, and three-dimensional arrays. To begin with, if A is declared $A[1..u_1]$, then assuming one word per element, it may be represented in sequential memory as in Figure 2.5. If α is the address of $A[1]$, then the address of an arbitrary element $A[i]$ is just $\alpha + i - 1$.

array element:	$A[1]$	$A[2]$	$A[3]$	$\cdots$	$A[i]$	$\cdots$	$A[u_1]$
address:	α	$\alpha+1$	$\alpha+2$	$\cdots$	$\alpha+i-1$	$\cdots$	$\alpha+u_1-1$

Figure 2.5 Sequential representation of $A[1..u_1]$

The two dimensional array $A[1..u_1, 1..u_2]$ may be interpreted as u_1 rows, $row_1, row_2, \ldots, row_{u_1}$, each row consisting of u_2 elements. In a row major representation, these rows would be represented in memory as in Figure 2.6.

Again, if α is the address of $A[1,1]$, then the address of $A[i,1]$ is $\alpha + (i-1)u_2$, as there are $i-1$ rows each of size u_2 preceding the first element in the i'th row. Knowing the address of $A[i,1]$, we can say that the address of $A[i,j]$ is then simply $\alpha + (i-1)u_2 + (j-1)$.

Figure 2.7 shows the representation of the three-dimensional array $A[1..u_1, 1..u_2, 1..u_3]$. This array is interpreted as u_1 two-dimensional arrays of dimension $u_2 \times u_3$. To locate $A[i,j,k]$, we first obtain $\alpha + (i-1)u_2 u_3$ as the address for $A[i,1,1]$ since there are $i-1$ two-dimensional arrays of size $u_2 \times u_3$ preceding this element. From this and the formula for addressing a two-dimensional array, we obtain $\alpha + (i-1)u_2 u_3 + (j-1)u_3 + (k-1)$ as the address of $A[i,j,k]$.

Generalizing on the preceding discussion, the addressing formula for any element $A[i_1, i_2, \ldots, i_n]$ in an n-dimensional array declared as $A[1..u_1, 1..u_2, \ldots, 1..u_n]$ may be easily obtained. If α is the address for $A[1,1,\ldots,1]$ then $\alpha + (i_1-1)u_2 u_3 \ldots u_n$ is the address for $A[i_1, 1, \ldots, 1]$. The address for $A[i_1, i_2, 1, \ldots, 1]$ is then $\alpha + (i_1-1)u_2 u_3 \ldots u_n + (i_2-1)u_3 u_4 \ldots u_n$.

Repeating in this way the address for $A[i_1, i_2, \ldots, i_n]$ is

$$\alpha + (i_1 - 1)u_2 u_3 \ldots u_n$$
$$+ (i_2 - 1)u_3 u_4 \ldots u_n$$
$$+ (i_3 - 1)u_4 u_5 \ldots u_n$$

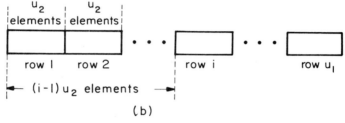

	col 1	col 2	...	col u_2
row 1	X	X	...	X
row 2	X	X	...	X
row 3	X	X	...	X
		⋮		
row u_1	X	X	...	X

(a)

(b)

Figure 2.6 Sequential representation of $A[1..u_1, 1..u_2]$.

$$\cdots$$

$$+ (i_{n-1} - 1)u_n$$
$$+ (i_n - 1)$$

$$= \alpha + \sum_{j=1}^{n} (i_j - 1)a_j \text{ where } \begin{cases} a_j = \prod_{k=j+1}^{n} u_k \quad 1 \le j < n \\ a_n = 1 \end{cases}$$

Note that a_j may be computed from a_{j+1}, $1 \le j < n$, using only one multiplication as $a_j = u_{j+1}a_{j+1}$. Thus, a compiler will initially take the declared bounds $u_1, \ldots, u_n$ and use them to compute the constants $a_1, \ldots, a_{n-1}$ using $n-2$ multiplications. The address of $A[i_1, \ldots, i_n]$ can then be found using the formula, requiring $n-1$ more multiplications and n additions and n subtractions.

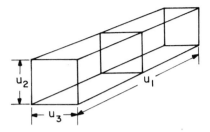

(a) 3-dimensional array $A[1..u_1, 1..u_2, 1..u_3]$ regarded as u_1 2-dimensional arrays.

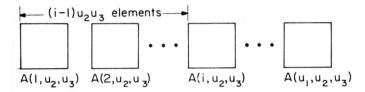

(b) Sequential row major representation of a 3-dimensional array. Each 2-dimensional array is represented as in Figure 2.6.

Figure 2.7 Sequential representation of $A[1..u_1, 1..u_2, 1..u_3]$

An alternative scheme for array representation, column major order, is considered in Exercise 19.

To review, in this chapter we have used arrays to represent ordered lists of polynomials and sparse matrices. In all cases we have been able to move values around, accessing arbitrary elements in a fixed amount of time, and this has given us efficient algorithms. However, several problems have been raised. First, by using a sequential mapping that associates a_i of $(a_1, \ldots, a_n)$ with the i'th element of the array, we are forced to move data around whenever an insert or delete operation is used. Second, once we adopt one ordering of the data, we sacrifice the ability to have a second ordering simultaneously.

2.5 EXERCISES

1. Write a Pascal procedure that multiplies two polynomials represented using the array *terms* of Section 2.2. What is the computing time of your procedure?

2. Write a Pascal procedure that evaluates a polynomial at a value x_0 using the representation of Exercise 1. Try to minimize the number of operations.

3. If $A = (a_1, \ldots, a_n)$ and $B = (b_1, \ldots, b_m)$ are ordered lists, then $A < B$ if $a_i = b_i$ for $1 \le i < j$ and $a_j < b_j$, or, if $a_i = b_i$ for $1 \le i \le n$ and $n < m$. Write a procedure which returns $-1, 0, +1$, depending upon whether $A < B$, $A = B$, or $A > B$. Assume you can compare atoms a_i and b_j.

4. Assume that n lists, $n > 1$, are being represented sequentially in the one-dimensional array *space* $[1..m]$. Let *front*$[i]$ be one less than the position of the first element in the i'th list and let *rear*$[i]$ point to the last element in the i'th list, $1 \le i \le n$. Assume that *rear*$[i] \le$ *front*$[i + 1]$, $1 \le i \le n$ and *front*$[n + 1] = m$. The functions to be performed on these lists are insertion and deletion.

    (a) Obtain suitable initial and boundary conditions for *front*$[i]$ and *rear*$[i]$.

    (b) Write a procedure *insert* $(i, j, item:$ **integer**$)$ to insert *item* after the $(j - 1)$'st element in list i. This procedure should fail to make an insertion only if there are already m elements in *space*.

5. Using the assumptions of Exercise 4 write a procedure *delete* $(i, j:$ **integer; var** *item*: **integer**$)$ that sets *item* to the j'th element of the i'th list and removes it. The i'th list should be maintained as sequentially stored.

6. The polynomials $A(x) = x^{2n} + x^{2n-2} + \ldots + x^2 + x^0$ and $B(x) = x^{2n+1} + x^{2n-1} + \ldots + x^3 + x$ cause *padd* to work very hard. For these polynomials, determine the exact number of times each statement will be executed.

7. Analyze carefully the computing time and storage requirements of algorithm *Fast-Transpose*. What can you say about the existence of an even faster algorithm?

8. Using the idea in *FastTranspose* of m row pointers, rewrite algorithm *mmult* to multiply two sparse matrices A and B represented as in Section 2.3 without transposing B. What is the computing time of your algorithm?

9. When all the elements either above or below the main diagonal of a square matrix are zero, then the matrix is said to be triangular. Figure 2.8 shows a lower and an upper triangular matrix. In a lower triangular matrix, A, with n rows, the maximum number of nonzero terms in row i is i. Hence, the total number of nonzero terms is $\Sigma_{i=1}^{n} i = n(n + 1)/2$. For large n it would be worthwhile to save the space taken by the zero entries in the upper triangle. Obtain an addressing formula for elements a_{ij} in the lower triangle if this lower triangle is stored by rows in an array

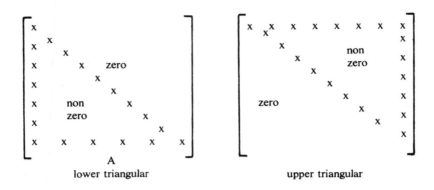

Figure 2.8 Lower and upper triangular matrices

$B[1..n(n+1)/2]$ with $A[1,1]$ being stored in $B[1]$. What is the relationship between i and j for elements in the zero part of A?

10. Let A and B be two lower triangular matrices, each with n rows. The total number of elements in the lower triangles is $n(n+1)$. Devise a scheme to represent both the triangles in an array $c[1..n, 1..n+1]$. [Hint: Represent the triangle of A as the lower triangle of c and the transpose of B as the upper triangle of c.] Write algorithms to determine the values of $A[i,j]$, $B[i,j]$, $1 \le i$, $j \le n$ from the array c.

11. Another kind of sparse matrix that arises often in numerical analysis is the tridiagonal matrix. In this square matrix, all elements other than those on the major diagonal and on the diagonals immediately above and below this one are zero (Figure 2.9). If the elements in the band formed by these three diagonals are represented row-wise in an array, b, with $A[1,1]$ being stored in $b[1]$, obtain an algorithm to determine the value of $A[i,j]$, $1 \le i$, $j \le n$ from the array b.

12. Define a square band matrix $A_{n,a}$ to be an $n \times n$ matrix in which all the nonzero terms lie in a band centered around the main diagonal. The band includes $a - 1$ diagonals below and above the main diagonal and also the main diagonal (Figure 2.10).

    (a) How many elements are there in the band of $A_{n,a}$?

    (b) What is the relationship between i and j for elements a_{ij} in the band of $A_{n,a}$?

    (c) Assume that the band of $A_{n,a}$ is stored sequentially in an array b by diagonals starting with the lowermost diagonal. Thus, $A_{4,3}$ above would have the

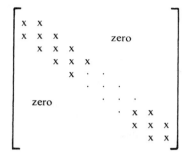

Figure 2.9 Tridiagonal matrix A

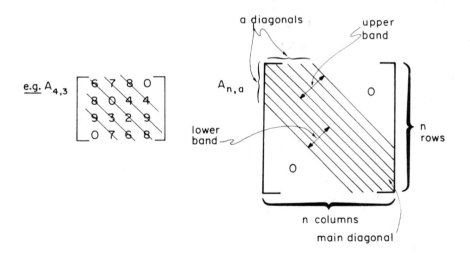

Figure 2.10 Square band matrix

following representation:

b[1]	b[2]	b[3]	b[4]	b[5]	b[6]	b[7]	b[8]	b[9] .	b[10]	b[11]	b[12]	b[13]	b[14]
9	7	8	3	6	6	0	2	8	7	4	9	8	4
a_{31}	a_{42}	a_{21}	a_{32}	a_{43}	a_{11}	a_{22}	a_{33}	a_{44}	a_{12}	a_{23}	a_{34}	a_{13}	a_{24}

Obtain an addressing formula for the location of an element a_{ij} in the lower band of $A_{n,a}$, e.g., $LOC(a_{31}) = 1$, $LOC(a_{42}) = 2$ in the example above.

13. A generalized band matrix $A_{n,a,b}$ is an $n \times n$ matrix A in which all the nonzero terms lie in a band made up of $a - 1$ diagonals below the main diagonal, the main diagonal, and $b - 1$ diagonals above the main diagonal (Figure 2.11)

(a) How many elements are there in the band of $A_{n,a,b}$?

(b) What is the relationship between i and j for elements a_{ij} in the band of $A_{n,a,b}$?

(c) Obtain a sequential representation of the band of $A_{n,a,b}$ in the one-dimensional array c. For this representation, write a Pascal procedure *value* (n,a,b,i,j,c) that determines the value of element a_{ij} in the matrix $A_{n,a,b}$. The band of $A_{n,a,b}$ is represented in the array c.

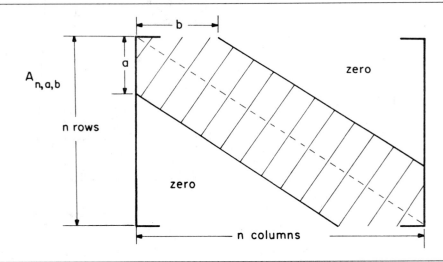

Figure 2.11 Generalized band matrix

14. How much time does it take to locate an arbitrary element $A[i,j]$ in the representation of Section 2.3 and to change its value?

15. A variation of the scheme discussed in Section 2.3 for sparse matrix representation involves representing only the nonzero terms in a one-dimensional array v in the order described. In addition, a strip of $n \times m$ bits, $bits[1..n, 1..m]$ is also kept. $bits[i,j] = 0$ if $A[i,j] = 0$ and $bits[i,j] = 1$ if $A[i,j] \neq 0$. The figure below illustrates the representation for the sparse matrix of Figure 2.3.

$$\begin{bmatrix} 1 & 0 & 0 & 1 & 0 & 1 \\ 0 & 1 & 1 & 0 & 0 & 0 \\ 0 & 0 & 0 & 1 & 0 & 0 \\ 0 & 0 & 0 & 0 & 0 & 0 \\ 1 & 0 & 0 & 0 & 0 & 0 \\ 0 & 0 & 1 & 0 & 0 & 0 \end{bmatrix} \quad \begin{bmatrix} 15 \\ 22 \\ -15 \\ 11 \\ 3 \\ -6 \\ 91 \\ 28 \end{bmatrix}$$

    (a) On a computer with w bits per word, how much storage is needed to represent a sparse matrix $A_{n \times m}$ with t nonzero terms?

    (b) Write an algorithm to add two sparse matrices A and C, represented as above, to obtain $D = A + C$. How much time does your algorithm take?

    (c) Discuss the merits of this representation versus the representation of Section 2.3. Consider space and time requirements for such operations as random access, add, multiply, and transpose. Note that the random access time can be improved somewhat by keeping another array ra such that $ra[i] = $ number of nonzero terms in rows 1 through $i - 1$.

16. A complex-valued matrix X is represented by a pair of matrices (A,B) where A and B contain real values. Write a program that computes the product of two complex-valued matrices (A,B) and (C,D), where $(A,B) * (C,D) = (A + iB) * (C + iD) = (AC - BD) + i(AD + BC)$. Determine the number of additions and multiplications if the matrices are all $n \times n$.

17. How many values can be held by an array with dimensions $a[0..n]$, $b[-1..n, 1..m]$, $c[-n..0, 1..2]$?

18. Obtain an addressing formula for the element $A[i_1, i_2, \ldots, i_n]$ in an array declared as $A[l_1..u_1, l_2..u_2, \ldots, l_n..u_n]$. Assume a row major representation of the array with one word per element and α the address of $A[l_1, l_2, \ldots, l_n]$.

19. Do Exercise 18 assuming a column major representation. In this representation, a two-dimensional array is stored sequentially by columns rather than by rows.

20. An $m \times n$ matrix is said to have a *saddle point* if some entry $A[i,j]$ is the smallest value in row i and the largest value in column j. Write a Pascal program which determines the location of a saddle point if one exists. What is the computing time of your method?

21. Given an array $a[1..n]$ produce the array $z[1..n]$ such that $z[1] = a[n]$, $z[2] = a[n-1], \ldots, z[n-1] = a[2], z[n] = a[1]$. Use a minimal amount of storage.

22. One possible set of axioms for an ordered list comes from the six operations of Section 2.2. This set is given in Structure 2.3. Use these axioms to describe the list $A = (a,b,c,d,e)$, and show what happens when $DEL(A, 2)$ is executed.

---

structure *ORDERED__LIST* (*atoms*)
   declare *MTLST* ( ) $\rightarrow$ *list*
        LEN (*list*) $\rightarrow$ *integer*
        RET (*list,integer*) $\rightarrow$ *atom*
        STO (*list,integer,atom*) $\rightarrow$ *list*
        INS (*list,integer,atom*) $\rightarrow$ *list*
        DEL (*list,integer*) $\rightarrow$ *list* ;
   for all $L \ \varepsilon \ list, \ i,j \varepsilon \ integer \ a,b \ \varepsilon \ atom$ **let**
    LEN (*MTLST*) :: = 0; *LEN* (*STO* (*L,i,a*)) ::= 1 + *LEN* (*L*)
    RET (*MTLST,j*) :: = *error*
    RET (*STO* (*L,i,a*),*j*) :: =
     if $i = j$ **then** a **else** *RET* (*L,j*)
    INS (*MTLST, j,b*) :: = *STO* (*MTLST, j,b*)
    INS (*STO* (*L,i,a*),*j,b*) ;; =
     if $i \geq j$ **then** *STO* (*INS* (*L,j,b*), $i + 1,a$)
          else *STO* (*INS* (*L,j,b*),*i,a*)
    DEL (*MTLST,j*) :: = *MTLST*
    DEL (*STO* (*L,i,a*),*j*) :: =
     if $i = j$ **then** *DEL* (*L,j*)
         else if $i > j$ **then** *STO* (*DEL* (*L,j*),$i - 1,a$)
             else *STO* (*DEL* (*L,j*),*i,a*)
   end
end *ORDERED__LIST*

Structure 2.3 Specification of an ordered list

23. There are a number of problems, known collectively as "random walk" problems, which have been of longstanding interest to the mathematical community. All but the most simple of these are extremely difficult to solve and for the most part they remain largely unsolved. One such problem may be stated as:

A (drunken) cockroach is placed on a given square in the middle of a tile floor in a rectangular room of size $n \times m$ tiles. The bug wanders (possibly in search of an aspirin) randomly from tile to tile throughout the room. Assuming that he may move from his present tile to any of the eight tiles surrounding him (unless he is against a wall) *with equal probability*, how long will it take him to touch every tile on the floor at least once?

Hard as this problem may be to solve by pure probability theory techniques, it is quite easy to solve using the computer. The technique for doing so is called "simulation". This technique is widely used in industry to predict traffic flow, inventory control, and so forth. The problem may be simulated using the following method:

An $n \times m$ array *count* is used to represent the number of times our cockroach has reached each tile on the floor. All the cells of this array are initialized to zero. The position of the bug on the floor is represented by the coordinates $(ibug, jbug)$. The eight possible moves of the bug are represented by the tiles located at $(ibug + imove [k], jbug + jmove [k])$, where $1 \le k \le 8$ and

$$
\begin{array}{ll}
imove[1] = -1 & jmove[1] = 1 \\
imove[2] = 0 & jmove[2] = 1 \\
imove[3] = 1 & jmove[3] = 1 \\
imove[4] = 1 & jmove[4] = 0 \\
imove[5] = 1 & jmove[5] = -1 \\
imove[6] = 0 & jmove[6] = -1 \\
imove[7] = -1 & jmove[7] = -1 \\
imove[8] = -1 & jmove[8] = 0
\end{array}
$$

A *random walk* to one of the eight given squares is simulated by generating a random value for k lying between 1 and 8. Of course the bug cannot move outside the room, so that coordinates that lead up a wall must be ignored and a new random combination formed. Each time a square is entered, the count for that square is incremented so that a nonzero entry shows the number of times the bug has landed on that square so far. When every square has been entered at least once, the experiment is complete.

Write a program to perform the specified simulation experiment. Your program *MUST*:

(a) handle all values of n and m, $2 < n \leq 40$, $2 \leq m \leq 20$;

(b) perform the experiment for: (1) $n = 15$, $m = 15$ starting point: (20,10), and (2) $n = 39$, $m = 19$ starting point: (1,1);

(c) have an iteration limit, that is, a maximum number of squares the bug may enter during the experiment (this assures that your program does not get "hung" in an "infinite" loop) a maximum of 50,000 is appropriate for this exercise; and

(d) for each experiment, print: (1) the total number of legal moves that the cockroach makes, and (2) the final *count* array (this will show the "density" of the walk, that is, the number of times each tile on the floor was touched during the experiment).

(Have an aspirin.) This exercise was contributed by Olson.

24. Chess provides the setting for many fascinating diversions that are quite independent of the game itself. Many of these are based on the strange "L-shaped" move of the knight. A classical example is the problem of the knight's tour, which has captured the attention of mathematicians and puzzle enthusiasts since the beginning of the eighteenth century. Briefly stated, the problem is to move the knight, beginning from any given square on the chessboard, in such a manner that it travels successively to all 64 squares, touching each square once and only once. It is convenient to represent a solution by placing the numbers 1, 2, ..., 64 in the squares of the chessboard indicating the order in which the squares are reached. Note that it is not required that the knight be able to reach the initial position by one more move; if this is possible the knight's tour is called re-entrant. One of the more ingenious methods for solving the problem of the knight's tour was that given by J. C. Warnsdorff in 1823. His rule was that the knight must always be moved to one of the squares from which there are the fewest exits to squares not already traversed.

The goal of this exercise is to write a computer program to implement Warnsdorff's rule. The ensuing discussion will be much easier to follow, however, if you first try to construct a particular solution to the problem by hand before reading any further.

The most important decisions to be made in solving a problem of this type are those concerning how the data is to be represented in the computer. Perhaps the most natural way to represent the chessboard is by an 8×8 array *board* as shown in Figure 2.12. The eight possible moves of a knight on square (5,3) are also shown in this figure. In general a knight at (i,j) may move to one of the squares $(i-2,j+1)$, $(i-1,j+2)$, $(i+1,j+2)$, $(i+2,j+1)$, $(i+2,j-1)$, $(i+1,j-2)$, $(i-1,j-2)$, $(i-2,j-1)$. Notice, however, that if (i,j) is located near one of the edges of the board, some of these possibilities could move the knight off the board, and, of course, this is not permitted. The eight possible knight moves may

	1	2	3	4	5	6	7	8
1								
2								
3		8		1				
4	7				2			
5			K					
6	6				3			
7		5		4				
8								

Figure 2.12 Legal moves for a knight

conveniently be represented by two arrays *ktmov1* and *ktmov2*, as shown below.

ktmov1	ktmov2
-2	1
-1	2
1	2
2	1
2	-1
1	-2
-1	-2
-2	-1

Then a knight at (i, j) may move to $(i + ktmov1[k], j + ktmov2[k])$, where k is some value between 1 and 8, provided that the new square lies on the chessboard.

Below is a description of an algorithm for solving the knight's tour problem using Warnsdoff's rule. The data representation discussed in the previous section is assumed.

(a)   [Initialize chessboard] For $1 \leq i, j \leq 8$ set *board* $[i, j]$ to 0.

(b)   [Set starting position] Read and print i, j and then set *board*$[i, j]$ to 1.

(c)   [Loop] For $2 \leq m \leq 64$, do steps (d) through (g).

(d)   [Form set of possible next squares] Test each of the eight squares one knight's move away from (i, j) and form a list of the possibilities for the next square (*nexti* $[l]$, *nextj* $[l]$). Let *npos* be the number of possibilities. (That is, after performing this step we will have *nexti* $[l] = i + ktmov1[k]$ and *nextj* $[l]$ $= j + ktmov2[k]$, for certain values of k between 1 and 8. Some of the squares $(i + ktmov1[k]$, $j + ktmov2[k])$ may be impossible for the next move either because they lie off the chessboard or because they have been previously occupied by the knight -- i.e., they contain a nonzero number. In every case we will have $0 \leq npos \leq 8$.)

(e)   [Test special cases] If *npos* = 0, the knight's tour has come to a premature end; report failure and then go to step (h). If *npos* = 1, there is only one possibility for the next move; set *min* = 1 and go right to step (g).

(f)   [Find next square with minimum number of exits] For $1 \leq l \leq npos$ set *exits*$[l]$ to the number of exits from square (*nexti* $[l]$, *nextj* $[l]$). That is, for each of the values of l, examine each of the next squares (*nexti* $[l]+ktmov1[k]$, *nextj* $[l] + ktmov2[k]$) to see if it is an exit from (*nexti* $[l]$, *nextj* $[l]$), and count the number of such exits in *exits* $[l]$. (Recall that a square is an exit if it lies on the chessboard and has not been previously occupied by the knight.) Finally, set *min* to the location of the minimum value of *exits*. (There may be more than one occurrence of the minimum value of *exits*. If this happens, it is convenient to let *min* denote the first such occurrence, although it is important to realize that by so doing we are not actually guaranteed finding a solution. Nevertheless, the chances of finding a complete knight's tour in this way are remarkably good, and that is sufficient for the purposes of this exercise.)

(g)   [Move knight] Set $i = nexti\,[min]$, $j = nextj\,[min]$, and *board*$[i, j] = m$. (Thus, (i, j) denotes the new position of the knight, and board$[i, j]$ records the move in proper sequence.)

(h)   [Print] Print out *board* showing the solution to the knight's tour, and then terminate the algorithm.

The problem is to write a Pascal program which corresponds to this algorithm. This exercise was contributed by Legenhausen and Rebman.

CHAPTER 3
STACKS AND QUEUES

3.1 FUNDAMENTALS

Two of the more common data objects found in computer algorithms are stacks and queues. They arise so often that we will discuss them separately before moving on to more complex objects. Both these data objects are special cases of the more general data object, ordered list, which we considered in the previous chapter. Recall that $A = (a_1, a_2, \ldots, a_n)$ is an ordered list of $N \geq 0$ elements. The a_i are referred to as atoms or elements which are taken from some set. The null or empty list has $n = 0$ elements.

A *stack* is an ordered list in which all insertions and deletions are at one end, called the *top*. A *queue* is an ordered list in which all insertions take place at one end, the *rear*, while all deletions take place at the other end, the *front*. See Figure 3.1 for an example of both. Given a stack $S = (a_1, \ldots, a_n)$, we say that a_1 is the *bottommost* element and element a_i is on *top* of element a_{i-1}, $1 < i \leq n$. When viewed as a queue with a_n as the *rear* element, we say that a_{i+1} is *behind* a_i, $1 \leq i < n$.

The restrictions on a stack imply that if the elements A, B, C, D, E are added to the stack, in that order, then the first element to be removed/deleted must be E. Equivalently we say that the last element to be inserted into the stack will be the first to be removed. For this reason stacks are sometimes referred to as *Last-In-First-Out* (LIFO) lists. The restrictions on a queue require that the first element which is inserted into the queue will be the first one to be removed. Thus A is the first letter to be removed, and queues are known as *First-In-First-Out* (FIFO) lists. Note that the data object queue defined here need not necessarily correspond to the mathematical concept of queue in which the insert/delete rules may be different.

One natural example of stacks which arises in computer programming is the processing of procedure calls and their terminations. Suppose we have four procedures as shown in Figure 3.2.

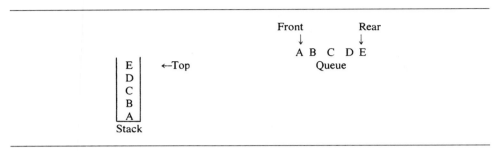

Figure 3.1 Example stack and queue

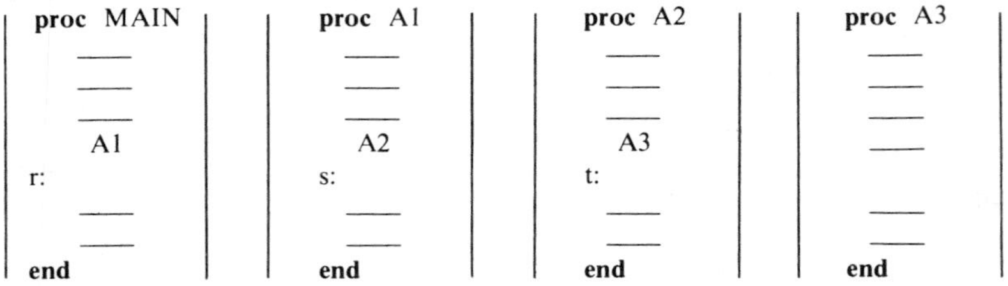

Figure 3.2 Sequence of subroutine calls

The MAIN procedure invokes procedure $A1$. On completion of $A1$, execution of MAIN will resume at location r. The address r is passed to $A1$, which saves it in some location for later processing. $A1$ then invokes $A2$, which in turn invokes $A3$. In each case the invoking procedure passes the return address to the invoked procedure. If we examine the memory while $A3$ is computing, there will be an implicit stack which looks like

$$(q,r,s,t)$$

The first entry, q, is the address to which MAIN returns control. This list operates as a stack since the returns will be made in the reverse order of the invocations. Thus, t is removed before s, s before r, and r before q. Equivalently, this means that $A3$ must finish processing before $A2$, $A2$ before $A1$, and $A1$ before MAIN. This list of return addresses need not be maintained in consecutive locations. For each procedure there is usually a single location associated with the machine code that is used to retain the return address. This can be severely limiting in the case of recursive and re-entrant procedures, since every time we invoke a procedure the new return address wipes out the old one. For example, if we inserted a call to $A1$ within procedure $A3$, expecting the return to be at location u, then at execution time the stack would become (q,u,s,t) and the return address r would be lost. When recursion is allowed, it is no longer adequate to reserve one location for the return address of each procedure. Since returns are made in the reverse order of calls, an elegant and natural solution to this procedure return problem is afforded through the explicit use of a stack of return addresses. Whenever a return is made, it is to the top address in the stack.

Associated with the object stack are several operations that are necessary:

$CREATE(S)$ which creates S as an empty stack

$ADD(i,S)$ which inserts the element i onto the stack S and returns the new stack

$DELETE(S)$ which removes the top element of stack S and returns the new stack

$TOP(S)$ which returns the top element of stack S

$ISEMTS(S)$ which returns ''true'' if S is empty, else ''false''

These five functions constitute a working definition of a stack. However we choose to represent a stack, it must be possible to build these operations. The structure $STACK$ is formally described in Structure 3.1.

---

structure $STACK$ $(item)$
1   **declare** $CREATE(\ ) \rightarrow stack$
2         $ADD(item,stack) \rightarrow stack$
3         $DELETE(stack) \rightarrow stack$
4         $TOP(stack) \rightarrow item$
5         $ISEMTS(stack) \rightarrow boolean$;
6   **for all** $S\ \varepsilon\ stack,\ i\ \varepsilon\ item$ **let**
7      $ISEMTS(CREATE)$ $::=$ **true**
8      $ISEMTS(ADD(i,S))$ $::=$ **false**
9      $DELETE(CREATE)$ $::= error$
10     $DELETE(ADD(i,S)) ::= S$
11     $TOP(CREATE)$ $::= error$
12     $TOP(ADD(i,S))$ $::= i$
13   **end**
14 **end** $STACK$

Structure 3.1 The data structure: $STACK$

The five functions with their domains and ranges are declared in lines 1 through 5. Lines 6 through 13 are the set of axioms that describe how the functions are related. Lines 10 and 12 are the essential ones that define the last-in-first-out behavior. The above definitions describe an infinite stack, for no upper bound on the number of elements is specified. This will be dealt with when we represent this structure in a computer.

The simplest way to represent a stack is by using a one-dimensional array, say $stack[1..n]$, where n is the maximum number of allowable entries. The first, or bottom, element in the stack will be stored at $stack[1]$, the second at $stack[2]$ and the i'th at $stack[i]$. Associated with the array will be a variable, top, which points to the top element in the stack. With this decision made, the following implementations result:

$$CREATE\,(stack) ::= \textbf{var}\; stack : \textbf{array}[1..n]\;\textbf{of}\; items\,; top : 0..n\,;$$
$$top := 0;$$
$$ISEMTS\,(stack) ::= \textbf{if}\; top = 0\;\textbf{then true}$$
$$\textbf{else false;}$$
$$TOP\,(stack) ::= \textbf{if}\; top = 0\;\textbf{then}\; error$$
$$\textbf{else}\; stack\,[top\,];$$

The implementations of these three operations using an array are so short that we needn't make them separate procedures but can just use them directly whenever we need to. The *ADD* and *DELETE* operations are only a bit more complex. The corresponding procedures (Programs 3.1 and 3.2) have been written assuming that *stack, top*, and *n* are global.

```
procedure add (item : items);
{add item to the global stack stack;
top is the current top of stack
and n is its maximum size}
begin
  if top = n then StackFull
          else begin
                top := top + 1;
                stack [top] := item;
             end;
end; {of add}
```

Program 3.1 Add to a stack

Programs 3.1 and 3.2 are so simple that they need little explanation. Procedure *delete* actually combines the functions TOP and DELETE. *Stackfull* and *StackEmpty* are procedures that we leave unspecified since they will depend upon the particular application. Often when a stack becomes full, the *StackFull* procedure will signal that more

```
procedure delete(var item : items);
{remove top element from the stack stack and put it in item}
begin
  if top = 0 then StackEmpty
         else begin
                  item := stack [top];
                  top := top − 1;
              end;
end; {of delete}
```

Program 3.2 Delete from a stack

storage needs to be allocated and the program rerun. *Stackempty* is often a meaningful condition. In Section 3.3 we will see a very important computer application of stacks where *StackEmpty* signals the end of processing.

The correctness of the stack implementation above may be established by showing that in this implementation, the stack axioms of lines 7-12 of the stack structure definition are true. Let us show this for the first three rules. The remainder of the axioms can be shown to hold similarly.

(1)   line 7: *ISEMTS (CREATE)* ::= **true**

Since CREATE results in top being initialized to zero, it follows from the implementation of ISEMTS that *ISEMTS(CREATE)* ::= **true**.

(2)   line 8: *ISEMTS (ADD (i,S)* ::= **false**

The value of *top* is changed only in procedures CREATE, *add* and *delete*. CREATE initializes *top* to zero while *add* increments it by 1 so long as *top* is less than *n* (this is necessary because we can implement only a finite stack). *delete* decreases *top* by 1 but never allows its value to become less than zero. Hence, *add(i)* either results in an error condition (*StackFull*), or leaves the value of *top* > 0. This then implies that *ISEMTS (ADD (i,s))* ::= **false**.

(3)   line 9: *DELETE (CREATE)* ::= *error*

This follows from the observation that *CREATE* sets *top* = 0, and the procedure *delete* signals the error condition *StackEmpty* when *top* = 0.

Queues, like stacks, also arise quite naturally in the computer solution of many problems. Perhaps the most common occurrence of a queue in computer applications is for the scheduling of jobs. In batch processing the jobs are ''queued-up'' as they are read in and executed, one after another, in the order they were received. This ignores the possible existence of priorities, in which case there will be one queue for each priority.

As mentioned earlier, when we talk of queues we talk about two distinct ends: the front and the rear. Additions to the queue take place at the rear. Deletions are made from the front. So, if a job is submitted for execution, it joins at the rear of the job queue. The job at the front of the queue is the next one to be executed. A minimal set of useful operations on a queue includes the following:

$CREATEQ(Q)$	which creates Q as an empty queue
$ADDQ(i,Q)$	which adds the element i to the rear of a queue and returns the new queue
$DELETEQ(Q)$	which removes the front element from the queue Q and returns the resulting queue
$FRONT(Q)$	which returns the front element of Q
$ISEMTQ(Q)$	which returns "true" if Q is empty, else "false"

A complete specification of this data structure is given in Structure 3.2.

```
     structure QUEUE (item)
1    declare CREATEQ ( ) → queue
2            ADDQ (item, queue) → queue
3            DELETEQ (queue) → queue
4            FRONT (queue → item
5            ISEMTQ (queue) → boolean ;
6    for all Q εqueue, i ε item let
7      ISEMTQ (CREATEQ) ::= true
8      ISEMTQ (ADD (i,Q)) ::= false
9      DELETEQ (CREATEQ) ::= error
10     DELETEQ (ADDQ (i,Q)) ::=
11       if ISEMTQ (Q) then CREATEQ
12                     else ADDQ (i,DELETEQ (Q))
13     FRONT (CREATEQ) ::= error
14     FRONT (ADDQ (i,Q)) ::=
15       if ISEMTQ (Q) then i else FRONT (Q)
16   end
17 end QUEUE
```

Structure 3.2 Specification of $QUEUE$

The axiom of lines 10-12 shows that deletions are made from the front of the queue.

The representation of a finite queue in sequential locations is somewhat more difficult than a stack. In addition to a one-dimensional array $q[1..n]$, we need two variables, *front* and *rear*. The conventions we shall adopt for these two variables are that *front* is always one less than the actual front of the queue and *rear* always points to the last element in the queue. Thus, *front* = *rear* if and only if there are no elements in the queue. The initial condition then is *front* = *rear* = 0. Figure 3.3 gives an example of queue insertion and deletion using these conventions. The queue is a job queue and Ji represents job i.

		$Q[1]$	[2]	[3]	[4]	[5]	[6]	[7]	...	remarks
front	rear									
0	0		queue		empty					initial
0	1	J1								Job 1 joins Q
0	2	J1	J2							Job 2 joins Q
0	3	J1	J2	J3						Job 3 joins Q
1	3		J2	J3						Job 1 leaves queue
1	4		J2	J3	J4					Job 4 joins Q
2	4			J3	J4					Job 2 leaves Q

Figure 3.3 Insertion and deletion from a queue

With this scheme, the following implementation of the *CREATEQ*, *ISEMTQ*, and *FRONT* operations is desired for a queue with capacity n:

$CREATEQ(q) ::=$ **var** q : **array** $[1..n]$ **of** *items* ; *front*, *rear* : $0..n$;
$\qquad$ *front* := 0; *rear* := 0;
$ISEMTQ(q) :=$ **if** *front* = *rear* **then true else false;**
$FRONT(q) \quad ::=$ **if** *ISEMTQ*(q) **then error else** $q[front + 1]$;

The procedures for *ADDQ* and *DELETEQ* are given as Programs 3.3 and 3.4.

The correctness of this implementation may be established in a manner akin to that used for stacks. With this set up, notice that unless the front regularly catches up with the rear and both pointers are reset to zero, the *QueueFull* signal does not necessarily imply that there are n elements in the queue. That is, the queue will gradually move to the right. One obvious thing to do when *QueueFull* is signaled is to move the entire queue to the left so that the first element is again at $q[1]$ and *front* = 0. This is time consuming, especially when there are many elements in the queue at the time of the *QueueFull* signal.

Let us look at an example (Figure 3.4), which shows what could happen, in the worst case, if each time a queue of size n becomes full we choose to move the entire queue left so that it starts at $q[1]$. To begin, assume there are n elements J1, ..., Jn in the

```
procedure addq (item : items);
{add item to the queue q}
{q, rear, and n are global variables}
begin
   if rear = n then QueueFull
            else begin
                    rear := rear + 1;
                    q [rear] := item;
                 end;
end; {of addq}
```

Program 3.3 Add to a queue

```
procedure deleteq(var item : items);
{delete from the front of q and put into item}
begin
if front = rear then QueueEmpty
            else begin
                    front := front + 1;
                    item := q [front];
                 end;
end; {of deleteq}
```

Program 3.4 Delete from a queue

queue and we next receive alternate requests to delete and add elements. Each time a new element is added, the entire queue of $n-1$ elements is moved left.

A more efficient queue representation is obtained by regarding the array $q [1..n]$ as circular. It now becomes more convenient to declare the array as $q [0..n-1]$. When $rear = n-1$, the next element is entered at $q [0]$ in case that spot is free. Using the same conventions as before, front will always point one position counterclockwise from the first element in the queue. Again, $front = rear$ if and only if the queue is empty. Initially we have $front = rear = 1$. Figure 3.5 illustrates some of the possible configurations for a circular queue containing the four elements J1-J4 with $n > 4$. The assumption of circularity changes the addq and deleteq procedures slightly. In order to add an element, it will be necessary to move rear one position clockwise, i.e.,

front	rear	q[1]	[2]	[3]	.....	[n]	next operation
0	n	J1	J2	J3	.....	Jn	initial state
1	n		J2	J3	.....	Jn	delete J1
0	n	J2	J3	J4	.....	Jn+1	add Jn+1 (jobs J2 through Jn are moved)
1	n		J3	J4	.....	Jn+1	delete J2
0	n	J3	J4	J5	.....	Jn+2	add Jn+2

Figure 3.4 Queue example

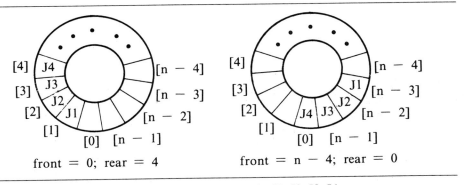

front = 0; rear = 4   front = n − 4; rear = 0

Figure 3.5 Circular queue of n elements and four jobs J1, J2, J3, J4

$$\textbf{if } rear = n - 1 \textbf{ then } rear := 0$$
$$\textbf{else } rear := rear + 1$$

Using the modulo operator which computes remainders, this is just $rear := (rear + 1)$ **mod** n. Similarly, it will be necessary to move *front* one position clockwise each time a deletion is made. Again, using the modulo operator, this can be accomplished by *front* $:= (front + 1)$**mod** n. An examination of the algorithms (Programs 3.5 and 3.6) indicates that addition and deletion can now be carried out in a fixed amount of time or O(1).

One surprising point in the two algorithms is that the test for queue full in *addq* and the test for queue empty in *deleteq* are the same. In the case of *addq*, however, when *front* = *rear* is evaluated and found to be true, there is actually one space free, i.e.,

---

procedure *addq* (*item* : *items*);
{insert *item* into the circular queue stored in $q[0..n-1]$}
begin
 rear := (*rear* + 1)**mod** *n*; {advance *rear* clockwise}
 if *front* = *rear* **then** *QueueFull*
                    else *q* [*rear*] := *item*; {insert}
end; {of *addq*}

Program 3.5 Add to a circular queue

---

procedure *deleteq*(**var** *item* : *items*);
{remove front element from *q* and put into *item*}
begin
 if *front* = *rear* **then** *QueueEmpty*
                else begin
                        front := (*front* + 1) **mod** *n*; {advance *front* clockwise}
                        item := *q* [*front*];
                    end;
end; {of *deleteq*}

Program 3.6 Delete from a circular queue

q [*rear*], since the first element in the queue is not at *q* [*front*] but is one position clockwise from this point. However, if we insert an item here, then we will not be able to distinguish between the cases full and empty, since this insertion would leave *front* = *rear*. To avoid this, we signal *QueueFull*, thus permitting a maximum of $n-1$ rather than n elements to be in the queue at any time. One way to use all n positions would be to use another variable, *tag*, to distinguish between the two situations, i.e., *tag* = 0 if and only if the queue is empty. This would, however, slow down the two procedures. Since the *addq* and *deleteq* procedures will be used many times in any problem involving queues, the loss of one queue position will be more than made up for by the reduction in computing time.

    The procedures *QueueFull* and *QueueEmpty* have been used without explanation, but they are similar to *StackFull* and *StackEmpty*. Their function will depend on the particular application. Note however that when *QueueFull* is invoked, the rear pointer has already been moved. This should be taken into account by this procedure.

3.2 A MAZING PROBLEM

The rat in a maze experiment is a classical one from experimental psychology. A rat (or mouse) is placed through the door of a large box without a top. Walls are set up so that movements in most directions are obstructed. The rat is carefully observed by several scientists as it makes its way through the maze until it eventually reaches the exit. There is only one way out, but at the end is a nice hunk of cheese. The idea is to run the experiment repeatedly until the rat will zip through the maze without taking a single false path. The trials yield its learning curve.

We can write a computer program for getting through a maze, and it will probably not be any smarter than the rat on its first try through. It may take many false paths before finding the right one. But the computer can remember the correct path far better than the rat. On its second try it should be able to go right to the end with no false paths taken, so there is no sense rerunning the program. Why don't you sit down and try to write this program yourself before you read on and look at our solution. Keep track of how many times you have to go back and correct something. This may give you an idea of your own learning curve as we rerun the experiment throughout the book.

Let us represent the maze by a two-dimensional array, $maze[1..m, 1..p]$, where a value of 1 implies a blocked path, while a 0 means one can walk right on through. We assume that the rat starts at $maze[1,1]$ and the exit is at $maze[m,p]$. An example is given in Figure 3.6.

```
entrance →  0 1 0 0 0 1 1 0 0 0 1 1 1 1 1
            1 0 0 0 1 1 0 1 1 1 0 0 1 1 1
            0 1 1 0 0 0 0 1 1 1 1 0 0 1 1
            1 1 0 1 1 1 1 0 1 1 0 1 1 0 0
            1 1 0 1 0 0 1 0 1 1 1 1 1 1 1
            0 0 1 1 0 1 1 1 0 1 0 0 1 0 1
            0 1 1 1 1 0 0 1 1 1 1 1 1 1 1
            0 0 1 1 0 1 1 0 1 1 1 1 1 0 1
            1 1 0 0 0 1 1 0 1 1 0 0 0 0 0
            0 0 1 1 1 1 1 0 0 0 1 1 1 1 0
            0 1 0 0 1 1 1 1 1 0 1 1 1 1 0  → exit
```

Figure 3.6 An example maze

With the maze represented as a two-dimensional array, the location of the rat in the maze can at any time be described by the row, i, and the column, j, of its position. Now let us consider the possible moves the rat can make at some point $[i,j]$ in the maze. Figure 3.7 shows the possible moves from any point $[i,j]$. The position $[i,j]$ is marked by an X. If all the surrounding squares have a 0, then the rat can choose any of these eight squares as its next position. We call these eight directions by the names of the points on a compass: north, northeast, east, southeast, south, southwest, west, and northwest, or N, NE, E, SE, S, SW, W, NW.

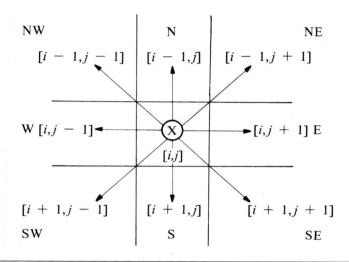

Figure 3.7 Allowable moves

We must be careful here because not every position has eight neighbors. If $[i,j]$ is on a border where either $i = 1$ or m, or $j = 1$ or p, then less than eight, and possibly only three, neighbors exist. To avoid checking for these border conditions we can surround the maze by a border of ones. The array will therefore be declared as $maze[0..m+1, 0..p+1]$.

Another device that will simplify the problem is to predefine the possible directions to move in a table, *move*, as in Figure 3.8. The data types needed are:

$$
\begin{aligned}
&\textbf{type } \textit{offsets} = \textbf{record}\\
&\qquad a : -1..1;\\
&\qquad b : -1..1;\\
&\qquad \textbf{end};\\
&\quad \textit{directions} = (\text{N, NE, E, SE, S, SW, W, NW});\\
&\textbf{var } \textit{move} : \textbf{array}[\textit{directions}] \textbf{ of } \textit{offsets};
\end{aligned}
$$

If we are at position $[i,j]$ in the maze and we wish to find the position $[g,h]$ that is southwest of us, then we set

$$g := i + move[\text{SW}].a;\quad h := j + move[\text{SW}].b;$$

q	$move\,[q\,].a$	$move\,[q\,].b$
N	-1	0
NE	-1	1
E	0	1
SE	1	1
S	1	0
SW	1	-1
W	0	-1
NW	-1	-1

Figure 3.8 Table of moves

For example, if we are at position [3,4], then position [3 + 1 = 4, 4 + (−1) = 3] is southwest.

As we move through the maze we may have the chance to go in several directions. Not knowing which one to choose, we pick one but save our current position and the direction of the last move in a list. This way, if we have taken a false path we can return and try another direction. With each new location we will examine the possibilities, starting from the north and looking clockwise. Finally, in order to prevent us from going down the same path twice we use another array, $mark[0:m+1,0:p+1]$, which is initially zero. $mark[i,j]$ is set to 1 once we arrive at that position. We assume $maze[m,p] = 0$, as otherwise there is no path to the exit. Program 3.7 is a first pass at an algorithm.

This is not a Pascal program and yet it describes the essential processing without too much detail. The use of indentation for delineating important blocks of code plus the use of Pascal reserved words make the looping and conditional tests transparent.

What remains to be pinned down? Using the three arrays *maze*, *mark*, and *move* we need only specify how to represent the list of new triples. Since the algorithm calls for removing first the most recently entered triple, this list should be a stack. We can use the sequential representation we saw before. All we need to know now is a reasonable bound on the size of this stack. Since each position in the maze is visited at most once, at most mp elements can be placed into the stack. Thus mp locations is a safe but somewhat conservative bound. The maze of Figure 3.9 has only one entrance to exit path. It has $\lceil m/2\rceil(p+1)$ positions.

Thus, mp is not too crude a bound. We are now ready to give a precise maze algorithm (Program 3.8).

While using nonnumeric indices for *move* keeps the correspondence with direction transparent, it makes the resulting Pascal program somewhat cumbersome. This is so because the predecessor of N and the successor of NW are not defined. For this reason, in writing procedure *path* (Program 3.8), we assume that *move* is actually declared as:

---

initialize *list* to the maze entrance coordinates and direction north;
while *list* is not empty **do**
begin
  (i, j, mov) := coordinates and direction from front of *list*;
  while there are more moves **do**
  begin
  (g, h) := coordinates of next move;
  if $(g = m)$ **and** $(h = p)$ **then** success;
  if *maze* $[g, h] = 0$ {legal move}
    and $(mark\,[g, h] = 0)$ {haven't been here before}
  then begin
      $mark\,[g, h] := 1$;
      add (i, j, mov) to front of *list*;
      $i := g;\ \ j := h;\ \ mov := 0$;
    end;
  end;
end;
writeln('no path found');

Program 3.7 First pass at maze algorithm

$$
\begin{bmatrix}
0 & 0 & 0 & 0 & 0 & 0 \\
1 & 1 & 1 & 1 & 0 \\
0 & 0 & 0 & 0 & 0 & 0 \\
0 & 1 & 1 & 1 & 1 & 1 \\
0 & 0 & 0 & 0 & 0 & 0 \\
1 & 1 & 1 & 1 & 0 \\
0 & 0 & 0 & 0 & 0 & 0 \\
0 & 1 & 1 & 1 & 1 & 1 \\
0 & 0 & 0 & 0 & 0 & 0
\end{bmatrix}
$$

Figure 3.9 Maze example with a long path

var *move*: **array**[1..8] **of** *offsets;*

The correspondence is $move[1] = move[N], \ldots, move[8] = move[NW]$.

    The arrays *maze, mark, move,* and *stack,* along with the variables or constants *top, m, p,* and *n,* are assumed global to *path*. Further, it is assumed that *stack* $[1..n]$ is an array of *items* where the type *items* is defined as:

```
type items = record
              x : 1..m;
              y : 1..p;
              dir : 1..9;
            end;
```

If n is at least mp, then the *StackFull* condition will never occur.

Now, what can we say about the computing time of this procedure? It is interesting that even though the problem is easy to grasp, it is difficult to make any but the most trivial statement about the computing time. The reason for this is because the number of iterations of the main **while** loop is entirely dependent upon the given maze. What we can say is that each new position $[i,j]$ that is visited gets marked, so paths are never taken twice. There are at most eight iterations of the inner **while** loop for each marked position. Each iteration of the inner **while** loop takes a fixed amount of time, O(1), and if the number of zeros in *maze* is z then at most z positions can get marked. Since z is bounded above by mp, the computing time is O(mp). (In actual experiments, however, the rat may be inspired by the watching psychologists and the invigorating odor from the cheese at the exit. It might reach its goal by examining far fewer paths than those examined by algorithm *path*. This may happen despite the fact that the rat has no pencil and only a very limited mental stack. It is difficult to incorporate the effect of the cheese odor and the cheering of the psychologists into a computer algorithm.) The array *mark* can be eliminated altogether and *maze*[g,h] changed to 1 instead of setting *mark*[g,h] to 1, but this will destroy the original maze.

3.3 EVALUATION OF EXPRESSIONS

When pioneering computer scientists conceived the idea of higher level programming languages, they were faced with many technical hurdles. One of the biggest was the question of how to generate machine language instructions that would properly evaluate any arithmetic expression. A complex assignment statement such as

$$X := A/B - C + D * E - A * C \qquad (3.1)$$

might have several meanings, and even if it were uniquely defined, say by a full use of parentheses, it still seemed a formidable task to generate a correct and reasonable instruction sequence. Fortunately the solution we have today is both elegant and simple. Moreover, it is so simple that this aspect of compiler writing is really one of the more minor issues.

```
procedure path;
{output a path (if any) in the maze. maze[0,i] = maze [m +1,i] =
maze [j,0] = maze [j,p +1] = 1, 0≤i≤p +1, 0≤j≤m+1}
var position : items; d,g,h,i,j,q : integer; found : boolean;
begin
  {start at (1,1)}
  mark[1,1] := 1; top := 1; found := false;
  with stack[1] do begin x := 1; y := 1; dir := 2; end;
  while (top > 0) and not found do {stack not empty}
  begin
    delete (position); {unstack}
    with position do begin i := x; j := y; d := dir; end;
    while (d <= 8) and not found do {move forward}
    begin
      g := i + move [d].a; h := j + move [d].b;
      if (g = m) and (h = p) then {reached exit}
                              begin {output path}
                                for q := 1 to top do
                                  writeln(stack [q]);
                                writeln(i,j); writeln(m,p);
                                found := true;
                              end {of then}
                        else
                              begin
                                if (maze [g,h] = 0) and mark [g,h] = 0)
                                then begin {new position}
                                        mark [g,h] := 1;
                                        with position do x := i; y := j; dir := d+1; end;
                                        add (position); {stack it}
                                        i := g; j := h; d := 1; {move to (g,h)}
                                     end
                                     else d := d+1; {try next direction}
                              end; {of else}
    end; {of while d <= 8}
  end; {of top > 0}
  if not found then writeln('no path in maze');
end; {of path}
```

Program 3.8 Procedure *path*

An expression is made up of operands, operators, and delimiters. The expression above has five operands: $A,B,C,D,$ and E. Though these are all one-letter variables, operands can be any legal variable name or constant in our programming language. In any expression the values that variables take must be consistent with the operations performed on them. These operations are described by the operators. In most programming languages there are several kinds of operators that correspond to the different kinds of data a variable can hold. First, there are the basic arithmetic operators: plus, minus, times, and divide $(+, -, *, /)$. Other arithmetic operators include unary minus, **mod**, and **div**. The latter two may sometimes be library subroutines rather than predefined operators. A second class is the relational operators: $<, <=, =, <>, >=, >$. These are usually defined to work for arithmetic operands, but they can just as easily work for character string data. ('CAT' is less than 'DOG' since it precedes 'DOG' in alphabetical order.) The result of an expression which contains relational operators is one of the two constants: **true** or **false**. Such an expression is called boolean, named after the mathematician George Boole, the father of symbolic logic. There also may be logical operators such as **and**, **or**, and **not**.

The first problem with understanding the meaning of an expression is to decide in what order the operations are carried out. This means that every language must uniquely define such an order. For instance, if $A = 4, B = C = 2, D = E = 3$, then in Eq.3.1 we might want X to be assigned the value

$$((4/2) - 2) + (3 * 3) - (4 * 2)$$
$$= 0 + 9 - 8$$
$$= 1$$

However, the true intention of the programmer might have been to assign X the value

$$(4/(2 - 2 + 3)) * (3 - 4) * 2$$
$$= (4/3) * (-1) * 2$$
$$= -0.6666666$$

Of course, the programmer could specify the latter order of evaluation by using parentheses:

$$X := ((A/(B - C + D)) * (E - A) * C$$

To fix the order of evaluation, we assign to each operator a priority. Then within any pair of parentheses we understand that operators with the highest priority will be evaluated first. A set of sample priorities from Turbo Pascal is given in Figure 3.10. The highest priority is 1. **shl** and **shr** stand for shift left and shift right. For example, 2 **shl** 5 = 64 and 64 **shl** 5 = 2.

priority	operator
1	unary minus
2	**not**
3	*, /, **div, mod, and, shl, shr**
4	+, −, **or, xor**
5	<, <=, =, <>, >=, >, **in**

Figure 3.10 Priority of operators in Turbo Pascal, version 3.0

Notice that all of the relational operators have the same priority. Unary minus has top priority, followed by boolean negation. When we have an expression where two adjacent operators have the same priority, we need a rule to tell us which one to perform first. For example, do we want the value of $-A+B$ to be understood as $(-A) + B$ or $-(A + B)$? Convince yourself that there will be a difference by trying $A = -1$ and $B = 2$. The Pascal rule is that for all priorities, evaluation of operators of the same priority will proceed left to right. Remember that by using parentheses we can override these rules, as expressions are always evaluated with the innermost parenthesized expression first.

Now that we have specified priorities and rules for breaking ties we know how $X := A/B - C + D*E - A*C$ will be evaluated, namely, as

$$X := (((A/B) - C) + (D * E)) - (A * C)$$

How can a compiler accept such an expression and produce correct code? The answer is given by reworking the expression into a form we call *postfix notation*. If e is an expression with operators and operands, the conventional way of writing e is called *infix*, because the operators come *in*-between the operands. (Unary operators precede their operand.) The *postfix* form of an expression calls for each operator to appear *after* its operands. For example,

infix: $A*B/C$ has postfix: $AB*C/$

If we study the postfix form of $A*B/C$ we see that the multiplication comes immediately after its two operands A and B. Now imagine that $A*B$ is computed and stored in T. Then we have the division operator, /, coming immediately after its two operands T and C.

Let us look at our previous example

infix: $A/B - C + D * E - A * C$

postfix: $AB/C - DE * + AC * -$

and trace out the meaning of the postfix.

Suppose that every time we compute a value, we store it in the temporary location T_i, $i \geq 1$. If we read the postfix expression left to right, the first operation is division. The two operands that precede this are A and B. So, the result of A/B is stored in T_1 and the postfix expression is modified as in Figure 3.11. This figure also gives the remaining sequence of operations. The result is stored in T_6. Notice that if we had parenthesized the expression, this would change the postfix only if the order of normal evaluation were altered. Thus, $(A/B) - C + (D * E) - A * C$ will have the same postfix form as the previous expression without parentheses. But $(A/B) - (C + D) * (E - A) * C$ will have the postfix form $AB/CD + EA - * C * -$.

operation	postfix
$T_1 := A/B$	$T_1 C - DE * + AC * -$
$T_2 := T_1 - C$	$T_2 DE * + AC * -$
$T_3 := D * E$	$T_2 T_3 + AC * -$
$T_4 := T_2 + T_3$	$T_4 AC * -$
$T_5 := A * C$	$T_4 T_5 -$
$T_6 := T_4 - T_5$	T_6

Figure 3.11 Postfix evaluation

Before attempting an algorithm to translate expressions from infix to postfix notation, let us make some observations regarding the virtues of postfix notation that enable easy evaluation of expressions. To begin with, the need for parentheses is eliminated. Second, the priority of the operators is no longer relevant. The expression may be evaluated by making a left to right scan, stacking operands, and evaluating operators using as operands the correct number from the stack and finally placing the result onto the stack (see Program 3.9). This evaluation process is much simpler than attempting direct evaluation from infix notation.

To see how to devise an algorithm for translating from infix to postfix, note that the order of the operands in both forms is the same. In fact, it is simple to describe an algorithm for producing postfix from infix:

---

procedure *eval* (*e* : *expression*);
{evaluate the postfix expression *e*. It is assumed that the last
token (a token is either an operator, operand, or '#')
in *e* is '#.' A procedure *NextToken* is used to extract from *e*
the next token. A one-dimensional array
stack[1..*n*] is used as a stack.}
var *x* : *token*;
begin
  top := 0; {initialize *stack*}
  x := *NextToken* (*e*);
  while *x* <> '#' **do**
  begin
    if *x* is an operand
    then *add* (*x*) {add to *stack*}
    else begin {operator}
        remove the correct number of operands for operator
        x from *stack*; perform the operation *x* and store the
        result (if any) onto the stack;
      end;
    x := *NextToken* (*e*);
  end; {of **while**}
end; {of *eval*}

Program 3.9 Algorithm to evaluate postfix expressions

(1)   Fully parenthesize the expression.

(2)   Move all operators so that they replace their corresponding right parentheses.

(3)   Delete all parentheses.

For example, $A / B - C + D * E - A * C$ when fully parenthesized yields

$$((((A / B) - C) + (D * E)) - A * C))$$

The arcs join an operator and its corresponding right parenthesis. Performing steps 2 and 3 gives

$$AB/C - DE * + AC * -$$

The problem with this as an algorithm is that it requires two passes: the first one reads the expression and parenthesizes it while the second actually moves the operators.

As we have already observed, the order of the operands is the same in infix and postfix. So as we scan an expression for the first time, we can form the postfix by immediately passing any operands to the output. Then it is just a matter of handling the operators. The solution is to store them in a stack until just the right moment and then to unstack and pass them to the output.

For example, since we want $A + B * C$ to yield $ABC * +$, our algorithm should perform the following sequence of stacking (these stacks will grow to the right):

next token	stack	output
none	empty	none
A	empty	A
$+$	$+$	A
B	$+$	AB

At this point the algorithm must determine if $*$ gets placed on top of the stack or if the $+$ gets taken off. Since $*$ has higher priority, we should stack $*$ producing

$*$	$+*$	AB
C	$+*$	ABC

Now the input expression is exhausted, so we output all remaining operators in the stack to get

$$ABC *+$$

For another example, $A *(B +C)*D$ has the postfix form $ABC +*D *$, and so the algorithm should behave as

next token	stack	output
none	empty	none
A	empty	*A*
*	*	*A*
(	*(	*A*
B	*(	*AB*
+	*(+	*AB*
C	*(+	*ABC*

At this point we want to unstack down to the corresponding left parenthesis, and then delete the left and right parentheses. This gives us:

)	*	*ABC* +
*	*	*ABC* +*
D	*	*ABC* +* *D*
done	empty	*ABC* +* *D* *

These examples motivate a priority-based scheme for stacking and unstacking operators. The left parenthesis complicates things as when it is not in the stack, it behaves as an operator with high priority, while once it gets in, it behaves as one with low priority (no operator other than the matching right parenthesis should cause it to get unstacked). We establish two priorities for operators: *isp* (in-stack priority) and *icp* (in-coming priority). The *isp* and *icp* of all operators in Figure 3.10 is the priority given in this figure. In addition, we define $isp\,['('] = 5$, $icp['('] = 0$, and $isp['\#'] = 5$. These priorities result in the following rule: *operators are taken out of the stack as long as their in-stack priority is numerically less than or equal to the in-coming priority of the new operator.* Our algorithm to transform from infix to postfix is given in Program 3.10.

As for the computing time, the algorithm makes only one pass across the input. If the expression has *n* symbols, then the number of operations is proportional to some constant times *n*.

```
procedure postfix(e : expression);
{output the postfix form of the infix expression e.
NextToken and stack are as in procedure eval. It is
assumed that the last token in e is '#.'  Also, '#' is used
at the bottom of the stack.}
var x,y : token;
begin
 stack[1] := '#'; top := 1; {initialize stack}
 x := NextToken (e);
 while x <> '#' do
 begin
   if x is an operand
   then write(x)
   else if x = ')'
        then begin {unstack until '('}
                 while stack [top] <> '(' do
                 begin delete (y); write(y); end;
                 delete (y); {delete '('}
              end
        else begin
                 while isp [stack [top]] <= icp [x] do
                 begin delete (y); write(y); end;
                 add (x);
              end;
    x := NextToken (e);
 end; {of while}
 {end of expression; empty stack}
 while top > 1 do
 begin delete (y); write(y); end;
 writeln('#');
end; {of postfix}
```

Program 3.10 Convert from infix to postfix form

3.4 MULTIPLE STACKS AND QUEUES

Until now we have been concerned only with the representations of a single stack or a single queue in the memory of a computer. For these two cases we have seen efficient sequential data representations. What happens when a data representation is needed for several stacks and queues? Let us once again limit ourselves to sequential mappings of these data objects into an array $v[1..m]$. If we have only two stacks to represent, then the solution is simple. We can use $v[1]$ for the bottommost element in stack 1 and $v[m]$ for the corresponding element in stack 2. Stack 1 can grow toward $v[m]$ and stack 2 toward $v[1]$. It is therefore possible to utilize efficiently all the available space. Can we do the same when more than two stacks are to be represented? The answer is no, because a one-dimensional array has only two fixed points, $v[1]$ and $v[m]$, and each stack requires a fixed point for its bottommost element. When more than two stacks, say n, are to be represented sequentially, we can initially divide out the available memory $v[1..m]$ into n segments and allocate one of these segments to each of the n stacks. This initial division of $v[1..m]$ into segments may be done in proportion to expected sizes of the various stacks if these are known. In the absence of such information, $v[1..m]$ may be divided into equal segments. For each stack i we shall use $b[i]$ to represent a position one less than the position in v for the bottommost element of that stack. $t[i], 1 \le i \le n$ will point to the topmost element of stack i. We shall use the boundary condition $b[i] = t[i]$ iff the i'th stack is empty. If we grow the i'th stack in lower memory indices than the $(i+1)$'th, then with roughly equal initial segments we have

$$b[i] = t[i] = \lfloor m/n \rfloor (i-1), \ 1 \le i \le n$$

as the initial values of $b[i]$ and $t[i]$ (see Figure 3.12). Stack i, $1 \le i \le n$ can grow from $b[i]+1$ up to $b[i+1]$ before it catches up with the $(i+1)$'th stack. It is convenient both for the discussion and the algorithms to define $b[n+1] = m$. Using this scheme, the *add* and *delete* algorithms of Programs 3.11 and 3.12 result.

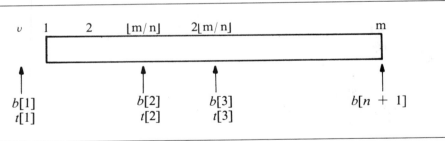

Figure 3.12 Initial configuration for n stacks in $v[1..m]$. All stacks are empty and memory is divided into roughly equal segments.

The algorithms to add and delete appear to be as simple as in the case of only one or two stacks. This really is not the case since the *StackFull* condition in algorithm *add* does not imply that all m locations of v are in use. In fact, there may be a lot of unused space between stacks j and $j+1$ for $1 \le j \le n$ and $j \ne i$ (Figure 3.13). The procedure *StackFull(i)* should therefore determine whether there is any free space in v and shift stacks around so as to make some of this free space available to the i'th stack.

procedure *add* (*i* : **integer**; *x* : *items*);
{add *x* to the *i*'th *stack*}
begin
  if *t* [*i*] = *b* [*i* +1] **then** *StackFull* (*i*)
              else begin
                    t [*i*] := *t* [*i*] + 1;
                    v [*t* [*i*]] := *x*; {add to *i*'th stack}
                  end;
end; {of *add*}

Program 3.11 Add to *i*'th stack

procedure *delete* (*i* : **integer**; **var** *x* : *items*);
{*delete* topmost item of stack *i*}
begin
  if *t* [*i*] = *b* [*i*] **then** *StackEmpty* (*i*)
              else begin
                    x := *v* [*t* [*i*]];
                    t [*i*] := *t* [*i*] − 1;
                  end;
end; {of *delete*}

Program 3.12 Delete from *i*'th stack

Several strategies are possible for the design of algorithm *StackFull*. We shall discuss one strategy in the text and look at some others in the exercises. The primary objective of algorithm *StackFull* is to permit the adding of elements to stacks so long as there is some free space in *v*. One way to guarantee this is to design *StackFull* along the following lines:

(1)   Determine the least, *j*, $i < j \leq n$ such that there is free space between stacks *j* and *j* + 1, i.e., $t[j] < b[j+1]$. If there is such a *j*, then move stacks $i + 1, i + 2, \ldots, j$ one position to the right (treating *v* [1] as leftmost and *v* [*m*] as rightmost), thereby creating a space between stacks *i* and *i* + 1.

(2)   If there is no *j* as in (1), then look to the left of stack *i*. Find the largest *j* such that $1 \leq j < i$ and there is space between stacks *j* and *j* + 1, i.e., $t[j] < b[j + 1]$. If there is such a *j*, then move stacks $j + 1, j + 2, \ldots, i$ one space left creating a free space between stacks *i* and *i* + 1.

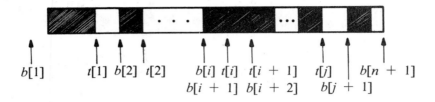

$b[1]$ $t[1]\ b[2]\ t[2]$ $b[i]\ t[i]\ t[i\ +\ 1]$ $t[j]$ $b[n\ +\ 1]$
$b[i\ +\ 1]\ b[i\ +\ 2]$ $b[j\ +\ 1]$

Figure 3.13 Configuration when stack i meets with stack $i + 1$ but there is still free space elsewhere in v

(3)   If there is no j satisfying either the conditions of (1) or (2), then all m spaces of v are utilized and there is no free space.

The writing of algorithm *StackFull* using the above strategy is left as an exercise. It should be clear that the worst case performance of this representation for the n stacks together with the above strategy for *StackFull* would be rather poor. In fact, in the worst case $O(m)$ time may be needed for each insertion (see exercises). In the next chapter we shall see that if we do not limit ourselves to sequential mappings of data objects into arrays, then we can obtain a data representation for m stacks that has a much better worst case performance than the representation described here. Sequential representations for n queues and other generalizations are discussed in the exercises.

3.5 EXERCISES

1.   Consider the railroad switching network given in Figure 3.14. Railroad cars numbered 1, 2, 3, . . ., n are at the right. Each car is brought into the stack and removed at any time. For instance, if $n = 3$, we could move 1 in, move 2 in, move 3 in, and then take the cars out producing the new order 3, 2, 1. For $n = 3$ and 4 what are the possible permutations of the cars that can be obtained? Are any permutations not possible?

2.   Using a boolean variable to distinguish between a circular queue being empty or full, write insert and delete procedures.

3.   Complete the correctness proof for the stack implementation of Section 3.1.

4.   Use the queue axioms to prove that the circular queue representation of Section 3.1 is correct.

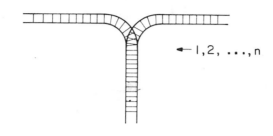

Figure 3.14 Railroad switching network

5. [Mystery function] Let f be an operation whose argument and result is a queue and which is defined by the axioms:

$f (CREATEQ) ::= CREATEQ$
$f (ADDQ (i,q)) := \textbf{if } ISEMTQ (q) \textbf{ then } ADDQ (i,q)$
$\qquad\qquad\qquad \textbf{else } ADDQ (FRONT (q), f (DELETEQ (ADDQ (i,q))))$

What does f do?

6. A double-ended queue (deque) is a linear list in which additions and deletions may be made at either end. Obtain a data representation mapping a deque into a one-dimensional array. Write algorithms to add and delete elements from either end of the deque.

7. A linear list is being maintained circularly in an array $c [0..n-1]$ with *front* and *rear* set up as for circular queues.

    (a) Obtain a formula in terms of *front*, *rear*, and n for the number of elements in the list.

    (b) Write an algorithm to delete the k'th element in the list.

    (c) Write an algorithm to insert an element y immediately after the k'th element.

    What is the time complexity of your algorithms for (b) and (c)?

8. Let $L = (a_1, a_2, \ldots, a_n)$ be a linear list represented in the array $v [1..n]$ using the mapping: the i'th element of L is stored in $v [i]$. Write an algorithm to make an in-place reversal of the order of elements in v. That is, the algorithm should transform v such that $v [i]$ contains the $(n - i + 1)$'th element of L. The only additional space available to your algorithm is that for simple variables. The input to the algorithm is v and n. How much time does your algorithm take to accomplish

the reversal?

9. (a) Find a path through the maze of Figure 3.15.

(b) Trace out the action of procedure *path* on the maze of Figure 3.15. Compare this to your own attempt in (a).

10. What is the maximum path length from start to finish for any maze of dimensions $n \times m$?

11. Write the postfix form of the following expressions:

(a) $A * B * C$

(b) $-A + B - C + D$

(c) $A * -B + C$

(d) $(A + B) * D + E/(F + A * D) + C$

(e) A **and** B **or** C **or** **not** $(E > F)$ (assuming Pascal precedence)

(f) **not** $(A$ **and** **not** $((B < C)$ **or** $(C > D)))$ **or** $(C < E)$

12. Use the priorities of Figure 3.10 together with those for '(' and '#' to answer the following:

(a) In algorithm *postfix*, what is the maximum number of elements that can be on the stack at any time if the input expression e has n operators and delimiters?

(b) What is the answer to (a) if e has n operators and the depth of nesting of parentheses is at most 6?

13. Another expression form that is easy to evaluate and is parenthesis-free is known as *prefix*. In this way of writing expressions, the operators precede their operands. For example:

infix	prefix
$A * B/C$	$/*ABC$
$A/B - C + D * E - A * C$	$- + - /ABC * DE * AC$
$A * (B + C)/D - G$	$-/* A + BCDG$

Notice that the order of operands is not changed in going from infix to prefix.

(a) What is the prefix form of the expressions in Exercise 11?

(b) Write an algorithm to evaluate a prefix expression, e. (Hint: Scan e right to left and assume that the leftmost token of e is '#.')

(c) Write an algorithm to transform an infix expression e into its prefix equivalent. Assume that the input expression e begins with a '#' and that the prefix expression should begin with a '#.'

What is the time complexity of your algorithms for (b) and (c)? How much space is needed by each of these algorithms?

14. Write an algorithm to transform from prefix to postfix. Carefully state any assumptions you make regarding the input. How much time and space does your algorithm take?

15. Do the preceding exercise, but this time for a transformation from postfix to prefix.

16. Write an algorithm to generate fully parenthesized infix expressions from their postfix form. What is the complexity (time and space) of your algorithm?

17. Do the preceding exercise starting from prefix form.

18. Two stacks are to be represented in an array $v[1..m]$ as described in Section 3.4. Write algorithms $add(i,x)$ and $delete(i)$ to add x and delete an element from stack i, $1 \le i \le 2$. Your algorithms should be able to add elements to the stacks so long as there are fewer than m elements in both stacks together.

19. Obtain a data representation mapping a stack s and a queue q into a single array $v[1..n]$. Write algorithms to add and delete elements from these two data objects. What can you say about the suitability of your data representation?

20. Write a Pascal procedure implementing the strategy for $StackFull(i)$ outlined in Section 3.4.

21. For the add and $delete$ algorithms of Section 3.4 and the $StackFull(i)$ algorithm of the preceding exercise, produce a sequence of adds and deletes that will require $O(m)$ time for each add. Use $n = 2$ and start from a configuration representing a full utilization of $v[1..m]$.

22. It has been empirically observed that most programs that get close to using all available space eventually run out of space. In the light of this observation, it seems futile to move stacks around providing space for other stacks to grow in if there is only a limited amount of space that is free. Rewrite the algorithm of the preceding exercise so that the algorithm terminates if there are fewer than c free spaces. c is an empirically determined constant that is provided to the algorithm.

23. Another strategy for the $StackFull(i)$ condition of Section 3.4 is to redistribute all the free space in proportion to the rate of growth of individual stacks since the last call to $StackFull$. This would require the use of another array $lt[1..n]$, where $lt[j]$ is the value of $t[j]$ at the last call to $StackFull$. Then the amount by which each stack has grown since the last call is $t[j] - lt[j]$. The amount for stack i is actually $t[i] - lt[i] + 1$, since we are not attempting to add another element to i.

    Write algorithm $StackFull(i)$ to redistribute all the stacks so that the free space between stacks j and $j + 1$ is in proportion to the growth of stack j since the last call to $StackFull$. $Stackfull(i)$ should assign at least one free location to stack i.

24. Design a data representation sequentially mapping n queues into an array $v[1..m]$. Represent each queue as a circular queue within v. Write procedures $addq$, $deleteq$, and $QueueFull$ for this representation.

25. Design a data representation, sequentially mapping n data objects into an array $v[1..m]$. n_1 of these data objects are stacks and the remaining $n_2 = n - n_1$ are queues. Write algorithms to add and delete elements from these objects. Use the same *spacefull* algorithm for both types of data objects. This algorithm should provide space for the i'th data object if there is some space not currently being used. Note that a circular queue with space for r elements can hold only $r - 1$.

26. [Landweber]
People have spent so much time playing card games of solitaire that the gambling casinos are now capitalizing on this human weakness. A form of solitaire is described below. Your assignment is to write a computer program to play the game, thus freeing hours of time for people to return to more useful endeavors.

To begin the game, 28 cards are dealt into seven piles. The leftmost pile has one card, the next two cards, and so forth, up to seven cards in the rightmost pile. Only the uppermost card of each of the seven piles is turned face-up. The cards are dealt left to right, one card to each pile, dealing to one less pile each time, and turning the first card in each round face-up. On the topmost face-up card of each pile you may build in descending sequences red on black or black on red. For example, on the 9 of spades you may place either the 8 of diamonds or the 8 of hearts. All face-up cards on a pile are moved as a unit and may be placed on another pile according to the bottommost face up card. For example, the 7 of clubs on the 8 of hearts may be moved as a unit onto the 9 of clubs or the 9 of spades.

Whenever a face-down card is uncovered, it is turned face-up. If one pile is removed completely, a face-up king may be moved from a pile (together with all cards above it) or the top of the waste pile (see below) into the vacated space. There are four output piles, one for each suit, and the object of the game is to get as many cards as possible into the output piles. Each time an ace appears at the top of a pile or the top of the stack it is moved into the appropriate output pile. Cards are added to the output piles in sequence, the suit for each pile being determined by the ace on the bottom.

From the rest of the deck, called the stock, cards are turned up one by one and placed face-up on a waste pile. You may always play cards off the top of the waste pile, but only one at a time. Begin by moving a card from the stock to the top of the waste pile. If there is ever more than one possible play to be made, the following order must be observed:

(a) Move a card from the top of a playing pile or from the top of the waste pile to an output pile. If the waste pile becomes empty, move a card from the stock to the waste pile.

(b)   Move a card from the top of the waste pile to the leftmost playing pile to which it can be moved. If the waste pile becomes empty, move a card from the stock to the waste pile.

(c)   Find the leftmost playing pile that can be moved and place it on top of the leftmost playing pile to which it can be moved.

(d)   Try (a), (b), and (c) in sequence, restarting with (a) whenever a move is made.

(e)   If no move is made via (a) through (d), move a card from the stock to the waste pile and retry (a).

Only the topmost card of the playing piles or the waste pile may be played to an output pile. Once played on an output pile, a card may not be withdrawn to help elsewhere. The game is over when either all the cards have been played to the output, or the stock pile has been exhausted and no more cards can be moved.

When played for money, the player pays the house $52 at the beginning, and wins $5 for every card played to the output piles. Write your program so that it will play several games and determine your net winnings. Use a random number generator to shuffle the deck. Output a complete record of two games in easily understood form. Include as output the number of games played and the net winnings (+ or −).

CHAPTER 4
LINKED LISTS

4.1 SINGLY LINKED LISTS

In the previous chapters, we studied the representation of simple data structures using an array and a sequential mapping. These representations had the property that successive nodes of the data object were stored a fixed distance apart. Thus, (1) if the element a_{ij} of a table was stored at location L_{ij}, then $a_{i,j+1}$ was at the location $L_{ij} + c$ for some constant c; (2) if the i'th node in a queue was at location L_i, then the $(i + 1)$'th node was at location $L_i + c$ mod n for the circular representation; (3) if the topmost node of a stack was at location L_T, then the node beneath it was at location $L_T - c$, etc. These sequential storage schemes proved adequate given the functions you wish to perform (access to an arbitrary node in a table, insertion or deletion of nodes within a stack or queue). However, when a sequential mapping is used for ordered lists, operations such as insertion and deletion of arbitrary elements become expensive. For example, consider the following list of three letter English words ending in AT:

(BAT, CAT, EAT, FAT, HAT, JAT, LAT, MAT,
OAT, PAT, RAT, SAT, TAT, VAT, WAT)

To make this list complete we naturally want to add the word GAT, which means gun or revolver. If we are using an array to keep this list, then the insertion of GAT will require us to move elements already in the list either one location higher or lower. We must either move HAT, JAT, LAT, . . ., WAT or else move BAT, CAT, EAT, and FAT. If we have to do many such insertions into the middle, then neither alternative is attractive because of the amount of data movement. On the other hand, suppose we decide to remove the word LAT which refers to the Latvian monetary unit. Then again, we have to move many elements so as to maintain the sequential representation of the list.

When our problem called for several ordered lists of varying sizes, sequential representation again proved to be inadequate. By storing each list in a different array of maximum size, storage may be wasted. By maintaining the lists in a single array a potentially large amount of data movement is needed. This was explicitly observed when we represented several stacks, queues, polynomials, and matrices. All these data objects are examples of ordered lists. Polynomials are ordered by exponent while matrices are ordered by rows and columns. In this chapter we shall present an alternate representation for ordered lists which will reduce the time needed for arbitrary insertion and deletion.

An elegant solution to this problem of data movement in *sequential* representations is achieved by using *linked* representations. Unlike a sequential representation where successive items of a list are located a fixed distance apart, in a linked representation these items may be placed anywhere in memory. Another way of saying this is that in a sequential representation the order of elements is the same as in the ordered list, while in a linked representation these two sequences need not be the same. To access elements in the list in the correct order, with each element we store the address or location of the next element in that list. Thus, associated with each data item in a linked representation is a pointer to the next item. This pointer is often referred to as a link. In general, a *node* is a collection of data, *data* 1, . . ., *datan* and links *link* 1, . . ., *linkm*. Each item in a node is called a *field*. A field contains either a data item or a link.

Figure 4.1 shows how some of the nodes of the list we considered before may be represented in memory by using pointers. The elements of the list are stored in a one-dimensional array called *data*. But the elements no longer occur in sequential order, BAT before CAT before EAT, etc. Instead we relax this restriction and allow them to appear anywhere in the array and in any order. To remind us of the real order, a second array, *link*, is added. The values in this array are pointers to elements in the *data* array. Since the list starts at *data*[8] = BAT, let us set a variable $f = 8$. *link*[8] has the value 3, which means it points to *data*[3] which contains CAT. The third element of the list is pointed at by *link*[3] which is EAT. By continuing in this way we can list all the words in the proper order. We recognize that we have come to the end when *link* has a value of zero.

Some of the values of *data* and *link* and undefined such as *data*[2], *link*[2], *data*[5], *link*[5], etc. We shall ignore this for the moment.

It is customary to draw linked lists as an ordered sequence of nodes with links being represented by arrows as in Figure 4.2. We shall use the name of the pointer variable that points to the list as the name of the entire list.

Thus the list of Figure 4.2 is the list *f*. Notice that we do not explicitly put in the values of the pointers but simply draw arrows to indicate they are there. This is so that we reinforce in our own mind the facts that (1) the nodes do not actually reside in sequential locations, and (2) the locations of nodes may change on different runs. Therefore, when we write a program which works with lists, we almost never look for a specific address except when we test for zero.

	data	link
1	HAT	15
2		
3	CAT	4
4	EAT	9
5		
6		
7	WAT	0
8	BAT	3
9	FAT	1
10		
11	VAT	7
.	.	.
.	.	.
.	.	.

Figure 4.1 Nonsequential list representation

Figure 4.2 Usual way to draw a linked list

Let us now see why it is easier to make arbitrary insertions and deletions using a linked list rather than a sequential list. To insert the data item GAT between FAT and HAT the following steps are adequate:

(1) Get a node which is currently unused; let its address be x.

(2) Set the *data* field of this node to GAT.

(3) Set the *link* field to x to point to the node after FAT which contains HAT.

(4) Set the *link* field of the node containing FAT to x.

Figure 4.3(a) shows how the arrays *data* and *link* will be changed after we insert GAT. Figure 4.3(b) shows how we can draw the insertion using our arrow notation. The new arrows are dashed. The important thing to notice is that when we insert GAT we do not have to move any elements which are already in the list. We have overcome the need to move data at the expense of the storage needed for the second field, *link*. But we will see that this is not too severe a penalty.

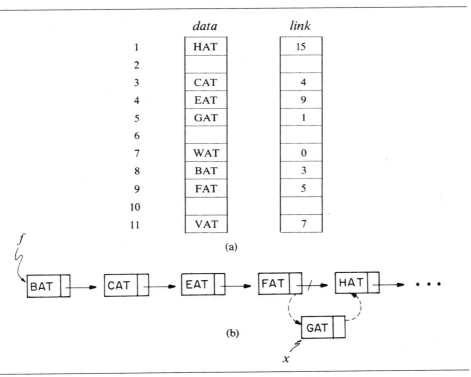

Figure 4.3 (a) Insert GAT into *data*[5]; (b) Insert node GAT into list

Now suppose we want to delete GAT from the list. All we need to do is find the element which immediately precedes GAT, which is FAT, and set *link*[9] to the position of HAT which is 1. Again, there is no need to move the data around. Even though the *link* field of GAT still contains a pointer to HAT, GAT is no longer in the list (see Figure 4.4).

From our brief discussion of linked lists, we see that the following capabilities are needed to make linked representations possible:

Figure 4.4 Delete GAT from list

(1)   a mechanism to define the structure of a node (i.e., the fields that it is composed of);

(2)   a means to create nodes as needed; and

(3)   a way to free nodes that are no longer in use.

These capabilities are provided in the programming language Pascal. To define a node structure, we need to know the **type** of each of its fields. The data field in the above example is simply an array of characters while the *link* field is a pointer to another node. In Pascal, pointer types are defined as:

$$\text{\textbf{type} } PointerType = \uparrow NodeType;$$

where *NodeType* refers to the type of nodes that the pointer may point to. *The symbol $\uparrow$ denotes the indirection operator ^. When keying in a Pascal program, you must use the ^ key where ever the symbol $\uparrow$ appears in this text. In texts, it is customary to use $\uparrow$ rather than ^ to denote a pointer.*

If the type of the nodes in our earlier example is denoted by *ThreeLetterNode* then *ptr*, defined below, gives the type of the *link* field of the nodes.

$$\text{\textbf{type} } ptr = \uparrow ThreeLetterNode;$$

The data type *ThreeLetterNode* may itself be defined as a record as below;

$$\text{\textbf{type} } ThreeLetterNode = \textbf{record}$$
$$data : \textbf{array}[1..3] \textbf{ of char};$$
$$link : ptr;$$
$$\textbf{end};$$

Note that the variable *f* in the *ThreeLetterNode* example is also a pointer and its type is to be declared as:

$$\textbf{var } f : ptr;$$

The fields of the node pointed to by *f* may be referenced in the following way:

$$f \uparrow . data, \ f \uparrow . link$$

and the components of the data field are referenced as:

$$f \uparrow . data \ [1], \ f \uparrow . data \ [2], \ f \uparrow . data \ [3]$$

This is shown diagrammatically in Figure 4.5.

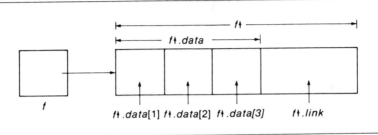

Figure 4.5 Referencing the fields of a node

Example 4.1: If a linked list is to consist of nodes that have a *data* field of type integer and a *link* field, the following type definition can be used:

> **type** *pointer* = ↑*ListNode*;
>   *ListNode* = **record**
>   *data* : **integer**;
>   *link* : *pointer*;
>   **end**;

The type definition

> **type** *ptra* = ↑*nodea*;
>   *ptrb* = ↑*nodeb*;
>   *nodea* = **record**
>   *data* 1 : **integer**;
>   *data* 2 : **char**;
>   *data* 3 : **real**;
>   *linka* : *ptra*;
>   *linkb* : *ptrb*;
>   **end**;

$$nodeb = \textbf{record}$$
$$data : \textbf{integer};$$
$$link : ptrb;$$
$$\textbf{end};$$

defines the type *nodea* to consist of three data fields and two link fields while nodes of type *nodeb* will consist of one data field and one link field. Note that the *linkb* field of nodes of type *nodea* must point to nodes of type *nodeb*. □

Nodes of a predefined type may be created using the procedure *new*. If f is of type *ptr* then following the call $new\,(f\,)$, $f\uparrow$ denotes the node (or variable) of type *ThreeLetter-Node* that is created. Similarly, if x, y, and z are, respectively, of type *pointer*, *ptra*, and *ptrb* (cf., Example 4.1), then following the sequence of calls

$$new(x); \; new(y); \; new(z);$$

$x\uparrow$, $y\uparrow$, and $z\uparrow$ will, respectively, denote the nodes of type *ListNode*, *nodea*, and *nodeb* that are created. These nodes may be disposed in the following way:

$$dispose(f); \; dispose(x); \; dispose(y); \; dispose(z);$$

Note that some implementations of Pascal do not provide a *dispose* function.

Pascal also provides a special constant **nil** that may be assigned to any pointer variable, regardless of type. This is generally used to denote a pointer field that points to no node (for example, the link field in the last node of Figure 4.3(b)) or an empty list (as in $f = \textbf{nil}$).

Arithmetic on pointer variables is not permitted. However, two pointer variables of the same type may be compared to see if both point to the same node. Thus if x and y are pointer variables of the same type then the expressions

$$x = y, x <> y, x = \textbf{nil}, \text{ and } x <> \textbf{nil}$$

are valid while the expressions

$$x + 1 \text{ and } y * 2$$

are invalid.

The effect of the assignments:

$$x := y \text{ and } x\uparrow := y\uparrow$$

on the initial configuration of Figure 4.6(a) is given in Figure 4.6(b) and (c). Note also that pointer values may neither be input nor output. In many applications, these restrictions on the use of pointers create no difficulties. In fact, in most applications, it does not even make sense to perform arithmetic on pointers. However, there are applications where we will want to perform arithmetic and/or input/output on pointers. We shall see applications where arithmetic on pointers is required in Sections 4.7 and 4.9. Applications requiring input/output of pointer values will be seen in Chapters 8 and 11. When arithmetic and/or input/output on pointers is to be performed, we can implement our own pointer type by using integers. This is discussed in Section 4.7.

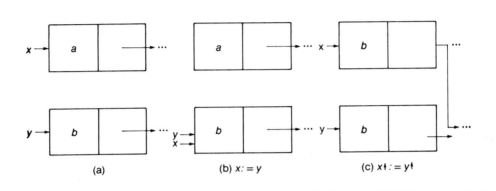

Figure 4.6 Effect of pointer assignments

Example 4.2: Procedure *create*2 (Program 4.1) creates a linked list with two nodes of type *ListNode* (cf., Example 4.1). The *data* field of the first node is set to 10 and that of the second to 20. *first* is a pointer to the first node. The resulting list structure is shown in Figure 4.7. □

```
procedure create 2(var first : pointer);
var second : pointer;
begin
  new (first);
  new (second);
  first ↑. link := second;  {link first node to second}
  second ↑. link := nil;  {last node}
  first ↑. data := 10;  {set data of first node}
  second ↑. data := 20;  {set data of second node}
end; {of create2}
```

Program 4.1 Create2

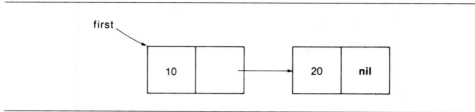

Figure 4.7 A two node list

Example 4.3: Let *first* be a pointer to a linked list as in Example 4.2. *first* = **nil** if the list is empty (i.e., there are no nodes on the list). Let *x* be a pointer to some arbitrary node in the list. Program 4.2 inserts a node with data field 50 following the node pointed at by *x*. The resulting list structures for the two cases *first* = **nil** and *first* ≠ **nil** are shown in Figure 4.8. □

```
procedure insert (var first : pointer ; x : pointer );
var t : pointer ;
begin
  new (t); {get a new node}
  t↑. data := 50; {set its data field}
  if first = nil then begin {insert into empty list}
                    first := t;
                  t↑. link := nil;
              end
  else begin {insert after x}
        t↑. link := x↑. link;
        x↑. link := t;
     end;
end; {of insert}
```

Program 4.2 Insert

Example 4.4: Let *first* and *x* be as in Example 4.3. Let *y* point to the node (if any) that precedes *x* and let *y* = **nil** if *x* = *first*. Procedure *delete* (Program 4.3) deletes node *x* from the list. □

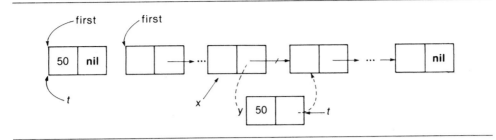

Figure 4.8 Lists for Example 4.3

```
procedure delete (x,y : pointer ; var first : pointer );
begin
  if y = nil then first := first↑. link
          else y ↑. link := x ↑. link;
  dispose (x); {return the node}
end; {of delete}
```

Program 4.3 Delete

4.2 LINKED STACKS AND QUEUES

We have already seen how to represent stacks and queues sequentially. Such a representation proved efficient if we had only one stack or one queue. However, when several stacks and queues coexist, there was no efficient way to represent them sequentially. In this section we present a good solution to this problem using linked lists. Figure 4.9 shows a linked stack and a linked queue.

Notice that the direction of links for both the stack and queue are such as to facilitate easy insertion and deletion of nodes. In the case of Figure 4.9(a), you can easily add a node at the top or delete one from the top. In Figure 4.9(b), you can easily add a node at the rear and both addition and deletion can be performed at the front, though for a queue we normally would not wish to add nodes at the front. If we wish to represent n stacks and m queues simultaneously, then the set of algorithms (Programs 4.4-4.7) will serve our purpose. The data type *pointer* is defined as:

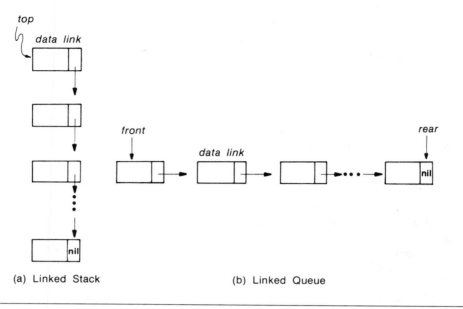

(a) Linked Stack   (b) Linked Queue

Figure 4.9 Linked stack and queue

$$\textbf{type } pointer = \uparrow node;$$
$$node = \textbf{record}$$
$$data : \textbf{integer};$$
$$link : pointer;$$
$$\textbf{end};$$

The following global arrays of type *pointer* are used:

$top[i]$ = node at top of *i*'th stack, $1 \leq i \leq n$
$front[i]$ = node at front of *i*'th queue, $1 \leq i \leq m$
$rear[i]$ = last node in *i*'th queue, $1 \leq i \leq m$

The initial conditions are

$top[i] = \textbf{nil}, 1 \leq i \leq n$
$front[i] = \textbf{nil}, 1 \leq i \leq m$

and the boundary conditions are

$top[i] = $ **nil** iff the i'th stack is empty
$front[i] = $ **nil** iff the i'th queue is empty

---

procedure *AddStack* (i,y : **integer**);
{add y to the i'th stack, $1 \le i \le n$}
var x : *pointer*;
begin
 new (x); {get a node}
 $x \uparrow . data := y$; {set its data field}
 $x \uparrow . link := top [i]$; {attach to top of i'th stack}
 $top [i] := x$; {update stack pointer}
end; {of *AddStack*}

Program 4.4 Add to a linked stack

---

procedure *DeleteStack* (i : **integer**; **var** y : **integer**);
{delete top node from stack i and set y
to be its data field, $1 \le i \le n$}
var x : *pointer*;
begin
 if $top [i] = $ **nil then** *StackEmpty*
          else begin
                  $x := top [i]$;
                  $y := x \uparrow . data$; {data field of top node}
                  $top [i] := x \uparrow . link$; {remove top node}
                  dispose (x); {free the node}
               end;
end; {of *DeleteStack*}

Program 4.5 Delete from a linked stack

The solution presented above to the n-stack, m-queue problem is seen to be both computationally and conceptually simple. There is no need to shift stacks or queues around to make space. Computation can proceed so long as there are free nodes. Though additional space is needed for the link field, the cost is no more than a factor of 2. Sometimes the *data* field does not use the whole word and it is possible to pack the *link* and *data* fields into the same word. In such a case the storage requirements for sequential and linked representations would be the same. For the use of linked lists to make sense, the overhead incurred by the storage for links must be overridden by (1) the virtue of being able to represent complex lists in a simple way, and (2) the computing time for manipulating the lists is less than for a sequential representation.

```
procedure AddQueue (i,y : integer);
{add y to queue i, 1≤i ≤m}
var x : pointer;
begin
  new (x);
  x↑.data := y; x↑.link := nil;
  if front[i ] = nil
  then front[i ] := x {empty queue}
  else rear [i ]↑.link := x;
  rear [i ] := x;
end; {of AddQueue}
```

Program 4.6 Add to a linked queue

```
procedure DeleteQueue (i : integer; var y : integer);
{delete the first node in queue i and set y
 to its data field, 1≤i ≤m}
var x : pointer;
begin
  if front[i ] = nil then QueueEmpty
              else begin
                    x := front[i ];
                    front[i ] := x↑.link; {delete first node}
                    y := x↑.data;
                    dispose (x); {free the node}
                  end;
end; {of DeleteQueue}
```

Program 4.7 Delete from a linked queue

4.3 POLYNOMIAL ADDITION

Let us tackle a reasonable size problem using linked lists. This problem, the manipulation of symbolic polynomials, has become a classical example of the use of list process.
As in Chapter 2, we wish to be able to represent any number of different polynomials as
long as their combined size does not exceed our block of memory. In general, we want
to represent the polynomial

$$A (x) = a_m x^{e_m} + \cdots + a_1 x^{e_1}$$

where the a_i are nonzero coefficients with exponents e_i such that $e_m > e_{m-1} > \ldots > e_2 > e_1 \geq 0$. Each term will be represented by a node. A node will be of fixed size having three fields which represent the coefficient and exponent of a term plus a pointer to the next term.

Assuming that all coefficients are integer, the required type declarations are

```
type PolyPointer = ↑PolyNode;
     PolyNode = record
                    coef : integer; {coefficient}
                    exp : integer; {exponent}
                    link : PolyPointer;
                end;
```

Polynodes will be drawn as:

coef	exp	link

For instance, the polynomials $a = 3x^{14} + 2x^8 + 1$ and $b = 8x^{14} - 3x^{10} + 10x^6$ would be stored as in Figure 4.10.

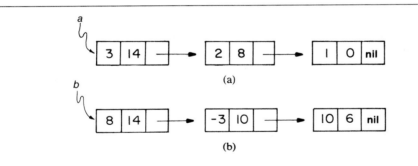

Figure 4.10 Polynomial representation

In order to add two polynomials together we examine their terms starting at the nodes pointed to by a and b. Two pointers p and q are used to move along the terms of a and b. If the exponents of two terms are equal, then the coefficients are added and a new term created for the result. If the exponent of the current term in a is less than the exponent of the current term of b, then a duplicate of the term of b is created and attached to c. The pointer q is advanced to the next term. Similar action is taken on a if $p{\uparrow}.\text{exp} > q{\uparrow}.\text{exp}$. Figure 4.11 illustrates this addition process on the polynomials a and b above.

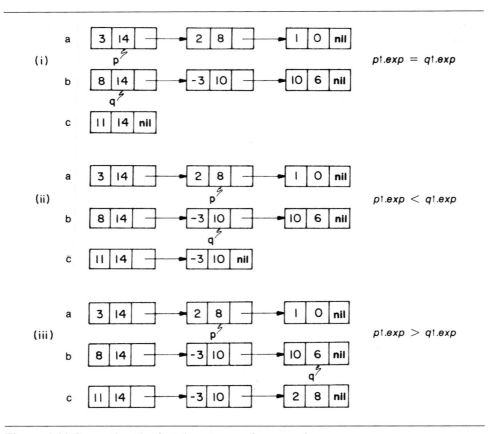

Figure 4.11 Generating the first three terms of $c = a + b$

Each time a new node is generated its *coef* and *exp* fields are set and it is appended to the end of the list c. In order to avoid having to search for the last node in c each time a new node is added, we keep a pointer d which points to the current last node in c. The complete addition algorithm is specified by the procedure *padd* (Program 4.9). *padd* makes use of a procedure *attach* (Program 4.8), which creates a new node and appends it to the end of c. To make things work out neatly, c is initially given a single node with no values which is deleted at the end of the algorithm. Though this is somewhat inelegant, it avoids more computation. As long as its purpose is clearly documented, such a tactic is permissible.

This is our first really complete example of the use of list processing, so it should be carefully studied. The basic algorithm is straightforward, using a merging process which streams along the two polynomials either copying terms or adding them to the

---

procedure *attach*(*c*,*e* : **integer**; **var** *d* : *PolyPointer*);
{create a new node with *coef*=*c*, and *exp*=*e* and attach it to the
node pointed at by *d*. *d* is updated to point to this new node.}
var *x* : *PolyPointer*;
begin
  new (*x*);
  with *x*↑ **do begin** *coef* := *c*; *exp* := *e*; **end**;
  d↑. *link* := *x*;
  d := *x*; {*d* points to new last node}
end; {of *attach*}

Program 4.8 Attach a node to the end of a list

result. Thus, the main **while** loop of lines 8-23 has three cases depending upon whether
the next pair of exponents are =, <, or >. Notice that there are five places where a new
term is created, justifying our use of the procedure *attach*.

Finally, some comments about the computing time of this algorithm. In order to
carry out a computing time analysis it is first necessary to determine which operations
contribute to the cost. For this algorithm there are several cost measures:

(1)   coefficient additions;

(2)   exponent comparisons;

(3)   additions/deletions to available space; and

(4)   creation of new nodes for *c*.

Let us assume that each of these four operations, if done once, takes a single unit of time.
The total time taken by algorithm *padd* is then determined by the number of times these
operations are performed. This number clearly depends on how many terms are present
in the polynomials *a* and *b*. Assume that *a* and *b* have *m* and *n* terms, respectively.

$$a(x) = a_m x^{e_m} + \ldots + a_1 x^{e_1}, \ b(x) = b_n x^{f_n} + \ldots + b_1 x^{f_1}$$

where

$$a_i, b_i \neq 0 \ \text{and} \ e_m > \ldots > e_1 \geq 0, f_n > \ldots > f_1 \geq 0$$

Then clearly the number of coefficient additions can vary as

$$0 \leq \text{coefficient additions} \leq \min\{m,n\}$$

```
1  procedure padd (a,b : PolyPointer; var c : PolyPointer);
2  {polynomials a and b represented as singly linked lists
3   are summed to form the new list named c}
4  var p,q,d : PolyPointer ; x  : integer;
5  begin
6    p := a ; q :=b; {p,q point to next term of a and b}
7    new (c); d := c; {initial node for c, returned later}
8    while (p <> nil) and (q <> nil) do
9      case compare (p ↑ .^exp, q↑. exp) of
10       '=':begin
11              x := p↑. coef + q↑. coef;
12              if x <> 0 then attach (x,p↑. exp,d);
13              p := p↑. link ; q :=q↑. link; {advance to next term}
14           end;
15       '<': begin
16              attach (q ↑. coef, q↑. exp,  d);
17              q := q↑. link; {next term of b}
18           end;
19       '>': begin
20              attach (p ↑. coef, p↑. exp,  d);
21              p := p↑. link; {next term of a}
22           end;
23     end; {of case and while}
24   while p <> nil do {copy rest of a}
25   begin
26     attach (p ↑. coef, p↑. exp,  d);
27     p := p↑. link;
28   end;
29   while q <> nil do {copy rest of b}
30   begin
31     attach (q ↑. coef, q↑. exp,  d);
32     q := q↑. link;
33   end;
34   d↑. link := nil; {last node}
35   {delete extra initial node}
36   p := c ; c := c↑. link ; dispose (p);
37  end; {of padd}
```

Program 4.9 Procedure to add two polynomials

The lower bound is achieved when none of the exponents are equal, while the upper bound is achieved when the exponents of one polynomial are a subset of the exponents of the other.

As for exponent comparisons, one comparison is made on each iteration of the **while** loop of lines 8-23. On each iteration either p or q or both move to the next term in their respective polynomials. Since the total number of terms is $m + n$, the number of iterations and hence the number of exponent comparisons is bounded by $m + n$. You can easily construct a case when $m + n - 1$ comparisons will be necessary: e.g., $m = n$ and

$$e_m > f_n > e_{m-1} > f_{n-1} > \ldots > f_2 > e_{n-m+2} > \ldots > e_1 > f_1$$

The maximum number of terms in c is $m + n$, and so no more than $m + n$ new nodes are created (this excludes the additional node which is attached to the front of c and later returned). In summary then, the maximum number of executions of any of the statements in *padd* is bounded above by $m + n$. Therefore, the computing time is $O(m + n)$. This means that if the algorithm is implemented and run on a computer, the time taken will be $c_1 m + c_2 n + c_3$ where c_1, c_2, c_3 are constants. Since any algorithm that adds two polynomials must look at each nonzero term at least once, algorithm *padd* is optimal to within a constant factor.

The use of linked lists is well suited to polynomial operations. We can easily imagine writing a collection of procedures for input, output, addition, subtraction, and multiplication of polynomials using linked lists as the means of representation. A hypothetical user wishing to read in polynomials $a(x)$, $b(x)$, and $c(x)$ and then compute $d(x) = a(x) * b(x) + c(x)$ would write in his or her main program

$$
\begin{aligned}
&read(a); \\
&read(b); \\
&read(c); \\
&t := pmul(a,b); \\
&d := padd(t,c); \\
&print(d);
\end{aligned}
$$

Now our user may wish to continue computing more polynomials. At this point it would be useful to reclaim the nodes which are being used to represent $t(x)$. This polynomial was created only as a partial result towards the answer $d(x)$. By returning the nodes of $t(x)$, they may be used to hold other polynomials.

Procedure *erase* (Program 4.10) frees up the nodes in t one by one. It is possible to free all the nodes in t in a more efficient way by modifying the list structure in such a way that the *link* field of the last node points to the first node in t (see Figure 4.12). A list in which the last node points back to the *first* is called a *circular* list. A singly linked list in which the last node has a **nil** link is called a *chain*.

```
procedure erase(var t : pointer);
{free all the nodes in the chain t}
var x : PolyPointer;
begin
   while t <> nil do
   begin
      x := t↑.link;
      dispose (t);
      t := x;
   end;
end; {of erase}
```

Program 4.10 Erasing a chain

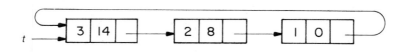

$$t$$

Figure 4.12 Circular list representation of $t = 3x^{14} + 2x^8 + 1$

The reason we dispose of nodes that are no longer in use is so that these nodes may be reused later. This objective, together with an efficient erase algorithm for circular lists, may be met by maintaining our own list (as a chain) of nodes that have been "disposed." When a new node is needed, we may examine this list. If this list is not empty, then one of the nodes on it may be made available for use. Only when this list is empty do we need to use procedure *new* to create a new node.

Let *av* be a variable of type *PolyPointer* that points to the first node in our list of nodes that have been "disposed." This list will henceforth be called the *available space list* or *av list*. Initially, $av = $ **nil**. Instead of using the procedures *new* and *dispose*, we shall now use the procedures *GetNode* (Program 4.11) and *retnode* (Program 4.12).

A circular list may now be erased in a fixed amount of time independent of the number of nodes on the list. Procedure *cerase* (Program 4.13) does this.

Figure 4.13 is a schematic showing the link changes involved in erasing a circular list.

A direct changeover to the structure of Figure 4.12, however, causes some problems during addition, etc., as the zero polynomial has to be handled as a special case. To avoid such special cases you may introduce a head node into each polynomial; i.e., each

```
procedure GetNode(var x : PolyPointer);
{provide a node for use}
begin
   if av = nil
   then new (x)
   else begin x := av ; av := av↑. link; end;
end; {of GetNode}
```

Program 4.11 Getnode

```
procedure retnode (x : PolyPointer);
{free the node pointed to by x}
begin
   x↑. link := av;
   av := x;
end; {of retnode}
```

Program 4.12 Return a node

```
procedure cerase ( var t : PolyPointer);
{erase the circular list t}
var second : PolyPointer;
begin
  if t <> nil
  then begin
          second := t↑. link; {second node}
          t↑. link := av; {first node linked to av}
          av := second; {second node of t becomes front of av list}
          t := nil;
       end;
end; {of cerase}
```

Program 4.13 Erasing a circular list

polynomial, zero or nonzero, will contain one additional node. The *exp* and *coef* fields of this node will not be relevant. Thus, the zero polynomial will have the representation of Figure 4.14(a) while $a = 3x^{14} + 2x^8 + 1$ will have the representation of Figure 4.14(b).

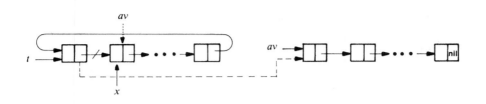

Figure 4.13 Dashes indicate changes involved in erasing a circular list

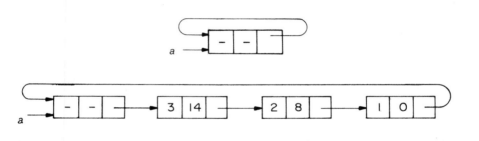

Figure 4.14 Representation of zero and $3x^{14} + 2x^8 + 1$

For this circular list with head node representation the test for $t =$ **nil** may be removed from *cerase*. The only changes to be made to algorithm *padd* are:

(1) Change line 6 to: $p := a\uparrow.link \,; q := b\uparrow.link \,;$
(2) Change line 8 to: **while** $(p <> a)$ **and** $(q <> b)$ **do**
(3) Change line 24 to: **while** $p <> a$ **do**
(4) Change line 29 to: **while** $q <> b$ **do**
(5) Delete lines 34 and 35
(6) Change line 36 to: $d\uparrow.link := c :$

Thus, the algorithm stays essentially the same. Zero polynomials are now handled in the same way as nonzero polynomials.

A further simplification in the addition algorithm is possible if the *exp* field of the head node is set to −1. Now when all nodes of a have been examined $p = a$ and $exp\,(p) = -1$. Since $-1 \le exp\,(q)$ the remaining terms of b can be copied by further executions of the case statement. The same is true if all nodes of b are examined before those of a. This implies that there is no need for additional code to copy the remaining terms as in *padd*. The final algorithm (*cpadd*) takes the simple form given in Program 4.14.

```
procedure cpadd (a,b : PolyPointer; var c : PolyPointer);
{polynomials a and b are represented as circular lists with head
nodes so that a↑.exp = b↑.exp = −1. Their sum, c, is returned
as a circular list.}
var p,q,d : PolyPointer ; x : integer; done : boolean;
begin
  p := a↑.link ; q := b↑.link;
  GetNode (c); c↑.exp := −1; {head node for c}
  d := c; {last node in c}; done := false
  repeat
    case compare (p↑.exp, q↑.exp) of
    '=': if p = a then done := true
        else begin
            x := p↑.coef + q↑.coef;
            if x <> 0 then attach (x, p↑.exp, d);
            p := p↑.link ; q := q↑.link;
          end;
    '<': begin
          attach (q↑.coef, q↑.exp, d);
          q := q↑.link;
        end;
    '>': begin
          attach (p↑.coef, p↑.exp, d);
          p := p↑.link;
        end;
    end; {of case}
  until done;
  d↑.link := c; {link last node to first}
end; {of cpadd}
```

Program 4.14 Adding circularly represented polynomials

Let us review what we have done so far. We have introduced the notions of a singly linked list, a chain, and a singly linked circular list. Each node on one of these lists consists of exactly one link field and some number of other fields. In all of our examples, all nodes on any given list had the same fields. The concept of a singly linked list does not require this and in subsequent sections, we shall see lists that violate this property.

In dealing with polynomials, we found it convenient to use circular lists. This required us to introduce the notion of an available space list. Such a list consists of all nodes that have been used at least once and are currently not in use. By using the available space list and the procedures *GetNode*, *retnode*, and *cerase*, it became possible to erase circular lists in constant time and also to reuse all nodes currently not in use. As we continue, we shall see more problems that call for variations in node structure and list representation because of the operations we wish to perform.

4.4 MORE ON LINKED LISTS

It is often necessary and desirable to build a variety of routines for manipulating singly linked lists. Some that we have already seen are (1) *GetNode* and (2) *retnode* which get and return nodes to *av*. Another useful operation is one which inverts a chain (Program 4.15). This routine is especially interesting because it can be done ''in place'' if we make use of three pointers.

```
procedure invert(var x : pointer );
{a chain pointed at by x is inverted so that if x=(a_1, ..., a_n)
then after execution x = (a_n, ..., a_1)}
var p,q,r : pointer;
begin
    p := x; q := nil; {q trails p}
    while p <> nil do
    begin
        r := q; q := p; {r trails q}
        p := p↑.link; {p moves to next node}
        q↑.link := r; {link q to preceding node}
    end;
    x := q;
end; {of invert}
```

Program 4.15 Invert a list

You should try this algorithm out on at least three examples, the empty list and lists of length 1 and 2, to convince yourself that you understand the mechanism. For a list of $m \geq 1$ nodes, the **while** loop is executed m times and so the computing time is linear or $O(m)$.

Another useful procedure is one which concatenates two chains x and y (Program 4.16). The complexity of this algorithm is also linear in the length of the list x.

```
procedure concatenate (x,y : pointer; var z : pointer);
{x = (a₁, ..., aₘ) and y=(b₁, ..., bₘ), m, n≥0
produces the new chain z = (a₁, ..., aₘ,b₁, ..., bₙ)}
var p : pointer;
begin
  if x = nil
  then z := y
  else begin
        z := x;
        if y <> nil
        then begin {find last node in x}
              p := x;
              while p↑.link <> nil do p := p↑.link;
              p↑.link := y; {link last of x to first of y}
            end;
      end;
end; {of concatenate}
```

Program 4.16 Concatenate

Now let us take another look at circular lists like the one in Figure 4.15.

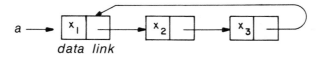

Figure 4.15 Example circular list

Suppose we want to insert a new node at the front of this list. We have to change the *link* field of the node containing x_3. This requires that we move down the entire length of *a* until we find the last node. It is more convenient if the name of a circular list points to the last node rather than the first (Figure 4.16). Now we can write procedures which insert a node at the front (Program 4.17) or at the rear of a circular list and take a fixed amount of time. To insert *x* at the rear, one only needs to add the additional statement *a* := *x* to the **else** clause of *InsertFront*.

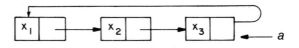

Figure 4.16 Pointing to the last node of a circular list

```
procedure InsertFront(var a : pointer ; x : pointer);
{insert the node pointed at by x at the "front" of the circular
list a, where a points to the last node in the list}
begin
  if a = nil
  then begin {empty list}
        a := x;
        x↑. link := x;
     end
  else begin
        x↑. link := a↑. link;
        a↑. link := x;
     end;
end; {of InsertFront}
```

Program 4.17 Insert at the front

As a last example of a simple procedure for circular lists, we write a function (Program 4.18) which determines the length of a such a list.

4.5 EQUIVALENCE RELATIONS

Let us put together some of these ideas on linked and sequential representations to solve a problem which arises in the design and manufacture of very large scale integrated (VLSI) circuits. One of the steps in the manufacture of a VLSI circuit involves exposing a silicon wafer using a series of masks. Each mask consists of several polygons. Polygons that overlap are electrically equivalent. Electrical equivalence specifies a relationship among mask polygons. This relation has several properties which it shares with

```
function length (a : pointer): integer;
{find the length of the circular list a}
var x : pointer;
begin
    length := 0;
    if a <> nil
    then begin
            x := a;
            repeat
              length := length + 1;
              x := x↑. link;
            until x = a;
        end;
end; {of length}
```

Program 4.18 Length

other relations such as the conventional mathematical equals. Suppose we denote an arbitrary relation by the symbol ≡ and suppose that:

(1)   For any polygon x, $x \equiv x$, e.g., x is electrically equivalent to itself. Thus, ≡ is *reflexive*.

(2)   For any two polygons x and y, if $x \equiv y$ then $y \equiv x$. Thus, the relation ≡ is *symmetric*.

(3)   For any three polygons x, y, and z, if $x \equiv y$ and $y \equiv z$ then $x \equiv z$, e.g., if x and y are electrically equivalent and y and z are also, then so also are x and z. The relation ≡ is *transitive*.

Definition: A relation, ≡, over a set S, is said to be an *equivalence relation* over S iff it is symmetric, reflexive, and transitive over S. □

Examples of equivalence relations are numerous. For example, the "equal to" (=) relationship is an equivalence relation since (1) $x = x$, (2) $x = y$ implies $y = x$, and (3) $x = y$ and $y = z$ implies $x = z$. One effect of an equivalence relation is to partition the set S into equivalence classes such that two members x and y of S are in the same equivalence class iff $x \equiv y$. For example, if we have 12 polygons numbered 1 through 12 and the following overlap pairs are defined:

$$1 \equiv 5, 4 \equiv 2, 7 \equiv 11, 9 \equiv 10, 8 \equiv 5, 7 \equiv 9, 4 \equiv 6, 3 \equiv 12, \text{ and } 12 \equiv 1$$

then, as a result of the reflexivity, symmetry, and transitivity of the relation ≡, we get the following partitioning of the 12 polygons into three equivalence classes:

$$\{1, 3, 5, 8, 12\}; \{2, 4, 6\}; \{7, 9, 10, 11\}$$

These equivalence classes are important as each such class defines a *signal net*. The signal nets can be used to verify the correctness of the masks.

The algorithm to determine equivalence classes works in essentially two phases. In the first phase the equivalence pairs (i, j) are read in and stored somewhere. In phase two we begin at 1 and find all pairs of the form $(1, j)$. The values 1 and j are in the same class. By transitivity, all pairs of the form (j, k) imply k is in the same class as 1. We continue in this way until the entire equivalence class containing 1 has been found, marked, and printed. Then we continue on.

```
procedure equivalence;
begin
    initialize;
    while more pairs do
    begin
        read the next pair (i, j);
        process this pair;
    end;
    initialize for output;
    repeat
        output a new equivalence class;
    until done;
end; {of equivalence}
```

Program 4.19 First pass at equivalence algorithm

The first design for this algorithm might go as in Program 4.19. Let m and n represent the number of related pairs and the number of objects, respectively. Now we need to determine which data structure should be used to hold these pairs. To determine this, we examine the operations that are required. The pair (i, j) is essentially two random integers in the range 1 to n. Easy random access would dictate an array, say $pairs[1..n, 1..m]$. The i'th row would contain the elements j which are paired directly to i in the input. However, this would potentially be very wasteful of space since very few of the array elements would be used. It might also require considerable time to insert a new pair, (i, k), into row i since we would have to scan the row for the next free location or use more storage.

These considerations lead us to consider a linked list to represent each row. Each node on the list requires only a *data* and a *link* field. However, we still need random access to the i'th row so a one-dimensional array, $seq[1..n]$ can be used as the head nodes of the n lists. Looking at the second phase of the algorithm we need a mechanism which tells us whether or not object i has yet to be printed. A boolean array, $out[1..n]$ can be used for this. The next refinement of the algorithm is Program 4.20. This refinement assumes that n is a global constant.

---

procedure *equivalence*;
declare *seq*, *out*, and other local variables;
begin
   initialize *seq* to **nil** and *out* to **true**;
   while more pairs **do** {input pairs}
   begin
     read the next pair (i,j);
     put j on the $seq[i]$ list;
     put i on the $seq[j]$ list;
   end;
   for $i := 1$ **to** n **do** {output equivalence classes}
     if $out[i]$ **then begin**
               $out[i] :=$ **false**;
               output this equivalence class;
            end;
end; {of *equivalence*}

Program 4.20 A more detailed version of equivalence algorithm

Let us simulate the algorithm as we have it so far, on the previous data set. After the **while** loop is completed the lists will look like as in Figure 4.17.

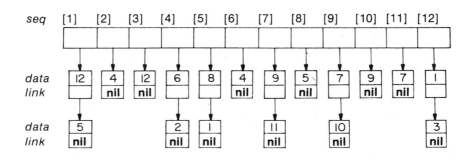

Figure 4.17 Lists after pairs input

For each relation $i \equiv j$, two nodes are used. *seq* [*i*] points to a list of nodes which contains every number which is directly equivalenced to *i* by an input relation.

In phase two we can scan the *seq* array and start with the first, *i*, $1 \leq i \leq n$ such that *out* [*i*] = **true**. Each element in the list *seq* [*i*] is printed. In order to process the remaining lists which, by transitivity, belong in the same class as *i*, a stack of their nodes is created. This is accomplished by changing the *link* fields so they point in the reverse direction. The complete procedure is given in Program 4.21.

```
procedure equivalence;
{input the equivalence pairs and output the equivalence classes}
type pointer = ↑node;
     node = record
                  data : 1..n;
                  link : pointer;
              end;
var  seq : array [1..n ] of pointer;
     out : array [1..n ] of boolean;
     i,j : integer;
     x,y,top : pointer;
     done : boolean;
begin
   {initialize seq and out}
   for i := 1 to n do begin seq [i ] := nil; out [i ] := true; end;
   {Phase 1: input equivalence pairs}
   while not eof (input) do
   begin
      readln(i, j);
      new (x); {add j to list seq [i ]}
      x↑.data := j; x↑.link := seq [i ]; seq [i ] :=x;
      new (x); {add i to list seq [j ]}
      x↑.data :=i; x↑.link := seq [j ]; seq [j]:=x;
   end;
   {Phase 2: output the equivalence classes}
   for i := 1 to n do
   if out [i ] {needs to be output}
   then begin
            writeln('A new class:', i);
            out [i ] := false;
            x := seq [i ]; top := nil; {init stack} done := false;
            repeat {find rest of class}
               while x <> nil do {process the list}
               begin
                  j := x↑.data;
                  if out [j ]
```

```
        then begin
                writeln(j); out [j] := false;
                y := x↑. link ; x↑. link := top;
                top := x; x := y;
            end
        else x := x↑. link;
    end; {of while x <> nil}
    if top = nil then done := true
    else begin
            x := seq [top↑. data ];
            top := top↑. link; {unstack}
        end;
    until done;
  end; {of if}
end; {of equivalence}
```

Program 4.21 Algorithm to find equivalence classes

Analysis of Procedure EQUIVALENCE

The initialization of *seq* and *out* takes $O(n)$ time. The processing of each input pair in phase 1 takes a constant amount of time. Hence, the total time for this phase is $O(m)$ where m is the number of input pairs. In phase 2 each node is put onto the linked stack at most once. Since there are only $2m$ nodes and the **for** loop is executed n times, the time for this phase is $O(m + n)$. Hence, the overall computing time is $O(m + n)$. Any algorithm which processes equivalence relations must look at all m equivalence pairs and also at all the n polygons at least once. Thus, there can be no algorithm with a computing time less than $O(m + n)$. This means that procedure *equivalence* is optimal to within a constant factor. Unfortunately, the space required by the algorithm is also $O(m + n)$. In Chapter 7 we shall see an alternate solution to this problem which requires only $O(n)$ space.

4.6 SPARSE MATRICES

In Chapter 2, we saw that when matrices were sparse (i.e., many of the entries were zero), then much space and computing time could be saved if only the nonzero terms were retained explicitly. In the case where these nonzero terms did not form any "nice" pattern such as a triangle or a band, we devised a sequential scheme in which each nonzero term was represented by a node with three fields: row, column, and value. These nodes were sequentially organized. However, as matrix operations such as addition, subtraction, and multiplication are performed, the number of nonzero terms in matrices will vary. Matrices representing partial computations (as in the case of polynomials) will be created and will have to be destroyed later on to make space for further matrices. Thus, sequential schemes for representing sparse matrices suffer from the same inadequacies as similar schemes for polynomials. In this section we shall study a very general linked list scheme for sparse matrix representation. As we have already seen, linked schemes facilitate efficient representation of varying size structures and here, too, our scheme will overcome the aforementioned shortcomings of the sequential representation studied in Chapter 2.

In the data representation we shall use, each column of a sparse matrix will be represented by a circularly linked list with a head node. In addition, each row will also be a circularly linked list with a head node.

Each node will have a field called *head*. This field will be used to distinguish between head nodes and nodes representing nonzero matrix elements. Each head node has three additional fields: *down*, *right*, and *next*. The total number of head nodes is max {number of rows, number of columns}. The head node for row i is also the head node for column i. The *down* field of a head node is used to link into a column list while the *right* field is used to link into a row list. The *next* field links the head nodes together.

Every other node has five additional fields: *row, col, down, right,* and *value* (Figure 4.18). The *down* field is used to link to the next nonzero term in the same column and the *right* field links to the next nonzero term in the same row. Thus if $a_{ij} \neq 0$, then there is a node with *head* = **false**, *value* = a_{ij}, *row* = i, and *col* = j. This node is linked into the circular linked lists for row i and column j. Hence, it is simultaneously in two different lists.

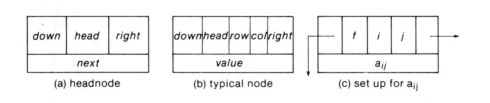

(a) headnode   (b) typical node   (c) set up for a_{ij}

Figure 4.18 Node structure for sparse matrices

As remarked earlier, each head node is in three lists: a row list, a column list, and a list of head nodes. The list of head nodes itself has a head node which is identical to the six field nodes used to represent nonzero elements. The *row* and *col* fields of this node are used to store the matrix dimensions.

The linked structure obtained for the 6×7 matrix, A, of Figure 4.19 is shown in Figure 4.20. While Figure 4.20 does not show the value of the *head* fields, these values are readily determined from the node structure shown. For each nonzero term of A, we have one six field node which is in exactly one column list and one row list. The head nodes are marked H1-H7. As can be seen from the figure, the *right* field of the head

$$\begin{array}{cc} 1\ 2 \\ 2\ 1 \end{array} \quad \begin{bmatrix} 0 & 0 & 11 & 0 & 0 & 13 & 0 \\ 12 & 0 & 0 & 0 & 0 & 0 & 14 \\ 0 & -4 & 0 & 0 & 0 & -8 & 0 \\ 0 & 0 & 0 & 0 & 0 & 0 & 0 \\ 0 & 0 & 0 & 0 & 0 & 0 & 0 \\ 0 & -9 & 0 & 0 & 0 & 0 & 0 \end{bmatrix}$$

Figure 4.19 6×7 sparse matrix A

node list header is used to link into the list of head nodes. Notice that the whole matrix may be referenced through the head node, a, of the list of head nodes.

If we wish to represent an $n \times m$ sparse matrix with r nonzero terms, then the number of nodes needed is $\max\{n,m\} + r + 1$. While each node may require several words of memory, the total storage needed will be less than nm for sufficiently small r.

Having arrived at this representation for sparse matrices, let us see how to manipulate it to perform efficiently some of the common operations on matrices. But first, let us see how the required node structure may be defined in Pascal. This time, we need to use variant records.

```
type MatrixPointer = ↑MatrixNode;
     MatrixNode = record
                     down : MatrixPointer;
                     right : MatrixPointer;
                     case head : boolean of
                        true: (next : MatrixPointer);
                        false: (value : integer;
                                row : integer;
                                col : integer);
                  end;
```

The first operation we shall consider is that of reading in a sparse matrix and obtaining its linked representation. We shall assume that the first input line consists of n (the number of rows), m (the number of columns), and r (the number of nonzero terms). The line is followed by r lines of input; each of these is a triple of the form (i,j,a_{ij}). These triples consist of the *row*, *col*, and *value* of the nonzero terms of the matrix. It is further assumed that these triples are ordered by rows and within rows by columns.

For example, the input for the 6×7 sparse matrix of Figure 4.18, which has seven nonzero terms, would take the form: 6,7,7; 1,3,11; 1,6,13; 2,1,12; 2,7,14; 3,2,-4; 3,6,-8; 6,2,-9. We shall not concern ourselves here with the actual format of this input on the input media (tapes, disk, terminal, etc.) but shall just assume we have some mechanism to get the next triple (see the exercises for one possible input format). The procedure *mread* will also make use of an auxiliary array *HeadNode*, which will be assumed to be

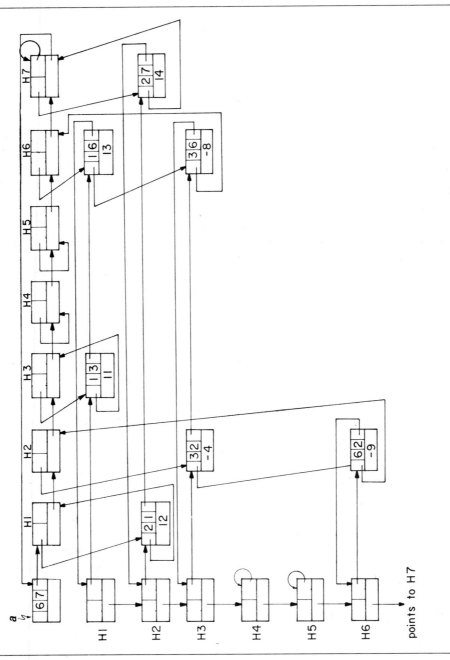

Figure 4.20 Linked representation of the sparse matrix A (the *head* field of a node is not shown; its value for each node should be clear from the node structure)

at least as large as the largest dimensioned matrix to be input. *headnode* [*i*] will be a pointer to the head node for column *i* and hence also for row *i*. This will permit us to efficiently access columns at random while setting up the input matrix. Procedure *mread* (Program 4.22) proceeds by first setting up all the head nodes and then setting up each row list, simultaneously building the column lists. The *next* field of head node *i* is initially used to keep track of the last node in column *i*. Eventually, in line 39, the head nodes are linked together through this field.

```
1  procedure mread (var a : MatrixPointer);
2  {read in a matrix and set up its linked representation.
3   An auxilliary global array hdnode is used}
4  var i,m,n,p,r,rrow,ccol,val,CurrentRow : integer;
5      x,last : MatrixPointer;

6  begin
7      readln(n,m,r); {matrix dimensions}
8      if m > n then p := m else p := n;

9      {set up head node for list of head nodes}
10     new (a); a↑. head := false ; a↑. row := n ; a↑. col := m;

11     if p = 0 then a↑. right := x;
12     else begin {at least one nonzero term}

13     for i := 1 to p do {initialize head nodes}
14     begin
15         new (x); hdnode [i ] := x;
16         with x↑ do begin head := true; right := x ; next := x; end;
17     end;
18     CurrentRow := 1; last := hdnode [1]; {last node in current row}

19     for i := 1 to r do {input triples}
20     begin
21         readln(rrow,ccol,val);
22         if rrow > CurrentRow
23         then begin {close current row}
24                 last↑. right := hdnode [CurrentRow ];
25                 CurrentRow := rrow ; last := hdnode [rrow ];
26             end;
27         new (x); {node for new triple}
28         with x↑ do begin head := false; row := rrow ; col := ccol ;
29                         value := val; end;
30         last↑. right := x ; last := x; {link into row list}
31         {link into column list}
```

```
32      hdnode [ccol ]↑. next↑. down := x ; hdnode [ccol ]↑. next := x;
33      end; {of input triples}

34      {close last row}
35      last↑. right := hdnode [CurrentRow ];

36      for i := 1 to m do {close all column lists}
37          hdnode [i ]↑. next↑. down := hdnode [i ];

38      {link the head nodes together}
39      for i := 1 to p − 1 do hdnode [i ]↑. next := hdnode [i + 1];
40      hdnode [p ]↑. next := a;
41      a↑. right := hdnode [1];
42      end; {of if p = 0}
43  end; {of mread}
```

Program 4.22 Read in a sparse matrix

Analysis of Algorithm MREAD

Since *new* works in a constant amount of time, all the head nodes may be set up in $O(\max\{n,m\})$ time, where n is the number of rows and m the number of columns in the matrix being input. Each nonzero term can be set up in a constant amount of time because of the use of the variable *last* and a random access scheme for the bottommost node in each column list. Hence, the **for** loop of lines 15-28 can be carried out in $O(r)$ time. The rest of the algorithm takes $O(\max\{n,m\})$ time. The total time is therefore $O(\max\{n,m\} + r) = O(n + m + r))$. Note that this is asymptotically better than the input time of $O(nm)$ for an $n \times m$ matrix using a two-dimensional array, but slightly worse than the sequential sparse method of Section 2.3.

Before closing this section, let us take a look at an algorithm to return all nodes of a sparse matrix. These nodes may be returned one at a time using *dispose*. A faster way to return the nodes is to set up an available space list as was done in Section 4.3 for polynomials. Assume that *av* points to the front of this list and that this list is linked through the field *right*. Procedure *merase* (Program 4.23) solves our problem in an efficient way.

Analysis of Procedure MERASE

Since each node is in exactly one row list, it is sufficient to just return all the row lists of the matrix *a*. Each row list is circularly linked through the field *right*. Thus, nodes need not be returned one by one as a circular list can be erased in a constant amount of time. The computing time for the algorithm is readily seen to be $O(n + m)$. Note, that even if the available space list had been linked through the field *down*, then erasing could still have been carried out in $O(n + m)$ time. The subject of manipulating these matrix structures is studied further in the exercises. The representation studied here is rather general. For most applications this generality is not needed. A simpler representation resulting in simpler algorithms is discussed in the exercises.

```
procedure merase(var a : MatrixPointer);
{Return all nodes of a to the av list.  This list is a chain linked
via the right field.  av points to its first node.}
var x,y : MatrixPointer;
begin
  x := a↑.right; a↑.right := av; av := a; {return a}
  while x < > a do {erase by rows}
  begin
    y := x↑.right;
    x↑.right := av;
    av := y;
    x := x↑.next; {next row}
  end;
  a := nil;
end; {of merase}
```

Program 4.23 Erasing a sparse matrix

4.7 DOUBLY LINKED LISTS AND DYNAMIC STORAGE MANAGEMENT

So far we have been working chiefly with singly linked linear lists. For some problems these would be too restrictive. One difficulty with these lists is that if we are pointing to a specific node, say p, then we can easily move only in the direction of the links. The only way to find the node which precedes p is to start back at the beginning of the list. The same problem arises when one wishes to delete an arbitrary node from a singly linked list. As can be seen from Example 4.4, in order to easily delete an arbitrary node you must know the preceding node. If we have a problem where moving in either direction is often necessary, then it is useful to have doubly linked lists. Each node now has two link fields, one linking in the forward direction and one in the backward direction.

A node in a doubly linked list has at least three fields, say *data, llink* (left link) and *rlink* (right link). A doubly linked list may or may not be circular. A sample doubly linked circular list with three nodes is given in Figure 4.21. Besides these three nodes a special node has been added called a head node. As was true in the earlier sections, head nodes are again convenient for the algorithms. The *data* field of the head node will usually contain no information. Now suppose that p points to any node in a doubly linked list. Then it is the case that

$$p = p↑.llink↑.rlink = p↑.rlink↑.llink$$

This formula reflects the essential virtue of this structure, namely, that one can go back and forth with equal ease. An empty list is not really empty since it will always have its

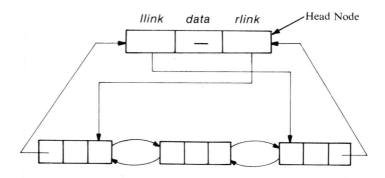

Figure 4.21 Doubly linked circular list with head node

head node and it will look as in Figure 4.22.

Figure 4.22 Empty doubly linked circular list with head node

Now to work with these lists we must be able to insert and delete nodes. Procedure *ddelete* (Program 4.24) deletes node *x* from list *l*. *x* now points to a node which is no longer part of the list *l*. Figure 4.23 shows how the method works on a doubly linked list with only a single node. Even though the *rlink* and *llink* fields of node *x* still point to the head node, this node has effectively been removed as there is no way to access *x* through *l*. Insertion is only slightly more complex (Program 4.25).

We shall now see an important problem from operating systems which is nicely solved by the use of doubly linked lists.

procedure *ddelete* (*x,l* : *dpointer*);
begin
   if *x* = *l* **then** *NomoreNodes*; {empty list}
   x↑. *llink*↑. *rlink* := *x*↑. *rlink*;
   x↑. *rlink*↑. *llink* := *x*↑. *llink*;
   dispose (*x*);
end; {of *ddelete*}

Program 4.24 Deleting from a doubly linked circular list

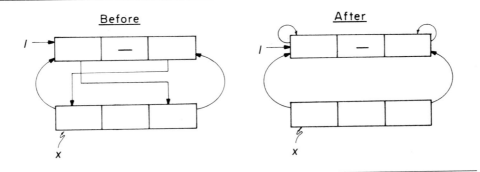

Figure 4.23 Deletion from a doubly linked circular list

procedure *dinsert* (*p, x* : *dpointer*);
{insert node *p* to the right of node *x*}
begin
   p↑. *llink* := *x* ; *p*↑. *rlink* := *x*↑. *rlink*;
   x↑. *rlink*↑. *llink* := *p* ; *x*↑. *rlink* := *p*;
end; {of *dinsert*}

Program 4.25 Insertion into a doubly linked circular list

Dynamic Storage Management

In a multiprocessing computer environment, several programs reside in memory at the same time. Different programs have different memory requirements. Thus, one program may require 60K of memory, another 100K, and yet another program may require 300K. Whenever the operating system needs to request memory, it must be able to allocate a block of contiguous storage of the right size. When the execution of a program is complete, it releases or frees the memory block allocated to it and this freed block may now be allocated to another program. In a dynamic environment the request sizes that will be made are not known ahead of time. Moreover, blocks of memory will in general, be freed in some order different form that in which they were allocated. At the start of the computer system no jobs are in memory and so the whole memory, say of size m words, is available for allocation to programs. Now jobs are submitted to the computer and requests are made for variable size blocks of memory. Assume we start off with 100,000 words of memory and five programs, $P1$, $P2$, $P3$, $P4$, and $P5$ make requests of size 10,000; 15,000; 6000; 8000; and 20,000, respectively. Figure 4.24 indicates the status of memory after storage for $P5$ has been allocated. The unshaded area indicates the memory that is currently not in use. Assume that programs $P4$ and $P2$ complete execution, freeing the memory used by them. Figure 4.25 shows the status of memory after the blocks for $P2$ and $P4$ are freed. We now have three blocks of contiguous memory that are in use and another three that are free. In order to make further allocations, it is necessary to keep track of those blocks that are not in use. This problem is similar to the one encountered in previous sections where we had to maintain a list of all free nodes. The difference between the situation then and the one we have now is that the free space consists of variable size blocks or nodes and that a request for a block of memory may now require allocation of only a portion of a node rather than the whole node. One of the functions of an operating system is to maintain a list of all blocks of storage currently not in use and then to allocate storage from this unused pool as required. One can adopt the chain structure used earlier to maintain the available space list. Now, in addition to linking all the free blocks together, it is necessary to retain information regarding the size of each block in this list of free nodes. Thus, each node on the free list has two fields in its first word, i.e., *size* and *link*. Figure 4.26 shows the free list that corresponds to Figure 4.25. The use of a head node simplifies later algorithms.

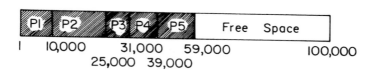

Figure 4.24 Memory after allocation to $P1$-$P5$

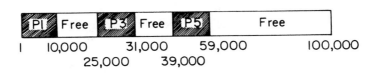

Figure 4.25 Status of memory after completion of *P* 2 and *P* 4

Note, however, that the storage management problem cannot be solved by defining a data type *block* with the fields *size*, *link*, and *UsableSpace*. This is so for the following reasons:

(1)   Different blocks are of different size.

(2)   We do not know how the usable space in each block is to be used. In general, this space will hold programs as well as data of varying type.

(3)   The use of a particular word in memory will change with time as this word will be a part of several different blocks as blocks continue to get allocated and freed.

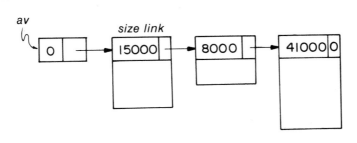

Figure 4.26 Free list with head node corresponding to Figure 4.25

Furthermore, the *link* field cannot be implemented as a Pascal pointer because the location of these fields in memory is not known and changes in time. In addition, we shall shortly see that in this application it does make sense to perform arithmetic on the link fields. In fact, without this capability, we shall have to sacrifice performance significantly.

Thus, the available memory to be managed is regarded simply as a one dimensional array of words. The array is indexed 1 through *m*. Each word is just a sequence of bits. We shall use the following procedures and functions to set and extract the *size* and *link* field of words:

$$SetSize(i, j) \dots \text{set the } size \text{ field of word } i \text{ to } j$$
$$SetLink(i, j) \dots \text{set the } link \text{ field of work } i \text{ to } j$$
$$size(i) \dots \text{extract the value in the } size \text{ field of word } i$$
$$link(i) \dots \text{extract the value in the } link \text{ field of word } i$$

Note that the *link* field contains an integer which is the index of the first word in the next block on the available space list. If there is no next block, then *link* = 0.

If we now receive a request for a block of memory of size *n*, then it is necessary to search down the list of free blocks finding the first block of size ≥*n* and allocating *n* words out of this block. Such an allocation strategy is called *FirstFit*. Procedure *FirstFit* (Program 4.26) makes storage allocations using the first fit strategy. An alternate strategy, *best fit*, calls for finding a free block whose size is as close to *n* as possible, but not less than *n*. This strategy is examined in the exercises.

```
procedure FirstFit(n : integer; var p : integer);
{Allocate a block of size n using first fit. p is set to 0 if there is no
block large enough, otherwise p is the start of the allocated block.}
var q : integer; NotDone : boolean;
begin
    p := link (av); q := av; {q trails p} NotDone := true;
    while (p <> 0) and NotDone do {examine free blocks}
        if size (p) ≥ n {block large enough}
        then begin {allocate from this block}
                SetSize (p, size (p) − n);
                if size (p) = 0 {allocate whole block}
                then SetLink (q, link (p))
                else p := p + size (p); {allocate last n words}
                NotDone := false
            end
        else begin
                q := p; p := link (p); {next block}
            end; {of if and while}
end; {of FirstFit}
```

Program 4.26 First fit allocation

Program 4.26 is simple enough to understand. In case only a portion of a free block is to be allocated, the allocation is made from the bottom of the block. This avoids changing any links in the free list unless an entire block is allocated. There are, however, two major problems with *FirstFit*. First, experiments have shown that after some processing time many small nodes are left in the available space list, these nodes being smaller than any requests that would be made. Thus, a request for 9900 words allocated from a block of size 10,000 would leave behind a block of size 100, which may be smaller than any request that will be made to the system. Retaining these small nodes on the available space list tends to slow down the allocation process as the time needed to make an allocation is proportional to the number of nodes on the available space list. To get around this, we choose some suitable constant ε such that if the allocation of a portion of a node leaves behind a node of size $< \varepsilon$, then the entire node is allocated. That is, we allocate more storage than requested in this case. The second problem arises from the fact that the search for a large enough node always begins at the front of the list. As a result of this, all the small nodes tend to collect at the front so that it is necessary to examine several nodes before an allocation for larger blocks can be made. In order to distribute small nodes evenly along the list, one can begin searching for a new node from a different point in the list each time a request is made. To implement this, the available space list is maintained as a circular list with a head node of size zero. *av* now points to the last node from which an allocation was made. We shall see what the new allocation algorithm looks like after we discuss what has to be done to free a block of storage.

The second operation is the freeing of blocks or returning nodes to *av*. Not only must we return the node, but we also want to recognize if its neighbors are also free so that they can be coalesced into a single block. Looking back at Figure 4.26, we see that if *P3* is the next program to terminate, then rather than just adding this node onto the free list to get the free list of Figure 4.27, it would be better to combine the adjacent free blocks corresponding to *P2* and *P4*, obtaining the free list of Figure 4.28. This combining of adjacent free bocks to get bigger free blocks is necessary. The block allocation algorithm splits big blocks while making allocations. As a result, available block sizes get smaller and smaller. Unless recombination takes place at some point, we will no longer be able to meet large requests for memory.

With the structure we have for the available space list, it is not easy to determine whether blocks adjacent to the block (n,p) (n = size of block and p = starting location) being returned are free. The only way to do this, at present, is to examine all the nodes in *av* to determine whether:

(1)   the left adjacent block is free, i.e., the block ending at $p - 1$

(2)   the right adjacent block is free, i.e., the block beginning at $p + n$

In order to determine (1) and (2) above without searching the available space list, we adopt the node structure of Figure 4.29 for allocated and free nodes.

The first and last words of each block are reserved for allocation information. The first word of each free block has four fields: *llink, rlink, tag* and *size*. Only the *tag* and *size* field are important for a block in use. The last word in each free block has two fields: *tag* and *UpLink*. Only the *tag* field is important for a block in use. Now by just examining the tags at $p - 1$ and $p + n$ one can determine whether the adjacent blocks are free. The *UpLink* field of a free block points to the start of the block. The available space list will now be a doubly linked circular list, linked through the fields *llink* and *rlink*. It will have a head node with *size* = 0. A doubly linked list is needed, as the return block algorithm will delete nodes at random from *av*. The need for *UpLink* will become

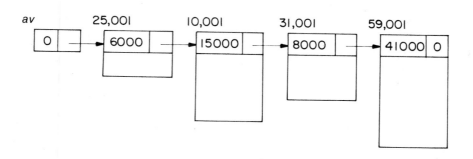

Figure 4.27 Available space list when adjacent free blocks are not coalesced

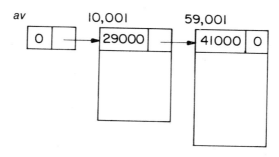

Figure 4.28 Available space list when adjacent free blocks are coalesced

clear when we study the freeing algorithm. Since the first and last nodes of each block have *tag* fields, this system of allocation and freeing is called the *boundary tag method*.

It should be noted that the *tag* fields in allocated and free blocks occupy the same bit position in the first and last words, respectively. This is not obvious from Figure 4.29 where the *llink* field precedes the *tag* field in a free node. The labeling of fields in this figure has been done so as to obtain clean diagrams for the available space list. The algorithms we shall obtain for the boundary tag method will assume that memory is numbered 1 to m and that $tag(0) = tag(m + 1) = 1$. This last requirement will enable us to free the block beginning at 1 and the one ending at m without having to test for these blocks as special cases. Such a test would otherwise have been necessary as the first of these blocks has no left adjacent block while the second has no right adjacent block.

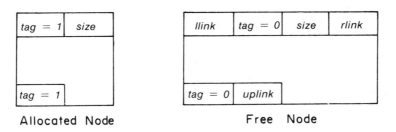

Figure 4.29 Node structure for allocated and free blocks

While the *tag* information is all that is needed in an allocated block, it is customary to also retain the size in the block. Hence, Figure 4.29 includes a *size* field in an allocated block.

Before presenting the allocate and free algorithms let us study the initial condition of the system when all of memory is free. Assuming memory begins at location 1 and ends at m, the *av* list initially looks as in Figure 4.30.

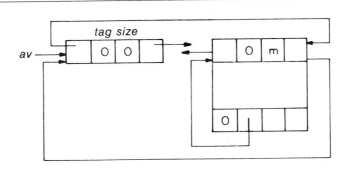

Figure 4.30 Initial configurartion of *av* list

The allocate (Program 4.27) and free procedures (Program 4.28) use the following functions and procedures. The implementation of these is left unspecified.

setxyz (i,j) ... set the *xyz* field of word i to j
xyz (i) ... extract the value in the *xyz* field of word i

```
 1  procedure allocate (n: integer; var p: integer);
 2  {Use next fit to allocate a block of size at least n.
 3   No blocks of size < eps are retained on the av list.
 4   p is set as in procedure firstfit.}
 5  label 99;
 6  var diff: integer;
 7  begin
 8    p := rlink (av); {start search at p}
 9    repeat
10      if size (p) >= n {block large enough} then
11      begin
12        diff := size (p)−n;
13        if diff < eps {allocate whole block}
14        then begin
15              SetRlink (llink (p),rlink (p)); {delete from list}
16              SetLlink (rlink (p),llink (p));
17              SetTag (p,1); SetTag (p +size (p)−1,1);
18              av := llink (p); {start next search here}
19              goto 99;
20            end
21        else begin {allocate last n words}
22              SetSize (p,diff); SetUpLink (p +diff −1,p);
23              SetTag (p +diff−1,0); av := p;
24              p := p +diff; SetSize (p,n);
25              SetTag (p,1); SetTag (p +n −1,1);
26              goto 99;
27            end;
28      end;
29      p := rlink (p); {examine next block}
30    until p = rlink (av);
31    p := 0; {no block large enough}
32  99: end; {of allocate}
```

Program 4.27 Allocate using next fit

While the allocate and free procedures (Programs 4.27 and 4.28) may appear complex, they are a direct consequence of the doubly linked list structure of the available space list and also of the node structure in use. Notice that the use of a head node eliminates the test for an empty list in both algorithms and hence simplifies them. The use of circular linking makes it easy to start the search for a large enough node at any point in the available space list. The *UpLink* field in a free block is needed only when returning a block whose left adjacent block is free (see lines 16 and 37 of procedure *free*). In lines 31 and 40 *av* is changed so that it always points to the start of a free block rather than into the middle of a free block. One may readily verify that the algorithms work for special cases such as when the available space list contains only the head node.

The best way to understand the algorithms is to simulate an example. Let us start with a memory of size 5000 from which the following allocations are made: $r_1 = 300$, $r_2 = 600$, $r_3 = 900$, $r_4 = 700$, $r_5 = 1500$ and $r_6 = 1000$. At this point the memory configuration is as in Figure 4.31. This figure also depicts the different blocks of storage and the available space list. Note that when a portion of a free block is allocated, the allocation is made from the bottom of the block so as to avoid unnecessary link changes in the av list. First block r_1 is freed. Since $tag(5000) = tag(4700) = 1$, no coalescing takes place and the block is inserted into the av list (Figure 4.32(a)). Next, block r_4 is returned. Since both its left adjacent block (r_5) and its right adjacent block (r_3) are in use at this time ($tag(2500) = tag(3201) = 1$), this block is just inserted into the free list to get the configuration of Figure 4.32(b). Block r_3 is next returned. Its left adjacent block is free, $tag(3200) = 0$; but its right adjacent block is not, $tag(4101) = 1$. So this block is just attached to the end of its adjacent free block without changing any link fields (Figure 4.32(c)). Block r_5 next becomes free. $tag(1000) = 1$ and $tag(2501) = 0$ and so this block is coalesced with its right adjacent block which is free and inserted into the spot previously occupied by this adjacent free block (Figure 4.32(d)). r_2 is freed next. Both its upper and lower adjacent blocks are free. The upperblock is deleted from the free space list and combined with r_2. This bigger block is now just appended to the end of the free block made up of r_3, r_4 and r_5 (Figure 4.32(e)).

```
 1  procedure free(p : integer);
 2  {return a block beginning at p and of size size (p)}
 3  var n,q: integer;
 4  begin
 5    n := size (p);
 6    if (tag (p − 1)=1) and (tag (p +n)=1)
 7    then begin {both adjacent blocks in use}
 8          SetTag (p,0); SetTag (p +n −1,0); {free the block}
 9          SetUpLink (p +n −1,p);
10          {insert at right of av}
11          SetLlink (p,av); SetRlink (p,rlink (av));
12          SetLlink (rlink (p),p); SetRlink (av,p);
13        end
14    else if (tag (p +n)=1) and (tag (p −1)=0)
15        then begin {only left block free}
16              q := UpLink (p −1); {start of left block}
17              SetSize (q,size (q)+n);
18              SetUpLink (p +n −1,q); SetTag (p +n −1,0);
19            end
20        else if (tag (p +n)=0) and (tag (p −1)=1)
21              then begin {only right block free}
```

```
22                      {replace block beginning at p +n by
23                      one beginning at p}
24                      SetRlink (llink (p +n),p);
25                      SetLlink (rlink (p +n),p);
26                      SetLlink (p,llink (p +n));
27                      SetRlink (p,rlink (p +n));
28                      SetSize (p,n +size (p +n));
29                      SetUpLink (p +size (p )−1,p);
30                      SetTag (p,0);
31                      av := p;
32                    end
33                  else begin {both adjacent blocks free}
34                      {delete right block from av list}
35                      SetRlink (llink (p +n),rlink (p +n));
36                      SetLlink (rlink (p +n),llink (p +n));
37                      q := UpLink (p −1);
38                      SetSize (q,size (q )+n +size (p +n));
39                      SetUpLink (q +size (q )−1,q);
40                      av := llink (p +n);
41                    end;
42  end; {of free}
```

Program 4.28 Free a block using boundry tags

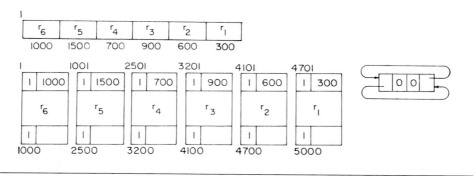

Figure 4.31 Memory configuration after the allocations $r_1, \ldots, r_6$

As for the computational complexity of the two algorithms, one may readily verify that the time required to free a block of storage is independent of the number of free blocks in *av*. Freeing a block takes a constant amount of time. In order to accomplish this we had to pay a price in terms of storage. The first and last words of each block in

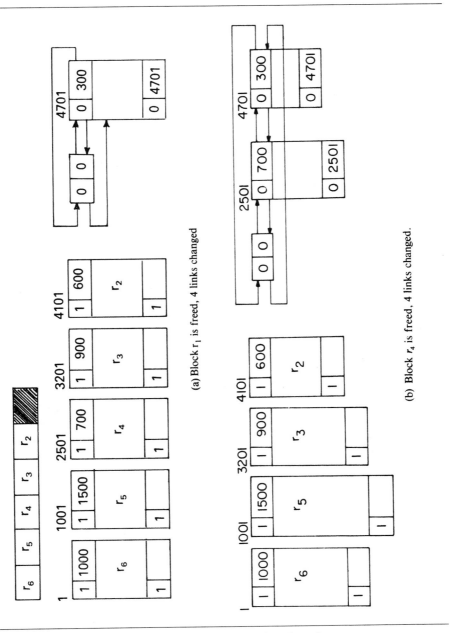

Figure 4.32 Freeing of blocks in boundary tag system (continued)

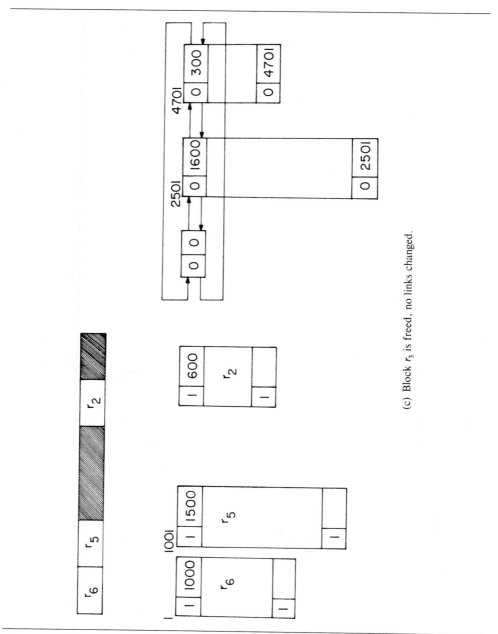

Figure 4.32 Freeing of blocks in boundary tag system (continued)

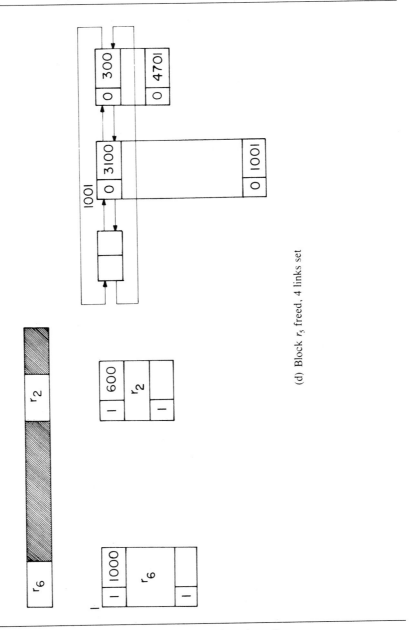

Figure 4.32 Freeing of blocks in boundary tag system (continued)

194 Linked Lists

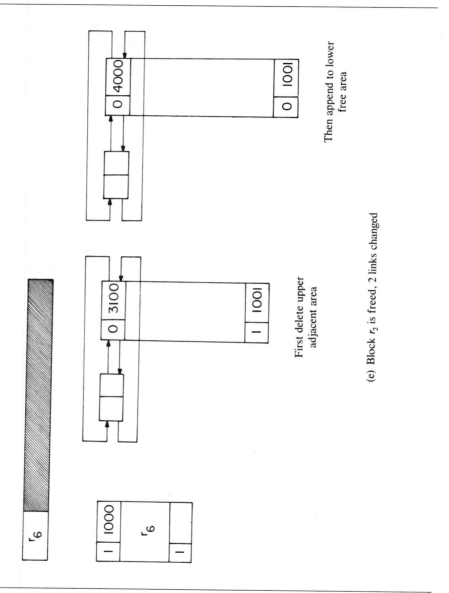

First delete upper adjacent area

Then append to lower free area

(e) Block r_2 is freed, 2 links changed

Figure 4.32 Freeing of blocks in boundary tag system

use are reserved for *tag* information. Though additional space is needed to maintain *av* as a doubly linked list, this is of no consequence as all storage in *av* is free in any case. The allocation of a block of storage still requires a search of the *av* list. In the worst case, all free blocks may be examined.

An alternative scheme for storage allocation, the "buddy system", is investigated in the exercises.

4.8 GENERALIZED LISTS

In Chapter 2, a linear list was defined to be a finite sequence of $n \geq 0$ elements, $\alpha_1, \ldots, \alpha_n$, which we write as $A = (\alpha_1, \ldots, \alpha_n)$. The elements of a linear list are restricted to be atoms and thus the only structural property a linear list has is the one of position, i.e., α_i precedes α_{i+1}, $1 \leq i < n$. It is sometimes useful to relax this restriction on the elements of a list, permitting them to have a structure of their own. This leads to the notion of a generalized list in which the elements α_i, $1 \leq i \leq n$ may be either atoms or lists.

Definition: A *generalized list, A*, is a finite sequence of $n \geq 0$ elements, $\alpha_1, \ldots, \alpha_n$, where the α_i are either atoms or lists. The elements α_i, $1 \leq i \leq n$ which are not atoms are said to be the *sublists* of *A*. ☐

The list *A* itself is written as $A = (\alpha_1, \ldots, \alpha_n)$. *A* is the *name* of the list $(\alpha_1, \ldots, \alpha_n)$ and *n* its *length*. By convention, all list names will be represented by capital letters. Lower case letters will be used to represent atoms. If $n \geq 1$, then α_1 is the *head* of *A* while $(\alpha_2, \ldots, \alpha_n)$ is the *tail* of *A*.

The above definition is our first example of a recursive definition so one should study it carefully. The definition is recursive because within our description of what a list is, we use the notion of a list. This may appear to be circular, but it is not. It is a compact way of describing a potentially large and varied structure. We will see more such definitions later on. Some examples of generalized lists are:

(1) $D = ()$ the null, or empty, list; its length is zero
(2) $A = (a,(b,c))$ a list of length two; its first element is the atom *a*, and its second element is the linear list (b,c)
(3) $B = (A,A,())$ a list of length three whose first two elements are the list *A*, and the third element is the null list
(4) $C = (a,C)$ a recursive list of length two; *C* corresponds to the infinite list $C = (a, (a, (a, \ldots)$

Example (1) is the empty list and is easily seen to agree with the definition. For list *A*, we have

$$head(A) = \text{`}a\text{'}, \ tail(A) = ((b,c))$$

The *tail* (A) also has a head and tail which are (b,c) and $(\ )$, respectively. Looking at list B, we see that

$$head(B) = A, tail(B) = (A,(\ ))$$

Continuing, we have

$$head\,(tail\,(B)) = A,\ tail\,(tail\,(B)) = ((\ ))$$

both of which are lists.

Two important consequences of our definition for a list are (1) lists may be shared by other lists as in example (3), where list A makes up two of the sublists of B; and (2) lists may be recursive as in example (4). The implications of these two consequences for the data structures needed to represent lists will become evident as we go along.

First, let us restrict ourselves to the situation where the lists being represented are neither shared nor recursive. To see where this notion of a list may be useful, consider how to represent polynomials in several variables. Suppose we need to devise a data representation for them and consider one typical example, the polynomial

$$P(x,y,z) = x^{10}y^3z^2 + 2x^8y^3z^2 + 3x^8y^2z^2 + x^4y^4z + 6x^3y^4z + 2yz$$

You can easily think of a sequential representation for P, say using nodes with four fields: *coef, expx, expy,* and *expz.* But this would mean that polynomials in a different number of variables would need a different number of fields, adding another conceptual inelegance to other difficulties we have already seen with the sequential representation of polynomials. If we used linear lists, we might conceive of a node of the form

coef	expx	expy
expz	link	

These nodes would have to vary in size depending on the number of variables, causing difficulties in storage management. The idea of using a general list structure with fixed size nodes arises naturally if we consider rewriting $P(x,y,z)$ as

$$((x^{10} + 2x^8)y^3 + 3x^8y^2)z^2 + ((x^4 + 6x^3)y^4 + 2y)z$$

Every polynomial can be written in this fashion, factoring out a main variable z, followed by a second variable y, etc. Looking carefully now at $P(x,y,z)$, we see that there are two terms in the variable z, $Cz^2 + Dz$, where C and D are polynomials themselves but in the variables x and y. Looking more closely at $C(x,y)$, we see that it is of the form

$Ey^3 + Fy^2$, where E and F are polynomials in x. Continuing in this way, we see that every polynomial consists of a variable plus coefficient exponent pairs. Each coefficient is itself a polynomial (in one less variable) if we regard a single numerical coefficient as a polynomial in zero variables.

From the preceding discussion, we see that every polynomial, regardless of the number of variables in it, can be represented using nodes of the type *PolyNode* defined as:

```
type triple = (variable, ptr, no);
     PolyPointer = ↑PolyNode;
     PolyNode = record
                    link : PolyPointer;
                    exp : integer;
                    case trio : triple of
                        variable : (vble : char);
                        ptr : (dlink : PolyPointer);
                        no : (coef : integer);
                end;
```

Note that the type of the field *vble* can be changed to **integer** in case all variables are kept in a table and *vble* just gives the corresponding table index.

The polynomial $P = 3x^2y$ now takes the representation given in Figure 4.33 while $P(x,y,z)$ defined before has the list representation shown in Figure 4.34. For simplicity, the *trio* field is omitted from Figure 4.34. The value of this field for each node is self evident.

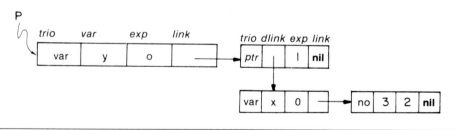

Figure 4.33 Representation of $3x^2y$

It is a little surprising that every generalized list can be represented using the node structure:

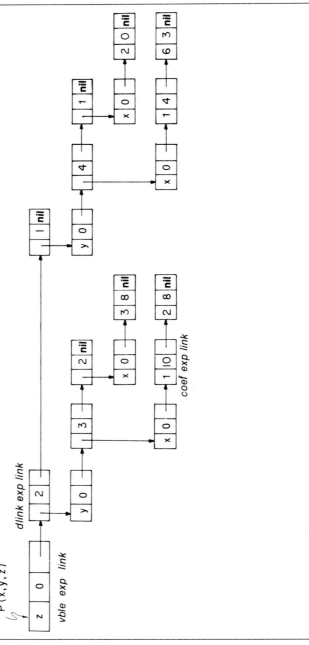

Figure 4.34 Representation of $P(x,y,z)$

tag = true/false	data/dlink	link

This structure may be defined in Pascal as:

type *ListPointer* = ↑*ListNode*;
    ListNode = **record**
        link : *ListPointer*;
        case *tag* : **boolean of**
          false : (*data* : **char**);
          true : (*dlink* : *ListPointer*);
        end;

where the type of the *data* field will change from one application to the next. You should convince yourself that this node structure is adequate for the representation of any list A. The *link* field may be used as a pointer to the tail of the list while the *data/dlink* field can hold an atom in case *head*(A) is an atom or be a pointer to the list representation of *head*(A) in case it is a list. Using this node structure, the example lists (1)-(4) have the representation shown in Figure 4.35. In these examples, the data field is of type **char**.

Recursive Algorithms for Lists

Now that we have seen a particular example where generalized lists are useful, let us return to their definition again. Whenever a data object is defined recursively, it is often easy to describe algorithms which work on these objects recursively. To see how recursion is useful, let us write a procedure (Program 4.29) which produces an exact copy of a nonrecursive list p in which no sublists are shared. We will assume the nodes of p are of type *ListNode* as defined earlier.

Program 4.29 reflects exactly the definition of a list. We immediately see that *copy* works correctly for an empty list. A simple proof using induction will verify the correctness of the entire procedure. Once we have established that the program is correct we may wish to remove the recursion for efficiency. This can be done using some straightforward rules. The following rules assume that the recursive procedure does not use the labels 1, 2, . . ., k, where k is one more than the number of places from which a recursive call is made.

(1)   At the beginning of the procedure or function, code is inserted which declares a stack (called recursion stack) and initializes it to be empty. In the most general case, the stack will be used to hold the values of parameters, local variables, and a return address for each recursive call. We might prefer to use a separate stack for each value.

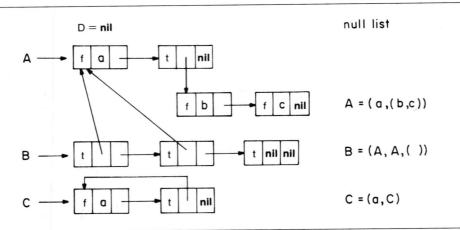

Figure 4.35 Representation of lists (1)-(4); an *f* in the *tag* field represents the value false while a *t* represents the value true

```
function copy (p: ListPointer): ListPointer;
{copy the nonrecursive list with no shared sublists
 pointed at by p}
var q: ListPointer;
begin
  q := nil;
  if p <> nil
  then begin
          new (q); q↑.tag := p↑.tag;
          if not p↑.tag then q↑.data := p↑.data
                        else q↑.dlink := copy (p↑.dlink);
          q↑.link := copy (p↑.link);
       end;
  copy := q;
end; {of copy}
```

Program 4.29 Copy a list

(2)   The label 1 is attached to the first executable statement.

(3)   If this is a function, then replace all appearances of the function name on the left hand side of assignment statements by a new variable, say z, of the same type as the function.

Now, each recursive call is replaced by a set of instructions that do the following:

(4)   Store the values of all pass by value parameters and local variables in the stack. The pointer to the top of the stack can be treated as global.

(5)   Create the i'th new label, i, and store i in the stack. The value i of this label will be used as the return address. This label is placed in the program as described in rule (7).

(6)   Evaluate the arguments of this call that correspond to pass by value parameters (they may be expressions) and assign these values to the appropriate formal parameters.

(7)   Insert an unconditional branch to the beginning of the procedure.

(8)   If this is a procedure, add the label created in (5) to the statement immediately following the unconditional branch. In case this statement already has a label, change it and all references to it to the label created in (5). If this is a function then follow the unconditional branch by code to use the value of the variable Z in the same way the function was used earlier. The first statement of this code is given the label that was created in (5).

These steps are sufficient to remove all recursive calls from the procedure or function. Finally, we need to precede the last **end** statement of the procedure or function by code to do the following:

(9)   If the recursion stack is empty, then assign the value of z to the function name and execute a normal **end** of function in case this a function. In the case of a procedure, we simply execute a normal **end** of procedure.

(10)   If the stack is not empty, then restore the value of all pass by value parameters that are not also pass by reference actual parameters and of all local variables. These are at the top of the stack. Use the return label from the top of the stack and execute a branch to this label. This can be done using a **case** statement as shown in the following example.

(11)   In addition, the label (if any) attached to the **end** of the procedure or function statement is moved to the first statement of the code for (9) and (10).

By following these rules carefully one can take any recursive program and produce a program which works in exactly the same way, yet which uses only iteration to control the flow of the program. On many compilers this resultant program will be much more efficient than its recursive version. On other compilers the times may be fairly close.

Once the transformation to iterative form has been accomplished, one can often simplify the program even further thereby producing even more gains in efficiency. These rules have been used to produce the iterative version of *copy* which appears in Program 4.30.

```
function  copy (p :ListPointer ): ListPointer ;
{copy the nonrecursive list with no shared sublists
pointed at by p}
label 1,2,3;
constant StackSize = 100;
var StackPointer: 0..100;
    qstack: array [1..StackSize] of ListPointer;
    pstack: array [1..StackSize] of ListPointer;
    LabelStack: array [1..StackSize] of integer;
    ReturnLabel: integer;
    q: ListPointer;
    z: ListPointer;
begin
    StackPointer := 0; {initialize stacks}
 1: q := nil;
    if p <> nil
    then begin
            new (q); q↑.tag := p↑.tag;
            if not p↑.tag then q↑.data := p↑.data
            else begin
                    StackPointer := StackPointer + 1;
                    if StackPointer > StackSize then StackFull;
                    qstack [StackPointer ] := q;
                    pstack [StackPointer ] := p;
                    LabelStack [StackPointer ] := 2;
                    p := p ↑.dlink;
                    goto 1;
                    2: q ↑.dlink := z;
                    end; {of if not p ↑.tag}
            StackPointer := StackPointer + 1;
            if StackPointer > StackSize then StackFull;
            qstack [StackPointer ] := q;
            pstack [StackPointer ] := p;
            LabelStack [StackPointer ] := 3;
            p := p ↑.link;
            goto 1;
            3: q ↑.link := z;
            end; {of if p <> nil}
    z := q;
```

```
      if StackPointer < > 0
      then begin {simulate an end of function}
              q := qstack [StackPointer ];
              p := pstack [StackPointer ];
              ReturnLabel := LabelStack [StackPointer ];
              StackPointer := StackPointer − 1;
              case ReturnLabel of
                 2: goto 2;
                 3: goto 3;
              end; {of case}
            end; {of if StackPointer < > 0}
     copy := z;
  end; {of copy}
```

Program 4.30 Nonrecursive version of *copy*

It is hard to believe that the nonrecursive version is any more intelligible than the recursive one. But it does show explicitly how to implement such an algorithm in, say, FORTRAN. The nonrecursive version does have some virtues, namely, it is more efficient. The overhead of parameter passing on most compilers is heavy. Moreover, there are optimizations that can be made on the latter version, but not on the former. Thus, both of these forms have their place. We will often use the recursive version for descriptive purposes.

Now let us consider the computing time of this algorithm. The null list takes a constant amount of time. For the list

$$A = ((a,b),((c,d),e))$$

which has the representation of Figure 4.36, p takes on the values given in Figure 4.37. The sequence of values should be read down the columns b, r, s, t, u, v, w, x are the addresses of the eight nodes of the list. From this particular example one should be able to see that nodes with $tag =$ **false** will be visited twice, while nodes with $tag =$ **true** will be visited three times. Thus, if a list has a total of m nodes, no more than $3m$ executions of any statement will occur. Hence, the algorithm is $O(m)$ or linear which is the best we could hope to achieve. Another factor of interest is the maximum depth of recursion or, equivalently, how many locations one will need for the recursion stack. Again, by carefully following the algorithm on the previous example we see that the maximum depth is a combination of the lengths and depths of all sublists. However, a simple upper bound to use is m, the total number of nodes. Though this bound will be extremely large in many cases, it is achievable, for instance, if

$$A = (((((a)))))$$

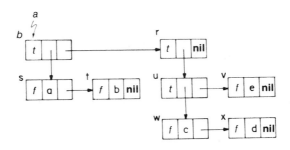

Figure 4.36 Linked representation for A

levels of recursion	value of p	continuing levels	p	continuing levels	p
1	b	2	r	3	u
2	s	3	u	4	v
3	t	4	w	5	o
4	o	5	x	4	v
3	t	6	o	3	u
2	s	5	x	2	r
1	b	4	w	3	o
				2	r
				1	b

Figure 4.37 Values of parameter in execution of *copy* (A)

Another procedure which is often useful is one which determines whether two lists are identical. This means they must have the same structure and the same data in corresponding fields. Again, using the recursive definition of a list we can write a short recursive procedure (Program 4.26) which accomplishes this task.

Procedure *equal* is a function which returns either the value **true** or **false**. Its computing time is clearly no more than linear when no sublists are shared since it looks at each node of s and t no more than three times. For unequal lists the procedure terminates as soon as it discovers that the lists are not identical.

Another handy operation on nonrecursive lists is the function which computes the depth of a list. The depth of the empty list is defined to be zero and in general

---

```
function equal (s,t : ListPointer): boolean;
{s and t are nonrecursive lists.  This function has value
 true iff the two lists are identical}
var x : boolean;
begin
 equal := false;
 if (s = nil) and (t = nil)
 then equal := true
 else if (s <> nil) and (t <> nil)
      then if s↑.tag = t↑.tag
           then begin
                if not s↑.tag
                then if s↑.data = t↑.data then x := true
                                          else x := false
                else x := equal (s↑.dlink,t↑.dlink);
                if x then equal := equal (s↑.link,t↑.link)
                end;
end; {of equal}
```

Program 4.31 Function *equal*

$$depth (s) = \begin{cases} 0 & \text{if } s \text{ is an atom} \\ 1 + \max \{depth (x_1), ..., depth (x_n)\} & \text{if } s \text{ is the list } (x_1, ..., x_n), n \ge 1 \end{cases}$$

Procedure *depth* (Program 4.32) is a very close transformation of the definition which is itself recursive. By now you have seen several programs of this type and you should be feeling more comfortable both reading and writing recursive algorithms.

Reference Counts, Shared and Recursive Lists

In this section we shall consider some of the problems that arise when lists are allowed to be shared by other lists and when recursive lists are permitted. Sharing of sublists can in some situations result in great savings in storage used, as identical sublists occupy the same space. In order to facilitate ease in specifying shared sublists, we extend the definition of a list to allow for naming of sublists. A sublist appearing within a list definition may be named through the use of a list name preceding it. For example, in the list $A = (a, (b,c))$, the sublist (b,c) could be assigned the name Z by writing $A = (a,Z(b,c))$. In fact, to be consistent we would then write $A(a,Z(b,c))$ which would define the list A as above.

```
function depth (s : ListPointer): integer;
{compute the depth of the nonrecursive list s}
var p : ListPointer; m,n : integer;
begin
  if s <> nil
  then begin
        p := s; m := 0;
        while p <> nil do
        begin
          if p↑.tag
          then begin
                  n := depth (p↑.dlink);
                  if m < n then m := n;
                end;
          p := p↑.link;
        end;
        depth := m + 1;
      end
  else depth := 0;
end; {of depth}
```

Program 4.32 Function *depth*

Lists that are shared by other lists, such as list *A* of Figure 4.35, create problems when you wish to add or delete a node at the front. If the first node of *A* is deleted, it is necessary to change the pointers from the list *B* to point to the second node. In case a new node is added then pointers from *B* have to be changed to point to the new first node. However, we normally do not know all the points from which a particular list is being referenced. (Even if you did have this information, addition and deletion of nodes could require a large amount of time.) This problem is easily solved through the use of head nodes. In case you expect to perform many add/deletes from the front of lists, then the use of a head node with each list or named sublist will eliminate the need to retain a list of all pointers to any specific list. If each list is to have a head node, then lists (1)-(4) are represented as in Figure 4.38. Even in situations where you do not wish to add or delete nodes from lists dynamically, as in the case of multivariate polynomials, head nodes prove useful in determining when the nodes of a particular structure may be returned to the storage pool. For example, let *t* and *u* be program variables pointing to the two polynomials $(3x^4 + 5x^3 + 7x)y^3$ and $(3x^4 + 5x^3 + 7x)y^6 + (6x)y$ of Figure 4.39. If *perase* is to erase a polynomial, then the invocation *perase*(*t*) should not return the nodes corresponding to the coefficient $3x^4 + 5x^3 + 7x$ since this sublist is also part of *u*.

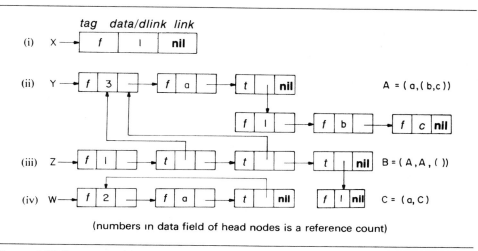

Figure 4.38 Structure with head nodes for lists (1)-(4)

Thus, whenever lists are being shared by other lists, we need a mechanism to help determine whether or not the list nodes may be physically returned to the available space list. This mechanism is generally provided through the use of a reference count maintained in the head node of each list. Since the *data* field of the head nodes is free, the reference count is maintained in this field. (Alternatively a third variant may be introduced with *tag* having three possible values 0, 1, 2.) This reference count of a list is the number of pointers (either program variables or pointers from other lists) to that list. If the lists (1)-(4) of Figure 4.38 are accessible via the program variables x, y, z, and w, then the reference counts for the lists are:

(1) $ref(x) = 1$ accessible only via x
(2) $ref(y) = 3$ pointed to by y and two pointers from z
(3) $ref(z) = 1$ accessible only via z
(4) $ref(w) = 2$ two pointers to list c

Now a call to *lerase*(t) (list erase) should result only in a decrementing by 1 of the reference counter of t. Only if the reference count becomes zero are the nodes of t to be physically returned to the available space list. The same is to be done to the sublists of t.

Assume that the data type *ListPointer* is defined as

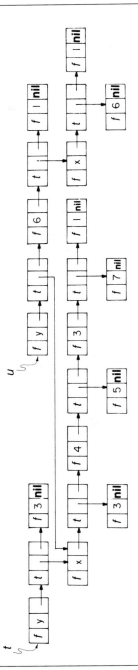

Figure 4.39 $T = (3x^4 + 5x^3 + 7x)y^3$, $U = (3x^4 + 5x^3 + 7x)y^6 + 6xy$

```
type ListPointer = ↑ListNode;
     three = 0..2;
     ListNode = record
                    link : ListPointer;
                    case tag : three of
                        0 : (data : integer);
                        1 : (dlink : ListPointer);
                        2 : (ref : integer);
                end;
```

An algorithm to erase a list x could proceed by examining the top level nodes of a list whose reference count has become zero. Any such sublists encountered are erased and finally, the top level nodes are linked into the available space list. The list erase algorithm is given in Program 4.33.

```
procedure lerase (var x : ListPointer);
{recursively erase a nonrecursive list. Each
head node has a reference count. We assume x ≠ nil.}
var y : ListPointer;
begin
  x↑.ref := x↑.ref−1; {decrement reference count}
  if x↑.ref = 0
  then begin
          y := x; {y traverses top level of x}
          while y↑.link <> nil do
          begin
            y := y↑.link;
            if y↑.tag then lerase (y↑.dlink);
          end;
          y↑.link := av; {attach top level nodes to av list}
          av := x;
       end;
  x := nil;
end; {of lerase}
```

Program 4.33 Procedure *lerase*

A call to *lerase*(y) will now only have the effect of decreasing the reference count of y to 2. Such a call followed by a call to *lerase*(z) will result in

(1)   reference count of z becomes zero;

(2)   next node is processed and $y\!\uparrow.ref$ reduces to 1;

(3) $y\!\uparrow.ref$ becomes zero and the five nodes of list $A\,(a,\,(b,c\,))$ are returned to the available space list; and

(4)   the top level nodes of z are linked into the available space list.

The use of head nodes with reference counts solves the problem of determining when nodes are to be physically freed in the case of shared sublists. However, for recursive lists, the reference count never becomes zero. $lerase(w)$ just results in $w\!\uparrow.ref$ becoming one. The reference count does not become zero even though this list is no longer accessible either through program variables or through other structures. The same is true in the case of indirect recursion (Figure 4.40). After calls to $lerase(r)$ and $lerase(s)$, $r\!\uparrow.ref=1$ and $s\!\uparrow.ref=2$ but the structure consisting of r and s is no longer being used and so it should have been returned to the available space list.

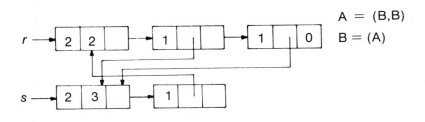

A = (B,B)
B = (A)

Figure 4.40 Indirect recursion of lists A and B pointed to by program variables r and s

Unfortunately, there is no simple way to supplement the list structure of Figure 4.40 so as to be able to determine when recursive lists may be physically erased. It is no longer possible to return all free nodes to the available space list when they become free. So when recursive lists are being used, it is possible to run out of available space even though not all nodes are in use. When this happens, it is possible to collect unused nodes (i.e., garbage nodes) through a process known as garbage collection. This will be described in the next section.

4.9 GARBAGE COLLECTION AND COMPACTION

As remarked at the close of the last section, garbage collection is the process of collecting all unused nodes and returning them to available space. This process is carried out in essentially two phases. In the first phase, known as the marking phase, all nodes in use are marked. In the second phase all unmarked nodes are returned to the available space list. This second phase is trivial when all nodes are of the same size. In this case, the second phase requires only the examination of each node to see whether or not it has been marked. If there are a total of n nodes, then the second phase of garbage collection can be carried out in $O(n)$ steps. In this situation it is only the first or marking phase that is of any interest in designing an algorithm. When variable size nodes are in use, it is desirable to compact memory so that all free nodes form a contiguous block of memory. In this case the second phase is referred to as memory compaction. Compaction of disk space to reduce average retrieval time is desirable even for fixed size nodes. In this section we shall study two marking algorithms and one compaction algorithm.

Marking

In order to be able to carry out the marking, we need a mark field in each node. It will be assumed that this mark field can be changed at any time by the marking algorithm. Marking algorithms mark all directly accessible nodes (i.e., nodes accessible through program variables referred to as pointer variables) and also all indirectly accessible nodes (i.e., nodes accessible through link fields of nodes in accessible lists). It is assumed that a certain set of variables has been specified as pointer variables and that these variables at all times are either **nil** (i.e., point to nothing) or are valid pointers to lists. It is also assumed that the link fields of nodes always contain valid link information.

Knowing which variables are pointer variables, it is easy to mark all directly accessible nodes. The indirectly accessible nodes are marked by systematically examining all nodes reachable from these directly accessible nodes. Before examining the marking algorithms let us review the node structure in use. Each node regardless of its usage will have two boolean fields: *mark* and *tag*. If *tag* = **false**, then the node contains only atomic information in a field called *data*. If *tag* = **true**, then the node has two link fields: *dlink* and *rlink*. Atomic information can be stored only in nodes that have *tag* = **false**. Such nodes are called *atomic* nodes. All other nodes are list nodes. This node structure is slightly different from the one used in the previous section where a node with *tag* = **false** contained atomic information as well as a *link*. With this new node structure, the list $(a, (b))$ is represented as in Figure 4.41. The type definition for the new nodes is given below:

type *ListPointer* = ↑*ListNode*;
      ListNode = **record**
                        mark : **boolean**;
                        case *tag* : **boolean of**
                              true : (*dlink* : *ListPointer*;
                                            rlink : *ListPointer*);
                              false : (*data* : **char**)
                  end;

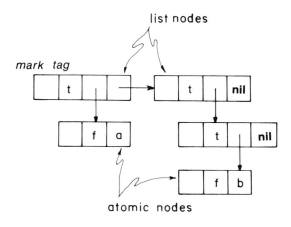

Figure 4.41 List (*a*, (*b*))

Both of the marking algorithms we shall discuss will require that all nodes be initially unmarked (i.e., $x\uparrow.mark =$ **false** for every node $x\uparrow$). Procedure *driver* (Program 4.34) will repeatedly call a marking algorithm to mark all nodes accessible from each of the pointer variables being used. In line 6, procedure *mark*1 is invoked. If we wish to use the second marking algorithm, then we need merely invoke *mark*2 instead of *mark*1. Both the marking algorithms have been written to work on arbitrary list structures (not just generalized lists as described here).

The first marking algorithm *mark*1 (Program 4.35) will start from the list node x and mark all nodes that can be reached from x via a sequence of *rlink*'s and *dlink*'s; examining all such paths will result in the examination of all reachable nodes. While examining any node of type list we will have a choice as to whether to move to the *dlink* or to the *rlink*. *mark*1 will move to the *dlink* but will at the same time place the *rlink* on a stack in case the *rlink* is a list node not yet marked. The use of this stack will enable us to return at a later point to the *rlink* and examine all paths from there. This strategy is

```
1 procedure driver
2 begin
3   for each pointer variable x that points to an unmarked node do
4   begin
5     x↑.mark := true;
6     if x↑.tag then mark1(x); {x is a list node}
7   end;
8 end; {of driver}
```

Program 4.34 Procedure *driver*

similar to the one used in the previous section for *lerase*.

Analysis of MARK1

In lines 12-14 of *mark*1 we check to see if $q = p↑.rlink$ can lead to other unmarked accessible nodes. If so, q is stacked. The examination of nodes continues with the node at $p↑.dlink$. When we have moved downwards as far as possible, we exit from the loop of lines 10-23. At this point we try out one of the alternative moves from the stack, line 9. You may verify that *mark*1 does indeed mark all previously unmarked nodes which are accessible from x.

In analyzing the computing time of this algorithm we observe that on each iteration (except for the last) of the loop of lines 10-23, at least one previously unmarked node gets marked (line 21). Thus, if the **while** loop, lines 7-25, is iterated r times and the total number of iterations of the **repeat** loop, lines 10-23, is u then at least $w = u - r$ previously unmarked nodes get marked by the algorithm. Let m be the number of new nodes marked. Then $m \geq w = u - r$. Also, the number of iterations of the loop of lines 7-25 is one plus the number of nodes that get stacked. The only nodes that can be stacked are those previously unmarked (line 14). Once a node is stacked it gets marked (line 15). Hence, $r \leq m + 1$. From this and the knowledge that $m \geq u - r$, we conclude that $u \leq 2m + 1$. The computing time of the algorithm is $O(u + r)$. Substituting for u and r, we obtain $O(m)$ as the computing time. The time is linear in the number of new nodes marked. Since any algorithm to mark nodes must spend at least one unit of time on each new node marked, it follows that there is no algorithm with a time less than $O(m)$. Hence, *mark*1 is optimal to within a constant factor (recall that $2m = O(m)$ and $10m = O(m)$).

Having observed that *mark*1 is optimal to within a constant factor you may be tempted to sit back in your arm chair and relish a moment of smugness. There is, unfortunately, a serious flaw with *mark*1. This flaw is sufficiently serious as to make the algorithm of little use in many garbage collection applications. Garbage collectors are invoked only when we have run out of space. This means that at the time *mark*1 is to

```
 1  procedure mark1(x : ListPointer);
 2  {mark all nodes accessible from the list node x. add and delete
 3   are the standard stack procedures. top points to the stack top.}
 4  var p,q : ListPointer; done : boolean;
 5  begin
 6     top := 0; add (x); {put x on the stack}
 7     while top > 0 do {stack not empty}
 8     begin
 9       delete (p); {unstack}; done := false;
10       repeat {move down stacking rlinks as needed}
11          q := p ↑.rlink;
12          if q <> nil
13          then begin
14                  if q ↑.tag and not q↑.mark then add (q); {unmarked list node}
15                  q↑.mark := true; {mark q}
16              end;
17          p := p ↑.dlink;
18          if p <> nil then
19             {a marked or atomic node cannot lead to new nodes}
20             if p↑.mark or not p ↑.tag then done := true
21                                  else p↑.mark := true;
22                         else done := true;
23       until done;
24       if p <> nil then p↑.mark := true;
25     end; {of while}
26  end; {of mark1}
```

Program 4.35 First marking algorithm

operate, we do not have an unlimited amount of space available in which to maintain the stack. In some applications each node might have a free field which can be used to maintain a linked stack. In fact, if variable size nodes are in use and storage compaction is to be carried out then such a field will be available (see the compaction algorithm *compact*). When fixed size nodes are in use, compaction can be efficiently carried out without this additional field and so we will not be able to maintain a linked stack (see exercises for another special case permitting the growth of a linked stack). Realizing this deficiency in *mark1*, let us proceed to another marking algorithm *mark2*. *mark2* will not require any additional space in which to maintain a stack. Its computing time is also $O(m)$ but the constant factor here is larger than that for *mark1*.

Unlike *mark1* which does not alter any of the links in the list *x*, the algorithm *mark2* will modify some of these links. However, by the time it finishes its task the list structure will be restored to its original form. Starting from a list node *x*, *mark2* traces all possible paths made up of *dlink*'s and *rlink*'s. Whenever a choice is to be made the *dlink* direction is explored first. Instead of maintaining a stack of alternative choices (as was done by *mark1*) we now maintain the path taken from x to the node p that is currently being examined. This path is maintained by changing some of the links along the path from x to p.

Consider the example list of Figure 4.42(a). Initially, all nodes except node A are unmarked and only node E is atomic. From node A we can either move down to node B or right to node I. *mark2* will always move down when faced with such a choice. We shall use p to point to the node currently being examined and t to point to the node preceding p in the path from x to p. The path t to x will be maintained as a chain comprised of the nodes on this $t-x$ path (read as "t to x"). If we advance from node p to node q then either $q = p\uparrow.rlink$ or $q = p\uparrow.dlink$ and q will become the node currently being examined. The node preceding q on the $x-q$ path is p and so the path list must be updated to represent the path from p to x. This is simply done by adding node p to the $t-x$ path already constructed. Nodes will be linked onto this path either through their *dlink* or *rlink* field. Only list nodes will be placed onto this path chain. When node p is being added to the path chain, p is linked to t via its *dlink* field if $q = p\uparrow.dlink$. When $q = p\uparrow.rlink$, p is linked to t via its *rlink* field. In order to be able to determine whether a node on the $t-x$ path list is linked through its *dlink* or *rlink* field, we make use of the *tag* field. Notice that since the $t-x$ path list will contain only list nodes, the tag on all these nodes will be **true**. When the *dlink* field is used for linking, this tag will be changed to **false**. Thus, for nodes on the $t-x$ path we have

$$tag = \begin{cases} \textbf{false} \text{ if the node is linked via its } dlink \text{ field} \\ \textbf{true} \text{ if the node is linked via its } rlink \text{ field} \end{cases}$$

The tag will be reset to true when the node gets off the $t-x$ path list. (While this use of the *tag* field represents a slight abuse of the language, it is preferable to introducing an additional field.)

Figure 4.42(b) shows the $t-x$ path list when node p is being examined. Nodes A, B, and C have a tag of zero (for false) indicating that linking on these nodes is via the *dlink* field. This also implies that in the original list structure, $B = A\uparrow.dlink$, $C = B\uparrow.dlink$ and $D = p = C\uparrow.dlink$. Thus, the link information destroyed while creating the $t-x$ path list is present in the path list. Nodes B, C, and D have already been marked by the algorithm. In exploring p we first attempt to move down to $q = p\uparrow.dlink = E$. E is an atomic node so it gets marked and we then attempt to move right from p. Now, $q = p\uparrow.rlink = F$. This is an unmarked list node. So, we add p to the path list and proceed to explore q. Since p is linked to q by its *rlink* field, the linking of p onto the $t-x$ path is made through its *rlink* field. Figure 4.42(c) shows the list structure at the time node G is being examined. Node G is a dead end. We cannot move further either down or right. At this time we move backwards on the $x-t$ path resetting links and tags until we reach a node whose *rlink* has not yet been examined. The marking continues from this node. Because nodes are removed from the $t-x$ path list in the reverse order in which they were added to it, this list behaves as a stack. The remaining details of *mark* 2 are spelled out in Program 4.36. The same driver as for *mark* 1 is assumed.

The procedure *mark2* given in Program 4.36(a) makes use of three other procedures which are given in Programs 4.36(b)-(d). These latter are to be physically placed between the **var** and first **begin** statement of *mark2*. Procedure *mark2* first attempts to move p one node down. If it cannot, then an attempt is made to move p one node to the right. If this cannot be done, then we attempt to backup on the $t-x$ list and move p to a node from which a rightward move may be possible. When even this backup is not possible, *mark2* terminates. The correctness of the procedures of Programs 4.36(a)-(d) is easily established.

Analysis of MARK2

Figure 4.42(e) shows the path taken by p on the list of Figure 4.42(a). It should be clear that a list node previously unmarked gets visited at most three times. Except for node x, each time a node already marked is reached at least one previously unmarked node is also examined (i.e., the one that led to this marked node). Hence the computing time of *mark2* is $O(m)$ where m is the number of newly marked nodes. The constant factor associated with m is, however, larger than that for *mark*1 but *mark2* does not require the stack space needed by *mark*1. A faster marking algorithm can be obtained by judiciously combining the strategies of *mark*1 and *mark2* (see the exercises).

When the node structure of Section 4.8 is in use, an additional boolean field in each node is needed to implement the strategy of *mark2*. This field is used to distinguish between the case when a *dlink* is used to link into the path list and when an *rlink* is used. The existing tag field cannot be used as some of the nodes on the $t-x$ path list will originally have *tag* = **true** while others will have *tag* = **false** and so it will not be possible to reset tag values correctly when nodes are removed from the $t-x$ list.

Storage Compaction

When all requests for storage are of a fixed size, it is enough to just link all unmarked (i.e., free) nodes together into an available space list. However, when storage requests may be for blocks of varying sizes, it is desirable to compact storage so that all the free space forms one contiguous block. Consider the memory configuration of Figure 4.43. Nodes in use have a *mark* field = t (for true), while free nodes have their *mark* field = f (for false). The nodes are labeled 1 through 8, with n_i, $1 \le i \le 8$ being the size of the i'th node.

The free nodes could be linked together to obtain the available space list of Figure 4.44. While the total amount of memory available is $n_1 + n_3 + n_5 + n_8$, a request for this much memory cannot be met since the memory is fragmented into four nonadjacent nodes. Further, with more and more use of these nodes, the size of free nodes will get

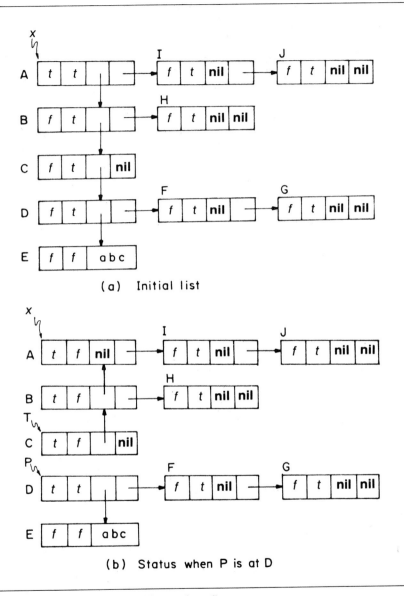

(a) Initial list

(b) Status when P is at D

Figure 4.42 Example list for *mark*2 (continued)

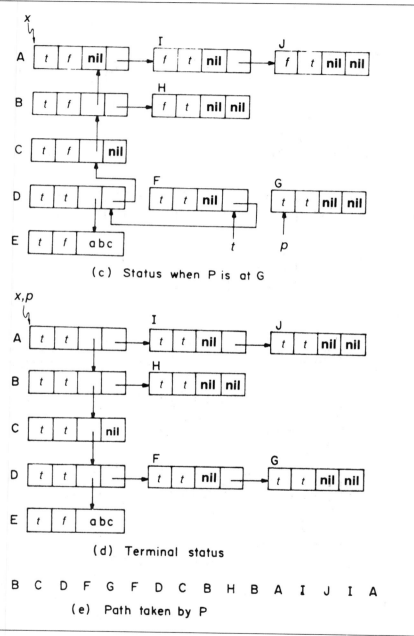

(c) Status when P is at G

(d) Terminal status

A B C D F G F D C B H B A I J I A

(e) Path taken by P

Figure 4.42 Example list for *mark2*

```
 1 procedure mark2(x : ListPointer);
 2 {same function as mark1}
 3 var p, q, t : ListPointer; failure : boolean;
 4 begin
 5   p := x; t := nil; {initialize t−x path list}
 6   repeat
 7     MoveDown;
 8     if failure then begin
 9                  MoveRight;
10                      if failure then backup;
11                  end;
12   until failure;
13 end; {of mark2}
```

Program 4.36 (a) Second marking algorithm

```
 1 procedure MoveDown;
 2 {Attempt to move p one node down}
 3 begin
 4   q := p↑.dlink; {go down list}; failure := true;
 5   if q <> nil
 6   then if not q↑.mark and q↑.tag
 7        then begin {unmarked list node}
 8               q↑.mark := true; p↑.tag := false;
 9               p↑.dlink := t; t := p; {add p to t−x path list}
10               p := q; failure := false;
11             end
12        else q↑.mark := true;
13 end; {of MoveDown}
```

Program 4.36(b) Procedure to move down one node

smaller and smaller. Ultimately, it will be impossible to meet requests for all but the smallest of nodes. In order to overcome this, it is necessary to reallocate the storage of the nodes in use so that the used part of memory (and hence also the free portion) forms a contiguous block at one end as in Figure 4.45. This reallocation of storage resulting in a partitioning of memory into two contiguous blocks (one used, the other free) is referred to as storage compaction. Since there will, in general, be links from one node to another, storage compaction must update these links to point to the relocated address of the respective node. If node n_i starts at location l_i before compaction and at $l_i{'}$ after

```
 1  procedure MoveRight;
 2  {Attempt to move p one node right}
 3  begin
 4      q := p↑.rlink; {move right}; failure := true;
 5      if q <> nil
 6      then if not q↑.mark and q↑.tag
 7          then begin {unmarked list node}
 8                  q↑.mark := true; p↑.rlink := t;
 9                  t := p; p := q; failure := false;
10              end
11          else q↑.mark := true;
12  end; {of MoveRight}
```

Program 4.36(c) Procedure to move right one node

```
 1  procedure backup;
 2  {Attempt to backup on t−x list}
 3  begin
 4      failure := true;
 5      while (t <> nil) and failure do
 6      begin
 7        q := t;
 8        if not q↑.tag
 9        then begin {linked via dlink}
10                t := q↑.dlink; q↑.dlink := p;
11                q↑.tag := true; p := q;
12                MoveRight;
13            end
14        else begin {linked via rlink}
15                {p is to right of q}
16                t := q↑.rlink; q↑.rlink := p;
17                p := q;
18            end;
19      end; {of while}
20  end; {of backup}
```

Program 4.36(d) Procedure to back up on the t−x list

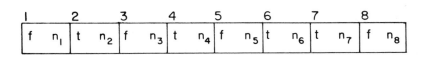

Figure 4.43 Memory configuraton after marking; free nodes have mark field = f

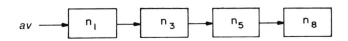

Figure 4.44 Available space list corresponding to Figure 4.43

compaction, then all link references to l_i must also be changed to l_i' in order not to disrupt the linked list structures existing in the system. Figure 4.46(a) shows a possible link configuration at the time the garbage collection process is invoked. Links are shown only for those nodes that were marked during the marking phase. It is assumed that there are only two links per node. Figure 4.46(b) shows the configuration following compaction. Note that the list structure is unchanged even though the actual addresses represented by the links have been changed.

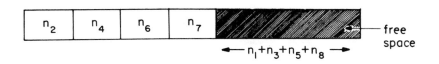

Figure 4.45 Memory configuraton after reallocating storage to nodes in use

With storage compaction we may identify three tasks: (1) determine new addresses for nodes in use; (2) update all links in nodes in use; and (3) relocate nodes to new addresses. Our storage compaction algorithm, *compact* (Program 4.37), is fairly straightforward, implementing each of these three tasks in a separate scan of memory. The algorithm assumes that each node, free or in use, has a *size* field giving the length of the node and an additional field, *NewAddr*, which may be used to store the relocated address of the node. Further, it is assumed that each node has two link fields *link*1 and *link*2. The extension of the algorithm to the most general situation in which nodes have a variable number of links is simple and requires only a modification of phase II. As in the case of the dynamic storage management algorithms of Section 4.7, the link fields contain integer values that give us the index of the first word in the node pointed at. 0 denotes a **nil** link. The fields in a node may be set and extracted using appropriate procedures and functions, respectively. In addition, we assume that the memory to be compacted is the array *memory* [1..*m*].

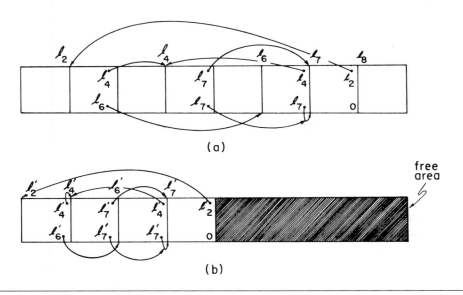

Figure 4.46 Configurations before and after compaction

```
procedure compact;
{compact the array memory [1..m]. Every node that is in
use has mark = true; a NewAddr field, and two link fields.
size (i) = number of words in the node.}
var i,j,k : integer;
begin
    {phase I: Scan memory left to right assigning new
    addresses to nodes in use. av = next available word.}
    av := 1; i := 1;
    while i <= m do
    begin
```

```
        if mark(i)
        then begin {assign new address}
                SetNewAddr (i) := av;
                av := av + size (i);
            end;
         i := i + size (i); {next node}
    end;
    {phase II: Update all links.  Assume that NewAddr (0) = 0}
    i := 1;
    while i <= m do
    begin
     if mark(i)
     then begin
                SetLink 1(i, NewAddr (link 1(i)));
                SetLink 2(i, NewAddr (link 2(i)));
            end;
      i := i + size (i);
    end;
    {phase III: relocate nodes}
    i := 1;
    while i <= m do
     if mark(i)
     then begin
                k := i − NewAddr (i); l := NewAddr (i);
                for j := i to i + size (i)−1 do
                  memory [j−k ] := memory [j ];
                i := i + size (l);
            end
     else i := i + size (i);
    end; {of compact}
```

Program 4.37 Memory compaction

In analyzing this algorithm, we see that if the number of nodes in memory is n, then phases I and II each require n iterations of their respective **while** loops. Since each iteration of these loops takes a fixed amount of time, the time for these two phases is $O(n)$. Phase III, however, will in general be more expensive. Though the **while** loop of this phase is also executed only n times, the time per iteration depends on the size of the node being relocated. If s is the amount of memory in use, then the time for this phase is $O(n + s)$. The overall computing time is, therefore, $O(n + s)$. The value of av at the end of phase I marks the beginning of the free space. At the termination of the algorithm the space $memory[av]$ to $memory[m]$ is free space. Finally, the physical relocation of nodes in phase III can be carried out using a long shift in case your computer has this facility.

In conclusion, we remark that both marking and storage compaction are slow processes. The time for the former is O(number of nodes) while the time for the latter is O(number of nodes + Σ(size of nodes relocated)). In the case of generalized lists, garbage collection is necessitated by the absence of any other efficient means to free storage when needed. Garbage collection has found use in some programming languages where it is desirable to free the user from the task of returning storage. In both situations, a disciplined use of pointer variables and link fields is required. Clever coding tricks involving illegal use of link fields could result in chaos during marking and compaction.

While compaction has been presented here primarily for use with generalized list systems using nodes of variable size, compaction can also be used in other environments such as the dynamic storage allocation environment of Section 4.7. Even though coalescing of adjacent free blocks takes place in algorithm *free* of Section 4.7, it is still possible to have several small nonadjacent blocks of memory free. The total size of these blocks may be large enough to meet a request and it may then be desirable to compact storage. The compaction algorithm in this case is simpler than the one described here. Since all addresses used within a block will be relative to the starting address rather than the absolute address, no updating of links within a block is required. Phases I and III can, therefore, be combined into one phase and phase II eliminated altogether. Since compaction is very slow, one would like to minimize the number of times it is carried out. With the introduction of compaction, several alternative schemes for dynamic storage management become viable. The exercises explore some of these alternatives.

4.10 STRINGS: A CASE STUDY

Suppose we have two character strings $S = `x_1 \ldots x_m`$ and $T = `y_i \ldots y_n`$. The characters x_i, y_j come from a set usually referred to as the *character set* of the programming language. The value n (or m) is the length of the character string T and is an integer which is greater than or equal to zero. In $n = 0$ then T is called the empty or *null string*. In this section we will discuss several alternate ways of implementing strings using the techniques of this chapter.

We begin by defining the data structure *STRING* using the axiomatic notation. For a set of operations we choose to model this structure after the string operations of PL/I. These include:

(1)   *NULL* produces an instance of the null string,

(2)   *ISNULL* returns **true** if the string is null, else **false**,

(3)   *IN* takes a string and a character and inserts it at the end of the string,

(4)   *LEN* returns the length of a string,

(5)   *CONCAT* places a second string at the end of the first string,

(6) *SUBSTR* returns any length of consecutive characters,

(7) *INDEX* determines the start of the rightmost substring of one string that equals another string.

This data structure is formally specified in Structure 4.1.

---

structure *STRING*
    declare *NULL* ( ) → *string* ; *ISNULL* (*string*) → *boolean*
        IN (*string*, *char*) → *string* ; *LEN* (*string*) → *integer*
        CONCAT (*string*, *string*) → *string*
        SUBSTR (*string*, *integer*, *integer*) → *string*;
        INDEX (*string*, *string*) → *integer*;
    for all *S,T* ε *string*, *i,j* ε *integer*, *c,d* ε *char* **let**
      ISNULL (*NULL*) ::= **true**; *ISNULL* (*IN* (*S,c*)) ::= **false**
      LEN (*NULL*) ::= 0; *LEN* (*IN* (*S,c*)) ::= 1 + *LEN* (*S*)
      CONCAT (*S,NULL*) ::= *S*
      CONCAT (*S,IN* (*T,c*)) ::= *IN* (*CONCAT* (*S,T*),*c*)
      SUBSTR (*NULL,i,j*) ::= *NULL*
      SUBSTR (*IN* (*S,c*),*i,j*) ::=
        if ($j = 0$) **or** ($i + j - 1 >$ *LEN* (*IN* (*S,c*))) **then** *NULL*
          else if ($i + j - 1 =$ *LEN* (*IN* (*S,c*)))
              then *IN* (*SUBSTR* (*S,i,j* $- 1$),*c*)
              else *SUBSTR* (*S,i,j*)
      INDEX (*S,NULL*) ::= *LEN* (*S*) + 1
      INDEX (*NULL,IN* (*T,d*)) ::= 0
      INDEX (*IN* (*S,c*),*IN* (*T,d*)) ::=
        if ($c = d$) **and** (*INDEX* (*S,T*) = *LEN* (*S*) $-$ *LEN* (*T*) + 1)
        then *INDEX* (*S,T*)
        else *INDEX* (*S,IN* (*T,d*))
    end
end *STRING*

Structure 4.1 Strings

As an example of how these axioms work, let $S =$ '*abcd*'. This will be represented as

$$IN (IN (IN (IN (NULL,a),b),c),d)$$

Now suppose we follow the axioms as they apply to *SUBSTR* (*S*,2,1). By the *SUBSTR* axioms we get

$$SUBSTR(S,2,1) \quad = SUBSTR(IN(IN(IN(NULL,a),b),c),2,1)$$
$$= SUBSTR(IN(IN(NULL,a),b),2,1)$$
$$= IN(SUBSTR(IN(NULL,a),2,0),b)$$
$$= IN(NULL,b)$$
$$= \text{`}b\text{'}$$

Suppose we try another example,

$$SUBSTR(S, 3, 2) \quad = IN(SUBSTR(IN(IN(IN(NULL,a),b),c),3,1),d)$$
$$= IN(IN(SUBSTR(IN(IN(NULL,a),b),3,0),c),d)$$
$$= IN(IN(NULL,c),d)$$
$$= \text{`}cd\text{'}$$

For your amusement try to simulate the steps taken for $INDEX(S,T)$ where $T = \text{`}bc\text{'} = IN(IN(NULL,b),c)$.

4.10.1 Data Representations for STRINGS

In deciding on a data representation for a given data object one must take into consideration the cost of performing different operations using that representation. In addition, a hidden cost resulting from the necessary storage management operations must also be taken into account. For strings, all three types of representation: sequential, linked list with fixed size nodes, and linked list with variable size nodes, are possible candidates. Let us look at the first two of these schemes and evaluate them with respect to storage management as well as efficiency of operation.

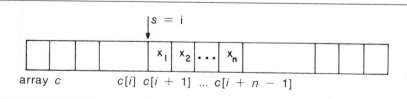

Figure 4.47 Sequential Representation of $s = \text{`}x_1 \ldots x_n\text{'}$

Sequential

   In this representation successive characters of a string will be placed in consecutive character positions in the array $c[1..m]$ (of type **char**). The string $s = 'x_1, \ldots, x_n'$ could then be represented as in Figure 4.47 with s a pointer to the first character. In order to facilitate easy length determination, the length of string s could be kept in another variable, sl. Thus, we would have $sl = n$. $SUBSTR(s,j,k-j+1)$ could be done now by copying over the characters $x_j, \ldots, x_k$ from locations $c[s+j-1]$ through $c[s+k-1]$ into a free space. The length of the string created would be $k-j+1$ and the time required $O(k-j+1)$ plus the time needed to locate a free space big enough to hold the string. $CONCAT(s,t)$ could similarly be carried out; the length of the resulting string would be $sl + tl$. For storage management two possibilities exist. The boundary tag scheme of Section 4.7 could be used in conjunction with the storage compaction strategies of Section 4.9. The storage overhead would be enormous for small strings. Alternatively, we could use garbage collection and compaction whenever more free space was needed. This would eliminate the need to return free spaces to an available space list and hence simplify the storage allocation process (see exercises).

   While a sequential representation of strings might be adequate for the functions discussed above, such a representation is not adequate when insertions and deletions into and from the middle of a string are carried out. An insertion of '$y_1, \ldots, y_n$' after the i-th character of s will, in general require copying over the characters $x_1, \ldots, x_i$ followed by $y_1, \ldots, y_m$ and then $x_{i+1}, \ldots, x_n$ into a new free area (see Figure 4.48). The time required for this is $O(n+m)$. Deletion of a substring may be carried out by either replacing the deleted characters by a special symbol, "~", or by compacting the space originally occupied by this substring (Figure 4.49). The former entails storage waste while the latter in the worst cases takes time proportional to $LENGTH(s)$. The replacement of a substring of s by another string t is efficient only if the length of the substring being replaced is equal to $LENGTH(t)$. If this is not the case, then some form of string movement will be required.

Linked List With Fixed Size Nodes

   An alternative to sequential string representation is linked list representation in which each node has two fields: *data* and *link*. The size of the node is the number of characters that can be stored in the *data* field. Let us assume that a link field need only be two characters long. Thus, on a computer that uses 6 bits per character, the link field will be 12 bits long. This permits link values in the range $[0, 2^{12} - 1]$. So, up to 2^{12} nodes maybe referenced. In the purest form of a linked list representation of strings, each node is of size 1 (i.e., the data field can hold only one character). Normally, this would represent extreme wastage of space. With a link field of size two characters, this would mean that only 1/3 of available memory would be available to store string information while the remaining 2/3 will be used only for link information. With a node size of 8, 80 percent of available memory could be used for string information. When using nodes of size > 1, it is possible that a string may need a fractional number of nodes. With a node size of 4, a string of length 13 will need only 3-1/4 nodes. Since fractional nodes cannot be allocated, 4 full nodes may be used with the last three characters of the last node set

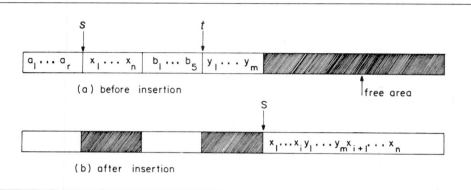

(a) before insertion

(b) after insertion

Figure 4.48 Insertion into a sequential string

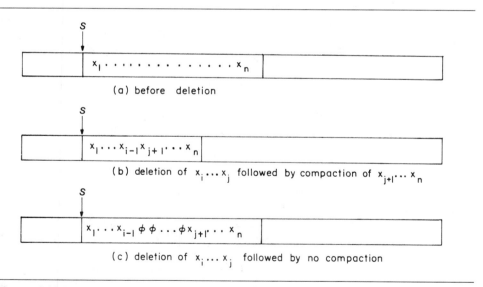

(a) before deletion

(b) deletion of $x_i \dots x_j$ followed by compaction of $x_{j+1} \dots x_n$

(c) deletion of $x_i \dots x_j$ followed by no compaction

Figure 4.49 Deletion of a substring

to ˜ (Figure 4.50(a)). An in place insertion might require one node to be split into two as in Figure 4.50(b). Deletion of a substring can be carried out by replacing all characters in this substring by ˜ and freeing nodes in which the *data* field consists only of ˜'s. In place replacement can be performed similarly. Storage compaction may be carried out when there are no free nodes. Strings containing many occurrences of ˜ could be compacted freeing several nodes. String representation with variable sized nodes is similar.

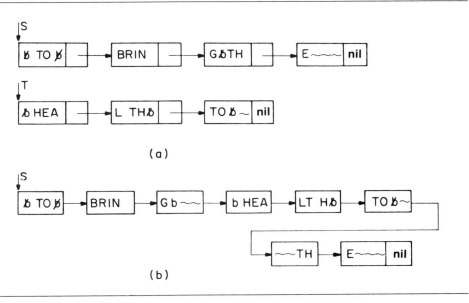

Figure 4.50 Linked list strings

When the node size is 1 things work out very smoothly. Insertion, deletion and concatenation are particularly easy. The length may be determined easily by retaining a head node with this information. Let us look more closely at the operations of insertion and concatenation when the node size is one and no head node is maintained. First, let us write a procedure, insert (Program 4.38) which takes two character strings and inserts the second after the *i*-th character of the first. Procedure *sinsert* assumes that the label 999 has been assigned to the last statement in the program. So a **goto** 999 terminates the program.

Examine how the algorithm works on the strings of Figure 4.51. *t* is to be inserted after the fifth character of *s* to give the result 'THIS NOW IS'. The fifth character in *s* and the last character of *t* are blanks. After line 18 is executed in *sinsert*, we have the configurations of Figure 4.52. In line 20, the last node of *t* is linked to the node pointed at by $iptr\uparrow.link$ and $iptr\uparrow.link$ is changed so as to point to node *t*.

The computing time of *sinsert* is proportional to $i+length\,(t)$. We can produce a more efficient algorithm by altering the data structure only slightly. If we use singly linked circular lists, then *s* and *t* will be represented as in Figure 4.53. The new version of *sinsert* is obtained by replacing lines 12-21 by the code given in Program 4.39. By

```
 1  procedure sinsert(var s: StringPointer; t: StringPointer; i: integer);
 2  {Insert string t after the i-th character of s.
 3  A new string s is created and t is destroyed.}
 4  var iptr, q: StringPointer; j: integer;
 5  begin
 6  if (i < 0) or (i > length (s)) then begin
 7                                    writeln('string length error');
 8                                    goto 999; {999 is program end}
 9                                  end;
10  if s = nil then s := t
11  else if t < > nil
12      then begin {0 ≤ i ≤ length (s) and length (t) > 0}
13            iptr := s;
14            for j := 1 to i −1 do {find i-th node of s}
15              iptr := iptr↑.link;
16            {find last node q in t}
17            q := t;
18            while q↑.link < > nil do q := q↑.link;
19            if i = 0 then begin q↑.link := s; s := t; end
20            else begin q↑.link := iptr↑.link; iptr↑.link := t; end;
21          end; {of if t < > nil}
22  end; {of sinsert}
```

Program 4.38 String insertion

using circular lists we avoided the need to find the end of list t. The computing time for this version is O(i) and is independent of the length of t.

4.10.2 Pattern Matching in STRINGS

Now let us develop an algorithm for a more sophisticated application of strings. Given two strings s and pat we regard the value of pat as a pattern to be searched for in s. If it occurs, then we want to know the node in s where pat begins. Procedure $find$ (Program 4.40) is a straightforward consequence of the data representation. Unfortunately, it is not very efficient. Suppose

$$s = \text{'}aaa \cdots a\text{'}; \, pat = \text{'}aaa \cdots ab\text{'}$$

where $lengths (s) = m$, $length (pat) = n$ and m is much larger than n. Then the first $n - 1$ letters of pat will match with the a's in string s but the n-th letter of pat will not. The

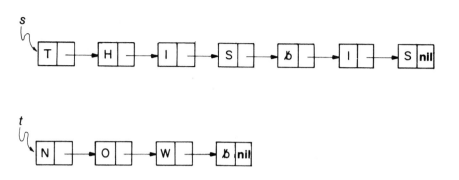

Figure 4.51 Example strings

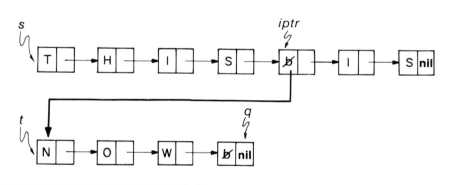

Figure 4.52 Configuration after line 18 of *sinsert*

pointer *p* will be moved to the second occurrence of 'a' and *s* and the $n - 1$ *a*'s of *pat* will match with *s* again. Proceeding in this way we see there will be $m - n + 1$ times that *s* and *pat* have $n - 1$ *a*'s in common. Therefore, algorithm *find* will require at least $(m - n + 1)(n - 1) = O(mn)$ operations. This makes the cost of *find* proportional to the product of the lengths of the two lists or quadratic rather than linear.

There are several improvements that can be made. One is to avoid the situation where *length*(*pat*) is greater than the remaining length of *s* but the algorithm is still searching for a match. Another improvement would be to check that the first and last

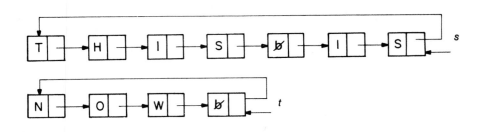

Figure 4.53 Circular representation of *s* and *t*

```
then begin
        iptr := s;
        for j := 1 to i do iptr := iptr↑.link;
        if i = 0
        then begin
                q := s↑.link; s↑.link := t↑.link; t↑.link := q;
            end
        else begin
                q := t↑.link; t↑.link := iptr↑.link; iptr↑.link := q;
            end;
    if (iptr = s) and (i < > 0) then s := t;
```

Program 4.39 Replacement code for *sinsert*

characters of *pat* are matched in *S* before checking the remaining characters. Of course, these improvements will speed up processing on the average. Procedure *nfind* (Program 4.41) incorporates these improvements.

If we apply *nfind* to the strings *s* = 'aa . . . a' and *pat* = 'a . . . ab', then the computing time for these inputs is O(*m*) where *m* = *length* (*s*) which is far better than *find* which required O(*mn*) time. However, the worst case computing time for *nfind* is still O(*mn*).

nfind is a reasonably complex program employing linked lists and it should be understood before one reads on. The use of pointers like *p, q, j, r* is very typical for programs using this data representation.

It would be far better if we could devise an algorithm which works in time O(*length* (*s*) + *length* (*pat*)), which is optimal for this problem since we must certainly look at all of *pat* and potentially all of *s*. Another desirable feature of any pattern finding

```
procedure find (s,pat : StringPointer; var i : StringPointer);
{i is set to nil if pat does not occur in s; otherwise i
 is set to point to the first node in s where pat begins.}
label 99;
var p,q : StringPointer;
begin
  if (pat < > nil) and (s < > nil)
  then begin
          i := s; p := s; q := pat; {i is starting point}
          repeat
            if p↑.data = q↑.data
            then begin {characters match}
                    q := q↑.link;
                    if q = nil then goto 99; {match found}
                    p := p↑.link; {next char in s}
                 end
            else begin {no match}
                    i := i↑.link; p := i; q := pat;
                 end;
          until p = nil;
       end;
    i := nil; {pat is nil or does not occur in s}
99: end; {of find}
```

Program 4.40 Find

algorithm is to avoid rescanning the string s. If s is so large that it cannot conveniently be stored in memory, then rescanning adds complications to the buffering operations. Such an algorithm has been developed by Knuth, Morris and Pratt. Using their example, suppose

$$pat = \text{`} a\,b\,c\,a\,b\,c\,a\,c\,a\,b \text{'}$$

Let $s = s_1\,s_2 \ldots s_m$ and assume that we are currently determining whether or not there is a match beginning at s_i. If $s_i \neq a$ then, clearly, we may proceed by comparing s_{i+1} and a. Similarly if $s_i = a$ and $s_{i+1} \neq b$ then we may proceed by comparing s_{i+1} and a. If $s_i s_{i+1} = ab$ and $s_{i+2} \neq c$ then we have the situation:

```
procedure nfind(s,pat : StringPointer; var i : StringPointer);
{pattern matching by first matching first and last
 characters of pat}
label 99;
var p,q,j,r : StringPointer; t : integer;
begin
  if (pat <> nil) and (s <> nil)
  then begin
          p := pat; q := p; t := 0;
          while q↑.link <> nil do {find end and length − 1 of pat}
          begin q := q↑.link; t := t+1; end;
          j := s; r := s; i := s;
          for k := 1 to t do {find t+1'st node of s}
            if j <> nil then j := j↑.link;
          while j <> nil do {j is t char from i}
          begin
            p := pat; r := i;
            if q↑.data = j↑.data {check last char of pat}
            then begin {check preceding char of pat}
                    while (p↑.data = r↑.data) and (p <> q) do
                    begin p := p↑.link; r := r↑.link; end;
                    if p = q then goto 99; {success}
                 end;
            i := i↑.link; j := j↑.link;
          end; {of while}
       end; {of if}
  i := nil; {pat = nil or no match}
99: end; {of nfind}
```

Program 4.41 Nfind

of *pat* with s_{i+1} as we already know that s_{i+1} is the same as the second character of *pat*, *b*, and so $s_{i+1} \neq a$. Let us try this again assuming a match of the first four characters in *pat* followed by a non-match, i.e., $s_{i+4} \neq b$. We now have the situation:

$$
\begin{array}{cccccccccc}
s = & \text{`-} & a & b & c & a & ? & ? & . & . & . & ?\text{'} \\
pat = & & \text{`}a & b & c & a & b & c & a & c & a & b\text{'}
\end{array}
$$

We observe that the search for a match can proceed by comparing s_{i+4} and the second character in *pat*, *b*. This is the first place a partial match can occur by sliding the pattern *pat* towards the right. Thus, by knowing the characters in the pattern and the position in

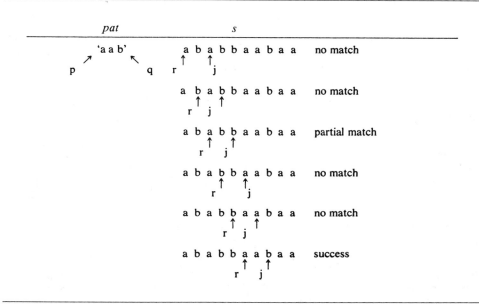

Figure 4.54 Action of *nfind* on *s* and *pat*

the pattern where a mismatch occurs with a charcter in *s* we can determine where in the pattern to continue the search for a match without moving backwards in *s*. To formalize this, we define a failure function for a pattern.

Definition: If $p = p_1 p_2 \ldots p_n$ is a pattern, then its *failure function, f,* is defined as:

$$f(j) = \begin{cases} \text{largest } i < j \text{ such that } p_1 p_2 \ldots p_i = p_{j-i+1}p_{j-i+2} \cdots p_j \text{ if such an } i \geq 1 \text{ exists} \\ 0 \qquad\qquad\qquad\qquad\qquad\qquad\qquad\qquad\qquad\qquad \text{otherwise} \end{cases}$$

□

For the example pattern above, *pat = abcabcacab*, we have

j	1	2	3	4	5	6	7	8	9	10

pat	a	b	c	a	b	c	a	c	a	b
f	0	0	0	1	2	3	4	0	1	2

From the definition of the failure function, we arrive at the following rule for pattern matching: *If a partial match is found such that $s_{i-j+1} \ldots s_{i-1} = p_1 p_2 \ldots p_{j-1}$ and $s_i \neq p_j$ then matching may be resumed by comparing s_i and $p_{f(j-1)+1}$ if $j \neq 1$. If $j = 1$, then we may continue by comparing s_{i+1} and p_1.*

In order to use the above rule when the pattern is represented as a linked list as per out earlier discussion, we include in every node representing the pattern, an additional field called *next*. If *loc* (j) is the node representing $p_j, 1 \leq j \leq n$, then we define

$$loc\,(j)\!\uparrow.\ next = \begin{cases} 0 & \text{if } j = 1 \\ loc\,(f(j-1)+1) & \text{if } j \neq 1 \end{cases}$$

Figure 4.55 shows the pattern *pat* with the *next* field included. With the definition for *next*, the pattern matching rule translates to procedure *pmatch* (Program 4.42).

The correctness of *pmatch* follows from the definitions of the failure function and of *next*. To determine the computing time, we observe that lines 9 and 15 can be executed for a total of at most $m = length\,(s)$ times as in each iteration p moves right on s but p never moves left in the algorithm. As a result q can move right on *pat* at most m times (lines 9 and 15). Since each execution of the **else** clause in line 12 moves q left on *pat*, it follows that this clause can be executed at most m times as otherwise q must fall off the left end of *pat*. As a result, the maximum number of iterations of the **while** loop of lines 6-17 is m and the computing time of *pmatch* is O(m). The performance of the algorithm may be improved by starting with a better failure function (see exercise 56).

The preceding discussion shows the *nfind* can be improved to an O(m) algorithm provided we are either given the failure function or *next*. We now look into the problem of determining f. Once f is known, it is easy to get *next*. From Exercise 55 we know that the failure function for any pattern $p_1 p_2 \ldots p_n$ is given by:

$$f(j) = \begin{cases} 0 & \text{if } j = 0, 1 \\ f^m(j-1) + 1 & \text{where } m \text{ is the least integer } k \text{ for which } p_{f^k(j-1)+1} = p_j \\ 0 & \text{if there is no } k \text{ satisfying the above} \end{cases}$$

(note that $f^1(j) = f\,(j)$ and $f^m(j) = f\,(f^{m-1}(j))$). This directly yields the procedure of Program 4.43 to compute f.

In analyzing the computing time of this algorithm we note that in each iteration of the **while** loop of line 9 the value of i decreases (by the definition of f). The variable i is reset at the beginning of each iteration of the **for** loop. However, it is either reset to 0 (when $j = 2$ or when the previous iteration went through line 11) or it is reset to a value

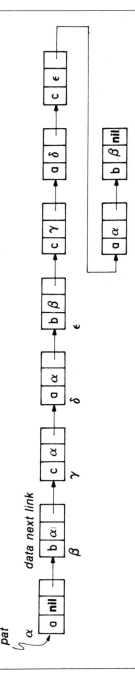

Figure 4.55 Augmented pattern *pat* with *next* field

```
 1 procedure pmatch (s, pat : StringPointer; var found: boolean);
 2 {determine if pat is a substring of s}
 3 var p,q : StringPointer;
 4 begin
 5    found := true; p := s ; q := pat;
 6    while (p < > nil) and (q < > nil) do
 7       if p↑.data = q↑.data
 8       then begin {character match}
 9              p := p↑.link ; q := q↑.link;
10           end
11       else if q := pat
12          then p := p↑.link
13          else q := q↑.next;
14    if q < > nil then found := false; {no match}
15 end; {of pmatch}
```

Program 4.42 Pmatch

```
 1 procedure fail (var p : pattern; var f : failure);
 2 {compute the failure function for the pattern p [1..n ]}
 3 var i,j : integer;
 4 begin
 5    f [1] := 0;
 6    for j := 2 to n do {compute f [j ]}
 7    begin
 8     i := f [j −1];
 9     while (p [j ] < > p [i +1]) and (i > 0) do i := f [i ];
10     if p [j ] = p [i +1] then f [j ] := i +1
11                          else f [j ] := 0;
12    end;
13 end; {of fail}
```

Program 4.43 Fail

1 greater than its terminal value on the previous iteration (i.e., when the previous iteration went through line 10). Since only $n-1$ executions of line 8 are made, the value of i therefore has a total increment of at most $n-1$. Hence it cannot be decremented more than $n-1$ times. Consequently the **while** loop of line 9 is iterated at most $n-1$ times over the whole algorithm and the computing time of *fail* is $O(n)$.

Even if we are not given the failure function for a pattern, pattern matching can be carried out in time $O(n + m)$. This is an improvement over *nfind*.

4.11 REFERENCES AND SELECTED READINGS

More list copying and marking algorithms may be found in: (1) "Copying list structures using bounded workspace," by G. Lindstrom, *CACM*, 17, 4, pp. 198-202, April 1974; (2) "A nonrecursive list moving algorithm," by E. Reingold, *CACM*, 16, 5, pp. 305-307, May 1973; and (3) "Bounded workspace garbage collection in an address-order preserving list processing environment," by D. Fisher, *Information Processing Letters*, 3, 1, pp. 29-32, July 1974.

For more Pascal implementations of lists, see *Sequential program structures*, by J. Welsh, J. Elder, and D. Bustard, Prentice-Hall International, London, 1984.

4.12 EXERCISES

Exercises 1-6 assume that each node has two fields: *data* and *link*.

1. Write an algorithm *length* to count the number of nodes in a singly linked list p, where p points to the first node in the list. The last node has link field **nil**.

2. Let p be a pointer to the first node in a singly linked list and x a pointer to an arbitrary node in this list. Write an algorithm to delete this node from the list. If $x=p$, then p should be reset to point to the new first node in the list.

3. Let $x = (x_1, x_2, \ldots, x_n)$ and $y = (y_1, y_2, \ldots, y_m)$ be two linked lists. Write an algorithm to merge the two lists together to obtain the linked list $z = (x_1, y_1, x_2, y_2, \ldots, x_m, y_m, x_{m+1}, \ldots, x_n)$ if $m \leq n$ and $z = (x_1, y_1, x_2, y_2, \ldots, x_n, y_n, y_{n+1}, \ldots, y_m)$ if $m > n$. No additional nodes may be used.

4. Do Exercise 1 for the case of circularly linked lists.

5. Do Exercise 2 for the case of circularly linked lists.

6. Do Exercise 3 for the case of circularly linked lists.

7. Devise a representation for a list where insertions and deletions can be made at either end. Such a structure is called a deque. Write a procedure for inserting at either end.

8. Consider the hypothetical data object $X2$. $X2$ is a linear list with the restriction that while additions to the list may be made at either end, deletions can be made from one end only. Design a linked list representation for $X2$. Write addition and deletion algorithms for $X2$. Specify initial and boundary conditions for your representation.

9. Give an algorithm for a singly linked circular list which reverses the direction of the links.

10. Let p be a pointer to a circularly linked list. Show how this list may be used as a queue. I.e., write algorithms to add and delete elements. Specify the value for p when the queue is empty.

11. It is possible to traverse a singly linked list in both directions (i.e., left to right and a restricted right-to-left traversal) by reversing the links during the left-to-right traversal. A possible configuration for a list p under this scheme is given in Figure 4.56.

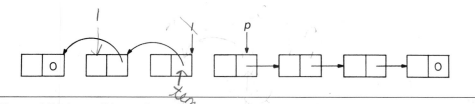

Figure 4.56 A possible configuration

p points to the node currently being examined and l to the node on its left. Note that all nodes to the left of p have their links reversed.

(a) Write an algorithm to move p, n nodes to the right from a given position (l,p).

(b) Write an algorithm to move p, n nodes left from any given position (l,p).

12. Write an algorithm $pread(x)$ to read in n pairs of coefficients and exponents, (c_i, e_i) $1 \leq i \leq n$ of a univariate polynomial, x, and to convert the polynomial into the circular linked list structure of Section 4.3. Assume $e_i > e_{i+1}$, $1 \leq i < n$, and that $c_i \neq 0$, $1 \leq i \leq n$. Your algorithm should leave x pointing to the head node. Show that this operation can be performed in time $O(n)$.

13. Let a and b be pointers to the head nodes of two polynomials represented as in Exercise 12. Write an algorithm to compute the product polynomial $c = a*b$. Your algorithm should leave a and b unaltered and create c as a new list. Show that if n and m are the number of terms in a and b, respectively, then this multiplication can be carried out in time $O(nm^2)$ or $O(mn^2)$. If a, b are dense show that the multiplication takes $O(mn)$.

14. Let a be a pointer to the head node of a univariate polynomial as in Section 4.3. Write an algorithm, $peval(a,x)$ to evaluate the polynomial a at the point x, where x is some real number.

In Exercises 15-19, the sparse matrices are represented as in Section 4.6.

15. Let a and b be two sparse matrices represented as in Section 4.6. Write an algorithm, $madd(a,b,c)$ *to create the matrix* $c = a + b$. *Your algorithm should leave the matrices a and b* unchanged and set up c as a new matrix in accordance with this data representation. Show that if a and b are $n \times m$ matrices with r_A and r_B nonzero terms, then this addition can be carried out in $O(n + m + r_A + r_B)$ time.

16. Let a and b be two sparse matrices. Write an algorithm $mmul\,(a,b,c)$ to set up the structure for $c = a*b$. Show that if a is an $n \times m$ matrix with r_A nonzero terms and if b is an $m \times p$ matrix with r_B nonzero terms, then c can be computed in time $O(pr_A + nr_B)$. Can you think of a way to compute c in $O(\min\{pr_A, nr_B\})$?

17. Write an algorithm to write out the terms of a sparse matrix a as triples (i,j,a_{ij}). The terms are to be output by rows and within rows by columns. Show that this operation can be performed in time $O(n + r_A)$ if there are r_A nonzero terms in a and a is an $n \times m$ matrix.

18. Write an algorithm $mtrp\,(a,b)$ to compute the matrix $b = a^T$, the transpose of the sparse matrix a. What is the computing time of your algorithm?

19. Design an algorithm to copy a sparse matrix. What is the computing time of your algorithm?

20. A simpler and more efficient representation for sparse matrices can be obtained when one is restricted to the operations of addition, subtraction, and multiplication. In this representaton, nodes have the fields *down, right, row, col,* and *value.* Each nonzero term is represented by a node. These nodes are linked together to form two circular lists. The first list, the row list, is made up by linking nodes by rows and within rows by columns. This is done via the *right* field. The second list, the column list, is made up by linking nodes via the *down* field. In this list, nodes are linked by columns and within columns by rows. These two lists share a common head node. In addition, a node is added to contain the dimensions of the matrix. The matrix a of Figure 4.19 has the representation shown in Figure 4.57.

Using the same assumptions as for algorithm *mread* of Section 4.6 write an algorithm to read in a matrix and set up its internal representation as above. How much time does your algorithm take? How much additional space is needed?

21. For the representation of Exercise 20 write algorithms to
    (a) erase a matrix
    (b) add two matrices
    (c) multiply two matrices
    (d) print out a matrix

For each of the above obtain computing times. How do these times compare with the corresponding times for the representation of Section 4.6?

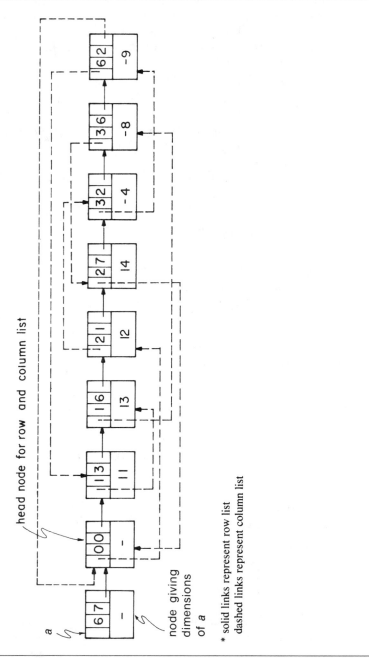

Figure 4.57 Representation of matrix *A* of Figure 4.19 using the scheme of Exercise 20

22. Compare the sparse representations of Exercise 20 and Section 4.6 with respect to some other operations. For example, how much time is needed to output the entries in an arbitrary row or column?

23. (a) Write an algorithm *BestFit(n,p)* similar to algorithm *FirstFit* of Section 4.7 to allocate a block of size *n* using the best fit strategy. Each block in the chain of available blocks has a *size* field giving the number of words in that block. The chain has a head node, *av* (see Figure 4.26). The best fit strategy examines each block in this chain. The allocation is made from the smallest block of size $\geq n$. *p* is set to the starting address of the space allocated.

    (b) Which of the algorithms *BestFit* and *FirstFit* takes less time?

    (c) Give an example of a sequence of requests for memory and memory freeing that can be met by *BestFit* but not by *FirstFit*.

24. Which of the two algorithms *allocate* and *free* of Section 4.7 require the condition $tag[0] = tag[m + 1] = 1$ in order to work right? Why?

25. Consider the operation XOR (exclusive OR, also written as $\oplus$) defined as below (for *i,j* binary):

$$i \oplus j = \begin{cases} 0 & \text{if } i \text{ and } j \text{ are identical} \\ 1 & \text{otherwise} \end{cases}$$

This differs from the usual OR of logic in that

$$i \text{ OR } j = \begin{cases} 0 & \text{if } i = j = 0 \\ 1 & \text{otherwise} \end{cases}$$

The definition can be extended to the case where *i* and *j* are binary strings (i.e., take the XOR of corresponding bits of *i* and *j*). So, for example, if $i = 10110$ and $j = 01100$, then $i \text{ XOR } j = i \oplus j = 11010$. Note that

$$a \oplus (a \oplus b) = (a \oplus a) \oplus b = b$$

and

$$(a \oplus b) \oplus b = a \oplus (b \oplus b) = a$$

This gives us a space saving device for storing the right and left links of a doubly linked list. The nodes will now have only two fields: *info* and *link*. If *l* is to the left of node *x* and *r* to its right, then $link(x) = l \oplus r$ (as in the case of the storage management algorithms, we assume that available memory is an array *memory* [1..n] *and that the link* field just gives us the next node's position in this array).

For the leftmost node $l = 0$ and for the rightmost node $r = 0$. Let (l,r) be a doubly linked list so represented, l points to the leftmost node and r to the right most node in the list.

(a) Write an algorithm to traverse the doubly linked list (l,r) from left to right listing out the contents of the *info* field of each node.

(b) Write an algorithm to traverse the list right to left listing out the contents of the *info* field of each node.

26. Design a storage management scheme for the case when all requests for memory are of the same size, say k. Is it necessary to coalesce adjacent blocks that are free? Write algorithms to free and allocate storage in this scheme.

27. Consider the dynamic storage management problem in which requests for memory are of varying sizes, as in Section 4.7. Assume that blocks of storage are freed according to the LAFF discipline (last-allocated-first-freed).

(a) Design a structure to represent the free space.

(b) Write an algorithm to allocate a block of storage of size n.

(c) Write an algorithm to free a block of storage of size n beginning at p.

28. In the case of static storage allocation all the requests are known in advance. If there are n requests $r_1, r_2, \ldots, r_n$ and $\Sigma r_i \le M$ where M is the total amount of memory available, then all requests can be met. So, assume $\Sigma r_i > M$.

(a) Which of these n requests should be satisfied if we wish to maximize the number of satisfied requests?

(b) Under the maximization criterion of (a), how small can the ratio $\dfrac{\text{storage allocated}}{M}$ get?

(c) Would this be a good criterion to use if jobs are charged a flat rate, say \$3 per job, independent of the size of the request?

(d) The pricing policy of (c) is unrealistic when there can be much variation in request size. A more realistic policy is to charge say x cents per unit of request. Is the criterion of (a) a good one for this pricing policy? What would be a good maximization criterion for storage allocation now? Write an algorithm to determine which requests are to be satisfied now. How much time does your algorithm take as a function of n, the number of requests? [If your algorithm takes a polynomial amount of time, and works correctly, take it to your instructor immediately. You have made a major discovery.]

29. [Buddy system] The text examined the boundary tag method for dynamic storage management. The next six exercises will examine an alternative approach in which only blocks of size a power of 2 will be allocated. Thus, if a request for a block of size n is made, then a block of size $\lceil \log_2 n \rceil$ is allocated. As a result of this, all free blocks are also of a size a power of 2. If the total memory size is 2^m

addressed from 0 to $2^m - 1$, then the possible sizes for free blocks are 2^k, $0 \le k \le m$. Free blocks of the same size will be maintained in the same available space list. Thus, this system will have $m+1$ available space lists. Each list is a doubly linked circular list and has a head node $avail[i]$, $0 \le i \le m$. Every free node has the structure of Figure 4.58. Initially all of memory is free and consists of one block beginning at 0 and of size 2^m. Write an algorithm to initialize all the available space lists.

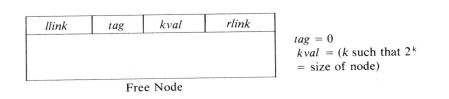

$$tag = 0$$
$$kval = (k \text{ such that } 2^k$$
$$= \text{size of node})$$

Free Node

Figure 4.58 Structure of a free node in the buddy system

30. [Buddy system allocation] Using the available space list structure of Exercise 29, write an algorithm to meet a request of size n if possible. Note that a request of size n is to be met by allocating a block of size 2^k, $k = \lceil \log_2 n \rceil$. To do this, examine the available space lists $avail[i]$, $k \le i \le m$ finding the smallest i for which $avail[i]$ is not empty. Remove one block from this list. Let p be the starting address of this block. If $i > k$, then the block is too big and is broken into two blocks of size 2^{i-1} beginning at p and $p + 2^{i-1}$, respectively. The block beginning at $p + 2^{i-1}$ is inserted into the corresponding available list. If $i - 1 > k$, then the block is to be further split and so on. Finally, a block of size 2^k beginning at p is allocated. A block in use has the form given in Figure 4.59.

(a) Write an algorithm using the strategy outlined above to allocate a block of storage to meet a request for n units of memory.

(b) For a memory of size $2^m = 16$, draw the binary tree representing the splitting of blocks taking place in satisfying 16 consecutive requests for memory of size 1. (Note that the use of the *tag* in the allocated block does not really create a problem in allocations of size 1 since memory would be allocated in units where 1 unit may be a few thousand words.) Label each node in this tree with its starting address and present *kval*, i.e., power of 2 representing its size.

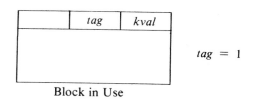

Block in Use

Figure 4.59 Structure of a block in use in buddy system

31. [Locating buddies] Two nodes in the tree of the preceding exercise are said to be buddies iff they are sibling nodes. Prove that two nodes starting at x and y, respectively, are buddies iff:

    (a) the *kvals* for x and y are the same; and

    (b) $x = y \oplus 2^k$, where $\oplus$ is the exclusive OR (XOR) operation defined in Exercise 25. The $\oplus$ is taken pairwise bitwise on the binary representation of y and 2^k.

32. [Freeing and coalescing blocks] When a block with *kval* k becomes free it is to be returned to the available space list. Free blocks are combined into bigger free blocks iff they are buddies. This combining follows the reverse process adopted during allocation. If a block beginning at p and of size k becomes free, it is to be combined with its buddy $p \oplus 2^k$ if the buddy is free. The new free block beginning at $l = \min\{p, p \oplus 2^k\}$ and of size $k + 1$ is to be combined with its buddy $l \oplus 2^{k+1}$ if free, and so on. Write an algorithm to free a block beginning at p and having *kval* $=k$ combining buddies that are free.

33. (a) Does the freeing algorithm of the preceding exercise always combine adjacent free blocks? If not, give a sequence of allocations and freeings of storage showing this to be the case.

    (b) How small can the ratio (storage requested)/(storage allocated) be for the buddy system? Storage requested $= \Sigma n_i$, where n_i is the actual amount requested. Give an example approaching this ratio.

    (c) How much time does the allocation algorithm take in the worst case to make an allocation if the total memory size is 2^m?

    (d) How much time does the allocation algorithm take in the worst case to free a block of storage?

34. [Buddy system when memory size is not a power of 2]

    (a)   How are the available space lists to be initialized if the total storage available is not a power of 2?

    (b)   What changes are to be made to the block freeing algorithm to take care of this case? Do any changes have to be made to the allocation algorithm?

35. Write a nonrecursive version of algorithm *lerase* (x) of Section 4.8.

36. Write a nonrecursive version of algorithm *equal* (s,t) of Section 4.8.

37. Write a nonrecursive version of algorithm *depth* (s) of Section 4.8.

38. Write a procedure which takes an arbitrary nonrecursive list l with no shared sublists and inverts it and all of its sublists. For example, if $l = (a, (b,c))$, then inverse $(l) = ((c,b),a)$.

39. Devise a procedure that produces the list representation of an arbitrary list given its linear form as a string of atoms, commas, blanks, and parentheses. For example, for the input $l = (a, (b,c))$, your procedure should produce the structure of Figure 4.60.

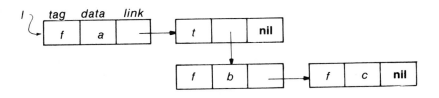

Figure 4.60 Structure for Exercise 39

40. One way to represent generalized lists is through the use of two field nodes and a symbol table which contains all atoms and list names together with pointers to these lists. Let the two fields of each node be named *alink* and *blink*. Then *blink* either points to the next node on the same level, if there is one, or is **nil**. The *alink* field either points to a node at a lower level or, in the case of an atom or list name, to the appropriate entry in the symbol table. For example, the list $B(A, (D,E),(\ ),B)$ would have the representation given in Figure 4.61. (The list names D and E were already in the table at the time the list B was input. A was not in the table and is assumed to be an atom.)

The symbol table retains a type bit for each entry. Type $= 1$ if the entry is a list name and type $= 0$ for atoms. The NIL atom may either be in the table or *alink* can be set to **nil** to represent the NIL atom. Write an algorithm to read in a list in

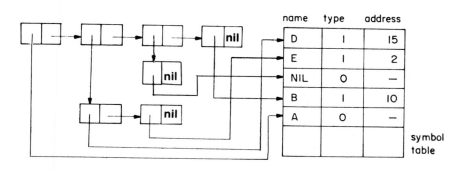

	name	type	address
	D	I	15
	E	I	2
	NIL	O	—
	B	I	10
	A	O	—

symbol table

Figure 4.61 Representation for Exercise 40

parentheses notation and to set up its linked representation as above with x set to point to the first node in the list. Note that no head nodes are in use. The following subalgorithms may be used by *lread*.

(a) *get(a,p)* searches the symbol table for the name a. p is set to 0 if a is not found in the table; otherwise, p is set to the position of a in the table.

(b) *put(a,t,p)* enters a into the table. p is the position at which a was entered. If a is already in the table, then the type and address fields of the old entry are changed. $t =$ **nil** to enter an atom or $t <>$ **nil** to enter a list with first node t. (*Note*: this permits definition of lists using indirect recursion.) The diagram is for the case when the addresses t are integers.

(c) *NextToken* gets next token in input list. (A token may be a list name, atom, '(',')' or ','. A '#' is returned if there are no more tokens.)

(d) *new(x)* gets a node for use.

You may assume that the input list is syntactically correct. In case a sublist is labeled as in the list $C(D,E(F,G))$ the structure should be set up as in the case $C(D, (F,G))$ and E should be entered into the symbol table as a list with the appropriate starting address.

41. Rewrite algorithm *mark*1 of Section 4.9 using the conventions of Section 4.8 for a tag field.

42. Rewrite algorithm *mark*1 of Section 4.9 for the case when each list and sublist has a head node. Assume that the *dlink* field of each head node is free and so may be used to maintain a linked stack without using any additional space. Show that the computing time is still $O(m)$.

43. When the *dlink* field of a node is used to retain atomic information as in Section 4.8, implementing the marking strategy of *mark*2 requires an additional bit in each node. In this exercise we shall explore a marking strategy which does not require this additional bit. Its worst case computing time will however be O(mn) where m is the number of nodes marked and n the total number of nodes in the system. Write a marking algorithm using the node structure and conventions of Section 4.8. Each node has the fields: *mark, tag, dlink* and *rlink*. Your marking algorithm will use variable p to point to the node currently being examined and *next* to point to the next node to be examined. If l is the address of the as yet unexplored list node with least address and p the address of the node currently being examined, then the value of *next* will be min $\{l, p + 1\}$. Show that the computing time of your algorithm is O(mn).

44. Prove that *mark*2(x) marks all unmarked nodes accessible from x.

45. Write a composite marking algorithm using *mark*1, *mark*2, and a fixed amount m of stack space. Stack nodes as in *mark*1 until the stack is full. When the stack becomes full, revert to the strategy of *mark*2. On completion of *mark*2, pick up a node from the stack and explore it using the composite algorithm. In case the stack never overflows, the composite algorithm will be as fast as mark1. When m = 0, the algorithm essentially becomes *mark*2. The computing time will in general be somewhere in between that of *mark*1 and *mark*2.

46. Write a storage compaction algorithm to be used following the marking phase of garbage collection. Assume that all nodes are of a fixed size and can be addressed as *node* [i], $1 \le i \le m$. Show that this can be done in two phases, where in the first phase a left-to-right scan for free nodes and a right to left scan for nodes in use is carried out. During this phase, used nodes from the right end of memory are moved to free positions at the left end. The relocated address of such nodes is noted in one of the fields of the old address. At the end of this phase all nodes in use occupy a contiguous chunk of memory at the left end. In the second phase, links to relocated nodes are updated.

47. Write a compaction algorithm to be used in conjunction with the boundary tag method for storage management. Show that this can be done in one left to right scan of memory blocks. Assume that memory blocks are independent and do not reference each other. Further assume that all memory references within a block are made relative to the start of the block. Assume the start of each block that is in use is in a table external to the space being allocated. Use procedure *FixTable* (i,j) to change the starting entry i to j.

48. Design a dynamic storage management system in which blocks are to be returned to the available space list only during compaction. At all other times, a *tag* is set to indicate the block has become free. Assume that initially all of memory is free and available as one block. Let memory be addressed 1 through m. For your design, write the following algorithms:

(a)   *allocate(n,p)* allocates a block of size *n*; *p* is set to its starting address. Assume that size *n* includes any space needed for control fields in your design.

(b)   *free(n,p)* frees a block of size *n* beginning *p*.

(c)   *compact* compacts memory and reinitializes the available space list. You may assume that all address references within a block are relative to the start of the block and so no link fields within blocks need to be changed. Also, there are no interblock references.

49. Write an algorithm to make an in place replacement of a substring of *x* by the string *y*. Assume that strings are represented using fixed size nodes and that each node in addition to a link field has space for four characters. Use ~ to fill up any unused space in a node.

50. Using the definition of *STRING* given in section 4.10, simulate the axioms as they would apply to (a) *CONCAT(S,T)*, (b) *SUBSTR(S,2,3)*, and (c) *INDEX(S,T)* where *S* = 'abcde' and *T* = 'cde'.

51. If $x = (x_1, \ldots, x_m)$ and $y = (y_1, \ldots, y_n)$ are strings where x_i and y_i are letters of the alphabet, then *x* is less than *y* if $x_i = y_i$ for $1 \le i \le j$ and $x_j < y_j$ or if $x_i = y_i$ for $1 \le i \le m$ and $m < n$. Write an algorithm which takes two strings *x,y* and returns either $-1, 0, +1$ if $x < y$, $x = y$ or $x > y$, respectively.

52. Let *x* and *y* be strings represented as singly linked lists. Write a procedure which finds the first character of *x* that does not occur in the string *y*.

53. Show that the computing time for procedure *nfind* is still O(*nm*). Find a string and a pattern for which this is true.

54. (a)   Compute the failure function for each of the following patterns: (1) *a a a a b*; (2) *a b a b a a*; and (3) *a b a a b a a b b*.

(b)   For each of the above patterns obtain the linked list representations including the field *next* as in Figure 4.55.

(c)   Let $p_1 p_2 \ldots p_n$ be a pattern of length *n*. Let *f* be its failure function. Define $f^1(j) = f(j)$ and $f^m(j) = f(f^{m-1}(j))$, $1 \le j \le n$ and $m > 1$. Show, using the definition of *f*, that:

$$f(j) = \begin{cases} 0 & \text{if } j = 1 \\ f^m(j-1)+1 & \text{where } m \text{ is the least integer } k \text{ for which } p_{f^k(j-1)+1} = p_j \\ 0 & \text{if there is no } k \text{ satisfying the above} \end{cases}$$

55. The definition of the failure function may be strengthened to

$$f(j) = \begin{cases} \text{largest } i < j \text{ such that } p_1 p_2 \ldots p_i = p_{j-i+1} \, p_{j-i+2} \ldots p_j \text{ and } p_{i+1} \ne p_{j+1} \\ 0 \qquad\qquad \text{if there is no } i \ge 1 \text{ satisfying above} \end{cases}$$

(a)   Obtain the new failure function for the pattern *pat* of the text.

(b)   Show that if this definition for f is used in the definition of *next* then algorithm *pmatch* still works correctly.

(c)   Modify algorithm *fail* to compute f under this definition. Show that the
computing time is still $O(m)$.

(d)   Are there any patterns for which the observed computing time of *pmatch* is
more with the new definition of f than with the old one? Are there any for
which it is less? Give examples.

56.   [Programming project] Design a linked allocation system to represent and manipulate univariate polynomials with integer coefficients (use circular linked lists with
head nodes). Each term of the polynomial will be represented as a node. Thus, a
node in this system will have three fields as below:

Exponent	Link
Coefficient	

In order to erase polynomials efficiently, we shall need to use an available space
list and associated procedures as described in Section 4.3. The external (i.e., for
input or output) representation of a univariate polynomial will be assumed to be a
sequence of integers of the form: $n, e_1, c_1, e_2, c_2, e_3, c_3 \ldots, e_n, c_n$, where the e_i
represent the exponents and the c_i the coefficients; n gives the number of terms in
the polynomial. The exponents are in decreasing order, i.e., $e_1 > e_2 > \ldots > e_n$.

Write and test the following procedures:

(a)   *pread(x)* Read in an input polynomial and convert it to its circular list
representation using a head node. x is set to point to the head node of this
polynomial.

(b)   *pwrite(x)* Convert the polynomial x from its linked list representation to its
external representation and output it.

(c)   *padd(x,y,z)* Compute $z = x + y$

(d)   *psub(x,y,z)* Compute $z = x - y$

(e)   *pmul(x,y,z)* Compute $z = x * y$

(f)   *peval(x,a,v)* a is a real constant and the polynomial x is evaluated at the
point a. v is set to this value.

Note: Procedures (c)-(f) should leave the input polynomials unaltered after completion of their respective tasks.

(g)   *perase*(x) Return the circular list x to the available space list.

57.   [Programming project] In this project, we shall implement a complete linked list system to perform arithmetic on sparse matrices using the representation of Section 4.6. First, design a convenient node structure assuming *value* is an integer.

Since we shall need to erase circular lists, we shall utilize the space list concept introduced in Section 4.3. So, we may begin by writing and testing the procedures associated with this list. Next, write and test the following procedures for matrix operations:

(a)   *mread* (a) Read matrix a and set up according to the representation of Section 4.6. The input has the following format:

line 1:   *n m r*   n = # or rows
                            m = # or columns
                            r = # of nonzero terms

line 2
  .
  .   } triples of (row, column, value)
  .

These triples are in increasing order by rows. Within rows, the triples are in increasing order of columns. The data is to be read in one line at a time and converted to internal representation. The variable a is set to point to the head node of the circular list of head nodes (as in the text).

(b)   *mwrite*(a) Print out the terms of a. To do this, you will have to design a suitable output format. In any case, the output should be ordered by rows and within rows by columns.

(c)   *merase*(a) Return all nodes of the sparse matrix a to the available space list.

(d)   *madd*(a,b,c) Create the sparse matrix $c = a + b$. a and b are to be left unaltered.

(e)   *msub*(a,b,c) $c = a - b$. a and b are to be left unaltered.

(f)   *mmult*(a,b,c) Create the sparse matrix $c = a * b$. a and b are to be left unaltered.

(g)   *mtrp*(a,b) Create the sparse matrix $b = a^t$. a is to be left unaltered.

58.   [Programming project] Do the project of Exercise 57 using the matrix representation of Exercise 20.

59.   [Landweber] This problem is to simulate an airport landing and takeoff pattern. The airport has three runways, runway 1, runway 2, and runway 3. There are four landing holding patterns, two for each of the first two runways. Arriving planes will enter one of the holding pattern queues, where the queues are to be as close in

size as possible. When a plane enters a holding queue, it is assigned an integer *id* number and an integer giving the number of time units the plane can remain in the queue before it must land (because of low fuel level). There is also a queue for takeoffs for each of the three runways. Planes arriving in a takeoff queue are also assigned an integer *id*. The takeoff queues should be kept approximately the same size.

At each time, up to three planes may arrive at the landing queues and up to three planes may arrive at the takeoff queues. Each runway can handle one takeoff or landing at each time slot. Runway 3 is to be used for takeoffs except when a plane is low on fuel. At each time unit, planes in either landing queue whose air time has reached zero must be given priority over other landings and takeoffs. If only one plane is in this category, runway 3 is to be used. If more than one, then the other runways are also used (at each time, at most, three planes can be serviced in this way).

Use successive even (odd) integers for *id*'s of planes arriving at takeoff (landing) queues. At each time unit assume that arriving planes are entered into queues before takeoffs or landings occur. Try to design your algorithm so that neither landing nor takeoff queues grow excessively. However, arriving planes must be placed at the ends of queues. Queues cannot be reordered.

The output should clearly indicate what occurs at each time unit. Periodically output (a) the contents of each queue; (b) the average takeoff waiting time; (c) the average landing waiting time; (d) the average flying time remaining on landing; and (e) the number of planes landing with no fuel reserve. (b) and (c) are for planes that have taken off or landed, respectively. The output should be self explanatory and easy to understand (and uncluttered).

The input can be from cards, a terminal, a file, or it can be generated by a random number generator. For each time unit the input is of the form:

col1	0-3	indicating the number of planes arriving at takeoff queues
col2	0-3	indicating # of planes arriving at landing queues
col4-5	1-20	
col6-7	1-20	units of flying time for planes arriving in landing queues
col8-9	1-20	(from col2)

CHAPTER 5
TREES

5.1 BASIC TERMINOLOGY

In this chapter we shall study a very important data object, trees. Intuitively, a tree structure means that the data are organized so that items of information are related by branches. One very common place where such a structure arises is in the investigation of genealogies. There are two types of genealogical charts which are used to present such data: the *pedigree* and the *lineal* chart. Figure 5.1 gives an example of each.

The pedigree chart of Figure 5.1(a) shows someone's ancestors, in this case those of Dusty, whose two parents are Honey Bear and Brandy. Brandy's parents are Nuggett and Coyote, who are Dusty's grandparents on her father's side. The chart continues one more generation farther back to the great-grandparents. By the nature of things, we know that the pedigree chart is normally two-way branching, though this does not allow for inbreeding. When that occurs we no longer have a tree structure unless we insist that each occurrence of breeding is separately listed. Inbreeding may occur frequently when describing family histories of flowers or animals.

The lineal chart of Figure 5.1(b), though it has nothing to do with people, is still a genealogy. It describes, in somewhat abbreviated form, the ancestry of the modern European languages. Thus, this is a chart of descendants rather than ancestors and each item can produce several others. Latin, for instance, is the forebear of Spanish, French, Italian, and Rumanian. Proto Indo-European is a prehistoric language presumed to have existed in the fifth millenium B.C. This tree does not have the regular structure of the pedigree chart, but it is a tree structure nevertheless.

With these two examples as motivation let us define formally what we mean by a tree.

Definition: A *tree* is a finite set of one or more nodes such that (1) there is a specially designated node called the *root*; (2) the remaining nodes are partitioned into $n \geq 0$

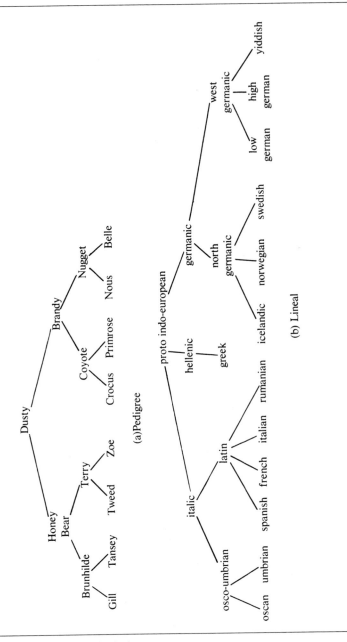

Figure 5.1 Two types of geneological charts

disjoint sets $T_1, \ldots, T_n$ where each of these sets is a tree. $T_1, \ldots, T_n$ are called the *sub-trees* of the root. □

Again we have an instance of a recursive definition (compare this with the definition of a generalized list in Section 4.8). If we return to Figure 5.1, we see that the roots of the trees are Dusty and Proto Indo-European. Tree (a) has two subtrees whose roots are Honey Bear and Brandy while tree (b) has three subtrees with roots Italic, Hellenic, and Germanic. The condition that $T_1, \ldots, T_n$ be disjoint sets prohibits subtrees from ever connecting together (no cross-breeding). It follows that every item in a tree is the root of some subtree of the whole. For instance, West Germanic is the root of a subtree of Germanic which itself has three subtrees with roots: Low German, High German, and Yiddish. Yiddish is a root of a tree with no subtrees.

There are many terms that are often used when referring to trees. A *node* stands for the item of information plus the branches to other nodes. Consider the tree in Figure 5.2. This tree has 13 nodes, each item of data being a single letter for convenience. The root is A and we will normally draw trees with the root at the top. The number of subtrees of a node is called its *degree*. The degree of A is 3, of C is 1, and of F is zero. Nodes that have degree zero are called *leaf* or *terminal* nodes. $\{K,L,F,G,M,I,J\}$ is the set of leaf nodes. Consequently, the other nodes are referred to as *nonterminals*. The roots of the subtrees of a node, X, are the *children* of X. X is the *parent* of its children. Thus, the children of D are H, I, J; the parent of D is A.

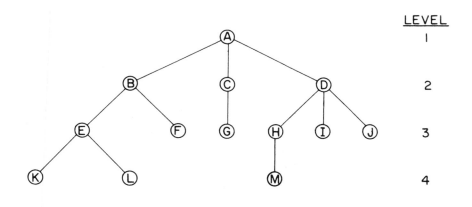

Figure 5.2 A sample tree

Children of the same parent are said to be *siblings*. H, I, and J are siblings. We can extend this terminology if we need to so that we can ask for the grandparent of M which is D, etc. The *degree of a tree* is the maximum degree of the nodes in a tree. The tree of Figure 5.2 has degree 3. The *ancestors* of a node are all the nodes along the path from the root to that node. The ancestors of *M* are *A*, *D*, and *H*.

The *level* of a node is defined by initially letting the root be at level one. If a node is at level *l*, then its children are at level *l* + 1. Figure 5.2 shows the levels of all nodes in that tree. The *height* or *depth* of a tree is defined to be the maximum level of any node in the tree.

A *forest* is a set of *n* ≥ 0 disjoint trees. The notion of a forest is very close to that of a tree because if we remove the root of a tree we get a forest. For example, in Figure 5.2 if we remove *A* we get a forest with three trees.

There are other ways to draw a tree. One useful way is as a list. The tree of Figure 5.2 could be written as the list

$$(A\,(B\,(E\,(K,L),F),C\,(G),D\,(H\,(M),I,J)))$$

The information in the root node comes first followed by a list of the subtrees of that node.

Now, how do we represent a tree in memory? If we wish to use linked lists, then a node must have a varying number of fields depending upon the number of branches.

DATA	LINK 1	LINK 2	...	LINK *n*

However, it is often simpler to write algorithms for a data representation when the node size is fixed. Using data and pointer fields we can represent a tree using the fixed node size list structure we devised in Chapter 4. The list representation for the tree of Figure 5.2 is shown in Figure 5.3. We can now make use of many of the general procedures that we originally wrote for handling lists. Thus, the data object tree is a special instance of the data object list and we can specialize the list representation scheme to them. In a later section we will see that another data object which can be used to represent a tree is the data object binary tree.

5.2 BINARY TREES

A binary tree is an important type of tree structure which occurs very often. It is characterized by the fact that any node can have at most two branches, i.e., there is no node with degree greater than two. For binary trees we distinguish between the subtree on the left and on the right, whereas for trees the order of the subtrees was irrelevant. Also a binary tree may have zero nodes. Thus a binary tree is really a different object than a tree.

Definition: A *binary tree* is a finite set of nodes which is either empty or consists of a

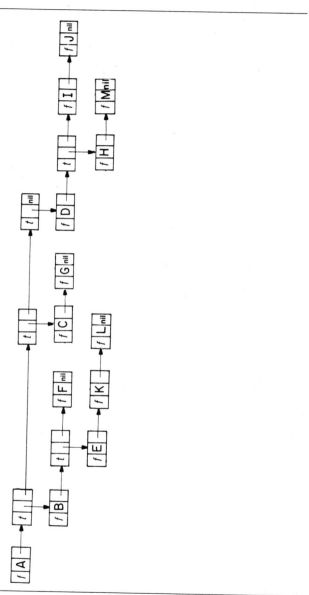

Figure 5.3 List representation of the tree of Figure 5.2

root and two disjoint binary trees called the *left subtree* and the *right subtree*.

Using the notation introduced in Chapter 1 we can define the data structure binary tree as in Structure 5.1.

---

structure *BTREE*
  declare   *CREATE* () → *btree*
           ISMTBT (*btree*) → *boolean*
           MAKEBT (*btree*,*item*,*btree*) → *btree*
           LCHILD (*btree*) → *btree*
           DATA (*btree*) →*item*
           RCHILD (*btree*) → *btree*
  for all *p,r*ε*btree*, *d*ε*item* **let**
    ISMTBT (*CREATE*)::= **true**
    ISMTBT (*MAKEBT* (*p,d,r*)) ::= **false**
    LCHILD (*MAKEBT* (*p,d,r*)) :: = *p* ; *LCHILD* (*CREATE*) :: = *error*
    DATA (*MAKEBT* (*p,d,r*)) :: = *d* ; *DATA* (*CREATE*) :: = *error*
    RCHILD (*MAKEBT* (*p,d,r*)) :: = *r* ; *RCHILD* (*CREATE*) :: = *error*
  end
end *BTREE*

Structure 5.1

This set of axioms defines only a minimal set of operations on binary trees. Other operations can usually be built in terms of these. See Exercise 35 for an example.

The distinctions between a binary tree and a tree should be analyzed. First of all there is no tree having zero nodes, but there is an empty binary tree. The two binary trees of Figure 5.4 are different. The first one has an empty right subtree while the second has an empty left subtree. If the above are regarded as trees, then they are the same despite the fact that they are drawn slightly differently.

Figure 5.4 Two different binary trees

Figure 5.5 shows two sample binary trees. These two trees are special kinds of binary trees. The first is a *skewed* tree, skewed to the left, and there is a corresponding one which skews to the right. Tree 5.3(b) is called a *complete* binary tree. This kind of binary tree will be defined formally later on. Notice that all terminal nodes are on adjacent levels. The terms that we introduced for trees such as degree, level, height, leaf, parent, and child all apply to binary trees in the natural way. Before examining data representations for binary trees, let us first make some relevant observations regarding such trees. First, what is the maximum number of nodes in a binary tree of depth k?

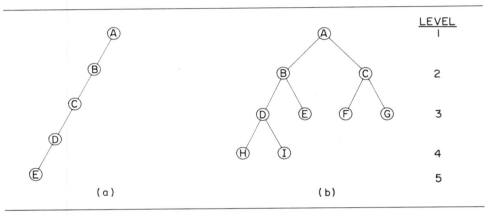

Figure 5.5 Two sample binary trees

Lemma 5.1: (1) The maximum number of nodes on level i of a binary tree is 2^{i-1}, $i \geq 1$, and (2) the maximum number of nodes in a binary tree of depth k is $2^k - 1$, $k \geq 1$.

Proof: (1) The proof is by induction on i.
Induction base: The root is the only node on level $i = 1$. Hence the maximum number of nodes on level $i = 1$ is $2^0 = 2^{i-1}$.
Induction hypothesis: For all j, $1 \leq j < i$, the maximum number of nodes on level j is 2^{j-1}.
Induction step: The maximum number of nodes on level $i-1$ is 2^{i-2}, by the induction hypothesis. Since each node in a binary tree has maximum degree 2, the maximum number of nodes on level i is 2 times the maximum number on level $i-1$ or 2^{i-1}.
(2) the maximum number of nodes in a binary tree of depth k is

$$\sum_{i=1}^{k} (\text{maximum number of nodes on level } i) = \sum_{i=1}^{k} 2^{i-1} = 2^k - 1. \quad \square$$

Next, let us examine the relationship between the number of terminal nodes and the number of nodes of degree 2 in a binary tree.

Lemma 5.2: For any nonempty binary tree, T, if n_0 is the number of terminal nodes and n_2 the number of nodes of degree 2, then $n_0 = n_2 + 1$.

Proof: Let n_1 be the number of nodes of degree 1 and n the total number of nodes. Since all nodes in T are of degree ≤ 2 we have

$$n = n_0 + n_1 + n_2 \qquad (5.1)$$

If we count the number of branches in a binary tree, we see that every node except for the root has a branch leading into it. If B is the number of branches, then $n = B + 1$. All branches emanate either from a node of degree 1 or from a node of degree 2. Thus, $B = n_1 + 2n_2$. Hence, we obtain

$$n = 1 + n_1 + 2n_2 \qquad (5.2)$$

Subtracting Eq. (5.2) from Eq. (5.1) and rearranging terms we get

$$n_0 = n_2 + 1 \quad \square$$

In Figure 5.5(a) $n_0 = 1$ and $n_2 = 0$ while in Figure 5.5(b) $n_0 = 5$ and $n_2 = 4$.

As we continue our discussion of binary trees, we shall derive some other interesting properties.

5.3 BINARY TREE REPRESENTATIONS

A *full* binary tree of depth k is a binary tree of depth k having $2^k - 1$ nodes. By Lemma 5.1, this is the maximum number of nodes such a binary tree can have. Figure 5.6 shows a full binary tree of depth 4. A very elegant sequential representation for such binary trees results from sequentially numbering the nodes, starting with nodes on level 1, then those on level 2 and so on. Nodes on any level are numbered from left to right (see Figure 5.6). This numbering scheme gives us the definition of a complete binary tree. A binary tree with n nodes and a depth k is *complete* iff its nodes correspond to the nodes numbered 1 to n in the full binary tree of depth k. The nodes may now be stored in a one dimensional array *tree*, with the node numbered i being stored in *tree*[i]. Lemma 5.3 enables us to determine easily the locations of the parent, left child, and right child of any node i in the binary tree.

Lemma 5.3: If a complete binary tree with n nodes (i.e., depth $= \lfloor \log_2 n \rfloor + 1$) is represented sequentially as above then for any node with index, i, $1 \leq i \leq n$ we have

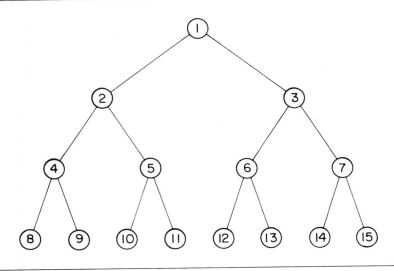

Figure 5.6 Full binary tree of depth 4 with sequential node numbers

(1) *parent(i)* is at $\lfloor i/2 \rfloor$ if $i \neq 1$. When $i = 1$, i is the root and has no parent.

(2) *lchild(i)* is at $2i$ if $2i \leq n$. If $2i > n$, then i has no left child.

(3) *rchild(i)* is at $2i + 1$ if $2i + 1 \leq n$. If $2i + 1 > n$, then i has no right child.

Proof: We prove (2). (3) is an immediate consequence of (2) and the numbering of nodes on the same level from left to right. (1) follows from (2) and (3). We prove (2) by induction on i. For $i = 1$, clearly the left child is at 2 unless $2 > n$ in which case 1 has no left child. Now assume that for all j, $1 \leq j \leq i$, *lchild(j)* is at $2j$. Then, the two nodes immediately preceding *lchild(i + 1)* in the representation are the right child of i and the left child of i. The left child of i is at $2i$. Hence, the left child of $i + 1$ is at $2i + 2 = 2(i + 1)$ unless $2(i + 1) > n$ in which case $i + 1$ has no left child. $\square$

This representation can clearly be used for all binary trees though in most cases there will be a lot of unutilized space. For complete binary trees the representation is ideal as no space is wasted. For the skewed tree of Figure 5.5(a) however, less than half the array is utilized. In the worst case a skewed tree of depth k will require $2^k - 1$ spaces. Of these only k will be occupied.

While the above representation appears to be good for complete binary trees it is wasteful for many other binary trees. In addition, the representation suffers from the general inadequacies of sequential representations. Insertion or deletion of nodes from the middle of a tree requires the movement of potentially many nodes to reflect the change in level number of these nodes. These problems can be easily overcome through

	tree		tree
[1]	A		A
[2]	B		B
[3]	—		C
[4]	C		D
[5]	—		E
[6]	—		F
[7]	—		G
[8]	D		H
[9]	—		I
.	.		
.	.		
.	.		
[16]	E		

Figure 5.7 Array representation of the binary trees of Figure 5.5

the use of a linked representation. Each node will have three fields, *LeftChild*, *data*, and *RightChild* and is defined in Pascal as

```
type TreePointer = ↑TreeRecord;
     TreeRecord = record
                    LeftChild : TreePointer;
                    data : char;
                    RightChild : TreePointer;
                  end;
```

We shall draw such a node using either of the representations of Figure 5.8.

While this node structure will make it difficult to determine the parent of a node, we shall see that for most applications, it is adequate. In case it is necessary to be able to determine the parent of random nodes, then a fourth field *parent* may be included. The representation of the binary tree of Figure 5.5 using this node structure is given in Figure 5.9. A tree is referred to by the variable that points to its root.

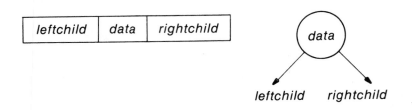

Figure 5.8 Node representations

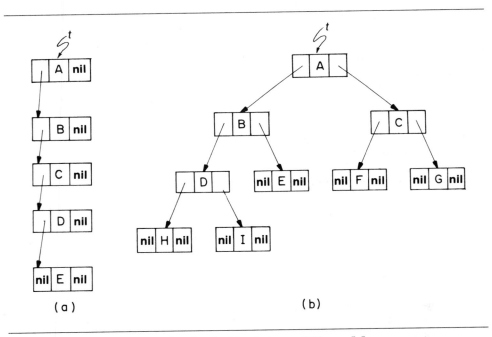

Figure 5.9 Linked representation for the binary trees of Figure 5.5

5.4 BINARY TREE TRAVERSAL

There are many operations that we often want to perform on trees. One notion that arises frequently is the idea of traversing a tree or visiting each node in the tree exactly once. A full traversal produces a linear order for the information in a tree. This linear order may be familiar and useful. When traversing a binary tree we want to treat each node and its subtrees in the same fashion. If we let *L, D, R* stand for moving left, printing the data, and moving right when at a node then there are six possible combinations of traversal: *LDR, LRD, DLR, DRL, RDL,* and *RLD*. If we adopt the convention that we traverse left before right then only three traversals remain: *LDR, LRD,* and *DLR*. To these we assign the names inorder, postorder, and preorder because there is a natural correspondence between these traversals and producing the infix, postfix, and prefix forms of an expression. Consider the binary tree of Figure 5.10. This tree contains an arithmetic expression with binary operators: add (+), multiply (*), divide (/), and variables A, B, C, D, and E. We will not worry for now how this binary tree was formed but assume that it is available. We will define three types of traversals, *inorder, preorder,* and *postorder*, and show the results for this tree.

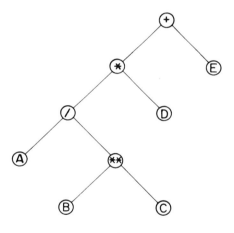

Figure 5.10 Binary tree with arithmetic expression

Informally, *inorder traversal*, calls for moving down the tree towards the left until you can go no farther. Then you "visit" the node, move one node to the right and continue again. If you cannot move to the right, go back one more node. A precise way of describing this traversal is to write it as a recursive procedure (Program 5.1).

Recursion is an elegant device for describing this traversal. Figure 5.11 is a trace of how **procedure** *inorder* (Program 5.1) works on the tree of Figure 5.10. You should first read down the left column and then the right one. Including the initial (MAIN) invocation, the procedure is invoked a total of 19 times. The elements get output in the order

```
 1 procedure inorder (CurrentNode : TreePointer );
 2 {CurrentNode is a pointer to a node in a binary tree.  For full
 3   tree traversal, pass inorder the pointer to the top of the tree}
 4 begin {inorder}
 5   if CurrentNode < > nil
 6   then
 7   begin
 8     inorder (CurrentNode ↑. LeftChild);
 9     write(CurrentNode ↑. data );
10     inorder (CurrentNode ↑. RightChild);
11   end
12 end; {of inorder}
```

Program 5.1 Algorithm *inorder*

$$A /B * C * D + E$$

which is the *in*fix form of the expression.

Call of *inorder*	Value in root	Action	Call of *inorder*	Value in root	
MAIN	+		10	C	
1	*		11	**nil**	
2	*		10	C	write('C')
3	/		12	**nil**	
4	A		1	*	write('*')
5	**nil**		13	D	
4	A	write('A')	14	**nil**	
6	**nil**		13	D	write('D')
3	/	write('/')	15	**nil**	
7	B		MAIN	+	write('+')
8	**nil**		16	E	
7	B	write ('B')	17	**nil**	
9	**nil**		16	E	write('E')
2	*	write('*')	18	**nil**	

Figure 5.11 Trace of Program 5.1

A second form of traversal is *preorder*. Program 5.2 is the Pascal code for this. In words we would say "visit a node, traverse left, and continue again. When you cannot continue, move right and begin again or move back until you can move right and resume." The nodes of Figure 5.10 would be output in *pre*order as

$$+ * * / A \; B \; C \; D \; E$$

which we recognize as the *pre*fix form of the expression.

```
 1  procedure preorder (CurrentNode : TreePointer );
 2  {CurrentNode is a pointer to a node in a binary tree. For full
 3   tree traversal, pass preorder the pointer to the top of the tree}
 4  begin {preorder}
 5    if CurrentNode < > nil
 6    then
 7    begin
 8      write(CurrentNode ↑. data );
 9      preorder (CurrentNode ↑. LeftChild );
10      preorder (CurrentNode ↑. RightChild );
11    end {of if}
12  end; {of preorder}
```

Program 5.2 Algorithm *preorder*

At this point it should be easy to guess the next traversal method which is called *postorder*. The output produced by **procedure** *postorder* (Program 5.3) is

$$A \; B \; / \; C * D * E +$$

which is the *post*fix of our expression.

Though we have written these three algorithms using recursion, it is very easy to produce equivalent nonrecursive versions. Let us take inorder as an example. To simulate the recursion we need two stacks, one which will hold values of *pointer* where *pointer* points to a node in the tree and one which holds return addresses to the place where the algorithm should resume after an end is encountered. We replace every recursive call by a mechanism which places the new pair (*pointer, ReturnAd*) onto the stacks and goes to the beginning; and where there is a return or end we insert code which deletes the top pair from the stacks if possible and either ends or branches to *ReturnAd* (see Section 4.8 for the exact details). Program 5.4 describes this algorithm fully.

```
1  procedure postorder (CurrentNode : TreePointer);
2  {CurrentNode is a pointer to a node in a binary tree.  For full
3   tree traversal, pass postorder the pointer to the top of the tree}
4  begin {postorder}
5   if CurrentNode < > nil
6   then
7   begin
8     postorder (CurrentNode↑.LeftChild);
9     postorder (CurrentNode↑.RightChild);
10    write(CurrentNode↑.data);
11   end {of if}
12  end; {of postorder}
```

Program 5.3 Algorithm postorder

```
1  procedure inorder1(CurrentNode : TreePointer);
2  {a nonrecursive version of inorder using two stacks of size
3   MaxStackSize}
4  label 1,2,3;
5  const MaxStackSize = 100;
6  var StackPointer : 0..MaxStackSize + 1;
7      ReturnAddressStack : array [1..MaxStackSize] of 2 ..3;
8      NodeStack : array [1..MaxStackSize] of treeepointer ;
9      AddressToReturnTo : integer;
10 begin
11  stackponter := 0; {initialize the stacks}
12 1: if CurrentNode < > nil
13  then
14  begin
15    StackPointer := StackPointer + 1;
16    if StackPointer > MaxStackSize then StackFull;
17    NodeStack [stackponter ] := CurrentNode ;
18    ReturnAddressStack [StackPointer ] := 2;
19    currentnode := currentnode↑.LeftChild;
20    goto 1;            {traverse left subtree}
21 2:   write (CurrentNode↑.data);
22    StackPointer := StackPointer + 1;
23    if StackPointer > MaxStackSize then StackFull;
24    NodeStack [StackPointer ] := CurrentNode :
25    ReturnAddressStack [StackPointer ] := 3;
26    CurrentNode :=CurrentNode↑.righthchild ;
```

```
27      goto 1;            {traverse right subtree}
28   end; {of if}
29   3:if StackPointer <> 0
30   then
31   begin {stack not empty, simulate a return}
32      CurrentNode := NodeStack [StackPointer ];
33      AddressToReturnTo := ReturnAddressStack [stackponter ];
34      StackPointer := StackPointer − 1;
35      case AddressToReturnTo of
36         2 : goto 2;
37         3 : goto 3;
38      end; {of case}
39   end; {of if}
40   end; {of inorder1}
```

Program 5.4 Inorder1

Though this procedure seems highly unstructured its virtue is that it is semiautomatic produced from the recursive version using a fixed set of rules. Our faith in the correctness of this program can be justified if we first prove the correctness of the original version and then prove that the transformation rules result in a correct and equivalent program. Also we can simplify this program after we make some observations about its behavior. For every pair (*CurrentNode*,3) in the two stacks when we come to label 3 this pair will be removed. All such consecutive pairs will be removed until either *StackPointer* gets set to zero or we reach a pair (*CurrentNode*,2). Therefore, the presence of label 3 pairs is useful in no way and we can delete that part of the algorithm. This means we can eliminate the lines 22-25. We next observe that this leaves us with only one return address, label 2, so we need not place that on the stack either. The new version is Program 5.5. This program is considerably simpler than the previous version, but it may still offend some people because of the seemingly undisciplined use of **goto**'s. Program 5.6 is a structured Pascal version.

What are the computing time and storage requirements of *inorder* 3? Let n be the number of nodes in the tree. If we consider the action of the above algorithm, we note that every node of the tree is placed on the stack once. Thus, the statements on lines 14-17 and 22-25 are executed n times. Moreover, *CurrentNode* will equal **nil** once for every **nil** link in the tree which is exactly

$$2n_0 + n_1 = n_0 + n_1 + n_2 + 1 = n + 1$$

So every step will be executed no more than some small constant times n or O(n). With some further modifications we can lower the constant (see exercises). The space required for the stack is equal to the depth of the tree. This is at most n.

```
 1  procedure inorder2(CurrentNode : TreePointer)
 2  {simpler, nonrecursive version using one stack of size MaxStackSize}
 3  const MaxStackSize = 100
 4  label 1,2;
 5  var StackPointer : integer;
 6      NodeStack : array [1..MaxStackSize] of TreePointer;
 7  begin
 8    StackPointer := 0; {initialize the stack}
 9  1: if CurrentNode < > nil
10    then
11    begin
12      StackPointer := StackPointer + 1;
13      if StackPointer > MaxStackSize then StackFull;
14      NodeStack [StackPointer ] := CurrentNode ;
15      CurrentNode := currentnode↑.LeftChild;
16      goto 1;            {traverse left subtree}
17  2:   write(CurrentNode↑.data);
18      CurrentNode := CurrentNode↑.RightChild ;
19      goto 1;            {traverse right subtree}
20    end;
21    if StackPointer <> 0
22    then
23    begin {stack not empty}
24      CurrentNode := NodeStack [StackPointer ];
25      stackponter := StackPointer − 1;
26      goto 2;
27    end {of if}
28  end; {of inorder2}
```

Program 5.5 Inorder2

Before we leave the topic of tree traversal, we shall consider one final question. Is it possible to traverse binary trees without the use of extra space for a stack? One simple solution is to add a *parent* field to each node. Then we can trace our way back up to any root and down again. Another solution which requires two bits per node is given in Section 5.6. If the allocation of this extra space is too costly then we can use the method of algorithm *mark*2 of Section 4.9. No extra storage is required since during processing the *LeftChild* and *RightChild* fields are used to maintain the paths back to the root. The stack of addresses is stored in the leaf nodes. The exercises examine this algorithm more closely.

```
 1  procedure inorder3(CurrentNode : TreePointer);
 2  {a nonrecursive, no goto version using a stack of size
 3    MaxStackSize}
 4  const MaxStackSize = 100;
 5  var done : boolean;
 6      stackponter : integer;
 7      NodeStack : array [1..MaxStackSize] of treeponter ;
 8  begin
 9    StackPointer := 0; {initialize the stack}
10    done := false; {initialize loop condition}
11    repeat
12      while CurrentNode <> nil do {move down LeftChild fields}
13      begin
14        StackPointer = StackPointer + 1
15        if StackPointer > MaxStackSize then StackFull;
16        NodeStack [stackponter ] := CurrentNode ;
17        CurrentNode :+ CurrentNode↑.LeftChild;
18      end; {of while}
19      if StackPointer <> 0
20      then
21      begin
22        CurrentNode := NodeStack [StackPointer ];
23        StackPointer := StackPointer − 1;
24        write(CurrentNode↑.data);
25        CurrentNode := CurrentNode↑.RightChild ;
26      end
27      else done := true;
28    until done;
29  end; {of inorder3}
```

Program 5.6 Inorder3

5.5 MORE ON BINARY TREES

Using the definition of a binary tree and the recursive version of the traversals, we can easily write other routines for working with binary trees. For instance, if we want to produce an exact copy of a given binary tree we can modify the postorder traversal algorithm only slightly to get Program 5.7.

Another problem that is especially easy to solve using recursion is determining the equivalence of two binary trees. Binary trees are equivalent if they have the same topology and the information in corresponding nodes is identical. By the same topology we

```
 1 function copy (OriginalTree : TreePointer) : treeponter ;
 2 {This function returns a pointer to an exact
 3   copy of the binary tree OriginalTree}
 4 var TempTree : TreePointer ;
 5 begin
 6   if OriginalTree <> nil
 7   then
 8   begin
 9      new(TempTree);
10      TempTree↑.LeftChild := copy (OriginalTree↑.LeftChild);
11      TempTree↑.RightChild := copy(OriginalTree↑.RightChild);
12      TempTree↑.data := TempTree ;
13      copy := TempTree ;
14   end
15   else copy := nil;
16 end {of copy}
```

Program 5.7 Algorithm *copy*

mean that every branch in one tree corresponds to a branch in the second in the same order and vice versa. Algorithm *equal*, Program 5.8, traverses the binary trees in preorder, though any order could be used.

As an example of the usefulness of binary trees, consider the set of formulas we can construct by taking variables $x_1, x_2, x_3, \ldots$, and the operators $\wedge$ (**and**), $\vee$ (**or**), and $\neg$ (**not**). These variables can only hold one of two possible values, true or false. The set of expressions which can be formed using these variables and operators is defined by the rules: (1) a variable is an expression; (2) if x and y are expressions then $x \wedge y$, $x \vee y$, $\neg x$ are expressions. Parentheses can be used to alter the normal order of evaluation which is **not** before **and** before **or**. This comprises the formulas in the *propositional calculus* (other operations such as implication can be expressed using $\wedge$, $\vee$, $\neg$). The expression

$$x_1 \vee (x_2 \wedge \neg x_3)$$

is a formula (read "x_1 or x_2 and not x_3"). If x_1 and x_3 are false and x_2 is true, then the value of this expression is

$$false \vee (true \wedge \neg false)$$

$$= false \vee true$$

$$= true$$

```
 1 function equal (firsttree, SecondTree : TreePointer) : boolean;
 2 {this procedure returns false if the binary trees firsttree and
 3 SecondTree are not equivalent.  Otherwise, it will return true}
 4 begin
 5   equal := false; {initialize answer}
 6   if ((firsttree = nil) and (SecondTree = nil))
 7   then equal := true
 8   else
 9     if ((firsttree < > nil) and (second < > nil))
10     then
11       if firsttree↑.data = SecondTree↑.data
12       then
13         if equal (firsttree↑.LeftChild, SecondTree↑.LeftChild)
14         then
15           equal := equal (firsttree↑.RightChild, SecondTree↑.RightChild);
16 end; {of equal}
```

Program 5.8 Algorithm *eval*

The *satisfiability problem* for formulas of the propositional calculus asks if there is an assignment of values to the variables which causes the value of the expression to be true. This problem is of great historical interest in computer science. It was originally used by Newell, Shaw, and Simon in the late 1950s to show the viability of heuristic programming (the Logic Theorist).

Again, let us assume that our formula is already in a binary tree, say

$$(x_1 \wedge \neg x_2) \vee (\neg x_1 \wedge x_3) \vee \neg x_3$$

in the tree of Figure 5.12. The inorder of this tree is

$$x_1 \wedge \neg x_2 \vee \neg x_1 \wedge x_3 \vee \neg x_3$$

which is the infix form of the expression. The most obvious algorithm to determine satisfiability is to let (x_1, x_2, x_3) take on all possible combinations of truth and a falsity and to check the formula for each combination. For n variables there are 2^n possible combinations of true $= t$ and false $= f$, e.g., for $n = 3$, the eight combinations are: (t,t,t), (t,t,f), (t,f,t), (t,f,f), (f,t,t), (f,t,f), (f,f,t), (f,f,f). The algorithm will take at least $O(g\,2^n)$ or exponential time where g is the time to substitute values for x_1, x_2, x_3 and evaluate the expression.

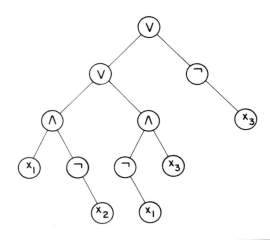

Figure 5.12 Propositional formula in a binary tree

To evaluate an expression one method would traverse the tree in postorder, evaluating subtrees until the entire expression is reduced to a single value. This corresponds to the postfix evaluation of an arithmetic expression that we saw earlier. Viewing this from the perspective of the tree representation, for every node we reach, the values of its arguments (or children) have already been computed. So when we reach the $\vee$ node on level 2, the values of $x_1 \wedge \neg x_2$ and $\neg x_1 \wedge x_3$ will already be available to us and we can apply the rule for **or**. Notice that a node containing $\neg$ has only a single right branch since **not** is a unary operator.

For the purposes of this algorithm we assume each node has four fields:

LeftChild	data	value	RightChild

where *LeftChild, data, RightChild* are as before and *value* is of type boolean. This node structure may be defined in Pascal as below:

type *TypesOfData* = (*LogicalNot, LogicalAnd, LogicalOr, LogicalTrue,*
$\qquad\qquad$ *logicalfalse*);
$\quad$ *TreePointer* = ↑*TreeRecord* ;
$\quad$ *TreeRecord* = **record**
$\qquad\qquad$ *LeftChild* $\quad$: *TreePointer* ;
$\qquad\qquad$ *data* $\qquad$: *TypesOfData*;
$\qquad\qquad$ *value* $\qquad$: **boolean**;
$\qquad\qquad$ *RightChild* : *TreePointer* ;
$\qquad$ **end**;

Also we assume that for leaf nodes t↑.*data* contains the current value of the variable represented at this node. With these preparations and assuming an expression with n variables pointed at by *tree* we can now write the first version of our algorithm for satisfiability. This is given in Program 5.9. Now let us concentrate on this modified version of postorder. Changing the original recursive version seems the simplest thing to do. We obtain the procedure of Program 5.10.

```
for all 2ⁿ possible combinations do
begin
    generate the next combination;
    replace the variables by their values;
    evaluate tree by traversing it in postorder;
    if tree↑.value
        then output combination and stop
end
writeln ("no satisfiable combination")
```

Program 5.9 First version of satisfiability algorithm

5.6 THREADED BINARY TREES

If we look carefully at the linked representation of any binary tree, we notice that there are more null links than actual pointers. As we saw before, there are $n+1$ null links and $2n$ total links. A clever way to make use of these null links has been devised by A. J. Perlis and C. Thornton. Their idea is to replace the null links by pointers, called threads, to other nodes in the tree. If p↑.*rchild* is normally equal to **nil**, we will replace it *by a pointer to the node which would be printed after p when traversing the tree in inorder.* A null *LeftChild* link at node p is replaced *by a pointer to the node which immediately precedes node p* in inorder. Figure 5.13 shows the binary tree of Figure 5.5(b) with its new threads drawn in as dotted lines.

```
1  procedure PostOrderEval (tree : TreePointer)
2  begin
3     if tree <> nil
4     then
5     begin
6        PostOrderEval (tree↑.LeftChild);
7        PostOrderEval (tree↑.RightChild);
8        case tree↑.data of
9          LogicalNot : tree↑.value := not tree↑.RightChild↑.value;
10         LogicalAnd : tree↑.value := tree↑.LeftChild↑.value and
11                         tree↑.RightChild↑.value ;
12         LogicalOr   : tree↑.value := tree↑.LeftChild↑.value or
13                         tree↑.RightChild↑.value ;
14         LogicalTrue: tree↑.value := true;
15         LogicalFalse tree↑.value := false;
16      end; {of case}
17   end; {of if}
18 end; {of PostOrderEval}
```

Program 5.10 Algorithm *PostOrderEval*

The tree *t* has 9 nodes and 10 null links which have been replaced by threads. If we traverse *t* in inorder, the nodes will be visited in the order *H, D, I, B, E, A, F, C, G*. For example, node *E* has a predecessor thread which points to *B* and a successor thread which points to *A*.

In the memory representation we must be able to distinguish between threads and normal pointers. This is done by adding two boolean fields to the record, *LeftThread* and *RightThread*.

If *tree↑.LeftThread* = true, the *tree↑.LeftChild* contains a thread and otherwise it contains a pointer to the LeftChild. Similarly if *tree↑.RightThread* = true, then *tree↑.RightChild* contains a thread and otherwise it contains a pointer to the RightChild.

This node structure is now given by the following Pascal type declaration:

```
type ThreadedPointer = ↑ThreadedTree ;
     ThreadedTree = record
                      LeftThread  : boolean;
                      LeftChild   : ThreadedPointer ;
                      data        : char;
                      RightChild  : ThreadedPointer ;
                      RightThread : boolean;
                    end;
```

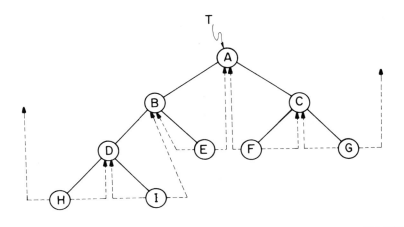

Figure 5.13 Threaded tree corresponding to Figure 5.5(b)

In Figure 5.13 we see that two threads have been left dangling in *LeftChild* of *H* and *RightChild* of *G*. In order that we leave no loose threads we will assume a head node for all threaded binary trees. An empty binary tree is represented by its head node as in Figure 5.14. The complete memory representation for the tree of Figure 5.13 is shown in Figure 5.15. The tree *t* is the left subtree of the head node.

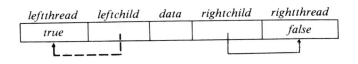

Figure 5.14 An empty threaded binary tree

This assumption will permit easy algorithm design. Now that we have made use of the old null links we will see that the algorithm for inorder traversal is simplified. First, we observe that for any node *x* in a binary tree, if $x\uparrow.RightThread$ = true, then the inorder successor of *x* is $x\uparrow.RightChild$ by definition of threads. Otherwise the inorder successor of *x* is obtained by following a path of left child links from the right child of *x* until a

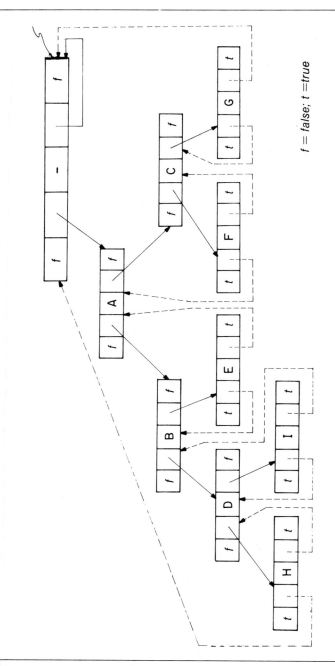

Figure 5.15 Memory representation of threaded tree

node with *LeftThread* = true is reached. The algorithm *insuc* (Program 5.7) finds the inorder successor of any node *x* in a threaded binary tree.

```
 1 function insuc (tree : ThreadedPointer) : ThreadedPointer ;
 2 {find the inorder successor of tree in a threaded binary tree}
 3 var temp : ThreadedPointer ;
 4 begin
 5     temp := tree↑.RightChild ;
 6     if not tree↑.RightThread
 7     then while not temp↑.LeftThread do
 8              temp := temp↑.LeftChild;
 9     insuc := temp ;
10 end; {of insuc}
```

Program 5.11 Algorithm *insuc*

The interesting thing to note about procedure *insuc* is that it is now possible to find the inorder successor of any arbitrary node in a threaded binary tree without using an additional stack. If we wish to list in inorder all the nodes in a threaded binary tree, then we can make repeated calls to the procedure *insuc*. Since the tree is the left subtree of the head node and because of the choice of *RightThread* = false for the head node, the inorder sequence of nodes for tree *t* is obtained by the procedure *tinorder* (Program 5.12).

```
 1 procedure tinorder (tree : ThreadedPointer);
 2 {traverse the threaded binary tree in inorder}
 3 var temp : ThreadedPointer :
 4 begin
 5     temp := tree ;
 6     repeat
 7        temp := insuc (temp );
 8        if temp <> tree
 9        then write(temp↑.data);
10     until temp = tree ;
11 end; {of tinoder}
```

Program 5.12 Algorithm *tinorder*

The computing time is still $O(n)$ for a binary tree with *n* nodes. The constant here will be somewhat smaller than for procedure *inorder*3.

We have seen how to use the threads of a threaded binary tree for inorder traversal. These threads also simplify the algorithms for preorder and postorder traversal. Before closing this section let us see how to make insertions into a threaded tree. This will give us a procedure for growing threaded trees. We shall study only the case of inserting a node t as the right child of a node s. The case of insertion of a left child is given as an exercise. If s has an empty right subtree, then the insertion is simple and diagrammed in Figure 5.16(a). If the right subtree of s is nonempty, then this right subtree is made the right subtree of t after insertion. When this is done, t becomes the inorder predecessor of a node which has a *LeftThread = true* field and consequently there is a thread which has to be updated to point to t. The node containing this thread was previously the inorder successor of s. Figure 5.16(b) illustrates the insertion for this case. In both cases s is the inorder predecessor of t. The details are spelled out in procedure *InsertRight*, Program 5.13.

5.7 BINARY TREE REPRESENTATION OF TREES

We have seen several representations for and uses of binary trees. In this section we will see that every tree can be represented as a binary tree. This is important because the methods for representing a tree as suggested in Section 5.1 had some undesirable features. One form of representation used variable size nodes. While the handling of nodes of variable size is not impossible, it is considerably more difficult than the handling of fixed size nodes. An alternative would be to use fixed size nodes, each node having k child fields, if k is the maximum degree of any node (see Figure 5.17). As Lemma 5.4 shows, this would be very wasteful in space.

Lemma 5.4: If T is a k-ary tree (i.e., a tree of degree k) with n nodes, each having a fixed size as in Figure 5.17, then $n(k-1)+1$ of the nk link fields are nil, $n \geq 1$.

Proof: Since each non-nil link points to a node and exactly one link points to each node other than the root, the number of non-nil links in an n node tree is exactly $n-1$. The total number of link fields in a k-ary tree with n nodes is nk. Hence, the number of null links is $nk - (n-1) = n(k-1)+1$. $\square$

Lemma 5.4 implies that for a 3-ary tree more than 2/3 of the link fields are nil. The proportion of nil links approaches 1 as the degree of the tree increases. The importance of using binary trees to represent trees is that for binary trees only about 1/2 of the link fields are nil.

In arriving at the binary tree representation of a tree we shall implicitly make use of the fact that the order of the children of a node is not important. Suppose we have the tree of Figure 5.18.

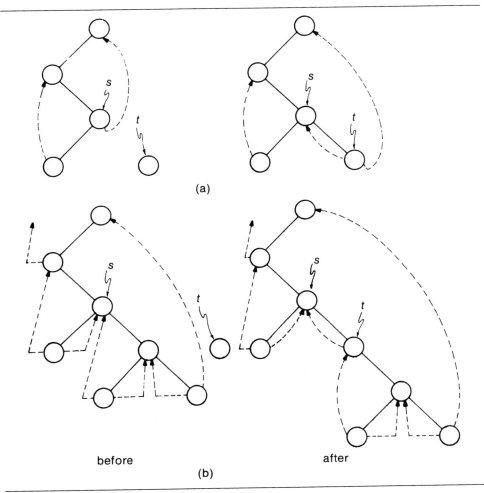

Figure 5.16 Insertion of *t* as a right child of *s* in a threaded binary tree

We observe that the reason we needed nodes with many link fields is that the prior representation was based on the parent-child relationship and a node can have any number of children. To obtain a binary tree representation, we need a relationship, between the nodes, that can be characterized by at most two quantities. One such relationship is the leftmost-child-next-right-sibling relationship. Every node has at most one leftmost child and at most one next right sibling. In the tree of Figure 5.18, the leftmost child of *B* is *E* and the next right sibling of *B* is *C*. Strictly speaking, since the order of children in a tree is not important, any of the children of a node could be its leftmost

```
 1  procedure InsertRight (s, t : ThreadedPointer );
 2  {insert node t as the right child of s in a threaded binary
 3  tree}
 4  var temp : ThreadedPointer ;
 5  begin
 6     t↑.RightChild := s↑.RightChild ;
 7     t↑.RightThread := s↑.RightThread ;
 8     t↑.LeftChild := s ;
 9     t↑.leftthread := true; {LeftChild is a thread}
10     s↑.RightChild := t; {attach t to s}
11     s↑.RightThread := false;
12     if not t↑.RightThread
13     then
14     begin
15        temp := insuc (t);
16        temp↑.LeftChild := t ;
17     end;
18  end; {of InsertRight}
```

Program 5.13 Algorithm *InsertRight*

DATA			
CHILD 1	CHILD 2	....	CHILD k

Figure 5.17 Possible node structure for a k-ary tree

child and any of its siblings could be its next right sibling. For the sake of definiteness, we choose the nodes based upon how the tree is drawn. The binary tree corresponding to the tree of Figure 5.18 is thus obtained by connecting together all siblings of a node and deleting all links from a node to its children except for the link to its leftmost child. The node structure corresponds to that of

DATA	
CHILD	SIBLING

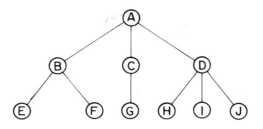

Figure 5.18 A sample tree

Using the transformation described above, we obtain the representation of Figure 5.19 for the tree of Figure 5.18.

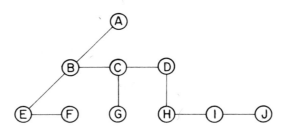

Figure 5.19 Representation of tree of Figure 5.18

This does not look like a binary tree, but if we tilt it roughly 45° clockwise, we get the tree of Figure 5.20. Some additional examples are given in Figure 5.21.

One thing to notice is that the *rchild* of the root node of every resulting binary tree will be empty. This is because the root of the tree we are transforming has no siblings. On the other hand, if we have a forest then these can all be transformed into a single binary tree by first obtaining the binary tree representation of each of the trees in the forest and then linking all the binary trees together through the *sibling* field of the root nodes. For instance, the forest with three trees (Figure 5.22) yields the binary tree of Figure 5.23.

We can define this transformation in a formal way as follows: If $T_1, \ldots, T_n$ is a forest of trees, then the binary tree corresponding to this forest, denoted by $B(T_1, \ldots, T_n)$ (1) is empty if $n = 0$, and (2) has root equal to root (T_1); has left subtree equal to $B(T_{11}, T_{12}, \ldots, T_{1m})$, where $T_{11}, \ldots, T_{1m}$ are the subtrees of root(T_1); and has

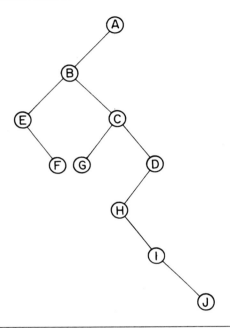

Figure 5.20 Associated binary tree for tree of Figure 5.18

right subtree $B(T_2, \ldots, T_n)$.

Preorder and inorder traversals of the corresponding binary tree T of a forest F have a natural correspondence with traversals on F. Preorder traversal of T is equivalent to visiting the nodes of F in *tree preorder*, which is defined by

(1) If F is empty then return.

(2) Visit the root of the first tree of F.

(3) Traverse the subtrees of the first tree in tree preorder.

(4) Traverse the remaining trees of F in preorder.

Inorder traversal of T is equivalent to visiting the nodes of F in *tree inorder* as defined by

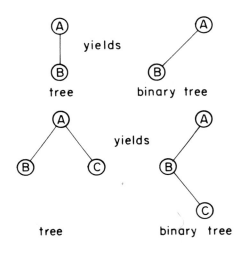

Figure 5.21 Binary tree transformations

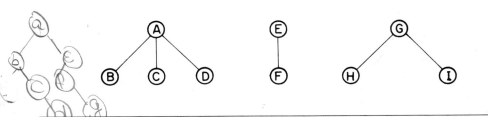

Figure 5.22 Three tree forest

(1)   If *F* is empty then return.

(2)   Traverse the subtrees of the first tree in tree inorder.

(3)   Visit the root of the first tree.

(4)   Traverse the remaining trees in tree inorder.

The above definitions for forest traversal will be referred to as preorder and inorder. The

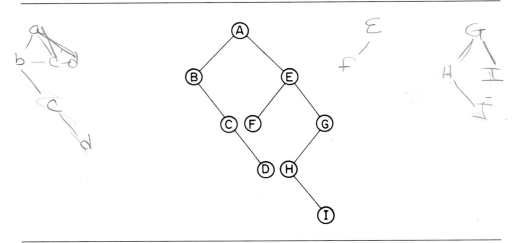

Figure 5.23 Binary tree representation of forest of Figure 5.22

proofs that preorder and inorder on the corresponding binary tree are the same as preorder and inorder on the forest are left as exercises. There is no natural analog for postorder traversal of the corresponding binary tree of a forest. Nevertheless, we can define the *postorder traversal of a forest* as

(1)   If F is empty then return.

(2)   Traverse the subtrees of the first tree of F in tree postorder.

(3)   Traverse the remaining trees of F in tree postorder.

(4)   Visit the root of the first tree of F.

This traversal is used later on in Section 5.10 to describe the minimax procedure.

5.8 SET REPRESENTATION

In this section we study the use of trees in the representation of sets. We shall assume that the elements of the sets are the numbers 1, 2, 3, . . ., n. These numbers might, in practice, be indices into a symbol table where the actual names of the elements are stored. We shall assume that the sets being represented are pairwise disjoint; i.e., if S_i and S_j, $i \neq j$, are two sets then there is no element which is in both S_i and S_j. For example, if we have 10 elements numbered 1 through 10, they may be partitioned into three disjoint sets, $S_1 = \{1, 7, 8, 9\}$, $S_2 = \{2, 5, 10\}$, and $S_3 = \{3, 4, 6\}$. The operations we wish to perform on these sets are

(1) Disjoint set union. If S_i and S_j are two disjoint sets, then their union $S_i \cup S_j = \{$all elements x such that x is in S_i or $S_j\}$. Thus, $S_1 \cup S_2 = \{1, 7, 8, 9, 2, 5, 10\}$. Since we have assumed that all sets are disjoint, following the union of S_i and S_j we can assume that the sets S_i and S_j no longer exist independently, i.e., they are replaced by $S_i \cup S_j$ in the collection of sets.

(2) Find (i). Find the set containing element i. Thus, 4 is in set S_3 and 9 is in set S_1.

The sets will be represented by trees. One possible representation for the sets S_1, S_2, and S_3 is given in Figure 5.24.

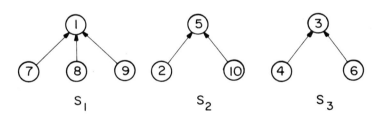

Figure 5.24 Possible tree representation of sets

Note that the nodes are linked on the parent relationship, i.e., each node other than the root is linked to its parent. The advantage of this will become apparent when we present the *union* and *find* algorithms. First, to take the union of S_1 and S_2 we simply make one of the trees a subtree of the other. $S_1 \cup S_2$ could then have one of the representations of Figure 5.25.

In order to find the union of two sets, all that has to be done is to set the parent field of one of the roots to the other root. This can be accomplished easily if, with each set name, we keep a pointer to the root of the tree representing that set. If, in addition, each root has a pointer to the set name, then to determine which set an element is

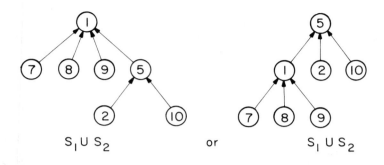

Figure 5.25 Possible representations of $S_1 \cup S_2$

currently in, we follow parent links to the root of its tree and use the pointer to the set name. The data representation for S_1, S_2, and S_3 may then take the form shown in Figure 5.26.

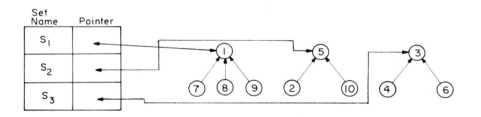

Figure 5.26 Data representation for S_1, S_2, and S_3

In presenting the *union* and *find* algorithms we shall ignore the actual set names and just identify sets by the roots of the trees representing them. This will simplify the discussion. The transition to set names is easy. If we determine that element i is in a tree with root j, and j has a pointer to entry k in the set name table, then the set name is just *name* [k]. If we wish to union sets S_i and S_j, then we wish to union the trees with roots *pointer*(S_i) and *pointer*(S_j). As we shall see, in many applications the set name is just the element at the root. The operation of *find*(i) now becomes: determine the root of the tree containing element i. *union*(i,j) requires two trees with roots i and j to be joined. We shall assume that the nodes in the trees are numbered 1 through n so that the node index corresponds to the element index. Thus, element 6 is represented by the node with index 6. Consequently, each node needs only one field: the *parent* field to link to its parent. Root nodes have a *parent* field of zero. Based on the above discussion, we see that the only data structure needed is an array, *parent* [*1 .. maxsets*] of type integer. *maxsets* is an upper bound on the number of elements we might have. Our first attempt at arriving at *union, find* algorithms would result in the algorithms *u* and *f* given in Program 5.14.

```
 1  procedure u (i,j : integer);
 2  {replace the disjoint sets with roots i and j, i ≠ j with
 3    their union}
 4  begin
 5    parent [i] := j;
 6  end; {of u}

 7  function f (i : integer) : integer;
 8  {find the root of the tree containing element i}
 9  var temp : integer;
10  begin
11    temp := i;
12    while parent [temp] > 0 do
13      temp := parent [temp];
14    f := temp;
15  end; {of f}
```

Program 5.14 Algorithm *u* and function *f*

While these two algorithms are very easy to state, their performance characteristics are not very good. For instance, if we start off with p elements each in a set of its own, i.e., $S_i = \{i\}$, $1 \le i \le p$, then the initial configuration consists of a forest with p nodes and *parent* $[i] = 0$, $1 \le i \le p$. Now let us process the following sequence of *union-find* operations:

$$u(1,2), f(1), u(2,3), f(1), u(3,4)$$
$$f(1), u(4,5), \ldots, f(1), u(n-1,n)$$

This sequence results in the degenerate tree of Figure 5.27. Since the time taken for a union is constant, all the $n - 1$ unions can be processed in time $O(n)$. However, each *find* requires following a chain of *parent* links from one to the root. The time required to process a *find* for an element at level i of a tree is $O(i)$. Hence, the total time needed to process the $n - 2$ finds is $O(\sum_{i=1}^{n-2} i) = O(n^2)$. We can do much better if care is taken to avoid the creation of degenerate trees. In order to accomplish this we shall make use of a *Weighting Rule for union (i, j)*. *If the number of nodes in tree i is less than the number in tree j, then make j the parent of i, otherwise make i the parent of j*. Using this rule on the

Figure 5.27 Degenerate tree

sequence of set unions given before we obtain the trees of Figure 5.28.

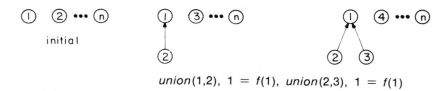

Figure 5.28 Trees obtained using the weighting rule

When the weighting rule is incorporated, the union procedure takes the form given in Program 5.15. Remember that the arguments of *union* must both be roots. The time required to process all the *n* finds is only O(*n*) since in this case the maximum level of any node is 2. This, however, is not the worst case. In Lemma 5.5 we show that using the weighting rule, the maximum level for any node is $\lfloor \log n \rfloor + 1$. First, let us see how easy it is to implement the weighting rule. We need to know how many nodes there are in every tree. To do this easily, we maintain a count field in the root of every tree. If *i* is a root node, then *count*[*i*] = number of nodes in that tree. The count can be maintained in the *parent* field as a negative number. This is equivalent to using one bit field to distinguish a count from a pointer. No confusion is created as for all other nodes the *parent* is positive.

```
 1  procedure union(i, j : integer);
 2  {union sets with roots i and j, i≠j, using the
 3    weighting rule. parent [i ] = − count [i ] and parent [j ]
 4    = −count [j ]}
 5  var temp : integer;
 6  begin
 7    temp := parent [i ] + parent [j ]
 8    if parent [i ] > parent [j ]
 9    then
10    begin        {i has fewer nodes}
11      parent [i ] := j ;
12      parent [j ] := temp ;
13    end
14    else
15    begin        {j has fewer nodes}
16      parent [j ] := i ;
17      parent [i ] := temp ;
18    end;
19  end; {of union}
```

Program 5.15 Algorithm *union*

The time required to perform a union has increased somewhat but is still bounded by a constant, i.e., it is O(1). The *find* algorithm remains unchanged. The maximum time to perform a find is determined by Lemma 5.5.

Lemma 5.5: Let *T* be a tree with *n* nodes created as a result of algorithm *union*. No node in *T* has level greater $\lfloor \log_2 n \rfloor + 1$.

Proof: The lemma is clearly true for $n = 1$. Assume it is true for all trees with i nodes, $i \leq n - 1$. We shall show that it is also true for $i = n$. Let T be a tree with n nodes created by the *union* algorithm. Consider the last union operation performed, *union*(k,j). Let m be the number of nodes in tree j and $n - m$ the number in k. Without loss of generality we may assume $1 \leq m \leq n/2$. Then the maximum level of any node in T is either the same as that in k or is one more than that in j. If the former is the case, then the maximum level in T is $\leq \lfloor \log_2 (n - m) \rfloor + 1 \leq \lfloor \log_2 n \rfloor + 1$. If the latter is the case, then the maximum level in T is $\leq \lfloor \log_2 m \rfloor + 2 \leq \lfloor \log_2 n/2 \rfloor + 2 \leq \lfloor \log_2 n \rfloor + 1$. $\square$

Example 5.1 shows that the bound of Lemma 5.5 is achievable for some sequence of unions.

Example 5.1: Consider the behavior of algorithm *union* on the following sequence of unions starting from the initial configuration *parent* $[i] = -count\,[i] = -1$, $1 \leq i \leq n = 2^3$:

$$union(1,2), \quad union(3,4), \quad union(5,6), \quad union(7,8),$$
$$union(1,3), \quad union(5,7), \quad union(1,5)$$

The trees of Figure 5.29 are obtained. As is evident, the maximum level in any tree is $\lfloor \log_2 m \rfloor + 1$ if the tree has m nodes. $\square$

As a result of Lemma 5.5, the maximum time to process a find is at most O($log\ n$) if there are n elements in a tree. If an intermixed sequence of $n - 1$ *union* and m *find* operations is to be processed, then the worst case time becomes O($n + m \log n$). Surprisingly, further improvement is possible. This time the modification will be made in the find algorithm using the *collapsing rule: If j is a node on the path from i to its root and parent* $[i] \neq root\,(i)$ *then set parent* $[j]$ *to root* (i). The new algorithm then becomes Program 5.16. This modification roughly doubles the time for an individual find. However, it reduces the worst case time over a sequence of finds.

Example 5.2: Consider the tree created by algorithm *union* on the sequence of unions of Example 5.1. Now process the following 8 finds:

$$find(8), find(8), \ldots, find(8)$$

Using the old version f of algorithm *find*, *find*(8) requires going up three parent link fields for a total of 24 moves to process all eight finds. In algorithm *find*, the first *find*(8) requires going up three links and then resetting two links. Each of the remaining seven finds requires going up only one link field. The total cost is now only 12 moves. $\square$

The worst case behavior of the *union-find* algorithms while processing a sequence of unions and finds is stated in Lemma 5.6. Before stating this lemma, let us introduce a very slow growing function $\alpha(m,n)$ which is related to a functional inverse of Ackermann's function $A\,(p,q)$. We have the following definition for $\alpha(m,n)$:

$$\alpha(m,n) = \min\{z \geq 1 \mid A\,(z,4\lceil m/n \rceil) > \log_2 n\}$$

The following trees are obtained:

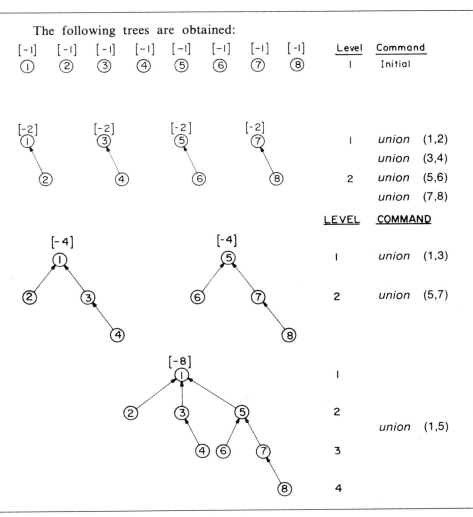

Figure 5.29 Trees achieving worst case bound

The definition of Ackermann's function used here is

$$A(p,q) = \begin{cases} 2q & p = 0 \\ 0 & q = 0 \text{ and } p \geq 1 \\ 0 & p \geq 1 \text{ and } p = 1 \\ A(p-1, A(p,q-1)) & p \geq 1 \text{ and } q \geq 2 \end{cases}$$

```
 1  function find (i : integer) : integer;
 2  {find the root of the tree containing element i. Use
 3     the collapsing rule to collapse all nodes from i to
 4     the root temp.}
 5  var temp : integer;
 6       temp 1 : integer;
 7       temp 2 : integer;
 8  begin
 9    temp := i;
10    while parent [temp ] > 0 do {find root}
11      temp := parent[temp ];
12    temp 2 := i;
13    while temp 2 < > temp do
14    begin
15      temp 1 := parent [temp 2];
16      parent [temp 2] := temp ;
17      temp 2 := temp 1;
18    end
19    find := temp ;
20  end; {of find}
```

Program 5.16 Algorithm *find*

The function $A(p,q)$ is a very rapidly growing function. You may prove the following three facts

$$(1) \quad A(3,4) = 2^{2^{\cdot^{\cdot^{\cdot^{2}}}}} \left. \right\} \quad 65{,}536 \text{ two's}$$

$$(2) \quad A(p,q + 1) > A(p,q)$$

$$(3) \quad A(p + 1,q) \geq A(p,q)$$

If we assume $m \neq 0$ then (2) and (3) together with the definition of $\alpha(m,n)$ imply that $\alpha(m,n) \leq 3$ for $\log_2 n < A(3,4)$. But from (1), $A(3,4)$ is a very large number indeed! In Lemma 5.6 n will be the number of *unions* performed. For all practical purposes we may assume $\log_2 n < A(3,4)$ and hence $\alpha(m,n) \leq 3$.

Lemma 5.6: [Tarjan] Let $T(m,n)$ be the maximum time required to process any inter-mixed sequence of $m \geq n$ *finds* and $n - 1$ *unions*. Then

$$k_1 m\alpha(m,n) \le T(m,n) \le k_2 m\alpha(m,n)$$

for some positive constants k_1 and k_2. □

Even though the function $\alpha(m,n)$ is a very slowly growing function, the complexity of *union-find* is not linear in m, the number of *finds*. As far as the space requirements are concerned, the space needed is one node for each element.

Let us look at an application of algorithms *union* and *find* to processing the equivalence pairs of Section 4.5. The equivalence classes to be generated may be regarded as sets. These sets are disjoint as no polygon can be in two equivalences classes. To begin with, all n polygons are in an equivalence class of their own; thus *parent[i]* $= -1, 1 \le i \le n$. If an equivalence pair, $i \equiv j$, is to be processed, we must first determine the sets containing i and j. If these are different, then the two sets are to be replaced by their union. If the two sets are the same, then nothing is to be done as the relation $i \equiv j$ is redundant; i and j are already in the same equivalence class. To process each equivalence pair we need to perform at most two finds and one union. Thus, if we have n polygons and $m \ge n$ equivalence pairs, the total processing time is at most $O(m\alpha(2m,m))$. While for very large n this is slightly worse than the algorithm of Section 4.5, it has the advantage of needing less space and also of being "on line." In Chapter 6 we shall see another application of the *union-find* algorithms.

Example 5.3: We shall use the *union-find* algorithms to process the set of equivalence pairs of Section 4.5. Initially, there are 12 trees, one for each variable. *parent[i]* $= -1, 1 \le i \le 12$. The tree configuraion following the processing of each equivalence pair is shown in Figure 5.30. Each tree represents an equivalence class. It is possible to determine if two elements are currently in the same equivalence class at each stage of the processing by simply making two finds. □

5.9 DECISION TREES

Another very useful application of trees is in decision making. Consider the well-known *eight coins* problem. Given coins a, b, c, d, e, f, g, h, we are told that one is a counterfeit and has a different weight than the others. We want to determine which coin it is, making use of an equal arm balance. We want to do so using a minimum number of comparisons and at the same time determine whether the false coin is heavier or lighter than the rest. The tree below represents a set of decisions by which we can get the answer to our problem. This is why it is called a decision tree. The use of capital H or L means that the counterfeit coin is *h*eavier or *l*ighter. Let us trace through one possible sequence. If $a + b + c < d + e + f$, then we know that the false coin is present among the six and is neither g nor h. If on our next measurement we find that $a + d < b + e$, then by interchanging d and b we have no change in the inequality. This tells us two things: (1) that c or f is not the culprit, and (2) that b or d is also not the culprit. If $a + d$ was equal to $b + e$, then c or f would be the counterfeit coin. Knowing at this point that

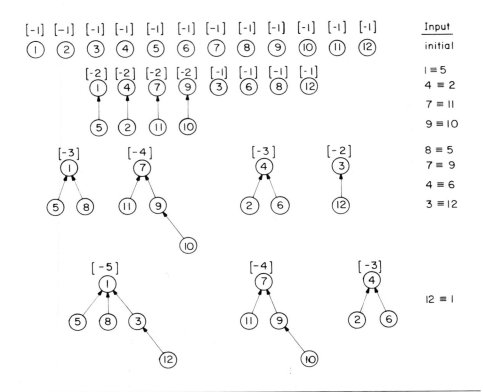

Figure 5.30 Trees for equivalence example

either *a* or *e* is the counterfeit, we compare *a* with a good coin, say *b*. If *a = b*, then *e* is heavy, otherwise *a* must be light.

By looking at this tree we see that all possibilities are covered, since there are eight coins which can be heavy or light and there are 16 terminal nodes. Every path requires exactly three comparisons. Though viewing this problem as a decision tree is very useful it does not immediately give us an algorithm. To solve the eight coins problem with a program, we must write a series of tests which mirror the structure of the tree. Moreover we must be sure that a single comparison yields one of three possibilities: =, >, or < . To perform the last comparison we will use the procedure *comp* (Program 5.17). To assure a three-way branch we assume the function *compare*(*a,b* : **integer**): **char** where the result is either '<,' '=,' or '>' with the obvious interpretations. The procedure *eightcoins* (Program 5.18) is now transparent and clearly mirrors the decision tree of Figure 5.31.

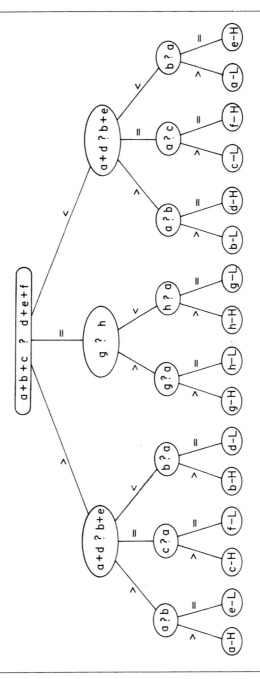

Figure 5.31 Eight coins decision tree

```
1 procedure comp (x,y,z : integer);
2 {x is compared against the standard coin z}
3 begin
4    if x > z then writeln (x, 'heavy')
5             else writeln (y, 'light');
6 end; {of comp}
```

Program 5.17 Algorithm *comp*

```
1 procedure eightcoins ;
2 {eight weights of coins are input; the illegal one
3   is discovered using only three comparisons}
4 var a, b, c, d, e, f, g, h : integer;
5 begin
6    read(a,b,c,d,e,f,g,h);
7    case compare (a + b + c, d + e + f ) of

8       '=' : if g > h then comp (g,h,a)
9                      else comp (h,g,a);
10      '=' : case compare (a + d, b + e) of
11                  '=' : comp (c,f,a);
12                  '>' : comp (a,e,b);
13                  '<' : comp (b,d,a);
14          end; {of case}
15      '<' : case compare (a + d, b + e) of
16                  '=' : comp (f,c,a);
17                  '>' : comp (d,b,a);
18                  '<' : comp (e,a,b);
19          end {of case}
20    end; {of case}
21 end; {of eightcoins}
```

Program 5.18 Algorithm *eightcoins*

5.10 GAME TREES

Another interesting application of trees is in the playing of games such as tic-tac-toe, chess, nim, kalah, checkers, go, etc. As an example, let us consider the game of nim. This game is played by two players A and B. The game itself is described by a *board* which initially contains a pile of n toothpicks. The players A and B make moves alternately with A making the first move. A *legal move* consists of removing either 1, 2, or 3 of the toothpicks from the pile. However, a player cannot remove more toothpicks than there are on the pile. The player who removes the last toothpick loses the game and the other player wins. The *board configuration* at any time is completely specified by the number of toothpicks remaining in the pile. At any time the game status is determined by the board configuration together with the player whose turn it is to make the next move. A *terminal board configuration* is one which represents either a *win, lose,* or *draw* situation. All other configurations are *nonterminal*. In nim there is only one terminal configuration: there are no toothpicks in the pile. This configuration is a win for player A if B made the last move, otherwise it is a win for B. The game of nim cannot end in a draw.

A sequence $C_1, \ldots, C_m$ of board configurations is said to be *valid* if:

(1) C_1 is the starting configuration of the game;

(2) $C_i, 0 < i < m$, are nonterminal configurations;

(3) C_{i+1} is obtained from C_i by a legal move made by player A if i is odd and by player B if i is even. It is assumed that there are only finitely many legal moves.

A valid sequence $C_1, \ldots, C_m$ of board configurations with C_m a terminal configuration is an *instance* of the game. The *length* of the sequence $C_1, C_2, \ldots, C_m$ is m. A *finite game* is one in which there are no valid sequences of infinite length. All possible instances of a finite game may be represented by a *game tree*. The tree of Figure 5.32 is the game tree for nim with $n = 6$. Each node of the tree represents a board configuration. The root node represents the starting configuration C_1. Transitions from one level to the next are made via a move of A or B. Transitions from an odd level represent moves made by A. All other transitions are the result of moves made by B. Square nodes have been used in Figure 5.32 to represent board configurations when it was A's turn to move. Circular nodes have been used for other configurations. The edges from level 1 nodes to level 2 nodes and from level 2 nodes to level 3 nodes have been labeled with the move made by A and B, respectively (for example, an edge labeled 1 means 1 toothpick is to be removed). It is easy to figure out the labels for the remaining edges of the tree. Terminal configurations are represented by leaf nodes. Leaf nodes have been labeled by the name of the player who wins when that configuration is reached. By the nature of the game of nim, player A can win only at leaf nodes on odd levels while B can win only at leaf nodes on even levels. The degree of any node in a game tree is at most equal to the number of distinct legal moves. In nim there are at

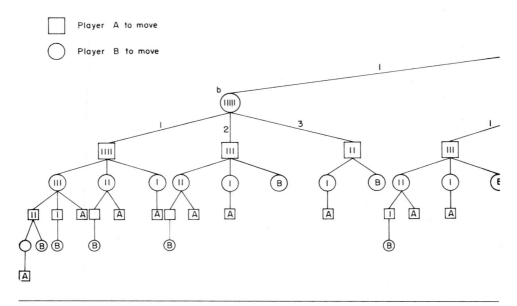

Player A to move

Player B to move

Figure 5.32 Complete game tree for nim with $n = 6$

most three legal moves from any configuration. By definition, the number of legal moves from any configuration is finite. The *depth* of a game tree is the length of a longest instance of the game. The depth of the nim tree of Figure 5.32 is 7. Hence, from start to finish this game involves at most six moves. It is not difficult to see how similar game trees may be constructed for other finite games such as chess, tic-tac-toe, kalah, etc. (Strictly speaking, chess is not a finite game as it is possible to repeat board configurations in the game. We can view chess as a finite game by disallowing this possibility. We could, for instance, define the repetition of a board configuration as resulting in a draw.)

Now that we have seen what a game tree is, the next question is "of what use are they?" Game trees are useful in determining the next move a player should make. Starting at the initial configuration represented by the root of Figure 5.32, player A is faced with the choice of making any one of three possible moves. Which one should he or she make? Assuming that player A wants to win the game, the move that maximizes the chances of winning should be made. For the simple tree of Figure 5.32 this move is not too difficult to determine. We can use an evaluation function $E(X)$ which assigns a numeric value to the board configuration X. This function is a measure of the value or worth of configuration X to player A. So, $E(X)$ is high for a configuration from which A has a good chance of winning and low for a configuration from which A has a good chance of losing. $E(X)$ has its maximum value for configurations that are either winning terminal configurations for A or configurations from which A is guaranteed to win

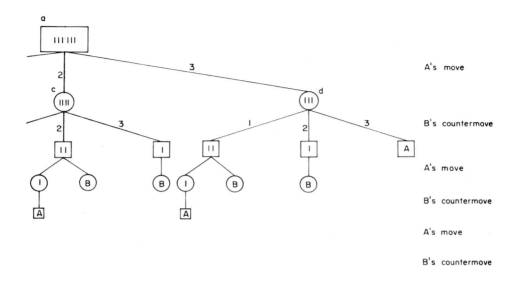

regardless of B's countermoves. $E(X)$ has its minimum value for configurations from which B is guaranteed to win.

For a game such as nim with $n = 6$ whose game tree has very few nodes, it is sufficient to define $E(X)$ only for terminal configurations. We could define $E(X)$ as

$$E(X) = \begin{cases} 1 & \text{if } X \text{ is a winning configuration for } A \\ -1 & \text{if } X \text{ is a losing configuration for } A \end{cases}$$

Using this evaluation function we wish to determine which of the configurations b, c, d player A should move the game into. Clearly, the choice is the one whose value is $\max \{V(b), V(c), V(d)\}$ where $V(x)$ is the value of configuration x. For leaf nodes x, $V(x)$ is taken to be $E(x)$. For all other nodes x let $d \geq 1$ be the degree of x and let $c_1, c_2, \ldots, c_d$ be the configurations represented by the children of x. Then $V(x)$ is defined by

$$V(x) = \begin{cases} \max_{1 \leq i \leq d} \{V(c_i)\} & \text{if } x \text{ is a square node} \\ \min_{1 \leq i \leq d} \{V(c_i)\} & \text{if } x \text{ is a circular node} \end{cases} \qquad (5.3)$$

The justification for Eq. (5.3) is fairly simple. If x is a square node, then it is at an odd level and it will be A's turn to move from here if the game ever reaches this node. Since A wants to win he or she will move to that child node with maximum value. In case x is a circular node it must be on an even level and if the game ever reaches this node, then it will be B's turn to move. Since B is out to win the game, B will (barring mistakes) make a move that will minimize A's chances of winning. In this case the next configuration will be $\min_{1 \le i \le d} \{V(c_i)\}$. Equation (5.3) defines the *minimax* procedure to determine the value of a configuration x. This is illustrated on the hypothetical game of Figure 5.33. P_{11} represents an arbitrary board configuration from which A has to make a move. The values of the leaf nodes are obtained by evaluating the function $E(x)$. The value of P_{11} is obtained by starting at the nodes on level 4 and computing their values using Eq. (5.3). Since level 4 is a level with circular nodes, all unknown values on this level may be obtained by taking the minimum of the children values. Next, values on levels 3, 2, and 1 may be computed in that order. The resulting value for P_{11} is 3. This means that starting from P_{11} the best A can hope to do is reach a configuration of value 3. Even though some nodes have value greater than 3, these nodes will not be reached, as B's countermoves will prevent the game from reaching any such configuration (assuming B's countermoves are optimal for B with respect to A's evaluation function). For example, if A made a move to P_{21}, hoping to win the game at P_{31}, A would indeed be surprised by B's countermove to P_{32} resulting in a loss to A. Given A's evaluation function and the game tree of Figure 5.33, the best move for A to make is to configuration P_{22}. Having made this move, the game may still not reach configuration P_{52} as B would, in general, be using a different evaluation function, which might give different values to various board configurations. In any case, the *minimax* procedure can be used to determine the best move a player can make given his evaluation function. Using the minimax procedure on the game tree for nim (Figure 5.32) we see that the value of the root node is $V(a) = 1$. Since $E(X)$ for this game was defined to be 1 if A was guaranteed to win, this means that if A makes the optimal move from node a then no matter what B's countermoves, A will win. The optimal move is to node b. One may readily verify that from b, A can win the game independent of B's countermove!

For games such as nim with $n = 6$, the game trees are sufficiently small that it is possible to generate the whole tree. Thus, it is a relatively simple matter to determine whether or not the game has a winning strategy. Moreover, for such games it is possible to make a decision on the next move by looking ahead all the way to terminal configurations. Games of this type are not very interesting since, assuming no errors are made by either player, the outcome of the game is predetermined and both players should use similar evaluation functions, i.e., $E_A(X) = 1$ for X a winning configuration and $E_A(X) = -1$ for X a losing configuration for A; $E_B(X) = -E_A(X)$.

Of greater interest are games such as chess where the game tree is too large to be generated in its entirety. It is estimated that the game tree for chess $> 10^{100}$ nodes. Even using a computer which is capable of generating 10^{11} nodes a second, the complete generation of the game tree for chess would require more than 10^{80} years. In games with large game trees the decision as to which move to make next can be made only by

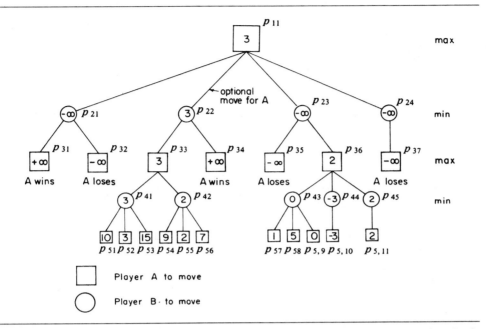

Figure 5.33 Portion of game tree for a hypothetical game; the value of terminal nodes is obtained from the evaluation function $E(x)$ for player A

looking at the game tree for the next few levels. The evaluation function $E(X)$ is used to get the values of the leaf nodes of the subtree generated, and then Eq. (5.3) can be used to get the values of the remaining nodes and hence to determine the next move. In a game such as chess it may be possible to generate only the next few levels (say six) of the tree. In such situations both the quality of the resulting game and its outcome will depend upon the quality of the evaluating functions being used by the two players as well as of the algorithm being used to determine $V(X)$ by minimax for the current game configuration. The efficiency of this algorithm will limit the number of nodes of the search tree that can be generated and so will have an effect on the quality of the game.

Let us assume that player A is a computer and attempt to write an algorithm that A can use to compute $V(X)$. It is clear that the procedure to compute $V(X)$ can also be used to determine the next move that A should make. A fairly simple recursive procedure to evaluate $V(X)$ using minimax can be obtained if we recast the definition of minimax into the following form:

$$
V'(X) = \begin{cases} e(X) & \text{if } X \text{ is a leaf of the subtree generated} \\ \max_{1 \le i \le d} \{-V'(c_i)\} & \text{if } X \text{ is not a leaf of the subtree generated and } c_i, \\ & 1 \le i \le d, \text{ are the children of } X \end{cases} \quad (5.4)
$$

where $e(X) = E(X)$ if X is a position from which A is to move and $e(X) = -E(X)$ otherwise.

Starting at a configuration X from which A is to move, one can easily prove that Eq. (5.4) computes $V'(X) = V(X)$ as given by Eq. (5.3). In fact, values for all nodes on levels from which A is to move are the same as given by Eq. (5.3) while values on other levels are the negative of those given by Eq. (5.3).

The recursive procedure to evaluate $V'(X)$ based on Eq. (5.4) is then $ve(X,l)$ (Program 5.19). This algorithm evaluates $V'(X)$ by generating only l levels of the game tree beginning with X as root. You may verify that this algorithm traverses the desired subtree of the game tree in postorder.

```
1  function ve (x : node ; l : integer) : integer;
2  {compute V'(n) by looking at most l moves ahead. e (x)
3   is the evaluation function for player A. For convenience,
4   it is assumed that starting from any board configuration x
5   the legal moves of the game permit a transition only to the
6   configurations c [1 .. d] if x is not a terminal
7   configuration.}
8  var ans : integer;
9      temp, i : integer;
10 begin
11    if terminal (x) or (l = 0)
12    then ve := e (x)
13    else
14    begin
15      ans := -ve (c [1], l - 1);
16      for i := 2 to d do
17      begin
18        temp := -ve (c [i ], l - 1)
19        if ans < temp then ans := temp
20      end;
21      ve := ans ;
22   end; {of if}
23 end; {of ve}
```

Program 5.19 Algorithm *ve*

An initial call to algorithm *ve* with $x = P_{11}$ and $l = 4$ for the hypothetical game of Figure 5.33 would result in the generation of the complete game tree. The values of various configurations would be determined in the order: $p_{31}, p_{32}, p_{21}, p_{51}, p_{52}, p_{53}, p_{41}, p_{54}, p_{55}, p_{56}, p_{42}, p_{33}, \ldots, p_{37}, p_{24}, p_{11}$. It is possible to introduce, with relative ease, some heuristics into algorithm *ve* that will result in the generation of only a portion of the possible configurations while still computing $V'(X)$ accurately.

Consider the game tree of Figure 5.33. After $V(p_{41})$ has been computed, it is known that $V(p_{33})$ is at least $V(p_{41}) = 3$. Next, when $V(p_{55})$ is determined to be 2, then we know then $V(p_{42})$ is at most 2. Since p_{33} is a max position, $V(p_{42})$ cannot affect $V(p_{33})$. Regardless of the values of the remaining children of p_{42}, the value of p_{33} is not determined by $V(p_{42})$ as $V(p_{42})$ cannot be more than $V(p_{41})$. This observation may be stated more formally as the following rule: The *alpha* value of a max position is defined to be the minimum possible value for that position. *If the value of a min position is determined to be less than or equal to the alpha value of its parent, then we may stop generation of the remaining children of this min position.* Termination of node generation under this rule is known as *alpha cutoff.* Once $V(p_{41})$ in Figure 5.33 is determined, the alpha value of p_{33} becomes 3. $V(p_{55}) \leq$ alpha value of p_{33} implies that p_{56} need not be generated.

A corresponding rule may be defined for min positions. The *beta* value of a min position is the maximum possible value for that position. *If the value of a max position is determined to be greater than or equal to the beta value of its parent node, then we may stop generation of the remaining children of this max position.* Termination of node generation under this rule is called *beta cutoff.* In Figure 5.33, once $V(p_{35})$ is determined, the beta value of p_{23} is known to be at most $-\infty$. Generation of p_{57}, p_{58}, p_{59} gives $V(p_{43}) = 0$. Thus, $V(p_{43})$ is greater than or equal to the beta value of p_{23} and we may terminate the generation of the remaining children of p_{36}. The two rules stated above may be combined together to get what is known as *alpha-beta pruning.* When alpha-beta pruning is used on Figure 5.33, the subtree with root p_{36} is not generated at all! This is because when the value of p_{23} is being determined the alpha value of p_{11} is 3. $V(p_{35})$ is less than the alpha value of p_{11} and so an alpha cutoff takes place. It should be emphasized that the alpha or beta value of a node is a dynamic quantity. Its value at any time during the game tree generation depends upon which nodes have so far been generated and evaluated.

In actually introducing alpha-beta pruning into algorithm *ve* it is necessary to restate this rule in terms of the values defined by Eq. (5.4). Under Eq. (5.4) all positions are max positions since the values of the min positions of Eq. (5.3) have been multiplied by -1. Let the *B*-value of a position be the minimum value that that position can have. The alpha-beta pruning rule now reduces to the following rule:

> *For any position X, let B be the B-value of its parent and let mb = −B. Then, if the value of X is determined to be greater than or equal to mb, we may terminate generation of the remaining children of X.*

Incorporating this rule into algorithm *ve* is fairly straightforward and results in algorithm *veb*. This algorithm has the additional parameter *mb* which is the negative of the *B*-value of the parent of *X*.

If *Y* is a position from which *A* is to move, then the initial call *veb* (*Y,l,maxinteger*) correctly computes $V'(Y)$ with an *l* move look ahead. Further pruning of the game tree may be achieved by realizing that the *B*-value of a node *X* places a lower bound on the value grandchildren of *X* must have in order to affect *X*'s value. Consider the subtree of

```
 1 function veb (x : node ; l,mb : integer) : integer;
 2 {determine V'(x) as in Eq. (5.4) using the B-rule and looking
 3   only l moves ahead.  Remaining assumptins and notations
 4   are the same as for algorithm ve. Configurations c [1..d] are global}
 5 var ans : integer;
 6     temp, i : integer;
 7 begin
 8 if terminal (x) or (l = 0)
 9   then veb := e (x)
10   else
11   begin
12      ans := -maxint
13      i := 1;
14      while (i ≤ d) and (ans < mb) do
15      begin
16         temp := -veb (c [i ], l − 1, −ans);
17         if ans < temp then ans := temp ;
18         i := i + 1;
19      end; {of if}
20      veb := ans ;
21   end; {of if}
22 end; {of veb}
```

Program 5.20 Algorithm veb

Figure 5.34(a). If $V'(GC(X)) \le B$ then $V'(C(X)) \ge -B$. Following the evaluation of $C(X)$, the B-value of X is max $\{B, -V'(C(X))\} = B$ as $V'(C(X)) \ge -B$. Hence unless $V'(GC(X)) > B$, it cannot affect $V'(X)$ and so B is a lower bound on the value $GC(X)$ should have. Incorporating this lower bound into algorithm veb yields algorithm ab (Program 5.21). The additional parameter lb is a lower bound on the value X should have.

We may easily verify that the initial call ab$(Y,l,mininteger,maxinteger)$ gives the same result as the call ve (Y,l).

Figure 5.34(b) shows a hypothetical game tree in which the use of algorithm ab results in greater pruning than achieved by algorithm veb. Let us first trace the action of veb on the tree of Figure 5.34(b). We assume the initial call to be veb $(p_1,l,$ **maxint**$)$ where l is the depth of the tree. After examining the left subtree of P_1, the B value of P_1 is set to 10 and nodes P_3, P_4, P_5, and P_6 are generated. Following this, $V'(P_6)$ is determined to be 9 and then the B-value of P_5 becomes -9. Using this, we continue to evaluate the node P_7. In the case of ab, however, since the B-value of P_1 is 10, the lower bound for P_4 is 10 and so the effective B-value of P_4 becomes 10. As a result the node P_7 is not generated since no matter what its value $V'(P_5) \ge -9$ and this will not enable

```
1  function ab (x : node ; l,lb,mb : integer) : integer;
2  {same as algorithm veb. lb is a lower bound on V´(x)}
3  var ans : integer;
4      temp,i : integer;
5  begin
6    if terminal (x) or (l = 0)
7    then ab := e (x)
8    else
9    begin
10     ans := lb ;
11     i := 1;
12     while (i ≤ d) and (ans < mb) do
13     begin
14       temp := −ab (c [i ], l − 1, −mb, −ans );
15       if ans < temp then ans := temp ;
16       i := i + 1;
17     end; {of while}
18     ab := ans ;
19   end; [of if}
20 end; {of ab}
```

Program 5.21 Algorithm *ab*

$V´(P_4)$ to reach its lower bound.

5.11 HEAPS

In Section 5.3, we defined a complete binary tree. In this section, we present a special form of a complete binary tree that is useful in many applications.

Definition: A *min tree* (*max tree*) is a tree in which the key value in each node is no larger (smaller) than the key values in its children (if any). □

Definition: A *max heap* is a complete binary tree that is also a max tree. A *min heap* is a complete binary tree that is also a min tree. □

Some example max heaps are shown in Figure 5.35 and some min heaps are shown in Figure 5.36. From the definitions it follows that the key in the root of a min tree is the smallest key in the tree while that in the root of a max tree is the largest.

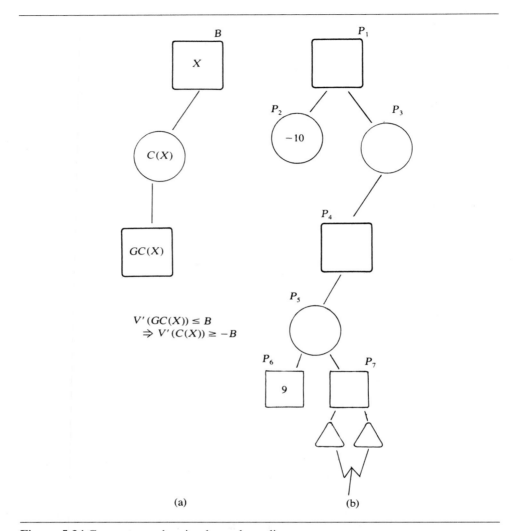

(a)   (b)

Figure 5.34 Games trees showing lower bounding

Heaps find application when a *priority queue* is to be maintained. In this kind of queue, the element to be deleted is the one with highest (or lowest) priority. At any time, an element with arbitrary priority can be inserted into the queue. In applications where an element with highest (lowest) priority is to be deleted each time, a max (min) heap may be used.

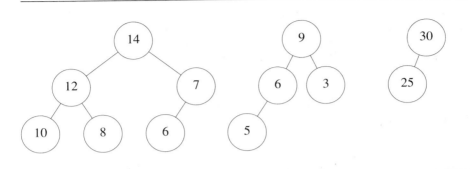

Figure 5.35 Max heaps

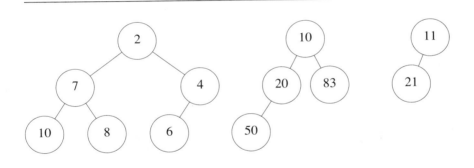

Figure 5.36 Min heaps

Example 5.4: Suppose that we are selling the services of a machine. Each user pays a fixed amount per use. However, the time needed by each user is different. We wish to maximize the returns from this machine under the assumption that the machine is not to be kept idle unless no user is available. This can be done by maintaining a priority queue of all persons waiting to use the machine. The value of the *key* field is the amount of time needed. Whenever the machine becomes available, the user with smallest time requirement is selected. Hence, a min heap is required. When a new user requests the machine, his/her request is put into the heap.

If each user needs the same amount of time on the machine but people are willing to pay different amounts for the service, then a priority queue on the amount of payment can be maintained. Whenever the machine becomes available, the user paying the most is selected. This requires a max heap. □

Example 5.5: Suppose that we are simulating a large factory. This factory has many machines and many jobs that require processing on some of these machines. An *event* is said to occur whenever a machine completes the processing of the job it is working on. When an event occurs, the job has to be moved to the queue for the next machine (if any) that it needs. If this queue is empty, the job can be assigned to the machine immediately. Also, a new job can be scheduled on the machine that has become idle (provided that its queue is not empty).

In order to determine the occurrence of events, a priority queue is used. This queue contains the finish time of all jobs that are presently being worked on. The next event occurs at the least time in the queue. So, a min heap can be used in this application. □

Before developing procedures to add to and delete from a heap, let us examine some other representations for a priority queue. We shall assume that each deletion removes the element with largest key value from the queue. The conclusions we draw are the same when the smallest element is to be deleted.

The simplest way to represent a priority queue is as an unordered linear list. Suppose that we have n elements each of size 1 in this queue. If the list is represented sequentially, additions are most easily performed at the end of this list. Hence, the insert time is $\Theta(1)$. A deletion requires a search for the element with largest key followed by its deletion. Since it takes $\Theta(n)$ time to find the largest element in an n element unordered list, the delete time is $\Theta(n)$. If a chain is used, additions can be performed at the front of the chain in $\Theta(1)$ time. Each deletion takes $\Theta(n)$ time. An alternative is to use an ordered linear list. The elements are in nondecreasing order in case a sequential representation is used and in nonincreasing order in case an ordered chain is used. The delete time for each representation is $\Theta(1)$ and the insert time $O(n)$. When a max heap is used, both additions and deletions can be performed in $O(\log n)$ time.

A max heap with five elements is shown in Figure 5.37(a). When an element is added to this heap, the resulting six element heap must have the structure shown in Figure 5.37(b). This is because a heap is a complete binary tree. If the element to be inserted has key value 1, it may be inserted as the left child of 2. If instead, the key value of the new element is 5, then this cannot be inserted as the left child of 2 (as otherwise, we will not have a max heap following the insertion). So, the 2 is moved down to its left child (Figure 5.37(c)) and we determine if placing the 5 at the old position of 2 results in a max heap. Since the parent element (20) is at least as large as the element (5) being inserted, it is all right to insert the new element at the position shown in the figure. Next, suppose that the new element has value 21 rather than 5. In this case, the 2 moves down to its left child as in Figure 5.37(c). The 21 cannot be inserted into the old position occupied by the 2 as the parent of this position is smaller than 21. Hence, the 20 is moved down to its right child and the 21 inserted in the root of the heap (Figure 5.37(d)).

To implement the insertion strategy described above, we need to go from an element to its parent. If a linked representation is used, an additional *parent* field is to be added to each node. However, since a heap is a complete binary tree, the formula based representation can be used. Lemma 5.3 enables us to locate the parent of any element

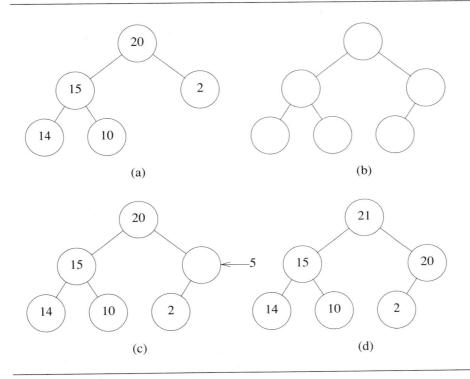

Figure 5.37 Insertion into a max heap

easily. Program 5.22 performs an insertion into a max heap that contains n elements. This assumes that *heap* is an array with allowable indexes in the range 1..*MaxElements*. Further, it is assumed that the type *element* is a record with a *key* field in addition to other fields. As a complete binary tree with n elements has a height $\lceil \log_2(n+1) \rceil$, the **while** loop of the insertion procedure is iterated O($\log n$) times.

When an element is to be deleted from a max heap, it is taken from the root of the heap. For instance, a deletion from the heap of Figure 5.37(d) results in the removal of the element 21. Since the resulting heap has only five elements in it, the binary tree of Figure 5.37(d) needs to be restructured to correspond to a complete binary tree with five elements. To do this, we remove the element in position 6, i.e., the element 2. Now, we have the right structure (Figure 5.38(a)) but the root is vacant and the element 2 is not in the heap. If the 2 is inserted into the root, the resulting binary tree is not a max heap. The element at the root should be the largest from among the 2 and the elements in the left and right children of the root. This element is 20. It is moved into the root thereby creating a vacancy in position 3. Since this position has no children, the 2 may be inserted here. The resulting heap is shown in Figure 5.37(a).

```
procedure InsertMaxHeap (x : element);
{Insert x into the global max heap heap [1..MaxElements ]}
{n is the present size of the heap}
var i : integer; NotDone : boolean;
begin
   if n = MaxElements then HeapFull
   else begin
         n := n +1; i := n; NotDone := true;
         while NotDone do
            if i := 1 then NotDone := false {at root}
            else if x.key <= heap [i div 2].key then NotDone := false
               else begin {move from parent to i}
                     heap [i ] := heap [i div 2];
                     i := i div 2;
                  end;
         heap [i ] := x;
      end; {of if n = MaxElemenets}
end; {of InsertMaxHeap}
```

Program 5.22 Insertion into a max heap

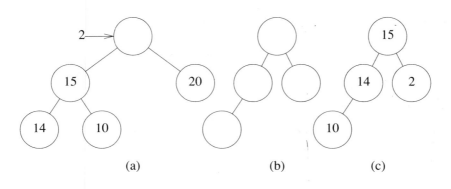

(a)   (b)   (c)

Figure 5.38 Deletion from a heap

Now, suppose we wish to perform another deletion. The 20 is to be deleted. Following the deletion, the heap has the binary tree structure shown in Figure 5.38(b). To get this structure, the 10 is removed from position 5. It cannot be inserted into the root as it is not large enough. The 15 moves to the root and we attempt to insert the 10 into position 2. This is, however, smaller than the 14 below it. So, the 14 is moved up and the 10 inserted into position 4. The resulting heap is shown in Figure 5.38(c).

Program 5.23 implements this strategy to delete from a heap. Once again, since the height of a heap with n elements is $\lceil \log_2(n+1) \rceil$, the **while** loop of this procedure is iterated $O(\log n)$ times. Hence the complexity of a deletion is $O(\log n)$.

```
procedure DeleteMaxHeap (var x : element);
{Delete from the max heap heap [1..MaxElements ]}
{n is the current heap size}
var i, r, j : integer; k : element; NotDone : boolean;
begin
    if n = 0 then HeapEmpty
    else begin
            NotDone := true; x := heap [1]; k := heap [n]; n := n − 1;
            i := 1; j := 2; {j is left child of i}
            while (j <= n) and NotDone do
            begin
                if j < n then if heap [j].key < heap [j +1].key then j := j +1;
                {j points to larger child}
                if k.key >= heap [j].key then NotDone := false
                                    else begin
                                            heap [i] := heap [j]; {move child up}
                                            {move i and j down}
                                            i := j; j := 2∗j;
                                        end;
            end;
            heap [i] := k;
        end;
end; {of DeleteMaxHeap}
```

Program 5.23 Deleting from a max heap

5.12 BINARY SEARCH TREES

While a heap is well suited for applications that require priority queues, it is not suited for applications in which arbitrary elements are to be deleted from the element list. Deletion of an arbitrary element from an n element heap takes $O(n)$ time. This is no better than the time needed for arbitrary deletions from an unordered linear list.

A *binary search tree* has a better performance than any of the data structures studied so far when the functions to be performed are search, insert, and delete. In fact, with a binary search tree, these functions can be performed both by key value and by rank (i.e., find an element with key x; find the fifth smallest element; delete the element with key x; delete the fifth smallest element; insert an element and determine its rank).

Definition: A *binary search tree* is a binary tree. It may be empty. If it is not empty then it satisfies the following properties:

(1)   Every element has a key and no two elements have the same key, i.e., all keys are distinct.

(2)   The keys (if any) in the left subtree are smaller than the key in the root.

(3)   The keys (if any) in the right subtree are larger than the key in the root.

(4)   The left and right subtrees are also binary search trees. □

There is some redundancy in the above definition. Properties (2), (3), and (4) together imply that the keys must be distinct. So, property (1) can be replaced by the property: The root has a key. The definition provided above is, however, clearer than the nonredundant version.

Some example binary trees in which the elements have distinct keys are shown in Figure 5.39. The tree of Figure 5.39(a) is not a binary search tree. This is so despite the fact that it satisfies properties (1), (2), and (3). The right subtree fails to satisfy property (4). This subtree is not a binary search tree as its right subtree has a key value (22) that is smaller than that in the subtree's root (25). The binary trees of Figure 5.39(b) and (c) are binary search trees.

Searching A Binary Search Tree

Since the definition of a binary search tree is recursive, it is easiest to describe a recursive search method. Suppose we wish to search for an element with key x. We begin at the root. If the root is **nil**, then the search tree contains no elements and the search is unsuccessful. Otherwise, we compare x with the key in the root. If x equals this key, then the search terminates successfully. If x is less than the key in the root, then no element in the right subtree can have key value x and only the left subtree is to be searched. If x is larger than the key in the root, only the right subtree needs to be searched. The subtrees may be searched recursively as in Program 5.24. This function assumes a linked representation for the search tree. Each node has the three fields: *LeftChild*, *RightChild*, and *data*. *data* is of type *element* and has at least the field *key* which is of type **integer**.

The recursion of Program 5.24 is easily replaced by a **while** loop as in Program 5.25.

In case we wish to search by rank, each node should have an additional field *LeftSize* which is one plus the number of elements in the left subtree of the node. For the search tree of Figure 5.39(b), the nodes with keys 2, 5, 30, and 40, respectively, have

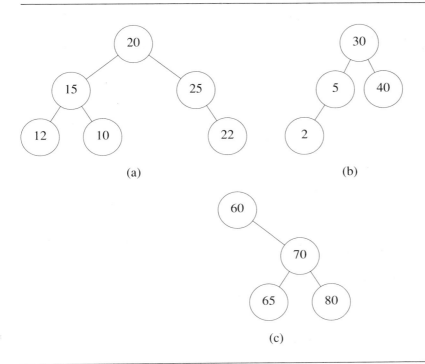

Figure 5.39 Binary trees

```
function search (t : TreePointer ; x : integer): TreePointer;
{Search the binary search tree t for an element with key x}
{Return a pointer to the element if it is found.  Return nil otherwise.}
begin
   if t = nil then search := nil
   else if x = t↑.data.key then search := t
       else if x < t↑.data.key then search := search (t↑.LeftChild, x)
           else search := search (t↑.RightChild, x);
end; {of search}
```

Program 5.24 Recursive search of a binary search tree

```
function search (t : TreePointer ; x : integer): TreePointer;
{Search the binary search tree t for an element with key x}
{Return a pointer to the element if it is found.  Return nil otherwise.}
var p : TreePointer; NotFound : boolean;
begin
  p := t; NotFound := true;

  while (p < > nil) and NotFound do
    if x = p↑.data.key then NotFound := false
    else if  x < p↑.data.key then p := p↑.LeftChild
                      else p := p↑.RightChild;

  if NotFound then search := nil
              else search := p;
end; {of search}
```

Program 5.25 Iterative search of a binary search tree

LeftSize equal to 1, 2, 3, and 1. Program 5.26 searches for the k'th smallest element.

```
function search (t : TreePointer ; k : integer): TreePointer;
{Search the binary search tree t for the kth smallest element}
{Return a pointer to the element if it is found.  Return nil otherwise.}
var p : TreePointer; NotFound : boolean; i : integer;
begin
  p := t; NotFound := true; i := k;

  while (p < > nil) and NotFound do
    if i = p↑.LeftSize then NotFound := false
    else if  i < p↑.LeftSize then p := p↑.LeftChild
        else begin
              i := i – LeftSize; {search for ith in right subtree}
              p := p↑.RightChild;
            end;

  if NotFound then search := nil
              else search := p;
end; {of search}
```

Program 5.26 Searching a binary search tree by rank

As can be seen, a binary search tree of height h can be searched by key as well as by rank in $O(h)$ time.

Insert

To insert a new element x, we must first verify that its key is different from those of existing elements. To do this a search is carried out. If the search is unsuccessful, then the element is inserted at the point the search terminated. For instance, to insert an element with key 80 into the tree of Figure 5.39(b), we first search for 80. This search terminates unsuccessfully and the last node examined is the one with key 40. The new element is inserted as the right child of this node. The resulting search tree is shown in Figure 5.40(a). Figure 5.40(b) shows the result of inserting the key 50 into the search tree of Figure 5.40(a).

Program 5.27 implements the insert strategy just described. In case nodes have a *LeftSize* field, then this is to be updated too. Regardless, the insertion can be performed in $O(h)$ time where h is the height of the search tree.

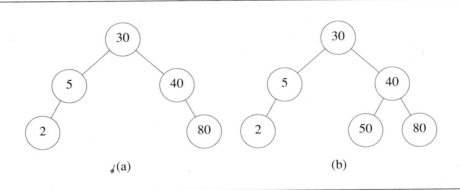

(a)   (b)

Figure 5.40 Inserting into a binary search tree

Delete

Deletion of a leaf element is quite easy. To delete 50 from the tree of Figure 5.40(b), the left child field of its parent is set to **nil** and the node disposed. This gives us the tree of Figure 5.40(a). To delete the 80, the right child field of 40 is set to **nil** obtaining the tree of Figure 5.39(b) and the node containing 80 disposed.

The deletion of a nonleaf element that has only one child is also easy. The node containing the element to be deleted is erased and the single child takes the place of the erased node. So, to delete the element 5 from the tree of Figure 5.40 (a), we simply change the pointer from the parent node (i.e., the node containing 30) to the single child node (i.e., the node containing 2).

```
procedure insert (var t : TreePointer ; x : element ; var success : boolean);
{Insert x into the binary search tree t}
var p, q : TreePointer; NotFound : boolean;
begin
   {Search for x.key.  q is parent of p}
   q := nil; p := t; NotDone := true;
   while (p < > nil) and NotFound do
      q := p;  {save p}
      if x.key = p↑.data.key then NotFound := false
      else if x.key < p↑.data.key then p :=p ↑.LeftChild
                              else p := p ↑.RightChild;

   {Perform insertion}
   if NotFound then success := false {x.key already in t}
   else begin {insert into t}
         new (p);
         with p↑ do
         begin
           LeftChild := nil; RightChild := nil; data := x;
         end;
         if q = nil
         then t := q
         else if x.key < q↑.data.key then q↑.LeftChild := p
                                 else q↑.RightChild := p;
         success := true;
      end;
end; {of insert}
```

Program 5.27 Insertion into a binary search tree

When the element to be deleted is in a nonleaf node that has two children, the element is replaced by either the largest element in its left subtree or the smallest one in its right subtree. Then we proceed to delete this replacing element from the subtree from which it was taken. For instance, if we wish to delete the element with key 30 from the tree of Figure 5.40(b), then we replace it by either the largest element, 5, in its left subtree or the smallest element, 40, in its right subtree. Suppose we opt for the largest element in the left subtree. The 5 is moved into the root and the tree of Figure 5.41(a) obtained. Now we must delete the second 5. Since this node has only one child, the pointer from its parent is changed to point to this child. The tree of Figure 5.41(b) obtained.

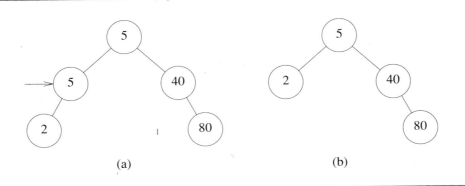

Figure 5.41 Deletion from a binary search tree

We leave the writing of the deletion procedure as an exercise. It should be evident that a deletion can be performed in O(h) time if the search tree has a height of h.

Height of a Binary Search Tree

Unless care is taken, the height of a binary search tree with n elements can become as large as n. This is the case, for instance, when Program 5.27 is used to insert the keys $[1, 2, 3, \ldots, n]$, in this order, into an initially empty binary search tree. It can, however, be shown that when insertions and deletions are made at random using the procedures given above, the height of the binary search tree is O(log n) on the average.

Search trees with a worst case height of O(log$n$) are called *balanced search trees*. Balanced search trees that permit searches, inserts, and deletes to be performed in O(h) time exist. Most notable among these are AVL and B trees. You are referred to the books by Knuth, Horowitz, and Sahni that are cited in the readings section for a discussion of these balanced search trees.

5.13 SELECTION TREES

Suppose we have k ordered sequences that are to be merged into a single ordered sequence. Each sequence consists of some number of records and is in nondecreasing order of a designated field called the *key*. An ordered sequence is called a *run*. Let n be the number of records in the k runs together. The merging task can be accomplished by repeatedly outputting the record with the smallest key. The smallest has to be found from k possibilities and it could be the leading record in any of the k-runs. The most direct way to merge k-runs would be to make $k - 1$ comparisons to determine the next record to output. For $k > 2$, we can achieve a reduction in the number of comparisons needed to find the next smallest element by using the idea of a selection tree. A *selection tree* is a binary tree where each node represents the smaller of its two children. Thus, the root node represents the smallest node in the tree. Figure 5.42 illustrates a selection tree for the case $k = 8$.

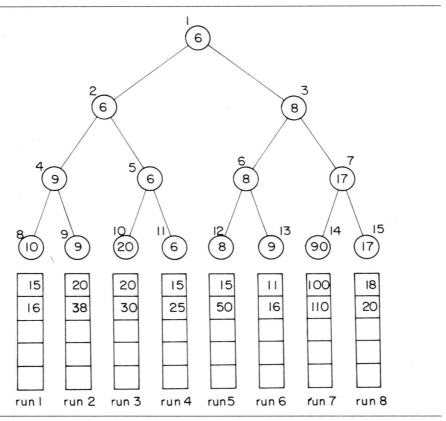

Figure 5.42 Selection tree for $k = 8$ showing the first three keys in each of the eight runs

    The construction of this selection tree may be compared to the playing of a tournament in which the winner is the record with the smaller key. Then, each nonleaf node in the tree represents the winner of a tournament and the root node represents the overall winner or the smallest key. A leaf node here represents the first record in the corresponding run. Since the records being merged are generally large, each node will contain only a pointer to the record it represents. Thus, the root node contains a pointer to the first record in run 4. The selection tree may be represented using the sequential allocation scheme for binary trees that results from Lemma 5.3. The number above each node in Figure 5.42 represents the address of the node in this sequential representation.

The record pointed to by the root has the smallest key and so may be output. Now, the next record from run 4 enters the selection tree. It has a key value of 15. To restructure the tree, the tournament has to be replayed only along the path from node 11 to the root. Thus, the winner from nodes 10 and 11 is again node 11 (15 < 20). The winner from nodes 4 and 5 is node 4 (9 < 15). The winner from 2 and 3 is node 3 (8 < 9). The new tree is shown in Figure 5.43. The tournament is played between sibling nodes and the result put in the parent node. Lemma 5.3 may be used to compute the address of sibling and parent nodes efficiently. After each comparison the next takes place at one higher level in the tree. The number of levels in the tree is $\lceil \log_2 k \rceil + 1$. So, the time to restruc-ture the tree is $O(\log_2 k)$. The tree has to be restructured each time a record is merged into the output file. Hence, the time required to merge all n records is $O(n \log_2 k)$. The time required to set up the selection tree the first time is $O(k)$. Hence, the total time needed to merge the k runs is $O(n \log_2 k)$.

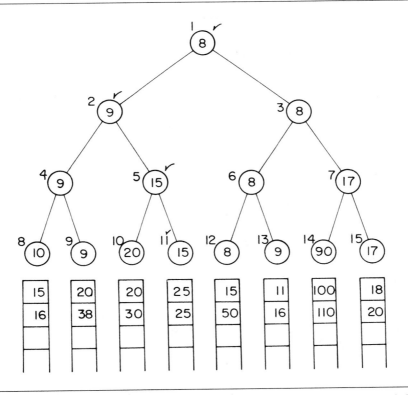

Figure 5.43 Selection tree of Figure 5.42 after one record has been output and the tree restructured (nodes that were changed are ticked)

A slightly faster algorithm results if each node represents the loser of the tournament rather than the winner. After the record with smallest key is output, the selection tree of Figure 5.42 is to be restructured. Since the record with the smallest key value is in run 4, this restructuring involves inserting the next record from this run into the tree. The next record has key value 15. Tournaments are played between sibling nodes along the path from node 11 to the root. Since these sibling nodes represent the losers of tournaments played earlier, we would simplify the restructuring process by placing in each nonleaf node a pointer to the record that loses the tournament rather than to the winner of the tournament. A tournament tree in which each nonleaf node retains a pointer to the loser is called a *tree of losers*. Figure 5.44 shows the tree of losers corresponding to the selection tree of Figure 5.42. For convenience, each node contains the key value of a record rather than a pointer to the record represented. The leaf nodes represent the first record in each run. An additional node, node 0, has been added to represent the overall winner of the tournament. Following the output of the overall winner, the tree is restructured by playing tournaments along the path from node 11 to node 1. The records with which these tournaments are to be played are readily available from the parent nodes.

5.14 COUNTING BINARY TREES

As a conclusion to our chapter on trees, we determine the number of distinct binary trees having n nodes. We know that if $n = 0$ or $n = 1$ there is one such tree. If $n = 2$, then there are two distinct binary trees (Figure 5.45) and if $n = 3$, there are five (Figure 5.46). How many distinct binary trees are there with n nodes?

Before solving this problem let us look at some other counting problems that are equivalent to this one.

In Section 5.4 we introduced the notion of preorder, inorder and postorder traversals. Suppose we are given the preorder sequence

$$A B C D E F G H I$$

and the inorder sequence

$$B C A E D G H F I$$

of the same binary tree. Does such a pair of sequences uniquely define a binary tree? Asked another way, can the above pair of sequences come from more than one binary tree? We can construct the binary tree which has these sequences by noticing that the first letter in preorder, A, must be the root and by definition of inorder all nodes preceding A must occur in the left subtree and the remaining nodes occur in the right subtree.

This gives us Figure 5.47(a) as our first approximation to the correct tree. Moving right in the preorder sequence we find B as the next root and from the inorder we see B has an empty left subtree and C is in its right subtree. This gives us Figure 5.47(b) as the

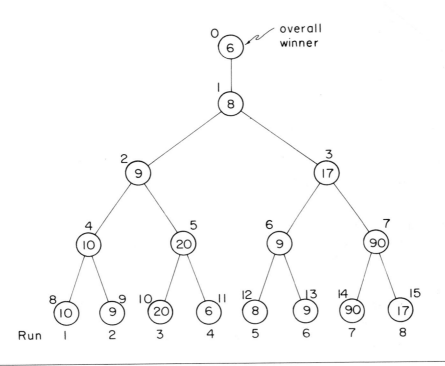

Figure 5.44 Tree of losers corresponding to Figure 5.42

and

Figure 5.45 Distinct binary trees with $n = 2$

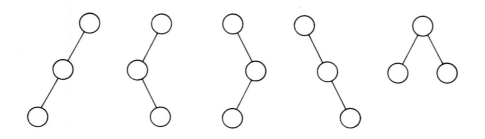

Figure 5.46 Distinct binary trees with $n = 3$

next approximation. Continuing in this way, we arrive at the binary tree of Figure 5.47(c). By formalizing this argument (see the exercises) we can verify that every binary tree has a unique pair of preorder-inorder sequences.

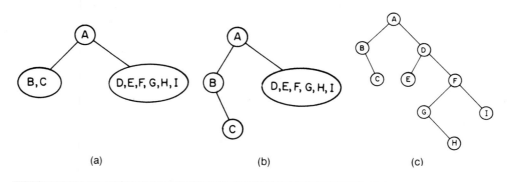

Figure 5.47 Constructing a binary tree from its inorder and preorder sequences

Let the nodes of an n node binary tree be numbered 1 to n. The *inorder permutation* defined by such a binary tree is the order in which its nodes are visited during an inorder traversal of the tree. A *preorder permutation* is similarly defined.

As an example, consider the binary tree of Figure 5.47(c) with the node numbering of Figure 5.48. Its preorder permutation is 1, 2, . . ., 9 and its inorder permutation is 2, 3, 1, 5, 4, 7, 8, 6, 9.

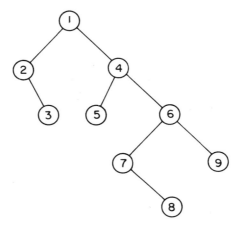

Figure 5.48 Binary tree of Figure 5.47(c) with its nodes numbered

If the nodes of a binary tree are numbered such that its preorder permutation is 1,2, ..., n, then from our earlier discussion it follows that distinct binary trees define distinct inorder permutations. The number of distinct binary trees is thus equal to the number of distinct inorder permutations obtainable from binary trees having the preorder permutation 1, 2, ..., n.

Using this concept of an inorder permutation, it is possible to show that the number of distinct permutations obtainable by passing the numbers 1 to n through a stack and deleting in all possible ways is equal to the number of distinct binary trees with n nodes (see the exercises). If we start with the numbers 1, 2, 3, then the possible permutations obtainable by a stack are

$$1,2,3; \; 1,3,2; \; 2,1,3; \; 2,3,1; \; 3,2,1;$$

It is not possible to obtain 3, 1, 2. Each of these five permutations corresponds to one of the five distinct binary trees with 3 nodes (Figure 5.49).

Another problem which surprisingly has connection with the previous two is the following: we have a product of n matrices

$$M_1 * M_2 * M_3 * \ldots * M_n$$

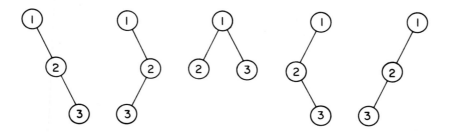

Figure 5.49 Binary trees corresponding to five permutations

that we wish to compute. We can perform these operations in any order because multiplication of matrices is associative. We ask the questions: how many different ways can we perform these multiplications? For example, if $n = 3$, there are two possibilities

$$(M_1 * M_2) * M_3 \text{ and } M_1 * (M_2 * M_3)$$

and if $n = 4$, there are five ways

$$((M_1 * M_2) * M_3) * M_4$$
$$(M_1 * (M_2 * M_3)) * M_4$$
$$M_1 * ((M_2 * M_3) * M_4)$$
$$(M_1 * (M_2 * (M_3 * M_4)))$$
$$((M_1 * M_2) * (M_3 * M_4))$$

Let b_n be the number of different ways to compute the product of n matrices. Then $b_2 = 1, b_3 = 2, b_4 = 5$. Let $M_{ij}, i \leq j$, be the product $M_i * M_{i+1} * \ldots * M_j$. The product we wish to compute is M_{1n}. M_{1n} may be computed by computing any one of the products $M_{1i} * M_{i+1,n}$ $1 \leq i < n$. The number of ways to obtain M_{1i} and $M_{i+1,n}$ are b_i and b_{n-i}, respectively. Therefore, letting $b_1 = 1$ we have:

$$b_n = \sum_{1 \leq i \leq n-1} b_i b_{n-i}, n > 1$$

If we can determine expression for b_n only in terms of n, then we have a solution to our problem. Now instead let b_n be the number of distinct binary trees with n nodes. Again an expression for b_n in terms of n is what we want. Then we see that b_n is the sum of all possible binary trees formed in the following way, a root and two subtrees with b_i and b_{n-i-1} nodes, for $0 \leq i \leq n - 1$ (Figure 5.50). This says that

$$b_n = \sum_{0 \leq i \leq n-1} b_i \, b_{n-i-1}, \, n \geq 1 \text{ and } b_0 = 1 \qquad (5.5)$$

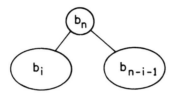

Figure 5.50 Decomposing b_n

This formula and the previous one are essentially the same.

So, *the number of binary trees with n nodes, the number of permutations of 1 to n obtainable with a stack, and the number of ways to multiply n + 1 matrices are all equal to the same number!*

To obtain this number we must solve the recurrence of Eq. (5.5). To begin we let

$$B(x) = \sum_{i \geq 0} b_i \, x^i \qquad (5.6)$$

which is the generating function for the number of binary trees. Next, observe that by the recurrence relation we get the identity

$$x \, B^2(x) = B(x) - 1$$

Using the formula to solve quadratics and the fact (Eq. (5.5)) that $B(0) = b_0 = 1$ we get:

$$B(x) = \frac{1 - \sqrt{1 - 4x}}{2x}$$

It is not clear at this point that we have made any progress but by using the binomial theorem to expand $(1 - 4x)^{1/2}$ we get

$$B(x) = \frac{1}{2x} \left[1 - \sum_{n \geq 0} \binom{1/2}{n} (-4x)^n \right]$$

(5.7)

$$= \sum_{m \geq 0} \binom{1/2}{m+1} (-1)^m 2^{2m+1} x^m$$

Comparing Eqs. (5.6) and (5.7) we see that b_n, which is the coefficient of x^n in $B(x)$, is:

$$\binom{1/2}{n+1} (-1)^n 2^{2n+1}$$

Some simplification yields the more compact form

$$b_n = \frac{1}{n+1} \binom{2n}{n}$$

which is approximately

$$b_n = O(4^n / n^{3/2})$$

5.15 REFERENCES AND SELECTED READINGS

For other representations of trees see: *The Art of Computer Programming: Fundamental Algorithms*, by D. Knuth, second edition, Addison-Wesley, Reading, 1973.

For the use of trees in generating optimal compiled code see: *Compilers: Principles, Techniques, and Tools*, by A. Aho, R. Sethi, and J. Ullman, Addison Wesley, Massachusetts, 1986.

Tree traversal algorithms may be found in: "Scanning list structures without stacks and tag bits," by G. Lindstrom, *Information Processing Letters*, vol. 2, no. 2, June 1973, pp. 47-51, and "Simple algorithms for traversing a tree without an auxiliary stack," by B. Dwyer, *Information Processing Letters*, vol. 2, no. 5, Dec. 1973, pp. 143-145.

For a further analysis of the set representation problem see: *Fundamentals of Computer Algorithms*, E. Horowitz and S. Sahni, Computer Science Press, Maryland, 1978.

The computing time analysis of the UNION-FIND algorithms may be found in: "Efficiency of a good but not linear set union algorithm," by R. Tarjan, *JACM*, vol. 22, no. 2, April 1975, pp. 215-225.

For more on game playing see: *Problem Solving Methods in Artificial Intelligence*, by N. Nilsson, McGraw-Hill, New York, 1971, and *Artificial Intelligence: The Heuristic Programming Approach*, by J. Slagle, McGraw-Hill, New York, 1971.

Additional data structures that employ trees may be found in: *Data Structures and Network Algorithms*, by R. Tarjan, Society for Industrial and Applied Mathematics, CBMS 44, 1983.

5.16 EXERCISES

1. For the binary tree of Figure 5.51 list the terminal nodes, the nonterminal nodes, and the level of each node.

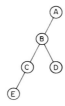

Figure 5.51 Binary tree for Exercise 1

2. Draw the internal memory representation of the above binary tree using (a) sequential, (b) linked, and (c) threaded linked representations.

3. Write a procedure which reads in a tree represented as a list as in Section 5.1 and creates its internal representation using nodes with three fields, *tag, data, link*.

4. Write a procedure which reverses the above process and takes a pointer to a tree and prints out its list representation.

5. Write a nonrecursive version of procedure *preorder*.

6. Write a nonrecursive version of procedure *postorder* without using **goto**s.

7. Rework *inorder3* so it is as fast as possible. (Hint: minimize the stacking and the testing within the loop.)

8. Write a nonrecursive version of procedure *postorder* using only a fixed amount of additional space. (See Exercise 36 for details.)

9. Do the preceding exercise for the case of *preorder*.

10. Given a tree of names constructed as described in Section 5.5 prove that an inorder traversal will always print the names in alphabetical order.

Exercises 11-13 assume a linked representation for a binary tree.

11. Write an algorithm to list the *data* fields of the nodes of a binary tree T by level. Within levels nodes are to be listed left to right.

12. Give an algorithm to count the number of leaf nodes in a binary tree T. What is its computing time?

13. Write an algorithm *swaptree* (t) which takes a binary tree and swaps the left and right children of every node. An example is given in Figure 5.52.

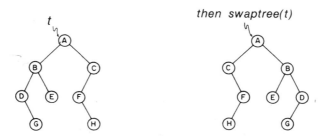

Figure 5.52 A *swaptree* example

14. Devise an external representation for formulas in the propositional calculus. Write a procedure which reads such a formula and creates a binary tree representation of it. How efficient is your procedure?

15. Procedure *PostOrderEval* must be able to distinguish between the symbols ∧, ∨, ¬, and a pointer in the *data* field of a node. How should this be done?

16. What is the computing time for *PostOrderEval*? First determine the logical parameters.

17. Write an algorithm which inserts a new node t as the left child of node s in a threaded binary tree. The left pointer of s becomes the left pointer of t.

18. Write a procedure which traverses a threaded binary tree in postorder. What are the time and space requirements of your method?

19. Define the inverse transformation of the one which creates the associated binary tree from a forest. Are these transformations unique?

20. Prove that preorder traversal on trees and preorder traversal on the associated binary tree gives the same result.

21. Prove that inorder traversal for trees and inorder traversal on the associated binary tree give the same result.

22. Using the result of Example 5.3, draw the trees after processing the instruction *union*(12,10).

23. Consider the hypothetical game tree of Figure 5.53.

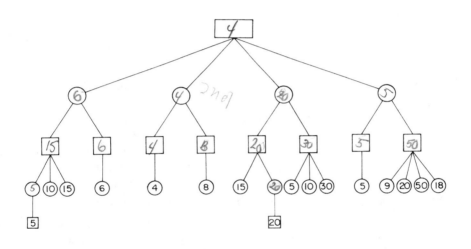

Figure 5.53 A hypothetical game tree

(a) Using the minimax technique, Eq. (5.3), obtain the value of the root node.

(b) What move should player *A* make?

(c) List the nodes of this game tree in the order in which their value is computed by algorithm *ve*.

(d) Using Eq. (5.4), compute $V'(X)$ for every node X in the tree.

(e) Which nodes of this tree are not evaluated during the computation of the value of the root node using algorithm *ab* with x = root, l = **maxint**, lb = −**maxint**, and mb = **maxint**?

24. Show that $V'(X)$ computed by Eq. (5.4) is the same as $V(X)$ computed by Eq. (5.3) for all nodes on levels from which A is to move. For all other nodes show that $V(X)$ computed by Eq. (5.3) is the negative of $V'(X)$ computed by Eq. (5.4).

25. Show that algorithm *ab* when initially called with $lb = -$**maxint**, and $mb =$ **maxint** yields the same results as *ve* does for the same X and l.

26. Prove that every binary tree is uniquely defined by its preorder and inorder sequences.

27. Do the inorder and postorder sequences of a binary tree uniquely define the binary tree? Prove your answer.

28. Answer the preceding exercise for preorder and postorder.

29. Write an algorithm to construct the binary tree with a given preorder and inorder sequence.

30. Do the preceding exercise for inorder and postorder.

31. Prove that the number of distinct permutations of $1,2,\ldots,n$ obtainable by a stack is equal to the number of distinct binary trees with n nodes. (Hint: Use the concept of an inorder permutation of a tree with preorder permutation $1,2,\ldots,n$).

32. Using Stirling's formula derive the more accurate value of the number of binary trees with n nodes,

$$b_n = (4^n/n^{3/2}\,\pi^{1/2})(1 + O(1/n))$$

33. Consider threading a binary tree using preorder threads rather than inorder threads as in the text. Is it possible to traverse a binary tree in preorder without a stack using these threads?

34. Write an algorithm for traversing an inorder threaded binary tree in preorder.

35. The operation $PREORD\,(btree) \rightarrow queue$ returns a queue whose elements are the data items of btree in preorder. Using the operation $APPENDQ\,(queue,\ queue) \rightarrow queue$ which concatenates two queues, $PREORD$ can be axiomatized by

        PREORD (CREATE) :: = MTQ
        PREORD (MAKEBT(p,d,r)) :: =
           APPENDQ (APPENDQ (ADDQ (MTQ,d),PREORD(p)), PREORD(r))

Devise similar axioms for inorder and postorder.

36. Program 5.28 performs an inorder traversal without using threads, a stack or a *parent* field. Verify that the algorithm is correct by running it on a variety of binary trees which cause every statement to execute at least once. Before attempting to study this algorithm be sure you understand *mark2* of Section 4.9.

```
 1  procedure inorder4(t : TreePointer);
 2  {inorder traversal of binary tree t using a fixed
 3  amount of additional storage}
 4  label 1, 80, 99;
 5  var top, LastRight : TreePointer;
 6  p, q, r, av, r1 : TreePointer;
 7  begin
 8  if t = nil then goto 99; {empty binary tree}
 9  top := nil; LastRight := nil; p := t: q := t;
10  repeat
11      repeat
12          if (p↑.LeftChild = nil) and (p↑.RightChild = nil
13          then {cannot move down}
14                  begin
15                  writeln(p↑.data); goto 1
16                  end
17          else if p↑.LeftChild = nil then {move to p↑.RightChild}
18                          begin
19                              writeln(p↑.data);
20                              r := p↑.RightChild; p↑.RightChild :=q;
21                              q := p; p := r;
22                          end
23                          else {move to p↑.LeftChild}
24                                  begin
25                                  r :=p↑.LeftChild;p↑.LeftChild := q;
26                                  q :=p; p := r;
27                                  end
28      until false;
29  {p is a leaf node, move upwards to a node whose right
30   subtree hasn't yet been examined}
31  1: av := p;
32      repeat
33          if p = t then goto 99;
34          if q↑.LeftChild = nil
35          then begin
36                  r := q↑.RightChild; q↑.RightChild := p;
37                  p := q; q := r;
38              end
39          else if q↑.RightChild = nil
40              then  begin {q is linked via LeftChild}
41                  r := q↑.LeftChild;q↑.lefchild := p;
42                  p := q; q := r; writeln(p↑.data);
43                      end
```

```
44            else {check if p is RightChild of q}
45            if q = LastRight then begin
46                 r := top ; LastRight := r↑.LeftChild;
47                 top := r↑.RightChild ;   {unstack}
48                 r↑.LeftChild := nil; r↑.RightChild := nil;
49                 r :=q↑.RightChild ; q↑.RightChild :=p ;
50                 p := q ; q :=r ; end
51            else begin {p is a LeftChild of q}
52                 writeln(q↑.data) {visit q}
53                 av↑.LeftChild := LastRight ; av↑.RightChild := top ;
54                 top := av ; LastRight ; av↑.RightChild := top ;
55                 r :=q↑.LeftChild; q↑.LeftChild := p ; {restore
                       link to p}
56                 r1 := q↑.RightChild ; q↑.RightChild := r ;
57                 p := r1; goto 80;
58                 {move right}
59                     end
60      until false;
61  80: {dummy statement}
62  until false;
63  99: end; {of inorder4}
```

Program 5.28 Inorder4

37. [Wilczynski] Following the conventions of LISP assume nodes with two fields:
     HEAD and *TAIL*. If $A = ((a(bc)))$ then $HEAD(A) = (a(bc))$, $TAIL(A) = NIL$,
     $HEAD(HEAD(A)) = a$, $TAIL(HEAD(A)) = ((bc))$. $CONS(A,B)$ gets a new node T,
     stores A in its *HEAD*, B in its *TAIL*, and returns T. B must always be a list. If
     $L = a$, $M = (bc)$ then $CONS(L,M) = (abc)$, $CONS(M,M) = ((bc)bc)$. Three other
     useful functions are: $ATOM(X)$ which is true if X is an atom else false, $NULL(X)$
     which is true if X is NIL else false, $EQUAL(X,Y)$ which is true if X and Y are the
     same atoms or equivalent lists else false.

     (a) Give a sequence of *HEAD*, *TAIL* operations for extracting a from the lists:
          $((cat)),((a)),((mart)),(((cb))a)$.

     (b) Write recursive procedures for *COPY, REVERSE, APPEND*.

     (c) Implement this "LISP" subsystem. Store atoms in an array, write pro-
          cedures *makelist* and *listprint* for input and output of lists.

38. Write a Pascal procedure to delete an element X from a binary search tree T.

39. Write a Pascal procedure to merge k runs using a tree of winners.

40. Write a Pascal procedure to merge k runs using a tree of losers. Compare the run time of this procedure with that for the procedure of the previous exercise.

41. Write an algorithm to construct a tree of losers for records R_i, $1 \le i \le k$, with key values K_i, $1 \le i \le k$. Let the tree nodes be T_i, $0 \le i < k$, with T_i, $1 \le i < k$, a pointer to the loser of a tournament and T_0 a pointer to the overall winner. Show that this construction can be carried out in time $O(k)$.

42. Write an algorithm, using a tree of losers, to carry out a k-way merge of k runs, $k \ge 2$. Show that if there are n records in the k runs together, then the computing time is $O(n \log_2 k)$.

43. Write a procedure to delete the element with key x from the binary search tree T. What is the time complexity of your procedure?

CHAPTER 6
GRAPHS

6.1 TERMINOLOGY AND REPRESENTATIONS

6.1.1 Introduction

The first recorded evidence of the use of graphs dates back to 1736 when Euler used them to solve the now classical Koenigsberg bridge problem. In the town of Koenigsberg (in Eastern Prussia) the river Pregal flows around the island Kneiphof and then divides into two. There are, therefore, four land areas that have this river on its borders (see Figure 6.1). These land areas are interconnected by means of seven bridges $a-g$. The land areas themselves are labeled $A-D$. The Koenigsberg bridge problem is to determine whether starting at some land area it is possible to walk across all the bridges exactly once returning to the starting land area. One possible walk would be to start from land area B; walk across bridge a to island A; take bridge e to area D; bridge g to C; bridge d to A; bridge b to B and bridge f to D. This walk does not go across all bridges exactly once, nor does it return to the starting land area B. Euler answered the Koenigsberg bridge problem in the negative: The people of Koenigsberg will not be able to walk across each bridge exactly once and return to the starting point. He solved the problem by representing the land areas as vertices and the bridges as edges in a graph (actually a multigraph) as in Figure 6.1(b). His solution is elegant and applies to all graphs. Defining the *degree* of a vertex to be the number of edges incident to it, Euler showed that there is a walk starting at any vertex, going through each edge exactly once and terminating at the start vertex iff the degree of each vertex is even. A walk which does this is called *Eulerian*. There is no Eulerian walk for the Koenigsberg bridge problem as all four vertices are of odd degree.

Since this first application of graphs, they have been used in a wide variety of applications. Some of these applications are: analysis of electrical circuits, finding shortest routes, project planning, identification of chemical compounds, statistical mechanics, genetics, cybernetics, linguistics, social sciences, etc. Indeed, it might well be said

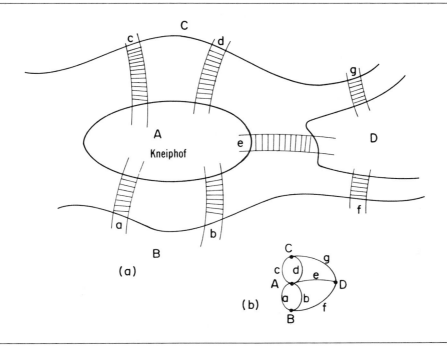

Figure 6.1 Section of the river Pregal in Koenigsberg and Euler´s graph

that of all mathematical structures, graphs are the most widely used.

6.1.2 Definitions and Terminology

A graph, G, consists of two sets V and E. V is a finite nonempty set of *vertices*. E is a set of pairs of vertices; these pairs are called *edges*. $V(G)$ and $E(G)$ will represent the sets of vertices and edges of graph G. We will also write $G = (V,E)$ to represent a graph. In an *undirected graph* the pair of vertices representing any edge is unordered. Thus, the pairs (v_1,v_2) and (v_2,v_1) represent the same edge. In a *directed graph* each edge is represented by a directed pair $<v_1,v_2>$; v_1 is the *tail* and v_2 the *head* of the edge. Therefore, $<v_2,v_1>$ and $<v_1,v_2>$ represent two different edges. Figure 6.2 shows three graphs G_1, G_2, and G_3. The graphs G_1 and G_2 are undirected. G_3 is a directed graph.

$V(G_1) = \{1,2,3,4\};$ $E(G_1) = \{(1,2),(1,3),(1,4),(2,3),(2,4),(3,4)\}$
$V(G_{2)} = \{1,2,3,4,5,6,7\};$ $E(G_2) = \{(1,2),(1,3),(2,4),(2,5),(3,6),(3,7)\}$
$V(G_3) = \{1,2,3\};$ $E(G_3) = \{<1,2>,<2,1>,<2,3>\}.$

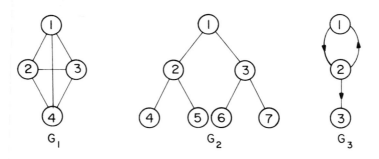

Figure 6.2 Three sample graphs

Note that the edges of a directed graph are drawn with an arrow from the tail to the head. The graph G_2 is also a tree while the graphs G_1 and G_3 are not. Trees can be defined as a special case of graphs, but we need more terminology for that. If (v_1,v_2) or $<v_1,v_2>$ is an edge in $E(G)$, then we require $v_1 \neq v_2$. In addition, since $E(G)$ is a set, a graph may not have multiple occurrences of the same edge. When this restriction is removed from a graph, the resulting data object is referred to as a multigraph. The data object of Figure 6.3 is a multigraph which is not a graph.

The number of distinct unordered pairs (v_i,v_j) with $v_i \neq v_j$ in a graph with n vertices is $n(n-1)/2$. This is the maximum number of edges in any n vertex undirected graph. An n vertex undirected graph with exactly $n(n-1)/2$ edges is said to be *complete*. G_1 is the complete graph on four vertices while G_2 and G_3 are not complete graphs. In the case of a directed graph on n vertices the maximum number of edges is $n(n-1)$.

If (v_1,v_2) is an edge in $E(G)$, then we shall say the vertices v_1 and v_2 are *adjacent* and that the edge (v_1,v_2) is *incident* on vertices v_1 and v_2. The vertices adjacent to vertex 2 in G_2 are 4, 5, and 1. The edges incident on vertex 3 in G_2 are (1,3), (3,6), and (3,7). If $<v_1,v_2>$ is a directed edge, then vertex v_1 will be said to be *adjacent to* v_2 while v_2 is *adjacent from* v_1. The edge $<v_1,v_2>$ is incident to v_1 and v_2. In G_3 the edges incident to vertex 2 are $<1,2>$, $<2,1>$, and $<2,3>$.

A *subgraph* of G is a graph G' such that $V(G') \subseteq V(G)$ and $E(G') \subseteq E(G)$. Figure 6.4 shows some of the subgraphs of G_1 and G_3.

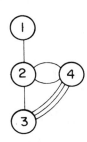

Figure 6.3 Example of a multigraph that is not a graph

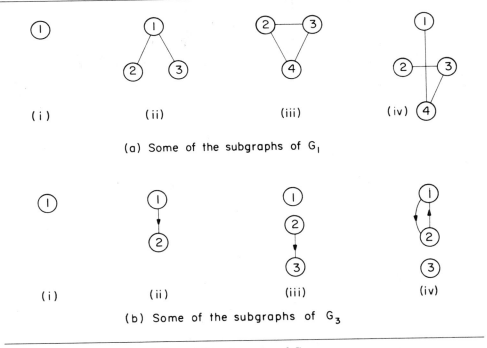

Figure 6.4 (a) Subgraphs of G_1 and (b) subgraphs of G_3

A *path* from vertex v_p to vertex v_q in graph G is a sequence of vertices $v_p, v_{i_1}, v_{i_2}, \ldots, v_{i_n}, v_q$ such that $(v_p,v_{i_1}), (v_{i_1},v_{i_2}), \ldots, (v_{i_n},v_q)$ are edges in $E(G)$. If G' is directed then the path consists of $<v_p,v_{i_1}>, <v_{i_1},v_{i_2}>, \ldots, <v_{i_n},v_q>$, edges in $E(G')$. The *length* of a path is the number of edges on it. A *simple path* is a path in which all vertices except possibly the first and last are distinct. A path such as (1,2), (2,4), (4,3), we write as 1,2,4,3. Paths 1,2,4,3 and 1,2,4,2 are both of length 3 in G_1. The first is a simple path while the second is not. 1,2,3 is a simple directed path in G_3. 1,2,3,2 is not a path in G_3 as the edge $<3,2>$ is not in $E(G_3)$. A *cycle* is a simple path in which the first and last vertices are the same. 1,2,3,1 is a cycle in G_1. 1,2,1 is a cycle in G_3. For the case of directed graphs we normally add on the prefix "directed" to the terms cycle and path. In an undirected graph, G, two vertices v_1 and v_2 are said to be *connected* if there is a path in G from v_1 to v_2 (since G is undirected, this means there must also be a path from v_2 to v_1). An undirected graph is said to be connected if for every pair of distinct vertices v_i, v_j in $V(G)$ there is a path from v_i to v_j in G. Graphs G_1 and G_2 are connected while G_4 of Figure 6.5 is not. A *connected component* or simply a component of an undirected graph is a *maximal* connected subgraph. G_4 has two components H_1 and H_2 (see Figure 6.5). A *tree* is a connected acyclic (i.e., has no cycles) graph. A directed graph G is said to be *strongly connected* if for every pair of distinct vertices v_i, v_j in $V(G)$ there is a directed path from v_i to v_j and also from v_j to v_i. The graph G_3 is not strongly connected as there is no path from v_3 to v_2. A *strongly connected component* is a maximal subgraph that is strongly connected. G_3 has two strongly connected components (see Figure 6.6).

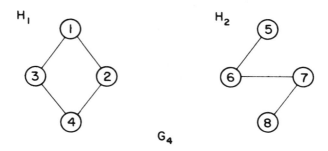

Figure 6.5 A graph with two connected components

The degree of a vertex is the number of edges incident to that vertex. The degree of vertex 1 in G_1 is 3. In case G is a directed graph, we define the *in-degree* of a vertex v to be the number of edges for which v is the head. The *out-degree* is defined to be the number of edges for which v is the tail. Vertex 2 of G_3 has in-degree 1, out-degree 2, and degree 3. If d_i is the degree of vertex i in a graph G with n vertices and e edges, then it is easy to see that $e = (\sum_{i=1}^{n} d_i)/2$.

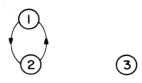

Figure 6.6 Strongly connected components of G_3

In the remainder of this chapter we shall refer to a directed graph as a *digraph*. An undirected graph will sometimes be referred to simply as a graph.

6.1.3 Graph Representations

While several representations for graphs are possible, we shall study only the three most commonly used: adjacency matrices, adjacency lists, and adjacency multilists. Once again, the choice of a particular representation will depend upon the application one has in mind and the functions one expects to perform on the graph.

Adjacency Matrix

Let $G = (V,E)$ be a graph with n vertices, $n \geq 1$. The adjacency matrix of G is a two-dimensional $n \times n$ array, say A, with the property that $A[i,j] = 1$ iff the edge (v_i, v_j) ($<v_i, v_j>$ for a directed graph) is in $E(G)$. $A[i,j] = 0$ if there is no such edge in G. The adjacency matrices for the graphs G_1, G_3, and G_4 are shown in Figure 6.7. The adjacency matrix for an undirected graph is symmetric as the edge (v_i, v_j) is in $E(G)$ iff the edge (v_j, v_i) is also in $E(G)$. The adjacency matrix for a directed graph need not be symmetric (as is the case for G_3). The space needed to represent a graph using its adjacency matrix is n^2 bits. About half this space can be saved in the case of undirected graphs by storing only the upper or lower triangle of the matrix.

From the adjacency matrix, one may readily determine if there is an edge connecting any two vertices i and j. For an undirected graph the degree of any vertex i is its row sum $\sum_{j=1}^{n} A[i,j]$. For a directed graph the row sum is the out-degree while the column sum is the in-degree. Suppose we want to answer a nontrivial question about graphs such as how many edges are there in G or is G connected. Using adjacency matrices all algorithms will require at least $O(n^2)$ time as $n^2 - n$ entries of the matrix (diagonal entries are zero) have to be examined. When graphs are sparse, i.e., most of the terms in the adjacency matrix are zero, one would expect that the former question would be

	1	2	3	4
1	0	1	1	1
2	1	0	1	1
3	1	1	0	1
4	1	1	1	0

(i)

	1	2	3
1	0	1	0
2	1	0	1
3	0	0	0

(ii)

	1	2	3	4	5	6	7	8
1	0	1	1	0	0	0	0	0
2	1	0	0	1	0	0	0	0
3	1	0	0	1	0	0	0	0
4	0	1	1	0	0	0	0	0
5	0	0	0	0	0	1	0	0
6	0	0	0	0	1	0	1	0
7	0	0	0	0	0	1	0	1
8	0	0	0	0	0	0	1	0

(iii)

Figure 6.7 Adjacency matrices for (i)G_1, (ii)G_3, and (iii)G_4

answerable in significantly less time, say O($e + n$) where e is the number of edges in G and $e << n^2/2$. Such a speed-up can be made possible through the use of linked lists in which only the edges that are in G are represented. This leads to the next representation for graphs.

Adjacency Lists

In this representation the n rows of the adjacency matrix are represented as n linked lists. There is one list for each vertex in G. The nodes in list i represent the vertices that are adjacent from vertex i. Each node has at least two fields: *vertex* and *link*. The *vertex* fields contain the indices of the vertices adjacent to vertex i. The adjacency lists for G_1, G_3, and G_4 are shown in Figure 6.8. Each list has a head node. The head nodes are sequential providing easy random access to the adjacency list for any particular vertex. The declarations in Pascal for the adjacency list representation would be

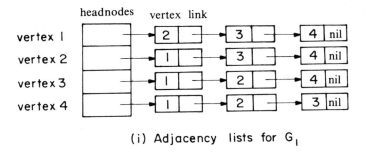

(i) Adjacency lists for G_1

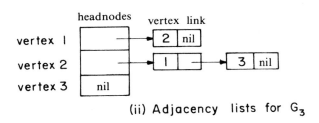

(ii) Adjacency lists for G_3

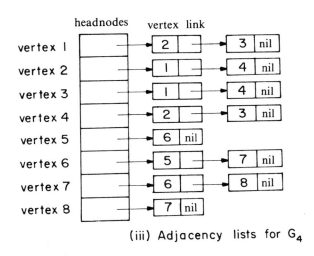

(iii) Adjacency lists for G_4

Figure 6.8 Adjacency lists

344 Graphs

```
type NextNode = ↑node ;
    node = record
            vertex : integer;
            link : NextNode ;
        end;
    HeadNodes : array[1..n ] of NextNode;
```

In the case of an undirected graph with n vertices and e edges, this representation requires n head nodes and $2e$ list nodes. Each list node has two fields. In terms of the number of bits of storage needed, this count should be multiplied by log n for the head nodes and log n + log e for the list nodes as it takes O(log m) bits to represent a number of value m. Often, you can sequentially pack the nodes on the adjacency lists, thereby eliminating the use of pointers. In this case, an array $node$ [1..n + 2e + 1] may be used. $node [i]$ gives the starting point of the list for vertex i, $1 \le i \le n$ and $node [n+1]$ is set to $n + 2e + 2$. The vertices from vertex i are stored in $node [i]$, . . ., $node [i + 1] - 1$, $1 \le i \le n$. Figure 6.9 gives such a sequential representation for the graph G_4 of Figure 6.5.

```
var nodes: array[1..n + 2e + 1] of integer;
```

[1] 10	[9] 24	[17] 3
[2] 12	[10] 2	[18] 6
[3] 14	[11] 3	[19] 5
[4] 16	[12] 1	[20] 7
[5] 18	[13] 4	[21] 6
[6] 19	[14] 1	[22] 8
[7] 21	[15] 4	[23] 7
[8] 23	[16] 2	

Figure 6.9 Sequential representation of graph G_4

The degree of any vertex in an undirected graph may be determined by just counting the number of nodes in its adjacency list. The total number of edges in G may, therefore, be determined in time O($n + e$). In the case of a digraph the number of list nodes is only e. The out-degree of any vertex may be determined by counting the number of nodes on its adjacency list. The total number of edges in G can, therefore, be determined in O($n + e$). Determining the in-degree of a vertex is a little more complex. In case there is a need to access repeatedly all vertices adjacent to another vertex then it may be worth the effort to keep another set of lists in addition to the adjacency lists. This set of lists, called *inverse adjacency lists*, will contain one list for each vertex. Each list will contain a node for each vertex adjacent to the vertex it represents (see Figure 6.10).

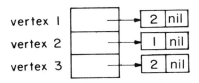

Figure 6.10 Inverse adjacency lists for G_3

Alternatively, one could adopt a simplified version of the list structure used for sparse matrix representation in Section 4.6. Each node would now have four fields and would represent one edge. The node structure would be

tail	head	column link for head	row link for tail

Figure 6.11 shows the resulting structure for the graph G_3. The head nodes are stored sequentially.

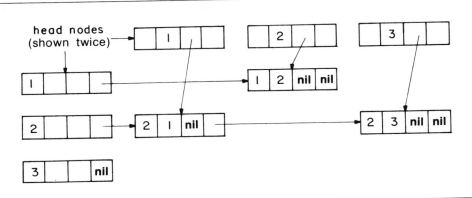

Figure 6.11 Orthogonal list representation for G_3

The nodes in the adjacency lists of Figure 6.8 were ordered by the indices of the vertices they represented. It is not necessary that lists be ordered in this way and, in general, the vertices may appear in any order. Thus, the adjacency lists of Figure 6.12 would be just as valid a representation of G_1.

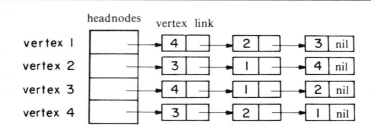

Figure 6.12 Alternate order adjacency list for G_1

Adjacency Multilists

In the adjacency list representation of an undirected graph each edge, (v_i, v_j) is represented by two entries, one on the list for v_i and the other on the list for v_j. As we shall see, in some situations it is necessary to be able to determine the second entry for a particular edge and mark that edge as already having been examined. This can be accomplished easily if the adjacency lists are actually maintained as multilists (i.e., lists in which nodes may be shared among several lists). For each edge there will be exactly one node, but this node will be in two lists, i.e., the adjacency lists for each of the two nodes it is incident to. The node structure now becomes

m	vertex1	vertex2	path1	path2

where m is a one bit mark field that may be used to indicate whether or not the edge has been examined. The declarations in Pascal are

type *nextedges* = ↑*edge* ;

edge = **record**

         m : **boolean**;

      vertex 1 : **integer**;

      vertex 2 : **integer**;

        path 1 : *nextedges*;

        path 2 : *nextedges*;

end;

var *headnodes* : **array**[1..*n*] **of** *nextedges*

The storage requirements are the same as for normal adjacency lists except for the addition of the mark bit *m*. Figure 6.13 shows the adjacency multilists for G_1. We shall study multilists in greater detail in Chapter 10.

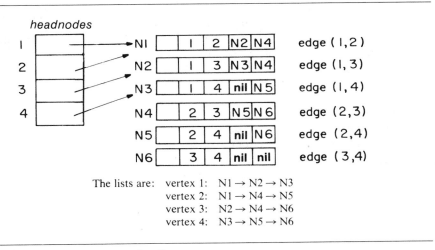

Figure 6.13 Adjacency multilists for G_1

Sometimes the edges of a graph have weights assigned to them. These weights may represent the distance from one vertex to another or the cost of going from one vertex to an adjacent vertex. In this case, the adjacency matrix entries $A[i,j]$ would keep this information too. In the case of adjacency lists this weight information may be kept in the list nodes by including an additional field. A graph with weighted edges is called a *network*.

6.2 TRAVERSALS, COMPONENTS, AND SPANNING TREES

Given the root nodes of a binary tree, one of the most common things one wishes to do is to traverse the tree and visit the nodes in some order. In the chapter on trees, we defined three ways (preorder, inorder, and postorder) for doing this. An analogous problem arises in the case of graphs. Given an undirected graph $G = (V, E)$ and a vertex v in $V(G)$, we are interested in visiting all vertices in G that are reachable from v (i.e., all vertices connected to v). We shall look at two ways of doing this: depth first search and breadth first search.

Depth First Search

Depth first search of an undirected graph proceeds as follows. The start vertex v is visited. Next an unvisited vertex w adjacent to v is selected and a depth first search from w initiated. When a vertex u is reached such that all its adjacent vertices have been visited, we back up to the last vertex visited which has an unvisited vertex w adjacent to it and initiate a depth first search from w. The search terminates when no unvisited vertex can be reached from any of the visited ones. This procedure is best described recursively as in Program 6.1. This procedure assumes a global array $visited[1..n]$ of type boolean that is initialized to **false**.

```
 1 procedure dfs(v : integer);
 2 {Given an undirected graph G = (V,E) with n vertices and an
 3  array visited[n] initially set to false, this algorithm visits
 4  all vertices reachable from v. visited is global.}
 5 var w : integer ;
 6 begin
 7    visited [v ] := true;
 8    for each vertex w adjacent to v do
 9       if not visited [w ] then dfs(w );
10 end; {of dfs}
```

Program 6.1 Algorithm *dfs*

In case G is represented by its adjacency lists then the vertices w adjacent to v can be determined by following a chain of links. Since the algorithm *dfs* would examine each node in the adjacency lists at most once and there are $2e$ list nodes, the time to complete the search is $O(e)$. If G is represented by its adjacency matrix, then the time to determine all vertices adjacent to v is $O(n)$. Since at most n vertices are visited, the total time is $O(n^2)$.

The graph G of Figure 6.14(a) is represented by its adjacency lists as in Figure 6.14(b). If a depth first search is initiated from vertex v_1, then the vertices of G are visited in the order: $v_1, v_2, v_4, v_8, v_5, v_6, v_3, v_7$. We can verify that $dfs(v_1)$ visits all vertices connected to v_1. So, all the vertices visited, together with all edges in G incident to these vertices, form a connected component of G.

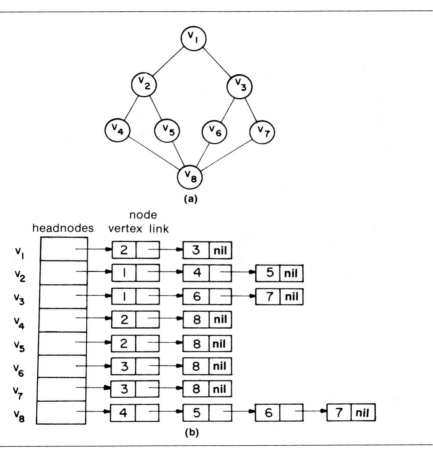

(a)

(b)

Figure 6.14 Graph G and its adjacency lists

Breadth First Search

Starting at vertex v and marking it as visited, breadth first search differs from depth first search in that all unvisited vertices adjacent to v are visited next. Then unvisited vertices adjacent to these vertices are visited and so on. A breadth first search beginning at vertex v_1 of the graph in Figure 6.14(a) would first visit v_1 and then v_2 and v_3. Next vertices v_4, v_5, v_6, and v_7 will be visited and finally v_8. Algorithm *bfs* (Program 6.2) gives the details.

```
 1  procedure bfs (v : integer);
 2  {A breadth first search of G is carried out beginning at vertex
 3   v. All vertices visited are marked as visited [i ] := true. The
 4   graph G and array visited are global and visited is initialized
 5   to false. InitializeQueue, AddQueue, EmptyQueue, and DeleteQueue
 6   are procedures/functions to handle queue operations}
 7  var w : integer,
 8      q : queue;
 9  begin
10     visited [v ] := true;
11     InitializeQueue (q);          {q is a queue}
12     AddQueue (q,v);               {add vertex to queue}
13     while not EmptyQueue (q) do
14     begin
15        DeleteQueue (q,v):         {remove from queue vertex v}
16        for all vertices w adjacent to v do
17           if not visited [w ]
18           then
19           begin
20              AddQueue (q,w);
21              visited [w ] := true;
22           end; {of if and for}
23     end; {of while}
24  end; {of bfs}
```

Program 6.2 Algorithm *bfs*

Each vertex visited gets into the queue exactly once, so the **while** loop is iterated at most n times. If an adjacency matrix is used, then the loop takes $O(n)$ time for each vertex visited. The total time is, therefore, $O(n^2)$. In case adjacency lists are used the loop has a total cost of $d_1 + \cdots + d_n = O(e)$ where $d_i = $ degree (v_i). Again, all vertices visited, together with all edges incident to them, form a connected component of G.

We now look at two simple applications of graph traversal: (1) finding the components of a graph, and (2) finding a spanning tree of a connected graph.

Connected Components

If G is an undirected graph, then one can determine whether or not it is connected by simply making a call to either *dfs* or *bfs* and then determining if there is any unvisited vertex. The time to do this is $O(n^2)$ if adjacency matrices are used and $O(e)$ if adjacency lists are used. A more interesting problem is to determine all the connected components of a graph. These may be obtained by making repeated calls to either *dfs(v)* or *bfs(v)*, with v a vertex not yet visited. This leads to algorithm *comp* (Program 6.3) which determines all the connected components of G. The algorithm uses *dfs*. *bfs* may be used instead if desired. The computing time is not affected.

```
 1  procedure comp (g : UndirectedGraph);
 2  {determine the connected components of g. g has n ≥ 1 vertices.
 3    visited is now a local array.}
 4  var visited : array [1..n] of boolean;
 5       i : integer;
 6  begin
 7    for i := 1 to n do
 8      visited [i] := false; {initialize all vertices as unvisted}
 9    for i := 1 to n do
10      if not visited [i]
11      then
12      begin
13        dfs(i); {find a component}
14        OutputNewVertices ; {output all newly visited vertices
15                          together with all edges incident to them}
16      end; {of if and for}
17  end; {of comp}
```

Program 6.3 Algorithm *comp*

If G is represented by its adjacency lists, then the total time taken by *dfs* is $O(e)$. The output can be completed in time $O(e)$ if *dfs* keeps a list of all newly visited vertices. Since the **for** loops take $O(n)$ time, the total time to generate all the connected components is $O(n + e)$.

By the definition of a connected component, there is a path between every pair of vertices in the component and there is no path in G from vertex v to w if v and w are in two different components. Hence, if A is the adjacency matrix of an undirected graph (i.e., A is symmetric) then its transitive closure A^+ may be determined in $O(n^2)$ time by first determining the connected components. $A^+[i,j] = 1$ iff there is a path from vertex i to j. For every pair of distinct vertices in the same component $A^+[i,j] = 1$. On the diagonal $A^+[i,i] = 1$ iff the component containing i has at least two vertices. We shall take a closer look at transitive closure in Section 6.3.

Biconnected Components

Let G be an undirected connected graph. A vertex v of G is an *articulation point* iff the deletion of v together with all edges incident to v leaves behind a graph that has at least two connected components. Vertices 2, 4, 6, and 8 are the articulation points of the connected graph of Figure 6.15(a).

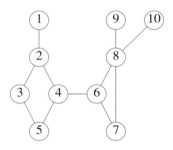

(a) An example connected graph

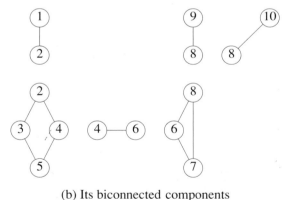

(b) Its biconnected components

Figure 6.15 A connected graph and its biconnected components

A *biconnected graph* is a connected graph that has no articulation points. The graph of Figure 6.15 is not biconnected and that of Figure 6.14(a) is. Articulation points are undesirable in graphs that represent communication networks. In such graphs the vertices represent communication stations and the edges represent communication links. The failure of a communication station that is an articulation point results in a loss of communication to stations other than the one that failed. If the communication graph is biconnected, then the failure of a single station results in a loss of communication to and from only that station.

A *biconnected component* of a connected graph G is a maximal biconnected subgraph H of G. By maximal, we mean that G contains no other subgraph that is both biconnected and properly contains H. The graph of Figure 6.15(a) contains six biconnected components. These are shown in Figure 6.15(b). Note that a biconnected graph has just one biconnected component; the whole graph. It is easy to verify that two biconnected components of the same graph can have at most one vertex in common. From this it follows that no edge can be in two or more biconnected components. Hence, the biconnected components of G partition the edges of G.

The biconnected components of a connected undirected graph G can be found by using any depth first spanning tree of G. For the example graph of Figure 6.15(a) a depth first spanning tree with root 4 is shown in Figure 6.16(a). This tree is redrawn in Figure 6.16(b) to better reveal the tree structure. This figure also shows the nontree edges of G by broken lines. The numbers outside the vertices give the sequence in which the vertices are visited during the depth first search. This number is called the *depth first number*, *dfn*, of the vertex. So, $dfn(1) = 5$, and $dfn(10) = 9$. Note that if u and v are two vertices such that u is an ancestor of v in the depth first spanning tree, then $dfn(u) < dfn(v)$.

A nontree edge (u, v) is a *back edge* with respect to a spanning tree T iff either u is an ancestor of v or v is an ancestor of u. A nontree edge that is not a back edge is called a *cross edge*. Both the nontree edges $(4, 2)$ and $(6, 8)$ are back edges. From the definition of a depth first search one can show that no graph can have cross edges with respect to any of its depth first spanning trees. From this, it follows that the root of the depth first spanning tree is an articulation point iff it has at least two children. Further, any other vertex u is an articulation point iff it has at least one child w such that it is not possible to reach an ancestor of u using a path composed solely of w, descendants of w, and a single back edge. These observations lead us to define a value *low* for each vertex of G such that $low(u)$ is the lowest depth first number that can be reached from u using a path of descendants followed by at most one back edge. $low(u)$ is given by the equation:

$$low(u) = \min\{dfn(u), \min\{low(w) \mid w \text{ is a child of } u\}, \\ \min\{dfn(w) \mid (u, w) \text{ is a back edge}\}\}$$

From the preceding discussion it follows that u is an articulation point iff u is either the root of the spanning tree and has two or more children or u is not the root and u has a child w such that $low(w) \geq dfn(u)$. For the spanning tree of Figure 6.16(b),

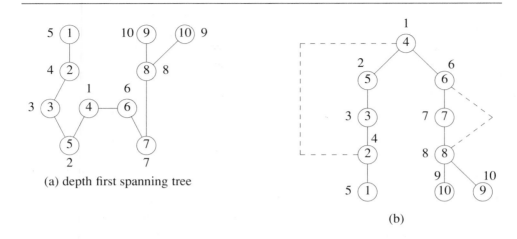

(a) depth first spanning tree

(b)

Figure 6.16 Depth first spanning tree of Figure 6.15 (a)

low (1..10) = (5, 4, 1, 1, 1, 6, 6, 8, 10, 9). Vertex 2 is an articulation point as it has a child 1 such that *low* (1) = 5 ≥ *dfn* (2) = 4. Vertex 8 is an articulation point as *low* (9) = 10 ≥ *dfn* (8) = 8; vertex 6 is an articulation point as *low* (7) = 6 ≥ *dfn* (6) = 6; vertex 4 is an articulation point as it is the root and has more than one child.

Procedure *dfs* is easily modified to compute *dfn* and *low* for each vertex of a connected graph. The result is procedure *DfnLow* of Program 6.4. This uses the function *min* 2 which returns the smaller of its two parameters. The procedure is invoked as *DfnLow* (x, 0) where x is the start vertex for the depth first search.

The edges of the connected graph may be partitioned into their biconnected components by adding some code to procedure *DfnLow*. First, note that following the return from *DfnLow* (w, u), *low* [w] has been computed. If *low* [w] ≥ (the current value of *low* [u]), then a new biconnected component has been identified. By using a stack to save edges when they are first encountered we can output all edges in a biconnected component as in Program 6.5. Proving the correctness of this procedure is left as an exercise. Its complexity is seen to be O(n +e). Note that procedure *bicon* assumes that the input connected graph has at least two vertices. Connected graphs with just one vertex contain no edges. By convention these are biconnected and a proper biconnected components procedure should handle these as a special case producing a single biconnected component as output.

---

procedure *DfnLow* (*u*, *v* : **integer**);
{Compute *dfn* and *low* while performing a depth first search beginning at vertex *u*.}
{*v* is the parent (if any) of *u* in the resulting spanning tree.}
{It is assumed that *dfn* [1..*n*] is initialized to zero and that *num* is initially 1.}
var *w* : **integer**;
begin
　dfn [*u*] := *num*; *low* [*u*] := *num*; *num* := *num* + 1;
　for each vertex *w* adjacent from *u* **do**
　　if *dfn* [*w*] = 0 **then begin**
　　　　　　　　　DfnLow (*w*, *u*); {*w* is an unvisited vertex}
　　　　　　　　　low [*u*] := *min* 2(*low* [*u*], *low* [*w*]);
　　　　　　end
　　　　　else if *w* < > *v* **then** *low* [*u*] := *min* 2(*low* [*u*], *dfn* [*w*]);
end;

Program 6.4 Procedure to compute *dfn* and *low*

Spanning Trees and Minimum Cost Spanning Trees

　　When the graph *G* is connected, a depth first or breadth first search starting at any vertex visits all the vertices in *G*. In this case the edges of *G* are partitioned into two sets *T* (for tree edges) and *B* (for back edges), where *T* is the set of edges used or traversed during the search and *B* the set of remaining edges. The set *T* may be determined by inserting the statement *T* := *T* ∪ {(*v*,*w*)} in the **then** clauses of *dfs* and *bfs*. The edges in *T* form a tree which includes all the vertices of *G*. Any tree consisting solely of edges in *G* and including all vertices in *G* is called a *spanning tree*. Figure 6.17 shows a graph and some of its spanning trees. When either *dfs* or *bfs* is used, the edges of *T* form a spanning tree. The spanning tree resulting from a call to *dfs* is known as a *depth first spanning tree*. When *bfs* is used, the resulting spanning tree is called a *breadth first spanning tree*.

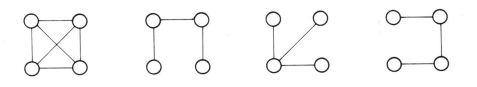

Figure 6.17 A complete graph and three of its spanning trees

```
procedure bicon (u, v : integer);
{Compute dfn and low, and output the edges of G by their biconnected components.}
{v is the parent (if any) of u in the resulting spanning tree.}
{It is assumed that dfn [1..n] is initialized to zero and that num is initially 1.}
{S is a global stack that is initially empty.}
var w : integer;
begin
    dfn [u] := num; low [u] := num; num := num + 1;
    for each vertex w adjacent from u do
    begin
        if (v < > w) and (dfn (w) < dfn (u)) then add (u, w) to stack S;
        if dfn [w] = 0 then begin
                            bicon (w, u); {w is an unvisited vertex}
                            low [u] := min 2(low [u], low [w]);
                            if low [w] >= dfn [u]
                            then begin
                                    writeln('New biconnected component');
                                    repeat
                                        delete an edge from the stack S;
                                        let this edge be (x, y);
                                        writeln(x, ', ',y);
                                    until (x, y) and (u, w) are the same edge;
                                end;
                        end
                    else if w < > v then low [u] := min 2(low [u], dfn [w]);
    end; {of for}
end;
```

Program 6.5 Procedure to output biconnected components when $n > 1$

Figure 6.18 shows the spanning trees resulting from a depth first and breadth first search starting at vertex v_1 in the graph of Figure 6.14. If any of the edges (v,w) in B (the set of back edges) is introduced into the spanning tree T, then a cycle is formed. This cycle consists of the edge (v,w) and all the edges on the path from w to v in T. If the edge (8,7) is introduced into the *dfs* spanning tree of Figure 6.18(a), then the resulting cycle is 8,7,3,6,8.

Spanning trees find application in obtaining an independent set of circuit equations for an electrical network. First, a spanning tree for the network is obtained. Then the edges in B (i.e., edges not in the spanning tree) are introduced one at a time. The introduction of each such edge results in a cycle. Kirchoff's second law is used on this cycle to obtain a circuit equation. The cycles obtained in this way are independent (i.e., none of these cycles can be obtained by taking a linear combination of the remaining

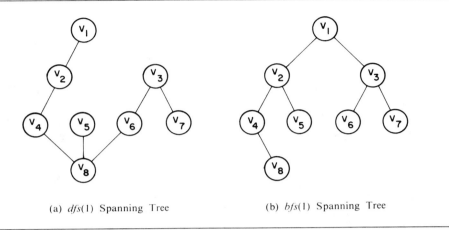

(a) *dfs*(1) Spanning Tree   (b) *bfs*(1) Spanning Tree

Figure 6.18 *dfs* and *bfs* spanning trees for graph of Figure 6.14

cycles) as each contains an edge from *B* which is not contained in any other cycle. Hence, the circuit equations so obtained are also independent. In fact, it may be shown that the cycles obtained by introducing the edges of *B* one at a time into the resulting spanning tree form a cycle basis and so all other cycles in the graph can be constructed by taking a linear combination of the cycles in the basis (see Harary in the references for further details).

It is not difficult to imagine other applications for spanning trees. One that is of interest arises from the property that a spanning tree is a minimal subgraph G' of G such that $V(G') = V(G)$ and G' is connected (by a minimal subgraph, we mean one with the fewest number of edges). Any connected graph with n vertices must have at least $n - 1$ edges and all connected graphs with $n - 1$ edges are trees. If the nodes of G represent cities and the edges represent possible communication links connecting two cities, then the minimum number of links needed to connect the n cities is $n - 1$. The spanning trees of G will represent all feasible choices. In any practical situation, however, the edges will have weights assigned to them. These weights might represent the cost of construction, the length of the link, etc. Given such a weighted graph one would then wish to select for construction a set of communication links that would connect all the cities and have minimum total cost or be of minimum total length. In either case, the links selected will have to form a tree (assuming all weights are positive). In case this is not so, then the selection of links contains a cycle. Removal of any one of the links on this cycle will result in a link selection of less cost connecting all cities. We are, therefore, interested in finding a spanning tree of G with minimum cost. The cost of a spanning tree is the sum of the costs of the edges in that tree.

The greedy method results in three different algorithms to obtain a minimum cost spanning tree of a connected undirected graph. We shall refer to these as Kruskal's algorithm, Prim's algorithm, and Sollin's algorithm. We begin by examining Kruskal's algorithm.

In Kruskal's algorithm a minimum cost spanning tree, T, is built edge by edge. Edges are considered for inclusion in T in nondecreasing order of their costs. An edge is included in T if it does not form a cycle with the edges already in T. Since G is connected and has $n > 0$ vertices, exactly $n - 1$ edges will be selected for inclusion in T.

Consider the connected graph of Figure 6.19(a). We begin with no edges selected. Figure 6.19(b) shows the current state of affairs. Edge (1,6) is the first edge picked. It is included into the spanning tree that is being built. This yields the graph of Figure 6.19(c). Next, the edge (3,4) is selected and included into the tree (Figure 6.19(d)). The next edge to be considered is (2,7). Its inclusion into the tree being built does not create a cycle. So, we get the graph of Figure 6.19(e). Edge (2,3) is considered next and included into the tree (Figure 6.19(f)). Of the edges not yet considered, (7,4) has the least cost. It is considered next. Its inclusion into the tree results in a cycle. So, this edge is discarded. Edge (5,4) is the next edge to be added to the tree being built. This results in the configuration of Figure 6.19(g). The next edge to be considered is the edge (7,5). It is discarded as its inclusion creates a cycle. Finally, edge (6,5) is considered and included into the tree being built. This completes the spanning tree (Figure 6.19(h)). The resulting tree has cost 99.

It is somewhat surprising that this straightforward approach should always result in a minimum spanning tree. We shall soon prove that this is indeed the case. First, let us look into the details of the algorithm. For clarity, the Kruskal algorithm is written out more formally in Program 6.6. Initially, E is the set of all edges in G. The only functions we wish to perform on this set are (1) determining an edge with minimum cost (line 3), and (2) deleting that edge (line 4). Both these functions can be performed efficiently if the edges in E are maintained as a sorted sequential list. In Chapter 7 we shall see how to sort these edges into nondecreasing order in time $O(e \log e)$, where e is the number of edges in E. Actually, it is not essential to sort all the edges so long as the next edges for line 3 can be determined easily. This is an instance where a min heap is ideal as it permits the next edge to be determined and deleted in $O(\log e)$ time. The construction of the heap itself takes $O(e)$ time.

In order to be able to perform steps 5 and 6 efficiently, the vertices in G should be grouped together in such a way that one may easily determine if the vertices v and w are already connected by the earlier selection of edges. In case they are, then the edge (v,w) is to be discarded. If they are not, then (v,w) is to be added to T. One possible grouping is to place all vertices in the same connected component of T into a set (all connected components of T will also be trees). Then, two vertices v,w are connected in T iff they are in the same set. For example, when the edge (4,3) is to be considered, the sets would be {1}, {2,3,4}, {5}, {6}. Vertices 4 and 3 are already in the same set and so the edge (4,3) is rejected. The next edge to be considered is (2,6). Since vertices 2 and 6 are in different sets, the edge is accepted. This edge connects the two components {2,3,4} and {6} together and so these two sets should be unioned to obtain the set representing the

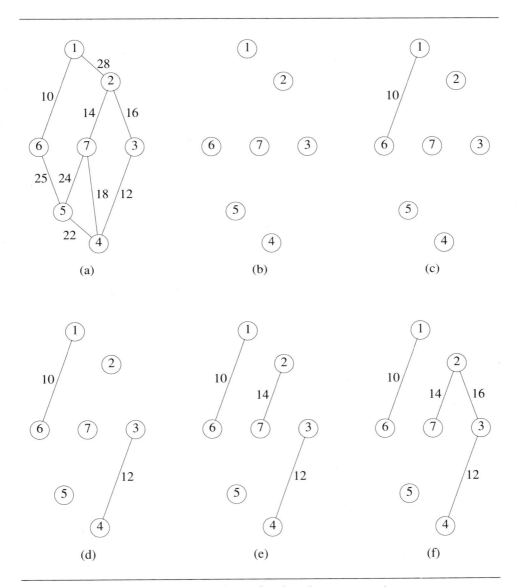

Figure 6.19 Stages in Kruskal's algorithm (Continued on next page)

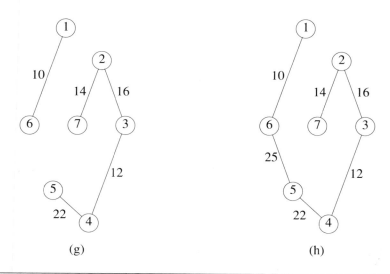

(g)   (h)

Figure 6.19 Stages in Kruskal's algorithm (Continued from previous page)

```
1 T := ∅
2 while T contains less than n − 1 edges and E not empty do begin
3     choose an edge (v,w) from E of lowest cost;
4     delete (v,w) from E;
5     if (v,w) does not create a cycle in T
6         then add (v,w) to T
7         else discard (v,w)
8 end
9 if T contains fewer than n − 1 edges then writeln ('no spanning tree')
```

Program 6.6 Kruskal's algorithm

new component. Using the set representation of Section 5.8 and the *find* and *union* algorithms of that section we can obtain an efficient implementation of lines 5 and 6. The computing time is, therefore, determined by the time for lines 3 and 4 which in the worst case is O($e \log e$). We leave the writing of the resulting algorithm as an exercise. Theorem 6.1 proves that the algorithm resulting from Program 6.6 does yield a minimum spanning tree of G.

Theorem 6.1: Let G be any undirected connected graph. Kruskal's algorithm generates a minimum cost spanning tree.

Proof: We shall show the following: (a) Kruskal's method results in a spanning tree whenever a spanning tree exists; and (b) the spanning tree generated is of minimum cost.

For (a), we note that the only edges that get discarded in Kruskal's method are those that result in a cycle. The deletion of a single edge that is on a cycle of a connected graph results in a graph that is also connected. Hence, if G is initially connected, the set of edges in T and E always form a connected graph. Consequently, if G is initially connected, the algorithm cannot terminate with $E = \varnothing$ and $i < n - 1$.

Now, let us proceed to establish that the constructed spanning tree, T, is of minimum cost. Since G has a finite number of spanning trees, it must have at least one of minimum cost. Let U be such a minimum cost spanning tree. Both T and U have exactly $n-1$ edges. If $T = U$, then T is of minimum cost and we have nothing to prove. So, assume that $T \neq U$. Let $k, k > 0$, be the number of edges in T that are not in U. Note that k is also the number of edges in U that are not in T.

We shall show that T and U have the same cost by transforming U into T. This transformation will be done in k steps. At each step, the number of edges in T that are not in U will be reduced by exactly 1. Further, the cost of U will not change as a result of the transformation. As a result, U after k steps of transformation will have the same cost as the initial U and will consist of exactly those edges that are in T. This implies that T is of minimum cost.

Each step of the transformation involves adding to U one edge from T and removing one edge, f, from U. The edges e and f are selected in the following way:

(1)   Let e be the least cost edge in T that is not in U. Such an edge must exist as $k > 0$.

(2)   When e is added to U, a unique cycle is created. Let f be any edge on this cycle that is not in T. Note that at least one of the edges on this cycle is not in T as T contains no cycles.

From the way e and f are selected, it follows that $V = U + \{e\} - \{f\}$ is a spanning tree and that T has exactly $k-1$ edges that are not in V. We need to show that the cost of V is the same as that of U. Clearly, the cost of V is the cost of U plus the cost of the edge e minus the cost of the edge f. The cost of e cannot be less than the cost of f as otherwise the spanning tree V has a smaller cost than the tree U. This is impossible. If e has a higher cost than f, then f is considered before e by Kruskal's algorithm. Since it is not in T, Kruskal's algorithm must have discarded this edge at this time. Hence, f together with edges in T having a cost less than or equal to the cost of f must form a cycle. By the choice of e, all these edges are also in U. Hence, U must also contain a cycle. But, it does not as it is a spanning tree. So, the assumption that e is of higher cost than f leads to a contradiction. The only possibility that remains is that e and f have the same cost. Hence, V has the same cost as U. $\square$

Prim's algorithm, like Kruskal's, constructs the minimum cost spanning tree edge by edge. However, at all times during the algorithm, the set of selected edges forms a tree. By contrast, the set of selected edges in Kruskal's algorithm forms a forest at all times. Prim's algorithm begins with a tree T that contains a single vertex. This can be any of the vertices in the original graph. Then we add a least cost edge (u, v) to T such that $T \cup \{(u, v)\}$ is also a tree. This edge addition step is repeated until T contains $n-1$ edges. Notice that edge (u, v) is always such that exactly one of u and v is in T. A high level description of Prim's algorithm is provided in Program 6.7. This description also provides for the possibility that the input graph may not be connected. In this case there is no spanning tree. Figure Figure 6.20 shows the progress of Prim's algorithm on the graph of Figure 6.19(a).

{Assume that G has at least one vertex}
$T := \emptyset$; $TV := \{1\}$; {start with vertex 1 and no edges}
done := **false**;
while T contains fewer than $n-1$ edges **and not** *done* **do**
begin
    Let (u, v) be a least cost edge such that $u \in TV$ and $v \notin TV$;
    if there is no such edge **then** *done* := **true**
                      else add v to TV and (u, v) to T;
end;
if T contains fewer than $n-1$ edges **then writeln** ('no spanning tree');

Program 6.7 Prim's minimum spanning tree algorithm

Prim's algorithm can be implemented to have a time complexity $O(n^2)$ if we associate with each vertex v not in VT a vertex $near(v)$ such that $near(v) \in VT$ and $cost(v, near(v))$ is minimum over all such choices for $near(v)$ (we assume that $cost(v, w) = \infty$ if $(v, w) \notin E$). The next edge to add to T is such that $cost(v, near(v))$ is minimum and $v \notin VT$. Asymptotically faster implementations are also possible. One of these results from the use of Fibonacci heaps which are studied in Chapter 10. A reference to the application of Fibonacci heaps to the implementation of Prim's algorithm is provided at the end of Chapter 10. Establishing the correctness of Prim's algorithm is left as an exercise.

Sollin's algorithm selects several edges at each stage. At the start of a stage the selected edges together with all n graph vertices form a spanning forest. During a stage we select one edge for each tree in this forest. This edge is a minimum cost edge that has exactly one vertex in the tree. The selected edges are added to the spanning tree being constructed. Note that it is possible for two trees in the forest to select the same edge. So, multiple copies of the same edge are to be eliminated. At the start of the first stage the set of selected edges is empty. The algorithm terminates when there is only one tree at end of a stage or when no edges remain to be selected.

Figure 6.21 shows the stages in Sollin's algorithm when it begins with the graph of Figure 6.19(a). The initial configuration of zero selected edges is the same as that shown in Figure 6.19(b). Each tree in this spanning forest is a single vertex. The edges selected by vertices 1, 2, . . ., 7 are, respectively, (1, 6), (2, 7), (3, 4), (4, 3), (5, 4), (6, 1), (7, 2). The distinct edges in this selection are: (1, 6), (2, 7), (3, 4), and (5, 4). Adding these to

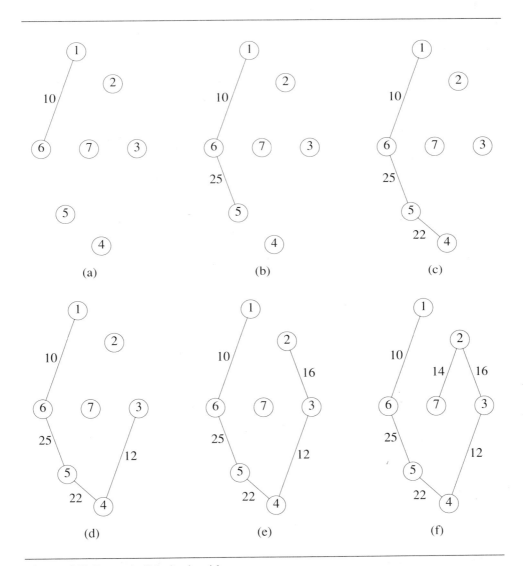

Figure 6.20 Stages in Prim's algorithm

the set of selected edges results in the configuration of Figure 6.21(a). In the next stage, the tree with vertex set {1, 6} selects edge (6, 5) and the remaining two trees select the edge (2, 3). Following the addition of these two edges to the set of selected edges the spanning tree construction is complete. The constructed spanning tree is shown in Figure 6.21(b). The development of Sollin's algorithm into a Pascal procedure and its correctness proof are left as exercises.

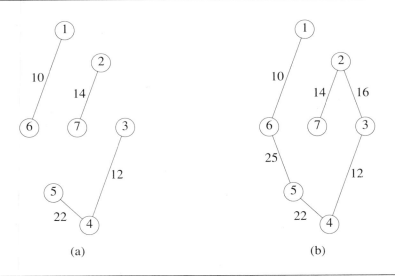

(a)   (b)

Figure 6.21 Stages in Sollin's algorithm

6.3 SHORTEST PATHS AND TRANSITIVE CLOSURE

Graphs may be used to represent the highway structure of a state or country with vertices representing cities and edges representing sections of highway. The edges may then be assigned weights which might be either the distance between the two cities connected by the edge or the average time to drive along that section of highway. A motorist wishing to drive from city A to city B would be interested in answers to the following questions:

(1)   Is there a path from A to B?

(2)   If there is more than one path from A to B, which is the shortest path?

The problems defined by (1) and (2) above are special cases of the path problems we shall be studying in this section. The length of a path is now defined to be the sum of the weights of the edges on that path rather than the number of edges. The starting vertex of the path will be referred to as the *source* and the last vertex the *destination*. The graphs will be digraphs to allow for one-way streets. Unless otherwise stated, we shall assume that all weights are positive.

Single Source All Destinations

In this problem we are given a directed graph $G = (V,E)$, a weighting function $w(e)$, $w(e) \geq 0$, for the edges of G and a source vertex v_0. The problem is to determine the shortest paths from v_0 to all the remaining vertices of G. It is assumed that all the weights are positive. As an example, consider the directed graph of Figure 6.22(a). The numbers on the edges are the weights. If v_0 is the source vertex, then the shortest path from v_0 to v_1 is v_0, v_2, v_3, v_1. The length of this path is $10 + 15 + 20 = 45$. Even though there are three edges on this path, it is shorter than the path $v_0 v_1$ which is of length 50. There is no path from v_0 to v_5. Figure 6.22(b) lists the shortest paths from v_0 to v_1, v_2, v_3, and v_4. The paths have been listed in nondecreasing order of path length. A greedy algorithm will generate the shortest paths in this order.

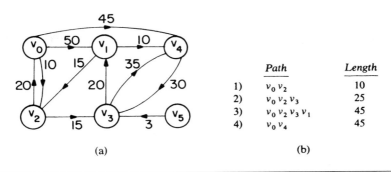

	Path	Length
1)	$v_0 v_2$	10
2)	$v_0 v_2 v_3$	25
3)	$v_0 v_2 v_3 v_1$	45
4)	$v_0 v_4$	45

(a)   (b)

Figure 6.22 Graph and shortest paths from v_0 to all destinations

Let S denote the set of vertices (including v_0) to which the shortest paths have already been found. For w not in S, let $dist[w]$ be the length of the shortest path starting from v_0 going through only those vertices which are in S and ending at w. We observe that when paths are generated in nondecreasing order of length:

(1) If the next shortest path is to vertex u, then the path begins at v_0, ends at u, and goes through only those vertices which are in S. To prove this we must show that all of the intermediate vertices on the shortest path to u must be in S. Assume there is a vertex w on this path that is not in S. Then, the v_0 to u path also contains a path from v_0 to w which is of length less than the v_0 to u path. By assumption the shortest paths are being generated in nondecreasing order of path length, and so the shorter path v_0 to w must already have been generated. Hence, there can be no intermediate vertex which is not in S.

(2) The destination of the next path generated must be that vertex u which has the minimum distance, $dist[u]$, among all vertices not in S. This follows from the definition of $dist$ and observation (1). In case there are several vertices not in S with the same $dist$, then any of these may be selected.

(3) Having selected a vertex u as in (2) and generated the shortest v_0 to u path, vertex u becomes a member of S. At this point, the length of the shortest paths starting at v_0, going through vertices only in S and ending at a vertex w not in S may decrease; i.e., the value of $dist[w]$ may change. If it does change, then it must be due to a shorter path starting at v_0 going to u and then to w. The intermediate vertices on the v_0 to u path and the u to w path must all be in S. Further, the v_0 to u path must be the shortest such path, otherwise $dist[w]$ is not defined properly. Also, the u to w path can be chosen so as to not contain any intermediate vertices. Therefore, we may conclude that if $dist[w]$ is to change (i.e., decrease), then it is because of the path from v_0 to u to w where the path from v_0 to u is the shortest such path and the path from u to w is the edge $<u,w>$. The length of this path is $dist[u] + $ length $(<u,w>)$.

The algorithm *ShortestPath* as first given by Dijkstra makes use of these observations to determine the cost of the shortest paths from v_0 to all other vertices in G. The actual generation of the paths is a minor extension of the algorithm and is left as an exercise. It is assumed that the n vertices of G are numbered 1 through n. The set s is maintained as a boolean array with $s[i] = $ **false** if vertex i is not in S and $s[i] = $ **true** if it is. It is assumed that the graph itself is represented by its cost adjacency matrix with $cost[i,j]$ being the weight of the edge $<i,j>$. $cost[i,j]$ will be set to some large number, **maxint**, in case the edge $<i,j>$ is not in $E(G)$. For $i = j$, $cost[i,j]$ may be set to any nonnegative number without affecting the outcome of the algorithm. Program 6.8 describes the algorithm completely. The data types *AdjacencyMatrix* and *distance* are as below.

$$\textbf{type } AdjacencyMatrix = \textbf{array } [1..maxn, 1..maxn] \textbf{ of integer};$$
$$distance = \textbf{array } [1..maxn] \textbf{ of integer};$$

Analysis of Algorithm *ShortestPath*

From our earlier discussion, it is easy to see that the algorithm works. The time taken by the algorithm on a graph with n vertices is $O(n^2)$. To see this, note that the **for** loop of line 12 takes $O(n)$ time. The **for** loop of line 19 is executed $n-2$ times. Each execution of this loop requires $O(n)$ time at line 21 to select the next vertex and again at lines 24-27 to update *dist*. So the total time for this loop is $O(n^2)$. In case a list of T vertices currently not in S is maintained, then the number of nodes on this list would at any time be $n-i$. This would speed up lines 21 and 24-27, but the asympototic time would remain $O(n^2)$. This and other variations of the algorithm are explored in the exercises.

Any shortest path algorithm must examine each edge in the graph at least once since any of the edges could be in a shortest path. Hence, the minimum possible time for such an algorithm would be $O(e)$. Since cost adjacency matrices were used to represent the graph, it takes $O(n^2)$ time just to determine which edges are in G and so any shortest path algorithm using this representation must take $O(n^2)$. For this representation, then, algorithm *ShortestPath* is optimal to within a constant factor. Even if a change to adjacency lists is made, only the overall time for the **for** loop of lines 24-27 can be brought down to $O(e)$ (since the *dist* can change only for those vertices adjacent from u). The

```
 1 procedure ShortestPath (v : integer; cost : AdjacencyMatrix ;
 2                         var dist : distance ; n : integer);
 3 {dist [j ], 1 ≤ j ≤n is set to the length of the shortest path
 4   from vertex v to vertex j in a digraph g with n vertices.
 5   dist [v ] is set to zero. g is represented by its cost adjacency
 6   matrix, cost [1 .. n, 1 .. n ]}
 7 var s : array [1 .. maxn] of boolean;
 8       i : integer;
 9       u : integer;
10      w : integer;
11 begin
12    for i := 1 to  n do {initialize set S to empty}
13    begin
14      s [i ] := false;
15      dist [i ] := cost [v,i ];
16    end;
17    s [v ] := true;
18    dist [v ] := 0;
19    for i := 1 to n − 2 do {determine n − 1 paths from vertex v}
20    begin
21      u := choose (dist,  n ); {choose returns a value u:
22              dist [u ] = minimum [dist [w ]] where s [w ] = false}
23      s [u ] := true;
24      for w := 1 to n do
25        if not s [w ] then
26          if dist [u ] + cost [u,w ] < dist [w ]
27            then dist [w ] := dist [u ] + cost [u,w ];
28    end; {of for i}
29 end; {of ShortestPath}
```

Program 6.8 Algorithm *ShortestPath*

total time for line 21 remains $O(n^2)$. A more efficient implementation of the greedy algorithm for the single source all destinations problem results from the use of Fibonacci heaps. This is discussed in Chapter 10.

Example 6.1: Consider the eight vertex digraph of Figure 6.23(a) with cost adjacency matrix as in 6.20(b). The values of *dist* and the vertices selected at each iteration of the **while** loop of line 21 for finding all the shortest paths from Boston are shown in Figure 6.24. Note that the algorithm terminates when only seven of the eight vertices are in S. By the definition of *dist*, the distance of the last vertex, in this case Los Angeles, is correct as the shortest path from Boston to Los Angeles can go through only the

remaining six vertices. □

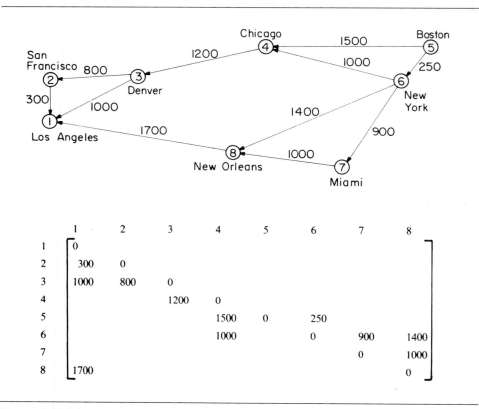

Figure 6.23 Digraph for Example 6.1

All Pairs Shortest Paths

The *all pairs shortest path problem* calls for finding the shortest paths between all pairs of vertices v_i, v_j, $i \neq j$. One possible solution to this is to apply the algorithm *ShortestPath* n times, once with each vertex in $V(G)$ as the source. The total time taken would be $O(n^3)$. For the all pairs problem, we can obtain a conceptually simpler algorithm which will work even when some edges in G have negative weights so long as G has no cycles with negative length. The computing time of this algorithm will still be $O(n^3)$ though the constant factor will be smaller. This new algorithm uses the dynamic programming approach to the design of algorithms.

Iteration	S	Vertex Selected	dist	LA [1]	SF [2]	D [3]	C [4]	B [5]	NY [6]	M [7]	NO [8]
Initial		—		$+\infty$	$+\infty$	$+\infty$	1500	0	250	$+\infty$	$+\infty$
1	5	6		$+\infty$	$+\infty$	$+\infty$	1250	0	250	1150	1650
2	5,6	7		$+\infty$	$+\infty$	$+\infty$	1250	0	250	1150	1650
3	5,6,7	4		$+\infty$	$+\infty$	2450	1250	0	250	1150	1650
4	5,6,7,4	8		3350	$+\infty$	2450	1250	0	250	1150	1650
5	5,6,7,4,8	3		3350	3250	2450	1250	0	250	1150	1650
6	5,6,7,4,8,3	2		3350	3250	2450	1250	0	250	1150	1650
	5,6,7,4,8,3,2										

Figure 6.24 Action of *ShortestPath*

The graph G is represented by its cost adjacency matrix with $cost[i,i] = 0$ and $cost[i,j] = \mathbf{maxint}$ in case edge $<i,j>$, $i \neq j$ is not in G. Define $A^k[i,j]$ to be the cost of the shortest path from i to j going through no intermediate vertex of index greater than k. Then, $A^n[i,j]$ will be the cost of the shortest i to j path in G since G contains no vertex with index greater than n. $A^0[i,j]$ is just $cost[i,j]$ since the only i to j paths allowed can have no intermediate vertices on them. The basic idea in the all pairs algorithm is to successively generate the matrices $A^0, A^1, A^2, \ldots, A^n$. If we have already generated A^{k-1}, then we may generate A^k by realizing that for any pair of vertices i, j either (1) the shortest path from i to j going through no vertex with index greater than k does not go through the vertex with index k and so its cost is $A^{k-1}[i,j]$; or (2) the shortest such path does go through vertex k. Such a path consists of a path from i to k and another one from k to j. These paths must be the shortest paths from i to k and from k to j going through no vertex with index greater than $k-1$, and so their costs are $A^{k-1}[i,k]$ and $A^{k-1}[k,j]$. Note that this is true only if G has no cycle with negative length containing vertex k. If this is not true, then the shortest i to j path going through no vertices of index greater than k may make several cycles from k to k and thus have a length substantially less than $A^{k-1}[i,k] + A^{k-1}[k,j]$ (see Example 6.2). Thus, we obtain the following formulas for $A^k[i,j]$:

$$A^k[i,j] = \min\{A^{k-1}[i,j], A^{k-1}[i,k] + A^{k-1}[k,j]\}, k \geq 1$$

and

$$A^0[i,j] = COST[i,j]$$

Example 6.2: Figure 6.25 shows a digraph together with its matrix A^0. For this graph

$A^2[1,3] \neq \min\{A^1[1,3], A^1[1,2] + A^1[2,3]\} = 2$. Instead we see that $A^2[1,3] = -\infty$ as the length of the path

$$1, 2, 1, 2, 1, 2, \ldots, 1, 2, 3$$

can be made arbitrarily small. This is so because of the presence of the cycle 1, 2, 1 which has a length of -1. $\square$

$$\begin{bmatrix} 0, & 1, & \infty \\ -2, & 0, & 1 \\ \infty, & \infty, & 0 \end{bmatrix}$$

Figure 6.25 Graph with negative cycle

The algorithm *AllCosts* (Program 6.9) computes $A^n[i,j]$. The computation is done in place using the array a. The reason this computation can be carried out in place is that $A^k[i,k] \doteq A^{k-1}[i,k]$ and $A^k[k,j] = A^{k-1}[k,j]$ and so the in place computation does not alter the outcome.

```
1 procedure AllCosts (cost, var a : AdjacencyMatrix; n : integer);
2 {cost [1 ..n, 1 .. n] is the cost adjacency matrix of a graph with n
3   vertices; a [i,j] is the cost of the shortest path between vertices
4   v_i, v_j  cost [i,i] = 0, 1 ≤ i ≤ n}
5 var i : integer;
6     j : integer;
7     k : integer;
8 begin
9   for i := 1 to n do
10    for j := 1 to n do
11      a [i,j] := cost [i,j]; {copy cost into a}
12    for k := 1 to n do {for a path with highest vertex index k}
13      for i := 1 to n do {for all possible pairs of vertices}
14        for j := 1 to n do
15          if (a [i,k] + a [k,j]) < a [i,j]
16              then a [i,j] := a [i,k] + a [k,j];
17 end; {of AllCosts}
```

Program 6.9 Algorithm *AllCosts*

This algorithm is especially easy to analyze because the looping is independent of the data in the matrix a.

The total time for procedure *AllCosts* is $O(n^3)$. An exercise examines the extensions needed to actually obtain the (i,j) paths with these lengths. Some speed up can be obtained by noticing that the innermost **for** loop needs be executed only when $a[i,k]$ and $a[k,j]$ are not equal to **maxint**.

Example 6.3: Using the graph of Figure 6.26(a), we obtain the cost matrix of Figure 6.26(b). The initial a matrix, A^0, plus its value after three iterations A^1, A^2, A^3 is given in Figure 6.27. □

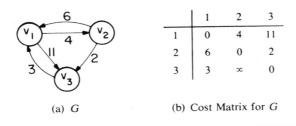

	1	2	3
1	0	4	11
2	6	0	2
3	3	∞	0

(a) G (b) Cost Matrix for G

Figure 6.26 Directed graph and its cost matrix

A^0	1	2	3
1	0	4	11
2	6	0	2
3	3	∞	0

A^1	1	2	3
1	0	4	11
2	6	0	2
3	3	7	0

A^2	1	2	3
1	0	4	6
2	6	0	2
3	3	7	0

A^3	1	2	3
1	0	4	6
2	5	0	2
3	3	7	0

Figure 6.27 Matrices A^k produced by *AllCosts* for the digraph of Figure 6.26

Transitive Closure

A problem related to the all pairs shortest path problem is that of determining for every pair of vertices i, j in G the existence of a path from i to j. Two cases are of interest, one when all path lengths (i.e., the number of edges on the path) are required to be positive and the other when path lengths are to be nonnegative. If A is the adjacency matrix of G, then the Matrix A^+ having the property $A^+[i,j] = 1$ if there is a path of length > 0 from i to j and 0 otherwise is called the *transitive closure* matrix of G. The matrix A^* with the property $A^*[i,j] = 1$, if there is a path of length ≥ 0 from i to j and 0 otherwise is the *reflexive transitive closure* matrix of G.

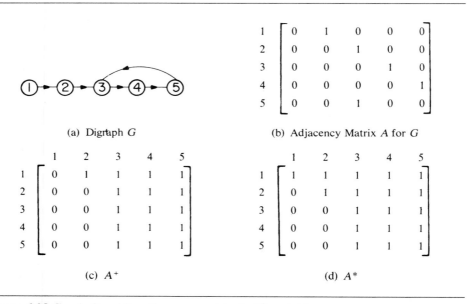

(a) Digraph G

(b) Adjacency Matrix A for G

(c) A^+

(d) A^*

Figure 6.28 Graph G and its adjacency matrix A, A^+ and A^*

Figure 6.28 shows A^+ and A^* for a digraph. Clearly, the only difference between A^* and A^+ is in the terms on the diagonal. $A^+[i,i] = 1$ iff there is a cycle of length >1 containing vertex i while $A^*[i,i]$ is always one as there is a path of length 0 from i to i. If we use algorithm *AllCosts* with $cost[i,j] = 1$ if $<i,j>$ is an edge in G and $cost[i,j]=+\infty$ if $<i,j>$ is not if G, then we can easily obtain A^+ from the final matrix A by letting $A^+[i,j] = 1$ iff $A[i,j]<+\infty$. A^* can be obtained from A^+ by setting all diagonal elements equal to 1. The total time is $O(n^3)$. Some simplification is achieved by slightly modifying the algorithm. In this modification the computation of lines 15 and 16 of *AllCosts* becomes $a[i,j] := a[i,j]$ **or** $(a[i,k]$ **and** $a[k,j])$ and $cost[i,j]$ is just the adjacency matrix of G. With this modification, a need only be a **boolean** matrix and then the final matrix A will be A^+.

6.4 ACTIVITY NETWORKS, TOPOLOGICAL SORT, AND CRITICAL PATHS

Topological Sort

All but the simplest of projects can be subdivided into several subprojects called activities. The successful completion of these activities will result in the completion of the entire project. A student working towards a degree in Computer Science will have to complete several courses successfully. The project in this case is to complete the major, and the activities are the individual courses that have to be taken. Figure 6.29 lists the courses needed for a computer science major at a hypothetical university. Some of these courses may be taken independently of others while other courses have prerequisites and can be taken only if all their prerequisites have already been taken. The data structures course cannot be started until certain programming and math courses have been completed. Thus, prerequisites define precedence relations between courses. The relationships defined may be more clearly represented using a directed graph in which the vertices represent courses and the directed edges represent prerequisites. This graph has an edge $<i, j>$ iff course i is a prerequisite for course j.

Definition: A directed graph G in which the vertices represent tasks or activities and the edges represent precedence relations between tasks is an *activity on vertex network* or AOV network. ☐

Definition: Vertex i in an AOV network G is a *predecessor* of vertex j iff there is a directed path from vertex i to vertex j. i is an *immediate predecessor* of j iff $<i,j>$ is an edge in G. If i is a predecessor of j, then j is a *successor* of i. If i is an immediate predecessor of j, then j is an *immediate successor* of i. ☐

Figure 6.29(b) is the AOV network corresponding to the courses of Figure 6.29(a). C3, C4, and C10 are the immediate predecessors of C7. C2, C3, and C4 are the immediate successors of C1. C12 is a successor of C4 but not an immediate successor. The precedence relation defined by the set of edges on the set of vertices is readily seen to be transitive. (Recall that a relation $\cdot$ is transitive iff it is the case that for all triples i,j,k, $i\cdot j$ and $j\cdot k \Rightarrow i\cdot k$.) In order for an AOV network to represent a feasible project, the precedence relation should also be irreflexive.

Definition: A relation $\cdot$ is *irreflexive* on a set S if for no element x in S it is the case that $x\cdot x$. A precedence relation which is both transitive and irreflexive is a *partial order*. ☐

If the precedence relation is not irreflexive, then there is an activity which is a predecessor of itself and so must be completed before it can be started. This is clearly impossible. When there are no inconsistencies of this type, the project is feasible. Given an AOV network one of our concerns would be to determine whether or not the precedence relation defined by its edges is irreflexive. This is identical to determining whether or not the network contains any directed cycles. A directed graph with no

Course Number	Course Name	Prerequisites
C1	Introduction to Programming	None
C2	Numerical Analysis	C1, C14
C3	Data Structures	C1, C14
C4	Assembly Language	C1, C13
C5	Automata Theory	C15
C6	Artificial Intelligence	C3
C7	Computer Graphics	C3, C4, C10
C8	Machine Arithmetic	C4
C9	Analysis of Algorithms	C3
C10	Higher Level Languages	C3, C4
C11	Compiler Writing	C10
C12	Operating Systems	C11
C13	Analytic Geometry and Calculus I	None
C14	Analytic Geometry and Calculus II	C13
C15	Linear Algebra	C14

(a) Courses Needed for a Computer Science Degree at Some Hypothetical University

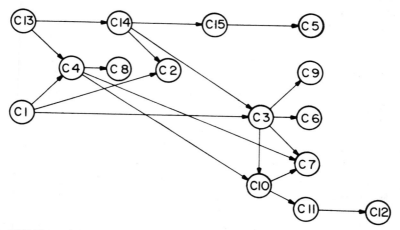

(b) AOV-Network Representing Courses as Vertices and Prerequisites as Edges

Figure 6.29 An activity on vertex network

directed cycles is an *acyclic* graph. Our algorithm to test an AOV network for feasibility will also generate a linear ordering, $v_{i_1}, v_{i_2}, \ldots, v_{i_n}$, of the vertices (activities). This linear ordering will have the property that if i is a predecessor of j in the network then i precedes j in the linear ordering. A linear ordering with this property is called a *topological order*. For the network of Figure 6.29(b) two of the possible topological orders are: C1, C13, C4, C8, C14, C15, C5, C2, C3, C10, C7, C11, C12, C6, C9 and C13, C14, C15,

C5, C1, C4, C8, C2, C3, C10, C7, C6, C9, C11, C12. If a student were taking just one course per term, then he would have to take them in topological order. If the AOV network represented the different tasks involved in assembling an automobile, then these tasks would be carried out in topological order on an assembly line. The algorithm to sort the tasks into topological order is straightforward and proceeds by listing out a vertex in the network that has no predecessor. Then, this vertex together with all edges leading out from it is deleted from the network. These two steps are repeated until either all vertices have been listed or all remaining vertices in the network have predecessors and so none can be removed. In this case there is a cycle in the network and the project is infeasible. Figure 6.30 is a crude form of the algorithm.

```
1  input the AOV network. Let n be the number of vertices.
2  for i := 1 to n do {output the vertices}
3  begin
4      if every vertex has a predecessor
5          then [the network has a cycle and is infeasible.  halt];
6      pick a vertex v which has no predecessors;
7      output v;
8      delete v and all edges leading out of v from the network;
9  end;
```

Figure 6.30 Design of a topological sorting algorithm

Trying this out on the network of Figure 6.31, we see that the first vertex to be picked in line 4 is v_1, as it is the only one with no predecessors. v_1 and the edges $<v_1,v_2>$, $<v_1,v_3>$, and $<v_1,v_4>$ are deleted. In the resulting network (Figure 6.31(b)), v_2, v_3, and v_4 have no predecessor. Any of these can be the next vertex in the topological order. Assume that v_4 is picked. Deletion of v_4 and the edges $<v_4,v_6>$ and $<v_4,v_5>$ results in the network of Figure 6.31(c). Either v_2 or v_3 may next be picked. Figure 6.31 shows the progress of the algorithm on the network. In order to obtain a complete algorithm that can be easily translated into a computer program, it is necessary to specify the data representation for the AOV network. The choice of a data representation, as always, depends on the functions you wish to perform. In this problem, the functions are: (1) decide whether a vertex has any predecessors (line 4), and (2) delete a vertex together with all its incident edges. Function 1 is efficiently done if for each vertex a count of the number of its immediate predecessors is kept. Function 2 is easily implemented if the network is represented by its adjacency lists. Then the deletion of all edges leading out of vertex v can be carried out by decreasing the predecessor count of all vertices on its adjacency list. Whenever the count of a vertex drops to zero, that vertex can be placed onto a list of vertices with a zero count. Then the selection in line 6 just requires removal of a vertex from this list. Filling in these details into the algorithm of Figure 6.30, we obtain the Pascal program *TopologicalOrder* (Program 6.10).

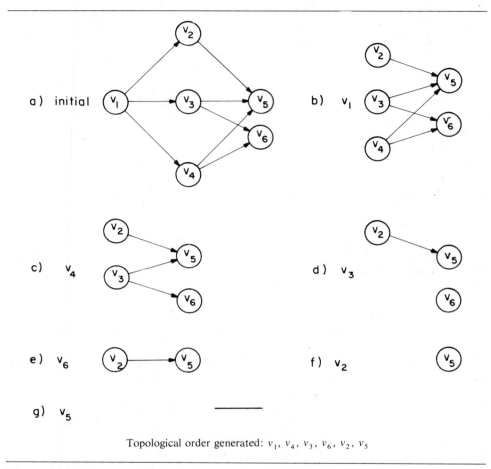

Topological order generated: v_1, v_4, v_3, v_6, v_2, v_5

Figure 6.31 Action of algorithm of Figure 6.30 on an AOV network

The algorithm assumes that the network is represented by adjacency lists. But now the head nodes of these lists contain two fields: *count* and *link*. The data types needed are

```
type NextNode = ↑node;
        node = record
                   vertex : integer;
                   link : NextNode;
               end;
```

```
 1  procedure TopologicalOrder (var AdList : AdjacencyLists ; n : integer);
 2  {The n vertices of an AOV network are listed in topological order.
 3    The network is represented as a set of adjacency lists with
 4    AdList [i].count = the in-degree of vertex i.}
 5  var i, j, k, top : integer;
 6       ptr : NextNode;
 7       done : boolean;
 8  begin
 9    top := 0; {initialize stack}
10    for := 1 to n do {create a linked stack of vertices with}
11      if AdList [i].count = 0 {no predecessors}
12      then begin
13              AdList [i].count := top; top := i;
14          end;
15    i := 1; done := false;
16    while ((i <= n) and not done) do
17        if top = 0 then begin
18                      writeln('network has a cycle'); done := true;
19                  end
20              else begin
21                      j := top; top := AdList [top].count ; {unstack a vertex}
22                      writeln (j);
23                      ptr := AdList [j].link;
24                      while ptr < > nil do
25                      begin {decrease the count of the successor vertices of j}
26                          k := ptr↑.vertex ; {k is a successor of j}
27                          AdList [k].count := AdList [k].count − 1; {decrease count}
28                          if AdList [k].count = 0
29                          then begin {add vertex k to stack}
30                                  AdList [k].count := top; top := k;
31                              end; {of if};
32                          ptr := ptr↑.link ;
33                      end; {of while ptr < > nil}
34                      i := i + 1;
35                  end; {of while (i ≤ n) and not done}
36  end; {of TopologicalOrder}
```

Program 6.10 Topological order

$$HeadNodes = \textbf{record}$$
$$count : \textbf{integer};$$
$$link : NextNode;$$
$$\textbf{end};$$
$$AdjacencyLists = \textbf{array } [1 .. n] \textbf{ of } HeadNodes;$$

The *count* field contains the in-degree of that vertex and *link* is a pointer to the first node on the adjacency list. Each list node has two fields: *vertex* and *link*. *count* fields can be easily set up at the time of input. When edge $<i,j>$ is input, the count of vertex j is incremented by 1. The list of vertices with zero count is maintained as a stack. A queue could have been used but a stack is slightly simpler. The stack is linked through the *count* field of the head nodes since this field is of no use after the *count* has become zero. Figure 6.32(a) shows the input to the algorithm in the case of the network of Figure 6.31(a).

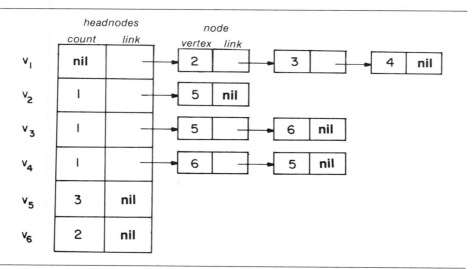

Figure 6.32 Input for procedure *TopologicalOrder*

As a result of a judicious choice of data structures the algorithm is very efficient. For a network with n vertices and e edges, the loop of lines 10-14 takes $O(n)$ time; lines 17-23 take $O(n)$ time over the entire algorithm; the **while** loop of lines 24-33 takes time $O(d_i)$ for each vertex i, where d_i is the out-degree of vertex i. Since this loop is encountered once for each vertex output, the total time for this part of the algorithm is $O((\sum_{i=1}^{n} d_i)+n) = O(e + n)$. Hence, the asymptotic computing time of the algorithm is $O(e+n)$. It is linear in the size of the problem!

Critical Paths

An activity network closely related to the AOV network is the activity on edge or AOE network. The tasks to be performed on a project are represented by directed edges. Vertices in the network represent events. Events signal the completion of certain activities. Activities represented by edges leaving a vertex cannot be started until the event at that vertex has occurred. An event occurs only when all activities entering it have been completed. Figure 6.33(a) is an AOE network for a hypothetical project with 11 tasks or activities $a_1, \ldots, a_{11}$. There are nine events $v_1, v_2, \ldots, v_9$. The events v_1 and v_9 may be interpreted as "start project" and "finish project," respectively. Figure 6.33(b) gives interpretations for some of the nine events. The number associated with each activity is the time needed to perform that activity. Thus, activity a_1 requires 6 days while a_{11} requires 4 days. Usually, these times are only estimates. Activities a_1, a_2, and a_3 may be carried out concurrently after the start of the project. a_4, a_5, and a_6 cannot be started until events v_2, v_3, and v_4, respectively, occur. a_7 and a_8 can be carried out concurrently after the occurrence of event v_5 (i.e., after a_4 and a_5 have been completed). In case additional ordering constraints are to be put on the activities, dummy activities whose time is zero may be introduced. Thus, if we desire that activities a_7 and a_8 not start until both events v_5 and v_6 have occurred, a dummy activity a_{12} represented by an

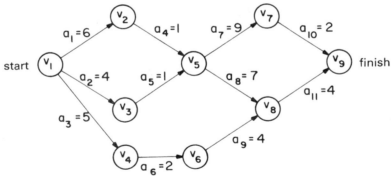

(a)   AOE Network. Activity Graph of a Hypothetical Project.

event	interpretation
v_1	start of project
v_2	completion of activity a_1
v_5	completion of activities a_4 and a_5
v_8	completion of activities a_8 and a_9
v_9	completion of project

(b)   Interpretation for Some of the Events in the Activity Graph of (a).

Figure 6.33 An AOE network

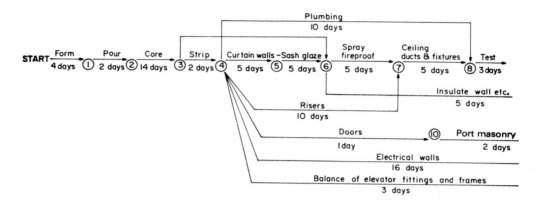

Figure 6.34 AOE network for the construction of a typical floor in a multistory building [Engineering News-Record (McGraw-Hill Book Company, Inc., Jan. 26, 1961).]

edge $<v_6, v_5>$ may be introduced. Activity networks of the AOE type have proved very useful in the performance evaluation of several types of projects. This evaluation includes determining such facts about the project as what is the least amount of time in which the project may be completed (assuming there are no cycles in the network); which activities should be speeded up in order to reduce completion time; etc.

Several sophisticated techniques such as PERT (performance evaluation and review technique), CPM (critical path method), and RAMPS (resource allocation and multiproject scheduling) have been developed to evaluate network models of projects. CPM was originally developed in connection with maintenance and construction projects. Figure 6.34 shows a network used by the Perinia Corporation of Boston in 1961 to model the construction of a floor in a multistory building. PERT was originally designed for use in the development of the Polaris missile system.

Since the activities in an AOE network can be carried out in parallel the minimum time to complete the project is the length of the longest path from the start vertex to the finish vertex (the length of a path is the sum of the times of activities on this path). A path of longest length is a *critical path*. The path v_1, v_2, v_5, v_7, v_9 is a critical path in the network of Figure 6.33(a). The length of this critical path is 18. A network may have more than one critical path (the path v_1, v_2, v_5, v_8, v_9 is also critical). The *earliest time* an event v_i can occur is the length of the longest path from the start vertex v_1 to the vertex v_i. The earliest time event v_5 can occur is 7. The earliest time an event can occur determines the *earliest start time* for all activities represented by edges leaving that vertex. Denote this time by $e(i)$ for activity a_i. For example, $e(7) = e(8) = 7$. For every

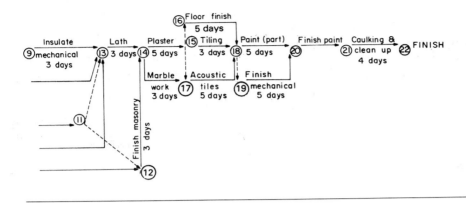

activity a_i, we may also define the *latest time*, $l(i)$, an activity may start without increasing the project duration (i.e., length of the longest path from start to finish). In Figure 6.33(a) we have $e(6)=5$ and $l(6)=8$, $e(8)=7$ and $l(8)=7$. All activities for which $e(i)=l(i)$ are called *critical activities*. The difference $l(i)-e(i)$ is a measure of the criticality of an activity. It gives the time by which an activity may be delayed or slowed without increasing the total time needed to finish the project. If activity a_6 is slowed down to take 2 extra days, this will not affect the project finish time. Clearly, all activities on a critical path are critical and speeding noncritical activities will not reduce the project duration.

The purpose of critical path analysis is to identify critical activities so that resources may be concentrated on these activities in an attempt to reduce project finish time. Speeding a critical activity will not result in a reduced project length unless that activity is on all critical paths. In Figure 6.33(a) the activity a_{11} is critical but speeding it up so that it takes only 3 days instead of 4 does not reduce the finish time to 17 days. This is so because there is another critical path v_1, v_2, v_5, v_7, v_9 that does not contain this activity. The activities a_1 and a_4 are on all critical paths. Speeding a_1 by 2 days reduces the critical path length to 16 days. Critical path methods have proved very valuable in evaluating project performance and identifying bottlenecks.

Critical path analysis can also be carried out with AOV networks. The length of a path would now be the sum of the activity times of the vertices on that path. For each activity or vertex, we could analogously define the quantities $e(i)$ and $l(i)$. Since the activity times are only estimates, it is necessary to re-evaluate the project during several stages of its completion as more accurate estimates of activity times become available. These changes in activity times could make previously noncritical activities critical and vice versa. Before ending our discussion on activity networks, let us design an algorithm to evaluate $e(i)$ and $l(i)$ for all activities in an AOE network. Once these quantities are known, then the critical activities may be easily identified. Deleting all noncritical activities from the AOE network, all critical paths may be found by just generating all paths from the start to finish vertex (all such paths will include only critical activities and so must be critical, and since no noncritical activity can be on a critical path, the network with noncritical activities removed contains all critical paths present in the original network).

In obtaining the $e(i)$ and $l(i)$ for the activities of an AOE network, it is easier to first obtain the earliest event occurrence time, $ee[j]$, and latest event occurrence time, $le[j]$, for all events, j, in the network. Then if activity a_i is represented by edge $<k,l>$, we can compute $e(i)$ and $l(i)$ from the formulas

$$e(i)=ee[k]$$

and $\qquad\qquad\qquad\qquad\qquad\qquad\qquad\qquad\qquad\qquad$ (6.1)

$$l(i)=le[l]-\text{duration of activity } a_i$$

The times $ee[j]$ and $le[j]$ are computed in two stages: a forward stage and a backward stage. During the forward stage we start with $ee[1]=0$ and compute the remaining early start times, using the formula

$$ee[j]=\max_{i\varepsilon P(j)}\{ee[i]+\text{duration of}<i,j>\} \qquad\qquad (6.2)$$

where $P(j)$ is the set of all vertices adjacent to vertex j. In case this computation is carried out in topological order, the early start times of all predecessors of j would have been computed prior to the computation of $ee[j]$. The algorithm to do this is obtained easily from algorithm *TopologicalOrder* by inserting the step

if $ee[k] < ee[j] + ptr\uparrow.dur$
$\qquad$ **then** $ee[k] := ee[j] + ptr\uparrow.dur;$

between lines 38 and 39. It is assumed that the array ee is initialized to zero and that dur is another field in the adjacency list nodes which contains the activity duration. This modification results in the evaluation of Eq. (6.2) in parallel with the generation of a topological order. $ee(j)$ is updated each time the $ee(i)$ of one of its predecessors is known (i.e., when i is ready for output). The step **writeln**(j) of line 33 may be omitted.

To illustrate the working of the modified *TopologicalOrder* algorithm let us try it out on the network of Figure 6.33(a). The adjacency lists for the network are shown in Figure 6.35(a). The order of nodes on these lists determines the order in which vertices will be considered by the algorithm. At the outset the early start time for all vertices is 0, and the start vertex is the only one in the stack. When the adjacency list for this vertex is

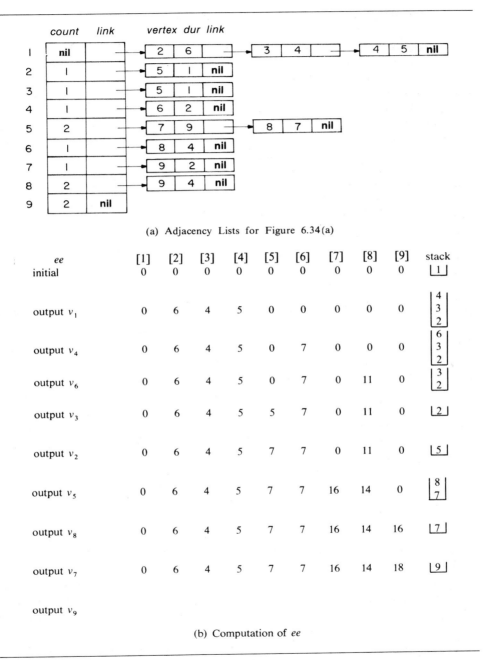

(a) Adjacency Lists for Figure 6.34(a)

	ee	[1]	[2]	[3]	[4]	[5]	[6]	[7]	[8]	[9]	stack
initial		0	0	0	0	0	0	0	0	0	1
output v_1		0	6	4	5	0	0	0	0	0	4 3 2
output v_4		0	6	4	5	0	7	0	0	0	6 3 2
output v_6		0	6	4	5	0	7	0	11	0	3 2
output v_3		0	6	4	5	5	7	0	11	0	2
output v_2		0	6	4	5	7	7	0	11	0	5
output v_5		0	6	4	5	7	7	16	14	0	8 7
output v_8		0	6	4	5	7	7	16	14	16	7
output v_7		0	6	4	5	7	7	16	14	18	9
output v_9											

(b) Computation of ee

Figure 6.35 Action of modified topological order

processed, the early start time of all vertices adjacent from v_1 is updated. Since vertices 2, 3 and 4 are now in the stack, all their predecessors have been processed and Eq. (6.2) evaluated for these three vertices. $ee[6]$ is the next one determined. When vertex v_6 is being processed, $ee[8]$ is updated to 11. This, however, is not the true value for $ee[8]$ since Eq. (6.2) has not been evaluated over all predecessors of v_8 (v_5 has not yet been considered). This does not matter since v_8 cannot get stacked until all its predecessors have been processed. $ee[5]$ is next updated to 5 and finally to 7. At this point $ee[5]$ has been determined as all the predecessors of v_5 have been examined. The values of $ee[7]$ and $ee[8]$ are next obtained. $ee[9]$ is ultimately determined to be 18, the length of a critical path. You may readily verify that when a vertex is put into the stack its early time has been correctly computed. The insertion of the new statement does not change the asymptotic computing time; it remains $O(e+n)$.

In the backward stage the values of $le[i]$ are computed using a procedure analogous to that used in the forward stage. We start with $le[n]=ee[n]$ and use the equation

$$le[j]=\min_{i \varepsilon S(j)} \{ le[i] - \text{duration of } <j,i> \} \qquad (6.3)$$

where $S(j)$ is the set of vertices adjacent from vertex j. The initial values for $le[i]$ may be set to $ee[n]$. Basically, Eq. (6.3) says that if $<j,i>$ is an activity and the latest start time for event i is $le[i]$, then event j must occur no later than $le[i] -$ duration of $<j,i>$. Before $le[j]$ can be computed for some event j, the latest event time for all successor events (i.e., events adjacent from j) must be computed. These times can be obtained in a manner identical to the computation of the early times by using inverse adjacency lists and inserting the step $le[k]:=\min\{le[k],le[j]-ptr\uparrow.dur\}$ at the same place as before in algorithm *TopologicalOrder*. The *count* field of a head node will initially be the out-degree of the vertex.

Figure 6.36 describes the process on the network of Figure 6.33(a). In case the forward stage has already been carried out and a topological ordering of the vertices obtained, then the values of $le[i]$ can be computed directly, using Eq. (6.3), by performing the computations in the reverse topological order. The topological order generated in Figure 6.35(b) is $v_1, v_4, v_6, v_3, v_2, v_5, v_8, v_7, v_9$. We may compute the values of $le[i]$ in the order 9, 7, 8, 5, 2, 3, 6, 4, 1 as all successors of an event precede that event in this order. In practice, one would usually compute both ee and le. The procedure would then be to compute ee first using algorithm *TopologicalOrder* modified as discussed for the forward stage and to then compute le directly from Eq. (6.3) in reverse topological order.

Using the values of ee (Figure 6.35) and of le (Figure 6.36 and Eq. (6.1)) we may compute the early and late times $e(i)$ and $l(i)$ and the degree of criticality of each task. Figure 6.37 gives the values. The critical activities are $a_1, a_4, a_7, a_8, a_{10}$, and a_{11}. Deleting all noncritical activities from the network we get the directed graph of Figure 6.38. All paths from v_1 to v_9 in this graph are critical paths and there are no critical paths in the original network that are not paths in the graph of Figure 6.38.

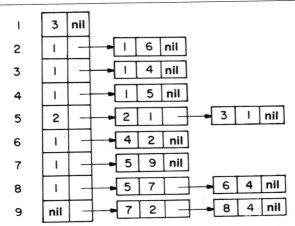

(a) Inverted Adjacency Lists for AOE Network of Figure 6.34(a).

le	[1]	[2]	[3]	[4]	[5]	[6]	[7]	[8]	[9]	stack
initial	18	18	18	18	18	18	18	18	18	9
output v_9	18	18	18	18	18	18	16	14	18	8 7
output v_8	18	18	18	18	7	10	16	14	18	6 7
output v_6	18	18	18	18	7	10	16	14	18	4 7
output v_4	3	18	18	8	7	10	16	14	18	7
output v_7	3	18	18	8	7	10	16	14	18	5
output v_5	3	6	6	8	7	10	16	14	18	3 2
output v_3	2	6	6	8	7	10	16	14	18	2
output v_2	0	6	6	8	7	10	16	14	18	1

(b) Computation of *topologicalorder* Modified to Compute Latest Event Times.

$$le[9] = ee[9] = 18$$
$$le[7] = \min\{le[9] - 2\} = 16$$
$$le[8] = \min\{le[9] - 4\} = 14$$
$$le[5] = \min\{le[7] - 9, le[8] - 7\} = 7$$
$$le[2] = \min\{le[5] - 1\} = 6$$
$$le[3] = \min\{le[5] - 1\} = 6$$
$$le[6] = \min\{le[8] - 4\} = 10$$
$$le[4] = \min\{le[6] - 2\} = 8$$
$$le[1] = \min\{le[2] - 6, le[3] - 4, le[4] - 5\} = 0$$

(c) Computation of *le* Directly from Equation (6.3) Using a Reverse Topological Order.

Figure 6.36 Computing *le* for AOE network of Figure 6.33(a)

activity	e	l	$l - e$
a_1	0	0	0
a_2	0	2	2
a_3	0	3	3
a_4	6	6	0
a_5	4	6	2
a_6	5	8	3
a_7	7	7	0
a_8	7	7	0
a_9	7	10	3
a_{10}	16	16	0
a_{11}	14	14	0

Figure 6.37 Early, late, and criticality values

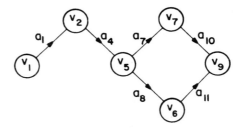

Figure 6.38 Graph obtained after deleting all noncritical activities

As a final remark on activity networks we note that the algorithm *Topological Order* detects only directed cycles in the network. There may be other flaws, such as vertices not reachable from the start vertex (Figure 6.39). When a critical path analysis is carried out on such networks, there will be several vertices with $ee[i] = 0$. Since all activity times are assumed >0, only the start vertex can have $ee[i] = 0$. Hence, critical path analysis can also be used to detect this kind of fault in project planning.

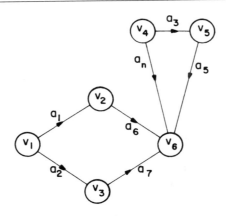

Figure 6.39 AOE network with some nonreachable activities

6.5 ENUMERATING ALL PATHS

In Section 6.3, we looked at the problem of finding a shortest path between two vertices. In this section we will be concerned with listing all possible simple paths between two vertices in order of nondecreasing path length. Such a listing could be of use, for example, in a situation where we are interested in obtaining the shortest path that satisfies some complex set of constraints. One possible solution to such a problem would be to generate in nondecreasing order of path length all paths between the two vertices. Each path generated could be tested against the other constraints and the first path satisfying all these constraints would be the path we were looking for.

Let $G=(V,E)$ be a digraph with n vertices. Let v_1 be the source vertex and v_n the destination vertex. We shall assume that every edge has a positive cost. Let $p_1 = r[0], r[1], \ldots, r[k]$ be a shortest path from v_1 to v_n; i.e., p_1 starts at $v_{r[0]} = v_1$, goes to $v_{r[1]}$ and then to $v_{r[2]}, \ldots, v_n = v_{r[k]}$. If P is the set of all simple v_1 to v_n paths in G, then it is easy to see that every path in $P - \{p_1\}$ differs from p_1 in exactly one of the following k ways:

(1) It contains the edges $(r[1],r[2]), \ldots, (r[k-1],r[k])$ but not $(r[0],r[1])$
(2) It contains the edges $(r[2],r[3]), \ldots, (r[k-1],r[k])$ but not $(r[1],r[2])$
.
.
.
(k) It does not contain the edge $(r[k-1],r[k])$

More compactly, for every path p in $P - \{p_1\}$ there is exactly one j, $1 \leq j \leq k$ such that p contains the edges

$$(r[j], r[j+1]), \ldots, (r[k-1], r[k]) \text{ but not } (r[j-1], r[j])$$

The set of paths $P - \{p_1\}$ may be partitioned into k disjoint sets $P^{(1)}, \ldots, P^{(k)}$ with set $P^{(j)}$ containing all paths in $P - \{p_1\}$ satisfying condition j above, $1 \leq j \leq k$.

Let $p^{(j)}$ be a shortest path in $P^{(j)}$ and let q be the shortest path from v_1 to $v_{r[j]}$ in the digraph obtained by deleting from G the edges $(r[j-1], r[j])$, $(r[j], r[j+1])$, $\ldots$, $(r[k-1], r[k])$. Then one readily obtains $p^{(j)} = q, r[j], r[j+1], \ldots, r[k] = n$. Let $p^{(l)}$ have the minimum length among $p^{(1)}, \ldots, p^{(k)}$. Then, $p^{(l)}$ also has the least length amongst all paths in $P - \{p_1\}$ and hence must be a second shortest path. The set $P^{(l)} - \{p^{(l)}\}$ may now be partitioned into disjoint subsets using a criterion identical to that used to partition $P - \{p_1\}$. If $p^{(l)}$ has k' edges, then this partitioning results in k' disjoint subsets. We next determine the shortest paths in each of these k' subsets. Consider the set Q which is the union of these k' shortest paths and the paths $p^{(1)}, \ldots, p^{(l-1)}, \ldots, p^{(k)}$. The path with minimum length in Q is a third shortest path p_3. The corresponding set may be further partitioned. In this way we may successively generate the v_1 to v_n paths in nondecreasing order of path length.

At this point, an example would be instructive. The generation of the v_1 to v_6 path of the graph of Figure 6.40 is shown in Figure 6.41. A very informal version of the algorithm appears as the procedure *mshortest* (Program 6.11).

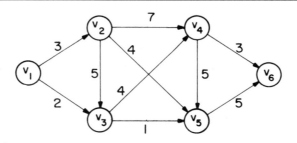

Figure 6.40 A graph

Since the number of v_1 to v_n paths in a digraph with n vertices ranges from 0 to $(n-1)!$, a worst case analysis of the computing time of *mshortest* is not very meaningful. Instead, we shall determine the time taken to generate the first m shortest paths. Line 5 of the **for** loop may require determining $n-1$ shortest paths in an n vertex graph. Using a modified version of algorithm *ShortestPath* this would take $O(n^3)$ for each iteration of the **for** loop. The total contribution of line 5 is therefore $O(mn^3)$. In the next chapter,

Shortest Path	Cost	Included Edges	Excluded Edges	New Path
$v_1v_3v_5v_6$	8	none	none	
		none	(v_5v_6)	$v_1v_3v_4v_6 = 9$
		(v_5v_6)	(v_3v_5)	$v_1v_2v_5v_6 = 12$
		$(v_3v_5)(v_5v_6)$	(v_1v_3)	$v_1v_2v_3v_5v_6 = 14$
$v_1v_3v_4v_6$	9	none	(v_5v_6)	
		none	$(v_4v_6)(v_5v_6)$	∞
		(v_4v_6)	$(v_3v_4)(v_5v_6)$	$v_1v_2v_4v_6 = 13$
		$(v_3v_4)(v_4v_6)$	$(v_1v_3)(v_5v_6)$	$v_1v_2v_3v_4v_6 = 15$
$v_1v_2v_5v_6$	12	(v_5v_6)	(v_3v_5)	
		(v_5v_6)	$(v_2v_5)(v_3v_5)$	$v_1v_3v_4v_5v_6 = 16$
		$(v_2v_5)(v_5v_6)$	$(v_1v_2)(v_3v_5)$	∞
$v_1v_2v_4v_6$	13	(v_4v_6)	$(v_3v_4)(v_5v_6)$	
		(v_4v_6)	$(v_2v_4)(v_3v_4)(v_5v_6)$	∞
		$(v_2v_4)(v_4v_6)$	$(v_1v_2)(v_3v_4)(v_5v_6)$	∞
$v_1v_2v_3v_5v_6$	14	$(v_3v_5)(v_5v_6)$	(v_1v_3)	
		$(v_3v_5)(v_5v_6)$	$(v_2v_3)(v_1v_3)$	∞
		$(v_2v_3)(v_3v_5)(v_5v_6)$	$(v_1v_2)(v_5v_6)$	
$v_1v_2v_3v_4v_6$	15	$(v_3v_4)(v_4v_6)$	$(v_1v_3)(v_5v_6)$	
		$(v_3v_4)(v_4v_6)$	$(v_2v_3)(v_1v_3)(v_5v_6)$	∞
		$(v_2v_3)(v_3v_5)(v_5v_6)$	$(v_1v_2)(v_1v_3)(v_5v_6)$	∞
$v_1v_3v_4v_5v_6$	16	(v_5v_6)	$(v_2v_5)(v_3v_5)$	
		(v_5v_6)	$(v_4v_5)(v_2v_5)(v_3v_5)$	∞
		$(v_4v_5)(v_5v_6)$	$(v_3v_4)(v_2v_5)(v_3v_5)$	$v_1v_2v_4v_5v_6 = 20$
		$(v_3v_4)(v_4v_5)(v_5v_6)$	$(v_1v_3)(v_2v_5)(v_3v_5)$	$v_1v_2v_3v_4v_5v_6 = 22$

Figure 6.41 Action of *mshortest*

when we study heap sort, we shall see that it is possible to maintain Q as a heap with the result that the total contribution of lines 3 and 6 is less than $O(mn^3)$. The total time to generate the m shortest paths is, therefore, $O(mn^3)$. The space needed is determined by the number of tuples in Q. Since at most $n - 1$ shortest paths are generated at each iteration of line 5, at most $O(mn)$ tuples get onto Q. Each path has at most $O(n)$ edges and the additional constraints take less space than this. Hence, the total space requirements are $O(mn^2)$.

---

procedure *mshortest* (*M*)

{Given a digraph *G* with positive edge weights this procedure outputs the *M* shortest paths from v_1 to v_n. *Q* contains tuples of the form (p,C) where p is a shortest path in *G* satisfying constraints *C*. These constraints either require certain edges to be included or excluded from the path}

    begin

1    $Q := \{(\text{shortest } v_1 \text{ to } v_n \text{ path}, \phi)\}$;

2   **for** $i := 1$ **to** *M* **do begin** {generate M shortest paths}

3   *let* (p,C) be the tuple in Q such that path p is of minimal length;

                                   {p is the i'th shortest path}

4   **writeln** path p; delete path p from *Q*;

5   determine the shortest paths in *G* under the constraints *C* and the additional constraints imposed by the partitioning described in the text;

6   add these shortest paths together with their constraints to *Q*;

7   **end**;

8   **end** {*mshortest*}

Program 6.11 Find the *M* shortest paths

6.6 REFERENCES AND SELECTED READINGS

Euler's original paper on the Koenigsberg bridge problem makes interesting reading. This paper has been reprinted in: ''Leonhard Euler and the Koenigsberg Bridges,'' *Scientific American*, vol. 189, no. 1, July 1953, pp. 66-70.

The biconnected component algorithm is due to Tarjan. This, together with a linear time algorithm to find the strongly connected components of a directed graph, appears in the paper: ''Depth-first search and linear graph algorithms,'' by R. Tarjan, *SIAM Journal on Computing*, vol. 1, no. 2, 1972, pp. 146-159.

Prim's minimum cost spanning algorithm was actually first proposed by Jarnik in 1930 and rediscovered by Prim in 1957. Since virtually all references to this algorithm give credit to Prim, we continue to refer to it as Prim's algorithm. Similarly the algorithm we refer to as Sollin's algorithm was first proposed by Boruvka in 1926 and rediscovered by Sollin several years later. For an interesting discussion of the history of the minimum spanning tree problem see: ''On the history of the minimum spanning tree problem,'' by R. Graham and P. Hell, *Annals of the History of Computing*, Vol 7, No 1, 1985, pp. 43-57.

Further algorithms on graphs may be found in: *The Design and Analysis of Computer Algorithms*, by A. Aho, J. Hopcroft and J. Ullman, Addison-Wesley, Reading, Massachusetts, 1974; *Graph Theory with Applications to Engineering and Computer*

Science, by N. Deo, Prentice-Hall, Englewood Cliffs, New Jersey, 1974; *Combinatorial Optimization*, by E. Lawler, Holt, Reinhart and Winston, 1976; *Flows in Networks*, by L. Ford and D. Fulkerson, Princeton University Press, 1962; and *Integer Programming and Network Flows*, by T.C. Hu, Addison-Wesley, Reading, Massachusetts, 1970.

For more on activity networks and critical path analysis see: *Project Management with CPM and PERT*, by Moder and C. Phillips, Van Nostrand Reinhold Co., 1970.

6.7 EXERCISES

1. Does the multigraph of Figure 6.42 have an Eulerian walk? If so, find one.

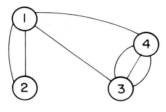

Figure 6.42 A multigraph

2. For the digraph of Figure 6.43 obtain:
    (a)   the in degree and out degree of each vertex
    (b)   its adjacency matrix
    (c)   its adjacency list representation
    (d)   its adjacency multilist representation
    (e)   its strongly connected components

3. Devise a suitable representation for graphs so they can be stored on disk. Write an algorithm which reads in such a graph and creates its adjacency matrix. Write another algorithm which creates the adjacency lists from the disk input.

4. Draw the complete undirected graphs on one, two, three, four, and five vertices. Prove that the number of edges in an n vertex complete graph is $n(n-1)/2$.

5. Is the directed graph of Figure 6.44 strongly connected? List all the simple paths.

6. Show how the graph above would look if represented by its adjacency matrix, adjacency lists, adjacency multilist.

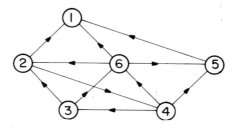

Figure 6.43 A digraph

Figure 6.44 A directed graph

7. For an undirected graph G with n vertices and e edges show that $\sum_{1}^{n} d_i = 2e$ where $d_i = $ degree of vertex i.

8. (a) Let G be a connected undirected graph on n vertices. Show that G must have at least $n - 1$ edges and that all connected undirected graphs with $n - 1$ edges are trees.

   (b) What is the minimum number of edges in a strongly connected digraph on n vertices? What shape do such digraphs have?

9. For an undirected graph G with n vertices prove that the following are equivalent:

   (a) G is a tree

   (b) G is connected, but if any edge is removed the resulting graph is not connected

   (c) For any distinct vertices $u \in V(G)$ and $v \in V(G)$ there is exactly one simple path from u to v

(d) G contains no cycles and has $n - 1$ edges

10.   Write a Pascal procedure to input the number of vertices in an undirected graph and its edges one by one and set up the linked adjacency list representation of the graph. You may assume that no edge is input twice. What is the run time of your procedure as a function of the number of vertices and the number of edges?

11.   Let G be a connected undirected graph. Show that no vertex of G can be in more than two biconnected components of H. Use this to show that no edge of G can be in two or more biconnected components of G.

12.   Let G be a connected graph and let T be any of its depth first spanning trees. Show that G has no cross edges relative to T.

13.   Prove that procedure *bicon* (Program 6.5) correctly partitions the edges of a connected graph into the biconnected components of the graph.

14.   A *bipartite graph* $G = (V,E)$ is an undirected graph whose vertices can be partitioned into two disjoint sets V_1 and $V_2 = V - V_1$ with the properties (a) no two vertices in V_1 are adjacent in G and (b) no two vertices in V_2 are adjacent in G. The graph G_4 of Figure 6.5 is bipartite. A possible partitioning of V is $V_1 = \{1,4,5,7\}$ and $V_2 = \{2,3,6,8\}$. Write an algorithm to determine whether a graph G is bipartite. In case G is bipartite your algorithm should obtain a partitioning of the vertices into two disjoint sets V_1 and V_2 satisfying properties (a) and (b) above. Show that if G is represented by its adjacency lists, then this algorithm can be made to work in time $O(n + e)$ where $n = |V|$ and $e = |E|$.

15.   Show that every tree is a bipartite graph.

16.   Prove that a graph G is bipartite iff it contains no cycles of odd length.

17.   Program 6.12 was obtained by Stephen Barnard to find an Eulerian circuit in an undirected graph in case there was such a circuit.

```
    function euler (v : vertex): path;
1 begin
2    path := {∅};
3    for all vertices w  adjacent to v and edge (v,w) not yet used do begin
4        mark edge (v,w) as used;
5        path := {(v,w)} ∪ euler (w) ∪ path;
6    end;
7        euler := path;
8 end {euler}
```

Program 6.12

(a) Show that if G is represented by its adjacency multilists and *path* by a linked list, then algorithm *euler* works in time $O(n + e)$.

(b) Prove by induction on the number of edges in G that the above algorithm does obtain an Euler circuit for all graphs G having such a circuit. The initial call to Euler can be made with any vertex v.

(c) At termination, what has to be done to determine whether or not G has an Euler circuit?

18. Apply depth first and breadth first search to the complete graph on four vertices. List the vertices in the order they would be visited.

19. Show how to modify algorithms *dfs* as it is used in *comp* to produce a list of all newly visited vertices.

20. Prove that when algorithm *dfs* is applied to a connected graph the edges of T form a tree.

21. Prove that when algorithm *bfs* is applied to a connected graph the edges of T form a tree.

22. An edge (u, v) of a connected undirected graph G is a *bridge* iff its deletion from G results in a graph that is not connected. In the graph of Figure 6.15, the edges $(1, 2)$, $(4, 6)$, $(8, 9)$, and $(8, 10)$ are bridges. Write an $O(n + e)$ time algorithm to find the bridges of G. n and e are, respectively, the number of vertices and edges of G. (Hint: use the ideas in procedure *biconnected* (Program 6.5).)

23. Prove that Prim's algorithm finds a minimum cost spanning tree for every connected undirected graph.

24. Refine Program 6.7 into a Pascal procedure to find a minimum cost spanning tree. The complexity of your procedure should be $O(n^2)$ where n is the number of vertices in the input graph. Show that this is the case.

25. Prove that Sollin's algorithm finds a minimum cost spanning tree for every connected undirected graph.

26. What is the maximum number of stages in Sollin's algorithm? Give this as a function of the number of vertices n in the graph.

27. Obtain a Pascal procedure to find a minimum cost spanning tree using Sollin's algorithm. What is the complexity of your procedure?

28. Show that $A^+ = A^* \times A$ where matrix multiplication of the two matrices is defined as $a_{ij}^+ = \vee_{k=1}^{n} a_{ik}^* \wedge a_{kj}$. $\vee$ is the logical *or* operation and $\wedge$ is the logical *and* operation.

29. Obtain the matrices A^+ and A^* for the digraph of Figure 6.44.

30. Another way to represent a graph is by its incidence matrix, INC. There is one row for each vertex and one column for each edge. Then $INC[i, j] = 1$ if edge j is incident to vertex i. The incidence matrix for the graph of Figure 6.14(a) is given in Figure 6.45. The edges of Figure 6.14(a) have been numbered from left to right,

$$
\begin{array}{c}
1\;2\;3\;4\;5\;6\;7\;8\;9\;10 \\
\begin{array}{c}
1 \\ 2 \\ 3 \\ 4 \\ 5 \\ 6 \\ 7 \\ 8
\end{array}
\left[
\begin{array}{cccccccccc}
1 & 1 & 0 & 0 & 0 & 0 & 0 & 0 & 0 & 0 \\
1 & 0 & 1 & 1 & 0 & 0 & 0 & 0 & 0 & 0 \\
0 & 1 & 0 & 0 & 1 & 1 & 0 & 0 & 0 & 0 \\
0 & 0 & 1 & 0 & 0 & 0 & 1 & 0 & 0 & 0 \\
0 & 0 & 0 & 1 & 0 & 0 & 0 & 1 & 0 & 0 \\
0 & 0 & 0 & 0 & 1 & 0 & 0 & 0 & 1 & 0 \\
0 & 0 & 0 & 0 & 0 & 1 & 0 & 0 & 0 & 1 \\
0 & 0 & 0 & 0 & 0 & 0 & 1 & 1 & 1 & 1
\end{array}
\right]
\end{array}
$$

Figure 6.45 Incidence matrix of graph of Figure 6.14(a)

top to bottom. Rewrite algorithm *dfs* so it works on a graph represented by its incidence matrix.

31. If ADJ is the adjacency matrix of a graph $G = (V,E)$ and INC is the incidence matrix, under what conditions will $ADJ = INC \times INC^T - I$ where INC^T is the transpose of matrix INC? Matrix multiplication is defined as in Exercise 28. I is the identity matrix.

32. Show that if T is a spanning tree for the undirected graph G, then the addition of an edge e, $e \notin E(T)$ and $e \in E(G)$, to T creates a unique cycle.

33. By considering the complete graph with n vertices, show that the number of spanning trees is at least $2^{n-1} - 1$.

34. The *radius* of a tree is the maximum distance from the root to a leaf. Given a connected, undirected graph write an algorithm for finding a spanning tree of minimum radius. (Hint: use breadth first search.) Prove that your algorithm is correct.

35. The *diameter* of a tree is the maximum distance between any two vertices. Given a connected, undirected graph write an algorithm for finding a spanning tree of minimum diameter. Prove the correctness of your algorithm.

36. Write out Kruskal's minimum spanning tree algorithm (Program 6.6) as a complete program. You may use as procedures the algorithms *union* and *find* of Chapter 5. Use algorithm *sort* to sort the edges into nondecreasing order by weight.

37. Using the idea of algorithm *ShortestPath*, give an algorithm to find a minimum spanning tree whose worst case time is $O(n^2)$.

38. Use algorithm *ShortestPath* to obtain in nondecreasing order the lengths of the shortest paths from vertex 1 to all remaining vertices in the digraph of Figure 6.46.

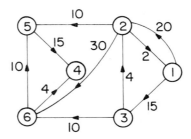

Figure 6.46 Digraph for shortest paths exercise

39. Rewrite algorithm *ShortestPath* under the following assumptions:

    (a)   *G* is represented by its adjacency lists, where each node has three fields: *vertex*, *cost*, and *link*. *cost* is the length of the corresponding edge and *n* the number of vertices in *G*.

    (b)   Instead of representing *S*, the set of vertices to which the shortest paths have already been found, the set $T = V(G) - S$ is represented using a linked list.
    What can you say about the computing time of your new algorithm relative to that of *ShortestPath*?

40. Modify algorithm *ShortestPath* so that it obtains the shortest paths in addition to the lengths of these paths. What is the computing time of your algorithm?

41. Using the directed graph of Figure 6.47, explain why *ShortestPath* will not work properly. What is the shortest path between vertices v_1 and v_7?

42. Modify algorithm *AllCosts* so that it obtains a shortest path for all pairs of vertices i, j. What is the computing time of your new algorithm?

43. By considering the complete graph with *n* vertices show that the maximum number of simple paths between two vertices is $O((n-1)!)$.

44. Use algorithm *AllCosts* to obtain the lengths of the shortest paths between all pairs of vertices in the graph of Figure 6.46. Does *AllCosts* give the right answers? Why?

45. Does the following set of precedence relations (<) define a partial order on the elements 1 thru 5? Why?

$$1 < 2; 2 < 4; 2 < 3; 3 < 4; 3 < 5; 5 < 1$$

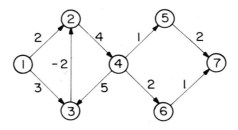

Figure 6.47 Directed graph on which *ShortestPath* does not work properly

46. (a) For the AOE network of Figure 6.48 obtain the early, $e(\ )$, and late, $l(\ )$, start times for each activity. Use the forward-backward approach.

(b) What is the earliest time the project can finish?

(c) Which activities are critical?

(d) Is there any single activity whose speed up would result in a reduction of the project length?

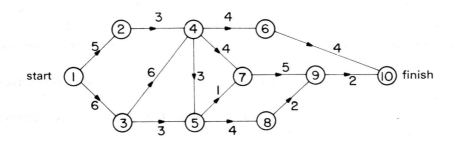

Figure 6.48 An AOE network

47. Define a critical AOE network to be an AOE network in which all activities are critical. Let G be the undirected graph obtained by removing the directions and weights from the edges of the network.

(a) Show that the project length can be decreased by speeding exactly one activity if there is an edge in G which lies on every path from the start vertex to the finish vertex. Such an edge is called a bridge. Deletion of a bridge from a connected graph disconnects the graph into two connected components.

(b) Write an $O(n + e)$ algorithm using adjacency lists to determine whether the connected graph G has a bridge. In case G has a bridge, your algorithm should output one such bridge.

48. Write a set of computer programs for manipulating graphs. Such a collection should allow input and output of arbitrary graphs, determining connected components and spanning trees. The capabililty of attaching weights to the edges should also be provided.

49. Make sure you can define the following terms:

adjacent (v) connected (v_p, v_q)
adjacent-to (v) connected (G)
adjacent-from (v) connected component
degree (v) strongly connected
in-degree (v) tree
out-degree (v) network
path   spanning tree
simple path
cycle
subgraph

CHAPTER 7
INTERNAL SORTING

7.1 SEARCHING

In this chapter, we use the term *file* to mean a collection of records, each record having one or more fields. This is to be distinguished from the use of this term in the Pascal language. The fields used to distinguish among the records are known as *keys*. Since the same file may be used for several different applications, the key fields for record identification will depend on the particular application. For instance, we may regard a telephone directory as a file, each record having three fields: name, address, and phone number. The key is usually the person's name. However, we may wish to locate the record corresponding to a given number, in which case the phone number field would be the key. In yet another application we may desire the phone number at a particular address, so this field too could be the key.

Once we have a collection of records there are at least two ways in which to store them: sequentially or nonsequentially. For the time being let us assume we have a sequential file f and we wish to retrieve a record with a certain key value k. If f has n records with $f[i].key$ the key value for record i, then we may carry out the retrieval by examining the key values $f[n].key, \ldots, f[1].key$ in that order, until the correct record is located. Such a search is known as sequential search since the records are examined sequentially. Program 7.1 gives a sequential search procedure that uses the following data types:

$$\textbf{type } records = \textbf{record}$$
$$key : \textbf{integer};$$
$$other : fields;$$
$$\textbf{end};$$
$$afile = \textbf{array } [0..n] \textbf{ of } records;$$

```
1 procedure SeqSearch (var f : afile; var i : integer; n,k : integer);
2 {search a file f with key values f[1] . key, . . ., f[n] . key for a record
3   such that f [i] . key = k. If there is no such record, i is set to 0.}
4 begin
5   f[0] . key := k;
6   i := n;
7   while f[i] . key < > k do
8     i := i − 1;
9 end; {of SeqSearch}
```

Program 7.1 Sequential search

Note that the introduction of the dummy record 0 with *key* $f[0] . key = k$ in f simplifies the search by eliminating the need for an end of file test ($i < 1$) in the **while** loop. While this might appear to be a minor improvement, it actually reduces the running time by 50% for large n. If no record in the file has key value k, then $i = 0$, and the above procedure requires $n + 1$ comparisons. The number of key comparisons made in case of a successful search depends on the position of the key in the file. If all keys are distinct and key $f[i] . key$ is being searched for, then $n − i + 1$ key comparisons are made. The average number of comparisons for a successful search is, therefore, $\sum_{1 \le i \le n} (n − i + 1)/n = (n + 1)/2$.

For large n this many comparisons is very inefficient. However, we all know that it is possible to do much better when looking up phone numbers. What enables us to make an efficient search? The fact that the entries in the file (i.e., the telephone directory) are in lexicographic order (on the name key) is what enables one to look up a number while examining only a very few entries in the file. So, if the file is ordered one should be able to search for specific records quickly.

One of the better known methods for searching an ordered sequential file is called binary search. In this method, the search begins by examining the record in the middle of the file rather than the one at one of the ends as in sequential search. Let us assume that the file being searched is ordered by nondecreasing values of the key (i.e., in alphabetical order for strings). Then, based on the results of the comparsion with the middle key, $f[m] . key$, one can draw one of the following conclusions:

(1)   if $k < f[m] . key$ then if the record being searched for is in the file, it must be in the lower numbered half of the file;

(2)   if $k = f[m] . key$ then the middle record is the one being searched for; and

(3)   if $k > f[m].key$ then if the record being searched for is in the file, it must be in the higher numbered half of the file.

Consequently, after each comparison either the search terminates successfully or the size of the file remaining to be searched is about one half of the original size (note that in the case of sequential search, after each comparison the size of the file remaining to be searched decreases by only 1). So, after j key comparisons the file remaining to be examined is of size at most $\lceil n/2^j \rceil$ (n is the number of records). Hence, in the worst case, this method requires O(log n) key comparisons to search a file. Algorithm *BinarySearch* implements the scheme just outlined.

```
1  procedure BinarySearch (var f : afile; var i : integer; n,k : integer);
2  {Search a file whose n records are ordered such that
3  f[1].key ≤ f[2].key ≤ ... ≤ f[n].key for a record i such that
4   f[i].key = k; i = 0 if there is no such record else f[i].key = k.
5   Throughout the algorithm, l is the smallest index such that
6   f[l].key may be k and u the largest index such
7   that f[u].key may be k.}
8  var done : boolean
9      l,u,m : integer;
10 begin
11    l := 1; u := n; i := 0;
12    done := false;
13    while ((l <= u) and (not done)) do
14    begin
15      m := (l + u) div 2; {compute index of middle record}
16      case compare (k, f[m].key) of
17          '>' : l := m + 1 {look in upper half}
18          '=' : begin
19                   i := m;
20                   done := true;
21                end;
22          '<' : u := m - 1; {look in lower half}
23      end; {of case}
24    end; {of while}
25 end; {of BinarySearch}
```

Program 7.2 Binary search

    In the binary search method described above, it is always the key in the middle of the subfile currently being examined that is used for comparison. This splitting process can be described by drawing a binary decision tree in which the value of a node is the index of the key being tested. Suppose there are 31 records, then the first key tested is

$f[16].key$ since $\lfloor(1 + 31)/2\rfloor = 16$. If k is less than $f[16].key$ then $f[8].key$ is tested next as $\lfloor(1 + 15)/2\rfloor = 8$; or if k is greater than $f[16].key$ then $f[24].key$ is tested. The binary tree describing this process is given in Figure 7.1. A path from the root to any node in the tree represents a sequence of comparisons made by *BinarySearch* to either find k or determine that it is not present. From the depth of this tree one can easily see that the algorithm makes no more than $O(\log_2 n)$ comparisons.

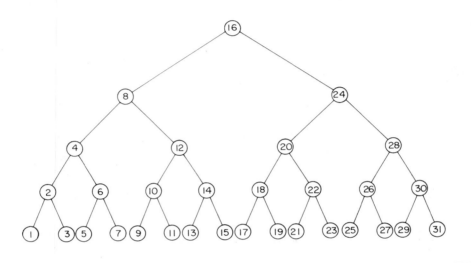

Figure 7.1 Binary decision tree for binary search

It is possible to consider other criteria than equal splitting for dividing the remaining file. An alternate method is Fibonacci search, which splits the subfile according to the Fibonacci sequence,

$$0, 1, 1, 2, 3, 5, 8, 13, 21, 34, \ldots$$

which is defined as $F_0 = 0$, $F_1 = 1$, and

$$F_i = F_{i-1} + F_{i-2}, \ i \geq 2$$

An advantage of Fibonacci search is that it involves only addition and subtraction rather than the division in *BinarySearch*. So its average performance is better than that of binary search on computers for which division takes sufficiently more time than addition/subtraction.

Suppose we begin by assuming that the number of records is one less than some Fibonacci number, $n = F_a - 1$. Then, the first comparsion of key k is made with $f[F_{a-1}].key$ with the following outcomes:

(1) $k < f[F_{a-1}].key$ in which case the subfile from 1 to $F_{a-1} - 1$ is searched and this file has one less than a Fibonacci number of records

(2) $k = f[F_{a-1}].key$ in which case the search terminates successfully

(3) $k = f[F_{a-1}].key$ in which case the subfile from $F_{a-1} + 1$ to $F_a - 1$ is searched and the size of this file is $F_a - 1 - (F_{a-1} + 1) + 1 = F_a - F_{a-1} - 1 = F_{a-2} - 1$.

Again it is helpful to think of this process as a binary decision tree; the resulting tree for $n = 33$ is given in Figure 7.2.

This tree is an example of a Fibonacci tree. Such a tree has $n = F_a - 1$ nodes, and its left and right subtrees are also Fibonacci trees with $F_{a-1} - 1$ and $F_{a-2} - 1$ nodes respectively. The values in the nodes show how the file will be broken up during the searching process. Note how the values of the children differ from the parent by the same amount. Moreover, this difference is a Fibonacci number. If we look at a grandparent, parent and two children where the parent is a left child, then if the difference from grandparent to parent is F_j, the next difference is F_{j-1}. If instead the parent is a right child, then the next difference is F_{j-2}. Program 7.3 implements this Fibonacci splitting idea.

Getting back to our example of the telephone directory, we notice that neither of the two ordered search methods suggested above corresponds to the one actually employed by humans in searching the directory. If we are looking for a name beginning with W, we start the search towards the end of the directory rather than at the middle. A search method based on this interpolation search would then begin by comparing key $f[i].key$ with $i = ((k - f[l].key)/(f[u].key - f[l].key)) * n$ ($f[l].key$ and $f[u].key$ are the values of the smallest and largest keys in the file). The behavior of such an algorithm will clearly depend on the distribution of the keys in the file.

We have seen that as far as the searching problem is concerned, something is to be gained by maintaining the file in an ordered manner if the file is to be searched repeatedly. Let us now look at another example where the use of ordered files greatly reduces the computational effort. The problem we are now concerned with is that of comparing two files of records containing data which is essentially the same data but has been obtained from two different sources. We are concerned with verifying that the two files contain the same data. Such a problem could arise, for instance, in the case of the U.S. Internal Revenue Service which might receive millions of forms from various employers stating how much they paid their employees and then another set of forms from individual employees stating how much they received. So we have two files of records, and we wish to verify that there is no discrepancy between the information in the files. Since the forms arrive at the IRS in essentially a random order, we may assume a random arrangement of the records in the files. The key here would probably be the social security numbers. Let the two files be $F1$ and $F2$ with keys $F1[i].key$ and $F2[i].key$. Let us make the following assumptions about the required verification: (1) if corresponding to

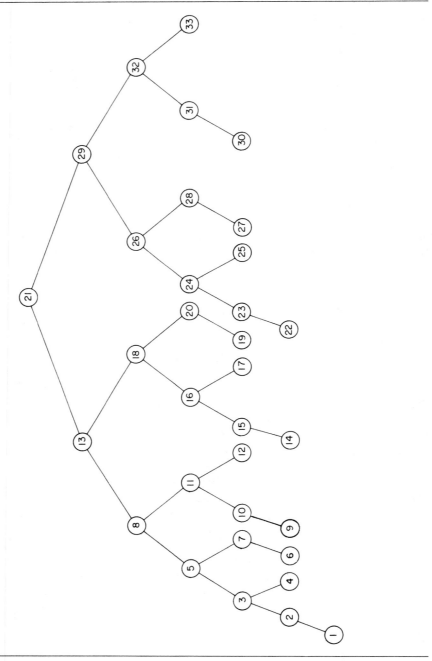

Figure 7.2 Binary decision tree for Fibonacci search with $n = 33$

```
 1  procedure FibSearch(g : afile: var i : integer; n,k : integer);
 2  {Search a file, g, stored in nondecreasing order by field key
 3   for a record i such that f[i].key = k. Assume that
 4   Fₐ + m = n + 1, m ≥ 0 and Fₐ₊₁ > n + 1.n
 5   is the number of records in g. Fₐ and Fₐ₊₁ are consecutive
 6   Fibonacci numbers. If k is not present i is set to 0.}
 7  var done : boolean
 8     p,q,t,a : integer;
 9  begin
10     a : fibindex(n + 1); {returns largest integer a : Fₐ ≤ n + 1}
11     i := fib(a − 1); {returns the a-1st Fibonacci number}
12     p := fib(a − 2);
13     q := fib(a − 3);
14     m := n + 1 − (i +p);
15     if k > g [i].key {set i so size of right subfile is p}
16     then i := i + m;
17     done := false;
18     while ((i <> 0) and (not done) do
19       case compare (k, g [i].key) of
20         '<' : if q = 0 then i := 0
21                    else
22                        begin
23                            i := i − q ;t := p ; p := q ; q := t − q;
24                        end
25         '>' : if p = 1 then i := 0
26                    else
27                        begin
28                            i := i + q ; p := p − q ; q := q − p;
29                        end
30         '=' : done := true; {found a match}
31     end; {of case  and while}
32  end; {of FibSearch}
```

Program 7.3 Fibonacci search

a key $F1[i].key$ in the employer file there is no record in the employee file, a message is
to be sent to the employee; and (2) if the reverse is true, then a message is to be sent to
the employer; and (3) if there is a discrepancy between two records with the same key a
message to that effect is to be output.

   If one proceeded to carry out the verification directly, one would probably end up
with an algorithm similar to *verify*1 (Program 7.4). One may readily verify that the worst
case asymptotic computing time of the Program 7.4 is O(mn).

```
 1  procedure verify1(F1, F2 : afile; l,n,m : integer);
 2  {Compare two unordered files F1 and F2 of size n and m, respectively.
 3   l is the maximum of m and n.  The output is
 4    (a)  all records found in F1 but not in F2
 5    (b)  all records found in F2 but not in F1
 6    (c)  all records that are in F1 and F2 with the same key
 7          but have different values for other fields}
 8  var i,j :integer;
 9    marked : array[1..n] of boolean;
10  begin
11    for i := 1 to l do marked[i] := false;
12    for i := 1 to n do
13    begin
14      SeqSearch (F2,j,m,F1[i].key);
15      if j = 0 then writeln(F1[i].key, 'not in F2.') {satisfies (a)}
16      else
17      begin
18        if F1[i].other < > F2[j].other
19        then {satisifies (c)}
20           writeln('discrepancy in ', F1[i].key,F1[i].other,F2[j].other);
21        marked[j] :=true; {mark the record as being seen}
22      end;
23    end
24    for i := 1 to m do
25      if not marked[i] then writeln (F2[i].key, 'not in F1.'); {satisfies (b)}
26  end; {of verify1}
```

Program 7.4 Verifying using a sequential search

On the other hand if we first ordered the two files and then made the comparison it would be possible to carry out the verification task in time $O(t_{sort}(n)+t_{sort}(m) + n + m)$ where $t_{sort}(n)$ is the time needed to sort a file of n records. As we shall see, it is possible to sort n records in $O(n\log n)$ time, so the computing time becomes $O(\max\{n\log n, m\log m\})$. The algorithm *verify2*, Program 7.5, achieves this.

We have seen two important uses of sorting: (1) as an aid in searching, and (2) as a means for matching entries in files. Sorting also finds application in the solution of many other more complex problems, e.g., from operations research and job scheduling. In fact, it is estimated that over 25 percent of all computing time is spent on sorting with some installations spending more than 50 percent of their computing time sorting files. Consequently, the problem of sorting has great relevance in the study of computing. Unfortunately, no one method is the "best" for all initial orderings of the file being sorted. We shall therefore study several methods, indicating when one is superior to the

```
 1  procedure verify2(var F1, F2 : afile; n,m : integer);
 2  {Same task as verify1. However this time sort F1 and F2 so that
 3  the keys are in increasing order in each file. We assume that the
 4  keys in each file are distinct}
 5  var i,j : integer
 6  begin
 7      sort (F1, n); {sort the file by key}
 8      sort (F2, m);
 9      i := 1; j := 1;
10      while ((i <= n) and (j <= m)) do
11          case compare (F1[i].key, F2[j].key) of
12          '<' : begin
13              writeln(F1[i].key, 'not in F2.');
14              i := i + 1;
15              end
16          '=' : begin
17                  if not (F1[i].other = F2[j].other)
18                  then
19                  writeln ('discrepancy in ', F1[i].other,F2[j].other);
20              i := i + 1; j := j + 1;
21          end;
22          '>' : begin
23                  writeln (F2[j].key,'not in F1.');
24                  j := j + 1;
25          end;
26      end; {of case and while}
27      if i <= n then PrintRest (F1, i, n, 1)
28      {PrintRest prints the records of the file that are missing}
29      else if j <= m then PrintRest (F2, j, m, 2);
30  end; {of verify2}
```

Program 7.5 Fast verification of two files

others.

First let us formally state the problem we are about to consider. We are given a file of records $(R_1, R_2, \ldots, R_n)$. Each record, R_i, has key value K_i. In addition we assume an ordering relation $(<)$ on the keys so that for any two key values x and y either $x = y$ or $x < y$ or $y < x$. The ordering relation $(<)$ is assumed to be transitive, i.e., for any three values x, y, and z, $x < y$ and $y < z$ implies $x < z$. The sorting problem then is that of finding a permutation, σ, such that $K_{\sigma(i)} \leq K_{\sigma(i+1)}$, $1 \leq i \leq n - 1$. The desired ordering is then $(R_{\sigma(1)}, R_{\sigma(2)}, \ldots, R_{\sigma(n)})$.

Note that in the case when the file has several key values that are identical, the permutation, σ, defined above is not unique. We shall distinguish one permutation, σ_s, from all the others that also order the file. Let σ_s be the permutation with the following properties:

(1) $K_{\sigma_s(i)} \leq K_{\sigma_s(i+1)}$, $1 \leq i \leq n - 1$

(2)   If $i < j$ and $K_i = K_j$ in the input file, then R_i precedes R_j in the sorted file

A sorting method generating the permutation σ_s will be said to be *stable*.

To begin with we characterize sorting methods into two broad categories: (1) internal methods, i.e., methods to be used when the file to be sorted is small enough so that the entire sort can be carried out in main memory; and (2) external methods, i.e., methods to be used on larger files. In this text we shall study internal sorting methods only. The following internal sorting methods will be developed: insertion sort, quick sort, merge sort, heap sort, and radix sort.

7.2 INSERTION SORT

The basic step in this method is to insert a record R into a sequence of ordered records, $R_1, R_2, \ldots, R_i,\ (K_1 \leq K_2, \ldots, \leq K_i)$ in such a way that the resulting sequence of size $i + 1$ is also ordered. Program 7.6 accomplishes this insertion. It assumes the existence of an artificial record R_0 with key $K_0 = -\textbf{maxint}$ (i.e, all keys are $\geq K_0$). Also the type *afile* is defined as

$$\textbf{type } afile = \textbf{array } [0 \mathinner{..} maxn] \textbf{ of } records;$$

Again, note that the use of R_0 enables us to simplify the **while** loop, avoiding a test for end of file, i.e., $j < 1$.

Insertion sort is carried out by beginning with the ordered sequence R_0, R_1 and then successively inserting the records $R_2, R_3, \ldots, R_n$ into the sequence. Since each insertion leaves the resultant sequence ordered, the file with n records can be ordered making $n - 1$ insertions. The details are given in algorithm *InsertionSort* (Program 7.7).

Analysis of Insertion Sort

In the worst case algorithm *insert* $(r, list, i)$ makes $i + 1$ comparisons before making the insertion. Hence the computing time for the insertion is $O(i)$. Procedure *InsertionSort* invokes procedure *insert* for $j = 1, 2, \ldots, n - 1$ resulting in an overall worst case time of $O(\sum_{j=1}^{n-1} j + 1) = O(n^2)$.

One may also obtain an estimate of the computing time of this method based upon the relative disorder in the input file. We shall say that the record R_i is *left out of order* (LOO) iff $R_i < \max_{1 \leq j < i}\{R_j\}$. Clearly, the insertion step has to be carried out only for those

```
 1 procedure insert (r : records ; var list : afile; i : integer);
 2 {Insert record r with key r . key into the ordered
 3   sequence list [0], . . ., list [i ]
 4   in such a way that the resulting sequence is
 5   also ordered on the field key.
 6   We assume that list contains a dummy record at index zero
 7   such that r . key ≥ list [0] . key for all i}
 8 var j : integer;
 9 begin
10    j := i;
11    while r . key < list [j ] . key do
12    begin
13      list [j + 1] := list [j ];
14      j := j − 1;
15    end;
16    list [j + 1] := r;
17 end; {of insert}
```

Program 7.6 Insertion into a sorted file

```
1 procedure InsertionSort(var list : afile; n : integer);
2 {sort list in nondecreasing value of the file key. Assume n > 0.}
3 var j : integer;
4 begin
5    list [0] . key := −maxint;
6    for j := 2 to n do
7      insert (list [j ],list,j − 1);
8 end; {of InsertionSort}
```

Program 7.7 Insertion sort

records that are LOO. If k is the number of records LOO, then the computing time is $O((k + 1)n)$. The worst case time is still $O(n^2)$. One can also show that the average time is also $O(n^2)$.

Example 7.1: Assume $n = 5$ and the input sequence is $(5, 4, 3, 2, 1)$ [note we assume for convenience that the records have only one field which also happens to be the key]. Then, after each insertion we have the following:

$$-\infty, 5, 4, 3, 2, 1 \qquad \text{[initial sequence]}$$
$$-\infty, 4, 5, 3, 2, 1 \qquad i = 2$$
$$-\infty, 3, 4, 5, 2, 1 \qquad i = 3$$
$$-\infty, 2, 3, 4, 5, 1 \qquad i = 4$$
$$-\infty, 1, 2, 3, 4, 5 \qquad i = 5$$

Note that $-\infty$ denotes $-$**maxint** and this is an example of the worst case behavior. □

Example 7.2: $n = 5$ and the input sequence is $(2, 3, 4, 5, 1)$. After each execution of *insert* we have:

$$-\infty, 2, 3, 4, 5, 1 \qquad \text{[initial]}$$
$$-\infty, 2, 3, 4, 5, 1 \qquad i = 2$$
$$-\infty, 2, 3, 4, 5, 1 \qquad i = 3$$
$$-\infty, 2, 3, 4, 5, 1 \qquad i = 4$$
$$-\infty, 1, 2, 3, 4, 5 \qquad i = 5$$

In this example only R_5 is LOO and the time for each $i = 2$, 3, and 4 is O(1) while for $i = 5$ it is O(n). □

It should be fairly obvious that this method is stable. The fact that the computing time is O(kn) makes this method very desirable in sorting sequences where only a very few records are LOO (i.e., $k<<n$). The simplicity of this scheme makes it about the fastest sorting method for $n \le 20 - 25$ elements, depending upon the implementation and machine properties. For variations on this method see Exercises 2 and 3.

7.3 QUICK SORT

We now turn our attention to a sorting scheme with a very good average behavior. The quick sort scheme developed by C. A. R. Hoare has the best average behavior among all the sorting methods we shall be studying. In Insertion Sort the key K_i currently controlling the insertion is placed into the right spot with respect to the sorted subfile $(R_1, \ldots, R_{i-1})$. Quick sort differs from insertion sort in that the key K_i controlling the process is placed at the right spot with respect to the whole file. Thus, if key K_i is placed in position $s(i)$, then $K_j \le K_{s(i)}$ for $j < s(i)$ and $K_j \ge K_{s(i)}$ for $j > s(i)$. Hence, after this positioning has been made, the original file is partitioned into two subfiles, one consisting of records $R_1, \ldots, R_{s(i)-1}$ and the other of records $R_{s(i)}+1, \ldots, R_n$. Since in the sorted sequence all records in the first subfile may appear to the left of $s(i)$ and all in the second subfile to the right of $s(i)$, these two subfiles may be sorted independently. The method is best stated recursively as Program 7.8. Procedure *InterChange* (x, y) performs $t := x; x := y; y := t$.

```
 1  procedure QuickSort(var list : afile; m,n : integer);
 2  {sort records list [m ], . . ., list [n ] into nondecreasing
 3   order on field key.
 4   Key k = list [m ] . key is arbitrarily chosen as the control key.
 5   Pointers i and j are used to partition the subfile so
 6   that at any time list [l ] . key ≤ k,l < i and
 7   list [l ] . key ≥ k, l > j.  It is assumed that
 8   list [m ] . key ≤ list [n + 1] . key}
 9  var i,j,k : integer;
10  begin
11    if m < n
12    then
13    begin
14      i := m ; j := n + 1; k := list [m ] . key;
15      repeat
16        repeat
17          i := i + 1;
18        until list [i ] . key >= k;
19        repeat
20          j := j − 1;
21        until list [j ] . key <= k;
22        if i < j
23        then InterChange (list [i ],list [j ]);
24      until i >= j;
25      InterChange (list [m ],list [j ]);
26      QuickSort (list,m,j − 1);
27      QuickSort (list,j + 1,n);
28    end; {of if}
29  end; {of QuickSort}
```

Program 7.8 Quick sort

Example 7.3: The input file has 10 records with keys (26, 5, 37, 1, 61, 11, 59, 15, 48, 19). The following table gives the status of the file at each call of *QuickSort*. Square brackets are used to demarcate subfiles yet to be sorted.

R_1	R_2	R_3	R_4	R_5	R_6	R_7	R_8	R_9	R_{10}	m	n
[26	5	37	1	61	11	59	15	48	19]	1	10
[11	5	19	1	15]	26	[59	61	48	37]	1	5
[1	5]	11	[19	15]	26	[59	61	48	37	1	2
1	5	11	[19	15]	26	[59	61	48	37]	4	5
1	5	11	15	19	26	[59	61	48	37]	7	10
1	5	11	15	19	26	[48	37]	59	[61]	7	8
1	5	11	15	19	26	37	48	59	[61]	10	10
1	5	11	15	19	26	37	48	59	61		

☐

Analysis of Quick Sort

The worst case behavior of this algorithm is examined in Exercise 4 and shown to be $O(n^2)$. However, if we are lucky then each time a record is correctly positioned, the subfile to its left will be of the same size as that to its right. This would leave us with the sorting of two subfiles each of size roughly $n/2$. The time required to position a record in a file of size n is $O(n)$. If $T(n)$ is the time taken to sort a file of n records, then when the file splits roughly into two equal parts each time a record is positioned correctly we have

$$T(n) \leq cn + 2T(n/2), \text{ for some constant } c$$

$$\leq cn + 2(cn/2 + 2T(n/4))$$

$$\leq 2cn + 4T(n/4)$$

.

.

.

$$\leq cn \log_2 n + nT(1) = O(n \log_2 n)$$

In our presentation of quick sort, the record whose position was being fixed with respect to the subfile currently being sorted was always chosen to be the first record in that subfile. Exercise 5 examines a better choice for this control record. Lemma 7.1 shows that the average computing time for quick sort is $O(n \log_2 n)$. Moreover, experimental results show that as far as average computing time is concerned, it is the best of the internal sorting methods we shall be studying.

Unlike insertion sort, where the only additional space needed was for one record, quick sort needs stack space to implement the recursion. In case the files split evenly as in the above analysis, the maximum recursion depth would be log n requiring a stack space of O(log n). The worst case occurs when the file is split into a left subfile of size $n - 1$ and a right subfile of size 0 at each level of recursion. In this case, the depth of recursion becomes n requiring stack space of O(n). The worst case stack space can be reduced by a factor of 4 by realizing that right subfiles of size less than 2 need not be stacked. An asymptotic reduction in stack space can be achieved by *sorting smaller subfiles first*. In this case the additional stack space is at most O(log n).

Lemma 7.1: Let $T_{avg}(n)$ be the expected time for procedure *QuickSort* to sort a file with n records. Then there exists a constant k such that $T_{avg}(n) \le kn\log_e n$ for $n \ge 2$.

Proof: In the call to *QuickSort* $(1, n)$, k_1 gets placed at position j. This leaves us with the problem of sorting two subfiles of size $j - 1$ and $n - j$. The expected time for this is $T_{avg}(j - 1) + T_{avg}(n - j)$. The remainder of the algorithm clearly takes at most cn time for some constant c. Since j may take on any of the values 1 to n with equal probability we have

$$T_{avg}(n) \le cn + \frac{1}{n}\sum_{j=1}^{n}(T_{avg}(j - 1) + T_{avg}(n - j)) = cn + \frac{2}{n}\sum_{j=0}^{n-1}T_{avg}(j), \; n \ge 2 \quad (7.1)$$

We may assume $T_{avg}(0) \le b$ and $T_{avg}(1) \le b$ for some constant b. We shall now show $T_{avg}(n) \le kn\log_e n$ for $n \ge 2$ and $k = 2(b + c)$. The proof is by induction on n.

Induction base: For $n = 2$ we have from Eq. (7.1)

$$T_{avg}(2) \le 2c + 2b \le kn\log_e 2$$

Induction hypothesis: Assume $T_{avg}(n) \le kn\log_e n$ for $1 \le n < m$

Induction step: From Eq. (7.1) and the induction hypothesis we have

$$T_{avg}(m) \le cm + \frac{4b}{m} + \frac{2}{m}\sum_{j=2}^{m-1}T_{avg}(j) \le cm + \frac{4b}{m} + \frac{2k}{m}\sum_{j=2}^{m-1}j\log_2 j \quad (7.2)$$

Since $j\log_e j$ is an increasing function of j, Eq. (7.2) yields

$$T_{avg}(m) \le cm + \frac{4b}{m} + \frac{2k}{m}\int_{2}^{m}x\log_e x \; dx = cm + \frac{4b}{m} + \frac{2k}{m}\left[\frac{m^2\log_e m}{2} - \frac{m^2}{4}\right]$$

$$= cm + \frac{4b}{m} + km\log_e m - \frac{km}{2} \leq km\log_e m, \ \text{for } m \geq 2 \ \square$$

7.4 HOW FAST CAN WE SORT?

Both of the sorting methods we have seen have a worst case behavior of $O(n^2)$. It is natural at this point to ask the question: '' What is the best computing time for sorting that we can hope for?'' The theorem we shall prove shows that if we restrict our question to algorithms for which the only operations permitted on keys are comparisons and interchanges then $O(n \log_2 n)$ is the best possible time.

The method we use is to consider a tree which describes the sorting process by having a vertex represent a key comparison and the branches indicate the result. Such a tree is called a *decision tree*. A path through a decision tree represents a possible sequence of computations that an algorithm could produce.

As an example of such a tree, let us look at the tree obtained for insertion sort working on a file with tree records in it. The input sequence is three records R_1, R_2, and R_3 so the root of the tree is labeled (1,2,3). Depending on the outcome of the comparison between keys K_1 and K_2, this sequence may or may not change. If $K_2 < K_1$, then the sequence becomes (2,1,3), otherwise it stays (1,2,3). The full tree resulting from these comparisons is shown below. The left nodes are number I-VI and are the only points at which the algorithm may terminate. Hence only six permutations of the input sequence are obtainable from this algorithm. Since all six of these are different and 3! = 6, it follows that this algorithm has enough leaves to constitute a valid sorting algorithm for three records. The maximum depth of this tree is 3. The table below gives six different orderings of key values 7, 9, 10 which show that all six permutations are possible. The tree is not a full binary tree of depth 3 and so it has fewer than $2^3 = 8$ leaves. The possible output permutations are

leaf	permutation	sample input key values which give the permutation
I	1 2 3	(7,9,10)
II	1 3 2	(7,10,9)
III	3 1 2	(9,10,7)
IV	2 1 3	(9,7,10)
V	2 3 1	(10,7,9)
VI	3 2 1	(10,9,7)

The decision tree is given in Figure 7.3.

Theorem 7.1: Any decision tree that sorts n distinct elements has a height of at least

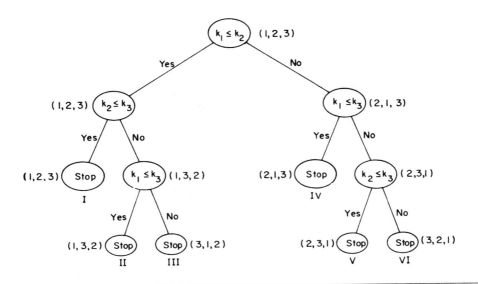

Figure 7.3 Decision tree for insertion sort

$\log_2(n!) + 1$.

Proof: When sorting n elements there are $n!$ different possible results. Thus, any decision tree must have $n!$ leaves. But a decision tree is also a binary tree which can have at most 2^{k-1} leaves if its height is k. Therefore, the height must be at least $\log_2 n! + 1$. $\square$

Corollary: Any algorithm which sorts by comparisons only must have a worst case computing time of $\Omega(n \log_2 n)$.

Proof: We must show that for every decision tree with $n!$ leaves there is a path of length $cn\log_2 n$, c a constant. By the theorem, there is a path of length $\log_2 n!$. Now

$$n! = n(n-1)(n-2)\ldots(3)(2)(1) \le (n/2)^{n/2}$$

so $\log_2 n! \ge (n/2)\log_2(n/2) = O(n\log_2 n)$. $\square$

7.5 MERGE SORT

Before looking at the merge sort algorithm to sort n records let us see how one may merge two sorted files to get a single sorted file. We shall examine two different algorithms for this. The first one, Program 7.9, is very simple and uses O(n) additional space. The two files two be merged are $(x_l, \ldots, x_m)$ and $(x_{m+1}, \ldots, x_n)$. The resulting merged file is $(z_l, \ldots, z_n)$.

At each iteration of the **while** loop, k increases by 1. The total increment in k is $n - l + 1$. Hence the **while** loop is iterated at most $n - l + 1$ times. The **if** statement moves at most one record per iteration. The total time is therefore O($n - l + 1$). If records are of length M, then the time is really O($M (n - l + 1)$). When M is greater than 1 we could use linked lists for $(x_1, \ldots, x_m)$ and $(x_{m+1}, \ldots, x_n)$ and obtain a new sorted linked list containing these $n - l + 1$ records. Now, we won't need the additional space for $n - l + 1$ records as needed above for Z. Instead, only space for $n - l + 1$ links is needed. The merge time becomes independent of M and O($n - l + 1$). Note that $n - l + 1$ is the number of records being merged.

The second merging algorithm we shall consider is more complex than that of Program 7.9. However, it requires only O(1) additional space. We assume that $l = 1$. With this assumption the total number of records in the two files being merged is n. Our discussion will make the further simplifying assumptions that n is a perfect square and the number of records in each of the two files to be merged is a multiple of $\sqrt{n}$. The development of the full algorithm with these assumptions removed is left as an exercise.

Suppose that $n = 36$ and that each of the two files to be merged has 18 records. The first line of Figure 7.4 gives a sample instance. Only the record keys are shown. We assume that the sorted key sequence is 0, 1, . . ., a, b, . . ., z. The vertical bar separates the two sorted files of size 18. Each file can be thought of as consisting of sorted blocks of size $\sqrt{n} = 6$. The first step in the O(1) merge is to create a block that consists of the $\sqrt{n}$ records with the largest keys. This is done by scanning the two sorted files from the right end to the left end. From this scan we discover that the $\sqrt{n}$ largest keys are those that are boxed in line 2 of Figure 7.4.

Next, the records from the second file that are in the set of $\sqrt{n}$ records with largest keys are exchanged with the same number of records just to the left of those in the first file that are in this set. This results in the configuration of line 3 of the figure. The vertical bars partition the n records into blocks of $\sqrt{n}$ consecutive records. Notice that the $\sqrt{n}$ records with largest keys form a single block. This block is now swapped with the leftmost block and the rightmost block is sorted to get line 4. The $\sqrt{n} - 1$ blocks excluding the one with the largest keys are sorted by their rightmost records to get line 5. This completes the preprocessing needed to commence the actual merge.

The actual merge consists of several merge sub steps in each of which two segments of records are merged together. The first segment is the longest sorted sequence of records beginning at block two. Observe that this will always end at a block boundary. The second sequence consists solely of the next block. In the case of line 5, both of these sequences conisist of exactly one block. A merge sub step uses three place

```
 1  procedure merge(var x,z : afile;l,m,n : integer);
 2  {(x [l ], . . . ,x [m ]) and (x [m + 1], . . ., x [n ]) are
 3    two sorted lists with keys
 4    such that x [l ] . key ≤ . . . ≤ x [m ] . key, and
 5    x [m + 1] . key ≤ . . . ≤ x [n ] . key.  These records are merged to
 6    obtain the sorted list (z [l ], . . ., z [n ]) such that
 7    z [l ] . key ≤ . . . ≤ z [n ] . key}
 8  var i,j,k,t : integer:
 9  begin
10    i := l;
11    k := l;
12    j := m + 1; {i, j, and k are positions in the three files}
13    while ((i <= m) and (j <= n)) do
14    begin
15      if x [i ] . key <= x [j ] . key
16      then
17      begin
18        z [k ] := x [i ];
19        i := i + 1;
20      end
21      else
22      begin
23        z [k ] := x [j ];
24        j := j + 1;
25      end;
26      k := k + 1;
27    end; {of while}
28    if i > m
29    then        {(z_k, . . ., z_n) := (x_j, . . ., x_n)}
30      for t := j to n do
31        z [k + t − j ] :=x [t ]
32    else        {(z_k, . . ., z_m) := (x_j, . . ., x_m)}
33      for t := i to m do
34        z [k + t − i ] := x [t ];
35  end; {of merge}
```

Program 7.9 Merging two sorted files

markers which are depicted in line 5 by the symbol ●. The leftmost one marks the position where the next merged record is to go. The second marker points to the next unmerged record of the first segment and the third marker points to the next unmerged record of the second segment. Initially these are, respectively, positioned at the first

0 2 4 6 8 a c e g i j k *l* m n t w z | 1 3 5 7 9 b d f h o p q r s u v x y

0 2 4 6 8 a c e g i j k *l* m n t ⟦w z⟧ | 1 3 5 7 9 b d f h o p q r s ⟦u v x y⟧

0 2 4 6 8 a | c e g i j k | u v x y w z | 1 3 5 7 9 b | d f h o p q | r s *l* m n t

u v x y w z | c e g i j k | 0 2 4 6 8 a | 1 3 5 7 9 b | d f h o p q | *l* m n r s t

u v x y w z 0 2 4 6 8 a | 1 3 5 7 9 b | c e g i j k | d f h o p q | *l* m n r s t

0 v x y w z u 2 4 6 8 a | 1 3 5 7 9 b | c e g i j k | d f h o p q | *l* m n r s t

0 1 x y w z u 2 4 6 8 a | v 3 5 7 9 b | c e g i j k | d f h o p q | *l* m n r s t

0 1 2 y w z u x 4 6 8 a | v 3 5 7 9 b | c e g i j k | d f h o p q | *l* m n r s t

Figure 7.4 First eight lines for O(1) space merge example

records of the largest block, segment one, and segment two. The two segments are merged by comparing the two keys pointed at by place markers two and three and exchanging the record with smaller key (in case of a tie, the record in the first segment is used) with the record pointed at by the first place marker. Following the first such exchange we get line 6. Lines 7 and 8 show the configuration following each of the next two exchanges. This merge exchanging continues until all of the first segment has been merged. In the case of our example eight more records get merged before the current merge sub step terminates. Line 1 of Figure 7.5 shows the configuration after the records with keys 3, 4, and 5 have been merged; line 2 shows the configuration following the merging of the records with keys 6, 7, and 8; and line 3 shows the status after segment one has been fully merged.

0 1 2 3 4 5 u x w 6 8 a | v y z 7 9 b | c e g i j k | d f h o p q | l m n r s t

0 1 2 3 4 5 6 7 8 u w a | v y z x 9 b | c e g i j k | d f h o p q | l m n r s t

0 1 2 3 4 5 6 7 8 9 a w | v y z x u b | c e g i j k | d f h o p q | l m n r s t

0 1 2 3 4 5 6 7 8 9 a w v y z x u b c e g i j k | d f h o p q | l m n r s t

0 1 2 3 4 5 6 7 8 9 a b c d e f g h i j k v z u | y x w o p q | l m n r s t

0 1 2 3 4 5 6 7 8 9 a b c d e f g h i j k v z u y x w o p q | l m n r s t

0 1 2 3 4 5 6 7 8 9 a b c d e f g h i j k l m n o p q y x w | v z u r s t

0 1 2 3 4 5 6 7 8 9 a b c d e f g h i j k l m n o p q r s t | v z u y x w

Figure 7.5 Last eight lines for O(1) space merge example

The following observations allow us to conclude that the merge of a merge sub step can always be done as described above without using extra space beyond that needed to exchange two records:

(1) There are $\sqrt{n}$ records from the initial position of the first place marker to that of the second place marker.

(2) The second segment has $\sqrt{n}$ records.

(3) Because of the tie breaker rule and the initial ordering of blocks by their last records, the first segment will be fully merged before the second.

When a merge sub step is complete the $\sqrt{n}$ records with largest keys are contiguous and the first place marker points to the first of these records. The third place marker points to the first unmerged record in the second segment. This record begins the first segment for the next merge sub step. This segment is the longest sorted segment that begins at this record. This always ends at a block boundary. The next block forms the second segment. In the case of our example, the first segment begins at the record with key b and the second begins at the record with key d. Line 4 of Figure 7.5 shows the initial positions of the three place markers. Line 5 shows the configuration after the first segment has been fully merged.

The first segment for the next merge sub step begins at the record pointed at by the third place marker. We find a longest sorted sequence that begins here. This consists of just three records. The next block forms the second sequence. The initial positions of the three place markers for the third sort sub step is shown in line 6 of the figure. Line 7 show the status after this sub step is complete. Now the longest sorted sequence that begins at the third place marker consists of the records with keys r, s, and t. As there is no next block, the second segment is empty. The last merge sub step results in the configuration of line 8. Since the second segment is empty to begin with, the last merge sub step can be performed using just two place markers that move rightwards one position at a time. We simply exchange the records pointed at by these two place markers.

Once the merge sub steps have been performed, the block of records with largest keys is at the right end and may be sorted using an $O(1)$ space sorting algorithm such as insertion sort. The steps involved in the $O(1)$ space merge algorithm just described are summarized in Program 7.10.

{Steps in an $O(1)$ space merge when the total number of records, n is a perfect square}
{and the number of records in each of the files to be merged is a multiple of $\sqrt{n}$}

Step 1: Identify the $\sqrt{n}$ records with largest keys. This is done by following right to left along the two files to be merged.

Step 2: Exchange the records of the second file that were identified in Step 1 with those just to the left of those identified from the first file so that the $\sqrt{n}$ records with largest keys form a contiguous block.

Step 3: Swap the block of $\sqrt{n}$ largest records with the leftmost block (unless it is already the leftmost block). Sort the rightmost block.

Step 4: Reorder the blocks excluding the block of largest records into nondecreasing order of the last key in the blocks.

Step 5: Perform as many merge sub steps as needed to merge the $\sqrt{n} - 1$ blocks other than the block with the largest keys.

Step 6: Sort the block with the largest keys.

Program 7.10 $O(1)$ space merge

For the complexity analysis, we see that steps 1 and 2, and the swapping of Step 3 each take $O(\sqrt{n})$ time and $O(1)$ space. The sort of Step 3 can be done in $O(n)$ time and $O(1)$ space using insertion sort. Step 4 can be done in $O(n)$ time and $O(1)$ space using a selection sort (see Chapter 1). Note that selection sort sorts m records using $O(m^2)$ key comparisons and $O(m)$ record moves. When selection sort is used to implement Step 4 of Program 7.10 each block of $\sqrt{n}$ records is regarded as a single record with key equal to that of the last record in the block. So, each record move of selection sort actually moves a block of size $\sqrt{n}$. The number of key comparisons is $O(n)$ and while the number of block moves is $O(\sqrt{n})$, the time needed for these is $O(n)$. Note that if insertion sort is used in place of selection sort, the time becomes $O(n^{1.5})$ as insertion sort makes $O(m^2)$ record moves when sorting m records. So, in this application insertion sort is inferior to selection sort. The total number of merge sub steps is at most $\sqrt{n} - 1$. The end point of the first segment for each merge sub step can be found in time proportional to the number of blocks in the segment as we need merely find the first block whose last key is greater than the first key of the next block. The time for each sub step is therefore linear in the number of records merged. Hence, the total Step 5 time is $O(n)$. The sort of Step 6 can be done in $O(n)$ time using either a selection or an insertion sort. When the steps of Program 7.10 are implemented as above the total time is $O(n)$ and the additional space used is $O(1)$.

We are now ready to develop the merge sort algorithm. This development may be done so as to result in either an iterative or a recursive sort algorithm. We shall see both versions here. The iterative version uses the simple merge method of Program 7.9 and the recursive version uses Program 7.9 modified to work with linked lists. We develop the iterative version of merge sort first. This version begins by interpreting the input as n sorted files each of length 1. These are merged pairwise to obtain $n/2$ files of size 2 (if n is odd, then one file is of size 1). These $n/2$ files are then merged pairwise and so on until we are left with only one file. The example below illustrates the process.

Example 7.4: The input file is (26, 5, 77, 1, 61, 11, 59, 15, 48, 19). The tree of Figure 7.6 illustrates the subfiles being merged at each pass. □

As is apparent from the example above, merge sort consists of several passes over the records being sorted. In the first pass, files of size 1 are merged. In the second, the size of the files being merged is 2. On the i'th pass the files being merged are of size 2^{i-1}. Consequently, a total of $\lceil \log_2 n \rceil$ passes are made over the data. Since two files can be merged in linear time (algorithm *merge*), each pass of merge sort takes $O(n)$time. As there are $\lceil \log_2 n \rceil$ passes, the total computing time is $O(n \log n)$.

In formally writing the algorithm for a merge, it is convenient to first present an algorithm (Program 7.11) to perform one merge pass of the merge sort.

It is easy to verify that the above algorithm results in a stable sorting procedure. Exercise 8 discusses a variation of the merge sort discussed above. In this variation the prevailing order within the input file is taken into account to obtain initially sorted subfiles of length ≥ 1.

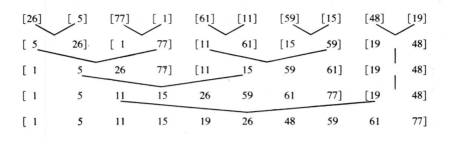

Figure 7.6 Merge tree

```
 1  procedure MergePass(var x,y : afile; n,l : integer);
 2  {This algorithm performs one pass of the merge sort.  It merges
 3   adjacent pairs of subfiles of length l from the list x to list
 4   y. n is the number of records in x.}
 5  var i, t : integer;
 6  begin
 7    i := 1;
 8    while i <= (n − 2∗l + 1) do
 9    begin
10      merge (x,y,i,i + l − 1, i + 2∗l − 1);
11      i := i + 2∗l;
12    end;
13    {merge remaining file of length < 2∗l}
14    if (i + l − 1) < n then merge (x,y,i,i + l − 1, n)
15    else
16      for t := i to n do
17         y [t] := x [t];
18  end; {of MergePass}
```

Program 7.11 Merge pass

Recursive Formulation of Merge Sort

Merge sort may also be arrived at recursively. In the recursive formulation we divide the file to be sorted into two roughly equal parts called the left and the right subfiles. These subfiles are sorted using the algorithm recursively and then the two subfiles are merged together to obtain the sorted file. First, let us see how this would work on our earlier example.

```
 1 procedure MergeSort(var x : afile; n : integer);
 2 {Sort the file x = (x[1], . . ., x[n]) into nondecreasing order on the
 3   keys x[1].key, . . ., x[n].key}
 4 var l : integer;
 5     y : afile;
 6 begin
 7    {l is the size of the subfile currently being merged}
 8    l := 1;
 9    while l < n do
10    begin
11      MergePass (x,y,n,l);
12      l := 2 * l;
13      MergePass (y,x,n,l); {interchange role of x and y}
14      l := 2 * l;
15    end
16 end; {of MergeSort}
```

Program 7.12 Merge sort

Example 7.5: The input file (26, 5, 77, 1, 61, 11, 59, 15, 49, 19) is to be sorted using the recursive formulation of merge sort. If the subfile from l to u is currently to be sorted then its two subfiles are indexed from l to $\lfloor (l + u)/2 \rfloor$ and from $\lfloor (l + u)/2 \rfloor + 1$ to u. The subfile partitioning that takes place is described by the binary tree of Figure 7.7. Note that the subfiles being merged are different from those being merged in algorithm *MergeSort*. □

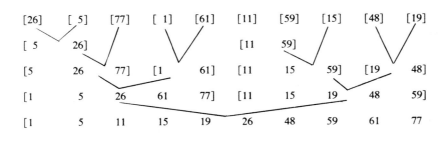

Figure 7.7 Subfile partitioning for recursive merge sort

From the preceding example we may draw the following conclusion. If algorithm *merge* is used to merge sorted subfiles from one array into another, then it is necessary to copy subfiles. For example to merge [5, 26] and [77] we would have to copy [77] into the same array as [5, 26]. To avoid this unnecessary copying of subfiles using sequential allocation, we look to a linked list representation for subfiles. This method of representation will permit the recursive version of merge sort to work efficiently.

Each record is assumed to have three fields: *link*, *key*, and *other*. The record structure is defined as

$$\textbf{type } records = \textbf{record}$$
$$key : \textbf{integer};$$
$$other : fields;$$
$$link : \textbf{integer};$$
$$\textbf{end};$$
$$afile = \textbf{array } [0 .. n] \textbf{ of } records;$$

$r[i].link$ and $r[i].key$ are the link and key value fields in record i, $1 \le i \le n$. Note that for this application, the *link* fields are of type **integer** and not of type **pointer**. We assume that initially $afile[i].link = 0$, $1 \le i \le n$. Thus, each record is initially in a chain containing only itself. Let q and r be pointers to two chains of records. The records on each chain are assumed linked in nondecreasing order of the key field. Let $ListMerge(q,r,p)$ be an algorithm to merge the two chains q and r to obtain p that is also linked in nondecreasing order of key values. Then the recursive version of merge sort is given by algorithm *rMergeSort* (Program 7.13). To sort the file $x_1, \ldots, x_n$ this algorithm is invoked as $rMergeSort(x,l,n,p)$. p is returned as the start of a chain ordered as described earlier. In case the file is to be physically rearranged into this order then one of the schemes discussed in Section 7.8 may be used. *ListMerge* is given in Program 7.14.

One may readily verify that this linked version of merge sort results in a stable sorting procedure and that the computing time is $O(n \log n)$.

7.6 HEAP SORT

While the merge sort scheme discussed in the previous section has a computing time of $O(n \log n)$ both in the worst case and as average behavior, it requires additional storage proportional to the number of records in the file being sorted. The sorting method we are about to study will require only a fixed amount of additional storage and at the same time will have as its worst case and average computing time $O(n \log n)$. In this method, we utilize a max-heap (see Section 5.11). The deletion and insertion algorithms associated with max-heaps directly yield an $O(n \log n)$ sorting method. The n records are first inserted into an initially empty heap. Next, the records are extracted from the heap one at a time. It is possible to create the heap of n records faster by using the procedure

---

```
 1  procedure rMergeSort(var x : afile; l,u : integer; var p:integer);
 2  {The list x = (x [l ], . . ., x [u ]) is to be sorted on the field key.
 3    link is a link field in each record and is initially set to 0.
 4    The sorted list is a chain beginning at p.
 5    x [0] is a record for intermediate results used only in ListMerge}
 6  var mid,q,r : integer;
 7  begin
 8    if l >= uthen p := l
 9    else begin
10      mid := (l + u) div 2;
11      rMergeSort (x,l,mid,q);
12      rMergeSort (x,mid +1,u,r);
13      ListMerge (x,q,r,p);
14    end; {of if}
15  end; {of rMergeSort}
```

Program 7.13 Recursive merge sort

adjust (Program 7.15). This procedure takes a binary tree T whose left and right subtrees satisfy the heap property but whose root may not and adjusts T so that the entire binary tree satisfies the heap property.

If the depth of the tree with root i is k, then the **while** loop is executed at most k times. Hence the computing time of the algortihm is $O(k)$.

The heap sort algorithm now takes the form given in Program 7.16.

Example 7.6: The input file is (26, 5, 77, 1, 61, 11, 59, 15, 48, 19). Interpreting this as a binary tree we have the transformations of Figure 7.8. Figure 7.9 depicts the heap after restructuring and the sorted part of the file. □

Analysis of Heap Sort

Suppose $2^{k-1} \leq n < 2^k$ so that the tree has k levels and the number of nodes on level i is 2^{i-1}. In the first **for** loop, *adjust* is called once for each node that has a child. Hence, the time required for this loop is the sum, over each level, of the number of nodes on a level times the maximum distance the node can move. This is no more than

$$\sum_{1 \leq i \leq k} 2^{i-1}(k-i) = \sum_{1 \leq i \leq i-1} 2^{k-i-1} i \leq n \sum_{1 \leq i \leq k-1} i/2^i < 2n = O(n)$$

In the next **for** loop, $n - 1$ applications of *adjust* are made with maximum depth

---

```
 1  procedure ListMerge (x : afile; u,y : integer; var z : integer);
 2  {The linked lists u and y are merged to obtain z.  In u, y,
 3    and z the records are linked in order of nondecreasing key
 4    values.  The file of records is named x of type afile.}
 5  var i,j : integer;
 6  begin
 7     i := u; j := y; z := 0;
 8     while ((i < > 0) and (j < > 0)) do
 9       if x [i]. key <= x [j]. key
10       then
11       begin
12         x [z].link := i;
13         z := i; i := x [i].link;
14       end
15       else
16       begin
17         x [z].link := j;
18         z := j; j := x [j].link;
19       end;
20     {move remainder}
21     if i = 0 then x [z].link := j
22             else x [z].link := i;
23     z := x [0].link;
24  end; {of ListMerge}
```

Program 7.14 Merging linked lists

$k = \lceil \log_2 (n + 1) \rceil$. Hence the computing time for this loop is $O(n \log n)$. Consequently, the total computing time is $O(n \log n)$. Note that apart from variables, the only additional space needed is space for one record to carry out the interchange in the second **for** loop.

7.7 SORTING ON SEVERAL KEYS

Let us now look at the problem of sorting records on several keys, $K^1, K^2, \ldots, K^r$ (K^1 is the most significant key and K^r the least). A file of records $R_1, \ldots, R_n$ will be said to be sorted with respect to the keys K^1, K^2, *to the r-tuple $(y_1, \ldots, y_r)$ iff either $x_i = y_i$, $1 \le i \le j$ and $x_{j+1} < y_{j+1}$ for some $j < r$ or $x_i = y_i$, $1 \le i \le r$.*

```
 1  procedure adjust(var tree : afile; i,n : integer);
 2  {Adjust the binary tree with root i to satisfy the heap property.
 3    The left and right subtrees of i, i.e., with root 2i and 2i + 1,
 4    already satisfy the heap property.  No node has index greater
 5    than n.}
 6  var j : integer;
 7        k : integer;
 8        r : records;
 9        done : boolean;
10  begin
11     done := false;
12     r := tree [i ];
13     k := tree [i ] . key;
14     j := 2 * i;
15     while ((j <= n) and not done) do
16     begin {first find max of left and right child}
17       if j < n then if  tree [j ] . key < tree [j + 1] . key then j := j + 1;
18       {compare max. child with k. If k is max, then done.}
19       if k >= tree [j ] . key
20       then
21         done := true
22       else
23       begin
24         tree [j div 2] := tree [j ]; {move j'th record up the tree}
25         j := 2*j;
26       end;
27     end;
28     tree [j div 2] := r;
29  end; { of adjust}
```

Program 7.15 Adjusting a max-heap

For example, the problem of sorting a deck of cards may be regarded as a sort on two keys, the suit and face values, with the following ordering relations

Suits: ♣ < ♦ < ♥ < ♠

```
 1  procedure HeapSort(var r : afile ; n : integer);
 2  {the file r = (r [1],. . ., r [n ]) is sorted into nondecreasing order on
 3    the field key}
 4  var i : integer;
 5       t : records;
 6  begin
 7    for i:= (n div 2) downto 1 do {convert r into a heap}
 8      adjust (r,i,n);
 9    for i := (n − 1) downto 1 do {sort r}
10    begin
11      t := r [i + 1]; {interchange r₁ and rⱼ₊₁}
12      r [i + 1] := r [1];
13      r [1] := t;
14      adjust (r, 1,i); {recreate heap}
15    end;
16  end; {of HeapSort}
```

Program 7.16 Heap sort

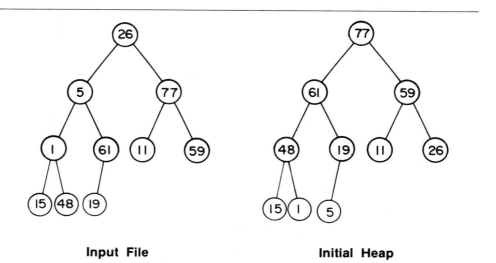

Input File   **Initial Heap**

Figure 7.8 Array interpreted as a binary tree

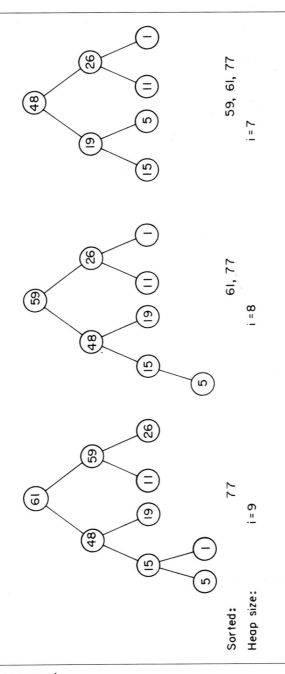

Figure 7.9 Heap sort example

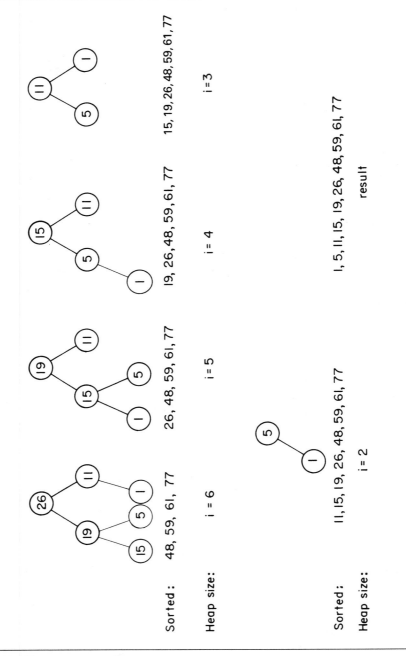

Figure 7.9 Heap sort example

Face values: $2 < 3 < 4 \ldots < 10 < J < Q < K < A$

There appears to be two popular ways to accomplish the sort. The first is to sort on the most significant key K^1 obtaining several ''piles'' of records each having the same value for K^1. Then each of these piles is independently sorted on the key K^2 into ''sub-piles'' such that all the records in the same subpile have the same values for K^1 and K^2. The subpiles are then sorted on K^3, etc., and the piles put together. In the example above this would mean first sorting the 52 cards into four piles, one for each of the suit values. Then sort each pile on the face value. Now place the piles on top of each other to obtain the ordering

$$2\clubsuit, \ldots, A\clubsuit, \ldots, 2\spadesuit, \ldots, A\spadesuit$$

A sort proceeding in this fashion will be referred to as a most significant digit first (MSD) sort. The second way, quite naturally, is to sort on the least significant digit first (LSD). This would mean sorting the cards first into 13 piles corresponding to their face values (key K^2). Then, place the 3's on top of the 2's, . . ., the kings on top of the queens, the aces on top of the kings; turn the deck upside down and sort on the suit (K^1) using some stable sorting method obtaining four piles, each of which is orderd on K^2; combine the piles to obtain the required ordering on the cards.

Comparing the two procedures outlined about (MSD and LSD) you notice that LSD is simpler as the piles and subpiles obtained do not have to be sorted independently (provided the sorting scheme used for sorting on key K^i, $1 \le i \le r$ is stable). This in turn implies less overhead.

LSD and MSD only specify the order in which the different keys are to be sorted on and not the sorting method to be used within each key. The technique generally used to sort cards is a MSD sort in which the sorting on suit is done by a bin sort (i.e., four ''bins'' are set up, one for each suit value and the cards are placed into their corresponding ''bins''). Next, the cards in each bin are sorted using an algorithm similar to Insertion Sort. However, there is another way to do this. First use a bin sort on the face value. To do this we need 13 bins, one for each distinct face value. Then collect all the cards together as described above and perform bin sort on the suits using four bins. Note that a bin sort requires only $O(n)$ time if the spread in key values is $O(n)$.

LSD or MSD sorting can be used to sort records on only one logical key by interpreting this key as being composed of several keys. For example, if the keys are numeric, then each decimal digit may be regarded as a key. So if all the keys are in the range $0 \le K \le 999$, then we can use either the LSD or MSD sorts for three keys (K^1, K^2, K^3), where K^1 is the digit in the hundredths place, K^2 the digit in the tens place, and K^3 the digit in the units place. Since all the keys lie in the range $0 \le K^i \le 9$, the sort within the keys can be carried out using a bin sort with 10 bins. This, in fact, is essentially the process used to sort records punched on cards using a card sorter. In this case, using the LSD process would be more convenient as it eliminates maintaining several independent subpiles. If the key is interpreted as above the resulting sort is called a radix 10 sort. If the key decomposition is carried out using the binary representation of the keys, then we obtain a radix 2 sort. In general, we could choose any radix r obtaining a radix r sort. The number of bins required is r.

Let us look in greater detail at the implementation of an LSD radix r sort. We assume that the records $R_1, \ldots, R_n$ have keys that are d-tuples $(x_1, x_2, \ldots, x_d)$ and $0 \leq x_i < r$. Thus, we shall need r bins. The records are assumed to have a *link* field. The records in each bin will be linked together into a linear linked list with $f[i]$, $0 \leq i \leq r$, a pointer to the first record in bin i and $e[i]$, a pointer to the last record in bin i. These lists will essentially be operated as queues. Procedure *RadixSort* formally presents the LSD radix r method in Program 7.17. This procedure assumes that *rminus1* is defined as a constant with value $r - 1$. Also it is assumed that the key field of each record is an array $key[1 .. d]$ with $0 \leq key[i] \leq kr = r - 1$.

Analysis of Radix Sort

The algorithm makes d passes over the data, each pass taking $O(n + r)$ time. Hence the total computing time is $O(d(n + r))$. In the sorting of numeric data, the value of d will depend on the choice of the radix r and also on the largest key. Different choices of r will yield different computing times.

Example 7.7: We shall illustrate the operation of algorithm *RadixSort* while sorting a file of 10 numbers in the range [0,999]. Each decimal digit in the key will be regarded as a subkey. So, the value of d is 3 and that of r is 10. The input file is linked and has the form given in Figure 7.10. The nodes are labeled $R_1, \ldots, R_{10}$. Figure 7.10 illustrates the $r = 10$ case and the list after the queues have been collected from the 10 bins at the end of each phase. By using essentially the method above but by varying the radix, we can obtain (see Exercises 11 and 12) linear time algorithms to sort n record files when the keys are in the range $0 \leq K_i < n^k$ for some constant k. □

7.8 PRACTICAL CONSIDERATIONS FOR INTERNAL SORTING

Apart from radix sort, all the sorting methods we have looked at require excessive data movement; i.e., as the result of a comparison, records may be physically moved. This tends to slow down the sorting process when records are large. In sorting files in which the records are large it is necessary to modify the sorting methods so as to minimize data movement. Methods such as insertion sort and merge sort can be easily modified to work with a linked file rather than a sequential file. In this case each record will require an additional link field. Instead of physically moving the record, its link field will be changed to reflect the change in the position of that record in the file. At the end of the sorting process, the records are linked together in the required order. In many applications (e.g., when we just want to sort files and then output them record by record on some external media in the sorted order) this is sufficient. However, in some applications it is

```
 1  procedure RadixSort(var r : afile;d,n : integer);
 2  {records r = (r [1], . . ., r [n ]) are sorted on the keys key [1], . . ., key [d ].
 3    The range of each key is 0≤key [i ]≤rminus1. rminus1 is a constant.
 4    Sorting within a key is done using a bin sort.}
 5  var e,f :array [0 .. rminus1] of integer; {queue pointers}
 6      i,j,p,t : integer;
 7      k : 0 .. kr;
 8  begin
 9  for i := 1 to  n do {link into a chain starting at p}
10      r [i ].link := i +1;
11  r [n ].link := 0; p := 1;
12  for i := d downto 1 do {sort on key [i ]}
13  begin
14      for j := 0 to rminus1 do {initialize bins to be empty queues}
15      f [j ] := 0;
16      while p < > 0 do {put records into queues}
17      begin
18      k := r [p ]↑. key [i ];
19      if f [k ] = 0 then f [k ] := p
20                   else r [e [k ]]↑. link := p;
21      e [k ] := p;
22      p := r [p ]↑. link; {get next record}
23      end; {of while}
24      j := 0;
25      while f [j ] = 0 do
26          j := j + 1; {find first nonempty queue}
27      p := f [j ]; t := e [j ];
28      for k := j +1 to rminus1 do {concatenate remaining queues}
29          if f [k ]< >0
30          then
31          begin
32              r [t ]↑. link := f [k ];
33              t := e [k ];
34          end; {of if and for}
35      r [t ]↑. link := 0;
36  end ; {of for of line 12}
37  end; {of RadixSort}
```

Program 7.17 LSD radix sort

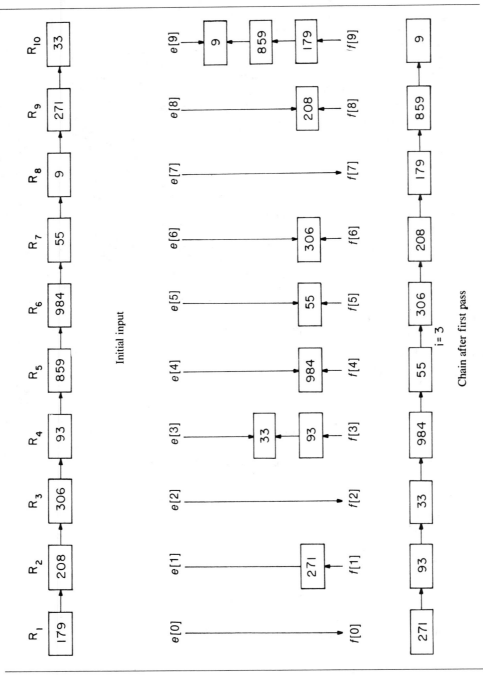

Figure 7.10 Radix sort example

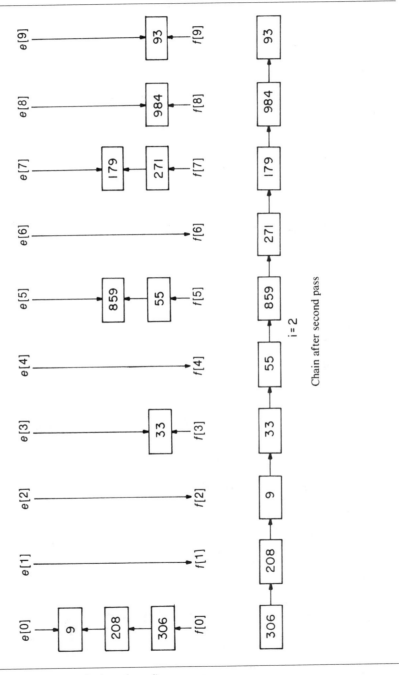

Figure 7.10 Radix sort example (continued)

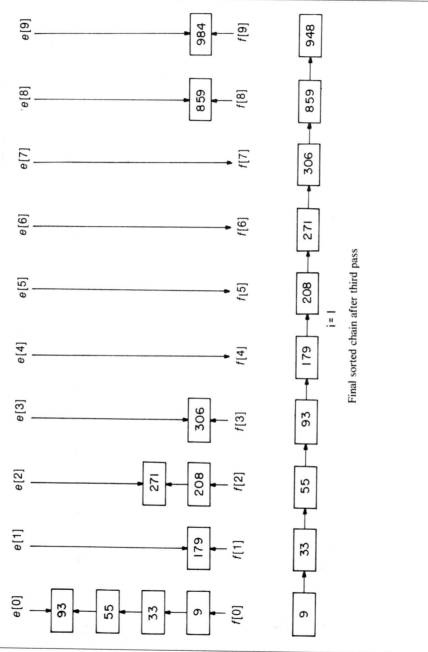

Figure 7.10 Radix sort example

necessary to physically rearrange the records *in place* so that they are in the required order. Even in such cases considerable savings can be achieved by first performing a linked list sort and then physically rearranging the records according to the order specified in the list. This rearranging can be accomplished in linear time using some additional space.

If the file, F, has been sorted so that at the end of the sort p is a pointer to the first record in a linked list of records, then each record in this list will have a key which is greater than or equal to the key of the previous record (if there is a previous record), see Figure 7.11. To physically rearrange these records into the order specified by the list, we begin by interchanging records R_1 and R_p. Now, the record in the position R_1 has the smallest key. If $p \neq 1$ then there is some record in the list with link field $= 1$. If we could change this link field to indicate the new position of the record previously as position 1 then we would be left with records $R_2, \ldots, R_n$ linked together in nondecreasing order. Repeating the above process will, after $n - 1$ iterations, result in the desired rearrangement. The snag, however, is that in a singly linked list we do not know the predecessor of a node. To overcome this difficulty, our first rearrangement algorithm *list*1 (Program 7.18), begins by converting the singly linked list p into a doubly linked list and then proceeds to move records into their correct places.

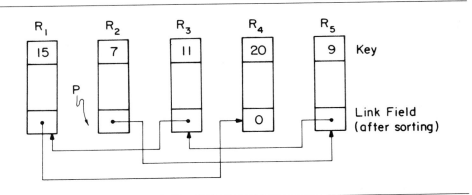

Figure 7.11 List sort

Example 7.8: After a list sort on the input file (35,18,12,42,26,14) has been made the file is linked as in Figure 7.12 (only three fields of each record are shown). Following the links starting at R_p we obtain the logical sequence of records R_3, R_6, R_2, R_5, R_1 and R_4 corresponding to the key sequence 12, 14, 18, 26, 35, and 42. Filling in the backward links, we get the doubly linked list of Figure 7.13. The configuration at the end of the first execution of the **for** loop is given in Figure 7.14. The logical sequence of the remaining list (LS) is: R_6, R_2, R_5, R_3, R_4. The remaining execution is illustrated in

```
 1  procedure list1(var r : afile; n : integer; p : integer);
 2  {p is a pointer to list of n sorted records linked together
 3   by the field link. linkb is assumed to be present in each
 4   record. The records are rearranged so that the resulting
 5   records r[1], ..., r[n] are consecutive and sorted.
 6   Type definitions are as for merge except for an extra link field}
 7  var i,u,s : integer;
 8      a : records;
 9  begin
10     u := 0; x := p;
11     while s < > 0 do {convert p into a doubly linked list using linkb}
12     begin
13       r[s].linkb := u;
14       u := s;
15       s := r[s].link;
16     end;
17     for i := 1 to n − 1 do {move rₚ to position i while}
18     begin                {maintaining the list}
19       if p < > i
20       then
21       begin
22         if r[i].link < > 0 then r[r[i].link].linkb := p;
23         r[r[i].linkb].link := p;
24         a := r[p]; r[p] := r[i]; r[i] := a;
25       end;
26       p := r[i].link;
27     end;
28  end; {of list1}
```

Program 7.18 List1

Figure 7.15. □

Analysis of Procedure *list*1

If there are n records in the file then the time required to convert the chain P into a doubly linked list is $O(n)$. The **for** loop is iterated $n - 1$ times. In each iteration at most two records are interchanged. This requires three records to move. If each record is m words long, then the cost per interchange is $3m$. The total time is therefore $O(nm)$. The worst case of $3(n - 1)$ record moves is achievable. For example, consider the input key sequence $R_1, R_2, \ldots, R_n$, with $R_2 < R_3 < \ldots < R_n$ and $R_1 > R_n$. For $n = 4$ and keys 4,1,2,3 the file after each iteration has the following form: $i = 1$: 1,4,2,3; $i = 2$: 1,2,4,3; $i = 3$: 1,2,3,4. A total of nine record moves is made.

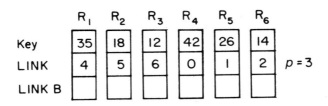

Figure 7.12 Linked list following a list sort

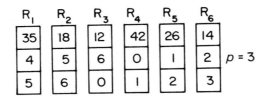

Figure 7.13 Doubly linked list resulting from list of Figure 7.12

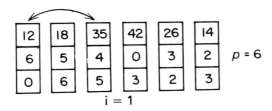

Figure 7.14 Configuration after first iteration of the **for** loop of procedure *list*1

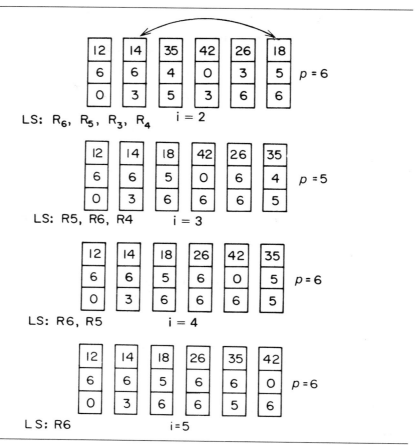

Figure 7.15 Example for procedure *list*1

Several modifications to algorithm *list*1 are possible. One that is of interest was given by M. D. MacLaren. This results in a rearrangement algorithm in which no additional link fields are necessary. In this algorithm (Program 7.19), after the record R_p is exchanged with R_i the link field of the new R_i is set to p to indicate that the original record was moved. This, together with the observation that p must always be $\geq i$, permits a correct reordering of the records. The computing time remains $O(nm)$.

Example 7.9: The data is the same as in Example 7.8. After the list sort we have the configuration of Figure 7.16. The configuration after each of the first two iterations of the **for** loop is shown in Figure 7.17. Now $p < 3$ and so it is advanced to $r[p].link = 6$. The configurations following iterations three and four are shown in Figure 7.18. Again

```
 1 procedure list2(var r :afile; n : integer; p : integer);
 2 {same function as list1 except that a second link field, linkb,
 3   is not required}
 4 var i,q : integer;
 5     t : records;
 6 begin
 7    for i := 1 to n − 1 do
 8    begin
 9      {find correct record to place into i-th position. The index
10       of this record must be ≥ i as records in positions
11       1, 2, . . ., i − 1 are already correctly positioned}
12      while p < i do
13        p := r [p ].link;
14        q := r [p ].link;       {r_q is next record with largest key}
15        if p < > i {interchange r_i and r_p moving r_p to its}
16        then          {correct spot as r_p has i-th smallest key.}
17        begin         {Also set link from old position of r_j to}
18          t := r [i ];                    {new one}
19          r [i ] := r [p ]; r [p ] := t ; r [i ].link := p;
20        end; {of if}
21        p := q;
22    end; {of for}
23 end; {of list2}
```

Program 7.19 List2

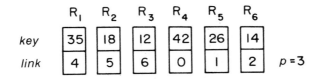

Figure 7.16 Configuration after a list sort

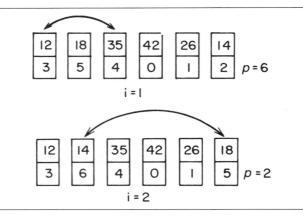

Figure 7.17 Configurations after iterations 1 and 2 of *list2*

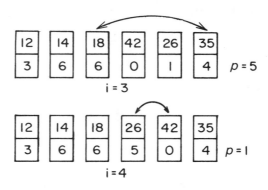

Figure 7.18 Configurations after iterations 3 and 4 of *list2*

$p < 5$ and following links from $r[p]$ we find $r[6]$ to be the record with fifth smallest key. The final configuration is given in Figure 7.19. □

Analysis of Procedure *list2*

The sequence of record moves for *list2* is identical to that for *list1*. Hence, in the worst case $3(n-1)$ record moves for a total cost of $O(nm)$ are made. No node is examined more than once in the **while** loop. So the total time for the **while** loop is $O(n)$. While the asymptotic computing time for both *list1* and *list2* is the same and the same

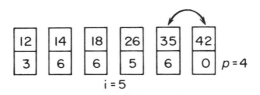

Figure 7.19 Final configuration for *list2*

number of record moves is made in either case, we would expect *list2* to be slightly faster than *list1* because each time two records are interchanged *list1* does more work than *list2* does. *list1* is inferior to *list2* on both space and time considerations.

The list sort technique discussed above does not appear to be well suited for use with sort methods such as quick sort and heap sort. The sequential representation of the heap is essential to heap sort. In such cases as well as in the methods suited to list sort, one can maintain an auxiliary table with one entry per record. The entries in this table serve as an indirect reference to the records. Let this table be type *TableList* which is defined as *TableList* = **array** [1..*maxn*] **of integer**. At the start of the sort $t[i] = i$, $1 \le i \le n$. If the sorting algorithm requires an interchange of R_i and R_j, then only the table entries need to be interchanged, i.e., $t[i]$ and $t[j]$. At the end of the sort, the record with the smallest key is $R_{t[1]}$ and that with the largest $R_{t[n]}$. In general, following a table sort $R_{t[i]}$ is the record with the i'th smallest key. The required permutation on the records is therefore $R_{t[1]}, R_{r[2]}, \ldots, R_{t[n]}$ (see Figure 7.20). This table is adequate even in situations such as binary search, where a sequentially ordered file is needed. In other situations, it may be necessary to physically rearrange the records according to the permutation specified by t.

The algorithm to rearrange records corresponding to the permutation $t[1], t[2], \ldots, t[n]$ is a rather interesting application of a theorem from mathematics: every permutation is made up of disjoint cycles. The cycle for any element i is made up of $i, t[i], t^2[i], \ldots, t^k[i]$, where $t^j[i] = t[t^{j-1}[i]]$ and $t^0[i] = i$ such that $t^k[i] = i$. Thus, the permutation t of Figure 7.20 has two cycles, the first involving R_1 and R_5 and the second involving R_4, R_3, and R_2. Procedure *table* (Program 7.20) utilizes this cyclic decomposition of a permutation. First, the cycle containing R_1 is followed and all records moved to their correct positions. The cycle containing R_2 is the next one examined unless this cycle has already been examined. The cycles for $R_3, R_4, \ldots, R_{n-1}$ are followed in that order, achieving a reordering of all the records. While processing a trivial cycle for R_1 (i.e., $t[i] = i$), no rearrangement involving records R_i is required since the condition $t[i] = i$ means that the records with the i'th smallest key is R_i. In processing a nontrivial cycle for record R_i (i.e., $t[i] \ne i$), R_i is moved to a temporary position p, then the record at $t[i]$ is moved to i; next the records at $t[t[i]]$ is moved to $t[i]$, and so on until the end of the cycle $t^k[i]$ is reached and the record at p is moved to

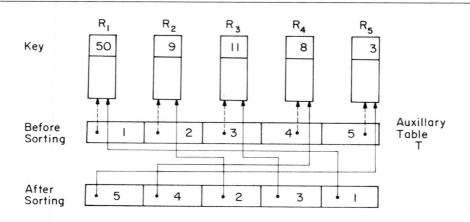

Figure 7.20 Table sort

$t^{k-1}[i]$.

Example 7.10: Following a table sort on the file f we have the following values for t (only the key values for the eight records of f are shown):

	R_1	R_2	R_3	R_4	R_5	R_6	R_7	R_8
f	35	14	12	42	26	50	31	18
t	3	2	8	5	7	1	4	6

There are two nontrivial cycles in the permutation specified by t. The first is R_1, R_3, R_8, R_6, and R_1. The second is R_4, R_5, R_7, R_4. During the first iteration ($i = 1$) of the **for** loop of algorithm *table*, the cycle R_1, $R_{t[1]}$, $R_{t^2[1]}$, $R_{t^3[1]}$, R_1 is followed. Record R_1 is moved to a temporary spot P; $R_{t[1]}$ (i.e., R_3) is moved to the position R_1; $R_{t^2[1]}$ (i.e., R_8) is moved to R_3; R_6 to R_8, and finally P to R_6. Thus, at the end of the first iteration we have

f	12	14	18	42	26	35	31	50
t	1	2	3	5	7	6	4	8

For $i = 2, 3$, $t[i] = i$, indicating that these records are already in their correct positions. When $i = 4$, the next nontrivial cycle is discovered and the records on this cycle R_4, R_5, R_7, R_4 are moved to their correct positions. Following this we have

```
 1 procedure table(var r : afile; n : integer; var t : TableList);
 2 {The records r[1], . . ., r[n] are rearranged to correspond to the
 3  sequence r[t[1]], . . ., r[t[n]], n ≥ 1}
 4 var i,j,k : integer;
 5    p : records;
 6 begin
 7   for i := 1 to n − 1 do
 8   if t[i] < > i
 9   then                {there is a nontrivial cycle starting at i}
10   begin               {move r[i] to a temporary spot p and follow}
11     p := r[i];        {cycle i,t[i], t[t[i]], . . ., until the correct spot}
12     j := i;
13     repeat
14       k := t[j];
15       r[j] := r[k];
16       t[j] := j;
17       j := k;
18     until t[j] = i;
19     r[j] := p; {j is position for record p}
20     t[j] := j;
21   end;
22 end; {of table}
```

Program 7.20 Table sort

f	12	14	18	26	31	35	42	50
t	1	2	3	4	5	6	7	8

For the remaining values of $i(i = 5, 6,$ and $7)$, $t[i] = i$, and no more nontrivial cycles are found. □

Analysis of Procedure table

If each record uses m words of storage, then the additional space needed is m words for p plus a few more for variables such as $i, j,$ and k. To obtain an estimate of the computing time we observe that the **for** loop is executed $n − 1$ times. If for some value of i, $t[i] \neq i$ then there is a nontrivial cycle including $k > 1$ distinct records $R_i, R_{t[i]}, \ldots, R_{t^{k-1}[i]}$. Rearranging these records requires $k + 1$ record moves. Following this, the records involved in this cycle are not moved again at any time in the algorithm since $t[j] = j$ for all such records R_j. Hence no record can be in two different nontrivial cycles. Let k_l be the number of records on a nontrivial cycle starting at R_l when $i = l$ in the algorithm. Let $k_l = 0$ for a trivial cycle. Then, the total number of record moves is

$$\sum_{\substack{l=0 \\ k_l \neq 0}}^{n-1} (k_l+1)$$

Since the records on nontrivial cycles must be different, $\sum k_l \leq n$. The total record moves is thus maximum when $\sum k_l = n$ and there are $\lfloor n/2 \rfloor$ cycles. When n is even, each cycle contains two records. Otherwise one contains three and the others two. In either case the number of record moves is $\lfloor 3n/2 \rfloor$. One record move costs O(m) time. The total computing time is therefore O(mn).

In comparing the algorithms *list2* and *table* for rearranging records we see that in the worst case *list2* makes $3(n-1)$ record moves while *table* makes only $\lfloor 3n/2 \rfloor$ record moves. For larger values of m it would therefore be worthwhile to make one pass over the sorted list of records creating a table t corresponding to a table sort. This would take O(n) time. Then algorithm *table* could be used to rearrange the records in the order specified by t.

Of the several sorting methods we have studied there is no one method that is best. Some methods are good for small n, others for large n. Insertion sort is good when the file is already partially ordered. Because of the low overhead of the method it is also the best sorting method for "small" n. Merge sort has the best worst case behavior but requires more storage than heap sort and has slightly more overhead than merge sort. Quick sort has the best average behavior but its worst case behavior is O(n^2). The behavior of radix sort depends on the size of the keys and the choice of r.

Figure 7.21 gives the average running times for *InsertionSort*, *QuickSort*, *MergeSort*, and *HeapSort*. Figure 7.22 is a plot of these times. As can be seen for n up to about 20, *InsertionSort* is the fastest. *QuickSort* is the fastest for values of n from about 20 to about 45. For larger values of n, *MergeSort* is the fastest. In practice, therefore, it would be worthwhile to combine *InsertionSort*, *QuickSort*, and *MergeSort* so that *MergeSort* uses *QuickSort* for subfiles of size less than about 45 and *QuickSort* uses *InsertionSort* when the subfile size is below about 20.

7.9 REFERENCES AND SELECTED READINGS

A comprehensive discussion of sorting and searching may be found in: *The Art of Computer Programming: Sorting and Searching*, by D. Knuth, vol. 3, Addison-Wesley, Reading, Massachusetts, 1973.

Two other useful references on sorting are: *Sorting and Sort Systems*, by H. Lorin, Addison-Wesley, Reading, Massachusetts, 1975, and *Internal Sorting Methods Illustrated with PL/1 Programs*, by R. Rich, Prentice-Hall, Englewood Cliffs, 1972.

Two references on quick sort are: "Quicksort," by C. A. R. Hoare, *The Computer Journal*, 5, 1962, pp. 10-15, and "The analysis of quicksort programs," by R. Sedgewick, *Acta Informatica*, 7, 1976/77, pp. 327-355.

n	quick	merge	heap	insert
0	0.041	0.027	0.034	0.032
10	1.064	1.524	1.482	0.775
20	2.343	3.700	3.680	2.253
30	3.700	5.587	6.153	4.430
40	5.085	7.800	8.815	7.275
50	6.542	9.892	11.583	10.892
60	7.987	11.947	14.427	15.013
70	9.587	15.893	17.427	20.000
80	11.167	18.217	20.517	25.450
90	12.633	20.417	23.717	31.767
100	14.275	22.950	26.775	38.325
200	30.775	48.475	60.550	148.300
300	48.171	81.600	96.657	319.657
400	65.914	109.829	134.971	567.629
500	84.400	138.033	174.100	874.600
600	102.900	171.167	214.400	
700	122.400	199.240	255.760	
800	142.160	230.480	297.480	
900	160.400	260.100	340.000	
1000	181.000	289.450	382.250	

Times in hundredths of a second

Figure 7.21 Average times for sort methods

Figure 7.21 and Figure 7.22 are taken from: *Software Development in Pascal*, by S. Sahni, Camelot Publishing Co., 1985.

The O(1) space linear time merge algorithm is from the paper: ''Practical in-place merging,'' by B. Huang and M. Langston, *CACM*, Vol 31, No 3, 1988, pp. 348-352.

7.10 EXERCISES

1. [Count sort] About the simplest known sorting method arises from the observation that the position of a record in a sorted file depends on the number of records with smaller keys. Associated with each record there is a *count* field used to determine the number of records which must precede this one in the sorted file. Write an algorithm to determine the *count* of each record in an unordered file. Show that if the file has n records, then all the *counts* can be determined by making at most $n(n-1)/2$ key comparisons.

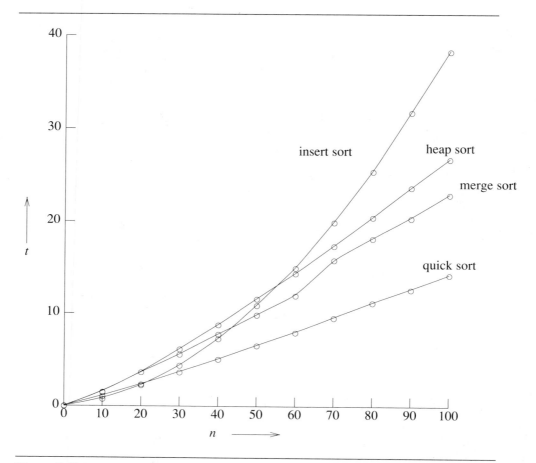

Figure 7.22 Plot of average times

2. The insertion of algorithm *insert* was carried out by (a) searching for the spot at which the insertion is to be made and (b) making the insertion. If as a result of the search it was decided that the insertion had to be made between R_i and R_{i+1}, then records $R_{i+1}, \ldots, R_n$ were moved one space to locations $R_{i+2}, \ldots, R_{n+1}$. This was carried out in parallel with the search of (a). (a) can be sped up using the idea of *BinarySearch*. Write an *insert* algorithm incorporating this.

3. Phase (b) (see Exercise 2) can be sped up by maintaining the sorted file as a linked list. In this case the insertion can be made without any accompanying movement of the other records. However, now (a) must be carried out sequentially as before. Such an insertion scheme is known as list insertion. Write an algorithm for list insertion. Note that the insertion algorithms of Exercises 3 and 4 can be used for a

sort without making any changes in *InsertionSort*.

4. Write a procedure for insertion sort that begins with a linked list of records and obtains a new linked list in which the records are in nondecreasing order of the field *key*. Assume that the records are linked by the field *link*.

5. (a) Show that algorithm *QuickSort* takes $O(n^2)$ time when the input file is already in sorted order.

   (b) Why is $K_m \leq K_{n+1}$ required in *QuickSort*?

6. (a) The quick sort algorithm *QuickSort* presented in Section 7.3 always fixes the position of the first record in the subfile currently being sorted. A better choice for this record is to choose the record with key value which is the median of the keys of the first, middle, and last record in the subfile. Thus, using this median of three rule we correctly fix the position of the record R_i with $K_i = $ median $\{K_m, K_{(m+n)/2}, K_n\}$; i.e., K_i is the second largest key, e.g., median $\{10, 5, 7\} = 7 = $ median $\{10, 7, 7\}$. Write a nonrecursive version of *QuickSort* incorporating this median of three rule to determine the record whose position is to be fixed. Also, adopt the suggestion of Section 7.8 and use insertion sort to sort subfiles of size less than 21. Show that this algorithm takes $O(n \log n)$ time on an already sorted file.

   (b) Show that if smaller subfiles are sorted first then the recursion in algorithm *QuickSort* can be simulated by a stack of depth $O(\log n)$.

7. Quick sort is an unstable sorting method. Give an example of an input file in which the order of records with equal keys is not preserved.

8. Suppose we use Program 7.10 to obtain a merge sort procedure. Is the resulting procedure a stable sort?

9. Write a procedure to shift the records $(x_1, \ldots, x_n)$ circularly right by p, $0 \leq p \leq n$ positions. Your procedure should have time complexity $O(n)$ and space complexity $O(1)$. (Hint: Use three segment reversals.)

10. The two sorted files $(x_1, \ldots, x_m)$ and $(x_{m+1}, \ldots, x_n)$ are to be merged to get the sorted file $(x_l, \ldots, x_n)$. Let $s = \lfloor \sqrt{n} \rfloor$.

    (a) Assume that one of these files has fewer than s records. Write a procedure to merge the two sorted files in $O(n)$ time while using only $O(1)$ additional space. Show that your procedure actually has these complexities. (Hint: If the first list has fewer than s elements then find the position, q, in the merged file of the first element of the first file; perform a circular shift of $q-1$ as in the preceding exercise. This circular shift involves only the records of the first file and the first $q-1$ records of the second. Following the circular shift the first q records are in their final merged positions. Repeat this process for the second, third, etc., elements of the initial first file.)

(b)   Assume that both files have at least s elements. Write a merge procedure with the same asymptotic complexity as that for (a). Show that your procedure actually has this complexity. (Hint: Partition the first file such that the first block has $s_1, 0 \leq s_1 < s$, records and the remainder have s records. Partition the second file so that the last block has $s_2, 0 \leq s_2 < s$ records. If $s_1 \neq 0$, then compare the first blocks of the two files to identify the s_1 records with smallest key. Perform a swap as in Step 2 of Program 7.10 so that these s_1 records are in the leftmost block of the first file. If $s_2 \neq 0$, then using a similar process we can get the s_2 records with largest keys into the rightmost block of the second file. Now, the leftmost block of size s_1 and the rightmost one of size s_2 are sorted. Following this, we may forget about them. The remaining blocks of the first and second files may be arranged in sorted order using the merge procedure of part (a). Next, Program 7.10 may be used to merge them.)

(c)   Use the procedures for (a) and (b) to obtain an $O(n)$ time and $O(1)$ space procedure to merge two files of arbitrary size.

(d)   Compare the run time of the merge procedure of (c) with that of Program 7.9. Use $m = n/2$ and the values $n = 100, 250, 500, 1000, 2000, 5000, 10000$. For each value of n use ten randomly generated pairs of sorted files and compute the average merge time. Plot these for the two merge procedures. What conclusions can you draw?

(e)   Modify your procedure for part (b) so that it does not use the procedure of (a) to rearrange records in the first and second files into sorted order. Rather, the last and first blocks of the first and second files, respectively, are sorted. To find the largest s records we need to look at the last two blocks of the first file and the last block of the second file. Program this procedure and obtain run times using the data of (d). Add these to your plot of (d).

(f)   Program the $O(1)$ space merge procedure as described by Huang and Langston in their paper cited in the references and selected readings section. This procedure begins by partitioning the first file as in (b). The second file is partitioned into blocks of size except for the last block whose size s_2 is such that $s \leq s_2 < 2*s$. The largest s records are found and placed in the rightmost block of the first file. This is called the merge buffer. The rightmost block of the second file (i.e., the one with size s_2) is sorted. If $s_1 > 0$, the leftmost block of the first file is merged with the leftmost block of the second file using the last s_1 positions of the merge buffer. A swap of the leftmost s_1 records and those in the rightmost s_1 positions of the merge buffer results in moving the s_1 smallest records to their final place and also restores the merge buffer to contain the largest s records. Now we can forget about the first s_1 records and proceed to move the merge buffer to the leftmost s size block and sort the remaining blocks by their last records. One of these blocks is of size s_2. The sort of the blocks needs to be a little careful about

this. Obtain the run times for this procedure using the data of (d). Add these results to your plot of (d). What conslusions can you draw?

11. (a) Prove that algorithm *MergeSort* is stable.

(b) Heap sort is unstable. Give an example of an input file in which the order of records with equal keys is not preserved.

12. In the merge sort scheme discussed in Section 7.5 the sort was started with n sorted files each of size 1. Another approach would be to first make one pass over the data determining sequences of records that are in order and then using these as the initially sorted files. In this case, a left-to-right pass over the data of Example 7.4 would result in the partitioning of Figure 7.23. This would be followed by pairwise merging of the files until only one file remains.

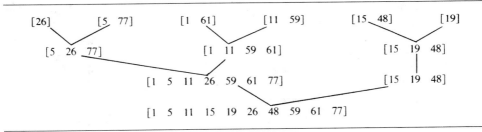

Figure 7.23 Merge sort starting with sorted sublists

Rewrite the merge sort algorithm to take into account the existing order in the records. How much time does this algorithm take on an initially sorted file? Note that the original algorithm took O(n log n) on such an input file. What is the worst case computing time of the new algorithm? How much additional space is needed? Use linked lists.

13. Does algorithm *RadixSort* result in a stable sort when used to sort numbers as in Example 7.7?

14. Write a sort algorithm to sort records $R_1, \ldots, R_n$ lexically on keys $(K^1, \ldots, K^r)$ for the case when the range of each key is much larger than n. In this case, the bin sort scheme used in *RadixSort* to sort within each key becomes inefficient (why?). What scheme would you use to sort within a key if we desired an algorithm with (a) good worst case behavior, (b) good average behavior, and (c) n is small, say <15?

15. If we have n records with integer keys in the range [0,n^2), then they may be sorted in O(n log n) time using heap or merge sort. Radix sort on a single key, i.e., $d = 1$ and $r = n^2$ takes O(n^2) time. Show how to interpret the keys as two subkeys so that radix sort will take only O(n) time to sort n records. (Hint: each key, K_i, may

be written as $K_i = K_i^1 n + K_i^2$ with K_i^1 and K_i^2 integers in the range $[0,n)$.)

16. Generalize the method of the previous exercise to the case of integer keys in the range $(0,n^p)$ obtaining an $O(pn)$ sorting method.

17. Write the status of the file $F = (12,2,16,30,8,28,4,10,20,6,18)$ at the end of each phase of the following algorithms:

   (a) *InsertionSort*

   (b) *QuickSort*

   (c) *MergeSort*

   (d) *HeapSort*

   (e) *RadixSort* – radix 10

18. Write a table sort version of quick sort. Now during the sort, records are not physically moved. Instead, $t[i]$ is the index of the record that would have been in position i if records were physically moved around as in algorithm *QuickSort*. To begin with $t[i] = i$, $1 \le i \le n$. At the end of the sort $t[i]$ is the index of the record that should be in the i'th position in the sorted file. So now algorithm *table* of Section 7.8 may be used to rearrange the records into the sorted order specified by t. Note that this reduces the amount of data movement taking place when compared to *QuickSort* for the case of large records.

19. Write an algorithm similar to algorithm *table* to rearrange the records of a file if with each record we have a *count* of the number of records preceding it in the sorted file (see Exercise 1).

20. Under what conditions would an MSD radix sort be more efficient than an LSD radix sort?

21. Assume you are given a list of five-letter English words and are faced with the problem of listing out these words in sequences such that the words in each sequence are anagrams, i.e., if x and y are in the same sequence, then word x is a permutation of word y. You are required to list out the fewest such sequences. With this restriction show that no word can appear in more than one sequence. How would you go about solving this problem?

22. Assume you are working in the census department of a small town where the number of records, about 3000, is small enough to fit into the internal memory of a computer. All the people currently living in this town were born in the United States. There is one record for each person in this town. Each record contains (a) the state in which the person was born, (b) county of birth, and (c) name of person.

   How would you produce a list of all persons living in this town? The list is to be ordered by state. Within each state the persons are to be listed by their counties, the counties being arranged in alphabetical order. Within each county, the names are also listed in alphabetical order. Justify any assumptions you may make.

23. The objective of this assignment is to come up with one composite sorting algorithm that is good on the worst time criterion. The candidate algorithms are:

(a) Insert Sort

(b) Quick Sort

(c) Merge Sort

(d) Heap Sort

To begin with, program these algorithms in your favorite high level programming language (make sure you have access to a time routine in this language before you start). In each case, assume that n integers are to be sorted. In the case of quick sort, use the median of 3 method. In the case of merge sort, use the iterative algorithm (as a separate exercise, you might wish to compare the run times of the iterative and recursive versions of merge sort and determine what the recursion penality is in your favorite language using your favorite compiler). Check out the correctness of the programs using some test data. Since quite detailed and working algorithms are given in the book, this part of the assignment should take little effort. In anycase, no points are earned until after this step.

To get reasonably accurate run times, you need to know the accuracy of the clock or timer you are using. Determine this by reading the appropriate manual. Let this be δ. Now, run a pilot test to determine ball-park-times for your 4 sorting procedures for $n = 5, 10, 20, 30, 40, 50,$ and 100. You will notice times of 0 for many of these values of n. The other times may not be much larger than the clock accuracy.

To time an event that is smaller than or near the clock accuracy, repeat it many times and divide the overall time by the number of repetitions. You should obtain times that are accurate to within 1%.

We need worst case data for each of the 4 sort methods. The worst case data for insert sort is easy to generate. Just use the sequence $n, n-1, n-2, \ldots, 1$. Worst case data for merge sort can be obtained by working backwards. Begin with the last merge your algorithm will perform and make this work hardest. Then look at the 2nd last merge, and so on. Use this logic to obtain a program that will generate worst case data for merge sort for each of the above values of n.

Generating worst case data for heap sort is the hardest. So, here we shall use a random permutation generator (a Pascal one is provided in Program 7.21). We shall generate random permutations of the desired size; clock heap sort on each of these; and use the max of these times as an approximation to the worst case time. You will be able to use more random permutations for smaller values of n than for larger. For no value of n should fewer than 10 permutations be used. Use the same technique to obtain worst case times for quick sort.

Having settled on the test data, we are ready to perform our experiment. Obtain the worst case times. From these times you will get a rough idea when one algorithm performs better than the other. Now, narrow the scope of your experiments and determine the exact value of n when one algorithm outperforms another. For some algorithms, this value may be 0. For instance, each of the other three algorithms may be faster than quick sort for all values of n.

Plot your findings on a single sheet of graph paper. Do you see the n^2 behavior of insert sort and quick sort; and the $n\log n$ behavior of the other two algorithms for suitably large n (about $n > 20$)? If not, there is something wrong with your test or your clock or with both. For each value of n determine the sort algorithm that is fastest (simply look at your graph). Write a composite algorithm with the best possible performance for all n. Clock this algorithm and plot the times on the same graph sheet you used earlier.

A word of **CAUTION**. If you are using a multi process computer, make all your final runs at about the same time. On these computers, the clocked time will vary significantly with the amount of computer work load. Comparing the run times of an insert sort run made at 2:00pm with the run times of a merge sort run made at 2:00am will not be very meaningful.

WHAT TO TURN IN
You are required to submit a report that states the clock accuracy; the number of random permutations tried for heap sort; the worst case data for merge sort and how you generated it; a table of times for the above values of n; the times for the narrowed ranges; the graph; and a table of times for the composite algorithm. In addition, your report must be accompanied by a complete listing of the program used by you (this includes the sorting procedures and the main program for timing and test data generation).

```
procedure permute(var a : ElementList ; n:integer);
{Random permutation generator}
var  i, j: integer; k: element;
begin
   for i := n downto 2 do
   begin
      j := random (i) + 1;  {j := random integer in the range [0, i−1]}
      k := a [j ]; a [j ] := a [i ]; a [i ] := k;
   end;
end; {of permute}
```

Program 7.21 Random permutation generator

24. Repeat the previous exercise for the case of average run times. Average case data is almost impossible to create. So, use random permutations. This time, however, don't repeat a permutation many times to overcome clock inaccuracies. Instead, use each permutation once and clock the time over all (for a fixed n).

25. Use the composing strategy outlined at the end of Section 7.8 to combine *Insertion Sort*, *QuickSort*, and *MergeSort* into a single sorting scheme. Compare the average run time of this with that of the individual sorting methods.

26. Experiment with *RadixSort* to see how it performs relative to the sorting procedures compared in Figure 7.21.

27. Obtain Figure 7.21 and Figure 7.22 for the case of worst case run time.

CHAPTER 8
EXTERNAL SORTING

In this chapter, we consider techniques to sort large files. The files are assumed to be so large that the whole file cannot be contained in the internal memory of a computer, making an internal sort impossible. Before discussing methods available for external sorting it is necessary first to study the characteristics of the external storage devices that can be used to accomplish the sort. External storage devices may broadly be categorized as either sequential access (e.g., tapes) or direct access (e.g., drums and disks). Section 8.1 presents a brief study of the properties of these devices. In Sections 8.2 and 8.3 we study sorting methods which make the best use of these external devices.

8.1 STORAGE DEVICES

8.1.1 Magnetic Tapes

Magnetic tape devices for computer input/output are similar in principle to audio tape recorders. The data is recorded on magnetic tape approximately 0.5 inches wide. The tape is wound around a spool. A new reel of tape is normally 2400 feet long (with use, the length of tape in a reel tends to decrease because of frequent cutting off of lengths of the tape). Tracks run across the length of the tape, with a tape having typically 7 to 9 tracks across its width. Depending on the direction of magnetization, a spot on the track can represent either a 0 or a 1 (i.e., a bit of information). At any point along the length of the tape, the combination of bits on the tracks represents a character (e.g., A–Z, 0–9, +, :, ;, etc.). The number of bits that can be written per inch of track is referred to as the tape density. Examples of standard track densities are 800 and 1600 bpi (bits per inch). Since there are enough tracks across the width of the tape to represent a character, this density also gives the number of characters per inch of tape. Figure 8.1 illustrates this. With the conventions of the figure, the code for the first character on the tape is 10010111 while that for the third character is 00011100. If the tape is written using a density of 800 bpi, then the length marked x in the figure is 3/800 inches.

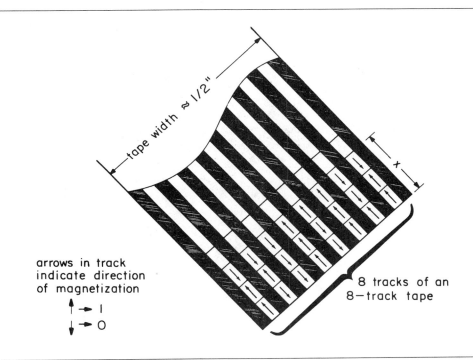

Figure 8.1 Segment of a magnetic tape

Reading from a magnetic tape or writing onto one is done from a tape drive, as shown if Figure 8.2. A tape drive consists of two spindles. On one of the spindles is mounted the source reel and on the other the take-up reel. During forward reading or forward writing, the tape is pulled from the source reel across the read/write heads and onto the take-up reel. Some tape drives also permit backward reading and writing of tapes; i.e., reading and writing can take place when tape is being moved from the take-up to the source reel.

If characters are packed onto a tape at a density of 800 bpi, then a 2400 foot tape would hold a little over 23×10^6 characters. A density of 1600 bpi would double this figure. However, it is necessary to block data on a tape since each read/write instruction transmits a whole block of information into/from memory. Since normally we would neither have enough space in memory for one full tape load nor would we wish to read the whole tape at once, the information on a tape will be grouped into several blocks.

These blocks may be of a variable or fixed size. In between blocks of data is an inter-block gap normally about 3/4 inches long. The interblock gap is long enough to permit the tape to accelerate from rest to the correct read/write heads. Figure 8.3 shows a segment of tape with blocked data.

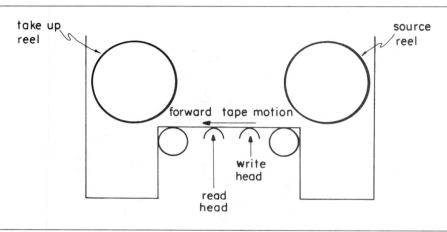

Figure 8.2 A tape drive

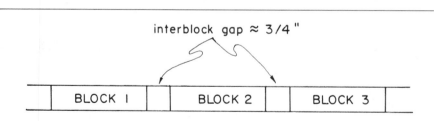

Figure 8.3 Blocked data on a tape

In order to read a block from a tape one specifies the length of the block and also the address, A, in memory where the block is to be transmitted. The block of data is packed into the words $A, A+1, A+2, \ldots$. Similarly, in order to write a block of data onto tape one specifies the starting address in memory and the number of consecutive words to be written. These input and output areas in memory will be referred to as buffers. Usually the block size will correspond to the size of the input/output buffers set up in memory. We would like these blocks to be as large as possible for the following reasons:

(1) Between any pair of blocks there is an interblock gap of 0.75 inches. With a track density of 800 bpi, this space is long enough to write 600 characters. Using a block length of 1 character/block on a 2400 foot tape would result in roughly 38,336 blocks or a total of 38,336 characters on the entire tape. Tape utilization is $1/601 < 0.17$ percent. With 600 characters per block, half the tape would be made up of interblock gaps. In this case, the tape would have only about 11.5×10^6 characters of information on it, representing a 50 percent utilization of tape. Thus, the longer the blocks the more characters we can write onto the tape.

(2) If the tape starts from rest when the input/output command is issued, the time required to write a block on n characters onto the tape is $t_a + n t_w$ where t_a is the delay time and t_w the time to transmit one character from memory to tape. The delay time is the time needed to cross the interblock gap. If the tape starts from rest, then t_a includes the time to accelerate to the correct tape speed. In this case t_a is larger than when the tape is already moving at the correct speed when a read/write command is issued. Assuming a tape speed of 150 inches per second during read/write and 800 bpi the time to read or write a character is 8.3×10^{-6} seconds. The transmission rate is therefore 12×10^4 characters/second. The delay time t_a may typically be about 10 milliseconds. If the entire tape consisted of just one long block, then it could be read in 2400 ft/150 in/sec + 10 msec $\approx$ 3 min 12 sec, thus effecting an average transmission rate of almost 12×10^4 charac/sec. If, on the other hand, each block were one character long, then the tape would have at most 38,336 characters or blocks. This would be the worst case and the read time would be about 6 min 24 sec or an average of 100 charac/sec. Note that if the read of the next block is initiated soon enough after the read of the present block, then the delay time would be reduced to 5 msec, corresponding to the time needed to get across the interblock gap of 0.75 inches at a tape speed of 150 in/sec. In this case, the time to read 38,336 one-character blocks would be 3 min 12 sec, corresponding to an average of about 200 charac/sec.

While large blocks are desirable from the standpoint of efficient tape usage as well as reduced input/output time, the amount of internal memory available for use as input/output buffers puts a limitation on block size.

Computer tape is the foremost example of a sequential access device. If the read head is positioned at the front of the tape and one wishes to read the information in a block 2000 ft down the tape, then it is necessary to forward space the tape the correct number of blocks. If now we wish to read the first block, the tape would have to be rewound 2000 ft to the front before the first block could be read. Typical rewind times over 2400 ft of tape could be around one minute.

Unless otherwise stated we will make the following assumptions about our tape drives:

(1)   Tapes can be written and read in the forward direction only.

(2)   The input/output channel of the computer is such as to permit the following three tasks to be carried out in parallel: writing onto one tape, reading from another and CPU operation.

(3)   If blocks $1, \ldots, i$ have been written on a tape, then the tape can be moved backwards block by block using a backspace command or moved to the first block via a rewind command. Overwriting block $i-1$ with another block of the same size destroys the leading portion of block i. While this latter assumption is not true of all tape drives, it is characteristic of most of them.

8.1.2 Disk Storage

As an example of direct access external storage, we consider disks. As in the case of tape storage, we have here two distinct components: (1) the disk module (or simply disk or disk pack) on which information is stored (this corresponds to a reel of tape in the case of tape storage) and (2) the disk drive (corresponding to the tape drive) which performs the function of reading and writing information onto disks. Like tapes, disks can be removed from or mounted onto a disk drive. A disk pack consists of several platters that are similar to phonograph records. The number of platters per pack varies and typically is about 6. Figure 8.4 shows a disk pack with 6 platters. Each platter has two surfaces on which information can be recorded. The outer surfaces of the top and bottom platters are not used. This gives the disk of Figure 8.4 a total of 10 surfaces on which information may be recorded. A disk drive consists of a spindle on which a disk may be mounted and a set of read/write heads. There is one read/write head for each surface. During a read/write the heads are held stationary over the position of the platter where the read/write is to be performed, while the disk itself rotates at high speeds (speeds of 2000-3000 rpm are fairly common). Thus, this device will read/write in concentric circles on each surface. The area that can be read from or written onto by a single stationary head is referred to as a *track*. Tracks are thus concentric circles, and each time the disk completes a revolution an entire track passes a read/write head. There may be from 100 to 1000 tracks on each surface of a platter. The collection of tracks simultaneously under a read/write head on the surfaces of all platters is called a *cylinder*. Tracks are divided into sectors. A *sector* is the smallest addressable segment of a track. Information is recorded along the tracks of a surface in blocks. In order to use a disk, one must specify the track or cylinder number, the sector number which is the start of the block and also the surface. The read/write head assembly is first positioned to the right cylinder. Before read/write can commence, one has to wait for the right sector to come beneath the read/write head. Once this has happened, data transmission can take place. Hence, there are three factors contributing to input/output for disks:

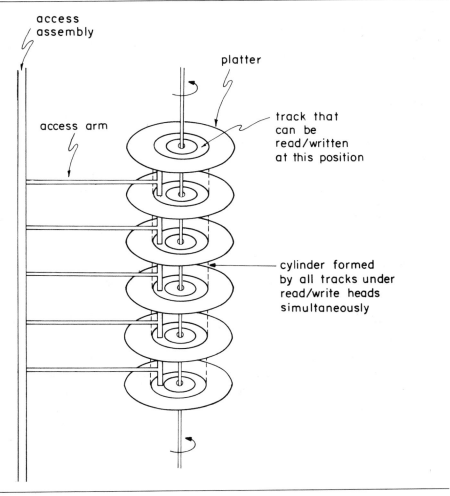

Figure 8.4 A disk drive with disk pack mounted (schematic)

(1)   *Seek time:* time taken to position the read/write heads to the correct cylinder. This will depend on the number of cylinders across which the heads have to move.

(2)   *Latency time:* time until the right sector of the track is under the read/write head.

(3)   *Transmission time:* time to transmit the block of data to/from the disk.

Maximum seek times on a disk are around 1/10 sec. A typical revolution speed for disks is 2400 rpm. Hence the latency time is at most 1/40 sec (the time for one revolution of the disk). Transmission rates are typically between 10^5 charac/sec and 5×10^5 charac/sec. The number of characters that can be written onto a disk depends on the number of surfaces and tracks per surface. This figure ranges from about 10^7 characters for small disks to about 5×10^8 characters for a large disk.

8.2 SORTING WITH DISKS

The most popular method for sorting on external storage devices is merge sort. This method consists of essentially two distinct phases. First, segments of the input file are sorted using a good internal sort method. These sorted segments, known as *runs*, are written out onto external storage as they are generated. Second, the runs generated in phase one are merged together following the merge tree pattern of Example 7.4, until only one run is left. Because the first merge algorithm (Program 7.9) of Section 7.5 requires only the leading records of the two runs being merged to be present in memory at one time, it is possible to merge large runs together. It is more difficult to adapt the other methods considered in Chapter 7 to external sorting. Let us look at an example to illustrate the basic external merge sort process and analyze the various contributions to the overall computing time. A file containing 4500 records, $A_1, \ldots, A_{4500}$, is to be sorted using a computer with an internal memory capable of sorting at most 750 records. The input file is maintained on disk and has a block length of 250 records. We have available another disk that may be used as a scratch pad. The input disk is not to be written on. One way to accomplish the sort using the general procedure outlined about is to:

(1) Internally sort three blocks at a time (i.e., 750 records) to obtain six runs R_1-R_6. A method such as heapsort or quicksort could be used. These six runs are written out onto the scratch disk (Figure 8.5).

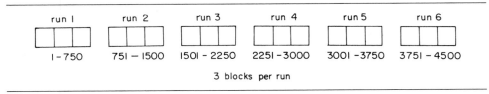

Figure 8.5 Blocked runs obtained after internal sorting

(2) Set aside three blocks of internal memory, each capable of holding 250 records. Two of these blocks will be used as input buffers and the third as an output buffer. Merge runs R_1 and R_2. This is carried out by first reading one block of each of these runs into input buffers. Blocks of runs are merged from the input buffers into the output buffer. When the output buffer gets full, it is written out onto disk. If an input

buffer gets empty, it is refilled with another block from the same run. After runs R_1 and R_2 are merged, R_3 and R_4 and finally R_5 and R_6 are merged. The result of this pass is 3 runs, each containing 1500 sorted records of 6 blocks. Two of these runs are now merged using the input/output buffers set up as above to obtain a run of size 3000. Finally, this run is merged with the remaining run of size 1500 to obtain the desired sorted file (Figure 8.6).

Let us now analyze the method described above to see how much time is required to sort these 4500 records. The analysis will use the following notation:

$$t_s = \text{maximum seek time}$$

$$t_l = \text{maximum latency time}$$

$$t_{rw} = \text{time to read or write one block of 250 records}$$

$$t_{IO} = t_s + t_l + t_{rw}$$

$$t_{IS} = \text{time to internally sort 750 records}$$

$$nt_m = \text{time to merge } n \text{ records from input buffers to the output buffer}$$

We shall assume that each time a block is read from or written onto the disk, the maximum seek and latency times are experienced. While this is not true in general, it will simplify the analysis. The computing times for the various operations are given in Figure 8.7.

Note that the contribution of seek time can be reduced by writing blocks on the same cylinder or on adjacent cylinders. A close look a the final computing time indicates that it depends chiefly on the number of passes made over the data. In addition to the intitial input pass made over the data for the internal sort, the merging of the runs requires 2-2/3 passes over the data (one pass to merge 6 runs of length 750 records, two thirds of a pass to merge two runs of length 1500 and one pass to merge one run of length 3000 and one of length 1500). Since one full pass covers 18 blocks, the input and output time is $2 \times (2\text{-}2/3 + 1) \times 18 \, t_{IO} = 132 t_{IO}$. The leading factor of 2 appears because each record that is read is also written out again. The merge time is 2-2/3 $\times 4500 t_m = 12{,}000 t_m$. Because of this close relationship between the overall computing time and the number of passes made over the data, future analysis will be concerned mainly with counting the number of passes being made. Another point to note regarding the above sort is that no attempt was made to use the computer's ability to carry out input/output and CPU operation in parallel and thus overlap some of the time. In the ideal situation we would overlap almost all the input/output time with CPU processing so that the real time would be approximately $132 \, t_{IO} \approx 12000 \, t_m + 6t_{IS}$.

If we had two disks, we could write on one while reading from the other and merging buffer loads already in memory all at the same time. In this case a proper choice of buffer lengths and buffer handling schemes would result in a time of almost $66t_{IO}$. This parallelism is an important consideration when sorting is being carried out in a non-

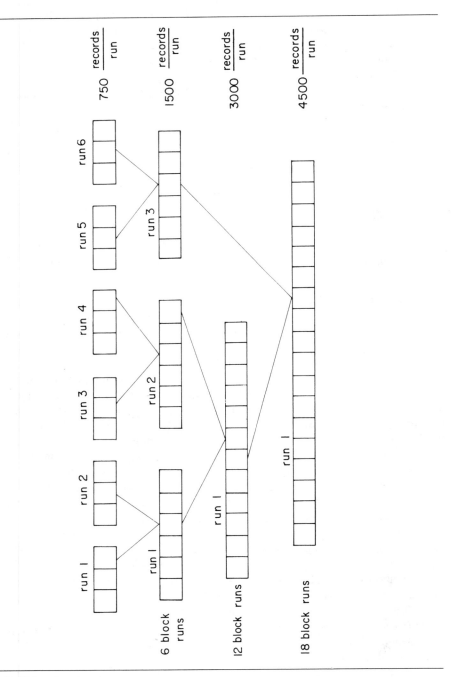

Figure 8.6 Merging the six runs

operation	time
(1) read 18 blocks of input, $18t_{IO}$, internally sort, $6t_{IS}$, write 18 blocks, $18t_{IO}$	$36t_{IO} + 6t_{IS}$
(2) merge runs 1-6 in pairs	$36t_{IO} + 4500t_m$
(3) merge two runs of 1500 records each, 12 blocks	$24t_{IO} + 3000t_m$
(4) merge one run of 3000 records with one run of 1500 records	$36t_{IO} + 4500t_m$
total time	$132t_{IO} + 12000t_m + 6t_{IS}$

Figure 8.7 Computing times for disk sort example

multi-programming environment. In this situation unless input/output and CPU processing is going on in parallel, the CPU is idle during input/oputput. In a multi-programming environment, however, the need for the sorting program to carry out input/output and CPU processing in parallel may not be so critical since the CPU can be busy working on another program (if there are other programs in the system at the time), while the sort program waits for the completion of its input/output. Indeed, in many multi-programming environments it may not even be possible to achieve parallel input, output and internal computing because of the structure of the operation system.

The remainder of this section will concern itself with: (1) reduction of the number of passes being made over the data and (2) efficient utilization of program buffers so that input, output and CPU processing is overlapped as much as possible. We shall assume that runs have already been created from the input file using some internal sort scheme. Later, we investigate a method for obtaining runs that are on the average about two times as long as those obtainable by the methods discussed in Chapter 7.

8.2.1 k-way Merging

The 2-way merge algorithm of Section 7.5 is almost identical to the merge procedure just described (Figure 8.6). In general, if we started with m runs, then the merge tree corresponding to Figure 8.6 would have $\lceil \log_2 m \rceil + 1$ levels for a total of $\lceil \log_2 m \rceil$ passes over the data file. The number of passes over the data can be reduced by using a higher order merge, i.e., k-way merge for $k \geq 2$. In this case, we would simultaneously merge k runs together. Figure 8.8 illustrates a 4-way merge on 16 runs. The number of passes over the data is now 2, versus 4 passes in the case of a 2-way merge. In general, a k-way merge on m runs requires at most $\lceil \log_k m \rceil$ passes over the data (Figure 8.9). Thus, the input/output time may be reduced by using a higher order merge.

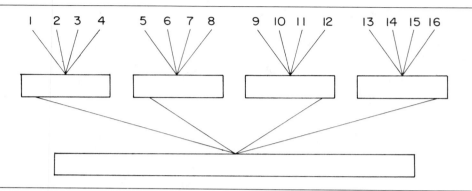

Figure 8.8 A 4-way merge on 16 runs

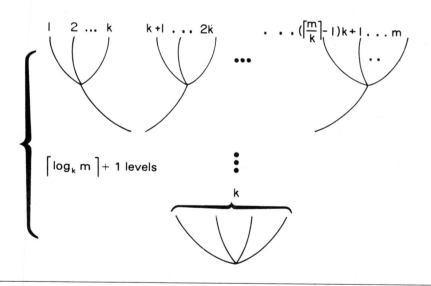

Figure 8.9 A k-way merge

The use of a higher order merge, however, has some other effects on the sort. To begin with, k-runs of size $S_1, S_2, S_3, \ldots, S_k$ can no longer be merged internally in $O(\Sigma_1^k S_i)$ time. In a k-merge, as in a 2-way merge, the next record to be output is the one with the smallest key. The smallest has now to be found from k possibilities and it could be the leading record in any of the k-runs. The most direct way to merge k-runs would be to make $k - 1$ comparisons to determine the next record to output. The computing time for this would be $O((k - 1) \Sigma_1^k S_i)$. Since $\log_k m$ passes are being made, the total number of key comparisons being made is $n(k - 1)\log_k m = n(k - 1)\log_2 m / \log_2 k$ where n is the number of records in the file. Hence, $(k - 1)/\log_2 k$ is the factor by which the number of key comparisons increases. As k increases, the reduction in input/output time will be overweighed by the resulting increase in CPU time needed to perform the k-way merge. For large k (say, $k \geq 6$) we can achieve a significant reduction in the number of comparisons needed to find the next smallest element by using a loser tree with k leaves (Chapter 5). In this case, the total time needed per level of the merge tree of Figure 8.9 is $O(n \log_2 k)$. Since the number of levels in this tree is $O(\log_k m)$, the asymptotic internal processing time becomes $O(n \log_2 k \log_k m) = O(n\log_2 m)$. The internal processing time is independent of k.

In going to a higher order merge, we save on the amount of input/output being carried out. There is no significant loss in internal processing speed. Even though the internal processing time is relatively insensitive to the order of the merge, the decrease in input/output time is not as much as indicated by the reduction to $\log_k m$ passes. This is so because the number of input buffers needed to carry out a k-way merge increases with k. Though $k + 1$ buffers are sufficient, we shall see in Section 8.2.2 that the use of $2k + 2$ buffers is more desirable. Since the internal memory available is fixed and independent of k, the buffer size must be reduced as k increases. This in turn implies a reduction in the block size on disk. With the reduced block size each pass over the data results in a greater number of blocks being written or read. This represents a potential increase in input/output time from the increased contribution of seek and latency times involved in reading a block of data. Hence, beyond a certain k value the input/output time would actually increase despite the decrease in the number of passes being made. The optimal value for k clearly depends on disk parameters and the amount of internal memory available for buffers (Exercise 1).

8.2.2 Buffer Handling for Parallel Operation

If k runs are being merged together by a k-way merge, then we clearly need at least k input buffers and one output buffer to carry out the merge. This, however, is not enough if input, output and internal merging are to be carried out in parallel. For instance, while the output buffer is being written out, internal merging has to be halted since there is no place to collect the merged records. This can be easily overcome through the use of two output buffers. While one is being written out, records are merged into the second. If buffer sizes are chosen correctly, then the time to output one buffer would be the same as the CPU time needed to fill the second buffer. With only k input buffers, internal merging will have to be held up whenever one of these input buffers becomes empty and another block from the corresponding run is being read in. This input delay can also be avoided if we have $2k$ input buffers. These $2k$ input buffers have to be cleverly used in order to avoid reaching a situation in which processing has to be held up because of lack of input records from any one run. Simply assigning two buffers per run does not solve the problem. To see this, consider the following example:

Example 8.1: Assume that a two way merge is being carried out using four input buffers, $in[i]$, $1 \le i \le 4$, and two output buffers, $ou[1]$ and $ou[2]$. Each buffer is capable of holding two records. The first few records of run 1 have key value 1, 3, 5, 7, 8, 9. The first few records of run 2 have key value 2, 4, 6, 15, 20, 25. Buffers $in[1]$ and $in[3]$ are assigned to run 1. The remaining two input buffers are assigned to run 2. We start the merging by reading in one buffer load from each of the two runs. At this time the buffers have the configuration of Figure 8.10(a). Now runs 1 and 2 are merged using records from $in[1]$ and $in[2]$. In parallel with this the next buffer load from run 1 is input. If we assume that buffer lengths have been chosen such that the times to input, output and generate an output buffer are all the same, then when $ou[1]$ is full we have the situation of Figure 8.10(b). Next, we simultaneously output $ou[1]$, input into $in[4]$ from run 2 and merge into $ou[2]$. When $ou[2]$ is full we are in the situation of Figure 8.10(c). Continuing in this way we reach the configuration of Figure 8.10(e). We now begin to output $ou[2]$, input from run 1 into $in[3]$ and merge into $ou[1]$. During the merge, all records from run 1 get exhausted before $ou[1]$ gets full. The generation of merged output must now be delayed until the inputting of another buffer load from run 1 is completed. □

Example 8.1 makes it clear that if $2k$ input buffers are to suffice then we cannot assign two buffers per run. Instead, the buffer must be floating in the sense that an individual buffer may be assigned to any run depending upon need. In the buffer assignment strategy we shall describe, for each run there will at any time be at least one input buffer containing records from that run. The remaining buffers will be filled on a priority basis; i.e., the run for which the k-way merging algorithm will run out of records first is the one from which the next buffer will be filled. One may easily predict which run's records will be exhausted first by simply comparing the keys of the last record read from each of the k runs. The smallest such key determines this run. We shall assume that in the case of equal keys, the merge process first merges the record from the run with least index. This means that if the key of the last record read from run i is equal to the key of the last record read from run j, and $i < j$, then the records read from i will be exhausted before those from j. So, it is possible that at any one time we might have more than two bufferloads from a given run and only one partially full buffer from another run. All bufferloads from the same run are queued together. Before formally presenting the algorithm for buffer utilization, we make the following assumptions about the parallel processing capabilities of the computer system available:

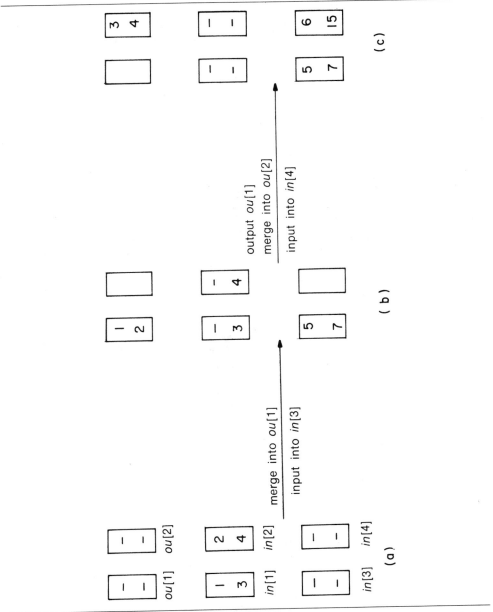

Figure 8.10 Example showing that two fixed buffers per run are not enough for continued parallel operation

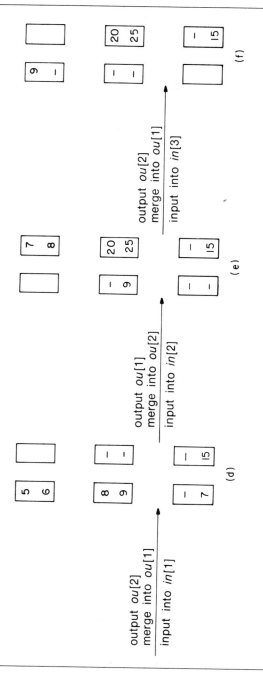

Figure 8.10 Example

(1)   We have two disk drives and the input/output channel is such that it is possible simultaneously to read from one disk and write onto the other.

(2)   While data transmission is taking place between an input/output device and a block of memory, the CPU cannot make references to that same block of memory. Thus, it is not possible to start filling the front of an output buffer while it is being written out. If this were possible, then by coordinating the transmission and merging rate only one output buffer would be needed. By the time the first record for the new output block was determined, the first record of the previous output block would have been written out.

(3)   To simplify the discussion we assume that input and output buffers are to be the same size.

Keeping these assumptions in mind, we first formally state the algorithm obtained using the strategy outlined earlier and then illustrate its working through an example. Our algorithm, Program 8.1, merges k-runs, $k \geq 2$, using a k-way merge. $2k$ input buffers and 2 output buffers are used. Each buffer is a contiguous block of memory. Input buffers are queued in k queues, one queue for each run. It is assumed that each input/output buffer is long enough to hold one block of records. Empty buffers are stacked with *av* pointing to the top buffer in this stack. The stack is a linked list. The following type definitions are made use of:

> **type** *buffer* = **array** [1..*maxbuffsize*] **of integer**;
> *InputBuffers* = **array** [1..*twok*] **of** *buffer*;
> *OutputBuffers* = **array** [0..1] **of** *buffer*;
> *FirstBuffers* = **array** [1..*k*] **of integer**;
> *EndBuffers* = **array** [1..*k*] **of integer**;
> *LinkFields* = **array** [1..*twok*] **of integer**;
> *LastValues* = **array** [1..*k*] **of integer**;

where k is a constant and *twok* = $2k$.

The algorithm also assumes that the end of each run has a sentinel record with a very large key, say *maxint*. It is assumed that all records other than the sentinel records have key value less than *maxint*. If block lengths, and hence buffer lengths, are chosen such that the time to merge one output buffer load equals the time to read a block, then almost all input, output, and computation will be carried out in parallel. It is also assumed that in the case of equal keys the k-way merge algorithm first outputs the record from the run with smallest index.

```
 1  procedure buffering;
 2  var
 3    in : InputBuffers;
 4    out : OutputBuffers;
 5    qfront : FirstBuffers;
 6    qend : EndBuffers;
 7    link : LinkFields;
 8    last : LastValues;
 9    i,j,ou,l,av : integer;
10    LastKeyMerged : integer;
11  begin{buffering}
12    for i := 1 to k do {input a block from each run}
13    begin {input first block of run i into in [i ]}
14      ReadBuff(i,i); {arguments are buffer and run number}
15      {ReadBuff is a procedure that inputs the next block of records}
16    end;
17    while input not complete do
18    begin {wait}
19    end;
20    for i := 1 to k do {initialize queues and free buffers}
21    begin
22      qfront[i ] := i ; qend [i ] := i ;
23      last [i ] := LastKey (in [i ]);
24      {LastKey is a function that returns the last key in a buffer}
25      link [k + i ] := k + i + 1; {stack free buffer}
26    end;
27    link [twok ] := 0; av := k + 1; ou := 0;
28    {first queue exhausted is the one whose last key is smallest}
29    j := findmin(last, 1,k );
30    {findmin is a function that finds j such that last [j ]=minimum (last [i ]),
       1 ≤ i ≤k}
31    l := av ; av := link [av]; {get next free buffer}
32    if last [j ] < > maxint then
33      {begin to read next block for run j into buffer in [l ]}
34      ReadBuff(l,j );
35    repeat
36    {kWayMerge merges records from the k buffers front[i ] into output
37    buffer ou until it is full.  If an input buffer becomes empty before
38    ou is filled, the next buffer in the queue for this run is used and
39    the empty buffer is stacked}
40      kWayMerge;
41      while input/output not complete do
42      begin {wait loop}
```

```
43      end;
44      if last [ j ] <> maxint then begin
45              link [end [ j ]] := l ; end [ j ] := l; last [ j ] := LastKey (in [ l ]);
46                                          {queue next block}
47              j := findmin(last, 1,k );
48              l := av ; av := link [av ]; {get next free buffer}
49          end;
50      LastKeyMerged := LastKey (out [ou ]);
51      if last [ j ] < > maxint then
52      begin
53          {begin to write out [ou ] and read next block of run j into in [ l ]}
54          WriteBuff(ou );
55          {WriteBuff is a procedure that outputs a block of records}
56          ReadBuff(l, j );
57      end
58      else
59      {begin to write out [ou ]}
60      WriteBuff(ou );
61      ou := 1 − ou;
62      until LastKeyMerged = maxint;
63      while outputincomplete do
64      begin {wait loop}
65      end;
66  end; {of buffering}
```

Program 8.1 Buffering

We make the following observations concerning procedure *buffering*:

(1) For large k, determination of the queue that will exhaust first can be made in $\log_2 k$ comparisons by setting up a selection tree for *last* [i], $1 \le i \le k$, rather than making $k - 1$ comparisons each time a buffer load is to be read in. The change in computing time will not be significant, since this queue selection represents only a very small fraction of the total time taken by the algorithm.

(2) For large k, the algorithm *kWayMerge* uses a tree of losers as discussed in Section 5.13

(3) All input/output except for the initial k blocks that are read and the last block output is done concurrently with computing. Since after k runs have been merged we would probably begin to merge another set of k runs, the input for the next set can commence during the final merge stages of the present set of runs. That is, when *last* [j] = **maxint** we begin reading one by one the first blocks from each of the next set of k runs to be merged. In this case, over the entire sorting of a file, the only time that is not overlapped with the internal merging time is the time for the

first *k* blocks of input and that for the last block of output.

(4)   The algorithm assumes that all blocks are of the same length. This may require inserting a few dummy records into the last block of each run following the sentinel record with key **maxint**.

Example 8.2: To illustrate the working of the above algorithm, let us trace through it while it performs a three-way merge on the three runs of Figure 8.11. Each run consists of four blocks of two records each; the last key in the fourth block of each of these three runs is **maxint** (shown as $+\infty$). We have six input buffers *in* [*i*], $1 \le i \le 6$, and two output buffers *out* [0] and *out* [1]. Figure 8.12 shows the status of the input buffer queues, the run from which the next block is being read and the output buffer being output at the beginning of each iteration of the **repeat-until** of the buffering algorithm.

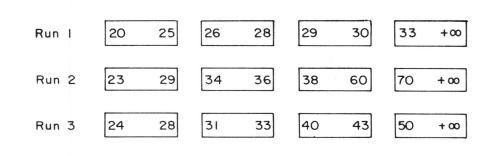

Figure 8.11 Three runs

From line 5 it is evident that during the *k*-way merge the test for "output buffer full?" should be carried out before the test "input buffer empty?", as the next input buffer for that run may not have been read in yet, and so there would be no next buffer in that queue. In lines 3 and 4 all 6 input buffers are in use and the stack of free buffers is empty. □

We end our discussion of buffer handling by proving that the algorithm *buffering* works. This is stated formally in Theorem 8.1.

Theorem 8.1: The following is true for algorithm *buffering*:

(1)   There is always a buffer available in which to begin reading the next block; and

(2)   during the *k*-way merge the next block in the queue has been read in by the time it is needed.

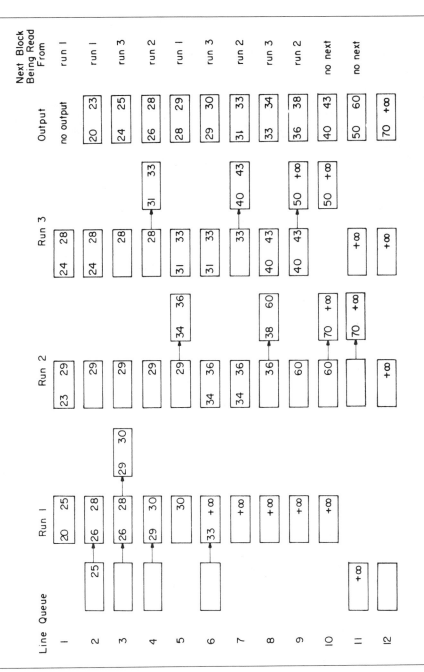

Figure 8.12 Buffering example

Proof: (1) Each time we get to line 48 of the algorithm there are at most $k+1$ buffer loads in memory, one of these being in an output buffer. For each queue there can be at most one buffer that is partially full. If no buffer is available for the next read, then the remaining k buffers must be full. This means that all the k partially full buffers are empty (as otherwise there will be more than $k+1$ buffer loads in memory). From the way the merge is set up, only one buffer can be both unavailable and empty. This may happen only if the output buffer gets full exactly when one input buffer becomes empty. But $k > 1$ contradicts this. So, there is always at least one buffer available when line 48 is being executed.

(2) Assume this is false. Let run R_i be the one whose queue becomes empty during *kWayMerge*. We may assume that the last key merged was not the sentinel key **maxint**, since otherwise *kWayMerge* would terminate the search rather then get another buffer for R_i. This means that there are more blocks of records for run R_i on the input file and *last* $[i] \neq$ **maxint**. Consequently, up to this time whenever a block was output another was simultaneously read in (see lines 54 and 56). Input/output therefore proceeded at the same rate and the number of available blocks of data is always k. An additional block is being read in, but it does not get queued until line 45. Since the queue for R_i has become empty first, the selection rule for the next run to read from ensures that there is at most one block of records for each of the remaining $k-1$ runs. Furthermore, the output buffer cannot be full at this time as this condition is tested for before the input buffer empty condition. Thus there are fewer than k blocks of data in memory. This contradicts our earlier assertion that there must be exactly k such blocks of data. $\square$

8.2.3 Run Generation

Using conventional internal sorting methods such as those of Chapter 7, it is possible to generate runs that are only as large as the number of records that can be held in internal memory at one time. Using a tree of losers, it is possible to do better than this. In fact, the algorithm we shall present will on the average generate runs that are twice as long as obtainable by conventional methods. This algorithm was devised by Walters, Painter, and Zalk. In addition to being capable of generating longer runs, this algorithm will allow for parallel input, output and internal processing. For almost all the internal sort methods discussed in Chapter 7, this parallelism is not possible. Heap sort is an exception to this. In describing the run generation algorithm, we shall not dwell too much upon the input/output buffering needed. It will be assumed that input/output buffers have been appropriately set up for maximum overlapping of input, output and internal processing. Wherever in the run generation algorithm there is an input/output instruction, it will be assumed that the operation takes place through the input/output buffers. We shall assume that there is enough space to construct a tree of losers for k records, $r[i]$, $0 \leq i < k$. This will require a loser tree with k nodes numbered 0 to $k - 1$. Each node, i, in this tree will have one field $l[i]$. $l[i]$, $1 \leq i < k$ represents the loser of the tournament played at node i. Node 0 represents the overall winner of the tournament. This node will not be explicitly present in the algorithm. Each of the k record positions $r[i]$ has a run number field $rn[i]$, $0 \le i < k$, associated with it. This field will enable us to determine whether or not $r[i]$ can be output as part of the run currently being generated. Whenever the tournament winner is output, a new record (if there is one) is input and the tournament replayed as discussed in Section 5.13. Algorithm *runs* is simply an implementation of the loser tree strategy discussed earlier. The variables used in this algorithm have the following significance:

$$r[i], 0 \le i < k \quad \text{...} \quad \text{the } k \text{ records in the tournament tree}$$
$$key[i], 0 \le i < k \quad \text{...} \quad \text{key value of record } r[i]$$
$$l[i], 0 \le i < k \quad \text{...} \quad \text{loser of the tournament played at node } i$$
$$rn[i], 0 \le i < k \quad \text{...} \quad \text{the run number to which } r[i] \text{ belongs}$$
$$rc \quad \text{...} \quad \text{run number of current run}$$
$$q \quad \text{...} \quad \text{overall tournament winner}$$
$$rq \quad \text{...} \quad \text{run number for } r[q]$$
$$rmax \quad \text{...} \quad \text{number of runs that will be generated}$$
$$LastKey \quad \text{...} \quad \text{key value of last record output}$$

The loop of lines 14-59 repeatedly plays the tournament outputting records. The only interesting thing about this algorithm is the way in which the tree of losers is initialized. This is done in lines 9-12 by setting up a fictitious run numbered 0. Thus, we have $rn[i] = 0$ for each of the k records $r[i]$. Since all but one of the records must be a loser exactly once, the initialization of $l[i] := i$ sets up a loser tree with $r[0]$ the winner. With this initialization the loop of lines 14-59 correctly sets up the loser tree for run 1. The test of line 26 suppresses the output of these k fictitious records making up run 0. The variable *LastKey* is made use of in line 39 to determine whether or not the new record input, $r[q]$, can be output as part of the current run. If $key(q) < LastKey$ then $r[q]$ cannot be output as part of the current run rc as a record with larger key value has already been output in this run. When the tree is being readjusted (lines 49-58), a record with lower run number wins over one with a higher run number. When run numbers are equal, the record with lower key value wins. This ensures that records come out of the tree in nondecreasing order of their run numbers. Within the same run, records come out of the tree in nondecreasing order of their key values. *rmax* is used to terminate the algorithm. In line 34, when we run out of input, a record with run number $rmax + 1$ is introduced. When this record is ready for output, the algorithm terminates from line 22. One may readily verify that when the input file is already sorted, only one run is generated. On the average, the run size is almost $2k$. The time required to generate all the runs for an n run file is $O(n \log k)$, as it takes $O(\log k)$ time to adjust the loser tree each time a record is output. The algorithm may be speeded slightly by explicitly initializing the loser tree using the first k records of the input file rather than k fictitious records as in lines 9-12. In this case, the conditional of line 26 may be removed as there will no longer be a need to suppress output of certain records. Program 8.2 implements this algorithm in Pascal. It is assumed that the data type *TreeRecord* is defined as:

```
                    type TreeRecord = record
                                          key : integer
                                          {other fields declared here}
                                      end;
```

```
 1 procedure runs;
 2 {generate runs using a tree of losers}
 3 label 99;
 4 var
 5     r : array[0..k] of TreeRecord ;
 6     key,l,rn : array [0..k] of integer;
 7     rc,q,rq,rmax,LastKey,temp,i,t : integer;
 8 begin {runs}
 9    for i := 1 to k - 1 do {set up fictitious run 0 to initialize tree}
10    begin
11        rn [i ] := 0; l [i ] := i ; key [i ] := 0;
12    end;
13    q := 0; rq := 0; rc := 0; rmax := 0; rn [0] := 0; LastKey := maxint;
14    while true do {output runs}
15    begin
16    if rq < > rc then {end of run}
17    begin
18     if rc < > 0 then
19     begin
20     output end of run marker
21     end;
22     if rq > rmax then goto 99
23                  else rc := rq ;
24    end;
25    {output record r [q ] if no fictitious}
26    if rq < > 0 then
27    begin
28     writerecord (r [q ]);
29     LastKey := key [q ];
30    end;
31    {input new record into tree}
32    if no more input then
33    begin
34        rq := rmax + 1; rn [q ] := rq ;
35    end
36    else
37    begin
38     ReadRecord (r [q ]);
```

```
39    if key [q ] < LastKey then
40    begin {new record belongs to next run}
41      rq := rq + 1;
42      rn [q ] := rq;
43      rmax := rq;
44    end
45      else
46        rn [q ] := rc ;
47      end;
48    {adjust losers}
49    t := (k + q) div 2; {t is parent of q}
50    while t < > 0 do
51    begin
52      if (rn [l [t ]] < rq) or ((rn [l [t ]] = rq) and (key [l [t ]] < key [q ])) then
53      begin
54        temp := q ; q := l [t ]; l [t ] := temp ;
55        rq := rn [q ];            {t is the winner}
56      end;
57      t := t div 2; {move up tree}
58    end;
59    end;
60 99: end; {of runs}
```

Program 8.2 Run generation using a loser tree

8.3 SORTING WITH TAPES

Sorting on tapes is carried out using the same basic steps as sorting on disks. Sections of the input file are internally sorted into runs which are written out onto tape. These runs are repeatedly merged together until there is only one run. The difference between disk and tape sorting lies essentially in the manner in which runs are maintained on the external storage media. In the case of disks, the seek and latency times are relatively insensitive to the specific location on the disk of the next block to be read with respect to the current position of the read/write heads. (The maximum seek and latency times were about 1/10 sec and 1/40 sec respectively.) This is not true for tapes. Tapes are sequential access. If the read/write head is currently positioned at the front of the tape and the next block to be read is near the end of the tape (say ~ 2400 feet away), then the seek time, i.e., the time to advance the correct block to the read/write head, is almost 3 min 2 sec (assuming a tape speed of 150 in/sec). This very high maximum seek time for tapes makes it essential that blocks on tape be arranged in such an order that they will be read in sequentially during the k-way merge of runs. Hence, while in the previous section we did not concern ourselves with the relative position of the blocks on disk, in this section, the distribution of blocks and runs will be our primary concern. We shall study two distribution schemes. Before doing this, let us look at an example to see the different factors involved in a tape sort.

Example 8.3: A file containing 4500 records, $R_1, \ldots, R_{4500}$, is to be sorted using a computer with an internal memory large enough to hold only 800 records. The available external storage consists of four tapes, $T1$, $T2$, $T3$, and $T4$. Each block on the input tape contains 250 records. The input tape is not to be destroyed during the sort. Initially, this tape is on one of the four available tape drives and so has to be dismounted and replaced by a work tape after all input records have been read. Let us look at the various steps involved in sorting this file. In order to simplify the discussion, we shall assume that the initial run generation is carried out using a conventional internal sort such as quicksort. In this case, three blocks of input can be read in at a time, sorted and output as a run. We shall also assume that no parallelism in input, output and CPU processing is possible. In this case we shall use only one output buffer and two input buffers. This requires only 750 record spaces. The computing time analysis of Figure 8.13 assumes that no operations are carried out in parallel. The analysis could be carried out further as in the case of disks to show the dependence of the sort time on the number of passes made over the data.

8.3.1 Balanced Merge Sorts

Example 8.3 performed a 2-way merge of the runs. As in the case of disk sorting, the computing time here too depends essentially on the number of passes being made over the data. Use of a higher order merge results in a decrease in the number of passes being made without significantly changing the internal merge time. Hence, we would like to use as high an order merge as possible. In the case of disks the order of merge was limited essentially by the amount of internal memory available for use as input/output buffers. A k-way merge required the use of $2k + 2$ buffers. While this is still true of tapes, another probably more severe restriction on the merge order k is the number of tapes available. In order to avoid excessive tape seek times, it is necessary that runs being merged together be on different tapes. Thus, a k-way tape merge requires at least k tapes for use as input tapes during the merge.

In addition, another tape is needed for the output generated during this merge. Hence, at least $k+1$ tapes must be available for a k-way tape merge (recall that in the case of a disk, one disk was enough for a k-way merge though two were needed to overlap input and output). Using $k+1$ tapes to perform a k-way merge requires an additional pass over the output tape to redistribute the runs onto k tapes for the next level of merges (see the merge tree of Figure 8.9). This redistribution pass can be avoided through the use of $2k$ tapes. During the k-way merge, k of these tapes are used as input tapes and the remaining k as output tapes. At the next merge level, the role in input-output tapes is interchanged as in Example 8.3, where in step 4, $T1$ and $T2$ are used as input tapes and

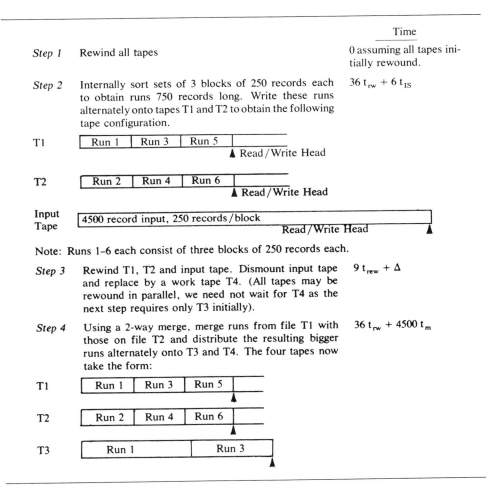

	Time

Step 1 Rewind all tapes — 0 assuming all tapes initially rewound.

Step 2 Internally sort sets of 3 blocks of 250 records each to obtain runs 750 records long. Write these runs alternately onto tapes T1 and T2 to obtain the following tape configuration. — $36\,t_{rw} + 6\,t_{IS}$

T1 — | Run 1 | Run 3 | Run 5 | — ▲ Read/Write Head

T2 — | Run 2 | Run 4 | Run 6 | — ▲ Read/Write Head

Input Tape — | 4500 record input, 250 records/block | — Read/Write Head ▲

Note: Runs 1–6 each consist of three blocks of 250 records each.

Step 3 Rewind T1, T2 and input tape. Dismount input tape and replace by a work tape T4. (All tapes may be rewound in parallel, we need not wait for T4 as the next step requires only T3 initially). — $9\,t_{rew} + \Delta$

Step 4 Using a 2-way merge, merge runs from file T1 with those on file T2 and distribute the resulting bigger runs alternately onto T3 and T4. The four tapes now take the form: — $36\,t_{rw} + 4500\,t_m$

T1 — | Run 1 | Run 3 | Run 5 | — ▲

T2 — | Run 2 | Run 4 | Run 6 | — ▲

T3 — | Run 1 | Run 3 | — ▲

Figure 8.13 Computing times for tape sort

$T3$ and $T4$ as output tapes while in step 6, $T3$ and $T4$ are the input tapes and $T1$ and $T2$ the output tapes (though there is no output for $T2$). These two approaches to a k-way merge are now examined. Algorithms $m1$ (Program 8.3) and $m2$ (Program 8.4) perform a k-way merge with the $k + 1$ tapes strategy while algorithm $m3$ performs a k-way merge using the $2k$ tapes strategy.

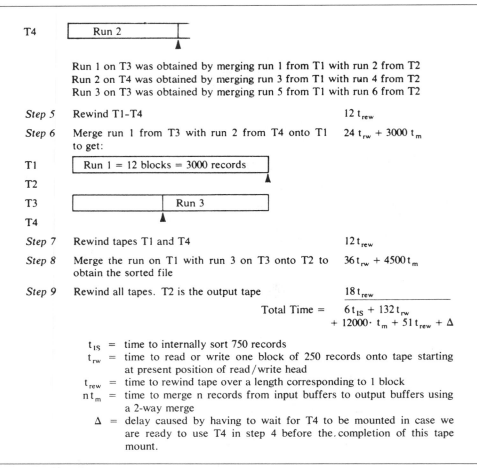

Step 5   Rewind T1-T4 $12\,t_{rew}$

Figure 8.13 Computing times for tape sort

Analysis of Algorithm $m1$

     To simplify the analysis we assume that the number of runs generated, m, is a power of k. Line 6 involves one pass over the entire file. One pass includes both reading and writing. In lines 11-19 the number of passes is $log_k m$ merge passes and $log_k m - 1$ redistribution passes. So, the total number of passes being made over the file is $2log_k m$. If the time to rewind the entire input take is t_{rew}, then the non-overlapping rewind time is roughly $2log_k m t_{rew}$.

     A somewhat more clever way to tackle the problem is to rotate the output tape, i.e., tapes are used as output tapes in the cyclic order, $k + 1, 1, 2, \ldots, k$. When this is done, the redistribution from the output tape makes less than a full pass over the file. Algorithm $m2$ formally describes the process. For simplicity the analysis of $m2$ assumes

```
 1  procedure m1;
 2  {sort a file of records from a given input tape using a k-way merge
 3  given tapes t₁, ..., t_{k+1} are available for the sort.}
 4  label 99;
 5  begin
 6     Create runs from the input tape distributing them evenly over
 7     tapes t₁, ..., t_k;
 8     Rewind t₁, ..., t_k and also the input tape;
 9     if there is only 1 run then goto 99; {the sorted file is on t₁}
10     replace input tape by t_{k+1};
11     while true do
12     {repeatedly merge onto t_{k+1} and redistribute back onto t₁, ..., t_k}
13     begin
14        merge runs from t₁, ..., t_k onto t_{k+1};
15        rewind t₁, ..., t_{k+1};
16        if number of runs on t_{k+1} = 1 then goto 99; {output on t_{k+1}}
17        evenly distribute from t_{k+1} onto t₁, ..., t_k;
18        rewind t₁, ..,t_{k+1};
19     end;
20  99: end; {of m1}
```

Program 8.3 $m1$

that m is a power of k. Program 8.4 is a pseudo-Pascal version of $m2$.

Analysis of Algorithm $m2$

The only difference between algorithms $m2$ and $m1$ is the redistributing time. Once again the redistributing is done $\log_k m - 1$ times. m is the number of runs generated in line 7. But now each redistributing pass reads and writes only $(k-1)/k$ of the file. Hence, the effective number of passes made over the data is $(2 - 1/k)\log_k m + 1/k$. For two-way merging on three tapes this means that algorithm $m2$ will make $3/2\log_k m + 1/2$ passes while $m1$ will make $2\log_k m$. If t_{rew} is the rewind time, then the non-overlappable rewind time for $m2$ is at most $(1 + 1/k)(\log_k m)t_{rew} + (1 - 1/k)t_{rew}$ as line 20 rewinds only $1/k$ of the file. Instead of distributing runs as in line 18 we could write the first m/k runs onto one tape, begin rewind, write the next m/k runs onto the second tape, begin rewind, etc. In this case, we can begin filling input buffers for the next merge level (line 15) while some of the tapes are still rewinding. This is so because the first few tapes written on would have completed rewinding before the distribution phase is complete (for $k > 2$).

```
 1  procedure m2;
 2  {Sort a file or records from a given input tape using a k-way merge
 3    given tapes t₁, ..., t_{k+1} are available for the sort.
 4    Same type definitions as m1}
 5  label 99;
 6  begin
 7    Create runs from the input file distributing them evenly over
 8    tapes t₁, ..., t_k;
 9    Rewind t₁, ..., t_k and also the input tape;
10    if there is only 1 run then goto 99; {sorted file on t₁}
11    replace input tape by t_{k+1};
12    i := k + 1; {i is index of output tape}
13    while true do
14    begin
15      merge runs from the k tapes t_j, 1<=j<=k + 1 and j < > i onto t_i;
16      rewind t₁, ..., t_{k+1};
17      if number of runs on t_i = 1 then goto 99; {output on t_i}
18      evenly distribute (k - 1)/k of the runs on t_i onto tape t_j,
19      1<=j<=k + 1 and j < >i and j < >i mod (k +1)+1;
20      rewind tapes t_j, 1 <= j <= k + 1 and j < > i;
21      i := i mod (k + 1) + 1;
22    end;
23    99: end; {of m2}
```

Program 8.4 $m2$

In case a k-way merge is made using $2k$ tapes, no redistribution is needed and so the number of passes being made over the file is only $\log_{km+1}$. This means that if we have $2k + 1$ tapes available, then a $2k$-way merge will make $(2 - 1/(2k))\log_{2km} + 1/(2k)$ passes while a k-way merge utilizing only $2k$ tapes will make $\log_k m + 1$ passes. Table 8.1 compares the number of passes being made in the two methods for some values of k. As is evident from the table, for $k > 2$ a k-way merge using only $2k$ tapes is better than a $2k$-way merge using $2k + 1$ tapes.

Algorithm $m3$ (Program 8.5) performs a k-way merge sort using $2k$ tapes.

Analysis of $m3$

To simplify the analysis assume that m is a power of k. In addition to the initial run creation pass, the algorithm makes $\log_k m$ merge passes. Let t_{rew} be the time to rewind the entire input file. The time for line 7 is t_{rew} and if m is a power of k then the rewind of line 15 takes t_{rew}/k for each but the last iteration of the **while** loop. The last rewind takes time t_{rew}. The total rewind is therefore bounded by $(2 + (\log_k m - 1)/k) t_{rew}$. Some of this may be overlapped using the strategy described in the analysis of algorithm

k	$2k$-way	k-way
1	$3/2\log_2 m + 1/2$	-
2	$7/8\log_2 m + 1/4$	$\log_2 m + 1$
3	$1.124\log_3 m + 1/6$	$\log_3 m + 1$
4	$1.25\log_4 m + 1/8$	$\log_4 m + 1$

Table 8.1 Number of passes using a $2k$-way merge versus a k-way merge on $2k + 1$ tapes

```
 1  procedure m3;
 2  {Sort a file of records from a given input tape using a k-way merge
 3    on 2k tapes t₁, ..., t₂ₖ}
 4  begin
 5    Create runs from the input file distributing them evenly
 6      over tapes t₁, ..., tₖ;
 7    rewind t₁, ..., tₖ; rewind the input tape;
 8    replace the input tape by tape t₂ₖ;
 9    i := 0;
10    while total number of runs on tᵢₖ₊₁, ..., tᵢₖ₊ₖ > 1 do
11      begin
12        j := 1 − i;
13        perform a k-way merge from tᵢₖ₊₁, ..., tᵢₖ₊ₖ evenly
14          distributing output runs onto tⱼₖ₊₁, ..., tⱼₖ₊ₖ;
15        rewind t₁, ..., t₂ₖ;
16        i := j; {switch input and output tapes}
17      end;
18    {sorted file is on tᵢₖ₊₁}
19  end; {of m3}
```

Program 8.5 $m3$

$m2$ (Exercise 4).

One should note that $m1$, $m2$, and $m3$ use the buffering algorithm of Section 8.2.2 during the k-way merge. This merge itself, for large k, would be carried out using a selection tree as discussed earlier. In both cases the proper choice of buffer lengths and the merge order (restricted by the the number of tape drives available) would result in an almost complete overlap of internal processing time with input/output time. At the end of each level of merge, processing will have to wait until the tapes rewind. Once again, this wait can be minimized if the run distribution strategy of Exercise 4 is used.

8.3.2 Polyphase Merge

Balanced k-way merging is characterized by a balanced or even distribution of the runs to be merged onto k input tapes. One consequence of this is that $2k$ tapes are needed to avoid wasteful passes over the data during which runs are just redistributed onto tapes in preparation for the next merge pass. It is possible to avoid altogether these wasteful redistribution passes when using fewer than $2k$ tape and a k-way merge, by distributing the "right number" of runs onto different tapes. We shall see one way to do this for a k-way merge utilizing $k + 1$ tapes. To begin, let us see how $m = 21$ runs may be merged using a 2-way merge with three tapes $T1$, $T2$, and $T3$. Lengths of runs obtained during the merge will be represented in terms of the length of initial runs created by the internal sort. Thus, the internal sort creates 21 runs of length 1 (the length of initial runs is the unit of measure). The runs on a tape will be denoted by s^n, where s is the run size and n, the number of runs of this size. If there are six runs of length 2 on a tape, we shall denote this by 2^6. The sort is carried out in several phases. In the first phase, the input file is sorted to obtain 21 runs. Thirteen of these are written onto $T1$ and eight onto $T2$. In phase 2, 8 runs from $T2$ are merged with 8 runs from $T1$ to get 8 runs of size 2 onto $T3$. In the next phase, the 5 runs of length 1 from $T1$ are merged with 5 runs of length 2 from $T3$ to obtain 5 runs of length 3 on $T2$. Figure 8.14 shows the seven phases involved in the sort.

phase	$T1$	$T2$	$T3$	fraction of total records read	
1	1^{13}	1^8	-	1	initial distribution
2	1^5	-	2^8	16/21	merge to $T3$
3	-	3^5	2^3	15/21	merge to $T2$
4	5^3	3^2	-	15/21	merge to $T1$
5	5^1	-	8^2	16/21	merge to $T3$
6	-	13^1	8^1	13/21	merge to $T2$
7	21^1	-	-	1	merge to $T1$

Figure 8.14 Polyphase merge on three tapes

Counting the number of passes made during each phase we get $1 + 16/21 + 15/21 + 15/21 + 16/21 + 13/21 + 1 = 5\text{-}4/7$ as a total number of passes needed to merge 21 runs. If algorithm $m2$ of Section 8.3.1 had been used with $k = 2$, then $3/2\lceil \log_2 21\rceil + 1/2 = 8$

passes would have been made. Algorithm $m3$ using 4 tapes would have made $\lceil \log_2 21 \rceil = 5$ passes. What makes this process work? Examination of Figure 8.14 shows that the trick is to distribute the runs initially in such a way that in all phases but the last only one tape becomes empty. In this case we can proceed to the next phase without redistribution of runs as we have two non-empty input tapes and one empty tape for output. To determine what the correct initial distribution is we work backwards from the last phase. Assume there are n phases. Then in phase n we wish to have exactly one run on $T1$ and no runs on $T2$ and $T3$. Hence, the sort will be complete at phase n. In order to achieve this, this run must be obtained by merging a run from $T2$ with a run from $T3$, and these must be the only runs on $T2$ and $T3$. Thus, in phase $n - 1$ we should have one run on each of $T2$ and $T3$. The run on $T2$ is obtained by merging a run from $T1$ with one from $T3$. Hence, in phase $n - 2$ we should have one run on $T1$ and two on $T3$.

Table 8.2 shows the distribution of runs needed in each phase so that merging can be carried out without any redistribution passes. Thus, if we have 987 runs, then a distribtuion of 377 runs onto $T1$ and 510 onto $T3$ at phase 1 would result in a 15 phase merge. At the end of the fifteenth phase the sorted file would be on $T1$. No redistribution passes would have been made. The number of runs needed for an n phase merge is readily seen to be $F_n + F_{n-1}$ where F_i is the i'th Fibonacci number (recall that $F_7 = 13$ and $F_6 = 8$ and that $F_{15} = 610$ and $F_{14} = 377$). For this reason this method of distributing runs is also known as Fibonacci merge. It can be shown that for three tapes this distribution of runs and resultant merge pattern requires only $1.04 \log_2 m + 0.99$ passes over the data. This compares very favorably with the $\log_2 m$ passes needed by algorithm $m3$ on four tapes using a balanced 2-way merge. The method can clearly be generalized to k-way merging on $k + 1$ tapes using generalized Fibonacci numbers. Table 8.3 gives the run distribution for 3-way merging on four tapes. In this case, it can be shown that the number of passes over the data is about $0.703\log_2 m + 0.96$.

Example 8.4: The intial internal sort of a file of records creates 57 runs. 4 tapes are availabe to carry out the merging of these runs. Figure 8.15 shows the status of the tapes using 3-way polyphase merge. The total number of passes over the data is $1+39/57+35/57+36/57+34/57+31/57+1 = 5\text{-}4/57$ compared to $\lceil \log_2 57 \rceil = 6$ passes for 2-way balanced merging on four tapes. $\square$

Remarks on Polyphase Merging

Our discussion of polyphase merging has ignored altogether the rewind time involved. Before one can begin the merge for the next phase it is necessary to rewind the output tape. During this rewind the computer is essentially idle. It is possible to modify the polyphase merge scheme discussed here so that essentially all rewind time is overlapped with internal processing and read/write on other tapes. This modification requires at least five tapes and can be found in Knuth, Vol. 3. Further, polyphase merging requires that the initial number of runs be a perfect Fibonacci number (or generalized Fibonacci number). In case this is not so, one can substitute dummy runs to obtain the required number of runs.

Phase	T1	T2	T3
n	1	0	0
$n-1$	0	1	1
$n-2$	1	0	2
$n-3$	3	2	0
$n-4$	0	5	3
$n-5$	5	0	8
$n-6$	13	8	0
$n-7$	0	21	13
$n-8$	21	0	34
$n-9$	55	34	0
$n-10$	0	89	55
$n-11$	89	0	144
$n-12$	233	144	0
$n-13$	0	377	233
$n-14$	377	0	610

Table 8.2 Run distribution for 3-tape polyphase merge

Several other ingenious merge schemes have been devised for tape sorts. Knuth, Vol. 3, contains an exhaustive study of these schemes.

8.3.3 Sorting with Fewer Than Three Tapes

Both the balanced merge scheme of Section 8.3.1 and the polyphase scheme of Section 8.3.2 required at least three tapes to carry out the sort. These methods are readily seen to require only $O(n\log n)$ time where n is the number of records. We state without proof the following results for sorting on one and two tapes.

Theorem 8.2: Any one tape algorithm that sorts n records must take time $\geq O(n^2)$. $\square$

Theorem 8.3: n records can be sorted on two tapes in $O(n\log n)$ time if it is possible to perform an inplace rewrite of a record without destroying adjacent records; i.e., if record R_2 in the sequence $R_1R_2R_3$ can be rewritten by an equal size record R'_2 to obtain $R_1R'_2R_3$. $\square$

Phase	T1	T2	T3	T4
n	1	0	0	0
$n-1$	0	1	1	1
$n-2$	1	0	2	2
$n-3$	3	2	0	4
$n-4$	7	6	4	0
$n-5$	0	13	11	7
$n-6$	13	0	24	20
$n-7$	37	24	0	44
$n-8$	81	68	44	0
$n-9$	0	149	125	81
$n-10$	149	0	274	230
$n-11$	423	274	0	504
$n-12$	927	778	504	0
$n-13$	0	1705	1431	927
$n-14$	1705	0	3136	2632

Table 8.3 Polyphase merge pattern for 3-way four tape merging

phase	$T1$	$T2$	$T3$	$T4$	fraction of total records read	
1	1^{13}	-	1^{24}	1^{20}	1	initial distribution
2	-	3^{13}	1^{11}	1^{7}	39/57	merge to $T2$
3	5^{7}	3^{6}	1^{4}	-	35/57	merge to $T1$
4	5^{3}	3^{2}	-	9^{4}	36/57	merge to $T4$
5	5^{1}	-	17^{2}	9^{2}	34/57	merge to $T3$
6	-	31^{1}	17^{1}	9^{1}	31/57	merge to $T2$
7	57^{1}	-	-	-	1	merge to $T1$

Figure 8.15 Four tape polyphase merge

8.4 REFERENCES AND SELECTED READINGS

The text by D. Knuth, cited in Chapter 7, contains a wealth of information on external sorting. The algorithm for Theorem 8.3 may be found in: ''A linear time two tape merge,'' by R. Floyd and A. Smith, *Information Processing Letters*, vol. 2, no. 5, December 1973, pp. 123-125.

8.5 EXERCISES

1. (a) n records are to be sorted on a computer with a memory capacity of S records ($S \ll n$). Assume that the entire S record capacity may be used for input/output buffers. The input is on disk and consists of m runs. Assume that each time a disk access in made the seek time is t_s and the latency time is t_l. The transmission time is t_t per record transmitted. What is the total input time for phase II of external sorting if a k-way merge is used with internal memory partitioned into I/O buffers so as to permit overlap of input, output and CPU processing as in algorithm *buffering*?

    (b) Let the CPU time needed to merge all the runs together be t_{CPU} (we may assume it is independent of k and hence constant). Let $t_s = 80$ ms, $t_l = 20ms$, $n = 200,000$, $m = 64$, $t_t = 10^{-3}$ sec/record, $S = 2000$. Obtain a rough plot of the total input time, t_{input}, versus k. Will there always be a value of k for which $t_{CPU} \approx t_{input}$?

2. (a) Modify algorithm $m3$ using the run distribution strategy described in the analysis of algorithm $m2$.

    (b) Let t_{rw} be the time to read/write a block and t_{rew} the time to rewind over one block length. If the initial run creation pass generates m runs for m a power of k, what is the time for a k-way merge using your algorithm? Compare this with the corresponding time for algorithm $m2$.

3. Obtain a table corresponding to Table 8.3 for the case of a 5-way polyphase merge on six tapes. Use this to obtain the correct initial distribution for 497 runs so that the sorted file will be on $T1$. How many passes are made over the data in achieving the sort? How many passes would have been made by a 5-way balanced merge sort on six tapes (algorithm $m2$)? How many passes would have been made by a 3-way balanced merge sort on six tapes (algorithm $m3$)?

4. In this exercise we shall investigate another run distribution strategy for sorting on tapes. Let us look at a 3-way merge on four tapes of 157 runs. These runs are initially distributed according to: 70 runs on $T1$, 56 on $T2$ and 31 on $T3$. The merging takes place according to Figure 8.16. That is, each phase consists of a 3-way merge followed by a 2-way merge and in each phase almost all the initial runs are processed.

Line	Phase	T1	T2	T3	T4	
1	1	1^{70}	1^{56}	1^{31}	—	initial distribution
2	2	1^{39}	1^{25}	—	3^{31}	merge on to T4
3	2	1^{14}	—	2^{25}	3^{31}	merge T1, T2 to T3
4	3	—	6^{14}	2^{11}	3^{17}	merge T1, T3, T4 to T2
5		5^{11}	6^{14}	—	3^{6}	merge T3, T4 to T1
6		5^{5}	6^{8}	14^{6}	—	merge T1, T2, T4 to T3
7	4	—	6^{3}	14^{6}	11^{5}	merge T1, T2 to T4
8	5	31^{3}	—	14^{3}	11^{2}	merge T2, T3, T4 to T1
9		31^{3}	25^{2}	14^{1}	—	merge T3, T4 to T2
10		31^{2}	25^{1}	—	70^{1}	merge T1, T2, T3 to T4
11	6	31^{1}	—	56^{1}	70^{1}	merge T1, T2 to T3
12	7	—	157^{1}	—	—	merge T1, T3, T4 to T2

Figure 8.16 Cascade merge example

(a) Show that the total number of passes made to sort 157 runs is 6-62/157.

(b) Using an initial distribution from Table 8.3 show that Fibonacci merge on four tapes makes 6-59/193 passes when the number of runs in 193.

The distribution required for the process discussed above corresponds to the cascade numbers which are obtained as in Figure 8.17 for a k-way merge. Each phase (except the last) in a k-way cascade merge consists of a k-way merge, followed by a $(k-1)$-way merge, followed by a $(k-2)$-way merge, . . ., a 2-way merge. The last phase consits of only a k-way merge. The table below gives the cascade numbers corresponding to a k-way merge. Each row represents a starting configuration for a merge phase. If at the start of a phase we have the distribution $n_1, n_2, \ldots, n_k$ where $n_i > n_{i+1}$, $1 \leq i < k$, then at the start of the previous phase we need $\sum_1^k n_i, \sum_1^{k-1} n_i, \ldots, n + n_2, n_1$ runs on the k input tapes respectively.

It can be shown that for a 4-way merge. Cascade merge results in more passes over the data than a 4-way Fibonacci merge.

5. (a) Generate the first 10 rows of the initial distribution table for a 5-way cascade merge using six tapes (see Exercise 4).

(b) Observe that 671 runs correspond to a perfect 5-way cascade distribution. How many passes are made in sorting the data using a 5-way cascade merge? (Ans: 5-561/671)

(c) How many passes are made by a 5-way Fibonacci merge starting with 497 runs and the distribution 120, 116, 108, 92, 61? (Ans: 5-400/497)

The number of passes is almost the same even though cascade merge started with

number of runs

1	0	0	. . .	0	0	1
1	1	1	. . .	1	1	k
.	.	.		.	.	
.	.	.		.	.	
.	.	.		.	.	
n_1	n_2	n_3	. . .	n_{k-1}	n_k	$\sum\limits_{1}^{k} n_i$
$\sum\limits_{1}^{k} n_i$	$\sum\limits_{1}^{k-1} n_i$	$\sum\limits_{1}^{k-2} n_i$	. . .	$n_1 + n_2$	n_1	

Figure 8.17 Initial distribution for a k-way cascade merge

35% more runs! In general, for ≥ 6 tapes, cascade merge makes fewer passes over the data than does Fibonacci merge.

6. List the runs output by algorithm *runs* using the following input file and $k = 4$.

$$100, 50, 18, 60, 2, 70, 30, 16, 20, 19, 99, 55, 20$$

7. For the example of Figure 8.14, compute the total rewind time. Compare this with the rewind time needed by algorithm *m2*.

CHAPTER 9
HASHING

9.1 SYMBOL TABLES

The notion of a symbol table arises frequently in computer science. When building loaders, assemblers, compilers, or any keyword driven translator a symbol table is used. In these contexts a symbol table is a *set of name-value pairs*. Associated with each name in the table is an attribute, a collection of attributes, or some direction about what further processing is needed. The operations that one generally wants to perform on symbol tables are: (1) ask if a particular name is already present, (2) retrieve the attributes of that name, (3) insert a new name and its value, and (4) delete a name and its value. In some applications, one wishes to perform only the first three of these operations. However, in its fullest generality we wish to study the representation of a structure which allows these four operations to be performed efficiently.

Is a symbol table necessarily a *set* of names or can the same name appear more than once? If we are translating a language with block structure (such as ALGOL or Pascal) then the variable X may be declared at several levels. Each new declaration of X implies that a new variable (with the same name) must be used. Thus, we may also need a mechanism to determine which of several occurrences of the same name has been the most recently introduced.

These considerations lead us to a specification of the structure *symbol table*. A set of axioms is given in Structure 9.1.

Consider the declarations of Program 9.1. The representation of part of the symbol table (ignoring procedure names and parameters) for these declarations would look like $S =$

$$INSERT\,(INSERT\,(INSERT\,(INSERT\,(CREATE,\ i, \textbf{integer}),\ j, \textbf{integer}),\ x, \textbf{real}),\ i, \textbf{real})$$

```
structure SYMBOL –TABLE
   declare CREATE ( ) → symtb
          INSERT (symtb,name, value ) → symtb
          DELETE (symtb,name ) → symtb
          FIND (symtb,name ) → value
          HAS (symtb,name ) → Boolean
          ISMTST (symtb ) → Boolean;
   for all S ε symtb, a,b ε name, r ε value let
     ISMTST (CREATE ) :: = true
     ISMTST (INSERT (S,a,r)) ::= false
     HAS (CREATE,a) :: = false
     HAS (INSERT (S,a,r),b) :: =
       if EQUAL (a,b) then true else HAS (S,b)
     DELETE (CREATE,a) :: = CREATE
     DELETE (INSERT (S,a,r),b) :: =
       if EQUAL (a,b) then S
       else INSERT (DELETE (S,b),a,r)
       FIND (CREATE,a) :: = error
       FIND (INSERT (S,a,r),b) :: = if EQUAL (a,b) then r
                                   else FIND (S,b)
   end
end SYMBOL_TABLE
```

Structure 9.1 Axioms for a symbol table

```
procedure x (a,b : integer);
   var i,j : integer;
   procedure y (c,d : real);
     var x, i : real;
   begin
   end;
begin
end;
```

Program 9.1 Sample procedure with declarations

Notice the identifier i which is declared twice with different attributes. Now, suppose we apply FIND(S,i). By the axioms EQUAL(i,i) is tested and has the value **true**. Thus the value **real** is returned as a result. If the function DELETE(S,i) is applied, then the result is the symbol table

$$INSERT\,(INSERT\,(INSERT\,(CREATE,\ i,\ \textbf{integer}),\ j,\ \textbf{integer}),\ x,\ \textbf{real})$$

If we wanted to change the specification of DELETE so that it removes all occurrences of i then one axiom needs to be redefined, namely

$$DELETE\,(INSERT\,(S,a,r),b)\ ::=\ \textbf{if}\ EQUAL\,(a,b)\ \textbf{then}\ DELETE\,(S,b)$$
$$\textbf{else}\ INSERT\,(DELETE\,(S,b),a,r)$$

In Section 5.12, we introduced the binary search tree as a data structure that can be used when we have a collection of distinct values or identifiers and the operations to be performed are search, insert, and delete. If n is the number of identifiers in the search tree, then the algortihms of Section 5 take O(n) time to perform a search, insert, or delete. In the next chapter, we consider several refinements of the binary search tree of Section 5.12. These refinements reduce the time per operation to O(log$n$). In this chapter, we examine the most practical of the techniques for dynamic search and insertion, hashing. Unlike search tree methods that rely on identifier comparisons to perform a search, hashing relies on a formula called the *hash function*. Oue discussion of hashing is divided into two parts: *static hashing* and *dynamic hashing*.

9.2 STATIC HASHING

9.2.1 Hash Tables

In *static hashing* the identifiers are stored in a fixed size table called the *hash table*. The address or location of an identifier, X, is obtained by computing some arithmetic function, f, of X. $f(X)$ gives the address of X in the table. This address will be referred to as the hash or home address of X. The memory available to maintain the symbol table is assumed to be sequential. This memory is referred to as the hash table, ht. The hash table is partitioned into b buckets, $ht[0], \ldots, ht[b-1]$. Each bucket is capable of holding s records. Thus, a bucket is said to consist of s slots, each slot being large enough to hold one record. Usually $s = 1$ and each bucket can hold exactly one record. A hashing function, $f(X)$, is used to perform an identifier transformation on X. $f(X)$ maps the set of possible identifiers onto the integers 0 through $b-1$. If the identifiers were restricted to be at most six characters long with the first one being a letter and the remaining either letters or decimal digits, then there would be $T = \sum_{0 \le i \le 5} 26 \times 36^i > 1.6 \times 10^9$ distinct possible values for X. Any reasonable application, however, would use far less than all of these identifiers.

The ratio n/T is the *identifier density*, while $\alpha = n/(sb)$ is the *loading density* or *loading factor*. Since the number of identifiers, n, in use is usually several orders of magnitude less than the total number of possible identifiers, T, the number of buckets, b, in the hash table is also much less than T. Therefore, the hash function f must map several different identifiers into the same bucket. Two identifiers, I_1, and I_2 are said to be *synonyms* with respect to f if $f(I_1) = f(I_2)$. Distinct synonyms are entered into the same bucket so long as all the s slots in that bucket have not been used. An *overflow* is said to occur when a new identifier I is mapped or hashed by f into a full bucket. A *collision* occurs when two nonidentical identifiers are hashed into the same bucket. When the bucket size s is 1, collisions and overflows occur simultaneously.

As an example, let us consider the hash table ht with $b = 26$ buckets, each bucket having exactly two slots, i.e., $s = 2$. Assume that there are $n = 10$ distinct identifiers in the program and that each identifier begins with a letter. The loading factor, α, for this table is $10/52 = 0.19$. The hash function f must map each of the possible identifiers into one of the numbers 1-26. If the internal binary representation for the letters A-Z corresponds to the numbers 1-26, respectively, then the function f defined by $f(X) = $ the first character of X will hash all identifiers X into the hash table. The identifiers GA, D, A, G, L, $A2$, $A1$, $A3$, $A4$, and E will be hashed into buckets 7, 4, 1, 7, 12, 1, 1, 1, 1, and 5, respectively, by this function. The identifiers A, $A1$, $A2$, $A3$, and $A4$ are synonyms. So also are G and GA. Figure 9.1 shows the identifiers GA, D, A, G, and $A2$ entered into the hash table.

	SLOT 1	SLOT 2
1	A	A2
2	0	0
3	0	0
4	D	0
5	0	0
6	0	0
7	GA	G
⋮	⋮	⋮
26	0	0

Zeros indicate empty slots

Figure 9.1 Hash table with 26 buckets and two slots per bucket

Note that GA and G are in the same bucket and each bucket has two slots. Similarly, the synonyms A and $A2$ are in the same bucket. The next identifier, $A1$, hashes into the bucket $ht[1]$. This bucket is full and a search of the bucket indicates that $A1$ is not in the bucket. An overflow has now occurred. Where in the table should $A1$ be entered so that it may be retrieved when needed? We will look into overflow handling strategies in Section 9.3. In the case where no overflows occur, the time required to enter or search for identifiers using hashing depends only on the time required to compute the hash function f and the time to search one bucket. Since the bucket size s is usually small (for internal tables s is usually 1) the search for an identifier within a bucket is carried out using sequential search. The time, then, is independent of n, the number of identifiers in use. For tree tables, this time was, on the average, log n. The hash function in the above example is not very well suited for the use we have in mind because of the very large number of collisions and resulting overflows that occur. This is so because it is not unusual to find programs in which many of the variables begin with the same letter. Ideally, we would like to choose a function f that is both easy to compute and results in very few collisions. Since the ratio b/T is usually very small, it is impossible to avoid collisions altogether.

In summary, hashing schemes perform an identifier transformation through the use of a hash function f. It is desirable to choose a function f that is easily computed and also minimizes the number of collisions. Since the size of the identifier space, T, is usually several orders of magnitude larger than the number of buckets b, and s is small, overflows necessarily occur. Hence a mechanism to handle overflows is also needed.

9.2.2 Hashing Functions

A hashing function, f, transforms an identifier X into a bucket address in the hash table. As mentioned earlier the desired properties of such a function are that it be easily computable and that it minimize the number of collisions. A function, such as the one discussed earlier, is not a very good choice for a hash function for symbol tables even though it is fairly easy to compute. The reason for this is that it depends only on the first character in the identifier. Since many programs use several identifiers with the same first letter, we expect several collisions to occur. In general, then, we would like the function to depend upon all the characters in the identifiers. In addition, we would like the hash function to be such that it does not result in a biased use of the hash table for random inputs; i.e., if X is an identifier chosen at random from the identifier space, then we want the probability that $f(X) = i$ to be $1/b$ for all buckets i. Then a random X has an equal chance of hashing into any of the b buckets. A hash function satisfying this property will be termed a *uniform hash function*.

Several kinds of uniform hash functions are in use. We shall describe four of these.

Mid-square

One hash function that has found much use in symbol table applications is the "middle of square" function. This function, f_m, is computed by squaring the identifier and then using an appropriate number of bits from the middle of the square to obtain the bucket address; the identifier is assumed to fit into one computer word. Since the middle bits of the square will usually depend upon all of the characters in the identifier, it is expected that different identifiers would result in different hash addresses with high probability even when some of the characters are the same. Figure 9.2 shows the bit configurations resulting from squaring some sample identifiers. The number of bits to be used to obtain the bucket address depends on the table size. If r bits are used, the range of values is 2^r, so the size of hash tables is chosen to be a power of 2 when this kind of scheme is used.

| IDENTIFIER | INTERNAL REPRESENTATION | |
X	X	X^2
A	1	1
A1	134	20420
A2	135	20711
A3	136	21204
A4	137	21501
A9	144	23420
B	2	4
C	3	11
G	7	61
DMAX	4150130	21526443617100
DMAX1	415013034	5264473522151420
AMAX	1150130	1345423617100
AMAX1	115013034	3454246522151420

Figure 9.2 Internal representations of X and X^2 in octal notation (X is input right justified, zero filled, six bits or two octal digits per character)

Division

Another simple choice for a hash function is obtained by using the modulo (**mod**) operator. The identifier X is divided by some number M and the remainder is used as the hash address for X.

$$f_D(X) = X \textbf{ mod } M$$

This gives bucket addresses in the range 0 through $(M - 1)$ and so the hash table is at least of size $b = M$. The choice of M is critical. If M is a power of 2, then $f_D(X)$ depends only on the least significant bits of X. For instance, if each character is represented by six bits and identifiers are stored right justified in a 60-bit word with leading bits filled with zeros (Figure 9.3) then with $M = 2^i$, $i \le 6$ the identifiers $A1$, $B1$, $C1$, $X41$, $DNTXY1$, etc., all have the same bucket address. With $M = 2^i$, $i \le 12$ the identifiers AXY, BXY, $WTXY$, etc., have the same bucket address.

Since programmers have a tendency to use many variables with the same suffix, the choice of M as a power of 2 would result in many collisions. This choice of M would have even more disastrous results if the identifier X is stored left justified zero filled. Then, all one-character identifiers would map to the same bucket, 0, for $M = 2^i$, $i \le 54$; all two-character identifiers would map to the bucket 0 for $M = 2^i$, $i \le 48$, etc. As a

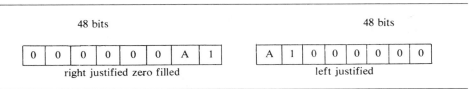

Figure 9.3 Identifier $A1$ right and left justified and zero filled (six bits per character)

result of this observation, we see that when the division function f_D is used as a hash function, the table size should not be a power of 2, while when the "middle of square" function f_m is used, the table size is a power of 2. If M is divisible by 2, then odd keys are mapped to odd buckets (as the remainder is odd) and even keys are mapped to even buckets. The use of the hash table is thus biased.

Let us try some other values for M and see what kind of identifiers get mapped to the same bucket, the goal being that we wish to avoid a choice of M that will lead to many collisions. This kind of analysis is possible as we have some idea as to the relationships between different variable names programmers tend to use. For instance, the knowledge that a program tends to have variables with the same suffix led us to reject $M = 2^i$. For similar reasons even values of M prove undesirable. Let $X = x_1 x_2$ and $Y = x_2 x_1$ be two identifiers each consisting of the characters x_1 and x_2. If the internal binary representation of x_1 has value $C(x_1)$ and that for x_2 has value $C(x_2)$ then if each character is represented by six bits, the numeric value of X is $2^6 C(x_1) + C(x_2)$ while that for Y is $2^6 C(x_2) + C(x_1)$. If p is a prime number dividing M then

$$(f_D(X) - f_D(Y)) \bmod p = (2^6 C(x_1) \bmod p + C(x_2) \bmod p$$
$$- 2^6 C(x_2) \bmod p - C(x_1) \bmod p) \bmod p$$

If $p = 3$, then

$$(f_D(X) - f_D(Y)) \bmod p = (64 \bmod 3 \ C(x_1) \bmod 3 + C(x_2) \bmod 3$$
$$- 64 \bmod 3 \ C(x_2) \bmod 3 - C(x_1) \bmod 3) \bmod 3$$
$$= C(x_1) \bmod 3 + C(x_2) \bmod 3 - C(x_2) \bmod 3 - C(x_1) \bmod 3$$
$$= 0 \bmod 3$$

i.e., permutations of the same set of characters are hashed at a distance a factor of 3 apart. Programs in which many variables are permutations of each other would again result in a biased use of the table and hence result in many collisions. This happens because 64 mod 3 = 1. The same behavior can be expected when 7 divides M as 64 mod 7 = 1. These difficulties can be avoided by choosing M as a prime number. Then, the only factors of M are M and 1. Knuth has shown that when M divides $r^k \pm a$ where k and a are small numbers and r is the radix of the character set (in the above example $r = 64$), then X mod M tends to be a simple superposition of the characters in X. Thus, a good choice for M would be: M *a prime number such that M does not divide $r^k \pm a$ for small k* and a. In Section 9.2.3 we shall see other reasons for choosing M as a prime number. In practice it has been observed that it is sufficient to choose M such that it has no prime divisors less than 20.

Folding

In this method the identifier X is partitioned into several parts, all but the last being of the same length. These parts are then added together to obtain the hash address for X. There are two ways of carrying out this addition. In the first, all but the last part are shifted so that the least significant bit of each part lines up with the corresponding bit of the last part (Figure 9.4(a)). The different parts are now added together to get $f(X)$. This method is known as *shift folding*. The other method of adding the parts is *folding at the boundaries*. In this method, the identifier is folded at the part boundaries and digits falling into the same position are added together (Figure 9.4(b)) to obtain $f(X)$.

$P_1 = 123$ $P_2 = 203$ $P_3 = 241$ $P_4 = 112$ $P_5 = 20$

	123
P_1	123
P_2	203
P_3	241
P_4	112
P_5	20
	699

(a) shift folding

P_1	123
P_2^r	302
P_3	241
P_4^r	211
P_5	20
	897

(b) folding at the boundaries $P_i^r =$ reverse of P_i

Figure 9.4 Two methods of folding

Digit Analysis

This method is particularly useful in the case of a static file where all the identifiers in the table are known in advance. Each identifier X is interpreted as a number using some radix r. The same radix is used for all the identifiers in the table. Using this radix, the digits of each identifier are examined. Digits having the most skewed distributions are deleted. Enough digits are deleted so that the number of digits left is small enough to give an address in the range of the hash table. The criterion used to find the digits to be used as addresses, based on the measure of uniformity in the distribution of values in each digit, is to keep those digits having no abnormally high peaks or valleys and those having small standard deviation. The same digits are used for all identifiers.

Experimental results presented in Section 9.3 suggest the use of the division method with a divisor M that has no prime factors less than 20 for general purpose applications.

9.2.3 Overflow Handling

In order to be able to detect collisions and overflows, it is necessary to initialize the hash table, ht, to represent the situation when all slots are empty. Assuming that no record has identifier zero, then all slots may be initialized to zero[1]. When a new identifier gets hashed into a full bucket, it is necessary to find another bucket for this identifier. The simplest solution would probably be to find the closest unfilled bucket. Let us illustrate this on a 26-bucket table with one slot per bucket. Assume the identifiers to be $GA, D, A, G, L, A2, A1, A3, A4, Z, ZA, E$. For simplicity we choose the hash function $f(X) = $ first character of X. Initially, all entries in the table are zero. $f(GA) = 7$, this bucket is empty, so GA and any other information making up the record are entered into $ht[7]$. D and A get entered into the buckets $ht[4]$ and $ht[1]$, respectively. The next identifier G has $f(G) = 7$. This slot is already used by GA. The next vacant slot is $ht[8]$ and so G is entered there. L enters $ht[12]$. $A2$ collides with A at $ht[1]$, the bucket overflows and $A2$ is entered at the next vacant slot $ht[2]$. $A1$, $A3$, and $A4$ are entered at $ht[3]$, $ht[5]$, and $ht[6]$, respectively. Z is entered at $ht[26]$, ZA at $ht[9]$ (the hash table is used circularly), and E collides with $A3$ at $ht[5]$ and is eventually entered at $ht[10]$. Figure 9.5 shows the resulting table. This method of resolving overflows is known as *linear probing* or *linear open addressing*.

In order to search the table for an identifier, x, it is necessary to first compute $f(x)$ and then examine keys at positions $ht[f(x)]$, $ht[f(x)+1]$, . . ., $ht[f(x)+j]$ such that $ht[f(x)+j]$ either equals x (x is in the table) or *BlankIdent* (x is not in the table) or we eventually return to $ht[f(x)]$ (the table is full). The resulting algorithm is Program 9.2. The data types used are

$$\textbf{type } \textit{identifier} = \textbf{packed array } [1..MaxChar] \textbf{ of char}$$
$$HashTable = \textbf{array}[1..MaxSize] \textbf{ of } \textit{identifer};$$

Our earlier example shows that when linear probing is used to resolve overflows, identifiers tend to cluster together, and moreover, adjacent clusters tend to coalesce, thus increasing the search time. To locate the identifier, ZA, in the table of Figure 9.5, it is necessary to examine $ht[26]$, $ht[1]$, . . ., $ht[9]$, a total of 10 comparisons. This is far worse than the worst case behavior for tree tables. If each of the identifiers in the table

---

1. A clever way to avoid initializing the hash table has been discovered by T. Gonzalez (see Exercise 6).

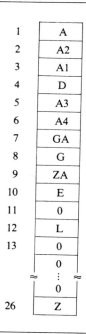

1	A
2	A2
3	A1
4	D
5	A3
6	A4
7	GA
8	G
9	ZA
10	E
11	0
12	L
13	0
	0
	⋮
	0
26	Z

Figure 9.5 Hash table with linear probing (26 buckets, 1 slot per bucket)

of Figure 9.1 was retrieved exactly once, then the number of buckets examined would be 1 for A, 2 for $A2$, 3 for $A1$, 1 for D, 5 for $A3$, 6 for $A4$, 1 for GA, 2 for G, 10 for ZA, 6 for E, 1 for L, and 1 for Z for a total of 39 buckets examined. The average number examined is 3.25 buckets per identifier. An analysis of the method shows that the expected average number of identifier comparisons, P, to look up an identifier is approximately $(2 - \alpha)/(2 - 2\alpha)$ where α is the loading density. This is the average over all possible sets of identifiers yielding the given loading density and using a uniform function f. In the above example $\alpha = 12/26 = .47$ and $P = 1.5$. Even though the average number of probes is small, the worst case can be quite large.

One of the problems with linear open addressing is that it tends to create clusters of identifiers. Moreover, these clusters tend to merge as more identifiers are entered, leading to bigger clusters. Some improvement in the growth of clusters and hence in the average number of probes needed for searching can be obtained by *quadratic probing*. Linear probing was characterized by searching the buckets $(f(x) + i)\bmod b$, $0 \le i \le b - 1$ where b is the number of buckets in the table. In quadratic probing, a quadratic function of i is used as the increment. In particular, the search is carried out by examining buckets $f(x)$, $(f(x) + i^2) \bmod b$, and $(f(x) - i^2) \bmod b$ for $1 \le i \le (b - 1)/2$.

```
 1  procedure LinearSearch (x : identifier; ht : HashTable; var j : integer;
                                                         b : integer);
 2  {Search the hash table ht [0..b − 1] (each bucket has exactly one
 3    slot) using linear probing. If ht [ j ] = BlankIdent then the j'th bucket
 4    is empty and x can be entered into the table. Otherwise ht [ j ] = x
 5    which is already in the table. f is the hash function.}
 6  var i : integer
 7  begin
 8    i := f (x); j := i;
 9    while (ht [ j ] < > x) and (ht [ j ] < > BlankIdent ) do
10    begin
11      j := (j + 1) mod b; {treat the table as circular}
12      if j = i then {no empty slots}
13                TableFull;
14    end;
15  end; {of LinearSearch}
```

Program 9.2 Linear search

When b is a prime number of the form $4j + 3$, for j an integer, the quadratic search described above examines every bucket in the table. The proof that when b is of the form $4j + 3$, quadratic probing examines all the buckets 0 to $b − 1$, relies on some results from number theory. We shall not go into the proof here. The interested reader should see Radke [1970] for a proof. Figure 9.6 lists some primes of the form $4j + 3$. Another possibility is to use a series of hash functions $f_1, f_2, \ldots, f_m$. This method is known as *rehashing*. Buckets $f_i(x)$, $1 \le i \le m$ are examined in that order. An alternate method for handling bucket overflow, random probing, is discussed in Exercise 3.

---

prime	j	prime	j
3	0	43	10
7	1	59	14
11	2	127	31
19	4	251	62
23	5	503	125
31	7	1019	254

Figure 9.6 Some primes of the form $4j + 3$

One of the reasons linear probing and its variations perform poorly is that searching for an identifier involves comparison of identifiers with different hash values. In the hash table of Figure 9.5, for instance, searching for the identifier ZA involved comparisons with the buckets ht [1] to ht [8], even though none of the identifiers in these buckets had a collision with ht [26] and so could not possibly be ZA. Many of the comparisons being made could be saved if we maintained lists of identifiers, one list per bucket, each list containing all the synonyms for that bucket. If this were done, a search would then involve computing the hash address $f(x)$ and examining only those identifiers in the list for $f(x)$. Since the sizes of these lists is not known in advance, the best way to maintain them is as linked chains. Additional space for a link is required in each slot. Each chain will have a headnode. The headnode, however, will usually be much smaller than the other nodes since it has to retain only a link. Since the lists are to be accessed at random, the headnodes should be sequential. We assume they are numbered 1 to M if the hash function f has range 1 to M.

Using chaining to resolve collisions and the hash function used to obtain Figure 9.5, the hash chains of Figure 9.7 are obtained. When a new identifier, x, is being inserted into a chain, the insertion can be made at either end. This is so because the address of the last node in the chain is known as a result of the search that determined x was not in the list for $f(x)$. In the example of Figure 9.7, new identifiers were inserted at the front of the chains. The number of probes needed to search for any of the identifiers is now one for each of $A4$, D, E, G, L, and ZA; two for each of $A3$, GA, and Z; three for $A1$; four for $A2$, and five for A, for a total of 24. The average is now two which is considerably less than for linear probing. Additional storage, however, is needed for links. The algorithm that results when chaining is used is given in Program 9.3. The data types are

```
type identifier = packed array[1..MaxChar ] of char;
     ListPointer = ↑ListNode;
     ListNode = record
                     ident = identifier;
                     link = ListPointer;
                end;
     HashTable = array[1..MaxSize ] of ListPointer;
```

The expected number of identifier comparisons can be shown to be $\sim 1 + \alpha/2$ where α is the loading density n/b (b = number of headnodes). For $\alpha = 0.5$ this figure is 1.25 and for $\alpha = 1$ it is about 1.5. This scheme has the additional advantage that only the b headnodes must be sequential and reserved at the beginning. Each headnode, however, will be at most one half to one word long. The other nodes will be much bigger and need be allocated only as needed. This could represent an overall reduction in space required for certain loading densities despite the links. If each record in the table is five words long, $n = 100$ and $\alpha = 0.5$, then the hash table will be of size $200 \times 5 = 1000$ words. Only 500 of these are used as $\alpha = 0.5$. On the other hand, if chaining is used with one full word per link, then 200 words are needed for the head nodes ($b = 200$). Each head

```
 1  procedure ChainSearch (x : identifier; var ht : HashTable;
 2                          b : integer; var i : ListPointer);
 3  {Search the hash table ht [0..b − 1] for x. Either ht [i ] = nil or it is a pointer to the
 4   list of identifiers x :f (x) = i. List nodes have the fields ident and link.
 5   Either j points to the node already containing x or j = nil.}
 6  var found : boolean;
 7  begin
 8   j := ht [f (x)]; {compute headnode address}
 9    {search the chain starting at j}
10    found := false;
11    while (j < > nil) and not found do
12      if j↑. ident = x then found := true
13                          else j := j↑. link;
14  end; {of ChainSearch}
```

Program 9.3 Chain search

node is one word long. One hundred nodes of six words each are needed for the records. The total space needed is thus 800 words, or 20 percent less than when no chaining was being used. Of course, when α is close to 1, the average number of probes using linear probing or its variations becomes quite large and the additional space used for chaining can be justified by the reduction in the expected number of probes needed for retrieval. If you wish to delete an entry from the table, then this can be done by just removing that node from its chain. The problem of deleting entries while using open addressing to resolve collisions is tackled in Exercise 1.

The results of this section tend to imply that the performance of a hash table depends only on the method used to handle overflows and is independent of the hash function so long as a uniform hash function is being used. While this is true when the identifiers are selected at random from the identifier space, it is not true in practice. In practice, there is a tendency to make a biased use of identifiers. Many identifiers in use have a common suffix or prefix or are simple permutations of other identifiers. Hence, in practice, we would expect different hash functions to result in different hash table performance. The table of Figure 9.8 presents the results of an empirical study conducted by Lum, Yuen, and Dodd. The values in each column give the average number of bucket accesses made in searching eight different tables with 33,575, 24,050, 4909, 3072, 2241, 930, 762, and 500 identifiers each. As expected, chaining outperforms linear open addressing as a method for overflow handling. In looking over the figures for the various hash functions, we see that division is generally superior to the other types of hash functions. For a general application, it is therefore recommended that the division method be used. The divisor should be a prime number, though it is sufficient to choose a divisor that has no prime factors less than 20. The table also gives the theoretical expected number of bucket accesses based on random keys.

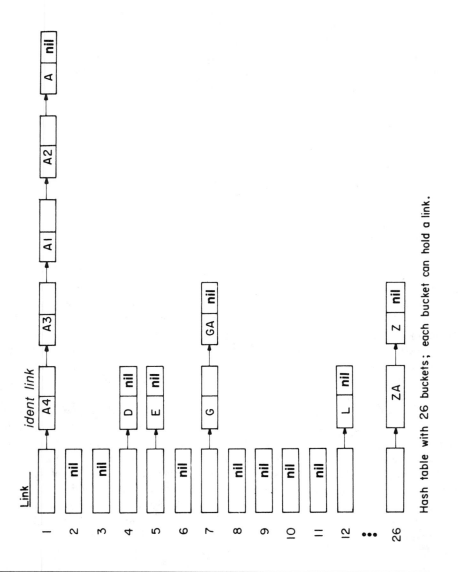

Figure 9.7 Hash chains corresponding to Figure 9.5

hash function type	α = n/b	.5		.75		.9		.95	
		C	L	C	L	C	L	C	L
MIDSQ		1.26	1.73	1.40	9.75	1.45	27.14	1.47	37.53
DIV		1.19	4.52	1.31	7.20	1.38	22.42	1.41	25.79
FOLD S		1.33	21.75	1.48	65.10	1.40	77.01	1.51	118.57
FOLD B		1.39	22.97	1.57	48.70	1.55	69.63	1.51	97.56
DA		1.35	4.55	1.49	30.62	1.52	89.20	1.52	125.59
THEO		1.25	1.50	1.37	2.50	1.45	5.50	1.48	10.50

Number of slots per bucket = 1

C = chaining
L = linear open addressing
α = loading density
MIDSQ = middle of square
DIV = division
FOLD S = shift folding
FOLD B = folding at boundaries
DA = digit analysis
THEO = theoretical expectation based on random keys

Figure 9.8 Average number of bucket accesses per identifier retrieved (condensed from Lum, Yuen, and Dodd, CACM, April 1971, Vol. 14, No. 4)

9.2.4 Theoretical Evaluation of Overflow Techniques

The experimental evaluation of hashing techniques indicates a very good performance over conventional techniques such as balanced trees. The worst case performance for hashing can, however, be very bad. In the worst case, an insertion or a search in a hash table with n identifiers may take $O(n)$ time. In this section, we present a probabilistic analysis for the expected performance of the chaining method and state without proof the results of similar analyses for the other overflow handling methods. First, we formalize what we mean by expected performance.

Let $HT[0: b-1]$ be a hash table with b buckets, each bucket having one slot. Let f be a uniform hash function with range $[0, b-1]$. If n identifiers $X_1, X_2, \ldots, X_n$ are entered into the hash table, then there are b^n distinct hash sequences $f(X_1), f(X_2), \ldots, f(X_n)$. Assume that each of these is equally likely to occur. Let S_n denote the expected number of identifier comparisons needed to locate a randomly chosen X_i, $1 \le i \le n$. Then, S_n is the average number of comparisons needed to find the j'th key X_j; averaged over $1 \le j \le n$ with each j equally likely and averaged over all b^n hash sequences assuming each of these to also be equally likely. Let U_n be the expected number of identifier comparisons when a search is made for an identifier not in the hash table. This hash table contains n identifiers. The quantity U_n may be defined in a manner analogous to that used for S_n.

Theorem 9.1 Let $\alpha = n/b$ be the loading density of a hash table using a uniform hashing function f. Then

(1) for linear open addressing

$$U_n \approx \frac{1}{2}\left[1 + \frac{1}{(1-\alpha)^2}\right]$$

$$S_n \approx \frac{1}{2}\left[1 + \frac{1}{1-\alpha}\right]$$

(2) for rehashing, random probing, and quadratic probing

$$U_n \approx 1/(1-\alpha)$$

$$S_n \approx -\left[\frac{1}{\alpha}\right]\log_e(1-\alpha)$$

(3) for chaining

$$U_n \approx \alpha$$

$$S_n \approx 1 + \alpha/2$$

Proof: Exact derivations of U_n and S_n are fairly involved and can be found in Knuth's book *The Art of Computer Programming: Sorting and Searching*. Here, we present a derivation of the approximate formulas for chaining. First, we must make clear our count for U_n and S_n. In case the identifier X being searched for has $f(X) = i$ and chain i has k nodes on it (not including the headnode) then k comparisons are needed if X is not on the chain. If X is j nodes away from the head node, $1 \le j \le k$, then j comparisons are needed.

When the n identifiers distribute uniformly over the b possible chains, the expected number in each chain is $n/b = \alpha$. Since U_n = expected number of identifiers on a chain, we get $U_n = \alpha$.

When the i'th identifier, X_i, is being entered into the table, the expected number of identifiers on any chain is $(i - 1)/b$. Hence, the expected number of comparisons needed to search for X_i after all n identifiers have been entered is $1 + (i - 1)/b$ (this assumes that new entries will be made at the end of the chain). We therefore get

$$S_n = \frac{1}{n} \sum_{i=1}^{n} \{1 + (i - 1)/b\} = 1 + \frac{n - 1}{2b} \approx 1 + \frac{\alpha}{2} \quad \square$$

9.3 DYNAMIC HASHING

9.3.1 Motivation for Dynamic Hashing

One of the most important classes of software is the database management system or DBMS. In a DBMS the user enters a query using some language (possibly SQL) and the system translates it and retrieves the resulting data. Fast access time is essential as a DBMS is typically used to hold large sets of information. Another key characteristic of a DBMS is that the amount of information can vary a great deal over time. Various data structures have been suggested for storing the data in a DBMS. In this section, we examine an extension of hashing that permits the technique to be used by a DBMS.

Traditional hashing schemes as described in the previous section are not ideal. This follows from the fact that one must statically allocate a portion of memory to hold the hash table. This hash table is used to point to the pages used to hold identifiers, or it may actually hold the identifiers themselves. In either case, if the table is allocated to be as large as possible, then space can be wasted. If it is allocated too small, then when the data exceeds the capacity of the hash table, the entire file must be restructured, a time consuming process. The purpose of *dynamic hashing*, (also referred to as *extendible hashing*) is to retain the fast retrieval time of conventional hashing while extending the technique so it can accommodate dynamically increasing and decreasing file size without penalty.

We assume that a file F is a collection of records R. Each record has a key field K by which it is identified. Records are stored in pages or buckets whose capacity is p. We will try to develop algorithms that minimize access to pages, since they are typically stored on disk and their retrieval into memory dominates any operation. The measure of space utilization is the ratio of the number of records, n, divided by the total space, mp, where m is the number of pages.

9.3.2 Dynamic Hashing Using Directories

Consider an example where an identifier consists of two characters and each character is represented by three bits. Figure 9.9 gives a list of some of these identifiers.

identifiers	binary represenation
A0	100 000
A1	100 001
B0	101 000
B1	101 001
C0	110 000
C1	110 001
C2	110 010
C3	110 011

Figure 9.9 Some identifiers requiring 3 bits per character

Consider placing these identifiers into a table that has four pages. Each page can hold at most two identifiers and each page is indexed by the two bit sequence 00, 01, 10, 11, respectively. We use the low order two bits of each identifier to determine in which page of the table to place it. The result of placing A0, B0, C2, A1, B1, and C3 is shown in Figure 9.10. Note that we select the bits from least significant to most significant.

You see in Figure 9.10(a) that A0 and B0 are in the first page. Since the first two low order bits of A0 and B0 are zero, these identifiers are placed in the first page. The second page contains only the single identifier C2 and its page is found by following its low order bits 0, 1. This type of binary tree, where locating an identifer is done by following its bit sequence, is called a *trie* and is described in more detail in Chapter 10. Note that this trie has nodes that always branch in two directions corresponding to 0 or 1. Only the leaf nodes of the trie contain a pointer to a page.

Now suppose we try to insert a new identifier, say C5 into Figure 9.10(a). Since the two low order bits of C5 are 1 and 0, and since we assume that a page can hold at most two identifiers, an overflow occurs. In this case a new page is added and the depth of the trie must be increased by one level. This is shown in Figure 9.10(b). Similary, if

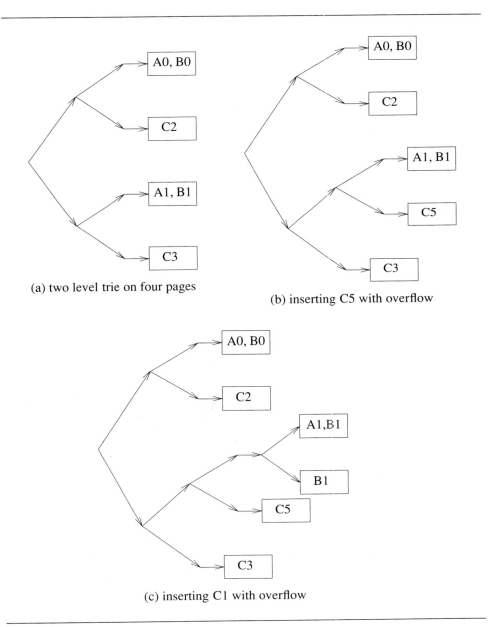

(a) two level trie on four pages

(b) inserting C5 with overflow

(c) inserting C1 with overflow

Figure 9.10 A trie to hold identifiers

we now try to insert the new identifier C1, that will cause an overflow of the page containing A1 and B1. A new page is obtained and the three identifiers are divided among the two pages according to their low order four bits.

From this example one can see that two major problems exist. The first is that the time to access a page depends upon the number of bits needed to distinguish the identifiers. Second, if the identifiers have a skewed distribution, then the depth of the tree will also be skewed, and as a result retrieval time will increase. Fagin et al.. present a method they call extendible hashing for solving these problems. To avoid the skewed distribution of identifiers, a hash function is used. This function takes the key and produces a random set of binary digits. To avoid the long search down the trie, a trie is mapped to a directory.

In Figure 9.11 you see three directories corresponding to the three tries in Figure 9.10. The first directory contains four entries indexed from 0 to 3. Each entry contains a pointer to a page. The second directory contains eight entries, indexed from 0 to 7, and the third has 16 entries indexed from 0 to 15. The second directory, Figure 9.11(b) has 5 pages. If we label the pages as $p0$, $p1$, $p2$, etc., reading down the column, then we see that page $p0$ has two directory entries pointing to it. Page $p1$ has one pointer to it, page $p2$ has two pointers, page $p3$ has one pointer, and page $p4$ has two pointers. In Figure 9.11(c) there are six pages with the following number of pointers respectively: 4, 1, 4, 2, 4, and 1.

Using the scheme of representing a trie by a directory, the table of identifiers can grow and shrink dynamically, assuming that the operating system can give us more pages or return pages to available storage with little or no difficulty. Moreover, the access time to get to any page is fixed at two. One step, the hashing, yields the address of the directory entry. The second step retrieves the page pointed at.

One important problem with this approach is that if the keys do not uniformly divide up among the pages, then the directory can grow quite large, but most of the entries will point to the same pages. Therefore, one cannot simply use the bit sequence of the keys themselves, but one must translate those bits into some random sequence. This is done using a *uniform hash function* as discussed in the previous section. But in contrast to the previous section we need a *family* of hashing functions, in that at any point we may require a different number of bits to distinguish the new key. One solution is the family:

$$hash_i: key \rightarrow \{0..2^{i-1}\}, \ 1 \leq i \leq d$$

where $hash_i$ is simply $hash_{i-1}$ with either a zero or one appended as the new leading bit of the result. So $hash(key, i)$ might be a function that produces a random number of i bits from the identifier *key*.

There are some important twists associated with this approach. For example, suppose a page is identified by i bits and that it overflows. A new page is allocated and all identifiers are rehashed into those two pages. All the identifiers in both pages have their low order i bits in common. These pages are referred to as *buddies*. When the number of identifiers in two buddy pages is less than the capacity of a single page, then

00 $\longrightarrow$ A0, B0	000 $\xrightarrow{a}$ A0, B0	0000 $\xrightarrow{a}$ A0, B0
01 $\longrightarrow$ A1, B1	001 $\xrightarrow{b}$ A1, B1	0001 $\xrightarrow{b}$ A1, B1
10 $\longrightarrow$ C2	010 $\xrightarrow{c}$ C2	0010 $\xrightarrow{c}$ C2
11 $\longrightarrow$ C3	011 $\longrightarrow$ e	0011 $\longrightarrow$ e
	100 $\longrightarrow$ a	0100 $\longrightarrow$ a
	101 $\xrightarrow{d}$ C5	0101 $\xrightarrow{d}$ C5
	110 $\longrightarrow$ c	0110 $\longrightarrow$ c
	111 $\xrightarrow{e}$ C3	0111 $\xrightarrow{e}$ C3
		1000 $\longrightarrow$ a
		1001 $\xrightarrow{f}$ B1
		1010 $\longrightarrow$ c
		1011 $\longrightarrow$ e
		1100 $\longrightarrow$ a
		1101 $\longrightarrow$ d
		1110 $\longrightarrow$ c
		1111 $\longrightarrow$ e
(a) 2 bits	(b) 3 bits	(c) 4 bits

Figure 9.11 Tries collapsed into directories

the two pages may be coalesced into one.

Suppose a page that can hold only p records now contains p records and a new one is to be added. A new page is allocated by the operating system. All $p + 1$ keys are rehashed, using one more bit and divided among the two pages. If the number of bits used is greater than the depth (the number of bits or $\log_2$ of the directory size) of the directory, the whole directory doubles in size and its depth increases by 1. If all $p + 1$ records are hashed to one of the two pages the split operation will have to be repeated. This is a very unlikely occurrence.

Program 9.4 contains a set of pseudo-Pascal programs that provide many of the details for implementing the directory version of dynamic hashing.

```
program dhashing (input, output);
const wdsize = 5; {maximum number of directory bits}
      psize = 10;  {maximum size of a page}
      maxdir = 32;  {maximum size of a directory}
type numbits = 1..wdsize;
     twochars = array[1..2] of char;  {holds an identifier}
     globaldepth = 1..wdsize; { 2^globaldepth = no. of directory entries}
     paddr = ↑ page;
     directory : array[0..maxdir] of paddr;
     page = record
                   localdepth : integer; {number of bits to distinquish ids}
                   names : array [1..psize] of twochars; {the actual identifiers}
                   numidents : integer; {number of identifiers in this page}
            end;
     brecord = record  { a sample record }
                   keyfield : twochars;
                   intdata : integer;
                   chardata : char;
               end;
var gdepth : globaldepth;
    rdirectory : directory; {will contain pointers to pages}

function hash (key : twochars ; precision : numbits) : paddr;
begin
   {Takes a two character identifier named key, and a precision of bits.}
   {The key is hashed using a uniform hash function and the low order}
   {precision bits are returned as a page address.}
end; {hash}

function buddy (index : paddr ; precision : numbits) : paddr;
begin
   {Takes an address of a page and a precision of bits and returns the page's buddy,}
   {namely the leading bit is complemented.}
end; {buddy}

function pgsearch (key : twochars ; index : paddr ; precision : numbits) : boolean;
begin
   {takes a key, the address of a page, and a precision of bits and searches}
   {for the key in the page returning either true or false.}
end; {pgsearch}
```

```
function convert (p : paddr) : integer;
begin
    {Converts a pointer to a page to an equivalent integer}
end; {convert}

procedure enter (r : brecord ; p : paddr);
begin
    {Inserts a new record into the page pointed at by p}
end; {enter}

procedure pgdelete (key : twochar ; p : pointer);
begin
    {Removes the record with key key from the page pointed at by p}
end; {pgdelete}

procedure find (r : brecord ; key : twochars ; var p : paddr ; found : boolean);
{Takes a record and its key and searches for this identifier in the file.}
{If found it sets found to true and returns the address of the page in p}
{If not found it sets found to false.}
var index, ptr : paddr ; intindex : integer;
begin
    index := hash (key,gdepth);
    intindex := convert (index); {change an address to an integer}
    ptr := rdirectory [intindex ]; {retrieve a pointer to a page}
    found := pgsearch (key, ptr, gdepth);
end; {find}

procedure insert (r : brecord, key : twochars);
{Inserts a new record into the file pointed at by the directory}
var found, done : boolean; p : paddr ;
label 99;
begin
    find (r, key, p, found) {check if key is present}
    if found then goto 99; {key already in}
    else if p ↑. numidents <> psize {page not full}
        then begin
                enter (r,p); p ↑. numidents := p ↑. numidents + 1; goto 99;
            end
        else if p ↑. localdepth = gdepth
            then if gdepth = wdsize
                then begin
                        writeln('table at max. capacity');
                        stop;
                    end
```

```
                else gdepth := gdepth + 1;
        done := false;
        repeat
            new (temp); {get large temp area}
            newpage (q);{get a new page called q}
            place all ids in p into temp, place r in temp
            rehash all ids in temp into p or q
            p ↑.localdepth := p ↑.localdepth + 1;
            q ↑.localdepth := p ↑.localdepth;
            if at least one identifier maps to p and q then done := true;
        until done;
        99:
end; {insert}


procedure delete (r : brecord ; key : twochars);
{Finds and deletes the record r from the file}
var found : boolean; p : paddr;
label 99;
begin
    find (r, key, p, found);
    if not found then goto 99
        else pgdelete (key, p);
    if size (p) + size (buddy (p)) <= psize /2 then coalesce (p, buddy (p));
end; {delete}
```

Program 9.4 Programs for extendible hashing

9.3.3 Analysis of Directory Dynamic Hashing

In terms of performance, the most important feature of this version of extendible hashing is that there is a guarantee of two disk accesses to get to any page. However, this does come at a price, namely the growth of the directory when we have to double the directory size, and the potentially wasted storage of many pointers pointing to the same page.

   A second criteria for judging hashing schemes is the space utilization. This is defined as the ratio of the number of records stored in the table divided by the total amount of space allocated. Several researchers (Fagin, Larson, and Mendelson), have analyzed this measure for different variations of dynamic hashing. They have all reached similar conclusions, namely that without any special strategies for handling overflows, the space utilization is approximately 69 percent Each of their derivations is quite complex and rely on assumptions about the distributions of the identifiers. Here we will follow the derivation given by Mendelson.

Let $L(k)$ stand for the expected number of leaf nodes needed to hold k records. When the number of records all fit in a single page, then $L(k) = 1$. The interesting case, is when k exceeds the page size. In this case the number of records in the two subtrees of the root have a symmetric binomial distribution. From this it follows that there will be j keys in the left subtree and $k - j$ records in the right tree, each with a given probability which is

$$\binom{k}{j} (1/2)^k$$

This implies that the number of leaf pages in the left subtree is $L(j)$ and the number in the right subtree is $L(k - j)$. Thus one can express $L(k)$ by the formula

$$L(k) = \sum_{0 \leq j \leq k} \binom{k}{j} \{L(j) + L(k-j)\} = 2^{1-k} \sum_{0 \leq j \leq k} \binom{k}{j} L(j)$$

Mendelson goes on to show that

$$L(k) \sim \frac{k}{p \ln 2}$$

It follows that the storage utilization is the number of records, k, divided by the product of the page size p and the number of leaf nodes $L(k)$ or that

$$utilization = \frac{k}{pL(k)} \sim \ln 2 \sim 0.69$$

To see that Mendelson's estimate is reasonable, suppose there is no overflow strategy other than doubling the directory size and a page is full with p records. An attempt is made to insert a $p+1$'st record and an overflow occurs. With a uniform hash function we will now have two pages each containing about $p/2$ identifiers, or a space utilization of 50 percent. After the process of inserting and deleting continues for a while, we would expect that a page is at least half full, having recently been split, or even fuller. Thus space utilization should be at least 50 percent but certainly less than 100 percent.

When a page overflows, it may cause a doubling of the directory size. To avoid this, the idea of using overflow pages has been introduced. Instead of increasing the directory, an overflow would cause a new page to be allocated and a pointer to that page is stored in the main page. All new identifiers wanting to be stored in the main page will be stored in the overflow page. We shall see that this will increase storage utilization, but at the expense of added retrieval time.

Assume an overflow page is the same size as a regular page and that both pages are full with p records, a total of $2p$ records. If one overflows, gets a new page, and distributes the keys among the three pages, then the utilization is $2p/3p$ or 66 percent. On the other hand, if the capacity of the overflow page is $p/2$ rather than p, and we split as before, then there are a total of $3p/2$ records divided over a capacity of $2p$, since the overflow page will no longer be needed and can be returned to the available storage list. This produces a utilization of $3/4 = 75$ percent. Thus, we see that overflow pages increase utilization but also increase retrieval time.

The issue of what is an ideal size for the overflow page has been investigated by Larson and others. His conclusion is that if it is sufficient to maintain space utilization below 80 percent, then the size of the overflow pages can vary widely, say from p to $p/2$. However, for higher utilizations, a successively narrow range of overflow page sizes becomes acceptable, due to the fact that utilization will begin to oscillate as well as decreasing significantly the access time. One technique is to monitor the space utilization of the file, so that when it achieves some predetermined amount, say the 80 percent ratio, the algorithm can resume splitting.

Another factor to analyze is the size of the directory given n records. Fagin estimated it as

$$2 \lceil \log \frac{n}{p \ln 2} \rceil$$

In Figure 9.12 we see a table given by Flajolet which shows for various numbers of records n and page size p the expected directory size. For example to store one million records using a page size sufficient for 50 records, a directory of size 62,500 would be needed. This is substantial and indicates that the directory may have to be stored using auxiliary storage.

n	5	10	p 20	50	100	200
10^3	1.5K	0.3K	0.1K	0.0K	0.0K	0.0K
10^4	25.6K	4.8K	1.7K	0.5K	0.2K	0.00K
10^5	424.1K	68.2K	16.8K	4.1K	2.0K	1.0K
10^6	6.9M	1.02M	0.26M	62.5K	16.8K	8.1K
10^7	111.11M	11.64M	2.25M	0.52M	0.26M	0.13M

Figure 9.12 Directory size given n records and p page size

In the event that the hash function does not evenly distribute the identifiers across the pages, more sophisticated techniques are required. Lomet has suggested that in the directory scheme pages not be viewed as being a fixed size, but they be permitted to grow. Thus any given page may be composed of several subpages and as more identifiers map to this page, its storage is expanded. This leads to different strategies for maintaining the identifiers within the page. The simplest strategy is to keep the identifiers in the order they were entered into the table. However, sequential searching is time consuming, especially as the identifier list gets long. An alternate is to treat each subpage as a dynamically hashed directoryless structure. Its maintenance is described in the next section.

Simulation

One important way to measure the performance of any new data structure is to carry out a series of experiments. Each experiment makes use of the algorithms that implement the data structure. Various distributions of identifiers are given to the algorithms with the resultant behavior tabulated. In the case of dynamic hashing, there are three factors that are especially important to monitor. These are: (1) access time, (2) insertion time, and (3) total space. The dependent parameters are: (1) the number of records, (2) the page size, (3) the directory size, (4) the size of main memory for holding the directory and identifiers, and (5) the time to process page faults.

Fagin et al., have done such a series of experiments. They found that in all cases extendible hashing performed at least as well or better than B-trees, a popular competitor. In the case of access time and insertion time, extendible hashing was clearly superior. For space utilization the two methods were about equal.

9.3.4 Directoryless Dynamic Hashing

The previous section assumed a directory existed that pointed to pages. One criticism of this approach is that at least one level of indirection is always required. It turns out that the directory can be eliminated if we assume that we have a contiguous address space that is large enough to hold all records. This, in effect, leaves it to the operating system to break the address space into pages and to manage moving them into and out of memory. This scheme is referred to as *directoryless hashing* or as *linear hashing*.

Consider the trie in Figure 9.10(a) which has two levels and indexes four pages. In the new method the two bit addresses are the actual addresses of these pages, (actually they are an offset of some base address). Thus the hash function will deliver the actual address of a page containing the key. Moreover, every value produced by the hash function must point to an actual page. In contrast to the directory scheme where a single page might be pointed at by several directory entries, in the directoryless scheme there must exist a unique page for every possible address. Figure 9.13 shows a simple trie and its mapping to contiguous memory without a directory.

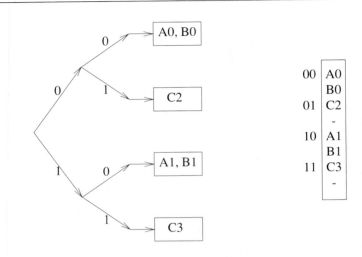

Figure 9.13 A trie mapped to a directoryless, contiguous storage

Now what happens when a page overflows? We could double the size of the address space, but this is quite wasteful. Instead, whenever an overflow occurs a new page is added to the end of the file and the identifiers in one of the pages is divided between its original page and the new page. This complicates the handling of the family of hash functions somewhat. But if we had simply added one bit to the result of the hash function, then the table would have to be doubled. By adding only a single page, the hash function must distinquish between pages addressed by r bits and those addressed by $r+1$. This will be shown in a moment.

In Figure 9.14 you see an example of directoryless hashing after two insertions. Initially, Figure 9.14(a) there are four pages each addressed by two bits. Two of the pages are full and two have one identifier each. When C5 is inserted, Figure 9.14(b), it hashes to the page whose address is 10. Since that page is full, an overflow node is allocated to hold C5. At the same time, a new page is added at the end of the storage and the identifiers in the first page are rehashed and split among the first and new page. Unfortunately none of the new identifiers go into the new page. The first page and the new page are now addressed by three bits, not two, as shown in part (b) of the figure. In the next step, the identifier C1 is inserted. This hashes to the same page as C5 and so another overflow node is used to store it. A new page is added to the end of the file and the identifiers in the second page are rehashed. Once again none go into the new page. (Note that this is largely a result of not using a uniform hash function). Now the first two pages and the two new pages are all addressed using three bits. Eventually one sees that the number of pages will double at which point a phase completes and a new phase begins.

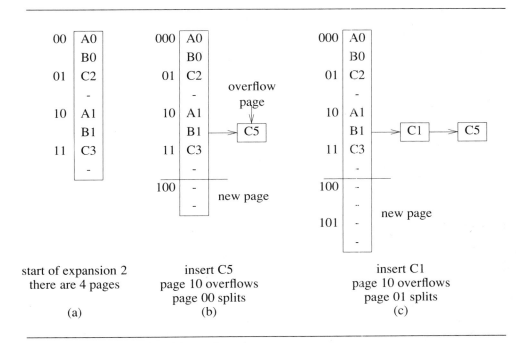

Figure 9.14 An example with two insertions

Consider Figure 9.15, which shows the state of file expansion during the r'th phase at some time q. At the beginning of the r'th phase, there are 2^r pages all addressed by r bits. In the figure, q new pages have been added. To the left of the q line are the pages that have already been split. To the right of the q line are the pages remaining to be split up to the line labeled r. To the right of the r line are the pages that have been added during this phase of the process. Each page in this section of the file is addressed by $r + 1$ bits. Note that the q line is an indicator of which page gets split next. The actual modified hash function is given in Program 9.5. All pages less than q require $r + 1$ bits. $hash\,(key,r)$ is in the range $\{0,2^{r-1}\}$ so, if the result is less than q, we rehash using $r + 1$ bits. This gives us either the pages to the left of q or above $2^r - 1$. The directoryless method always requires overflows.

One sees that for many retrievals the time will be one access, namely for those identifiers that are in the page directly addressed by the hash function. However, for others substantially more than two accesses might be required as one moves along the overflow chain. When a new page is added and the identifiers split across the two pages, all identifiers including the overflows are rehashed.

Another fact about this method is that space utilization is not good. As can be seen from Figure 9.14, some extra pages are empty and yet overflow pages are being

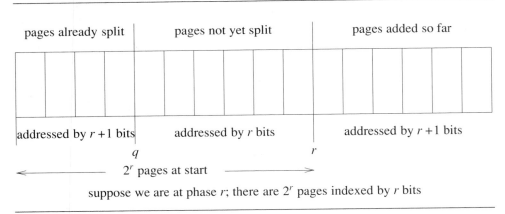

Figure 9.15 During the r'th phase of expansion of directoryless method

if $hash(key,r) < q$ **then** $page := hash(key,r+1)$
else $page := hash(key,r)$;
if needed, then follow overflow pointers.

Program 9.5 Modified hash function

used. Litwin has shown that space utilization is approximately 60 percent. He offers an alternate strategy pursued in the exercises. The term controlled splitting refers to splitting the ''next page'' only when storage utilization exceeds a predefined amount. Litwin suggests that until 80 percent utilization is reached, other pages continue to overflow.

A natural way to handle overflows is to use one of the traditional hashing schemes discussed earlier, such as open addressing. Recall that open addressing searches the file linearly from the point where the identifier hashes, either looking for the identifier or for an open spot.

From the example, one sees that the longest overflow chains will occur for those pages that are near the end of the expansion phase as they are the last to be split. In contrast, those pages that are split early are generally underfull.

9.4 REFERENCES AND SELECTED READINGS

Several interesting and enlightening works on hash tables exist. Some of these are: ''Scatter storage techniques,'' by R. Morris, *CACM*, vol. 11, no. 1, January 1968, pp. 38-44; ''Key to address transform techniques: A fundamental performance study on large existing formatted files,'' by V. Lum, P. Yuen, and M. Dodd, *CACM*, vol. 14, no. 4, April 1971, pp. 228-239; ''The quadratic quotient method: A hash code eliminating secondary clustering,'' by J. Bell, *CACM*, vol. 13, no. 2, February 1970, pp. 107-109; ''Full table quadratic searching for scatter storage,'' by A. Day, *CACM*, vol. 13, no. 8, August 1970, pp. 481-482; ''Identifier search mechanisms: A survey and generalized model,'' by D. Severence, *ACM Computing Surveys*, vol. 6, no. 3, September 1974, pp. 175-194; ''Hash table methods,'' by W. Mauer and T. Lewis, *ACM Computing Surveys*, vol. 7, no. 1, March 1975, pp. 5-20; *The Art of Computer Programming: Sorting and Searching*, by D. Knuth, Addison-Wesley, Reading, Massachusetts, 1973; ''Reducing the retrieval time of scatter storage techniques,'' by R. Brent, *CACM*, vol. 16, no. 2, February 1973, pp. 105-109; ''General performance analysis of key-to-address transformation methods using an abstract file concept,'' by V. Lum, *CACM*, vol. 16, no. 10, October 1973, pp. 603-612; and ''The use of quadratic residue research,'' by C. E. Radke, *CACM*, vol. 13, no. 2, Feb. 1970, pp. 103-105.

In the literature Larson was the first to introduce a method he called dynamic hashing. Litwin followed. Fagin, et al., called their method extendible hashing. Fagin uses a directory scheme that doubles in size on expansion. Larson used a linked tree structure as the representation of the directory with pointers to pages in the leaves. The references are: Larson, P. ''Dynamic Hashing,'' *BIT*, vol. 18, 1978, 184-201; Litwin, W. ''Virtual hashing: a dynamically changing hashing,'' *Proc. Int. Conf. on Very Large Databases*, Berlin, 1978, 517-523; and Fagin, R., Nievergelt, J., Pippenger, N., and Strong, H.R., ''Extendible hashing - a fast access method for dynamic files,'' *ACM Trans. on Database Systems*, vol. 4, no. 3, Sept. 1979, 315-344.

An excellent overview of dynamic hashing techniques and variations can be found in: Enbody, R.J. and Du, H.C., ''Dynamic Hashing Schemes,'' *ACM Computing Surveys*, vol. 20, no 2, June 1988, 85-113.

Some other papers on dynamic hashing are: Flajolet, P. ''On the performance evaluation of extendible hashing and trie searching'', *Acta Informatica*, 20, 1983, 345-369; Lomet, D.B. ''Bounded Index Exponential Hashing,'' *ACM Trans. on Database Systems*, vol. 8, no. 1, March 1983, 136-165; Mendelson, H. ''Analysis of Extendible Hashing,'' *IEEE Trans. on Software Engineering*, vol. se-8, no. 6, November 1982, 611-619; and Ramamohanarao, K. and Lloyd, J.W. ''Dynamic Hashing Schemes,'' *The Computer Journal*, vol. 25, no. 4, 1982, 478-485.

Scholl introduces two methods to improve storage utilization by deferring the splitting of pages and handling overflows internally. This gives a tradeoff between storage utilization and access time. See: Scholl, M. ''New File Organizations Based on Dynamic Hashing'', *ACM Trans. of Database Systems*, vol. 6, no. 1, 1981, 194-211.

9.5 EXERCISES

1. Write an algorithm to delete identifier x from a hash table which uses hash function f and linear open addressing to resolve collisions. Show that simply setting the slot previously occupied by x to *BlankIdent* does not solve the problem. How must algorithm *LinearSearch* be modified so that a correct search is made in the situation when deletions are permitted? Where can a new identifier be inserted?

2. (a) Show that if quadratic searching is carried out in the sequence $(f(x) + q^2)$, $(f(x) + (q-1)^2)$, . . ., $(f(x) + 1)$, $f(x)$, $(f(x) - 1)$, . . ., $(f(x) - q^2)$ with $q = (b-1)/2$ then the address difference mod b between successive buckets being examined is

$$b - 2, \; b - 4, \; b - 6, \; . . ., \; 5, \; 3, \; 1, \; 1, \; 3, \; 5, \; . . ., \; b - 6, \; b - 4, \; b - 2$$

   (b) Write an algorithm to search a hash table $ht[0:b-1]$ of size b for the identifier x. Use f as the hash function and the quadratic probe scheme discussed in the text to resolve overflows. In case x is not in the table, it is to be entered. Use the results of part (a) to reduce the computations.

3. [Morris 1968] In random probing, the search for an identifier, X, in a hash table with b buckets is carried out by examining buckets $f(x)$, $f(x)+S(i)$, $1 \le i \le b-1$ where $S(i)$ is a pseudo random number. The random number generator must satisfy the property that every number from 1 to $b - 1$ must be generated exactly once.

   (a) Show that for a table of size 2^r, the following sequence of computations generates numbers with this property:

   Initialize R to 1 each time the search routine is called.
   On successive calls for a random number do the following:
   $R := R * 5$
   $R := \log \text{order } r + 2 \text{ bits of } R$
   $S(i) := R/4$

   (b) Write an algorithm, incorporating the above random number generator, to search and insert into a hash table using random probing and the middle of square hash function, f_m.

   It can be shown that for this method, the expected value for the average number of comparisons needed to search for X is $-(1/\alpha)\log(1 - \alpha)$ for large table sizes. α is the loading factor.

4. Write an algorithm to list all the identifiers in a hash table in lexicographic order. Assume the hash function f is $f(x) =$ first character of X and linear probing is used. How much time does your algorithm take?

5. Let the binary representation of identifier X be x_1x_2. Let $|x|$ denote the number of bits in x and let the first bit of x_1 be 1. Let $|x_1| = \lceil |x|/2 \rceil$ and $|x_2| = \lfloor |x|/2 \rfloor$. Consider the following hash function

$$F(x) = \text{middle } k \text{ bits of } (x_1 \text{ XOR } x_2)$$

where XOR is the exclusive or operator. Is this a uniform hash function if identifiers are drawn at random from the space of allowable Pascal identifiers? What can you say about the behavior of this hash function in a real symbol table usage?

6. [T. Gonzalez] Design a symbol table representation which allows you to search, insert, and delete an identifier x in $O(1)$ time. Assume that $1 \leq x \leq m$ and that $m + n$ units of space are available where n is the number of insertions to be made. (Hint: use two arrays $a[1..n]$ and $b[1..m]$ where $a[i]$ will be the i'th identifier inserted into the table. If x is the i'th identifier inserted then $b[x] = i$.) Write algorithms to search, insert and delete identifiers. Note that you cannot initialize either a or b to zero as this would take $O(n + m)$ time. Note that x is an integer.

7. [T. Gonzalez] Let $S = \{x_1, x_2, \ldots, x_n\}$ and $T = \{y_1, y_2, \ldots, y_r\}$ be two sets. Assume $1 \leq x_i \leq m, 1 \leq i \leq n$ and $1 \leq y_i \leq m, 1 \leq i \leq r$. Using the idea of Exercise 6 write an algorithm to determine if $S \subseteq T$. Your algorithm should work in $O(r + n)$ time. Since $S \equiv T$ iff $S \subseteq T$ and $T \subseteq S$, this implies that one can determine in linear time if two sets are equivalent. How much space is needed by your algorithm?

8. [T. Gonzalez] Using the idea of Exercise 6 write an $O(n + m)$ time algorithm to carry out the function of algorithm *verify2* of Section 7.1. How much space does your algorithm need?

9. Using the notation of Section 9.2.4 show that when linear open addressing is used

$$S_n = \frac{1}{n} \sum_{i=0}^{n-1} U_i$$

Using this equation and the approximate equality

$$U_n \approx \frac{1}{2} \left[1 + \frac{1}{(1-\alpha)^2} \right] \quad \text{where } \alpha = \frac{n}{b}$$

show that

$$S_n \approx \frac{1}{2}\left[1 + \frac{1}{(1 - \alpha)}\right]$$

10. [Guttag] The following set of operations defines a symbol table that handles a langauge with block structure. Give a set of axioms for these operations:

> *INIT* - creates an empty table;
> *ENTERB* - indicates a new block has been entered;
> *ADD* - places an identifier and its attributes in the table;
> *LEAVEB* - deletes all identifiers which are defined in the innermost block;
> *RETRIEVE* - returns the attributes of the most recently defined identifier;
> *ISINB* - returns true if the identifer is defined in the innermost block else false.

11. The text points out that nonuniform distributions of keys will cause a skewed directory and a waste of directory space. One way to avoid this problem in the directory scheme is to not store the directory as a table but as a forest of tries. A new key is hashed to one of the tries and then its nodes are traversed to a leaf node which points to a page containing the desired record. Splitting is still required. The tries grow and contract with respect to the file. Write out the algorithms for maintaining a trie as a directory.

12. In extendible hashing, given a directory of size d, suppose two pointers point to the same page. All identifiers will share a number of low order bits in common. How many? If four pointers point to the same page, how many bits do the identifiers have in common?

13. Another way of handling overflows in directory dynamic hashing is to permit a page to be divided into as many multiple pages as necessary to hold all identifiers that hash to that page. Then you assign a limit on the size of the directory you are willing to accept and once that size has been reached, a page just continues to grow. Modify the algorithms in Program 9.4 to implement this strategy.

14. Prove that in directory-based dynamic hashing a page can be pointed at by a number of pointers which is a power of 2.

15. We have not talked much about how to organize the identifiers within a page for fast retrieval. Consider an unordered list, an ordered list, and hashing and compare their merits.

16. Procedure *insert* is almost a complete Pascal program except for a few lines of pseudo code. Replace the pseudo code by actual Pascal code that places all identifiers in page p into the *temp* area and then rehashes those identifiers back into either page p or q.

17. Program 9.4 contains a reference to a procedure *coalesce* that combines the identifiers in two pages into a single page. Using the types and procedures already defined, write a Pascal version of this procedure.

18. Take the formula given by Mendelson for the number of leaf pages required to store k records in a directory-based dynamic hashing scheme and formally derive the approximation that $L(k)$ is about equal to $k/(p\ln 2)$ where p is the page size.

19. Larson has suggested using open addressing in a directoryless dynamic hashing method to handle overflows. The problem is that those pages that have yet to be split will have the most overflows, but these pages are stored contiguously. Instead, he suggests that pages be alternately split, so next to an unsplit page is a split page. Show how the hashing function must be rewritten to handle this scheme.

CHAPTER 10
ADVANCED TREE STRUCTURES

10.1 MIN-MAX HEAPS

A *double-ended priority queue* is a data structure that supports the following operations:

(1)   Insert an element with arbitrary key.

(2)   Delete an element with the largest key.

(3)   Delete an element with the smallest key.

When only insertion and one of the above two deletion operations are to be supported, a min heap or a max heap may be used (see Chapter 5). A min-max heap supports all of the above operations.

Definition A *min-max heap* is a complete binary tree such that if it is not empty, each element has a field called *key*. Alternating levels of this tree are min levels and max levels, respectively. The root is on a min level. Let x be any node in a min-max heap. If x is on a min (max) level then the element in x has the minimum (maximum) key from amongst all elements in the subtree with root x. A node on a min (max) level is called a *min* (*max*) node.

An example 12 element min-max heap is shown in Figure 10.1. The value in each node is the key of the element in that node.

Suppose we wish to insert the element with key 5 into this min-max heap. Following the insertion, we will have a 13 element min-max heap. This has the shape shown in Figure 10.2. As in the case of heaps, the insertion algorithm for min-max heaps follows the path from the new node j to the root. Comparing the new key 5 with the key 10 that is in the parent of j, we see that since the node with key 10 is on a min level and $5 < 10$, 5 is guaranteed to be smaller than all keys in nodes that are both on max levels and on the path from j to the root. Hence, the min-max heap property is to be verified only with respect to min nodes on the path from j to the root. First, the element with key 10 is

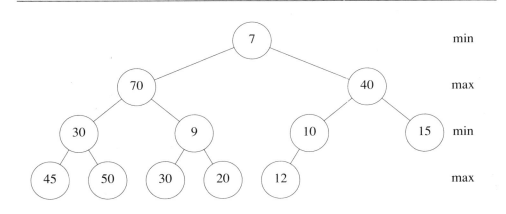

Figure 10.1 A 12 element min-max heap

moved to node j. Then the element with key 7 is moved to the former position of 10. Finally, the new element with key 5 is inserted into the root. The min-max heap following the insertion is shown in Figure 10.3(a).

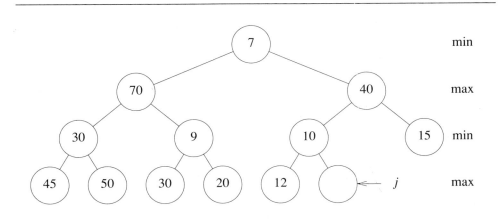

Figure 10.2 Min-max heap of Figure 10.1 with new node j

Next, suppose we wish to insert an element with key 80 into the min-max heap of Figure 10.1. The resulting min-max heap has 13 elements and has the shape shown in Figure 10.2. Since $80 > 10$ and 10 is on a min level, we are assured that 80 is larger than all keys in nodes that are both on min levels and on the path from j to the root. Hence,

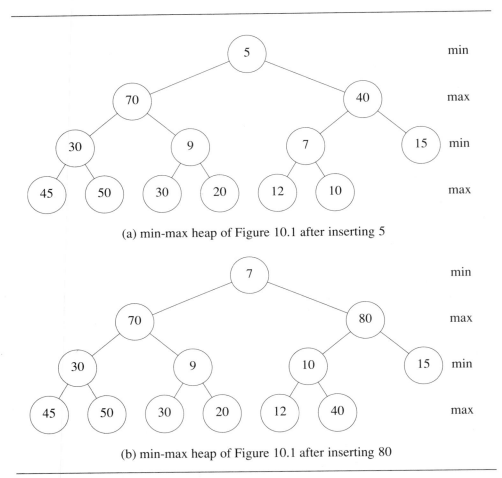

(a) min-max heap of Figure 10.1 after inserting 5

(b) min-max heap of Figure 10.1 after inserting 80

Figure 10.3 Insertion into a min-max heap

the min-max heap property is to be verified only with respect to max nodes on the path from j to the root. There is only one such node in the min-max heap of Figure 10.1. This node has key 40. The element with key 40 is moved to j and the new element inserted into the node formerly occupied by this element. The resulting min-max heap is shown in Figure 10.3(b).

The preceding insertion examples lead to the insertion procedure *MinMaxInsert* (Program 10.1). The data type *MinMaxHeap* is defined as:

type *MinMaxHeap* = **array** [1.. *MaxElements*] of *element*;

and *element* has at least the field *key*. A min-max heap is stored in a one dimensional array using the standard array representation of a complete binary tree (see Section 5.3). Procedure *MinMaxInsert* makes use of the two procedures *VerifyMax* and *VerifyMin* and the function *level*. The procedure *VerifyMax* (Program 10.2) begins at a max node *i* and follows along the path of max nodes from *i* to the root of the min-max heap *h*. It searches for the correct node to insert the element *x*. This node has the property that all max nodes above it and on the path to the root have key values at least as large as *x. key*. Further, all max nodes below it and on the path from *i* have key values smaller than *x. key*. During the search, max nodes with key smaller than *x. key* are moved one max level down. The procedure *VerifyMin* is quite similar to *VerifyMax* except that it begins at a min node *i* and follows along the path of min nodes from *i* to the root. *x* is inserted into one of the encountered min nodes so as to preserve the min-max heap property. The function *level* determines whether a node is on a min or a max level of a min-max heap. The formal development of *VerifyMin* and *level* is left as an exercise.

```
procedure MinMaxInsert (var h : MinMaxHeap ; var n : integer ; x : element );
{Insert x into the min-max heap h which presently has n elements}
var p : integer;
begin
    if n = MaxElements then MinMaxFull
    else begin
        n := n + 1; p := n div 2; {p is the parent of the new node}
        if p = 0 then h [1] := x {insertion into an initially empty heap}
        else case level (p) of
            min: if x. key < h [p ]. key
                then begin {follow min levels}
                    h [n ] := h [p ];
                    VerifyMin (h, p, x);
                end
                else VerifyMax (h, n, x); {follow max levels}
            max: if x. key > h [p ]. key
                then begin {follow max levels}
                    h [n ] := h [p ];
                    VerifyMax (h, p, x);
                end
                else VerifyMin (h, n, x); {follow min levels}
            end; {of case and if p = 0}
    end; {of if n = MaxElements}
end;
```

Program 10.1 Procedure to insert into a min-max heap

---

procedure *VerifyMax* (**var** *h* : *MinMaxHeap* ; *i* : **integer** ; *x* : *element*);
{Follow max nodes from the max node *i* to the root and insert *x* at proper place}
var *gp* : **integer**;
begin
   gp := *i* **div** 4; {grandparent of *i*}
   while *gp* < > 0 **do**
    if *x. key* > *h* [*gp*]. *key* **then begin** {move *h* [*gp*] to *h* [*p*]}
                h [*i*] := *h* [*gp*];
                i := *gp*; *gp* := *gp* **div** 4;
            end
         else *gp* := 0; {**x is to be inserted into node *i***}
   h [*i*] := *x*;
end;

Program 10.2 Procedure *VerifyMax*

The correctness of *MinMaxInsert* is easily established. Further, since a min-max heap with *n* elements has O(log*n*) levels, the complexity of procedure *MinMaxInsert* is O(log*n*).

Let us now take a look at deletion from a min-max heap. If we wish to delete the element with smallest key, then this element is in the root. In the case of the min-max heap of Figure 10.1, we are to delete the element with key 7. Following the deletion, we will be left with a min-max heap that has 11 elements. Its shape is that shown in Figure 10.4. The node with key 12 is deleted from the heap and the element with key 12 is reinserted into the heap. As in the case of deletion from a min or max heap, the reinsertion is done by examining the nodes of Figure 10.4 from the root down towards the leaves.

In a general situation, we are to reinsert an element *x* into a min-max heap, *h*, whose root is empty. We consider the two cases:

(1)   *The root has no children.* In this case *x* is to be inserted into the root.

(2)   *The root has at least one child.* Now, the smallest key in the min-max heap is in one of the children or grandchildren of the root. We determine which of these nodes has the smallest key. Let this be node *k*. The following possibilities need to be considered:

    (a)   *x. key* ≤ *h* [*k*]. *key*. *x* may be inserted into the root as there is no element in *h* with key smaller than *x. key*.

    (b)   *x. key* > *h* [*k*]. *key* and *k* is a child of the root. Since *k* is a max node, it has no descendants with key larger than *h* [*k*]. *key*. Hence, node *k* has no descendants with key larger than *x. key*. So, the element *h* [*k*] may be moved to the root and *x* inserted into node *k*.

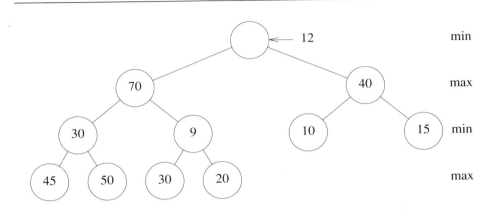

Figure 10.4 Shape of Figure 10.1 following a delete min

(c) $x.key > h[k].key$ and k is a grandchild of the root. In this case too, $h[k]$ may be moved to the root. Let p be the parent of k. If $x.key > h[p].key$, then $h[p]$ and x are to be interchanged. This ensures that the max node p contains the largest key in the sub-heap with root p. At this point, we are faced with the problem of inserting x into the sub-heap with root p. The root of this sub-min-max heap is presently empty. This is quite similar to our initial situation where we were to insert x into the min-max heap h with root 1 and node 1 is initially empty. Hence, we may iterate on the above.

In the case of our example, $x.key = 12$ and the smallest key in the children and grandchildren of the root node is 9. Let k denote the node that contains this key. Let p be its parent. Since, $9 < 12$ and k is a grandchild of the root, we are in case 2 (c). The element with key 9 (i.e., $h[k]$) is moved to the root. Since $x.key = 12 < 70 = h[p].key$, we do not perform the interchange between x and $h[p]$. The present configuration is shown in Figure 10.5. We must now reinsert x into the sub-min-max heap with root k. The node with the smallest key from among the children and grandchildren of node k has the key 20. Since $12 < 20$, we are in case 2 (a) and the element x is inserted into $h[k]$.

The preceding discussion results in the procedure *DeleteMin* (Program 10.3). This procedure uses a function *MinChildGrandChild* (i) that determines the child or grandchild of the node i that has the smallest key. In case both a child and a grandchild of i have the smallest key, it is preferable that *MinChildGrandChild* return the address of the child as this prevents further iterations of the **while** loop of *DeleteMin*. Notice that even though *DeleteMin* does not explicitly check for the case when $n = 1$ initially, this is handled correctly and an empty min-max heap results from the deletion.

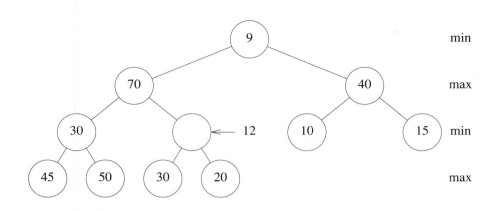

Figure 10.5 Figure 10.4 following the move of the element with key 9

In each iteration of the **while** loop of *DeleteMin* a constant amount of work is done. Also, in each iteration (except possibly the last), *i* moves down two levels. Since a min-max heap is a complete binary tree, *h* has O(log*n*) levels. Hence, the complexity of *DeleteMin* is O(log*n*).

The procedure to delete the element with maximum key is similar *DeleteMin*. We leave its development as an exercise.

10.2 DEAPS

A deap is a double-ended heap that supports the double-ended priority queue operations of insert, delete min, and delete max. As in the case of the min-max heap, these operations take logarithmic time on a deap. However, the deap is faster by a constant factor and the algorithms are simpler.

Definition: A *deap* is a complete binary tree which is either empty or satisfies the following properties:

(1)   The root contains no element.

(2)   The left subtree is a min-heap.

(3)   The right subtree is a max-heap.

(4)   If the right subtree is not empty, then let *i* be any node in the left subtree. Let *j* be the corresponding node in the right subtree. If such a *j* does not exist, then let *j* be the node in the right subtree that corresponds to the parent of *i*. The key in node *i* is less than or equal to that in *j*. □

```
procedure DeleteMin (var h : MinMaxHeap ; var y : element ; var n : integer);
{Delete an element with minimum key in the min-max heap h.}
{n is the number of elements in h.  The deleted element is returned in y.}
var i, j, k, p : integer;
    x, t : element;
    NotDone : boolean;
begin
  if n = 0 then EmptyMinMaxHeap
  else begin
          {Save root and last elements and update heap size}
          y := h [1]; x := h [n ]; n := n−1;

          {Initialize for reinsertion of x}
          NotDone := true; i := 1; {empty node} j := n div 2; {last node with a child}

          {Find place to insert x}
          while (i <= j) and NotDone do
          begin {i has a child, case (2)}
              k := MinChildGrandChild (i);
              if x. key <= h [k]. key
              then NotDone := false {case 2(a), x is to be inserted into h [i]}
              else begin {case 2(b) or (c)}
                      h [i] := h [k];
                      if k <= 2*i +1
                      then NotDone := false {k is a child of i, case 2(a)}
                      else begin {k is a grandchild of i, case 2(c)}
                              p := k div 2; {parent of k}
                              if x. .key > h [p ]. key
                              then begin t := h [p ]; h [p ] := x ; x := t; end;
                          end; {of if k <= 2*i +1}
                      i := k;
                  end; {of if x. key <= h [k]. key}
          end; {of while}
          h [i] := x; {insert x}
      end; {of if n = 0}
end; {of procedure DeleteMin}
```

Program 10.3 Procedure to delete the element with minimum key

An example 11 element deap is shown in Figure 10.6. The root of the min-heap contains 5 while that of the max-heap contains 45. The min-heap node with 10 corresponds to the max-heap node with 25 while the min-heap node with 15 corresponds to the max-heap node with 20. For the node containing 9, the node j defined in property (4) of the deap definition is the max-heap node that contains 40.

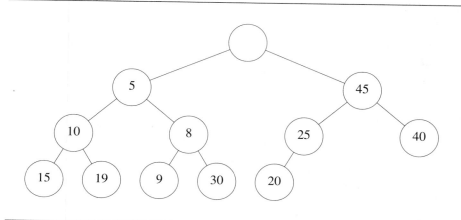

Figure 10.6 An 11 element deap

From the definition of a deap, it is evident that in an n element deap, $n > 1$, the min element is in the root of the min-heap while the max element is in the root of the max-heap. If $n = 1$, then the min and max elements are the same and are in the root of the min-heap. Since a deap is a complete binary tree, it may stored as an implicit data structure in a one dimensional array much the same way as min-, max-, and min-max heaps are stored. In the case of a deap, position 1 of the array is not utilized (we may simply begin the array indexing at 2 rather than at 1). Let n denote the last occupied position in this array. Then the number of elements in the deap is $n - 1$. If i is a node in the min-heap, then its corresponding node in the max heap is $i + 2^{\lfloor \log_2 i \rfloor - 1}$. Hence the j defined in property (4) of the definition is given by:

$$j := i + 2^{\lfloor \log_2 i \rfloor - 1};$$
$$\textbf{if } j > n \textbf{ then } j := j \textbf{ div } 2;$$

Notice that if property (4) of the deap definition is satisfied by all leaf nodes i of the min-heap, then it is satisfied by all remaining nodes of the min-heap too.

The double-ended priority queue operations are particularly easy to implement on a deap. The complexity of each operation is bounded by the height of the deap which is logarithmic in the number of elements in the deap. First, consider inserting an element into a deap. Suppose we wish to insert an element with key 4 into the deap of Figure

10.6. Following this insertion, the deap will have 12 elements in it and will thus have the shape shown in Figure 10.7. *j* points to the new node in the deap.

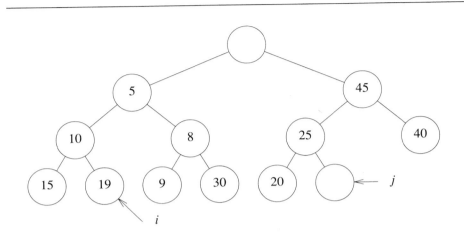

Figure 10.7 Shape of a 12 element deap

The insertion process begins by comparing the key 4 to the key in *j*'s corresponding node, *i*, in the min-heap. This node contains a 19. To satisfy property (4), we move the 19 to node *j*. Now, if we use the min-heap insertion algorithm to insert 4 into position *i*, we get the deap of Figure 10.8.

If instead of inserting a 4, we were to insert a 30 into the deap of Figure 10.6, then the resulting deap has the same shape as in Figure 10.7. Comparing 30 with the key 19 in the corresponding node *i*, we see that property (4) may be satisfied by using the max-heap insertion algorithm to insert 30 into position *j*. This results in the deap of Figure 10.9.

The case when the new node, *j*, is a node of the min-heap is symmetric to the case just discussed. The procedure to insert into a deap is given in Program 10.4. The data type *deap* is defined to be an array [2 .. *MaxElements*] of *element*. *n* is the position of the last element in the deap. *n* =1 denotes an empty deap.

The procedures and functions used by *DeapInsert* are specified below:

(1) *DeapFull*. This signals an error. The insertion cannot proceed as there is no space in the deap to accommodate the additional element.

(2) *MaxHeap*. This is a boolean valued function that returns the value **true** iff *n* is a position in the max-heap of the deap.

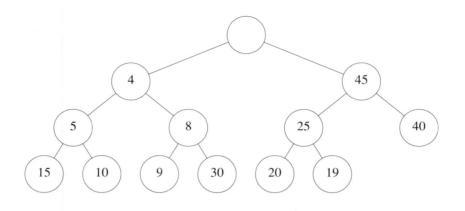

Figure 10.8 Deap of Figure 10.6 following the insertion of 4

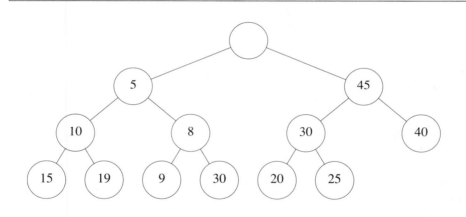

Figure 10.9 Deap of Figure 10.6 following the insertion of 30

(3) *MinPartner*. This function computes the min-heap node that corresponds to the max-heap position n. This is given by $n - 2^{\lfloor \log_2 n \rfloor - 1}$.

(4) *MaxPartner*. This function computes the max-heap node that corresponds to the parent of the min-heap position n. This is given by $(n + 2^{\lfloor \log_2 n \rfloor - 1})$ **div** 2.

```
procedure DeapInsert (var d : deap ; var n : integer ; x : element );
{Insert x into the deap d of size n −1}
var i : integer;
begin
    if n =MaxElements then DeapFull
    else begin
            n :=n +1;
            if n = 2 then d [2] := x {insertion into an initially empty deap}
            else case MaxHeap (n) of
                    true: begin {n is a position in the max-heap}
                            i := MinPartner (n);
                            if x. key < d [i ]. key
                            then begin
                                    d [n ] := d [i ];
                                    MinInsert (d, i, x);
                                end
                            else MaxInsert (d, n, x);
                    false: begin {n is a position in the min-heap}
                            i := MaxPartner (n);
                            if x. key > d [i ]. key
                            then begin
                                    d [n ] := d [i ];
                                    MaxInsert (d, i, x);
                                end
                            else MinInsert (d, n, x);
                end; {of case and if n = 2}
    end; {of if n = MaxElements}
end;
```

Program 10.4 Procedure to insert into a deap

(5)   The procedures *InsertMin* and *InsertMax* insert an element into a specified position of a min- and max-heap, respectively. This is done by following the path from this position towards the root of the respective heap. Elements are moved down as necessary until the correct place to insert the new element is found. This process differs from that used in Chapter 5 to insert into a min- or max-heap only in that the root is now at position 2 or 3 rather than at 1.

Now consider the delete min operation. A high level description of the deletion process is given in Program 10.5. The strategy is to first transform the deletion of the element from the root of the min-heap to the deletion of an element from a leaf position in the min-heap. This is done by following a root to leaf path in the min-heap ensuring that the min-heap properties are satisfied on the preceding levels of the heap. This process has the effect of shifting the empty position initially at the min-heap root to a leaf node p. This leaf node is then filled by the element, t, initially in the last position of the deap. The insertion of t into position p of the min-heap is done as in *DeapInsert* except that the specification of *MaxPartner* (i) is changed to:

$$j := i + 2^{\lfloor \log_2 i \rfloor - 1};$$
$$\textbf{if } j > n \textbf{ then } j := j \textbf{ div } 2;$$

---

procedure *DeapDeleteMin* (**var** d : *deap* ; **var** n : **integer** ; **var** x : *element*);
{Delete the min element from the deap d. The deleted element is returned in x.}
var i : **integer**;
    t : *element*;
begin
  if $n < 2$ **then** *DeapEmpty*
  else begin
        $x := d[2]$;
        $t := d[n]; n := n-1$;
        $i := 2$;
        while i has a child **do**
        begin
          Let j be the child with smaller key;
          $d[i] := d[j]$;
          $i := j$;
        end;
        Do a deap insertion of t at position i;
      end; {of **if** $n < 2$}
end;

Program 10.5 Delete min

Consider the deap of Figure 10.6. We remove the last element (i.e., the one with key 20) from the deap. Next, the vacancy created in position 2 by the deletion of the min element is filled by moving from position 2 to a leaf. Each move is preceded by a step that moves the smaller of the elements in the children of the current node up. Then, we move to the position previously occupied by the moved element. First, the 8 is moved up. Then the 9 is moved to its parent. Now we have an empty leaf. To do a deap insertion at the leaf formerly occupied by the 9, we compare 20 with the key 40 in its max partner. Since 20 < 40, no exchange is needed and we proceed to insert the 20 into the min-heap beginning at the empty position. This results in the deap of Figure 10.10.

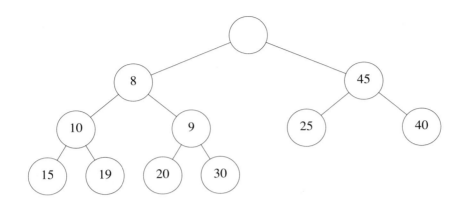

Figure 10.10 Deap of Figure 10.6 following a delete min

One may verify that Program 10.5 works correctly regardless of whether the last position in the deap is in the min- or max-heap. The delete max operation is performed in a similar manner.

10.3 LEFTIST TREES

In the preceding section we extended the definition of a priority queue by requiring that both delete max and delete min operations be permissible. In this section, we consider a different extension. Suppose that in addition to the normal priority queue operations, we are also required to support the operation of *combine*. This requires us to combine two priority queues into a single priority queue. One application for this is when the server for one priority queue shuts down. At this time, it is necessary to combine its priority queue with that of a functioning server.

Let n be the total number of elements in the two priority queues that are to be combined. If heaps are used to represent priority queues, then the combine operation takes $O(n)$ time. Using a leftist tree, the combine operation as well as the normal priority queue operations take logarithmic time.

In order to define a leftist tree, we need to introduce the concept of an extended binary tree. An *extended binary* tree is a binary tree in which all empty binary subtrees have been replaced by a square node. Figure 10.11 shows two example binary trees. Their corresponding extended binary trees are shown in Figure 10.12. The square nodes in an extended binary tree are called *external nodes*. The original (circular) nodes of the binary tree are called *internal nodes*.

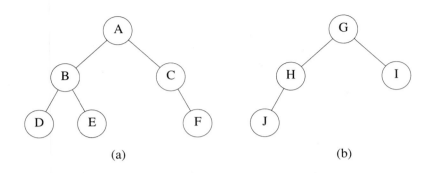

Figure 10.11 Two binary trees

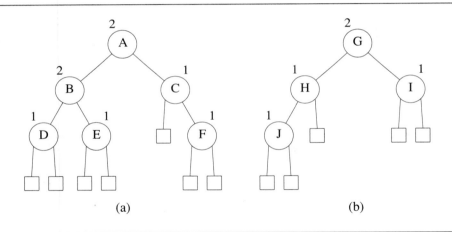

Figure 10.12 Extended binary trees corresponding to Figure 10.11

Let x be a node in an extended binary tree. Let *LeftChild* (x) and *RightChild* (x), respectively, denote the left and right children of the internal node x. Define *shortest* (x) to be the length of a shortest path from x to an external node. It is easy to see that *shortest* (x) satisfies the following recurrence:

$$shortest\,(x) = \begin{cases} 0 \text{ if } x \text{ is an external node} \\ 1 + \min\,\{shortest\,(LeftChild\,(x)),\, shortest\,(RightChild\,(x))\} \text{ otherwise} \end{cases}$$

The number outside each internal node x of Figure 10.12 is the value of *shortest* (x).

Definition: A *leftist tree* is a binary tree such that if it is not empty, then

$$shortest\,(LeftChild\,(x)) \geq shortest\,(RightChild\,(x))$$

for every internal node x. □

The binary tree of Figure 10.11(a) which corresponds to the extended binary tree of Figure 10.12(a) is not a leftist tree as $shortest\,(LeftChild\,(C)) = 0$ while $shortest\,(RightChild(C)) = 1$. The binary tree of Figure 10.11(b) is a leftist tree.

Lemma 10.1: Let x be the root of a leftist tree that has n (internal) nodes.

(a) $n \geq 2^{shortest(x)} - 1$

(b)   The rightmost root to external node path is the shortest root to external node path. Its length is *shortest* (x).

Proof: (a) From the definition of *shortest* (x) it follows that there are no external nodes on the first *shortest* (x) levels of the leftist tree. Hence, the leftist tree has at least

$$\sum_{i=1}^{shortest(x)} 2^{i-1} = 2^{shortest(x)} - 1$$

internal nodes.

(b) This follows directly from the definition of a leftist tree. □

Leftist trees are represented using nodes that have the fields: *LeftChild*, *RightChild*, *shortest*, and *data*. We assume that *data* is a record type with at least the field *key*. We note that the concept of an external node is introduced merely to arrive at clean definitions. The external nodes are never physically present in the representation of a leftist tree. Rather the appropriate child field of the parent of an external node is set to **nil**.

Definition: A *min-leftist tree* (*max leftist tree*) is a leftist tree in which the key value in each node is no larger (smaller) than the key values in its children (if any). In other words, a min (max) leftist tree is a leftist tree that is also a min (max) tree. □

Two min leftist trees are shown in Figure 10.13. The number inside a node x is the key of the element in x and the number outside x is *shortest* (x). The operations insert, delete min (delete max), and combine can be performed in logarithmic time using a min (max) leftist tree. We shall continue our discussion using min leftist trees.

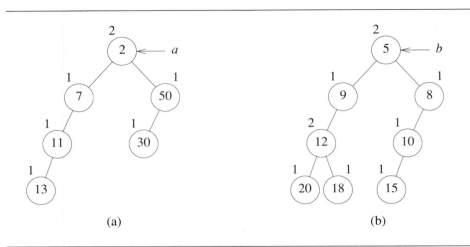

(a)   (b)

Figure 10.13 Example min leftist trees

The insert and delete min operations can both be performed by using the combine operation. To insert an element x into a min leftist tree a, we first create a min leftist tree b that contains the single element x. Then we combine the min leftist trees a and b. To delete the min element from a non empty min leftist tree a, we combine the min leftist trees $a \uparrow . LeftChild$ and $a \uparrow . RightChild$ and delete the node a.

The combine operation is itself quite simple. Suppose that the min leftist trees a and b are to be combined. First a new binary tree containing all elements in a and b is obtained by following the rightmost paths in a and/or b. This binary tree has the property that the key in each node is no larger than the keys in its children (if any). Next, the left and right subtrees of nodes are interchanged as necessary to convert this binary tree into a leftist tree.

As an example, consider combining the min leftist trees a and b of Figure 10.13. To obtain a binary tree that contains all the elements in a and b and that satisfies the required relationship between parent and child keys, we first compare the root keys 2 and 5. Since $2 < 5$, the new binary tree should have 2 in its root. We shall leave the left subtree of a unchanged and combine the right subtree of a and the entire binary tree b. The resulting binary tree will become the new right subtree of a. When combining the right subtree of a and the binary tree b, we notice that $5 < 50$. So, 5 should be in the root of the combined tree. Now, we proceed to combine the subtrees with root 8 and 50. Since $8 < 50$ and 8 has no right subtree, we can make the subtree with root 50 the right subtree of 8. This gives us the binary tree of Figure 10.14(a). Hence, the result of combining the right subtree of a and the tree b is the tree of Figure 10.14(b). When this is made the right subtree of a, we get the binary tree of Figure 10.14(c). To convert this into a leftist tree, we begin at the last modified root (i.e., 8) and trace back to the overall root ensuring that *shortest* (*LeftChild* ( )) ≥ *shortest* (*RightChild* ( )). This inequality holds at 8 but not at 5 and 2. Simply interchanging the left and right subtrees at these nodes causes the inequality to hold. The result is the leftist tree of Figure 10.14(d).

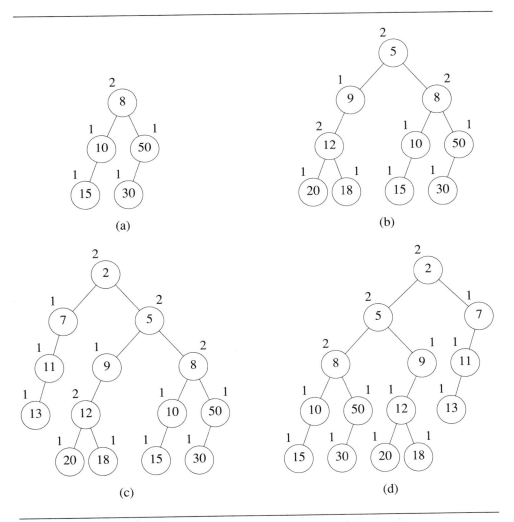

(a)

(b)

(c)

(d)

Figure 10.14 Combining the min leftist trees of Figure 10.13

The procedure to combine two leftist trees is given in Program 10.6. This makes use of the recursive procedure *MinUnion* that actually combines two nonempty leftist trees. This procedure intertwines the two steps: (1) create a binary tree that contains all

```
procedure MinCombine (var a, b : LeftistTree);
{Combine the two min leftist trees a and b.  The resulting min leftist}
{tree is returned in a and b is set to nil.}
begin
    if a = nil then a := b
                else if b < > nil then  MinUnion (a, b);
    b := nil;
end; {of MinCombine}

procedure MinUnion (var a, b : LeftistTree);
{Recursive procedure to combine two nonempty min leftist trees}
var u : element; t : LeftistTree;
begin
    {Set a to be min leftist tree with smaller root}
    if a ↑. data . key > b ↑. data . key
    then begin t := a; a := b; b := t; end;

    {Create binary tree such that the smallest key in each subtree is in the root}
    if a ↑. RightChild = nil
    then a ↑. RightChild := b
    else MinUnion (a ↑. RightChild,  b);

    {Leftist tree property}
    if a ↑. LeftChild = nil
    then begin {interchange subtrees}
            a ↑. LeftChild := a ↑. RightChild; a ↑. RightChild := nil;
        end
    else if a ↑. LeftChild ↑. shortest < a ↑. RightChild ↑. shortest
    then begin {interchange a's subtrees}
            u := a ↑. LeftChild; a ↑. LeftChild := a ↑. RightChild; a ↑. RightChild := u;
        end;

    {Set shortest field of a}
    if a ↑. RightChild = nil
    then a ↑. shortest := 1
    else a ↑. shortest := a ↑. RightChild ↑. shortest + 1;
end; {of MinUnion}
```

Program 10.6 Combining two min leftist trees

the elements and such that the root of each subtree has the largest key in that subtree; and (2) ensure that each node has a left subtree whose *shortest* value is greater than or equal to that of its right subtree. Since *MinUnion* moves down the leftmost paths in the two leftist trees being combined and since the lengths of these paths is at most logarithmic in the number of elements in each tree, the combining of two leftist trees with a total of n elements is done in time O(log$n$).

10.4 FIBONNACI HEAPS

A Fibonacci heap is a data structure that supports efficiently all the leftist tree operations as well as two other operations to be specified later. Unlike leftist trees where an individual operation can be performed in O(log$n$) time, it is possible that certain individual operations performed on a Fibonacci heap may take O(n) time. However, if we amortize part of the cost of expensive operations over the inexpensive ones, then the amortized complexity of an individual operation is either O(1) or O(log$n$) depending on the type (insert, combine, delete min, etc.) of the operation.

Let us examine the concept of cost (we shall use the terms *cost* and *complexity* interchangeably) amortization more closely. Suppose that a sequence I1, I2, D1, I3, I4, I5, I6, D2, I7 of insert and delete min operations is performed. Assume that the *actual cost* of each of the seven inserts is one. By this, we mean that each insert takes one unit of time. Further, suppose that the delete min operations D1 and D2 have an actual cost of eight and ten, respectively. The total cost of the sequence of operations is therefore 25. In an amortization scheme we charge some of the actual cost of an operation to other operations. This reduces the charged cost of some operations and increases that of others. The *amortized cost* of an operation is the total cost charged to it. The cost transferring (amortization) scheme is required to be such that the sum of the amortized costs of the operations is greater than or equal to the sum of their actual costs. If we charge one unit of the cost of a delete min to each of the inserts since the last delete min (if any), then two units of the cost of D1 get transferred to I1 and I2 (the charged cost of each increases by one) and four units of the cost of D2 get transferred to I3 - I6. The amortized cost of each of I1 - I6 becomes two, that of I7 is equal to its actual cost (i.e., one), and that of each of D1 and D2 becomes 6. The sum of the amortized costs is 25 which is the same as the sum of the actual costs.

Now suppose we can prove that no matter what sequence of insert and delete min operations is performed, we can charge costs in such a way that the amortized cost of each insert is no more than two and that of each delete min is no more than six. This will enable us to make the claim that the actual cost of any insert / delete min sequence is no more that $2*i+6*d$ where i and d are, respectively, the number of insert and delete min operations in the sequence. Suppose that the actual cost of a delete min is no more than ten, while that of an insert is one. Using actual costs, we can conclude that the sequence cost is no more than $i + 10 * d$. Combining these two bounds, we obtain min$\{2 * i + 6 * d, i + 10 * d\}$ as a bound on the sequence cost. Hence, using the notion of cost amortization it is possible to obtain tighter bounds on the complexity of a sequence of operations. We shall use the notion of cost amortization to show that while individual delete operations on an F-heap may be expensive, the cost of any sequence of F-heap operations is actually quite small.

As in the case of heaps and leftist trees, there are two varieties of Fibonacci heaps: min and max. A *min-Fibonacci heap* is a collection of min-trees while a *max-Fibonacci heap* is a collection of max-trees. We shall explicitly consider min Fibonacci heaps only. These will be referred to as *F-heaps*. Figure 10.15 shows an example F-heap that is comprised of three min-trees.

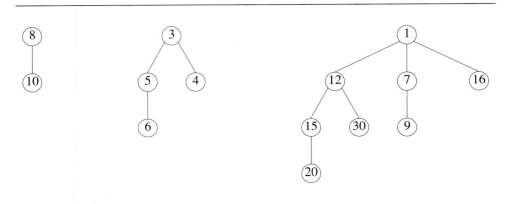

Figure 10.15 An F-heap with three min-trees

Using F-heaps, we can perform an insert and a combine in O(1) actual and amortized time and a delete min in O(log$n$) amortized time. Our initial discussion will be limited to these three F-heap operations. Later, we shall introduce the operations: (1) *decrease key*, decrease the key of a specified node by a given positive amount and (2) *delete*, delete the element in a specified node. The first of these can be done in O(1) amortized time and the second in O(log$n$) amortized time. An application of the decrease key operation will be studied at the end of this section.

F-heaps are represented using nodes that have the fields: *degree, child, LeftLink, RightLink,* and *data* (later, when we consider the two additional F-heap operations, we shall need the additional fields *parent* and *ChildCut*). The *parent* field is used to point to the node's parent (if any); the *degree* of a node is the number of children it has; the *child* field is used to point to any one of its children (if any); the *LeftLink* and *RightLink* fields are used to maintain doubly linked circular lists of siblings. The definition of the *Child-Cut* field is provided later. All the children of a node form a doubly linked circular list and the node points to one of these children. Additionally, the roots of the min-trees that comprise an F-heap are linked to form a doubly linked circular list. The F-heap is then pointed at by a single pointer to the min-tree root with smallest key.

Figure 10.16 shows the representation for the example of Figure 10.15. *child* fields are shown by broken arrows and *parent* fields by solid arrows. To enhance the readability of this figure, we have used bidirectional arrows to join together nodes that are in the same doubly linked circular list. When such a list contains only one node, no such arrows are drawn. Each of the key sets: {10}, {6}, {5,4}, {20}, {15, 30}, {9}, {12, 7, 16}, and {8, 1, 3} denotes the keys in one of the doubly linked circular lists of Figure 10.16. *a* is the pointer to the F-heap. Note that an empty F-heap has a **nil** pointer.

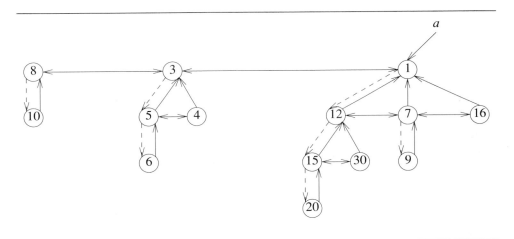

Figure 10.16 F-heap of Figure 10.15 showing parent pointers and sibling lists

An element x may be inserted into an F-heap a by first putting x into a new node and then inserting this node into the doubly linked circular list pointed at by a. The pointer a is reset to this new node only if a is either **nil** or the key of x is smaller than the key in the node pointed at by a. It is evident that these insertion steps can be performed in O(1) time.

To combine two nonempty F-heaps a and b, we combine the top doubly linked circular lists of a and b into a single doubly linked circular list. The new F-heap pointer is either a or b depending on which has the smaller key. This can be determined with a single comparison. Since two doubly linked circular lists can be combined into a single one in O(1) time, a combine takes only O(1) time.

Now, let's take a look at the delete min operation. Let a be the pointer of the F-heap from which the min element is to be deleted. If a is **nil**, then the F-heap is empty and a deletion cannot be performed. Assume that a is not **nil**. a points to the node that contains the min element. This node is deleted from its doubly linked circular list. The new F-heap consists of the remaining min-trees and the sub min-trees of the deleted root. Figure 10.17 shows the situation for the example of Figure 10.15.

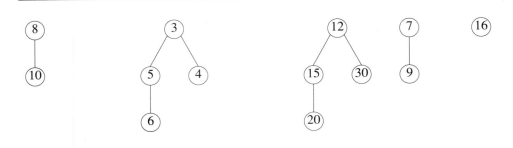

Figure 10.17 The F-heap of Figure 10.15 following the deletion of the min element

Before forming the doubly linked circular list of min-tree roots, we repeatedly combine together pairs of min-trees that have the same degree (the degree of a nonempty min-tree is the degree of its root). *This min-tree combining is done by making the min-tree whose root has larger key a subtree of the other (ties are broken arbitrarily).* When two min-trees are combined, the degree of the resulting min-tree is one larger than the original degree of each min-tree and the number of min-trees decreases by one. For our example, we may first combine either the min-trees with roots 8 and 7 or those with roots 3 and 12. If the first pair is combined, the min-tree with root 8 is made a subtree of the min-tree with root 7. We now have the min-tree collection of Figure 10.18. There are three min-trees of degree two in this collection. If the pair with roots 7 and 3 is picked for combining, the resulting min-tree collection is that of Figure 10.19. Since the min-trees in this collection have different degrees, the min-tree combining process terminates.

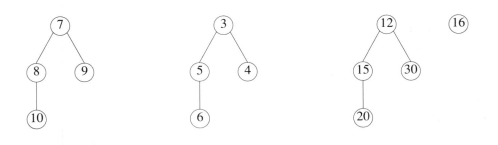

Figure 10.18 The F-heap of Figure 10.17 following the combining of the two degree one min-trees

The min-tree combining step is followed by a step in which the min-tree roots are linked together to form a doubly linked circular list and the F-heap pointer is reset so as

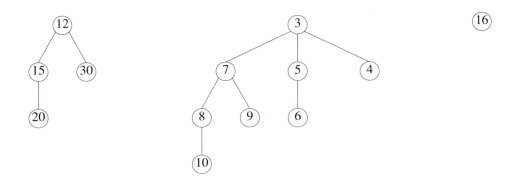

Figure 10.19 The F-heap of Figure 10.18 following the combining of two degree two min-trees

to point to the min-tree root with smallest key. The steps involved in a delete min operation are summarized in Program 10.7.

{Delete the min element from an F-heap a, this element is returned in x}

Step 1: [Handle empty F-heap] **if** $a = $ **nil then** *DeletionError* **else** perform Steps 2 - 4;

Step 2: [Deletion from nonempty F-heap] $x := a \uparrow. data$; $y := a \uparrow. child$; Delete a from its doubly linked circular list; Following this deletion, a points to any remaining node in the resulting list; If there is no such node, then $a = $ **nil**;

Step 3: [Min-tree combining] Consider the min-trees in the lists a and y; Combine together pairs of min-trees of the same degree until all remaining min-trees have different degree;

Step 4: [Form min-tree root list] Link the roots of the remaining min-trees (if any) together to form a doubly linked circular list; Set a to point to the root (if any) with minimum key;

Program 10.7 Steps in a delete min

Steps 1 and 2 take O(1) time. Step 3 may be implemented by using an array *tree* indexed from 0 to the maximum possible degree, *MaxDegree*, of a min-tree. Initially all entries in this array are **nil**. Let s be the number of min-trees in a and y. The lists a and y created in step 2 are scanned. For each min-tree p in the lists a and y created in step 2, the code of Program 10.8 is executed. The procedure *CombineMinTrees* makes the input tree with larger root a sub tree of the other tree. The resulting tree is returned in the first parameter. In the end, the array *tree* contains pointers to the min-trees that are to be combined in step 4. Since each time a pair of min-trees is combined the total number of min-trees decreases by one, the number of combines is at most $s-1$. Hence, the complexity of step 3 is O(*MaxDegree* $+s$). Step 4 is accomplished by scanning *tree* [0 .. *MaxDegree*] and linking together the min-trees found. During this scan, the min-tree with minimum key may also be determined. The complexity of step 4 is O(*MaxDegree*).

```
d := p ↑. degree;
while tree [d ] < > nil do
begin
    CombineMinTrees (p, tree [d ]);
    tree [d ] := nil;
    d := d +1;
end;
tree [d ] := p;
```

Program 10.8 Code to handle min-tree p encountered during a scan of lists a and y

Definition: The *binomial tree, B_k, of degree k* is a tree such that if $k = 0$, then the tree has exactly one node and if $k > 0$, then it consists of a root whose degree is k and whose subtrees are $B_0, B_1, \ldots, B_{k-1}$. □

The min-trees of Figure 10.15 are B_1, B_2, and B_3, respectively. One may verify that B_k has exactly 2^k nodes. Further, if we start with a collection of empty F-heaps and perform only the operations insert, combine, and delete min, then the min-trees in each F-heap are binomial trees. These observations enable us to prove that when only inserts, combines, and delete mins are performed, we can amortize costs such that the amortized cost of each insert and combine is O(1) and of each delete min is O(log$n$).

Lemma 10.2: Let a be an F-heap with n elements that results from a sequence of insert, combine, and delete min operations performed on initially empty F-heaps. Each min-tree in a has degree $\leq \log_2 n$. Consequently, *MaxDegree* $\leq \lfloor \log_2 n \rfloor$ and the actual cost of a delete min is O(log$n$ + s).

Proof: Since each of the min-trees in a is a binomial tree with at most n nodes, none can have degree greater than $\lfloor \log_2 n \rfloor$. □

Theorem 10.1: If a sequence of n insert, combine, and delete min operations is performed on initially empty F-heaps, then we can amortize costs such that the amortized time complexity of each insert and combine is O(1) and that of each delete min is O(log$n$).

Proof: For each F-heap define the quantities *#insert* and *LastSize* in the following way. When an initially empty F-heap is created or when a delete min is performed on an F-heap, its *#insert* value is set to zero. Each time an insert is done on an F-heap, its *#insert* value is increased by one. When two F-heaps are combined, the *#insert* value of the resulting F-heap is the sum of the *#insert* values of the F-heaps combined. Hence *#insert* counts the number of inserts performed on an F-heap or its constituent F-heaps since the last delete min performed in each. When an initially empty F-heap is created its *LastSize* value is zero. When a delete min is performed on an F-heap its *LastSize* is set to the number of min-trees it contains following this delete min. When two F-heaps are combined the *LastSize* value for the resulting F-heap is the sum of the *LastSize* values in the two F-heaps that were combined. One may verify that the number of min-trees in an F-heap is always equal to *#insert* + *LastSize*.

Consider any individual delete min in the operation sequence. Assume this is from the F-heap *a*. Observe that the total number of elements in all the F-heaps is at most *n* as only inserts add elements and at most *n* inserts can be present in a sequence of *n* operations. Let $u = a \uparrow. degree \leq \log_2 n$.

From Lemma 10.2, the actual cost of this delete min is O($\log n + s$). The $\log n$ term is due to *MaxDegree* and represents the time needed to initialize the array *tree* and the step 4 time. The *s* term represents the time to scan the lists *a* and *y* and to perform the at most $s - 1$ min-tree combines. We see that $s = \textit{#insert} + \textit{LastSize} + u - 1$. If we charge *#insert* units of cost to the insert operations that contribute to the count *#insert* and *LastSize* units to the delete mins that contribute to the count *LastSize* (each such delete min gets charged a number of cost units equal to the number of min-trees it left behind), then only $u - 1$ of the *s* cost units remain. Since $u \leq \log_2 n$ and since the number of min-trees in an F-heap immediately following a delete min is $\leq \log_2 n$, the amortized cost of a delete min becomes O($\log_2 n$).

Since the above charging scheme adds at most one unit to the cost of any insert, the amortized cost of an insert becomes O(1). The amortization scheme used does not charge anything extra to a combine. So the actual and amortized cost of a combine are also O(1). □

From the preceding theorem and the definition of cost amortization, it follows that the actual cost of any sequence of *i* inserts, *c* combines, and *dm* delete mins is O($i + c + dm \log i$).

Having seen how to perform the basic min-leftist tree operations using an F-heap, let us examine the operations: (1) delete an arbitrary node *b* from the F-heap *a*, and (2) decrease the key in the arbitrary node *b* by a positive amount.

The delete operation may be carried out as follows:

(1)   If $a = b$, then do a delete min; otherwise do steps 2, 3, and 4 below.

(2)   Delete *b* from the doubly linked list it is in.

(3)   Combine the doubly linked list of *b*'s children with the doubly linked list of the *a*'s min-tree roots. This is done by simply joining the two linked lists together. Trees of equal degree are not combined in a delete min.

(4)   Dispose of node *b*.

For example, if we delete the node containing 12 from the F-heap of Figure 10.15, we get the F-heap of Figure 10.20. The actual cost of an arbitrary delete is O(1) unless the min element is being deleted. In this case the deletion time is the time for a delete min operation.

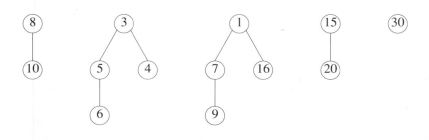

Figure 10.20 F-heap of Figure 10.15 following the deletion of 12

To decrease the key in node *b* we do the following:

(1)   Reduce the key in *b*.

(2)   If *b* is not a min-tree root and its key is smaller than that in its parent, then delete *b* from its doubly linked list and insert it into the doubly linked list of min-tree roots.

(3)   Change *a* to point to *b* in case the key in *b* is smaller than that in *a*.

Suppose we decrease the key 15 in the F-heap of Figure 10.15 by 4. The resulting F-heap is shown in Figure 10.21. The cost of performing a decrease key is O(1).

With the addition of the delete and decrease key operations, the min-trees in an F-heap need no longer be binomial trees. In fact, it is possible to have degree k min-trees with as few as $k+1$ nodes. As a result, the analysis of Theorem 10.1 is no longer valid. The analysis of Theorem 10.1 requires that each min-tree of degree k have an exponential (in k) number of nodes. When decrease key and delete operations are performed as described above, this is no longer true. To ensure that each min-tree of degree k has at least c^k nodes for some c, $c > 1$, each delete and decrease key operation must be followed by a *cascading cut* step. For this, we add the boolean field *ChildCut* to each node. The value of this field is useful only when x is not a min-tree root. In this case, *ChildCut*

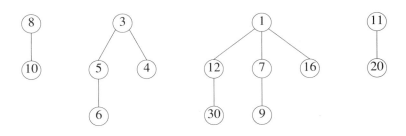

Figure 10.21 F-heap of Figure 10.15 following the reduction of 15 by 8

has the value **true** iff one of the children of x was cut off (i.e., removed) after the most recent time x was made the child of its current parent. This means that each time two min-trees are combined in a delete min operation, the *ChildCut* field of the root with larger key should be set to **false**. Further, whenever a delete or decrease key operation deletes a node q that is not a min-tree root from its doubly linked list (step 1 of delete and step 2 of decrease key), then the cascading cut step is invoked. During this, we examine the nodes on the path from the parent p of the deleted node q up to the nearest ancestor of the deleted node with *ChildCut* = **false**. In case there is no such ancestor, then the path goes from p to the root of the min-tree containing p. All non root nodes on this path with *ChildCut* field **true** are deleted from their respective doubly linked lists and added to the doubly linked list of min-tree root nodes of the F-heap. If the path has a node with *ChildCut* field **false**, this field is changed to **true**.

Figure 10.22 gives an example of a cascading cut. Figure 10.22(a) is the min-tree containing 14 before a decrease key operation that reduces this key by 4. The *ChildCut* fields are shown only for the nodes on the path from the parent of 14 to its nearest ancestor with *ChildCut* = **false**. A **true** value is indicated by T and a **false** one by F. During the decrease key operation, the min-tree with root 14 is deleted from the min-tree of Figure 10.22(a) and becomes a min-tree of the F-heap. Its root now has key 10. This is the first min-tree of Figure 10.22(b). During the cascading cut, the min-trees with roots 12, 10, 8, and 6 are cut off from the min tree with root 2. Thus the single min-tree of Figure 10.22(a) becomes six min-trees of the resulting F-heap. The *ChildCut* value of 4 becomes **true**. All other *ChildCut* values are unchanged.

Lemma 10.3: Let a be an F-heap with n elements that results from a sequence of insert, combine, delete min, delete, and decrease key operations performed on initially empty F-heaps.

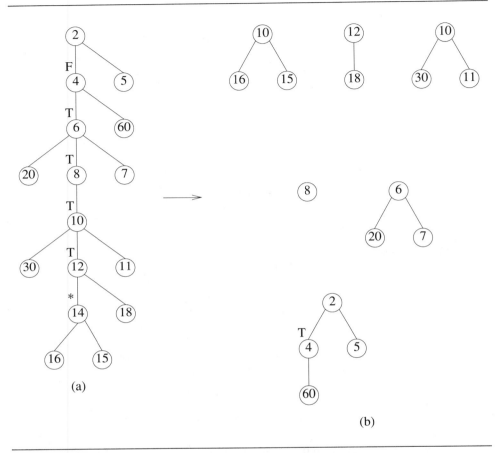

Figure 10.22 A cascading cut following a decrease of key 14 by 4

(a)   Let b be any node in any of the min-trees of a. The degree of b is at most $\log_\phi m$, where $\phi = (1+\sqrt{5})/2$ and m is the number of elements in the subtree with root b.

(b)   *MaxDegree* $\leq \lfloor \log_\phi n \rfloor$ and the actual cost of a delete min is O($\log n + s$).

Proof: We shall prove (a) by induction on the degree of b. Let N_i be the minimum number of elements in the subtree with root b when b has degree i. We see that $N_0 = 1$ and $N_1 = 2$. So, the inequality of (a) holds for degrees 0 and 1. For $i > 1$, let $c_1, \ldots, c_i$ be the i children of b. Assume that c_j was made a child of b before c_{j+1}, $j < i$. Hence, when c_k, $k \leq i$ was made a child of b, the degree of b was at least $k-1$. The only F-heap operation that makes one node a child of another is delete min. Here, during a combine min-tree step, one min-tree is made a sub tree of another min-tree of equal degree. Hence, at the time of combining, the degree of c_k must have been equal to that of b. Subsequent to combining, its degree can decrease as a result of a delete or decrease key operation. However, following such a combine, the degree of c_k can decrease by at most one as an attempt to cut off a second child of c_k results in a cascading cut at c_k. Such a cut causes c_k to become the root of a min-tree of the F-heap. Hence, the degree, d_k, of c_k is at least $\max\{0, k-2\}$. So, the number of elements in c_k is at least N_{d_k}. This implies that

$$N_i = N_0 + \sum_{k=0}^{i-2} N_k + 1 = \sum_{k=0}^{i-2} N_k + 2$$

One may show (see the exercises) that the Fibonacci numbers satisfy the equality

$$F_h = \sum_{k=0}^{h-2} F_k + 1, h > 1, F_0 = 0, \text{ and } F_1 = 1$$

From this we may obtain the equality $N_i = F_{i+2}, i \geq 0$. Further, since $F_{i+2} \geq \phi^i, N_i \geq \phi^i$. Hence, $i \leq \log_\phi m$.

(b) is a direct consequence of (a). $\square$

Theorem 10.2: If a sequence of n insert, combine, delete min, delete, and decrease key operations is performed on an initially empty F-heap, then we can amortize costs such that the amortized time complexity of each insert, combine, and decrease key operation is $O(1)$ and that of each delete min and delete is $O(\log n)$. The total time complexity of the entire sequence is the sum of the amortized complexities of the individual operations in the sequence.

Proof: The proof is quite similar to that of Theorem 10.1. The definition of *#insert* is unchanged. However, that of *LastSize* is augmented by requiring that following each delete and decrease key *LastSize* be changed by the net change in the number of min-trees in the F-heap (in the example of Figure 10.22 *LastSize* is increased by 5). With this modification, we see that at the time of a delete min operation $s = $ *#insert* $+$ *LastSize* $+ u - 1$. *#insert* units of cost may me charged, one each, to the *#insert* insert operations that contribute to this count and *LastSize* units may be charged to the delete min, delete, and decrease key operations that contribute to this count. This results in an additional charge of at most $\log_2 \phi$ to each contributing delete min and delete operation and of one to each contributing decrease key operation. As a result, the amortized cost of a delete min is $O(\log n)$.

Since the total number of cascading cuts is limited by the total number of deletes and decrease key operations (as these are the only operations that can set *ChildCut* to **true**), the cost of these cuts may be amortized over the delete and decrease key operations by adding one to their amortized costs. The amortized cost of a delete becomes O(log$n$) as its actual cost is O(1) (excluding the cost of the cascading cut sequence that may be performed); at most one unit is charged to it from the amortization of all the cascading cuts; and at most log$_\phi n$ units are charged to it from a delete min.

The amortized cost of a decrease key operation is O(1) as its actual cost is O(1) (excluding the cost of the ensuing cascading cut); at most one unit is charged to it from the amortization of all cascading cuts; and at most one unit is charged from a delete min.

The amortized cost of an insert is O(1) as its actual cost is one and at most one cost unit is charged to it from a delete min. Since the amortization scheme transfers no charge to a combine, its actual and amortized costs are the same. This cost is O(1). □

From the preceding theorem, it follows that the complexity of any sequence of F-heap operations is O(i +c +dk +(dm +d)log$i$) where i, c, dk, dm, and d are, respectively, the number of insert, combine, decrease key, delete min, and delete operations in the sequence.

We conclude this section on F-heaps by considering their application to the single source all destinations algorithm of Chapter 6. Let S be the set of vertices to which a shortest path has been found and let $dest(i)$ be the length of a shortest path from the source vertex to vertex i, $i \in \bar{S}$, that goes through only vertices in S. On each iteration of the shortest path algorithm, we need to determine an i, $i \in \bar{S}$, such that $dest(i)$ is minimum and add this i to S. This corresponds to a delete min operation on $\bar{S}$. Further, the $dest$ values of the remaining vertices in $\bar{S}$ may decrease. This corresponds to a decrease key operation on each of the affected vertices. The total number of decrease key operations is bounded by the number of edges in the graph and the number of delete min operations is $n - 2$. $\bar{S}$ begins with $n - 1$ vertices. If we implement $\bar{S}$ as an F-heap using $dest$ as the key, then $n - 1$ inserts are needed to initialize the F-heap. Additionally, $n - 2$ delete min operations and at most e decrease key operations are needed. The total time for all these operations is the sum of the amortized costs for each. This is O($n$log$n$ + e). The remainder of the algorithm takes O(n) time. Hence if an F-heap is used to represent S, the complexity of the shortest path algorithm becomes O($n$log$n$ + e). This is an asymptotic improvement over the implementation discussed in Chapter 6 if the graph does not have $\Omega(n^2)$ edges. If this single source algorithm is used n times, once with each of the n vertices in the graph as the source, then we can find a shortest path between every pair of vertices in O(n^2log$n$ + ne) time. Once again, this represents an asymptotic improvement over the O(n^3) dynamic programming algorithm of Chapter 6 for graphs that do not have $\Omega(n^2)$ edges. It is interesting to note that O($n$log$n$ + e) is the best possible implementation of the single source algorithm of Chapter 6 as the algorithm must examine each edge and may be used to sort n numbers.

10.5 HUFFMAN TREES

Binary search trees were introduced in Chapter 5. In this section, we consider the construction of binary search trees for a static set of identifiers. That is, no additions and/or deletions are made from the set. Only searches are performed.

In our study of binary search in Chapter 7, we saw that every sorted file corresponded to a binary search tree. For instance, a binary search on the file (**do, if, read**) corresponds to using algorithm *search* on the binary search tree of Figure 10.23. While this tree is a full binary tree, it need not be optimal over all binary search trees for this file when the identifiers are searched for with different probabilities. In order to determine an optimal binary search tree for a given static file, we must first decide on a cost measure for search trees. In searching for an identifier at level k using algorithm *search* (Program 5.25), k iterations of the **while** loop of lines 2-8 are made. In general, the number of iterations of this loop equals the level number of the identifier being searched. Further, since this **while** loop determines the cost of the search, it is reasonable to use the level number of a node as its cost.

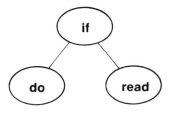

Figure 10.23 Binary search tree corresponding to a binary search on the file (**do, if, read**)

Consider the two search trees of Figure 10.24. The second of these requires at most three comparisons to decide whether the identifier being searched for is in the tree. The first binary tree may require four comparisons, since any identifier which alphabetically comes after **if** but precedes **repeat** will test four nodes. Thus, as far as worst case search time is concerned, this makes the second binary tree more desirable than the first. To search for an identifier in the first tree takes one comparison for the **if**, two for each of **for** and **while**, three for **repeat** and four for **read**. Assuming each is searched for with equal probability, the average number of comparisons for a successful search is 2.4. For the second binary search tree this amount is 2.2. Thus, the second tree has a better average behavior, too.

In evaluating binary search trees, it is useful to add a special "square" node at every place there is a null link. Doing this to the trees of Figure 10.24 yields the trees of Figure 10.25. Remember that every binary tree with n nodes has $n + 1$ null links and

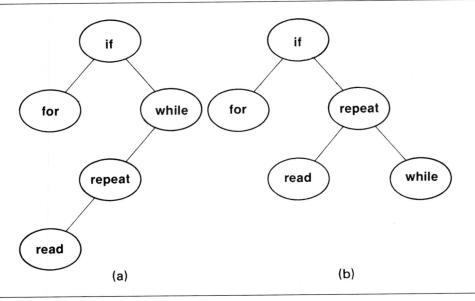

Figure 10.24 Two possible binary search trees

hence it will have $n + 1$ square nodes. We shall call these nodes *external* nodes because they are not part of the orginal tree. The remaining nodes will be called *internal* nodes. Each time a binary search tree is examined for an identifier which is not in the tree, the search terminates at an external node. Since all such searchers represent unsuccessful searches, external nodes will also be referred to as *failure* nodes. A binary tree with external nodes added is an *extended binary tree*. Figure 10.25 shows the extended binary trees corresponding to the search trees of Figure 10.24.

     We define the *external path length* of a binary tree to be the sum over all external nodes of the lengths of the paths from the root to those nodes. Analogously, the *internal path length* is defined to be the sum over all internal nodes of the lengths of the paths from the root to those nodes. For the tree of Figure 10.25(a) we obtain its internal path length, I, to be:

$$I = 0 + 1 + 1 + 2 + 3 = 7$$

Its external path length, E, is:

$$E = 2 + 2 + 4 + 4 + 4 + 3 + 2 = 17$$

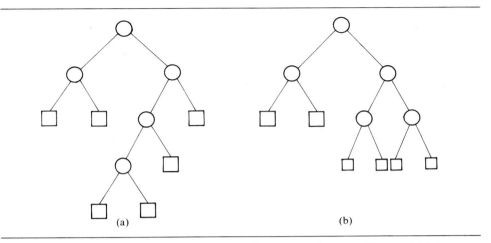

Figure 10.25 Extended binary trees corresponding to search trees of Figure 10.24

Exercise 21 shows that the internal and external path lengths of a binary tree with n internal nodes are related by the formula $E = I + 2n$. Hence, binary trees with the maximum E also have maximum I. Over all binary trees with n internal nodes what are the maximum and minimum possible values for I? The worst case, clearly, is when the tree is skewed (i.e., when the tree has a depth of n). In this case,

$$I = \sum_{i=0}^{n-1} i = n(n-1)/2$$

To obtain trees with minimal I, we must have as many internal nodes as close to the root as possible. We can have at most 2 nodes at distance 1, 4 at distance 2, and in general the smallest value for I is

$$0 + 2 \cdot 1 + 4 \cdot 2 + 8 \cdot 3 + \ldots +$$

This can be more compactly written as

$$\sum_{i \le k \le n} \lfloor log_2 k \rfloor = O(n log_2 n)$$

One tree with minimal internal path length is the complete binary tree defined in Section 5.2.

Before attempting to use these ideas of internal and external path lengths to obtain optimal binary search trees, let us look at a related but simpler problem. We are given a set of $n + 1$ positive weights $q_1, \ldots, q_{n+1}$. Exactly one of these weights is to be associated with each of the $n + 1$ external nodes in a binary tree with n internal nodes. The *weighted external path length* of such a binary tree is defined to be

$$\sum_{1 \le i \le n + 1} q_i k_i$$

where k_i is the distance from the root node to the external node with weight q_i. The problem is to determine a binary tree with minimal weighted external path length. Note that here no information is contained within internal nodes.

For example, suppose $n = 3$ and we are given the four weights: $q_1 = 15$, $q_2 = 2$, $q_3 = 4$, and $q_4 = 5$. Figure 10.26 shows two possible trees.

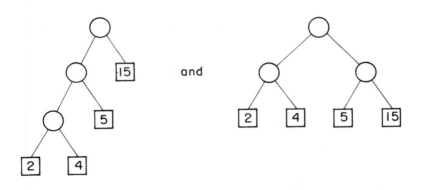

Figure 10.26 Example trees

Their respective weighted external path lengths are:

$$2 \cdot 3 + 4 \cdot 3 + 5 \cdot 2 + 15 \cdot 1 = 43$$

and

$$2 \cdot 2 + 4 \cdot 2 + 2 + 5 \cdot 2 + 15 \cdot 2 = 52.$$

Binary trees with minimal weighted external path length find application in several areas. One application is to determine an optimal merge pattern for $n + 1$ runs using a 2-way merge. If we have four runs, R_1-R_4 with q_i being the number of records in run R_i, $1 \leq i \leq 4$, then the skewed binary tree above defines the following merge pattern: merge R_2 and R_3; merge the result of this with R_4; and finally merge with R_1. Since two runs with n and m records each can be merged in time $O(n + m)$ (see Section 7.5), the merge time following the pattern of the above skewed tree is proportional to $(q_2+q_3) + \{(q_2+q_3)+q_4\} + \{q_1+q_2+q_3+q_4\}$. This is just the weighted external path length of the tree. In general, if the external node for run R_i is at a distance k_i from the root of the merge tree, then the cost of the merge will be proportional to $\sum q_i k_i$ which is the weighted external path length.

Another application of binary trees with minimal external path length is to obtain an optimal set of codes for messages $M_1, \ldots, M_{n+1}$. Each code is a binary string which will be used for transmission of the corresponding message. At the receiving end the code will be decoded using a decode tree. A decode tree is a binary tree in which external nodes represent messages. The binary bits in the code word for a message determine the branching needed at each level of the decode tree to reach the correct external node. For example, if we interpret a zero as a left branch and a one as a right branch, then the decode tree of Figure 10.27 corresponds to codes 000, 001, 01, and 1 for messages M_1, M_2, M_3, and M_4, respectively. These codes are called Huffman codes. The cost of decoding a code word is proportional to the number of bits in the code. This number is equal to the distance of the corresponding external node from the root node. If q_i is the relative frequency with which message M_i will be transmitted, then the expected decode time is

$$\sum_{1 \leq i \leq n+1} q_i d_i$$

where d_i is the distance of the external node for message M_i from the root node. The expected decode time is minimized by choosing code words resulting in a decode tree with minimal weighted external path length.

A very nice solution to the problem of finding a binary tree with minimum weighted external path length has been given by D. Huffman. We simply state his algorithm and leave the correctness proof as an exercise. The following type declarations are assumed:

```
type TreePointer = ↑TreeRecord;
     TreeRecord = record
                      LeftChild : TreePointer;
                      weight : integer;
                      RightChild : TreePointer;
                  end;
```

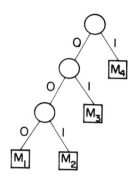

Figure 10.27 A decode tree

The algorithm *huffman* (Program 10.9) makes use of a list *l* of extended binary trees. Each node in a tree has three fields: *weight*, *LeftChild* and *RightChild*. Initially, all trees in *l* have only one node. For each tree this node is an external node, and its weight is one of the provided q_i's. During the course of the algorithm, for any tree in *l* with root node *t* and depth greater than 1, $t\uparrow.weight$ is the sum of weights of all external nodes in *t*. Algorithm *huffman* uses the subalgorithms *least* and *insert*. *least* determines a tree in *l* with minimum *weight* and removes it from *l*. *insert* adds a new tree to the list *l*.

```
 1 procedure huffman (var l : ListPointer ; n : integer);
 2 {l is a list of n single node binary trees as described above.}
 3 var t : TreePointer ;
 4     i : integer;
 5 begin
 6   for i := 1 to n − 1 do                {loop n −1 times}
 7   begin
 8     new(t);                             {Create a new binary tree}
 9     t↑.LeftChild := least (l);          {by combining the trees}
10     t↑.RightChild := least (l);         {with the two smallest weights}
11     t↑.weight := r↑.LeftChild↑.weight + t↑.RightChild↑.weights ;
12     insert (l,t);
13   end;
14 end; {of huffman}
```

Program 10.9 Huffman

We illustrate the way this algorithm works by an example. Suppose we have the weights $q_1 = 2$, $q_2 = 3$, $q_3 = 5$, $q_4 = 7$, $q_5 = 9$, $q_6 = 13$. Then the sequence of trees we would get is given in Figure 10.28 (the number in a circular node represents the sum of the weights of external nodes in that subtree).

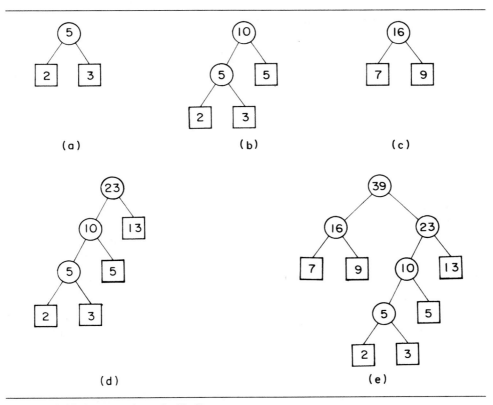

Figure 10.28 Construction of a Huffman tree

The weighted external path length of this tree is

$$2 \cdot 4 + 3 \cdot 4 + 5 \cdot 3 + 13 \cdot 2 + 7 \cdot 2 + 9 \cdot 2 = 93$$

In comparison, the best complete binary tree has weighted path length 95.

Analysis of Algorithm *huffman*

The main loop is executed $n-1$ times. If l is maintained as a heap (Section 5.11) then each call to *least* and *insert* requires only O($\log n$) time. Hence, the asymptotic computing time for the algorithm is O($n \log n$).

10.6 OPTIMAL BINARY SEARCH TREES

Let us now return to our original problem of representing a symbol table as a binary search tree. If the binary search tree contains the identifiers $a_1, a_2, \ldots, a_n$ with $a_1 < a_2 < \ldots < a_n$ and the probability of searching for each a_i is p_i, then the total cost of any binary search tree is

$$\sum_{1 \leq i \leq n} p_i \cdot \text{level}(a_i)$$

when only successful searches are made. Since unsuccessful searches, i.e., searches for identifiers not in the table, will also be made, we should include the cost of these searches in our cost measure, too. Unsuccessful searches terminate with *RetPointer* := **nil** in algorithm *search*. Every node with a null subtree defines a point at which such a termination can take place. Let us replace every null subtree by a failure node. The identifiers not in the binary search tree may be partitioned into $n + 1$ classes E_i, $0 \leq i \leq n$. E_0 contains all identifiers X such that $X < a_1$. E_i contains all identifiers X such that $a_i < X < a_{i+1}$, $1 \leq i < n$ and E_n contains all identifiers $X, X > a_n$. It is easy to see that for all identifiers in a particular class E_i, the search terminates at the same failure node and it terminates at different failure nodes for identifiers in different classes. The failure nodes may be numbered 0 to n with i being the failure node for class E_i, $0 \leq i \leq n$. If q_i is the probability that the identifier being searched for is in E_i, then the cost of the failure nodes is

$$\sum_{0 \leq i \leq n} q_i \cdot (\text{level(failure node } i) - 1)$$

The total cost of a binary search tree is therefore:

$$\sum_{1 \leq i \leq n} p_i \cdot \text{level}(a_i) + \sum_{0 \leq i \leq n} q_i \cdot (\text{level (failure node } i)-1) \tag{10.1}$$

An *optimal binary search tree* for the identifier set $a_1, \ldots, a_n$ is one which minimizes Eq.(10.1) over all possible binary search trees for this identifier set. Note that since all searches must terminate either successfully or unsuccessfully we have

$$\sum_{1 \le i \le n} p_i + \sum_{0 \le i \le n} q_i = 1$$

Example 10.1: Figure 10.29 shows the possible binary search trees for the identifier set $(a_1, a_2, a_3) = (\textbf{do, if, read})$.

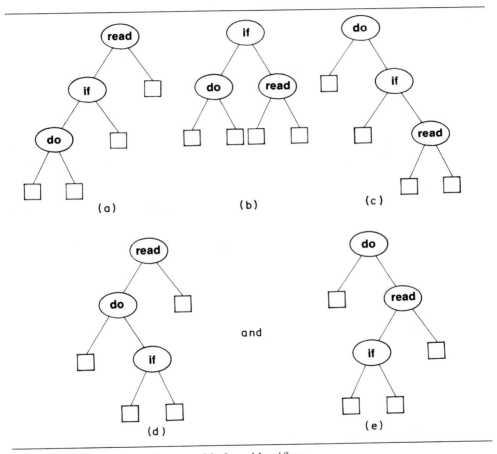

(a)

(b)

(c)

and

(d)

(e)

Figure 10.29 Binary search trees with three identifiers

With equal probabilities $p_i = a_j = 1/7$ for all i and j we have:

cost (tree a) = 15/7; cost (tree b) = 13/7
cost (tree c) = 15/7; cost (tree d) = 15/7
cost (tree e) = 15/7

As expected, tree b is optimal. With $p_1 = .5$, $p_2 = .1$, $p_3 = .05$, $q_0 = .15$, $q_1 = .1$, $q_2 = .05$, and $q_3 = .05$ we have

$$\text{cost (tree } a) = 2.65; \text{ cost (tree } b) = 1.9$$
$$\text{cost (tree } c) = 1.5; \text{ cost (tree } d) = 2.05$$
$$\text{cost (tree } e) = 1.6$$

Tree c is optimal with this assignment of p's and q's. $\square$

From among all the possible binary search trees, how does one determine the optimal tree? One possibility would be to proceed as in Example 10.1 and explicitly generate all possible binary search trees. The cost of each such tree could be computed and an optimal tree determined. The cost of each of the binary search trees can be determined in time $O(n)$ for an n node tree. If $N(n)$ is the total number of distinct binary search trees with n identifiers, then the complexity of the algorithm becomes $O(n\ N(n))$. From Section 5.14 we know that $N(n)$ grows too rapidly with increasing n to make this brute force algorithm of any practical significance. Instead, we can find a fairly efficient algorithm by making some observations regarding the properties of optimal binary search trees.

Let $a_1 < a_2 < \ldots < a_n$ be the n identifiers to be represented in a binary search tree. Let us denote by T_{ij} an optimal binary search tree for $a_{i+1}, \ldots, a_j, i < j$. We shall adopt the convention that T_{ii} is an empty tree for $0 \le i \le n$ and that T_{ij} is not defined for $i > j$. We shall denote by c_{ij} the cost of the search tree T_{ij}. By definition c_{ii} will be 0. r_{ij} will denote the root of T_{ij}; and

$$w_{ij} = q_i + \sum_{k=i+1}^{j} (q_k + p_k)$$

will denote the weight of T_{ij}. By definition we will have $r_{ii} = 0$ and $w_{ii} = q_i$, $0 \le i \le n$. An optimal binary search tree for $a_1, \ldots, a_n$ is therefore T_{on}, its cost c_{on}, its weight w_{on}, and its root r_{on}.

If T_{ij} is an optimal binary search tree for $a_{i+1}, \ldots, a_j$ and $r_{ij} = k$, $i < k \le j$, then T_{ij} has two subtrees L and R. L is the left subtree and contains the identifiers $a_{i+1}, \ldots, a_{k-1}$ and R is the right subtree and contains the identifiers $a_{k+1}, \ldots, a_j$ (Figure 10.30). The cost c_{ij} of T_{ij} is

$$c_{ij} = p_k + \text{cost } (L) + \text{cost } (R) + \text{weight } (L) + \text{weight } (R) \qquad (10.2)$$

where weight (L) = weight $(T_{i,k-1})$ = $w_{i,k-1}$, and weight (R) = weight (T_{kj}) = w_{kj}.

From Eq. (10.2) it is clear that if c_{ij} is to be minimal, then cost$(L) = c_{i,k-1}$ and cost$(R) = c_{kj}$, as otherwise we could replace either L or R by a subtree of lower cost, thus getting a binary search tree for $a_{i+1}, \ldots, a_j$ with lower cost than c_{ij}. This would violate

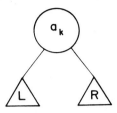

Figure 10.30 An optimal binary search tree T_{ij}

the assumption that T_{ij} was optimal. Hence, Eq. (10.2) becomes:

$$c_{ij} = p_k + c_{i,k-1} + c_{kj} + w_{i,k-1} + w_{kj}$$

$$= w_{ij} + c_{i,k-1} + c_{kj} \tag{10.3}$$

Since T_{ij} is optimal, it follows from Eq. (10.3) that $r_{ij} = k$ is such that

$$w_{ij} + c_{i,k-1} + c_{kj} = \min_{i < l \le j}\{w_{ij} + c_{i,l-1} + c_{lj}\}$$

or

$$c_{i,k-1} + c_{kj} = \min_{i < l \le j}\{c_{i,l-1} + c_{lj}\} \tag{10.4}$$

Equation (10.4) gives us a means of obtaining T_{on} and c_{on}, starting from the knowledge that $T_{ii} = \phi$ and $c_{ii} = 0$.

Example 10.2: Let $n = 4$ and $(a_1, a_2, a_3, a_4) = $ (**do, if, read, while**). Let $(p_1, p_2, p_3, p_4) = (3, 3, 1, 1)$ and $(q_0, q_1, q_2, q_3, q_4) = (2, 3, 1, 1, 1)$. The p's and q's have been multiplied by 16 for convenience. Initially, we have $w_{i,i} = q_i$, $c_{ii} = 0$, and $r_{ii} = 0$, $0 \le i \le 4$. Using Eqs. (10.3) and (10.4) we get:

$$w_{01} = p_1 + w_{00} + w_{11} = p_1 + q_1 + w_{00} = 8$$
$$c_{01} = w_{01} + \min\{c_{00} + c_{11}\} = 8$$
$$r_{01} = 1$$
$$w_{12} = p_2 + w_{11} + w_{22} = p_2 + q_2 + w_{11} = 7$$
$$c_{12} = w_{12} + \min\{c_{11} + c_{22}\} = 7$$
$$r_{12} = 2$$
$$w_{23} = p_3 + w_{22} + w_{33} = p_3 + q_3 + w_{22} = 3$$
$$c_{23} = w_{23} + \min\{c_{22} + c_{33}\} = 3$$
$$r_{23} = 3$$
$$w_{34} = p_4 + w_{33} + w_{44} = p_4 + q_4 + w_{33} = 3$$
$$c_{34} = w_{34} + \min\{c_{33} + c_{44}\} = 3$$
$$r_{34} = 4$$

Knowing $w_{i,i+1}$ and $c_{i,i+1}$, $0 \leq i < 4$ we can again use Eqs. (10.3) and (10.4) to compute $w_{i,i+2}$, $c_{i,i+2}$, $r_{i,i+2}$, $0 \leq i < 3$. This process may be repeated until w_{04}, c_{04}, and r_{04} are obtained. The table of Figure 10.31 shows the results of this computation. From the table, we see that $c_{04} = 32$ is the minimal cost of a binary search tree for a_1 to a_4. The root of tree T_{04} is a_2. Hence, the left subtree is T_{01} and the right subtree T_{24}. T_{01} has root a_1 and subtrees T_{00} and T_{11}. T_{24} has root a_3; its left subtree is therefore T_{22} and right subtree T_{34}. Thus, with the data in the table it is possible to reconstruct T_{04}. Figure 10.32 shows T_{04}. □

The above example illustrates how Equation (10.4) may be used to determine the c's and r's and also how to reconstruct T_{on} knowing the r's. Let us examine the complexity of this procedure to evaluate the c's and r's. The evaluation procedure described in the above example requires us to compute c_{ij} for $(j - i) = 1, 2, \ldots, n$ in that order. When $j - i = m$ there are $n - m + 1$ c_{ij}'s to compute. The computation of each of these c_{ij}'s requires us to find the minimum of m quantities (see Equation (10.4)). Hence, each such c_{ij} can be computed in time $O(m)$. The total time for all c_{ij}'s with $j - i = m$ is therefore $O(nm - m^2)$. The total time to evaluate all the c_{ij}'s and r_{ij}'s is therefore

$$\sum_{1 \leq m \leq n} (nm - m^2) = O(n^3)$$

Actually we can do better than this using a result due to D. E. Knuth which states that the optimal l in Eq. (10.4) may be found by limiting the search to the range $r_{i,j-1} \leq l \leq r_{i+1,j}$. In this case, the computing time becomes $O(n^2)$ (Exercise 24). Algorithm *obst* (Program 10.10) uses this result to obtain in $O(n^2)$ time the values of w_{ij}, r_{ij}, and c_{ij}, $0 \leq i \leq j \leq n$. The actual tree T_{0n} may be constructed from the values of r_{ij} in

	0	1	2	3	4
0	$w_{00}=2$ $c_{00}=0$ $r_{00}=0$	$w_{11}=3$ $c_{11}=0$ $r_{11}=0$	$w_{22}=1$ $c_{22}=0$ $r_{22}=0$	$w_{33}=1$ $c_{33}=0$ $r_{33}=0$	$w_{44}=1$ $c_{44}=0$ $r_{44}=0$
1	$w_{01}=8$ $c_{01}=8$ $r_{01}=1$	$w_{12}=7$ $c_{12}=7$ $r_{12}=2$	$w_{23}=3$ $c_{23}=3$ $r_{23}=3$	$w_{34}=3$ $c_{34}=3$ $r_{34}=4$	
2	$w_{02}=12$ $c_{02}=19$ $r_{02}=1$	$w_{13}=9$ $c_{13}=12$ $r_{13}=2$	$w_{24}=5$ $c_{24}=8$ $r_{24}=3$		
3	$w_{03}=14$ $c_{03}=25$ $r_{03}=2$	$w_{14}=11$ $c_{14}=19$ $r_{14}=2$			
4	$w_{04}=16$ $c_{04}=32$ $r_{04}=2$				

Figure 10.31 Computation of c_{04}, and r_{04}. The computation is carried out row wise from row 0 to row 4

$O(n)$ time. The algorithm for this is left as an exercise. The data types used by *obst* are:

```
type  identifier = packed array [1..MaxChar] of char;
      IdentArray = array{1..n] of identifier;
      parray  = array[1..n] of integer;
      qarray  = array[0..n] of integer;
      carray  = array[0..n,0..n] of integer;
```

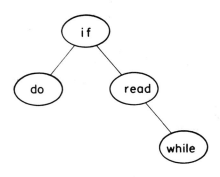

Figure 10.32 Optimal search tree for Example 10.2

10.7 AVL TREES

Dynamic tables may also be maintained as binary search trees. In Chapter 5, we saw how insertions and deletions can be performed on binary search trees. Figure 10.33 shows the binary search tree obtained by entering the months JANUARY to DECEMBER in that order into an initially empty binary search tree. Procedure *insert* (Program 5.27) is used.

The maximum number of comparisons needed to search for any identifier in the tree of Figure 10.33 is six for NOVEMBER. The average number of comparisons is (1 for JANUARY + 2 each for FEBRUARY and MARCH + 3 each for APRIL, JUNE and MAY + . . . + 6 for NOVEMBER)/12 = 42/12 = 3.5. If the months are entered in the order JULY, FEBRUARY, MAY, AUGUST, DECEMBER, MARCH, OCTOBER, APRIL, JANUARY, JUNE, SEPTEMBER and NOVEMBER, then the tree of Figure 10.34 is obtained. This tree is well balanced and does not have any paths to a node with a null link that are much longer than others. This is not true of the tree of Figure 10.33 which has six nodes on the path from the root to NOVEMBER and only two nodes, JANUARY and FEBRUARY, on another path to a null link. Moreover, during the construction of the tree of Figure 10.34 all intermediate trees obtained are also well balanced. The maximum number of identifier comparisons needed to find any identifier is now 4 and the average is 37/12 ≈ 3.1. If instead the months are entered in lexicographic order, the tree degenerates to a chain as in Figure 10.35. The maximum search time is now 12 identifier comparisons and the average is 6.5. Thus, in the worst case, binary search trees correspond to sequential searching in an ordered file. When the identifiers are entered in a random order, the tree tends to be balanced as in Figure 10.34. If all permutations are equiprobable, then it can be shown the average search and insertion time is $O(\log n)$ for an n node binary search tree.

```
 1  procedure obst (p : parray; q : qarray; a : IdentArray; var c,r,w : carray);
 2  {Given n distinct identifiers a₁ < a₂ < · · · < aₙ and probabilities
 3    pⱼ, 1 ≤ i ≤ n and qᵢ, 0≤ i ≤n this algorithm computes the
 4    cost cᵢⱼ of optimal binary search trees tᵢⱼ for identifiers aᵢ₊₁,...,aⱼ.
 5    It also computes rᵢⱼ, the root of tᵢⱼ. wᵢⱼ is the weight of tᵢⱼ.}
 6  var i,j,k,l,m : integer;
 7  begin
 8     for i := 0 to n − 1 do
 9     begin
10        w [i,j] := q [i]; r [i.j] = 0; c [i,i] := 0; {initialize}
11        w [i, i +1]:=q [i]+q [i +1]+p [i +1]; {optimal trees with one node}
12        r [i, i + 1] := i + 1;
13        c [i, i + 1] := q [i] + q [i + 1] + p [i + 1];
14     end;
15     w [n,n] := q [n]; r [n,n] := 0; c [n,n] := 0;
16     for m := 2 to n do {find optimal trees with m nodes}
17        for i := 0 to n − m do
18        begin
19           j := i + m;
20           w [i,j] := w [i, j − 1] + p [j] + q [j];
21           k := KnuthMin (c,r,i,j);
22           {KnuthMin returns a value k in the range [r [i, j − 1];
23           r [i + 1,j] minimizing c [i, k − 1] + c [k,j]}
24           c [i,j] := w [i,j] + c [i, k − 1] + c [k,j]; {Eq. 10.3)}
25           r [i,j] := k
26        end;
27  end; {of obst}
```

Program 10.10 Procedure to find an optimal binary search tree

From our earlier study of binary trees, we know that both the average and maximum search time will be minimized if the binary search tree is maintained as a complete binary tree at all times. However, since we are dealing with a dynamic situation, identifiers are being searched for while the table is being built and so it is difficult to achieve this ideal without making the time required to add new entries very high. This is so because in some cases it would be necessary to restructure the whole tree to accommodate the new entry and at the same time have a complete binary search tree. It is, however, possible to keep the trees balanced so as to ensure both an average and worst case retrieval time of O(log$n$) for a tree with n nodes. We shall study one method of growing balanced binary trees. These balanced trees will have satisfactory search and insertion time properties.

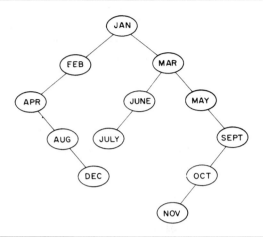

Figure 10.33 Binary search tree obtained for the months of the year

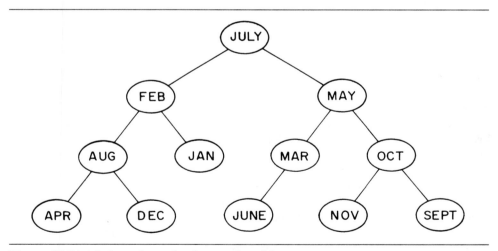

Figure 10.34 A balanced tree for the months of the year

In 1962, Adelson-Velskii and Landis introduced a binary tree structure that is balanced with respect to the heights of subtrees. As a result of the balanced nature of this type of tree, dynamic retrievals can be performed in O(log$n$) time if the tree has n nodes in it. At the same time, a new identifier can be entered or deleted from such a tree in time O(log n). The resulting tree remains height balanced. The tree structure introduced by them is given the name AVL-tree. As with binary trees, it is natural to define AVL trees recursively.

Definition: An empty tree is height balanced. If T is a nonempty binary tree with T_L and T_R as its left and right subtrees, the T is *height balanced* iff (1) T_L and T_R are height balanced and (2) $|h_L - h_R| \leq 1$ where h_L and h_R are the heights of T_L and T_R, respectively. □

The definition of a height balanced binary tree requires that every subtree also be height balanced. The binary tree of Figure 10.33 is not height balanced since the height of the left subtree of the tree with root 'APRIL' is 0 while that of the right subtree is 2. The tree of Figure 10.34 is height balanced while that of Figure 10.35 is not. To illustrate the processes involved in maintaining a height balanced binary search tree, let us try to construct such a tree for the months of the year. This time let us assume that the insertions are made in the order MARCH, MAY, NOVEMBER, AUGUST, APRIL, JANUARY, DECEMBER, JULY, FEBRUARY, JUNE, OCTOBER, and SEPTEMBER. Figure 10.36 shows the tree as it grows and the restructuring involved in keeping the tree balanced. The numbers within each node represent the difference in heights between the left and right subtrees of that node. This number is referred to as the balance factor of the node.

Definition: The *balance factor*, $BF(T)$, of a node T in a binary tree is defined to be $h_L - h_R$ where h_L and h_R are the heights of the left and right subtrees of T. For any node T in an AVL tree $BF(T) = -1, 0,$ or 1. □

Inserting MARCH and MAY results in the binary search trees (i) and (ii) of Figure 10.36. When NOVEMBER is inserted into the tree, the height of the right subtree of MARCH becomes 2, while that of the left subtree is 0. The tree has become unbalanced. In order to rebalance the tree, a rotation is performed. MARCH is made the left child of MAY, and MAY becomes the root. The introduction of AUGUST leaves the tree balanced. However, the next insertion, APRIL, causes the tree to become unbalanced again. To rebalance the tree, another rotation is performed. This time, it is a clockwise rotation. MARCH is made the right child of AUGUST, and AUGUST becomes the root of the subtree (Figure 10.36(v)). Note that both the previous rotations were carried out with respect to the closest parent of the new node having a balance factor of ±2. The insertion of JANUARY results in an unbalanced tree. This time, however, the rotation involved is somewhat more complex than in the earlier situations. The common point, however, is that it is still carried out with respect to the nearest parent of JANUARY with balance factor ±2. MARCH becomes the new root. AUGUST together with its left

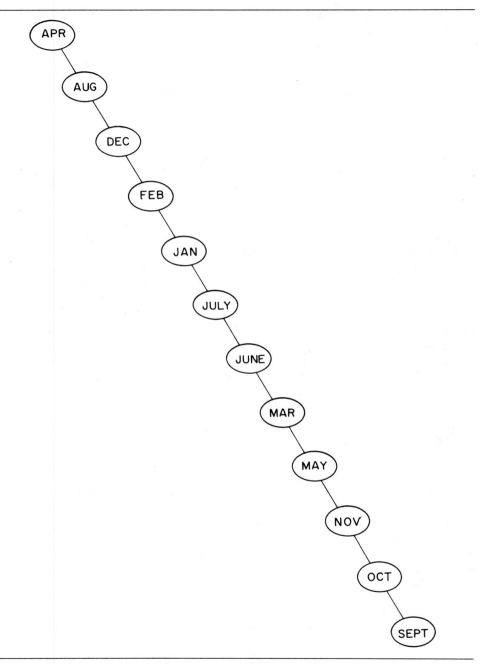

Figure 10.35 Degenerate binary search tree

subtree becomes the left subtree of MARCH. The left subtree of MARCH becomes the right subtree of AUGUST. MAY and its right subtree, which have identifiers greater than MARCH, become the right subtree of MARCH. If MARCH had a non-empty right subtree, this could have become the left subtree of MAY, since all identifiers would have been less than MAY.

Inserting DECEMBER and JULY necessitates no rebalancing. When FEBRUARY is inserted, the tree again becomes unbalanced. The rebalancing process is very similar to that used when JANUARY was inserted. The nearest parent with balance factor ±2 is AUGUST. DECEMBER becomes the new root of that subtree. AUGUST with its left subtree becomes the left subtree. JANUARY and its right subtree becomes the right subtree of DECEMBER, while FEBRUARY becomes the left subtree of JANUARY. If DECEMBER had had a left subtree, it would have become the right subtree of AUGUST. The insertion of JUNE requires the same rebalancing as in Figure 10.36(vi). The rebalancing following the insertion of OCTOBER is identical to that following the insertion of NOVEMBER. Inserting SEPTEMBER leaves the tree balanced.

In the preceding example we saw that the addition of a node to a balanced binary search tree could unbalance it. The rebalancing was carried out using essentially four different kinds of rotations LL, RR, LR, and RL (Figure 10.36 (v), (iii), (vi), and (ix), respectively). LL and RR are symmetric as are LR and RL. These rotations are characterized by the nearest ancestor, A, of the inserted node, Y, whose balance factor becomes ±2. The following characterization of rotation types is obtained:

LL: new node Y is inserted in the left subtree of the left subtree of A

LR: Y is inserted in the right subtree of the left subtree of A

RR: Y is inserted in the right subtree of the right subtree of A

RL: Y is inserted in the left subtree of the right subtree of A

Figures 10.37 and 10.38 show these rotations in terms of abstract binary trees. The root node in each of the trees of the figures represents the nearest ancestor whose balance factor has become ±2 as a result of the insertion. A moment's reflection will show that if a height balanced binary tree becomes unbalanced as a result of an insertion, then these are the only four cases possible for rebalancing (if a moment's reflection doesn't convince you, then try Exercise 26). In both the example of Figure 10.36 and the rotations of Figures 10.37 and 10.38. notice that the height of the subtree involved in the rotation is the same after rebalancing as it was before the insertion. This means that once the rebalancing has been carried out on the subtree in question, it is not necessary to examine the remaining tree. The only nodes whose balance factors can change are those in the subtree that is rotated.

In order to be able to carry out the rebalancing of Figure 10.37 and Figure 10.38 it is necessary to locate the node A around which the rotation is to be performed. As remarked earlier, this is the nearest ancestor of the newly inserted node whose balance factor becomes ±2. In order for a node's balance factor to become ±2, its balance factor

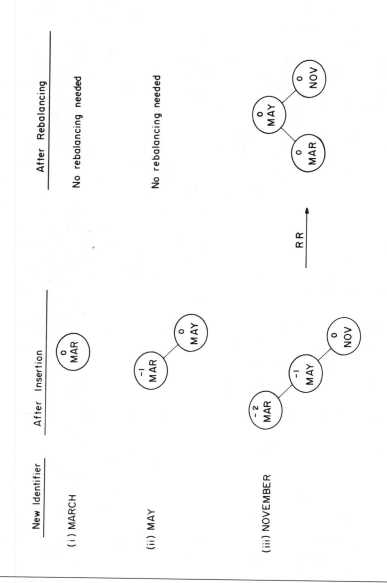

Figure 10.36 Balanced trees obtained for the months of the year

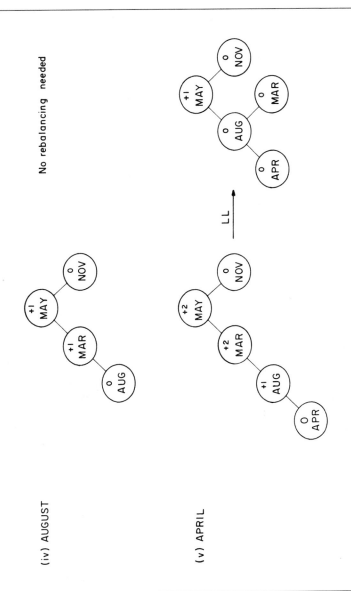

(iv) AUGUST

(v) APRIL

No rebalancing needed

LL

Figure 10.36 (continued)

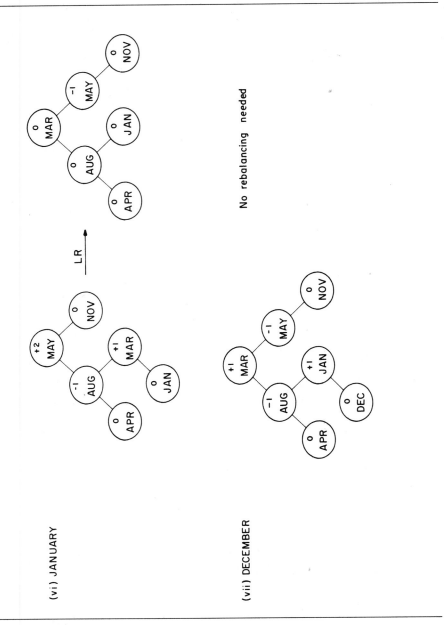

(vi) JANUARY

LR

No rebalancing needed

(vii) DECEMBER

Figure 10.36 (continued)

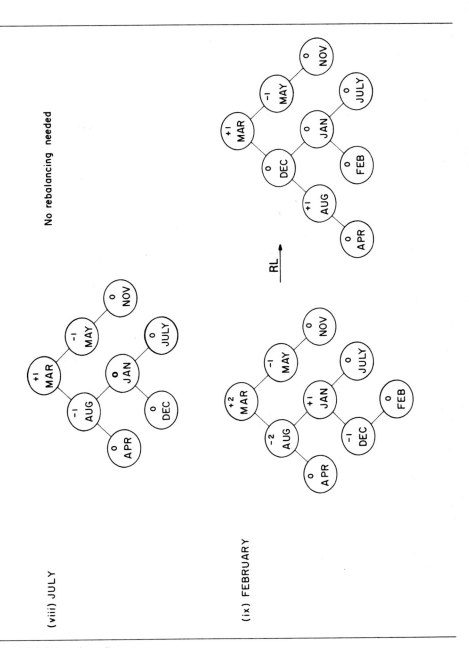

(viii) JULY

(ix) FEBRUARY

No rebalancing needed

Figure 10.36 (continued)

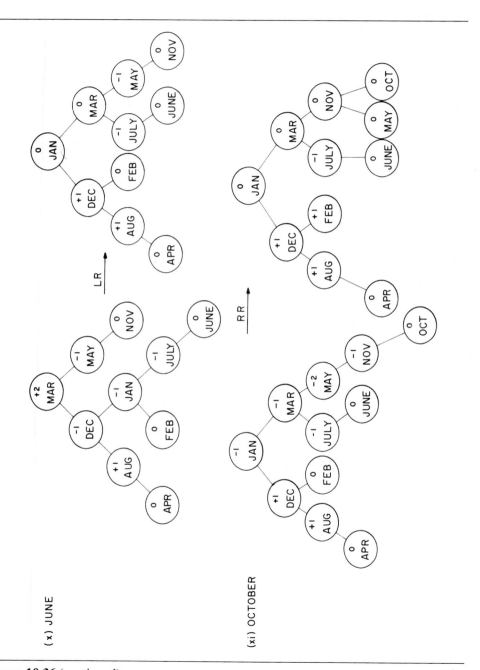

(x) JUNE

(xi) OCTOBER

Figure 10.36 (continued)

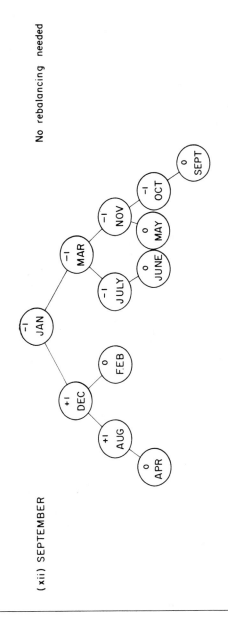

(xii) SEPTEMBER

No rebalancing needed

Figure 10.36

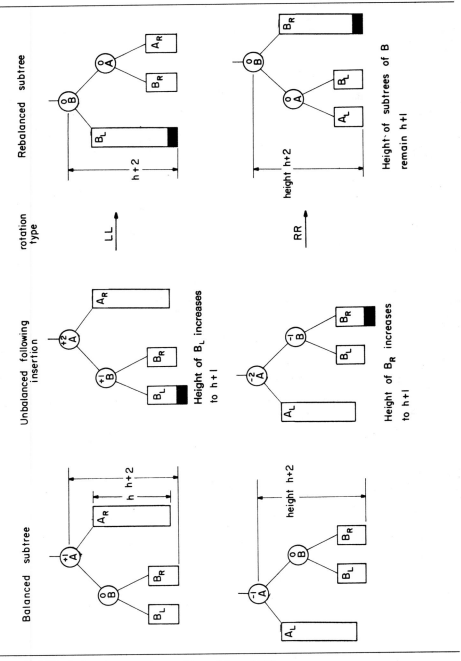

Figure 10.37 Rebalancing rotations of type LL and RR

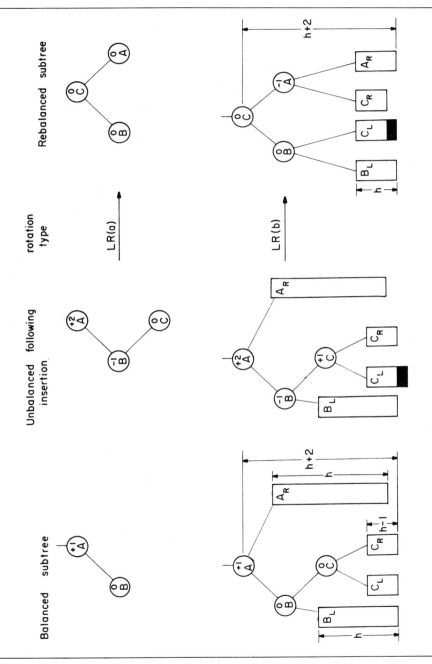

Figure 10.38 Rebalancing rotations of type LR and RL (continued)

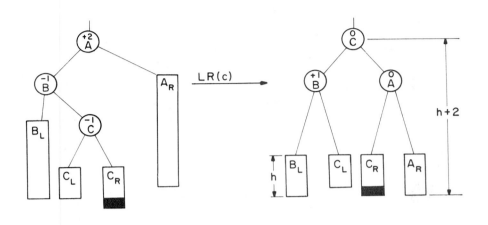

Figure 10.38 Rebalancing rotations on type LR and RL

must have been ±1 before the insertion. Therefore, before the insertion, the balance factors of all nodes on the path from A to the new insertion point must have been 0. With this information, the node A is readily determined to be the nearest ancestor of the new node having a balance factor ±1 before insertion. To complete the rotations the address of F, the parent of A, is also needed. The changes in the balance factors of the relevant nodes are shown in Figure 10.37 and Figure 10.38. Knowing F and A, all these changes can easily be carried out. What happens when the insertion of a node does not result in an unbalanced tree (Figure 10.36 (i), (ii), (iv), (vii), (viii), and (xii))? While no restructuring of the tree is needed, the balance factors of several nodes change. Let A be the nearest ancestor of the new node with balance factor ±1 before insertion. If as a result of the insertion the tree did not get unbalanced even though some path length increased by 1, it must be that the new balance factor of A is 0. In case there is no ancestor A with balance factor ±1 (as in Figure 10.36 (i), (ii), (iv), (vii), and (xii)), let A be the root. The balance factors of nodes from A to the parent of the new node will change to ±1 (see Figure 10.36 (viii), $A =$ JANUARY). Note that in both cases the procedure for determining A is the same as when rebalancing is needed. The remaining details of the insertion-rebalancing process are spelled out in algorithm *avlinsert*, Program 10.11. The type definitions in use are:

```
type identifier = packed array [1..MaxChar] of char;
     TreePointer = ↑TreeRecord;
     TreeRecord = record
                      LeftChild : TreePointer;
                      ident : identifier;
                      RightChild : TreePointer;
                      bf : − 1..1;
                  end;
```

```
 1 procedure avlinsert (x : identifier; var y,t : TreePointer);
 2 {the identifier x is inserted into the AVL tree with root t.
 3  Each node is assumed to have an identifier field ident, left
 4  and right child fields LeftChild and RightChild and a two bit
 5  balance factor field bf. p↑.bf = height of p↑.LeftChild −
 6  height of p↑.RightChild. y is set such that y↑.ident = x.}
 7 var a,b,c,f,p,q,clchild,crchild : TreePointer;
 8     found, unbalanced : boolean;
 9     d : integer;
10 begin {avlinsert}
11   if t = nil then {special case: empty tree t = 0}
12     begin
13       new(y); y↑.ident := x: t := y; t↑.bf := 0;
14       t↑.LeftChild := nil; t↑.RightChild := nil;
15     end
16   end
17   begin
18     {phase 1: Locate insertion pointer for x. a keeps track of
19       most recent node with balance factor ±1 and f is the
20       parent of a. q follows p through the tree.}
21     f := nil; a := t: p := t; q :=nil; found := false;
22     while (p < > nil) and (not found) do
23         begin {search t for insertion pointer for x}
24         if p↑.bf < > 0 then
25         begin
26             a := p; f := q;
27         end;
28         if x < p↑.ident then {take left branch}
29             begin
30                 q := p; p := p↑.LeftChild;
31             end
32         else if x > p↑.ident then {take right branch}
33             begin
```

```
34                    q := p; p := p ↑. RightChild;
35                end
36            else            {x is in t}
37                begin
38                    y := p; found :=true;
39                end;
40        end; {of while}
41        if not found then
42        begin
43        {phase 2: insert and rebalance. x is not in t and
44            may be inserted as the appropriate child of q.}
45        new(y); y ↑. ident := x; y ↑. LeftChild :=nil;
46        y ↑. RightChild :=nil; y ↑. bf := 0;
47        if x < q ↑. ident then {insert as left child}
48                            q ↑. LeftChild:=y
49                    else {insert as right child}
50                        q ↑. RightChild := y;
51        {adjust balance factors of nodes on path from a to q.
52            note that by the definition of a, all nodes on this
53            path must have balance factors of 0 and so will change
54            to ±1. d = + 1 implies x is inserted in left subtree
55            of a.d = − 1 implies x is inserted in right subtree of a.}
56        if x > a ↑. ident then
57                begin
58                    p := a ↑. RightChild; b := p; d := −1;
59                end
60            else
61                begin
62                    p := a ↑. LeftChild; b := p; d := +1
63                end;
64        while p < > y do
65            if x > p ↑. ident then {height of right increases by 1}
66            begin
67                p ↑. bf := −1; p := p ↑. RightChild;
68            end
69                else            {height of left increases by 1}
70            begin
71                p ↑. bf := +1; p := p ↑. LeftChild;
72            end;
73        {Is tree unbalanced?}
74        unbalanced := true;
75        if a ↑. bf = 0 then {tree still balanced}
76                begin
77                    a ↑. bf := d; unbalanced := false;
```

```
78    end;
79    if a↑.bf + d = 0 then {tree still balanced}
80        begin
81            a↑.bf := 0; unbalanced := false;
82        end;
83    if unbalanced then {tree unbalanced, determine rotation type}
84        begin
85            if d = +1 then {left imbalance}
86        begin
87            if b↑.bf = +1 then {rotation type LL}
88                begin
89                    a↑.LeftChild := b↑.RightChild;
90                    b↑.RightChild := a; a↑.bf := 0; b↑.bf := 0;
91                end
92            else
93                begin
94                    a := b↑.RightChild;
95                    b↑.RightChild = c↑.LeftChild;
96                    a↑.LeftChild := c↑.RightChild;
97                    c↑.LeftChild := b;
98                    c↑.RightChild := a;
99                    case c↑.bf of
100                       +1 : begin {LR(b)}
101                           a↑.bf := -1 ; b↑.bf := 0;
102                       end
103                       -1 : begin {LR(c)}
104                           b↑.bf := 1; a↑.bf := 0;
105                       end;
106                        0 : begin {LR(z)}
107                           b↑.bf := 0; a↑.bf := 0;
108                           end;
109                    end;
110                    c↑.bf := 0; b := c :{b is a new root}
111            end {of if b↑.bf = +1}
112        end {of then left imbalance}
113            else {right imbalance: this is symmetric to left
114                imbalance and is left as an exercise.}
115        begin
116        end;
117            {Subtree with root b has been rebalanced and
118            is the new subtree.}
119            if f = nil then
120                t := b
121            else if a = f↑.LeftChild then
```

```
122                              f ↑. LeftChild := b
123                    else if a = f ↑. RightChild then
124                              f ↑. RightChild := b;
125                   end; {of if unbalanced}
126      end; {of if not found}
127   end; {of if T = nil}
128 end; {of avlinsert}
```

Program 10.11 Insertion into an AVL tree

In order to really understand the insertion algorithm, the reader should try it out on the example of Figure 10.36. Once you are convinced that it does keep the tree balanced, then the next question is how much time does it take to make an insertion? An analysis of the algorithm reveals that if h is the height of the tree before insertion, then the time to insert a new identifier is $O(h)$. This is the same as for unbalanced binary serach trees, though the overhead is significantly greater now. In the case of binary search trees, however, if there were n nodes in the tree, then h could, in the worst case, be n (Figure 10.35) and the worst case insertion time was $O(n)$. In the case of AVL trees, however, h can be at most $O(\log n)$, and so the worst case insertion time is $O(\log n)$. To see this, let N_h be the minimum number of nodes in a height balanced tree of height h. In the worst case, the height of one of the subtrees will be $h - 1$ and of the other $h - 2$. Both these subtrees are also height balanced. Hence, $N_h = N_{h-1} + N_{h-2} + 1$ and $N_0 = 0$, $N_1 = 1$ and $N_2 = 2$. Note the similarity between this recursive definition for N_h and that for the Fibonacci numbers $F_n = F_{n-1} + F_{n-2}$, $F_0 = 0$ and $F_1 = 1$. In fact, we can show (Exercise 36) that $N_h = F_{h+2} - 1$ for $h \geq 0$. From Fibonacci number theory it is known that $F_h \approx \phi^h / \sqrt{5}$ where $\phi = (1 + \sqrt{5})/2$. Hence, $N_h \approx \phi^{n+2} / \sqrt{5} - 1$. This means that if there are n nodes in the tree, then its height, h, is at most $\log\phi (\sqrt{5}(n + 1)) - 2$. The worst case insertion time for a height balanced tree with n nodes is, therefore, $O(\log n)$.

Exercises 29-33 show that it is possible to find and delete a node with identifier X and to find and delete the k-th node from a height balanced tree in $O(\log n)$ time. Results of an empirical study of deletion in height balanced trees may be found in the paper by Karlton et al. Their study indicates that a random insertion requires no rebalancing, a rebalancing rotation of type LL or RR, and a rebalancing rotation of type LR and RL with probabilities .5349, .2327, and .2324, respectively. Table 10.1 compares the worst case times of certain operations on sorted sequential lists, sorted linked lists, and AVL-trees.

operation	sequential list	linked list	AVL-tree
search for X	$O(\log n)$	$O(n)$	$O(\log n)$
search for k'th item	$O(1)$	$O(k)$	$O(\log n)$
delete X	$O(n)$	$O(1)$ (doubly linked list and position of X known)	$O(\log n)$
delete k'th item	$O(n-k)$	$O(k)$	$O(\log n)$
insert X	$O(n)$	$O(1)$ (if position for insertion is known	$O(\log n)$
output in order	$O(n)$	$O(n)$	$O(n)$

Table 10.1 Comparison of various structures

10.8 2-3 TREES

By considering search trees of degree greater than 2, we can arrive at tree structures for which the insertion and deletion algorithms are simpler than that for AVL trees. Yet, these algorithms have $O(\log n)$ complexity. In this section, we shall look at a special case of B-trees. General B-trees are studied in the next chapter. The special case we shall consider here is called a 2-3 tree. This name derives from the fact that each internal node in a 2-3 tree has degree two or three. A degree two node is called a 2-*node* while a degree three node is called a 3-*node*.

Definition: A 2-3 tree is a search tree that is either empty or satisfies the following properties:

(1) Each internal node is either a 2-node or a 3-node. A 2-node has one element while a 3-node has two elements.

(2) Let *LeftChild* and *MiddleChild* denote the children of a 2-node. Let *dataL* be the element in this node and let *dataL. key* be its key. All elements in the sub 2-3 tree with root *LeftChild* have key less than *dataL. key*, while all elements in the sub 2-3 tree with root *MiddleChild* have key greater than *dataL. key*.

(3) Let *LeftChild*, *MiddleChild*, and *RightChild* denote the children of a 3-node. Let *dataL* and *dataR* be the two elements in this node. Then, *dataL. key* < *dataR. key*; all keys in the sub 2-3 tree with root *LeftChild* are less than *dataL. key*; all keys in the sub 2-3 tree with root *MiddleChild* are less than *dataR. key* and greater than *dataL. key*; and all keys in the sub 2-3 tree with root *RightChild* are greater than *dataR. key*.

(4) All external nodes are at the same level. □

An example 2-3 tree is given in Figure 10.39. As in the case of leftist trees, external nodes are introduced only to make it easier to define and talk about 2-3 trees. External nodes are not physically represented inside a computer. Rather, the corresponding child field of the parent of each external node is set to **nil**.

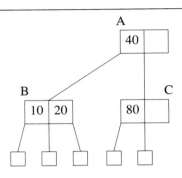

Figure 10.39 An example 2-3 tree

The number of elements in a 2-3 tree with height h (i.e., the external nodes are at level $h+1$) is between $2^h - 1$ and $3^h - 1$. To see this, note that the first bound applies when each internal node is a 2-node while the second bound applies when each internal node is a 3-node. These two cases represent the two extremes. A 2-3 tree with some 2-nodes and some 3-nodes will have a number of elements somewhere between these two bounds. Hence, the height of a 2-3 tree with n elements is between $\lceil \log_3(n+1) \rceil$ and $\lceil \log_2(n+1) \rceil$.

A 2-3 tree may be represented using nodes of the type *TwoThreePtr* defined as:

```
type TwoThreePtr = ↑ TwoThree;
     TwoThree = record
                     dataL : element;
                     dataR : element;
                     LeftChild : TwoThreePtr;
                     MiddleChild : TwoThreePtr;
                     RightChild : TwoThreePtr;
                 end;
```

We shall assume that no element has key **maxint** and shall adopt the convention that a 2-node will have *dataR. key* = **maxint**. Its single element is kept in *dataL* and *LeftChild* and *MiddleChild* point to its two children. Its *RightChild* field may be assigned any arbitrary value.

The search algorithm for binary search trees is easily extended to obtain the search procedure *search* 23 (Program 10.12) that searches a 2-3 tree *t* for a node that contains an element with key *x*. This uses a function *compare* that compares a key *x* with the keys in a given node *p*. It returns the value 1, 2, 3, or 4, respectively, depending upon whether *x* is less than the first key, between the first and second keys, greater than the second key, or equal to one of the keys in node *p*. The number of iterations of the **while** loop is bounded by the height of the 2-3 tree *t*. Hence if *t* has *n* nodes, the complexity of *search* 23 is $O(\log n)$.

---

procedure *search* 23(*t* : *TwoThreePtr* ; *x* : **integer** ; **var** *p* : *TwoThreePtr*);
{Search the 2-3 tree *t* for an element with key *x*. If this key is not in the tree,}
{then return **nil** in *p*. Otherwise, return a pointer to the node that contains this key.}
var *NotDone* : **boolean** ;
begin
  NotDone := **true**; *p* := *t*;
  while (*p* < > **nil**) **and** *NotDone* **do**
  case *compare* (*x*, *p*) **of**
    1: {*x* < *p* ↑. *dataL* . *key*}
      p := *p* ↑. *LeftChild*;
    2: {*p* ↑. *dataL* . *key* < *x* < *p* ↑. *dataR* . *key*}
      p := *p* ↑. *MiddleChild*;
    3: {*x* > *p* ↑. *dataR* . *key*}
      p := *p* ↑. *RightChild*;
    4: {*x* is one of the keys in *p*}
      NotDone := **false**;
  end; {of **case** and **while**}
end; {of *search* 23}

Program 10.12 Procedure to search a 2-3 tree

Insertion into a 2-3 tree is fairly simple. Consider inserting an element with key 70 into the 2-3 tree of Figure 10.39. First we search for this key. If the key is already in the tree then the insertion fails as all keys in a 2-3 tree are distinct. Since 70 is not in our example 2-3 tree, it may be inserted. For this, we need to know the leaf node encountered during the search for 70. Note that whenever we search for a key that is not in the 2-3 tree, the search encounters a unique leaf node. The leaf node encountered during the search for 70 is the node C with key 80. Since this node has only one element, the new element may be inserted here. The resulting 2-3 tree is shown in Figure 10.40(a).

Next, consider inserting an element *x* with key 30. This time the search encounters the leaf node B. Since B is a 3-node, it is necessary to create a new node D. D will contain the element that has the largest key from amongst the two elements currently in B and *x*. The element with the smallest key will be in B and the element with the median key together with a pointer to D will be inserted into the parent A of B.

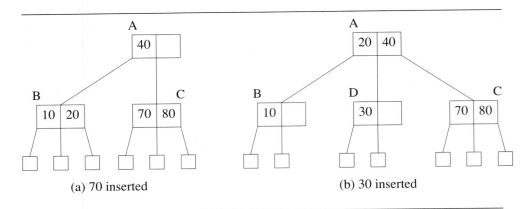

(a) 70 inserted (b) 30 inserted

Figure 10.40 Insertion into the 2-3 tree of Figure 10.39

The resulting 2-3 tree is shown in Figure 10.40(b).

As a final example, consider the insertion of an element x with key 60 into the 2-3 tree of Figure 10.40(b). The leaf node encountered during the search for 60 is node C. Since C is a 3-node, a new node E is created. This contains the element with largest key (80). Node C contains the element with smallest key (60). The element with the median key (70) together with a pointer to the new node E are to be inserted into the parent A of C. Again, since A is a 3-node, a new node F containing the element with largest key amongst {20, 40, 70} is created. As before, A contains the element with the smallest key. B and D become the left and middle children of A, respectively and C and E become these children of F. If A had a parent, then the element with the median key 40 and a pointer to the new node F would be inserted into this parent node. Since A does not have a parent, we create a new root G for the 2-3 tree. This contains the element with key 40 together with a left child pointer to A and a middle child pointer to F. The new 2-3 tree is as shown in Figure 10.41.

Each time an attempt is made to add an element into a 3-node p, a new node q is created. This is referred to as a node *split*. We say that node p is split into p, q, and the median element. Putting the ideas in the preceding discussion together, we get the insertion procedure of Program 10.13.

This procedure makes use of several procedures whose development is left as an exercise. We specify the task performed by each below:

(1) *NewRoot*. This is invoked when the root of t is to change. The inputs to this procedure are the left child of the new root, its single element, and its middle child. A pointer to the new root is returned in the first of these parameters.

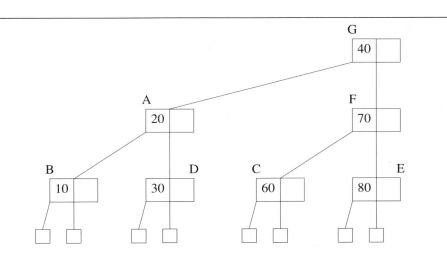

Figure 10.41 Insertion of 60 into the 2-3 tree of Figure 10.40(b)

(2)   *FindNode*. This is a modified version of *search* 23. It searches a nonempty 2-3 tree *t* for the presence of an element with key *y. key*. If this key is present in *t*, then *p* is set to **nil**. Otherwise, *p* is set to point to the leaf node encountered in the search. Additionally, *FindNode* creates a global data structure that enables us to follow back from *p* to the root *t*. This data structure could be a list of the nodes on the path form *t* to *p*. Such a list is needed as following a node split it is necessary to access the parent of the node that was split.

(3)   *InsertionError*. When an attempt to insert an element whose key corresponds to that of an element already in the 2-3 tree is made an insertion error occurs. This procedure is to signal an error and cause the program to terminate.

(4)   *PutIn*. This procedure is used to insert an element *y* into a node *p* that has exactly one element in it. The subtree *a* is to be placed immediately to the right of *y*. So, if *y* becomes *dataL*, then *a* becomes *MiddleChild* and the previous values of *dataL* and *MiddleChild* move to *dataR* and *RightChild*. If *y* becomes *dataR*, then *a* becomes *RightChild*.

(5)   *split*. This takes a node *p* that has two elements in it and creates a new node. The new node will contain the record with largest key from amongst the elements initially in *p* and the element *y*. The element with smallest key will be the only element left in *p*. The three original children pointers of *p* and the pointer *a* will occupy the four children fields that need to be defined in *p* and the new node. On return, *y* is the element with median key and *a* points the newly formed node.

```
procedure insert 23(var t : TwoThreePtr ; y : element );
{Insert the element y into the 2-3 tree t provided that t doesn't}
{already contain an element with the same key.}
var a, p : TwoThreePtr ;
    NotDone : boolean ;
begin
  if t = nil then NewRoot (t, y, nil)
  else begin {insertion into a nonempty 2-3 tree}
          p := FindNode (t, y . key);
          if p = nil then InsertionError {key already in t}
          else begin {y . key not in t}
                  a := nil; NotDone := true;
                  while NotDone do
                    if p ↑ . dataR . key = maxint
                    then begin {p is a 2-node}
                            PutIn (p, y, a);
                            NotDone := false;
                        end
                    else begin {p is a 3-node}
                            split (p, y, a);
                            if p = t then begin {root has been split}
                                        NewRoot (t, y, a);
                                        NotDone := false;
                                    end
                                    else p := parent of p;
                        end; {of p has two elements}
              end; {of y . key not in t}
      end; {of insertion into a nonempty 2-3 tree}
end; {of insert 23}
```

Program 10.13 Insertion into a 2-3 tree

In *insert* 23, y denotes the element to be inserted into node p and a denotes the node that was newly created at the last iteration of the **while** loop. As for the complexity analysis, we see that the total time taken is proportional to the height of the 2-3 tree t. Hence, insertion into a 2-3 tree with n elements takes $O(\log n)$ time.

Deletion from a 2-3 tree is conceptually no harder than insertion. In case we are deleting an element that is not in a leaf node, then we transform this into a deletion from a leaf node by replacing the deleted element by a suitable element that is in a leaf. For example, if we are to delete the element with key 50 that is in the root of Figure 10.42(a), then this element may be replaced by either the element with key 20 or the element with key 60. Both are in leaf nodes. In a general situation, we may use either the element with largest key in the subtree on the left or the element with smallest key in the subtree on the right of the element being deleted.

Henceforth, we shall consider only the case of deletion from a leaf node. Let us begin with the tree of Figure 10.42(a). To delete the element with key 70, we need merely set *dataR.key* = **maxint** in node C. The result is shown in Figure 10.42(b). To delete the element with key 90 from the 2-3 tree of Figure 10.42(b), we need to shift *dataR* to *dataL* and set *data 2.key* = **maxint** in node D. This results in the 2-3 tree of Figure 10.42(c).

Next consider the deletion of the element with key 60. This leaves node C empty. Since the left sibling B of C is a 3-node, we can move the element with key 20 into the *dataL* position of the parent node A and move the element with key 50 from the parent to the node C. After setting *dataR.key* = **maxint** in B, the 2-3 tree takes the form shown in Figure 10.42(d). This data movement operation is called a *rotation*. When the element with key 95 is deleted, node D becomes empty. The rotation performed when the 60 was deleted isn't possible now as the left sibling C is a 2-node. This time, we move the 80 into the left sibling C and delete the node D. We shall refer to this operation as a *combine*. In a combine one node is deleted, while no nodes are deleted in a rotation. The deletion of 95 results in the 2-3 tree of Figure 10.42(e). Deleting the element with key 50 from this tree results in the 2-3 tree of Figure 10.42(f). Now consider deleting the element with key 10 from this tree. Node B becomes empty. At this time, we examine B's right sibling C to see if it is a 2-node or a 3-node. If it is a 3-node, we can perform a rotation similar to that done during the deletion of 60. If it is a 2-node, then a combine is performed. Since C is a 2-node, we proceed in a manner similar to the deletion of 95. This time, the elements with keys 20 and 80 are moved into B and the node C deleted. This, however, causes the parent node A to have no elements. If the parent had not been a root, we would examine its left or right sibling as we did when nodes C (deletion of 60) and D (deletion of 95) became empty. Since A is the root, it is simply deleted and B becomes the new root (Figure 10.42(g)).

The steps involved in deletion from a leaf node p of a 2-3 tree t are summarized in Program 10.14.

For a rotation, there are essentially three cases depending on whether p is the left, middle, or right child of its parent r. If p is the left child of r, then let q be the right sibling of p. Otherwise, let q be the left sibling of p. Note that regardless of whether r is a 2-node or a 3-node, q is well defined. The three rotation cases are shown pictorially in Figure 10.43. A ''?'' denotes a don't care situation. a, b, c, and d denote the children (i.e., roots of subtrees) of nodes.

Figure 10.44 shows the two cases for a combine when p is the left child of r. We leave it as an exercise to obtain the figures for the cases when p is a middle child and when p is a right child.

The refinement of step 1 of Program 10.14 into Pascal code is shown in Program 10.15. The codes for rotation and combine for the case when p is the left child of r are given in Program 10.16 and Program 10.17, respectively. We leave the development of the complete deletion procedure as an exercise.

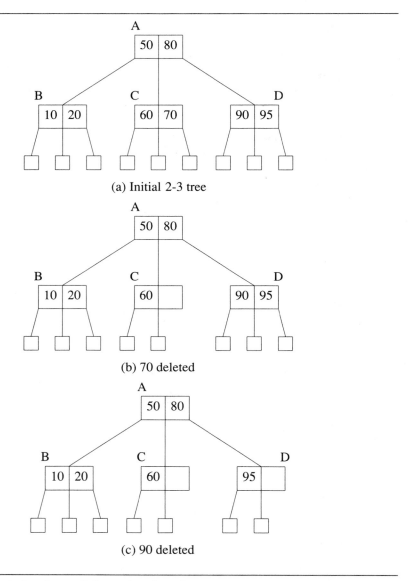

(a) Initial 2-3 tree

(b) 70 deleted

(c) 90 deleted

Figure 10.42 Deletion from a 2-3 tree (continued)

It should be evident that an individual rotation or combine takes $O(1)$ time. If a rotation is performed, deletion is completed. If a combine is performed, p moves up one level in the 2-3 tree. Hence, the number of combines that can be performed during a

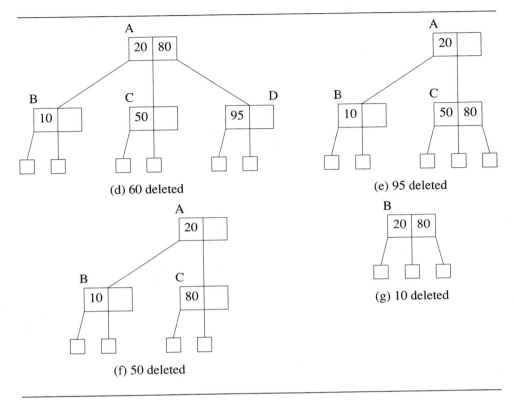

(d) 60 deleted

(e) 95 deleted

(f) 50 deleted

(g) 10 deleted

Figure 10.42 Deletion from a 2-3 tree

deletion cannot exceed the height of the 2-3 tree. Consequently, deletion from a 2-3 tree with n elements takes O($\log n$) time.

10.9 2-3-4 TREES

A 2-3-4 tree is an extension of a 2-3 tree to the case where 4-nodes (i.e., nodes with four children) are also permitted.

Definition: A 2-3-4 tree is a search tree that is either empty or satisfies the following properties:

Step 1: Modify node *p* as necessary to reflect its status after the desired element has been deleted.

Step 2: **while** *p* has zero elements and *p* is not the root **do**
  begin
   let *r* be the parent of *p* and let *q* be the left or right sibling of *p* (as appropriate);
   if *q* is a 3-node
   then perform a rotation
   else perform a combine;
   $p := r$;
  end;

Step 3: If *p* has zero elements, then *p* must be the root. The left child of *p* becomes the new root and the node *p* is deleted.

Program 10.14 Steps in deleting from a leaf of a 2-3 tree

(1) Each internal node is a 2-, 3-, or 4-node. A 2-node has one element; a 3-node has two elements; and a 4-node has three elements.

(2) Let *LeftChild* and *LeftMidChild* denote the children of a 2-node. Let *dataL* be the element in this node and let *dataL*. *key* be its key. All elements in the sub 2-3-4 tree with root *LeftChild* have key less than *dataL*. *key*, while all elements in the sub 2-3-4 tree with root *LeftMidChild* have key greater than *dataL*. *key*.

(3) Let *LeftChild*, *LeftMidChild*, and *RightMidChild* denote the children of a 3-node. Let *dataL* and *dataM* be the two elements in this node. Then, *dataL*. *key* < *dataM*. *key*; all keys in the sub 2-3-4 tree with root *LeftChild* are less than *dataL*. *key*; all keys in the sub 2-3-4 tree with root *LeftMidChild* are less than *dataM*. *key* and greater than *dataL*. *key*; and all keys in the sub 2-3-4 tree with root *RightMidChild* are greater than *dataM*. *key*.

(4) Let *LeftChild*, *LeftMidChild*, *RightMidChild* and *RightChild* denote the children of a 4-node. Let *dataL*, *dataM* and *dataR* be the three elements in this node. Then, *dataL*. *key* < *dataM*. *key* < *dataR*. *key*; all keys in the sub 2-3-4 tree with root *LeftChild* are less than *dataL*. *key*; all keys in the sub 2-3-4 tree with root *LeftMid-Child* are less than *dataM*. *key* and greater than *dataL*. *key*; all keys in the sub 2-3-4 tree with root *RightMidChild* are greater than *dataM*. *key* but less than *dataR*. *key*; and all keys in the sub 2-3-4 tree with root *RightChild* are greater than *dataR*. *key*.

(5) All external nodes are at the same level.

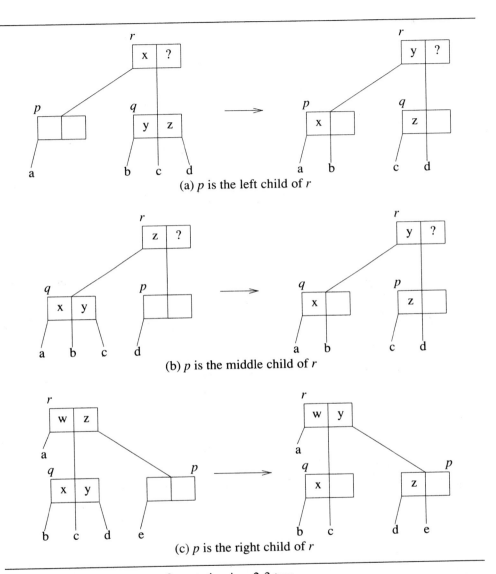

(a) *p* is the left child of *r*

(b) *p* is the middle child of *r*

(c) *p* is the right child of *r*

Figure 10.43 The three cases for rotation in a 2-3 tree

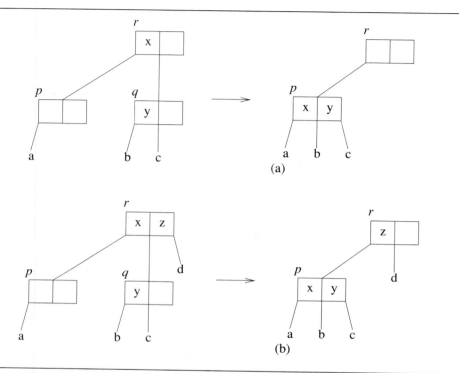

Figure 10.44 Combining in a 2-3 tree when p is a the left child of r

```
{Code for Step 1 of Program 10.14}
{Key x is to be deleted from the leaf node p}
with p do
    if x = dataL. key {delete first element}
    then if p ↑ . dataR. key < > maxint
        then begin {p is a 3-node}
                dataL := dataR; dataR. key := maxint;
             end
        else dataL. key := −maxint {p is a 2-node}
    else dataR. key := maxint; {delete second element}
```

Program 10.15 Refinement of step 1 of Program 10.14

{Rotation when p is the left child of r}
{q is the middle child of r}
$p\uparrow.dataL := r\uparrow.dataL$;
$p\uparrow.MiddleChild := q\uparrow.LeftChild$;
$r\uparrow.dataL := q\uparrow.dataL$;
with q **do**
begin
  $dataL := dataR$;
  $LeftChild := MiddleChild$;
  $MiddleChild := RightChild$;
  $dataR.key := $ **maxint**;
end;

Program 10.16 Pascal code for a rotation when p is the left child of r

{Combine when p is the left child of r}
{q is the right sibling of p}
with p **do**
begin
  $dataL := r\uparrow.dataL$;
  $dataR := q\uparrow.dataL$;
  $MiddleChild := q\uparrow.LeftChild$;
  $RightChild := q\uparrow.MiddleChild$;
end;
with r **do**
  if $dataR.key = $ **maxint** {r was a 2-node}
  then $dataL.key = $ **maxint**
  else begin
      $dataL := dataR$;
      $dataR.key := $ **maxint**;
      $MiddleChild := RightChild$;
    end;

Program 10.17 Code to perform a combine when p is a left child

A 2-3-4 tree may be represented using nodes of the type *TwoThreeFourPtr* defined as:

type *TwoThreeFourPtr* = ↑ *TwoThreeFour*;
    TwoThreeFour = **record**
                dataL : *element*;
                dataM : *element*;
                dataR : *element*;
                LeftChild : *TwoThreeFourPtr*;
                LeftMidChild : *TwoThreeFourPtr*;
                RightMidChild : *TwoThreeFourPtr*;
                RightChild : *TwoThreeFourPtr*;
    end;

As in the case of 2-3 trees, we shall assume that no element has key **maxint**. We shall adopt the convention that a 2-node will have *dataM. key* = **maxint**. The single element is kept in *dataL* and *LeftChild* and *LeftMidChild* point to its two children. A 3-node has *dataR. key* = **maxint** and the *LeftChild*, *LeftMidChild*, and *RightMidChild* fields point to its three subtrees. An example 2-3-4 tree using these conventions and nodes of type *TwoThreeFour* is shown in Figure 10.45.

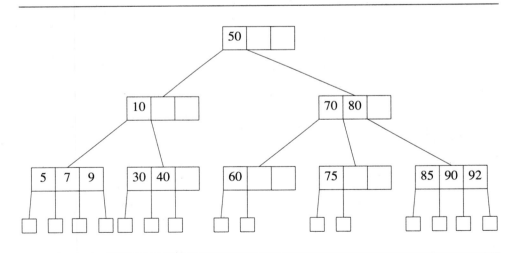

Figure 10.45 An example 2-3-4 tree

If a 2-3-4 tree of height h has only 2-nodes, then it contains $2^h - 1$ elements. If it contains only 4-nodes, then the number of elements is $4^h - 1$. A height h 2-3-4 tree with a mixture of 2-, 3-, and 4-nodes has between $2^h - 1$ and $4^h - 1$ elements. In other words, the height of a 2-3-4 tree with n elements is between $\lceil \log_4(n+1) \rceil$ and $\lceil \log_2(n+1) \rceil$.

2-3-4 trees have an advantage over 2-3 trees in that insertion and deletion can be performed by a single root to leaf pass rather than by a forward root to leaf pass followed by a backward leaf to root pass. As a result, the corresponding algorithms are simpler. More interestingly, a 2-3-4 tree can be efficiently represented as a binary tree (called a red-black tree). This results in a more efficient utilization of space than results from the use of nodes of type *TwoThree* in the case of 2-3 trees and of type *TwoThreeFour* in the case of 2-3-4 trees. Note that modifying the definitions of the types *TwoThree* and *TwoThreeFour*, to use variant records that have only as many fields as necessary for the variant in use, doesn't improve the efficiency of space utilization, as enough space to accomodate the largest variant is allocated whenever a variable of variant type is created. Using different record types for 2-nodes, 3-nodes, and 4-nodes improves space utilization, but introduces additional complexity in terms of memory management and requiring pointer fields that can point to three different types of nodes.

We shall examine the representation of 2-3-4 trees as binary trees in the next section. In this section, we shall see how insertions and deletions can be performed by making a single top-down root to leaf pass over the 2-3-4 tree. First, let us consider the insertion operation. If the leaf node into which the element is to be inserted is a 4-node, then this node splits and a backward leaf to root pass is initiated. This backward pass terminates when either a 2- or 3-node is encountered or when the root is split. To avoid the backward leaf to root pass, we split 4-nodes on the way down the tree. As a result, the leaf node into which the insertion is to be made is guaranteed to be a 2- or 3-node. The element to be inserted may be added to this node without any further node splitting.

There are essentially three different situations to consider for a 4-node:

(1)   it is the root of the 2-3-4 tree

(2)   its parent is a 2-node

(3)   its parent is a 3-node

The splitting transformations for cases (1) and (2) are shown in Figure 10.46 and Figure 10.47, respectively. For case (3), Figure 10.48 shows the transformation when the 4-node is the left child of the 3-node and Figure 10.49 shows it for the case when the 4-node is the left middle child. The remaining case when the 4-node is the right middle child of the 3-node is symmetric to the case when it is the left child and is left as an exercise. It is easy to see that if the transformations of Figure 10.46, Figure 10.47, and Figure 10.48 are used to split 4-nodes on the way down the 2-3-4 tree, then whenever a non root 4-node is encountered, its parent cannot be a 4-node. Notice that the transformation for a root 4-node increases the height of the 2-3-4 tree by one, while the remaining transformations do not affect its height.

The procedure to insert element *y* into the 2-3-4 tree *t* represented with nodes of type *TwoThreeFour* takes the form given in Program 10.18. The procedures and functions used by *insert* 234 are specified below:

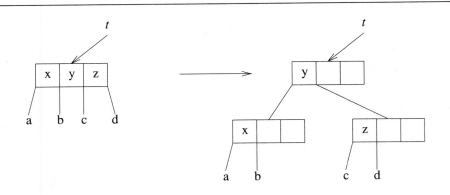

Figure 10.46 Transformation when the 4-node is the root

(1) *NewRoot*. This creates a single node 2-3-4 tree t with only the element y in it.

(2) *FourNode*. This is a boolean valued function which returns the value **true** iff the given node is a 4-node.

(3) *SplitRoot*. This uses the transformation of Figure 10.46 to split a root that is a 4-node.

(4) *NodeType*. This function returns the value TwoNode if the given node is a 2-node and the value ThreeNode otherwise.

(5) *SplitChildOf2*. The transformation of Figure 10.47 is used to split a 4-node that is a child of a 2-node.

(6) *SplitChildOf3*. The transformation of Figure 10.48 is used to split a 4-node that is a child of a 3-node.

(7) *compare*. The key of the given element y is compared with the keys in the given node p. The possible outputs from this function and the corresponding conditions are:

   (a) equal. $y.key$ equals the key of one of the elements in p

   (b) leaf. p is a leaf node

   (c) lChild. $y.key < p\uparrow.dataL.key$

   (d) lmChild. $p\uparrow.dataL.key < y.key < p\uparrow.dataM.key$

   (e) rmChild. $p\uparrow.dataM.key < y.key < p\uparrow.dataR.key$

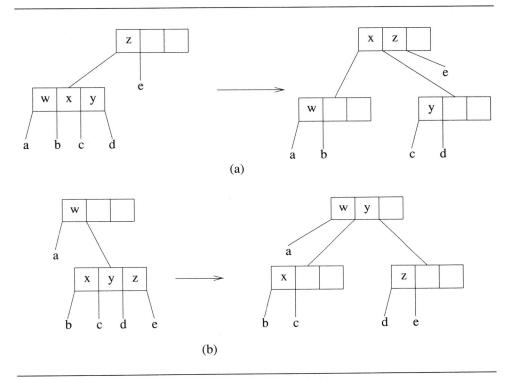

Figure 10.47 Transformation when the 4-node is the child of a 2-node

    (f)   rChild. $y . key > p \uparrow . dataR . key$

If y and p satisfy more than one of the above conditions, then the first is used.

(8)   *InsertionError*. This handles the case when the element y to be inserted has a key equal to that of an element already in the 2-3-4 tree.

(9)   *PutIn*. The element to be inserted is added to the given leaf node. This leaf node is either a 2-node or a 3-node.

    The complexity of *insert* 234 is readily seen to be O($\log n$), where n is the number of elements in t.

    As in the case of 2-3 trees, the deletion of an arbitrary element may be reduced to that of a deletion of an element that is in a leaf node. If the element to be deleted is in a leaf that is a 3-node or a 4-node, then its deletion leaves behind a 2-node or a 3-node. In this case, no restructuring work is required. Hence, to avoid a backward leaf to root restructuring path (as performed in the case of 2-3 trees) it is necessary to ensure that at the

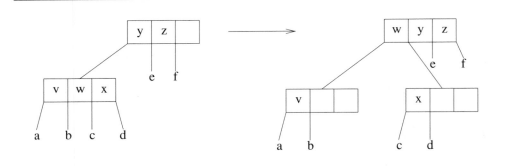

Figure 10.48 Transformation when the 4-node is the left child of a 3-node

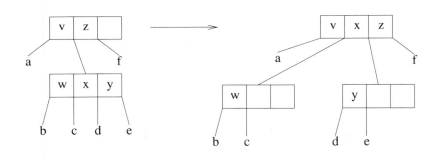

Figure 10.49 Transformation when the 4-node is the left middle child of a 3-node

time of deletion, the element to be deleted is in a 3-node or a 4-node. This is accomplished by restructuring the 2-3-4 tree during the downward root to leaf pass.

The restructuring strategy requires that whenever the search moves to a node on the next level, this node must be a 3-node or a 4-node. Suppose the search is presently at node p and will move next to node q. Note that q is a child of p and is determined by the relationship between the key of the element to be deleted and the keys of the elements in p. The following cases are to be considered:

(1) p is a leaf. In this case, the element to be deleted is either in p or not in the tree. If the element to be deleted is not in p, then the deletion is unsuccessful. Assume this is not the case. By the nature of the restructuring process, p can be a 2-node only if it is also the root. The deletion results in an empty tree.

```
procedure insert 234(var t : TwoThreeFourPtr ; y : element );
{Insert element y into the 2-3-4 tree t}
var p, q : TwoThreeFourPtr;
    NotDone : boolean;
begin
  if t = nil then NewRoot (t, y)  {insertion into an empty 2-3-4 tree}
  else begin
        if FourNode (t) then SplitRoot (t);
        p := t; q := nil;  {q is parent of p}
        NotDone := true;
        while NotDone do
        begin
          if FourNode (p)
          then begin
                if NodeType (q) =  TwoNode then SplitChildOf2(p, q)
                                           else SplitChildOf3(p, q);
                p := q; {back up to parent for next comparison}
              end; {of FourNode (p)}
          case compare (y, p) of
            equal: InsertionError; {key is duplicated}
            leaf: begin PutIn (y, p); NotDone := false; end;
            lChild: p := p ↑. LeftChild;
            lmChild: p := p ↑. LeftMidChild;
            rmChild: p := p ↑. RightMidChild;
            rChild: p := p ↑. RightChild;
          end; {of case}
        end; {of while}
      end; {of else begin}
end; {of insert 234}
```

Program 10.18 Insertion into a 2-3-4 tree

(2) q is not a 2-node. In this case, the search moves to q and no restructuring is needed.

(3) q is a 2-node and its nearest sibling r is also a 2-node (if q is the left child of p, then its nearest sibling is the left middle child of p; otherwise, the nearest sibling is its left sibling). Now, if p is a 2-node, it must be the root and we perform the transformation of Figure 10.46 in reverse. That is, p, q, and r are combined to form a 4-node and the height of the tree decreases by 1. If p is a 3-node or a 4-node, then we perform, in reverse, the 4-node splitting transformation for the corresponding case (Figure 10.47 through Figure 10.49).

(4) q is a 2-node and its nearest sibling r is a 3-node. In this case, we perform the transformation of Figure 10.50. This figure only shows the transformations for the case when q is the left child of a 3-node p. The cases when q is the left middle child, right middle child, or right child and when p is a 2-node (in this case p is the root) or a 4-node are symmetric.

(5) q is a 2-node and its nearest sibling r is a 4-node. This is similar to the case when r is a 3-node.

The above transformations guarantee that a backward restructuring pass is not needed following the deletion from a leaf node. We leave the development of the deletion procedure as an exercise.

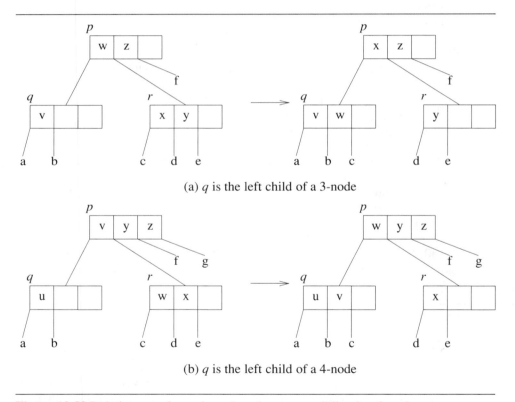

(a) q is the left child of a 3-node

(b) q is the left child of a 4-node

Figure 10.50 Deletion transformation when the nearest sibling is a 3-node

10.10 RED-BLACK TREES

A *red-black* tree is a binary tree representation of a 2-3-4 tree. The child pointers of a node in a red-black tree are of two types: red and black. If the child pointer was present in the original 2-3-4 tree, it is a black pointer. Otherwise, it is a red pointer. The node structure, *RedBlack*, used is defined as:

$$
\begin{aligned}
&\textbf{type } color = (red, black); \\
&\quad RedBlackPtr = \uparrow RedBlack; \\
&\quad RedBlack = \textbf{record} \\
&\qquad\qquad data : element; \\
&\qquad\qquad LeftChild : RedBlackPtr; \\
&\qquad\qquad RightChild : RedBlackPtr; \\
&\qquad\qquad LeftColor : color; \\
&\qquad\qquad RightColor : color; \\
&\qquad\textbf{end};
\end{aligned}
$$

It is possible to use an alternate node structure in which each node has a single color field. The value of this field is the color of the pointer from the node's parent. We examine this structure in the exercises. The former structure is better suited for top down insertion and deletion while the latter is better suited for algorithms that make a bottom to top restructuring pass. When drawing a red-black tree, we shall use a solid line to represent a black pointer and a broken one to represent a red pointer. A 2-3-4 tree represented using nodes of type *TwoThreeFour* is transformed into its red-black representation as follows:

(1)   A 2-node p is represented by a *RedBlack* node q with both its color fields black and $data = dataL$; $q\uparrow.LeftChild = p\uparrow.LeftChild$, and $q\uparrow.RightChild = p\uparrow.LeftMidChild$.

(2)   A 3-node p is represented by two *RedBlack* nodes connected by a red pointer. There are two ways in which this may be done (see Figure 10.51, color fields are not shown).

(3)   A 4-node is represented by three *RedBlack* nodes one of which is connected to the remaining two by red pointers (see Figure 10.52, color fields are not shown).

The red-black tree representation of the 2-3-4 tree of Figure 10.45 is given in Figure 10.53. External nodes and color fields are not shown. One may verify that a red-black tree satisfies the following properties:

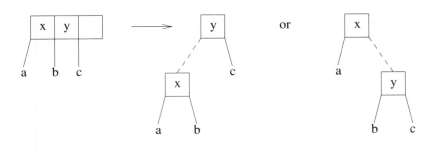

Figure 10.51 Transforming a 3-node into two *RedBlack* nodes

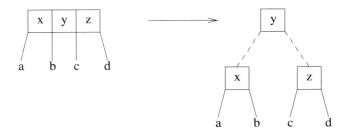

Figure 10.52 Transforming a 4-node into three *RedBlack* nodes

(1)   It is a binary search tree.

(2)   Every root to leaf path has the same number of black links (this follows from the fact that all external nodes of the original 2-3-4 tree are on the same level and black pointers represent original pointers).

(3)   No root to leaf path has two or more consecutive red pointers (this follows from the nature of the transformations of Figure 10.51 and Figure 10.52).

    As a result of property (1), a red-black tree can be searched using exactly the same algorithm as used to search an ordinary binary search tree. The pointer colors are not used during this search. An insertion can be carried out in one of two ways: top down and bottom up. In a top down insertion a single root to leaf pass is made over the red-black tree. A bottom up insertion makes both a root to leaf and a leaf to root pass. Let us examine the top down insertion method first.

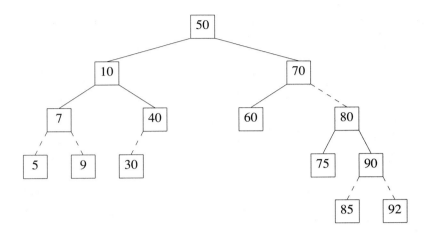

Figure 10.53 Red-black representation of 2-3-4 tree of Figure 10.45

To make a top down insertion, we use the 4-node splitting transformations described in Figure 10.46 through Figure 10.49. In terms of red-black trees, these take the form given in Figure 10.54 through Figure 10.57. The case when a 4-node is the right middle child of a 3-node is symmetric to the case when it is the left child (Figure 10.56).

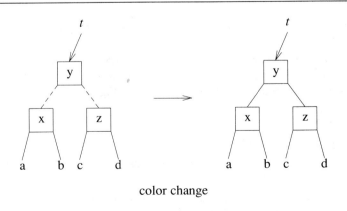

color change

Figure 10.54 Transformation for a root 4-node

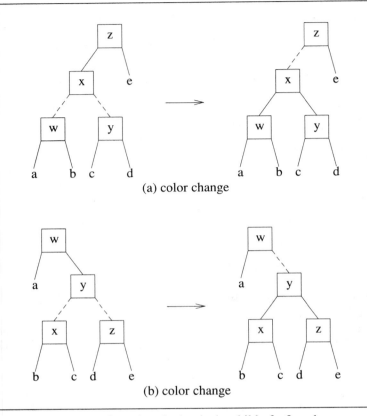

(a) color change

(b) color change

Figure 10.55 Transformation for a 4-node that is the child of a 2-node

We can detect a 4-node by simply looking for nodes q for which both color fields are red. Such nodes together with their two children form a 4-node. When such a q is detected, the transformations of Figure 10.54 through Figure 10.57 are accomplished as below:

(1)   Change both the colors of q to black.

(2)   If q is the left (right) child of its parent, then change the left (right) color of its parent to red.

(3)   If we now have two consecutive red pointers, then one is from the grandparent, gp, of q to the parent, p of q and the other from p to q. Let the direction of the first of these be X and that of the second be Y. We shall use L (R) to denote a left (right) direction. $XY =$ LL, LR, and RL in the case of Figures 10.56(a), 10.57(a), and

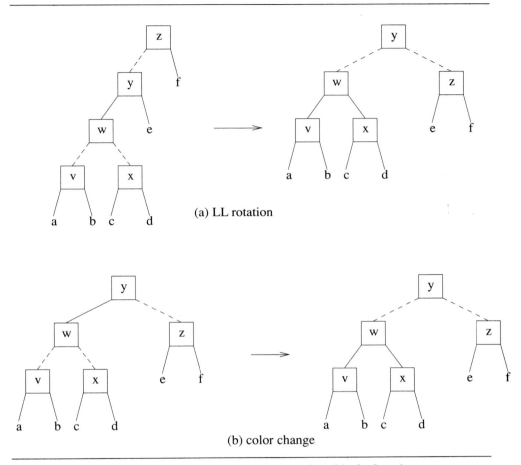

(a) LL rotation

(b) color change

Figure 10.56 Transformation for a 4-node that is the left child of a 3-node

10.57(b), respectively. For the case symmetric to Figure 10.56(a) that arises when the 4-node is a right middle child of a 3-node, $XY = RR$. A rotation similar to that performed in AVL trees is needed. We describe the rotation for the case $XY = LL$. Now, node p takes the place previously occupied by pp; the right child of p becomes the left child of pp and pp becomes the right child of p.

It is interesting to note that when the 4-node to be split is a root or the child of a 2-node or that of a "nicely" oriented 3-node (as in Figure 10.56(b), color changes suffice. Pointers need to be changed only when the 4-node is the child of a 3-node that is not "nicely" oriented (as in Figures 10.56(a) and 10.57). We leave the development of

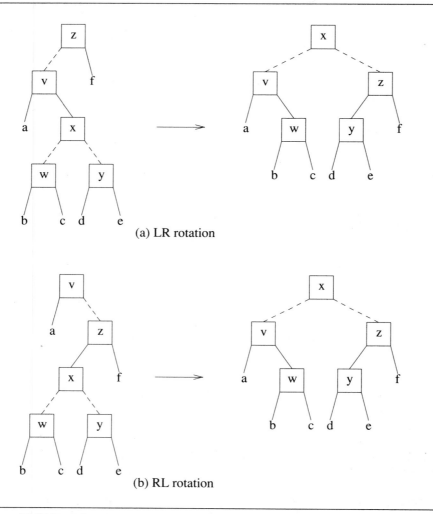

(a) LR rotation

(b) RL rotation

Figure 10.57 Transformation for a 4-node that is the left middle child of a 3-node

the formal insertion procedure as an exercise.

In a bottom-up insertion, we search the red-black tree for the key to be inserted. This search is unsuccessful. No transformations are made during this downward pass. The element to be inserted is added as the appropriate child of the node last encountered. A red pointer is used to join the new node to its parent. Following this, all root to leaf paths have the same number of black pointers. However, it is possible for one such path to have two consecutive red pointers. This violates the red-black property that no root to leaf path has two consecutive red pointers. Let these two pointers be $<p, q>$ and $<q, r>$. The first is from node p to node q and the second from node q to node r. Let s be the sibling (if any) of node q. $s = $ nil, if q has no sibling. The violation is classified as an XYZ violation where X = L if $<p, q>$ is a left pointer and X = R otherwise; Y = L if $<q, r>$ is a left pointer and Y = R otherwise; and Z = r if $s \neq$ nil and $<p, s>$ is a red pointer and Z = b otherwise.

The color change transformation of Figure 10.58 handles the violation cases LLr and LRr. Similar transforms handle the cases RRr and RLr. In these figures the subtrees a, b, c, d, and e may be empty and the pointer from the parent of y nonexistent (in case y is the root). These color changes potentially propagate the violation up the tree and may need to be reapplied several times. Note that the color change does not affect the number of black pointers on a root to leaf path. Figure 10.59 shows the rotations needed for the cases LLb and LRb. The cases RRb and RLb are symmetric. The rotations of this figure do not propagate the violation. Hence, at most one rotation can be performed. Once again, we observe that the above rotations do not affect the number of black pointers on any root to leaf path.

In comparing the top down and the bottom up insertion methods, we note that in the top down method O(log$n$) rotations can be performed while only one rotation is possible in the bottom up method. Both methods may perform O(log$n$) color changes. However, the top down method can be used in pipeline mode to perform several insertions in sequence. The bottom up method cannot be so used.

For top down deletion from a leaf, we note that if the leaf from which the deletion is to occur is the root, then the result is an empty red-black tree. If the leaf is connected to its parent by a red pointer, then it is part of a 3-node or a 4-node and the leaf may be deleted from the tree. If the pointer from the parent to the leaf is a black pointer, then the leaf is a 2-node. Deletion from a 2-node requires a backward restructuring pass. To avoid this, we ensure that the deletion leaf has a red pointer from its parent. This is accomplished by using the insertion transformations in the reverse direction together with red-black transformations corresponding to the 2-3-4 deletion transformations (3) and (4) (q is a 2-node whose nearest sibling is a 3- or 4-node), and a 3-node transformation that switches from one 3-node representation to the other as necessary to ensure that the search for the element to be deleted moves down a red pointer.

Since most of the insertion and deletion transformations can be accomplished by color changes and require no pointer changes or data shifts, these operations actually take less time using red-black trees than when a 2-3-4 tree is represented using nodes of type *TwoThreeFour*.

The development of the bottom up deletion transformations is left as an exercise.

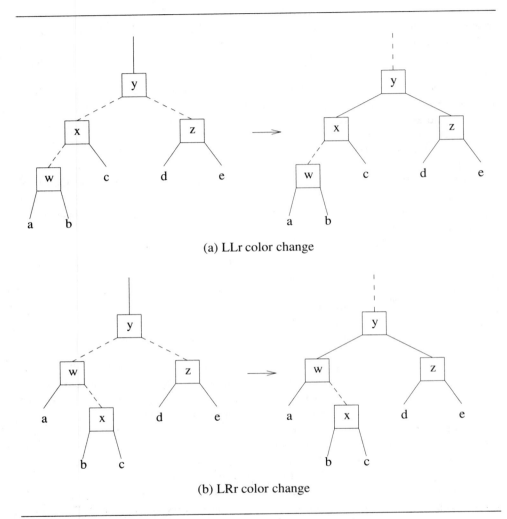

(a) LLr color change

(b) LRr color change

Figure 10.58 LLr and LRr color changes for bottom up insertion

10.11 SPLAY TREES

AVL, 2-3, 2-3-4, and red-black trees allow one to perform the search tree operations: insert, delete, and search in $O(\log n)$ worst case time per operation. In the case of priority queues we saw that if we are interested in amortized complexity rather than worst case complexity, simpler structures can be used. This is true even for search trees. Using a splay tree the search tree operations can be performed in $O(\log n)$ amortized time per

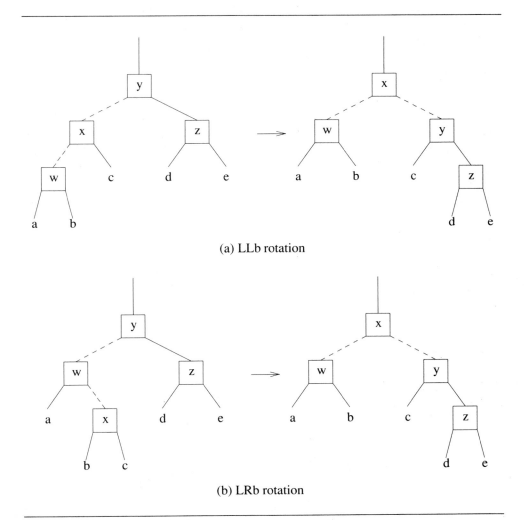

(a) LLb rotation

(b) LRb rotation

Figure 10.59 LLb and LRb rotations for bottom up insertion

operation.

A *splay tree* is a binary search tree in which each search, insert, and delete is performed in the same way as in an ordinary binary search tree (Chapter 5). However, each of these operations is followed by a *splay*. A splay consists of a sequence of rotations. For simplicity, we assume that each of the three operations is always successful. A failure can be modeled as a different successful operation. For example, an unsuccesful search may be modeled as a search for the element in the last node encountered in the unsuccessful search and an unsuccessful insert may be modeled as a successful search. With this assumption, the starting node for a splay is obtained as follows:

(1)   search. The splay starts at the node containing the searched for element.

(2)   insert. The start node for the splay is the newly inserted node.

(3)   delete. The parent of the physically deleted node is used as the start node for the splay. If this node is the root, then the splay start node is **nil**.

Splay rotations are performed along the path from the start node to the root of the binary search tree. These rotations are similar to those performed for AVL trees and red-black trees. Let q be the node at which the splay is being performed. Initially, q is the splay start node. The following steps define a splay:

(1)   If q is either **nil** or the root, then the splay terminates.

(2)   If q has a parent p but no grandparent, then the rotation of Figure 10.60 is performed and the splay terminates.

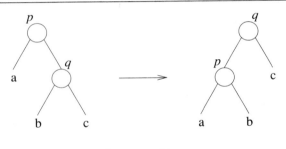

a, b, c are subtrees

Figure 10.60 Rotation when q is a right child and has no grandparent

(3)   If q has a parent p, and a grandparent gp, then the rotation is classified as LL (p is the left child of gp and q is the left child of p), LR (p is the left child of gp and q is the right child of p), RR, or RL. The RR and RL rotations are shown in Figure 10.61. LL and LR rotations are symmetric to these. The splay is repeated at the new location of q.

Notice that all rotations move q up the tree and that following a splay q becomes the new root of the search tree. Figure 10.62 shows an example binary search tree before, during, and after a splay at node *.

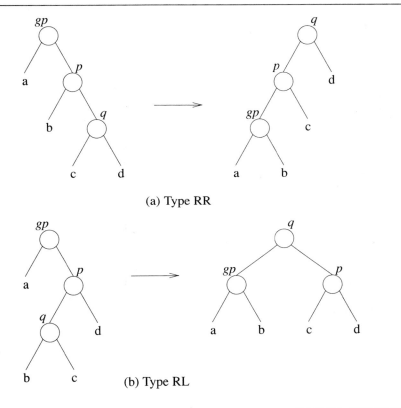

(a) Type RR

(b) Type RL

Figure 10.61 RR and RL rotations

In the case of Fibonnaci heaps, we obtained the amortized complexity of an operation by using an explicit cross charging scheme. The analysis for splay trees will use a *potential* technique. Let P_0 be the initial potential of the search tree and let P_i be its potential following the i'th operation in a sequence of n operations. The amortized time for the i'th operation is defined to be:

$$\text{(actual time for the } i\text{'th operation)} + P_i - P_{i-1}$$

That is, the amortized time is the actual time plus the change in the potential. Rearranging terms, we see that the actual time for the i'th operation is

$$\text{(amortized time for the } i\text{'th operation)} + P_{i-1} - P_i$$

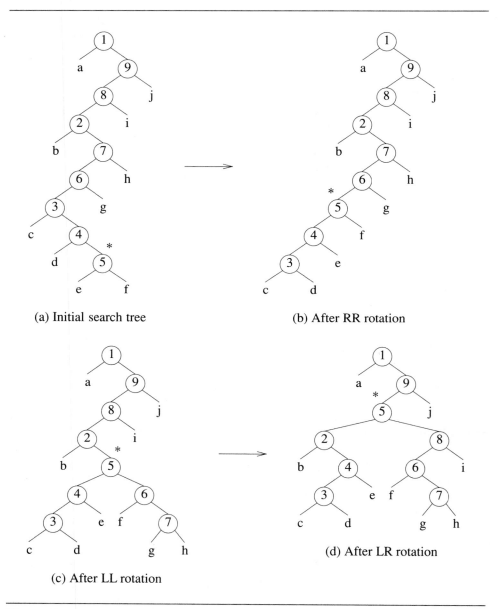

(a) Initial search tree

(b) After RR rotation

(c) After LL rotation

(d) After LR rotation

Figure 10.62 Rotations in a splay beginning at node * (continued)

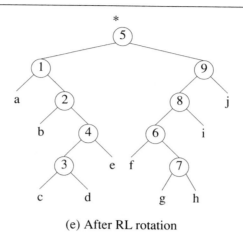

(e) After RL rotation

Figure 10.62 Rotations in a splay beginning at node *

Hence, the actual time needed to perform the n operations in the sequence is

$$\sum_i (\text{amortized time for the } i\text{'th operation}) + P_0 - P_n$$

Since each operation is followed by a splay whose actual complexity is of the same order as that of the whole operation, it is sufficient to consider only the time spent performing splays. Each splay consists of several rotations. We shall assign to each rotation a fixed cost of one unit. The choice of a potential function is rather arbitrary. The objective is to use one that results in as small a bound on the time complexity as is possible. The potential function we shall use is obtained in the following way. Let the size, $s(i)$, of the subtree with root i be the total number of nodes in it. The rank, $r(i)$, of node i is equal to $\log_2 s(i)$. The potential of the tree is $\sum_i r(i)$. The potential of an empty tree is defined to be zero. Suppose that in the tree of Figure 10.62(a), the subtrees a, b, . . ., j are all empty. Then, $(s(1), \ldots, s(9)) = (9, 6, 3, 2, 1, 4, 5, 7, 8)$; $r(4) = 1, r(5) = 0$, and $r(9) = 3$. In the following lemma we use r and r' to, respectively, denote the rank of a node before and after a rotation.

Lemma 10.4: Consider a binary search that has n elements / nodes. The amortized cost of a splay operation that begins at node q is at most $3(\log_2 n - r(q)) + 1$.

Proof: Consider the three steps in the definition of a splay.

(1) In this case, q is either **nil** or is the root. This step does not alter the potential of the tree. So its amortized and actual costs are the same. This cost is 1.

(2) In this step, the rotation of Figure 10.60 (or the symmetric rotation for the case q is the left child of p) is performed. Since only the ranks of p and q are affected, the potential change is $r'(p)+r'(q)-r(p)-r(q)$. Further, since $r'(p) < r(p)$ the potential change is less than $r'(q)-r(q)$. The amortized cost of this step (actual cost plus potential change) is, therefore, no more than $1+r'(q)-r(q)$.

(3) In this step only the ranks of q, p, and gp change. So, the potential change is $r'(q) + r'(p) + r'(gp) - r(q) - r(p) - r(gp)$. Consider an RR rotation. From Figure 10.61(a), we see that $r(gp) = r'(q), r'(q) > r'(p)$, and $r(p) > r(q)$. Using these in the equation for potential change, we see that the potential change cannot exceed $r'(q) + r'(gp) - 2r(q)$. This is at most $3(r'(q)-r(q))-2$. To prove this, we need to show that $2r'(q) - r'(gp) - r(q) \geq 2$. Let s and s', respectively, denote the size function before and after the rotation. So, $2r'(q) - r'(gp) - r(q) = 2\log_2 s'(q) - \log_2 s'(gp) - \log_2 s(q) = -(\log_2 A + \log_2 B)$, where $A = s'(gp)/s'(q)$ and $B = s(q)/s'(q))$. From Figure 10.61, we see that $a + b < 1$. So, $\log_2 A + \log_2 B \leq -2$. Hence, the amortized cost of an RR rotation is at most $1+3(r'(q)-r(q))-2 = 3(r'(q)-r(q))-1$. This bound may similarly be obtained for LL, LR, and RL rotations.

The lemma now follows by observing that steps 1 and 2 are mutually exclusive and can occur at most once. Step 3 occurs zero or more times. Summing up over the amortized cost of a single occurrence of steps 1 or 2 and all occurrences of step 3 we obtain the bound of the lemma. □

Theorem 10.3: The total time needed for a sequence of n search, insert, and delete operations performed on an initially empty splay tree is $O(n\log i)$ where $i, i > 0$, is the number of inserts in the sequence.

Proof: From our definition of the amortized cost of a splay operation, it follows that the time for the sequence of operations is the sum of the amortized costs of the splays and the potential change, $P_0 - P_n$. From Lemma 10.4, it follows that the sum of the amortized costs is $O(n\log i)$. The initial potential, P_0, is 0 and the final potential P_n is ≥ 0. So, the total time is $O(n\log i)$. □

10.12 DIGITAL SEARCH TREES

A *digital search tree* is a binary tree in which each node contains one element. The element to node assignment is determined by the binary representation of the element keys. Suppose that we number the bits in the binary representation of a key left to right beginning at one. Then bit one of 1000 is 1, while bits two, three, and four are 0. All keys in the left subtree of a node at level i have bit i equal to zero while those in the right subtree of nodes at this level have bit $i = 1$. Figure 10.63 shows an example digital search tree. This contains the keys 1000, 0010, 1001, 0001, 1100, and 0000.

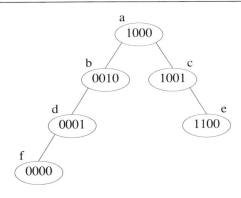

Figure 10.63 Example digital search tree

A search in a digital search tree is performed in the following way. Suppose we are to search for the key $k = 0011$ in the tree of Figure 10.63. k is first compared with the key in the root. Since k is different from the key in the root and since bit one of k is 0, we move to the left child, b, of the root. Now, since k is different from the key in node b and bit two of k is 0, we move to the left child, d, of b. As k is different from the key in node d and since bit three of k is one, we move to the right child of d. Node d has no right child to move to. From this we conclude that 1100 is not in the search tree. If we wish to insert k into the tree, then it is to be added as the right child of d. When this is done, we get the digital search tree of Figure 10.64.

The digital search tree procedures to search, insert, and delete are quite similar to the corresponding procedures for binary search trees. The essential difference is that the subtree to move to is determined by a bit in the search key rather than by the result of the comparison of the search key and the key in the current node. We leave the formal development of these procedures as an exercise.

Each of the above search tree operations can be performed in $O(h)$ time where h is the height of the digital search tree. If each key in a digital search tree has *KeySize* bits, then the height of the digital search tree is at most *KeySize* + 1.

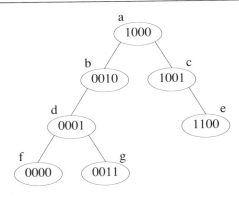

Figure 10.64 Digital search tree of Figure 10.63 following insertion of 0011

When we are dealing with very long keys, the cost of a key comparison is high. We can reduce the number of key comparisons to one by using a related structure called *Patricia* (*P*ractical *a*lgorithm *t*o *r*etrieve *i*nformation *c*oded *i*n *a*lphanumeric). We shall develop this structure in three steps. First, we introduce a structure called a binary trie. Then we transform binary tries into compressed binary tries. Finally, from compressed binary tries we obtain Patricia. Since binary tries and compressed binary tries are introduced only as a means of arriving at Patricia, we do not dwell much on how to manipulate these structures. A more general version of binary tries (called a trie) is considered in the next chapter.

A *binary trie* is a binary tree which has two kinds of nodes: *branch nodes* and *elements nodes*. A branch node has the two fields: *LeftChild* and *RightChild*. It has no *data* field. An element node has the single field *data*. Branch nodes are used to build a binary tree search structure similar to that of a digital search tree. This search structure leads to element nodes.

Figure 10.65 shows a six-element binary trie. To search for an element with key k, we use a branching pattern determined by the bits of k. The i'th bit of k is used at level i. If it is zero, the search moves to the left subtree. Otherwise, it moves to the right subtree. To search for 0010 we first follow the left child, then again the left child, and finally the right child.

Observe that a successful search in a binary trie always ends at an element node. Once this element node is reached, the key in this node is compared with the key we are searching for. This is the only key comparison that takes place. An unsuccessful search may terminate at either an element node or at a **nil** pointer.

The binary trie of Figure 10.65 contains branch nodes whose degree is one. By adding another field *BitNumber* to each branch node, we can eliminate all degree one branch nodes from the trie. The *BitNumber* field of a branch node gives the bit number

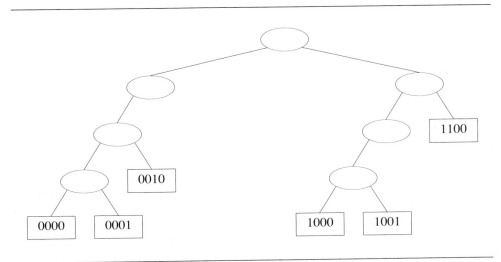

Figure 10.65 Example binary trie

of the key that is to be used at this node. Figure 10.66 gives the binary trie that results from the elimination of degree one branch nodes from the binary trie of Figure 10.65. The number outside a node is its *BitNumber*. A binary trie that has been modified in this way to contain no branch nodes of degree one is called a *compressed binary trie*.

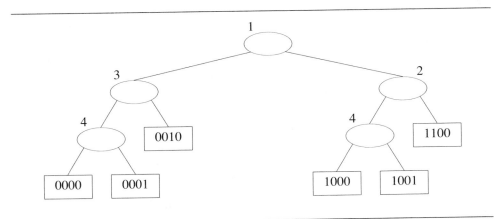

Figure 10.66 Binary trie of Figure 10.65 with degree one nodes eliminated

Compressed binary tries may be represented using nodes of a single type. The new nodes, called *augmented branch nodes* are the original branch nodes augmented by the field *data*. The resulting structure is called *Patricia* and is obtained from a compressed binary trie in the following way:

(1)   Replace each branch node by an augmented branch node.

(2)   Eliminate the element nodes.

(3)   Store the data previously in the element nodes in the data fields of the augmented branch nodes. Since every non empty compressed binary trie has one fewer branch node than it has element nodes, it is necessary to add one augmented branch node. This node is called the *head node*. The remaining structure is the left subtree of the head node. The head node has *BitNumber* equal to zero. Its right child field is not used. The assignment of data to augmented branch nodes is done in such a way that the *BitNumber* in the augmented branch node is less than or equal to that in the parent of the element node that contained this data.

(4)   Replace the original pointers to element nodes by pointers to the respective augmented branch nodes.

When the above transformations are performed on the compressed trie of Figure 10.66, we get the structure of Figure 10.67. Let *t* be an instance of Patricia. *t* is **nil** iff the instance is empty. An instance, *t*, with one element is represented by a head node whose left child field points to itself (Figure 10.68(a)).

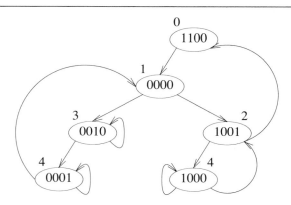

Figure 10.67 An example of Patricia

We can distinguish between pointers that were originally to branch nodes and those that were to element nodes by noting that, in Patricia, the former pointers are directed to nodes with a greater *BitNumber* value, while pointers of the latter type are directed to nodes whose *BitNumber* value is either equal to or less that that in the node where the pointer originates.

To search for an element with key *k* we begin at the head node and follow a path determined by the bits in *k*. When an element pointer is followed, the key in the reached node is compared with *k*. This is the only key comparison made. No comparisons are made on the way down. Suppose we wish to search for *k* = 0000 in the Patricia instance of Figure 10.67. We begin at the head node and follow the left child pointer to the node with 0000. The bit number field of this node is 1. Since bit one of *k* is 0, we follow the left child pointer to the node with 0010. Now bit three of *k* is used. Since this is 0, the search moves to the node with 0001. The bit number field of this node is 4. The fourth bit of *k* is zero, so we follow the left child field. This gets us to a node with bit number field less than that of the node we moved from. Hence, an element pointer was used. Comparing the key in this node with *k* we find a match and the search is successful.

Next, suppose that we are to search for *k* = 1011. We begin at the head node. The search successively moves to the nodes with 0000, 1001, 1000, 1001. *k* is compared with 1001. Since *k* is not equal to 1001, we conclude that there is no element with this key. The procedure to search an instance *t* of Patricia is given in Program 10.19. This procedure returns, in *y*, a pointer to the last node encountered in the search. If the key in this node is *k*, the search is successful. Otherwise, *t* contains no element with key *k*. The function *bit* (*i*, *j*) returns the *j*'th bit (the leftmost bit is bit one) of *i*.

```
procedure PatriciaSearch (t : Patricia ; k : KeyType ; var y : Patricia );
{Search t for the key k. y is set to point to the last node encountered}
var p : Patricia ;
begin
    if t = nil
    then y := nil {t is empty}
    else begin
            y := t ↑.LeftChild; {move to left child of head node}
            p := t; {p is the parent of y}
            while y ↑.BitNumber > p ↑.BitNumber do
            begin {follow a branch pointer}
                p := y;
                if bit (k, y ↑.BitNumber) = 0 then y := y ↑.LeftChild
                                             else y := y ↑.RightChild;
            end;
        end;
end;
```

Program 10.19 Searching Patricia

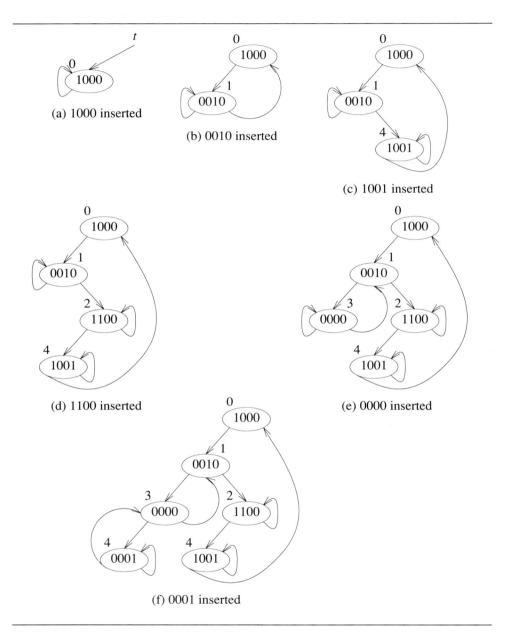

Figure 10.68 Insertion into Patricia

Let us now examine how we can insert new elements. Suppose we begin with an empty instance and wish to insert an element with key 1000. The result is an instance that has only a head node (Figure 10.68(a)). Next, consider inserting an element with key $k = 0010$. First, we search for this key using procedure *PatriciaSearch*. The search terminates at the head node. Since 0010 is not equal to the key $q = 1000$ in this node, we know that 0010 isn't currently in the Patricia instance and so the element may be inserted. For this, the keys k and q are compared to determine the first (i.e., leftmost) bit at which they differ. This is bit one. A new node containing the element with key k is added as the left child of the head node. Since bit one of k is zero, the left child field of this new node points to itself and its right child field points to the head node. The bit number field is set to 1. The resulting Patricia instance is shown in Figure 10.68(b).

Suppose that the next element to be inserted has $k = 1001$. The search for this key ends at the node with $q = 1000$. The first bit where k and q differ is bit $j = 4$. Now we search the instance of Figure 10.68(b) using only the first $j-1 = 3$ bits of k. The last move is from the node with 0010 to that with 1000. Since this is a right child move, a new node containing the element with key k is to be inserted as the right child of 0010. The bit number field of this node is set to $j = 4$. As bit four of k is 1, the right child field of the new node points to itself and its left child field points to the node with q. Figure 10.68(c) shows the resulting structure.

To insert $k = 1100$ into Figure 10.68(c), we first search for this key. Once again, $q = 1000$. The first bit where k and q differ is $j = 2$. The search using only the first $j-1$ bits ends at the node with 1001. The last move is a right child move from 0010. A new node containing the element with key k and bit number field $j = 2$ is added as the right child of 0010. Since bit j of k is one, the right child field of the new node points to itself. Its left child field points to the node with 1001 (this was previously the right child of 0010). The new Patricia instance is shown in Figure 10.68(d). Figure 10.68(e) shows the result of inserting an element with key 0000, and Figure 10.68(f) shows the Patrcia instance following the insertion of 0001.

The preceding discussion leads to the insertion procedure *PatriciaInsert* of Program 10.20. Its complexity is seen to be $O(h)$ where h is the height of t. h can be as large as min$\{KeySize + 1, n\}$ where *KeySize* is the number of bits in a key and n is the number of elements. When the keys are uniformly distributed the height is $O(\log n)$. We leave the development of the deletion procedure as an exercise.

10.13 REFERENCES AND SELECTED READINGS

Min-max heaps were developed in: ''Min-max heaps and generalized priority queues,'' by M. Atkinson, J. Sack, N. Santoro, and T. Strothotte, *Communications of the ACM*, pp. 996-1000, 29, 10, Oct. 1986. This paper also contains extensions of min-max heaps.

The deap data structure was invented by Svante Carlsson. The reference is: ''The deap - A double-ended heap to implement double-ended priority queues,'' *Information Processing Letters*, 26, pp. 33-36, 1987.

---

procedure *PatriciaInsert* (**var** *t* : *Patricia* ; *x* : *element*) ;
{Insert *x* into the Patricia instance *t*}
var *p*, *s*, *y*, *z* : *Patricia* ; *j* : **integer** ; *k* : *KeyType* ;
begin
  if *t* = **nil**
  then begin {*t* is empty}
       new (*t*); *t* ↑. *BitNumber* := 0; *t* ↑. *data* := *x*; *t* ↑.*LeftChild* := *t*;
     end
  else begin
      k := *x* . *key* ;
      PatriciaSearch (*t*, *k*, *y*);
      if *k* = *y* ↑. *key* **then** *InsertionError*
      else begin
         {find first bit where *k* and *y* ↑. *key* differ}
         j := 1; **while** *bit* (*k*, *j*) = *bit* (*y* ↑. *key*, *j*) **do** *j* := *j* +1 ;

         {Search *t* using first *j* −1 bits of *k*}
         s := *t* ↑. *LeftChild*; *p* := *t*;
         while (*s* ↑. *BitNumber* > *p* ↑. *BitNumber*) **and** (*s* ↑. *BitNumber* < *j*) **do**
         begin
           p := *s* ;
           if *bit* (*k*, *s* ↑. *BitNumber*) = 0 **then** *s* := *s* ↑. *LeftChild*
                             else *s* := *s* ↑. *RightChild* ;
         end;

         {Insert *x* as a child of *p*}
         new (*z*);
         with *z* **do**
         begin
           data := *x* ; *BitNumber* := *j* ;
           if *bit* (*k*, *j*) = 0 **then begin** *LeftChild* := *z* ; *RightChild* := *s* ; **end**
                            else begin *LeftChild* := *s* ; *RightChild* := *z* ; **end**;
         end;
         if *s* = *p* ↑. *LeftChild* **then** *p* ↑. *LeftChild* := *z*
                       else *p* ↑. *RightChild* := *z*;
      end;
    end;
end;

Program 10.20 Insertion procedure for Patricia

Leftist trees were invented by C. Crane: *Linear lists and priority queues as balanced binary trees*, Technical report CS-72-259, Computer Science Dept., Stanford University, CA, 1972.

Further discussion of leftist trees may be found in: *Data structures and network algorithms*, by R. Tarjan, SIAM, Philadelphia, PA, 1983.

The exercise on lazy deletion is from: ''Finding minimum spanning trees,'' by D. Cheriton and R. Tarjan, *SIAM Jr on Computing*, 5, 1976, pp. 724-742.

F-heaps were invented by M. Fredman and R. Tarjan. Their work is reported in the paper: ''Fibonacci heaps and their uses in improved network optimization algorithms,'' *JACM*, 34, 3, July 1987, pp. 596-615. This paper also describes several variants of the basic F-heap as discussed here as well as the application of F-heaps to the assignment problem and to the problem of finding a minimum cost spanning tree. Their result is that using F-heaps, minimum cost spanning trees can be found in $O(e\beta(e,n))$ time where $\beta(e,n) \leq \log^*n$ when $e \geq n$. $\log^*n = \min\{i \mid \log^{(i)}n \leq 1\}$, $\log^{(0)}n = n$, and $\log^{(i)}n = \log(\log^{(i-1)}n)$. The complexity of finding minimum cost spanning trees has been further reduced to $O(e\log\beta(e,n))$. The reference for this is: ''Efficient algorithms for finding minimum spanning trees in undirected and directed graphs,'' by H. Gabow, Z. Galil, T. Spencer, and R. Tarjan, *Combinatorica*, 6, 2, 1986, pp. 109-122.

The $O(n^2)$ optimum binary search tree algorithm is from: ''Optimum Binary Search Trees,'' by D. Knuth, *Acta Informatica*, 1, 1, 1971, pp. 14-25.

For a discussion of heuristics that obtain in $O(n \log n)$ time nearly optimal binary search trees see: ''Nearly Optimal Binary Search Trees,'' by K. Melhorn, *Acta Informatica*, 5, 1975, pp. 287-295; and ''Binary Search Trees and File Organization,'' by J. Nievergelt, *ACM Computing Surveys*, Vol.6, No. 3, Sept. 1974, pp. 195-207.

For more on Huffman codes see: ''An Optimum Encoding with Minimum Longest Code and Total Number of Digits,'' by E. Schwartz, *Information and Control*, 7, 1964, pp. 37-44.

The original paper on AVL trees by G. M. Adelson-Velskii and E. M. Landis appears in *Dokl. Acad. Nauk.*, SSR (Soviet Math), 3, 1962, pp. 1259-1263. Additional algorithms to manipulate AVL trees may be found in: ''Linear lists and priority queues as balanced binary trees,'' by C. Crane, STAN-CS-72-259, Computer Science Department, Stanford University, February 1972, and *The Art of Computer Programming: Sorting and Searching* by D. Knuth, Addison-Wesley, Reading, Massachusetts, 1973 (Section 6.2.3).

Results of an empirical study of height balanced trees appear in: ''Performance of Height-Balanced Trees,'' by P. L. Karlton, S. H. Fuller, R. E. Scroggs and E. B. Koehler, *CACM*, 19, 1, Jan. 1976, pp. 23-28.

2-3 trees and 2-3-4 trees are a special case of B-trees. References to B-trees are provided in the next chapter. The variations of 2-3 trees referred to in the exercises are from: *The design and analysis of computer algorithms*, by A. Aho, J. Hopcroft, and J. Ullman, Addison-Wesley, Reading, MA, 1974, and *Data structures and algorithms*, by A. Aho, J. Hopcroft, and J. Ullman, Addison-Wesley, Reading, MA, 1983.

Red-black trees were invented by R. Bayer. The reference is: "Symmetric binary B-trees: data structure and maintenence," *Acta. Infor.*, Vol 1, No 4, 1972, pp. 290-306.

Our treatment of red-black trees is due to Guibas and Sedgewick. The top-down single pass insertion and deletion algorithms for 2-3-4 trees are also due to them. The reference is: "A dichromatic framework for balanced trees," by L. Guibas and R. Sedgewick, *Proceedings 19th IEEE symposium on foundations of computer science*, pp. 8-21, 1978.

Bottom up insertion and deletion algorithms for red-black trees were proposed by R. Tarjan in the paper: "Updating a balanced search tree in O(1) rotations," *Info. Process. Letters*, 16, 5, 1983, pp. 253-257.

The paper: "Planar point location using persistent search trees," by N. Sarnak and R. Tarjan, *CACM*, 27, 9, 1986, pp. 669-679, develops a persistent variety of red-black trees. A persistent data structure is one which all previous versions plus the current version of the data structure can be accessed efficiently. The above paper also applies persistent red-black trees to the planar point location problem.

Splay trees were invented by D. Sleator and R. Tarjan. Their paper: "Self-adjusting binary search trees," *JACM*, 32, 3, July 1985, pp. 652-686, provides several other analyses of splay trees as well as variants of the basic splaying technique discussed in the text. There are several other data structures that provide good amortized performance for priority queue and search tree operations. The exercises examine some of these. The references for these additional structures are: "Self-adjusting heaps," by D. Sleator and R. Tarjan, *SIAM Jr. on Computing*, 15, 1, Feb 1986, pp. 52-69, and "Biased search trees," by S. Bent, D. Sleator, and R. Tarjan, *SIAM Jr. on Computing*, 14, 3, Aug 1985, pp. 545-568.

Digital search trees were first proposed by E. Coffman and J. Eve in *CACM*, 13, 1970, pp. 427-432.

References on tries are provided in the next chapter. The structure Patricia is due to D. Morrison. Digital search trees, tries, and Patricia are analyzed in the book: *The Art of Computer Programming: Sorting and Searching* by D. Knuth, Addison-Wesley, Reading, Massachusetts, 1973 (Section 6.3).

10.14 EXERCISES

1. Write the procedure *VerifyMin* defined in connection with insertion into a min-max heap.

2. Write the function *level* (i) which determines whether node i of a min-max heap is on a min or a max level

3. Write the function *MinChildGrandChild* (i) which returns the child or grandchild of node i of a min-max heap that has the smallest key. You may assume that i has at least one child.

4. Write a procedure *DeleteMax* to delete the element with maximum key in a min-max heap. Your algorithm should run in $O(\log n)$ time for a min-max heap with n elements.

5. Write a procedure to initialize a min-max heap with n elements. Do this using the idea used to initialize a min (or max) heap using a series of adjusts. Show that your procedure takes $O(n)$ time rather than the $O(n \log n)$ time that would be taken if initialization is done by performing n insertions into an initially empty heap.

6. Complete procedure *DeapInsert* (Program 10.4) by writing all the procedures and functions it uses. Test the insertion procedure by running it on a computer. Generate your own test data.

7. Refine procedure *DeapDeleteMin* (Program 10.5) into a Pascal procedure. Test the correctness of your procedure running the procedure on a computer using test data of your choice.

8. Write a procedure to initialize a deap with n elements. Your procedure must run in $O(n)$ time. Show that your procedure actually has this running time. (Hint: Proceed as in the initialization of a min-heap or max-heap.)

9. Write the procedures to perform all double-ended priority queue operations both for a min-max heap and for a deap.

   (a) Use suitable test data to test the correctness of your procedures.

   (b) Create a random list of n elements and a random sequence of insert, delete min, and delete max operations of length m. This latter sequence is created such that the probability of an insert is approximately .5 while that of each type of delete is approximately .25. Initialize a min-max heap and a deap to contain the n elements in the first random list. Now, measure the time to perform the m operations using the min-max heap as well as the deap. Divide this time by m to get the average time per operation. Do this for $n =$ 100, 500, 1000, 2000, . . ., 5000. Let m be 5000. Tabulate your computing times.

   (c) Based on your experiments, what can you say about the relative merits of the two double ended priority queue schemes?

10. Obtain an exact count of the worst case number of key comparisons that can be made during each of the double-ended priority queue operations when a min-max heap is used. Do this also for the case when a deap is used. What can you say about the expected worst case performance of these two methods? Can you think of a way to reduce the worst case number of comparisons using a binary search (this will not affect the number of element moves though)?

11. Let t be an arbitrary binary tree represented using the node structure for a leftist tree.

      (a)   Write a procedure to initialize the *shortest* field of each node in *t*.

      (b)   Write a procedure to convert *t* into a leftist tree.

      (c)   What is the complexity of each of the above two procedures?

12.   Write a procedure to initialize a min leftist tree with *n* elements. Assume that nodes have the same structure as used in the text. Your procedure must run in $\Theta(n)$ time. Show that this is the case. Can you think of a way to do this initialization in $\Theta(n)$ time, and such that the resulting min leftist tree is also a complete binary tree?

13.   Write a procedure to delete the element in node *x* of the min leftist tree *a*. Assume that each node has the fields: *LeftChild*, *RightChild*, *parent*, *shortest*, and *data*. The *parent* field of a node points to its parent in the leftist tree. Show that this deletion can be performed in $O(\log n)$, where *n* is the number of elements in *a*.

14.   [Lazy deletion] Another way to handle the deletion of arbitrary elements from a min leftist heap is to use a boolean field, *deleted*, in place of the parent field of the previous exercise. When an element is deleted, its *deleted* field is set to **true**. However, the node is not physically deleted. When a delete min operation is performed, we first search for the minimum element not deleted by performing a limited preorder search. This preorder search traverses only the upper part of the tree as needed to identify the min element. All deleted elements encountered are physically deleted and their subtrees combined to obtain the new min leftist tree.

      (a)   Write a procedure to delete the element in node *x* of the min leftist tree *a*.

      (b)   Write another procedure to delete the min element from a min leftist tree from which several elements have been deleted using the former procedure.

      (c)   What is the complexity of this latter procedure as a function of the number of deleted elements encountered and the number of elements in the entire tree?

15.   Prove that the binomial tree B_k has 2^k nodes, $k \geq 0$.

16.   Prove that if we start with empty F-heaps and perform only the operations insert, combine, and delete min, then all min-trees in the F-heaps are binomial trees.

17.   Show that if we start with empty F-heaps and do not perform cascading cuts, then it is possible for a sequence of F-heap operations to result in degree *k* min-trees that have only $k + 1$ nodes, $k \geq 1$.

18.   Write Pascal procedures to do the following:

      (a)   Create an empty F-heap

      (b)   Insert element *x* into an F-heap

      (c)   Perform a delete min from an F-heap. The deleted element is to be returned in *z*

(d)   Delete the element in node b of an F-heap a. The deleted element is to be returned in z

(e)   Decrease the key in the node b of an F-heap a by some positive amount c.

Note that all operations must leave behind properly structured F-heaps. Your procedures for (d) and (e) must perform cascading cuts. Test the correctness of your procedures by running them on a computer using suitable test data.

19.   For the Fibonacci numbers F_k and the numbers N_i of Lemma 10.3, prove the following:

(a) $F_h = \sum_{k=0}^{h-2} F_k + 1, h > 1$

(b)   Use (a) to show that $N_i = F_{i+2}, i \geq 0$.

(c)   Use the equality $F_k = \frac{1}{\sqrt{5}}(\frac{1+\sqrt{5}}{2})^k - \frac{1}{\sqrt{5}}(\frac{1-\sqrt{5}}{2})^k, k \geq 0$ to show that $F_{k+2} \geq \phi^k, k \geq 0$, where $\phi = (1+\sqrt{5})/2$.

20.   Implement the single source shortest path algorithm of Chapter 6 using the data structures recommended there as well as using F-heaps. Generate 10 connected undirected graphs with different edge densities (say 10%, 20%, . . ., 100% of maximum) for each of the cases $n = 100, 200, . . ., 500$. Assign random costs to the edges (use a uniform random number generator in the range [1, 1000]). Measure the run times of the two implementations of the shortest path algorithms. Plot the average times for each n.

21.   (a)   Prove by induction that if T is a binary tree with n internal nodes, I its internal path length and E its external path length, then $E = I + 2n, n \geq 0$.

(b)   Using the result of (a), show that the average number of comparisons s in a successful search is related to the average number of comparions, u, in an unsuccessful search by the formula

$$s = (1 + 1/n)u - 1, \ n \geq 1$$

22.   (a)   Show that algorithm *huffman* correctly generates a binary tree of minimal weighted external path length.

(b)   When n runs are to be merged together using an m-way merge, Huffman's method generalizes to the following rule: "First add $(1 - n) \bmod (m - 1)$ runs of length zero to the set of runs. Then repeatedly merge together the m shortest remaining runs until only one run is left." Show that this rule yields an optimal merge pattern for m-way merging.

23.   Using algorithm *obst*, compute w_{ij}, r_{ij}, and c_{ij}, $0 \leq i < j \leq 4$ for the identifier set $(a_1, a_2, a_3, a_4) = (\textbf{end}, \textbf{goto}, \textbf{print}, \textbf{read})$ with $p_1 = 1/20$, $p_2 = 1/5$, $p_3 = 1/10$, $p_4 = 1/20$, $q_0 = 1/5$, $q_1 = 1/10$, $q_2 = 1/5$, $q_3 = 1/20$, $q_4 = 1/20$. Using the r_{ij}'s, construct the optimal binary search tree.

24.   (a)   Show that the computing time of algorithm *obst* is $O(n^2)$.

    (b)   Write an algorithm to construct the optimal binary search tree T_{on} given the roots r_{ij} , $0 \leq i < j \leq n$. Show that this can be done in time $O(n)$.

25.   Since, often, only the approximate values of the p's and q's are known, it is perhaps just as meaningful to find a binary search tree that is nearly optimal; i.e., its cost, Eq. (10.1), is almost minimal for the given p's and q's. This exercise explores an $O(n \log n)$ algorithm that results in nearly optimal binary search trees. The search tree heuristic we shall study is:

Choose the root A_k such that $|w_{0,k-1} - w_{k,n}|$ is as small as possible. Repeat this procedure to find the left and right subtrees of A_k.

    (a)   Using this heuristic obtain the resulting binary search tree for the data of Exercise 3. What is its cost?

    (b)   Write a Pascal algorithm implementing the above heuristic. Your algorithm should have a time complexity of at most $O(n \log n)$.

An analysis of the performance of this heuristic may be found in the paper by Melhorn.

26.   (a)   Convince yourself that Figures 10.37 and 10.38 take care of all the possible situations that may arise when a height balanced binary tree becomes unbalanced as a result of an insertion. Alternately, come up with an example that is not covered by any of the cases in these figures.

    (b)   Complete Figure 10.38 by drawing the tree configurations for the rotations RL (a), (b) and (c).

27.   Complete algorithm *avlinsert* by filling in the steps needed to rebalance the tree in case the imbalance is of type *RL*.

28.   Obtain the height balanced trees corresponding to those of Figure 10.36 using algorithm *avlinsert*, starting with an empty tree, on the following sequence of insertions:

DECEMBER, JANUARY, APRIL, MARCH, JULY, AUGUST,
OCTOBER, FEBRUARY, NOVEMBER, MAY, JUNE

Label the rotations according to type.

29.   Assume that each node in an AVL tree t has the field *lsize*. For any node, a, $a \uparrow. lsize$ is the number of nodes in its left subtree +1. Write an algorithm *avlfind* (t,k) to locate the k-th smallest identifier in the subtree t. Show that this can be done in $O(\log n)$ time if there are n nodes in t.

30.   Rewrite algorithm *avlinsert* with the added assumption that each node has a *lsize* field as in Exercise 29. Show that the insertion time remains $O(\log n)$.

31. Write an algorithm to list the nodes of an AVL-tree T in ascending order of *ident* fields. Show that this can be done in O(n) time if T has n nodes.

32. Write an algorithm to delete the node with identifier x from an AVL tree t. The resulting tree should be restructured if necessary. Show that the time required for this is O(log n) when there are n nodes in t.

33. Do Exercise 32 for the case when each node has a *lsize* field and the k-th smallest identifier is to be deleted.

34. Write an algorithm to merge the nodes of the two AVL trees T_1 and T_2 together to obtain a new AVL tree. What is the computing time of your algorithm?

35. Write an algorithm to split an AVL tree, T, into two AVL trees T_1 and T_2 such that all identifiers in T_1 are $\leq x$ and all those in T_2 are $> x$.

36. Prove by induction that the minimum number of nodes in an AVL tree of height h is $N_h = F_{h+2} - 1$, $h \geq 0$.

37. Complete Table 10.1 by adding a column for hashing.

38. For a fixed k, $k \geq 1$, we define a height balanced tree $HB(k)$ as below:

    Definition An empty binary tree is a $HB(k)$ tree. If T is a non-empty binary tree with T_L and T_R as its left and right subtrees, then T is $HB(k)$ iff (a) T_L and T_R are $HB(k)$ and (b) $|h_L - h_R| \leq k$, where h_L and h_R are the heights of T_L and T_R, respectively. $\square$

    For the case of $HB(2)$ trees, obtain the rebalancing transformations.

39. Write an insertion algorithm for $HB(2)$ trees.

40. Write the function *compare* used in Program 10.12.

41. Develop the procedures *FindNode*, *NewRoot*, *PutIn*, and *split* used by procedure *insert* 23 (Program 10.13). Put these together and test the correctness of procedure *insert* 23. Next use random insertions and measure the height of the resulting 2-3 trees with $n = 100$, 1000, and 10,000 elements.

42. Complete Figure 10.44 by providing the figures for the case p is a middle child and p is a right child.

43. Develop a complete Pascal procedure to delete the element with key x from the 2-3 tree t. Test this procedure using at least five different 2-3 trees of your choice. For each of these perform at least six successive deletions.

44. Consider a variation of a 2-3 tree in which elements are kept only in leaf nodes. Each leaf has exactly one element. The remaining nodes are 2-nodes or 3-nodes. Each such node keeps only the values *largeA* = largest key in any leaf in its left subtree and *largeB* = largest key in any leaf in its middle subtree. As before, all external nodes are at the same level.

(a) Define two node structures such that one is suitable to represent a leaf node and other to represent a nonleaf node.

(b) Write a procedure to search such a 2-3 tree represented in this way.

(c) Write a procedure to insert an element x into this tree.

(d) Write a deletion procedure for such a 2-3 tree.

(e) Show that each of the above operations can be performed in $O(\log n)$ time where n is the number of elements (i.e., leaf nodes) in the tree.

45. Complete Figure 10.48 by drawing the splitting transformations for the cases when the 4-node is the left middle child and the right middle child of a 3-node.

46. Complete procedure *insert* 234 (Program 10.18) by writing the code for all the procedures and functions used. Test your procedure using randomly generated keys.

47. Use the deletion transformations described in the text to obtain a procedure to delete an element y from a 2-3-4 tree represented using nodes of type *TwoThreeFour*. Show that the complexity of you algorithm is $O(\log n)$, where n is the number of elements initially in the tree.

48. Rewrite procedure *insert* 234 (Program 10.18) so that it inserts an element into a 2-3-4 tree represented as a red-black tree.

49. Obtain the symmetric transforms for Figure 10.58 and Figure 10.59.

50. Show that it isn't possible to implement the single source shortest path algorithm of Chapter 6 so as to have complexity less than $O(e + n\log n)$.

51. Obtain a procedure to delete an element y from a 2-3-4 tree represented as a red-black tree. Use the top down method. Test the correctness of this procedure by running it on a computer. Generate your own test data.

52. Do the preceding exercise using the bottom up method.

53. The number of color fields in a node of a red-black tree may be reduced to one. In this case the color of a node represents the color of the pointer (if any) from the node's parent to that node. Write the corresponding insert and delete procedures using the top down approach. How would this change in the node structure affect the efficiency of the insert and delete procedures?

54. Do the previous exercise for the bottom up approach.

55. [Skewed heaps] A *skewed heap* is a min-tree which supports the min leftist tree operations: insert, delete min, and combine in amortized time $O(\log n)$ per operation. As in the case of min leftist trees, inserts and deletes are performed using the combine operation which is carried out by following the rightmost paths in the two heaps being combined. However, unlike min leftist trees, the left and right subtrees of all nodes (except the last) on the rightmost path in the resulting heap are interchanged.

(a) Write insert, delete min, and combine procedures for skewed heaps.

(b) Compare the running times of these with those for the same operations on a min leftist tree. Use random sequences of insert, delete min, and combine operations.

56. Obtain figures corresponding to Figure 10.60 and Figure 10.61 for the symmetric splay rotations.

57. Complete the proof of Lemma 10.4 by providing the proof for the case of an RL rotation. Note that the proofs for LL and LR rotations are similar to those for RR and RL rotations, respectively, as the rotations are symmetric.

58. [Sleator and Tarjan] Suppose we modify the definition of $s(i)$ used in connection with the complexity analysis of splay trees. Let each node i have a positive weight $w(i)$. Let $s(i)$ be the sum of the weights of all nodes in the subtree with root i. The rank of a i is $\log_2 s(i)$.

(a) Let t be a splay tree. Show that the amortized cost of a splay that begins at node q is at most $3(r(t)-r(q))+1$ where r is the rank just before the splay.

(b) Let S be a sequence of n inserts and m searches. Assume that each of the n inserts adds a new element to the splay tree and that all searches are successful. Let $p(i), p(i) > 0$, be the number of times element i is searched for. The $p(i)$'s satisfy the equality

$$\sum_{i=1}^{n} p(i) = m$$

Show that the total time spent on the m searches is

$$O(m + \sum_{i=1}^{n} p(i)\log(m/p(i)))$$

Note that since $\Omega(m + \sum_{i=1}^{n} p(i)\log(m/p(i)))$ is an information theoretic bound on the search time in a static search tree (the OBST of this chapter is an example of such a tree), splay trees are optimal to within a constant factor for the representation of a static set of elements.

59. Write the digital search tree procedures for the search, insert, and delete operations. Assume that each key has *KeySize* bits and that the function $bit(k, i)$ returns the i'th (from the left) bit of the key k. Show that each of your procedures has complexity O(h) where h is the height of the digital search tree.

60. Write the binary trie procedures for the search, insert, and delete operations. Assume that each key has *KeySize* bits and that the function $bit(k, i)$ returns the i'th (from the left) bit of the key k. Show that each of your procedures has complexity O(h) where h is the height of the binary trie.

61. Write the compressed binary trie procedures for the search, insert, and delete operations. Assume that each key has *KeySize* bits and that the function *bit* (k, i) returns the i'th (from the left) bit of the key k. Show that each of your procedures has complexity $O(h)$, where h is the height of the compressed binary trie.

62. Write a procedure to delete the element with key k from the Patricia instance t. The complexity of your algorithm should be $O(h)$, where h is the height of t. Show that this is the case.

CHAPTER 11
FILES

11.1 FILES, QUERIES, AND SEQUENTIAL ORGANIZATIONS

A file, as described in earlier chapters (and as distinct from the **file** type in Pascal), is a collection of records where each record consists of one or more fields. For example, the records in an employee file could contain these fields:

> Employee Number (E#)
> Name
> Occupation
> Degree (Highest Degree Obtained)
> Sex
> Location
> Martial Status (MS)
> Salary

Sample data for such a file is provided in Figure 11.1. The primary objective of file organization is to provide a means for record retrieval and update. The update of a record could involve its deletion, changes in some of its fields or the insertion of an entirely new record. Certain fields in the record are designated as key fields. Records may be retrieved by specifying values for some or all of these keys. A combination of key values specified for retrieval will be termed a *query*. Let us assume that in the employee file of Figure 11.1 the field Employee Number, Occupation, Sex, and Salary have been designated as key fields. Then, some of the valid queries to the file are:

Retrieve the records of all employees with

Record	E#	Name	Occupation	Degree	Sex	Location	MS	Salary
A	800	HAWKINS	programmer	B.S.	M	Los Angeles	S	10,000
B	510	WILLIAMS	analys.	B.S.	F	Los Angeles	M	15,000
C	950	FRAWLEY	analyst	M.S.	F	Minneapolis	S	12,000
D	750	AUSTIN	programmer	B.S.	F	Los Angeles	S	12,000
E	620	MESSER	programmer	B.S.	M	Minneapolis	M	9,000

Figure 11.1 Sample data for employee file

Q1: Sex = M
Q2: Salary > 9,000
Q3: Salary > average salary of all employees
Q4: (Sex = M **and** Occupation = Programmer) **or**
(Employee Number > 700 **and** Sex = F)

One invalid query to the file would be to specify location = Los Angeles, as the location field was not designated as a key field. While it might appear that the functions one wishes to perform on a file are the same as those performed on a symbol table (Chapter 9), several complications are introduced by the fact that the files we are considering in this chapter are too large to be held in internal memory. The tables of Chapter 9 were small enough that all processing could be carried out without accessing external storage devices such as disks and tapes.

In this chapter, we are concerned with obtaining data representations for files on external storage devices so that required functions (e.g., retrieval, update) may be carried out efficiently. The particular organizaton most suitable for any application will depend upon such factors as the kind of external storage device available, type of queries allowed, number of keys, mode of retrieval and mode of update. Let us elaborate on these factors.

Storage Device Types

We shall be concerned primarily with direct access storage devices (DASD) as exemplified by disks. Some discussion of tape files will also be made.

Query Types

The examples Q1-Q4 above, typify the kinds of queries one may wish to make. The four query types are:

Q1: Simple Query: The value of a single key is specified.

Q2: Range Query: A range of values for a single key is specified.

Q3: Functional Query: Some function of key values in the file is specified (e.g., average or median).

Q4: Boolean Query: A boolean combination of Q1-Q3 using the logical operators **and, or, not**.

Number of Keys

The chief distinction here will be between having only one key and files with more than one key.

Mode of Retrieval

The mode of retrieval may be either real time or batched. In real time retrieval, the response time for any query should be minimal (say a few seconds from the time the query is made). In a bank, the accounts file has a mode of retrieval that is real time, since requests to determine a balance must be satisfied quickly. Similarly, in an airline reservation system we must be able to determine the status of a flight (i.e., number of seats vacant) in a matter of a few seconds. In the batched mode of retrieval, the response time is not very significant. Requests for retrieval are batched together on a ''transaction file'' until either enough requests have been received or a suitable amount of time has passed. Then all queries on the transaction file are processed.

Mode of Update

The mode of update may, again, be either real time or batched. Real time update is needed, for example, in a reservation system. As soon as a seat on a flight is reserved, the file must be changed to indicate the new status. Batched update would be suitable in a bank account system where all deposits and withdrawals made on a particular day could be collected on a transaction file and the updates made at the end of the day. In the case of batched update one may consider two files: the Master File and the Transactions File. The Master File represents the file status after the previous update run. The transactions file holds all update requests that haven't yet been reflected in the master file. Thus, in the case of batched update, the master file is always 'out of date' to the extent that update requests have been batched on the transaction file. In the case of a bank file using real time retrieval and batched update, this would mean that only account balances at the end of the previous business day could be determined, since today's deposits and withdrawls haven't yet been incorporated into the master file.

The simplest situation is one in which there is only one key, the only queries allowed are of type $Q1$ (simple query), and all retrievals and updates are batched. For this situation tapes are an adequate storage medium. All the required functions can be carried out efficiently by maintaining the master file on a tape. The records in the file are ordered by the key field. Requests for retrieval and update are batched onto a transaction tape. When it is time to process the transactions, the transactions are sorted into order by the key field and an update process similar to algorithm *verify2* of Section 7.1 is carried out, creating a new master file. All records in the old master file are examined, changed if necesssary, and then written out onto a new master file. The time required for the whole process is essentially $O(n+m\log m)$, where n and m are the number of records in the master and transaction files, respectively (to be more accurate this has to be multiplied by the record length). This procedure is good only when the number of transactions that have been batched is reasonably large. If $m=1$ and $n=10^6$, then clearly it is very wasteful to process the entire master file. In the case of tapes, however, this is the best we can do since it is usually not possible to alter a record in the middle of a tape without destroying information in an adjacent record. The file organization described above for tape files will be referred to as *sequentially ordered*.

In this organization, records are placed sequentially onto the storage media, (i.e., they occupy consecutive locations and in the case of a tape this would mean placing records adjacent to each other). In addition, the physical sequence of records is ordered on some key, called the *primary key*. For example, if the file of Figure 11.1 were stored on a tape in the sequence A, B, C, D, E, then we would have a sequential file. This file, however, is unordered. If the primary key is Employee Number, then physical storage of the file in the sequence B, E, D, A, C, would result in an ordered sequential file. For batched retrieval and update, ordered sequential files are preferred over unordered sequential files since they are easier to process (compare *verify2* with *verify1* of Section 7.1).

Sequential organization is also possible in the case of a DASD such as a disk. Even though disk storage is really two dimensional (cylinder × surface) it may be mapped down into a one dimensional memory using the technique of Section 2.4. If the disk has c cylinders and s surfaces, one possibility would be to view disk memory sequentially as in Figure 11.2. Using the notation t_{ij} to represent the j'th track of the i'th surface, the sequence is $t_{1,1}, t_{2,1}, t_{3,1}, \ldots, t_{s,1}, t_{1,2}, \ldots, t_{s,2}$ etc.

If each employee record in the file of Figure 11.1 were one track long, then a possible sequential organization would store the records A, B, C, D, and E, onto tracks $t_{3,4}$, $t_{4,4}, t_{5,4}, t_{6,4}$, and $t_{7,4}$, respectively (assuming $c \geq 4$ and $s \geq 7$). Using the interpretation of Figure 11.2, the physical sequence in which the records have been stored is A, B, C, D, E. If the primary key is Employee Number then the logical sequence for the records is B, E, D, A, C as $E\#(B) < E\#(E) < \ldots < E\#(C)$. This would thus correspond to an unordered sequential file. In case the records are stored in the physical sequence B, E, D, A, C, then the file is ordered on the primary key, the logical and physical record sequences are the same, and the organization is that of a sequentially ordered file. Batched retrieval and update can be carried out essentially in the same way as for a sequentially ordered tape file by setting up input and output buffers and reading in, perhaps, one track of the master and transaction files at a time (the transaction file should be sorted on the primary key before beginning the master file processing). If updates do not change the size of records and no insertions are involved, then the updated track may be written back onto the old master file. The sequential interpretation of Figure 11.2 is particularly efficient for batched update and retrieval as the tracks are to be accessed in the order: all tracks on cylinder 1 followed by all tracks on cylinder 2, etc. As a result of this, the read/write heads are moved one cylinder at a time and this movement is necessitated only once for every s tracks read (s = number of surfaces). The alternative sequential interpretation (Figure 11.3) would require accessing tracks in the order: all tracks on surface 1, all tracks on surface 2, etc. In this case, a head movement would be necessitated for each track being read (except for tracks 1 and c).

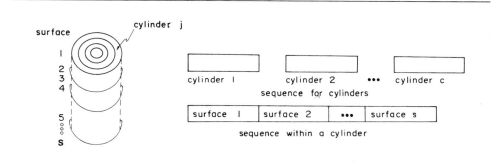

Figure 11.2 Interpreting disk memory as sequential memory

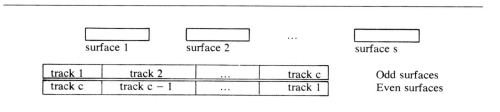

Figure 11.3 Alternative sequential interpretation of disk memory

Since, in batched update and retrieval, the entire master file is scanned (typical files might contain 10^5 or more records), enough transactions must be batched for this to be cost effective. In the case of disks, it is possible to extend this sequential ordered organization for use even in situations where the number of transactions batched is not enough to justify scanning the entire master file. First, take the case of a retrieval. If the records are of a fixed size, then it is possible to use binary search to obtain the record with the desired key value. For a file containing n records, this would mean at most $\lceil \log_2 n \rceil$ accesses would have to be made to retrieve the record. For a file with 10^5

records of length 300 characters, this would mean a maximum of 17 accesses. On a disk with maximum seek time 1/10 sec, latency time of 1/40 sec and a track density of 5000 characters/track this would mean a retrieval time of at most

$$17\left[1/10 + 1/40 + \frac{300}{5000}\times\frac{1}{40}\right] \text{ sec} \approx 2.15 \text{ sec}$$

Retrieving an arbitrary record from the same file stored on a tape with density 1600 bpi and a tape speed of 150 in/sec would in the worst case require 125 sec, as the entire file must be read to access the last record (this does not include the time to cross interblock gaps and to restart tape motion, etc. The actual time needed will be more than 125 sec).

When records are of variable size, binary search can no longer be used, as, given the address of the first and last records in a file, one can no longer calculate the address of the middle record. The retrieval time can be considerably reduced by maintaining an index to guide the search. An index is just a collection of key value and address pairs. In the case of the file of Figure 11.1 stored in the physical sequence B, E, D, A, C, at addresses $t_{1,2}$, $t_{2,2}$, $t_{3,2}$, $t_{4,2}$, and $t_{5,2}$, the index could contain five entries, one for each record in the file. The entries would be the pairs $(510, t_{1,2})$, $(620, t_{2,2})$, $(750, t_{3,2})$, $(800, t_{4,2})$, and $(900, t_{5,2})$. An index which contains one entry for every record in the file will be referred to as a *dense index*. If a dense index is maintained for the primary key, then retrieval of a record with primary key $= x$ could be carried out by first looking into the index and finding the pair $(x, addr)$. The desired record would then be retrieved from the location *addr*. The total number of accesses needed to retrieve a record would now be one plus the number of accesses needed to locate the tuple $(x, addr)$ in the index. In Section 11.2, we shall look at efficient indexing techniques that allow index searches to be carried out using at most three accesses even for reasonably large files. This means that a retrieval from the file of 10^5 records discussed earlier could be carried out making at most four accesses, rather than the seventeen accesses needed by a binary search. Since all addresses are kept in the index, it is not necessary to have fixed size records.

Sequential file organizations on a disk suffer from the same deficiencies as sequential organizations in internal memory. Insertion and deletion of records require moving large amounts of data in order to create space for the new record or to utilize the space used by the record being deleted. In practice, these difficulties can be overcome to some extent by marking deleted records as having been deleted and not physically deleting the record. If a record is to be inserted, it can be placed into some ''overflow'' area rather than in its correct place in the sequentially ordered file. The entire file will have to be periodically reorganized. Reorganization will take place when a sufficient number of overflow records have accumulated and when many ''deletions'' have been made. While this method of handling insertions and deletions results in a degradation of system performance, as far as further retrievals and updates is concerned, it is preferable to copying over large sections of the file each time an update is made. In situations where the update rate is very high or when the file size is too large to allow for periodic file reorganization (which would require processing the whole file), other organizations are called for. These will be studied in a later section.

So far, we have discussed only file organization when the number of keys is one. What happens when there is more than one key? A sequential file, clearly, can be ordered on only one key, the primary key. If an employee file is maintained on a disk using sequential organization with Employee Number as the primary key, then how does one retrieve all records with occupation = programmer? One obvious, and inefficient, way would be to process the entire file, outputting all records that satisfy this query. Another, possibly more efficient way would be to maintain a dense index on the occupation field, search this index and retrieve the necessary records. In fact, one could maintain a dense index on every key. This and other possibilities will be studied in Section 11.3.

Let us summarize the ideas we have discussed. File organization is concerned with representing data records on external storage media. The choice of a representation depends on the environment in which the file is to operate, e.g., real time, batched, simple query, one key, multiple keys, etc. When there is only one key, the records may be sorted on this key and stored sequentially either on tape or disk. This results in a sequentially ordered file. This organization is good for files operating in batched retrieval and update mode when the number of transactions batched is large enough to make processing the entire file cost effective. When the number of keys is more than one or when real time responses are needed, a sequential organization in itself is not adequate. In a general situation several indexes may have to be maintained. In these cases, file organization breaks down into two more or less distinct aspects: (1) the directory (i.e., collection of indexes) and (2) the physical organization of the records themselves. This will be referred to as the physical file. We have already discussed one possible physical organization, i.e., sequential (ordered and unordered). In this general framework, processing a query or update request would proceed in two steps. First, the indexes would be interrogated to determine the parts of the physical file that are to be searched. Second, these parts of the physical file will be searched. Depending upon the kinds of indexes maintained, this second stage may involve only the accessing of records satisfying the query or may involve retrieving nonrelevant records too.

11.2 INDEX TECHNIQUES

One of the important components of a file is the directory. A directory is a collection of indexes. The directory may contain one index for every key or may contain an index for only some of the keys. Some of the indexes may be dense (i.e., contain an entry for every record) while others may be non-dense (i.e., contain an entry for only some of the records). In some cases all the indexes may be integrated into one large index. Whatever the situation, the index may be thought of as a collection of pairs of the form (key value, address). If the records A, B, C, D, E, of Figure 11.1 are stored on disk addresses $a_1, a_2, \ldots, a_5$, respectively, then an index for the key Employee Number would have entries $(800, a_1)$; $(510, a_2)$; $(950, a_3)$; $(750, a_4)$; and $(620, a_5)$. The index would be dense since it contains an entry for each of the records in the file. We shall assume that all the key values in an index are distinct. This may appear to be restrictive since several records may have the same key value as in the case of the Occupation key in Figure 11.1. Records A, D, E, all have the value 'programmer' for the Occupation key. This difficulty can be overcome easily by keeping in the address field of each distinct key value a pointer to another address where we shall maintain a list of addresses of all records having this value. If at address b_1 we stored the list of addresses of all programmer records, i.e., a_1, a_4, and a_5, and at b_2 stored the address list for all analysts, i.e., a_2 and a_3, then we could achieve the effect of a dense index for Occupation by maintaining an index with entries ('programmer', b_1) and ('analyst', b_2).

An alternative to this is to change the format of entries in an index to (key value, address 1, address 2, . . ., address n). In both cases, different entries will have distinct key values. The second alternative requires the use of variable size nodes. The use of variable size nodes calls for complex storage management schemes (see Section 4.7), and so we would normally prefer the first alternative. An index, then, consists of pairs of the type (key value, address), the key values being distinct. The functions one wishes to perform on an index are: search for a key value; insert a new pair; delete a pair from the index; modify or update an existing entry. These functions are the same as those one had to perform on a dynamic table (Section 9.1). An index differs from a table essentially in its size. While a table was small enough to fit into available internal memory, an index is too large for this and has to be maintained on external storage (say, a disk). As we shall see, the techniques for maintaining an index are rather different from those used in Chapter 9 to maintain a table. The reason for this is the difference in the amount of time needed to access information from a disk and that needed to access information from internal memory. Accessing a word of information from internal memory takes typically about 10^{-8} seconds, while accessing the same word from a disk could take about 10^{-1} seconds.

11.2.1 Cylinder-Surface Indexing

The simplest type of index organization is the cylinder-surface index. It is useful only for the primary key index of a sequentially ordered file. It assumes that the sequential interpretation of disk memory is that of Figure 11.2, and that records are stored sequentially in increasing order of the primary key. The index consists of a cylinder index and several surface indexes. If the file requires c cylinders (1 through c) for storage, then the cylinder index contains c entires. There is one entry corresponding to the largest key value in each cylinder. Figure 11.4 shows a sample file together with its cylinder index (Figure 11.4(b)). Associated with each of the c cylinders is a surface index. If the disk has s usable surfaces, then each surface index has s entries. The i'th entry in the surface index for cylinder j is the value of the largest key on the j'th track of the i'th surface. The total number of surface index entries is therefore $c \cdot s$. Figure 11.4(c) shows the surface index for cylinder 5 of the file of Figure 11.4(a). A search for a record with a particular key value X is carried out by first reading into memory the cylinder index. Since the number of cylinders in a disk is only a few hundred, the cylinder index typically occupies only one track. The cylinder index is searched to determine which cylinder possibly contains the desired record. This search can be carried out using binary search in case each entry requires a fixed number of words. If this is not feasible, the cylinder index can consist of an array of pointers to the starting point of individual key values as in Figure 11.5. In either case the search can be carried out in $O(\log c)$ time. Once the cylinder index has been searched and the appropraite cylinder determined, the surface index corresponding to that cylinder is retrieved from the disk.

The number of surfaces on a disk is usually very small (say 10) so that the best way to search a surface index would be to use a sequential search. Having determined which surface and cylinder is to be accessed, this track is read in and searched for the record with key X. In case the track contains only one record, the search is trivial. In the example file, a search for the record corresponding to the Japanese torpedo bomber Nakajima B5N2 which was used at Pearl Harbor proceeds as follows: the cylinder index is accessed and searched. It is now determined that the desired record is either in cylinder 5, or it is not in the file. The surface index to be retrieved is that for cylinder 5. A search of this index results in the information that the correct surface number is 3. Track $t_{5,3}$ is now input and searched. The desired record is found on this track. The total number of disk accesses needed for retrieval is three (one to access the cylinder index, one for the surface index and one to get the track of records). When track sizes are very large, it may not be feasible to read in the whole track. In this case the disk will usually be sector addressable and so an extra level of indexing will be needed: the sector index. In this case the number of accesses needed to retrieve a record will increase to four. When the file extends over several disks, a disk index is also maintained. This is still a great improvement over the seventeen accesses needed to make a binary search of the sequential file.

This method of maintaining a file and index is referred to as ISAM (indexed sequential access method). It is probably the most popular and simplest file organization in use for single key files. When the file contains more than one key, it is not possible to use this index organization for the remaining keys (though it can still be used for the key on which the records are sorted in case of a sequential file).

11.2.2 Hashed Indexes

The principles involved in maintaining hashed indexes are essentially the same as those discussed for hash tables Chapter 9. The same hash functions and overflow handling techniques are available. Since the index is to be maintained on a disk and disk access times are generally several orders of magnitude larger than internal memory access times, much consideration must be given to hash table design and the choice of an overflow handling technique. Let us reconsider these two aspects of hash system design, giving special consideration to the fact that the hash table and overflow area will be on a

#	Aircraft	Nation	Type	Speed Max mph	Speed Cruising mph	Range miles	Max Altitude feet	Crew	Guns	Bombs	C	S
1	Amiot 143	France	NB	193	155	746	25,920	5	4	y	1	1
2	Avenger	USA	TB	271	145	2530	22,400	3	3	y	1	1
3	Avro Lancaster	GB	HB	287	210	1660	24,500	7	10	y	1	2
4	Barracuda Mk II	GB	TB	228	—	686	16,600	3	2	y	1	2
5	Black Widow	USA	NF	366	—	2500	33,100	3	8	y	1	3
6	Bloch MB-152	France	Fr	302	279	398	33,000	1	4	N	1	3
7	Boomerang	Aus.	Fr	295	—	932	29,000	1	6	y	1	4
8	Bregeut 691	France	AB	298	186	839	13,100	2	5	y	1	4
9	Caproni	Italy	MB	165	143	839	18,000	3	4	y	2	1
10	Caudron	France	Fr	303	199	559	29,855	1	4	N	2	1
11	Devastator	USA	TB	266	128	1000	19,700	3	2	y	2	2
12	Droop Snoot	USA	FB	414	290	450	44,000	1	5	y	2	2
13	Fiat Centauro	Italy	Fr	385	348	1025	42,650	1	5	N	2	3
14	Flying Fortress	USA	Br	317	210	2400	36,600	10	13	y	2	3
15	Hawker Tempest	GB	FB	436	391	740	36,500	1	4	y	2	4
16	Heinkel III H	Ger.	MB	252	211	1280	27,900	5	7	y	2	4
17	Heinkel 162A	Ger.	Fr	553	—	606	39,370	1	2	N	3	1
18	Heinkel 177 A-1	Ger.	HB	317	267	3480	22,970	5	6	y	3	1
19	Heinkel 219 A-5	Ger.	NF	416	336	1243	39,600	2	6	N	3	2
20	Helldiver	USA	Br	295	158	1925	29,100	2	4	y	3	2
21	Ilushin Il-4	USSR	MB	277	—	1616	33,000	4	3	y	3	3

Figure 11.4(a) World War II aircraft

#	Aircraft	Nation	Type	Speed Max mph	Speed Cruising mph	Range miles	Max Altitude feet	Crew	Guns	Bombs	C	S
22	Ilyushin Shturmovik	USSR	AB	251	199	466	24,600	2	5	y	3	3
23	Invader	USA	LB	355	284	1400	22,100	3	10	y	3	4
24	Junkers 188 E-1	Ger.	MB	311	233	1209	30,660	4	5	y	3	4
25	Kawanishi N1K2-J	Japan	Fr	370	230	1065	35,300	1	4	N	4	1
26	Kingcobra	USA	FB	408	378	450	43,000	1	5	y	4	1
27	Lavochkin La-9	USSR	Fr	429	311	1078	36,515	1	4	N	4	2
28	Macchi Veltro	Italy	Fr	391	—	612	36,910	1	5	N	4	2
29	Marauder	USA	LB	283	216	1100	19,800	7	11	y	4	3
30	Messerschmitt Hornisse	Ger.	HF	388	367	1050	33,000	2	8	N	4	3
31	Messerschmitt Komet	Ger.	Fr	597	—	—	39,500	1	2	N	4	4
32	Messerschmitt Sturmvogel	Ger.	Fr	541	—	652	37,565	1	4	N	4	4
33	MIG-5	USSR	FB	370	—	—	—	1	4	y	5	1
34	Mitsubishi G4M1	Japan	MB	267	196	3750	29,000	7	5	y	5	1
35	Mitsubishi Ki-67	Japan	HB	378	249	2361	31,070	6	5	y	5	2
36	Mosquito Mk VI	GB	FB	378	255	1855	33,000	2	8	y	5	2
37	Mustang P-51D	USA	Fr	437	362	950	41,900	1	6	y	5	3
38	Nakajima B5N2	Japan	TB	236	162	1237	27,100	3	2	y	5	3
39	Petlyakov Pe-8	USSR	HB	276	224	2300	25,920	11	6	y	5	4
40	Spitfire Mk XVI	GB	Fr	405	328	980	42,500	1	6	N	5	4
41	Superfortress	USA	HB	357	230	3250	31,850	10	13	y	6	1
42	Sykhoi Su-2	USSR	LB	302	—	746	28,870	2	5	y	6	1

Figure 11.4(a) Wordl War II aircraft (continued)

#	Aircraft	Nation	Type	Speed		Range miles	Max Altitude feet	Crew	Guns	Bombs	C	S
				Max mph	Cruising mph							
43	Tupolev Tu-2	USSR	Br	345	258	1555	33,000	4	7	y	6	2
44	Vengeance	USA	Br	279	230	2000	22,300	2	6	y	6	2

Abbreviations

Aus.	Australia	HF	heavy fighter
AB	attack bomber	LB	light bomber
Br	bomber	MB	medium bomber
C	cylinder	NB	night bomber
FB	fighter bomber	NF	night fighter
Fr	fighter	N	no
GB	Great Britain	S	surface
Ger.	Germany	y	yes
HB	heavy bomber		

Figure 11.4(a) World War II aircraft

cylinder	highest key value
1	Bregeut 691
2	Heinkel III H
3	Junkers 188 E-1
4	Messerschmitt Sturmvogel
5	Spitfire Mk XVI
6	Vengeance

Figure 11.4(b) Cylinder index for file of Figure 11.4(a)

surface	highest key value
1	Mitsubishi G 4M1
2	Mosquito MkV1
3	Nakajima B5N2
4	Spitfire MkXVI

Figure 11.4(c) Surface index for cylinder 5

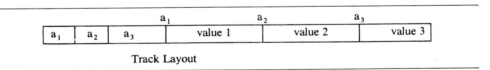

Track Layout

Figure 11.5 Using an array of pointers to permit binary search with variable length key values

disk.

Overflow Handling Techniques

The overflow handling techniques discussed in Chapter 9 are:

(1)   rehashing

(2)   open addressing

    (a)   random

    (b)   quadratic

    (c)   linear

(3)   chaining

The expected number of bucket access when $s = 1$ is roughly the same for methods (1), (2a), and (2b). Since the hash table is on a disk, and these overflow techniques tend to randomize the use of the hash table, we can expect each bucket access to take almost the maximum seek time. In the case of (2c), however, overflow buckets are adjacent to the home bucket and so their retrieval will require minimum seek time. While using chaining, we can minimize the tendency to randomize use of the overflow area by designating certain tracks as overflow tracks for particular buckets. In this case, successive buckets on a chain may be retrieved with little or no additional seek time. To the extent that this is possible, we may regard one bucket access to be equally expensive using methods (2c) and (3). Bucket accesses using the other methods are more expensive, and since the average number of buckets retrieved isn't any better than (3), we shall not discuss these further.

Hash Table

    Let b, s, α and n be as defined in Section 9.2.1. For a given α and n, we have $\alpha = n/(bs)$, and so the product bs is determined. In the case of a hash table maintained in internal memory we chose the number of slots per bucket, s, to be 1. With this choice of s, the expected number of buckets accessed when open linear addresssing is used, is $(2 - \alpha)/(2 - 2\alpha)$, and $1 + \alpha/2$ when chaining is used to resolve overflows. Since individual bucket accesses from a disk are expensive, we wish to explore the possibility of reducing the number of buckets accessed by increasing s. This would of necessity decrease b, the number of buckets, as bs is fixed. We shall assume that when chaining is used, the home bucket can be retrieved with one access. The hash table for chaining is similar to that for linear open addressing. Each bucket in the hash table, i.e., each home bucket, has s slots. Each such bucket also has a link field. This differs from the organization of Section 9.2.3, where $s = 0$ for home buckets using chaining. Remaining buckets on individual chains have only one slot each and require additional access. Thus, if the key value X is in the i'th node on a chain (the home bucket being the first node in the chain), the number of accesses needed to retrieve X is i. In the case of linear open addressing, if X is i buckets away from the home bucket, $f(x)$, then the number of accesses to retrieve X is $1 + i$.

    By way of example, consider the hash function $f(x) =$ first character of X and the values $B, B1, B2, B3, A$. Using a hash table with $b = 6$ and $S = 1$, the assignment of Figure 11.6(a) is obtained, if overflows are handled via linear open addressing. If each of the values is searched for once, then the total number of bucket retrievals is 1 (for A) + 1 (for B) + 2 (for $B1$) + 3 (for $B2$) + 4 (for $B3$) = 11. When the same table space is divided into three buckets each with two slots and $f'(x) = [f(X)/2]$, the assignment of key values to buckets is as in Figure 11.6(b). The number of bucket retrievals needed now is 1 (for each of B and $B1$) + 2 (for each of $B2$ and $B3$) + 3 (for A) = 9. Thus, the average number of buckets retrieved is reduced from 11/5 per search to 9/5 per search. The buckets of Figure 11.6(b) are twice as big as those of Figure 11.6(a). However, unless the bucket size becomes very large, the time to retrieve a bucket from disk will be dominated largely by the seek and latency time. Thus, the time to retrieve a bucket in each of the two cases discussed above would be approximately the same. Since the total average search time is made up of two components--first, the time, t_r, to read in buckets from disk and second, the time, t_p, to search each bucket in internal memory--we should choose b and s so as to minimize $a(t_r + t_p)$, where a = average number of buckets retrieved.

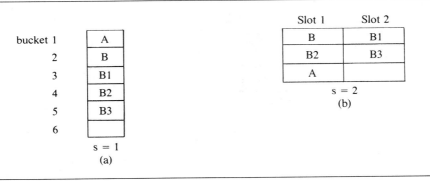

Figure 11.6 Hash tables with $s = 1$ and 2

Using a sequential search within buckets, the time t_p is proportional to s. Thus, the average t_p, for Figure 11.6(b), is one and a half times that for Figure 11.6(a). When s is small and the hash table is on a disk, we have $t_r \gg t_p$ and it is sufficient to minimize $a \cdot t_r$. Let us contrast this to the situation in Section 9.2 where t_r and t_p are comparable. The table of Figure 11.6(a) can be searched with an average of 11/5 key comparisons and accesses. The table of Figure 11.6(b) requires one comparison to find B, 2 for $B1$, 3 for $B2$, 4 for $B3$ and 5 for A, for a total of 15 comparisons. This implies an average of three comparisons per search. In this case, the search time has actually increased with the increase in s. But, when the table is on disk, the average times are roughly $11t_r/5$ and $9t_r/5$, and the table with $s = 2$ gives better performance. In general, we can conclude that increasing s while maintaining $b \cdot s$ fixed, reduces a (see Figure 11.7). The table of Figure 11.8 shows the results of some experiments conducted on existing hashed files maintained on disk. As is evident from this table, for a fixed α, the average number of bucket accesses decreases with increasing s. Moreover, for $s \geq 10$, the average number of accesses for open linear addresssing is roughly the same as for chaining. This, together with our earlier observation that unless care is taken while using chaining, successive accesses will access random parts of the disk, while in the case of open linear addressing consecutive disk segments would be accessed, leads us to the conclusion that with suitable α and s, linear addressing will outperform chaining (contrast this with the case of internal tables).

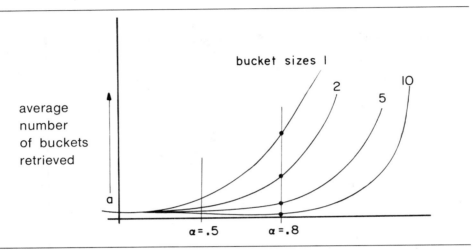

Figure 11.7 $\alpha = .5$

While both the data of Figures 11.7 and 11.8 might suggest a choice for $b = 1$ (thus maximizing the value of s), such a choice for s clearly is not best. The optimal value of s will depend very much on the values of the latency time, seek time and transmission rates of the disk drive in use. We may rewrite the retrieval time per bucket, t_r, as $t_s + t_l + s \cdot t_t$ where t_s, t_l and t_t are the seek time, latency time and transmission time per slot, respectively. When the seek time is very large relative to t_t, the optimal s would tend to be larger than when t_s is very small compared to t_t (as in the case of a drum). Another consideration is the size of the input buffer avaiable. Since the bucket has to be read into some part of internal memory, we must set aside enough space to accommodate a bucket load of data.

Loading Order
    As in the case of internal tables, the order in which key values are entered into the hash table is important. To the extent possible, an attempt should be made to enter these values in order of nonincreasing frequency of search. When this is done, new entries should be added to the end of the overflow chain rather than at the front.

Bucket size, s →	1		2		5		10		20		50	
Hash function →	D	M	D	M	D	M	D	M	D	M	D	M
Loading factor α ↓												
α = .5 C	1.19	1.26	1.09	1.14	1.02	1.03	—	1.01	—	—	—	—
α = .5 L	4.52	1.73	1.17	1.20	1.02	1.03	—	—	—	—	—	—
α = .75 C	1.31	1.40	1.19	1.29	1.11	1.16	1.07	1.09	1.03	1.03	—	1.03
α = .75 L	7.2	9.75	3.35	1.80	1.29	1.20	1.04	1.06	1.01	1.02	—	1
α = .9 C	1.38	1.45	1.30	1.37	1.24	1.27	1.16	1.28	1.09	1.15	1.03	1.07
α = .9 L	22.42	27.14	4.80	6.54	1.94	1.81	1.32	1.30	1.08	1.11	1.01	1.03
α = .95 C	1.41	1.47	1.34	1.39	1.25	1.32	1.20	1.28	1.17	1.28	1.08	1.15
α = .95 L	25.79	37.53	10.80	10.80	4.47	2.62	2.32	1.29	1.25	1.29	1.03	1.08

D = division
M = middle of square
C = chaining
L = linear open addressing
α = loading factor = (number of entries)/(number of slots in hash table)
Note For the same α C uses more space than L as overflows are handled in a separate area.

Figure 11.8 Observed average number of bucket accesses for different α and *s*. (Condensed from Lum, Yuen, and Dodd)

11.2.3 Tree Indexing: B-Trees

The balanced search trees of Chapter 10 (AVL, 2-3, 2-3-4, and red-black) provide a means to search, insert and delete entries from a table of size n using at most O(log n) time. Since these same functions are to be carried out in an index, one could use these tree structures for this application too. Suppose that an AVL tree is used. This would reside on a disk. If nodes are retrieved from the disk, one at a time, then a search of an index with n entries would require at most 1.4 log n disk accesses (the maximum depth of an AVL tree is 1.4 log n). For an index with a million entries, this would mean about 23 accesses in the worst case. This is a lot worse than the cylinder sector index scheme of Section 11.2.1. We can do slightly better using a 2-3 or 2-3-4 tree. We can do much better than 23 accesses by using a balanced tree based upon an m-way search tree for large m rather than one based on a search tree with small m (AVL trees are balanced m-way search trees with $m = 2$; for a 2-3 tree $m = 3$; and for a 2-3-4 tree $m = 4$).

Definiton: An *m-way search tree, T,* is a tree in which all nodes are of degree $\leq m$. If T is empty, (i.e., $T = $ **nil**) then T is an m-way search tree. When T is not empty it has the following properties;

(1) T is a node of the type

$$n, A_0, (K_1,A_1), (K_2,A_2), \ldots, (K_n,A_n)$$

where the A_i, $0 \leq i \leq n$ are pointers to the subtrees of T and the K_i, $1 \leq i \leq n$ are key values; and $1 \leq n < m$.

(2) $K_i < K_{i+1}$, $1 \leq i < n$.

(3)   All key values in the subtree A_i are less than K_{i+1} and greater than K_{i-1}, $0 < i < n$.

(4)   All key values in the subtree A_n are greater than K_n and those in A_0 are less than K_1.

(5)   The subtrees A_i, $0 \leq i \leq n$ are also m-way search trees. □

As an example of a 3-way search tree, consider the tree of Figure 11.9 for key values 10, 15, 20, 25, 30, 35, 40, 45, and 50. One may easily verify that it satisifes all the requirements of a 3-way search tree. In order to search for any key value x in this tree, we first "look into" the root node t at address a and determine the value of i for which $K_i \leq x < K_{i+1}$ (for convenience we use $K_0 = minint$ and $K_{n+1} = maxint$ where $minint$ is smaller than all legal key values and $maxint$ is larger than all legal key values). In case $x = K_i$, then the search is complete. If $x \neq K_i$, then by the definition of an m-way search tree, x must be in subtree A_i, if it is in the tree. When n (the number of keys in a node) is "large," the search for the appropriate value of i above may be carried out using binary search. For "small" n a sequential search is more appropriate. In the example, if $x = 35$, then a search in the root node indicates that the appropriate subtree to be searched is the one with root A_1 at address c. A search of this root node indicates that the next node to search is at address *e*. The key value 35 is found in this node and the search terminates. If this search tree resides on a disk, then the search for $x = 35$ would require accessing the nodes of addresses *a*, *c* and *e* for a total of three disk accesses. This is the maximum number of accesses needed for a search in the tree of Figure 11.9. The best binary search tree for this set of key values requires four disk accesses in the worst case. One such binary tree is shown in Figure 11.10.

Algorithm *msearch* (Program 11.1) searches an *m*-way search tree *t* for key value *x* using the scheme described above. In practice, when the search tree represents an index, the tuples (K_i, A_i) in each of the nodes will really be 3-tuples (K_i, A_i, B_i) where B_i is the address in the file of the record with key K_i. This address would consist of the cylinder and surface numbers of the track to be accessed to retrieve this record (for some disks this address may also include the sector number). The A_i, $0 \leq i \leq n$ are the addresses of root nodes of subtrees. Since these nodes are also on a disk, the A_i are cylinder and surface numbers. We assume that $A_i = 0$ is a null address.

```
 1  procedure msearch (t : mtree ; x : integer; var p : mtree ; var i, j : integer);
 2  {Search the m-way search tree t residing on disk for the key value x.
 3     Individual node format is n, A₀, (K₁, A₁), . . ., (Kₙ, Aₙ), n < m. A triple
 4     (p, i, j) is returned.  j=1 implies x is found at node location p with key Kᵢ.
 5     Else j=0 and p is the location of the node into which x can be inserted.}
 6  label 99;
 7  begin
 8     p := t ; K₀ := −maxint; q := nil; j := 1; {q is the parent of p}
 9     while p < >0 do
10        begin
11        input node located at p from disk;
12        let this node define n, A₀, (K₁, A₁), . . ., (Kₙ, Aₙ);
13        Kₙ₊₁ := maxint;
14        let i be such that Kᵢ <=x < Kᵢ₊₁;
15        if x = Kᵢ then {x has been found; return (p, i, 1)} goto 99;
16        q := p ; p := Aᵢ;
17        end;
18     {x is not in t; return location of node into which insertion can take
            place}
19     p := q ; j := 0; {return q, i, 0;}
20  99: end; {of msearch}
```

Program 11.1 Searching an *m*-way search tree

Analyzing algorithm *msearch* is fairly straightforward. The maximum number of disk accesses made is equal to the height of the tree *t*. Since individual disk accesses are very expensive relative to the time needed to process a node (i.e., determine the next node to access lines 14-16) we are concerned with minimizing the number of accesses

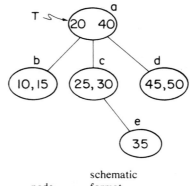

node	schematic format
a	2,b,(20,c),(40,d)
b	2,0,(10,0),(15,0)
c	2,0,(25,0),(30,e)
d	2,0,(45,0),(50,0)
e	1,0,(35,0)

Figure 11.9 Example of a 3-way search tree

needed to carry out a search. This is equivalent to minimizing the height of the search tree. In a tree of degree m and height $h \geq 1$ the maximum number of nodes is $\sum_{0 \leq i \leq h-1} m^i = (m^h - 1)/(m - 1)$. Since each node has at most $m - 1$ keys, the maximum number of entries in an m-way tree index of height h would be $m^h - 1$. For a binary tree with $h = 3$ this figure is 7. For a 200-way tree with $h = 3$ we have $m^h - 1 = 8 * 10^6 - 1$.

Clearly, the potentials of high order search trees are much greater than those of low order search trees. To achieve a performance close to that of the best m-way search trees for a given number of entries n, it is necessary that the search tree be balanced. The particular variety of balanced m-way search trees we shall consider here is known as a B-tree. In defining a B-tree, it is convenient to reintroduce the concept of failure nodes as used for optimal binary search trees in Section 10.6. A failure node represents a node which can be reached during a search only if the value x being searched for is not in the tree. Every subtree with root = **nil** is a point that is reached during the search iff x is not in the tree. For convenience, these empty subtrees will be replaced by hypothetical nodes called failure nodes. These nodes will be drawn square and marked with an F. The actual tree structure does not contain any such nodes but only the value **nil** where such a node occurs. Figure 11.11 shows the 3-way search tree of Figure 11.9 with failure nodes. Failure nodes are the only nodes that have no children.

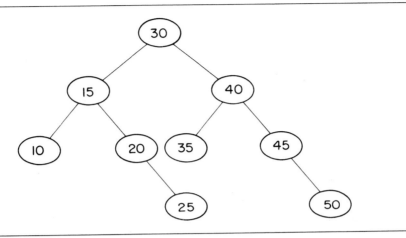

Figure 11.10 Best AVL-tree for data of Figure 11.9

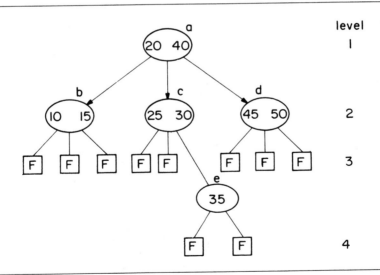

Figure 11.11 Search tree of Figure 11.9 with failure nodes shown

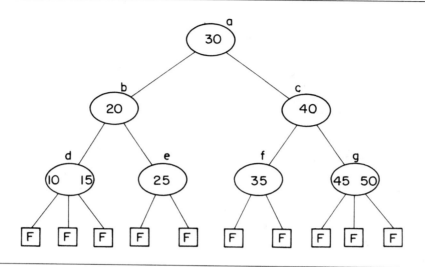

Figure 11.12 B-tree of order 3 for data of Figure 11.9

Definition: A B-tree, t, of order m is an m-way search tree that is either empty or is of height ≥ 1 and satisfies the following properties:

(1)   The root node has at least 2 children.

(2)   All nodes other than the root node and failure nodes have at least $\lceil m/2 \rceil$ children.

(3)   All failure nodes are at the same level. $\square$

The 3-way search tree of Figure 11.11 is not a B-tree since it has failure nodes at levels 3 and 4. This violates requirement (3). One possible B-tree of order 3 for the data of Figure 11.9 is shown if Figure 11.12. Notice that all nonfailure nodes are either of degree 2 or 3. In fact, for a B-tree of order 3, requirements (1), (2), and the definition of an m-way search tree together imply that all nonfailure nodes must be of degree 2 or 3. For this reason, B-trees of order 3 are also known as 2–3 trees. Observe that the definitions of a 2-3 tree and a 2-3-4 tree provided in Chapter 10 are equivalent to those of B-trees with $m = 3$ and 4, respectively.

While the total number of nonfailure nodes in a B-tree of a given order may be greater than the number of such nodes in the best possible search tree of that order (the 2–3 tree of Figure 11.12 has seven nodes while the 3-way search tree of Figure 11.9 has only five), we shall see later that it is easier to insert and delete nodes into a B-tree retaining the B-tree properties than it is to maintain the best possible m-way search tree at all times. Thus, the reasons for using B-trees rather than optimal m-way search trees for indexes are the same as those for using AVL trees as opposed to optimal binary search trees when maintaining dynamic internal tables.

Number of Key Values in a B-Tree

If t is a B-tree of order m in which all failure nodes are at level $l+1$, then we know that the maximum number of index entries in t is $m^l - 1$. What is the minumum number, N, of entries in t? From the definition of a B-tree we know that if $l > 1$, the root node has at least two children. Hence, there are at least two nodes at level 2. Each of these nodes must have at least $\lceil m/2 \rceil$ children. Thus, there are at least $2\lceil m/2 \rceil$ nodes at level 3. At level 4 there must be at least $2\lceil m/2 \rceil^2$ nodes, and continuing this argument, we see that there are at least $2\lceil m/2 \rceil^{l-2}$ nodes at level l when $l > 1$. All of these nodes are nonfailure nodes. If the key values in the tree are $K_1, K_2, \ldots, K_N$ and $K_i < K_{i+1}$, $1 \le i < N$, then the number of failure nodes is $N + 1$. This is so because failures occur for $K_i < X < K_{i+1}$, $0 \le i \le N$ and $K_0 = -\mathbf{maxint}$, $K_{N+1} = \mathbf{maxint}$. This results in $N + 1$ different nodes that one could reach while searching for a key value x not in t. Therefore, we have,

$$
\begin{aligned}
N + 1 &= \text{number of failure nodes in } t \\
&= \text{number of nodes at level } l + 1 \\
&\ge 2\lceil m/2 \rceil^{l-1}
\end{aligned}
$$

and so, $N \ge 2\lceil m/2 \rceil^{l-1} - 1$, $l \ge 1$.

This in turn implies that if there are N key values in a B-tree of order m, then all nonfailure nodes are at levels less than or equal to l, $l \le \log_{\lceil m/2 \rceil}\{(N + 1)/2\} + 1$. The maximum number of accesses that have to be made for a search is l. Using a B-tree of order $m = 200$, an index with $N \le 2 \times 10^6 - 2$ will have $l \le \log_{100}\{(N + 1)/2\} + 1$. Since l is integer, we obtain $l \le 3$. For $n \le 2 \times 10^8 - 2$ we get $l \le 4$. Thus, the use of a high order B-tree results in a tree index that can be searched making a very small number of disk accesses even when the number of entries is very large.

Choice of m

B-trees of high order are desirable since they result in a reduction in the number of disk accesses needed to search an index. If the index has N entries, then a B-tree of order $m = N + 1$ would have only one level. This choice of m clearly is not reasonable, since by assumption the index is too large to fit in internal memory. Consequently, the single node representing the index cannot be read into memory and processed. In arriving at a reasonable choice for m, we must keep in mind that we are really interested in minimizing the total amount of time needed to search the B-tree for a value x. This time has two components, one, the time for reading in the node from the disk and, two, the time needed to search this node for x. Let us assume that each node of a B-tree of order m is of a fixed size and is large enough to accomodate n, A_0 and $m-1$ values for (K_i, A_i, B_i), $1 \le j < m$. If the K_i are at most α characters long and the A_i and B_i each β characters long, then the size of a node is approximately $m(\alpha + 2\beta)$ characters. The time, t_i, required to read in a node is therefore:

$$t_i = t_s + t_l + m(\alpha + 2\beta)\, t_c$$
$$= a + bm$$

where

$a = t_s + t_l = $ seek time + latency time
$b = (\alpha + 2\beta)t_c$ and $t_c = $ transmission time per character

If binary search is used to carry out the search of line 14 of algorithm *msearch* then the internal processing time per node is $c \log_2 m + d$ for some constants c and d. The total processing time per node is thus,

$$\tau = a + bm + c \log_2 m + d \tag{11.1}$$

For an index with N entries, the number of levels, l, is bounded by:

$$l \leq \log_{\lceil m/2 \rceil} \{(N+1)/2\} + 1$$

$$\leq f \frac{\log_2 \{(N+1)/2\}}{\log_2 m} \quad \text{for some constant } f$$

The maximum search time is therefore given by Eq. (11.2).

$$\text{maximum search time} = g \left\{ \frac{a+d}{\log_2 m} + \frac{bm}{\log_2 m} + c \right\} \text{ seconds} \tag{11.2}$$

where $g = f * \log_2 \{(N + 1)/2\}$.

We therefore desire a value of m that minimizes (11.2). Assuming that the disk drive available has a $t_s = 1/100$ sec and $t_l = 1/40$ sec we get $a = 0.035$ sec. Since d will typically be a few microseconds, we may ignore it in comparison with a. Hence, $a + d \approx a = 0.035$ sec. Assuming each key value is at most six characters long and that each A_i and B_i is three characters long, $\alpha = 6$ and $\beta = 3$. If the transmission rate $t_c = 5 \times 10^{-6}$ sec/charac (corresponding to a track capacity of 5000 characters), $b = (\alpha + 2\beta)t_c = 6 \times 10^{-5}$ sec. The right hand side of Eq. (11.2) evaluates to

$$g \left\{ \frac{35}{\log_2 m} + \frac{0.06m}{\log_2 m} + 1000c \right\} \text{ milliseconds} \tag{11.3}$$

Plotting this function gives us the graph of Figure 11.13. From this plot it is evident that there is a wide range of values of m for which nearly optimal performance is achieved. This corresponds to the almost flat region $m \, \varepsilon \, [50,400]$. In case the lowest value of m in this region results in a node size greater than the allowable capacity of an input buffer, the value of m will be determined by the buffer size.

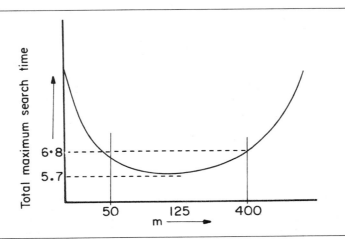

Figure 11.13 Plot of $(35+.06m)/\log_2 m$

Insertion

In addition to searching an index for a particular key value x, we also wish to insert and delete entries. We shall now focus attention on the problem of inserting a new key value x into a B-tree. The insertion is to be carried out in such a way that the tree obtained following the insertion is also a B-tree. As we shall see, the algorithm for doing this is conceptually much simpler than the corresponding insertion algorithm for AVL trees.

In attempting to discover the operations needed to carry out the insertion, let us insert $x = 38$ into the 2-3 tree of Figure 11.12. First, a search of the tree is carried out to determine where the 38 is to be inserted. The failure node that is reached during this search for $x = 38$ is the fourth from the right. Its parent node is f. The node f contains only one key value and thus has space for another. The 38 may therefore be entered here, and the tree of Figure 11.14(a) is obtained. In making this insertion, the tree nodes a, c and f were accessed from the disk during the search. In addition, the new node f had to be written back onto the disk. The total number of accesses is therefore four. Next, let us insert $x = 55$. A search into the B-tree of Figure 11.14(a) indicates that this key value should go into the node g. There is no space in this node, since it already contains $m - 1$ key values. Symbolically inserting the new key value at its appropriate position in a node that previously had $m - 1$ key values would yield a node, p, with the following format:

$$m, A_0, (K_1, A_1), \ldots, (K_m, A_m), \quad \text{and} \quad K_i < K_{i+1}, \ 1 \le i < m$$

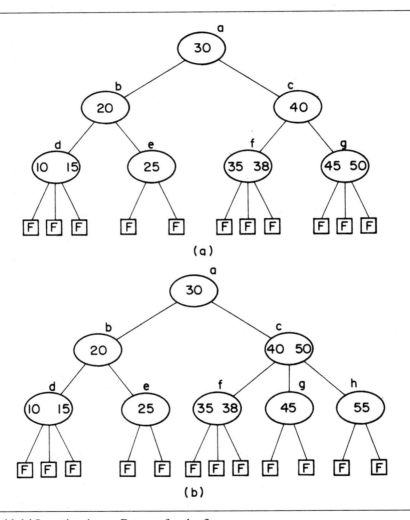

Figure 11.14 Insertion into a B-tree of order 3

This node may be split into two nodes p and q with the following formats:

$$\text{node } p: \lceil m/2 \rceil - 1, A_0, (K_1 A_1), \ldots, (K_{\lceil m/2 \rceil - 1}, A_{\lceil m/2 \rceil - 1}) \tag{11.4}$$

$$\text{node } q: m - \lceil m/2 \rceil, A_{\lceil m/2 \rceil}, (K_{\lceil m/2 \rceil + 1}, A_{\lceil m/2 \rceil + 1}), \ldots, (K_m, A_m)$$

The remaining value $K_{\lceil m/2 \rceil}$ and the new node q form a tuple $(K_{\lceil m/2 \rceil}, q)$, and an attempt is made to insert this tuple into the parent of p. In the current example, the node g splits into two nodes g and h. The tuple $(50, h)$ is inserted into the parent of g, i.e., node c. Since c has only one key value in it, this insertion can be carried out easily. This time, three accesses were made to determine that $x = 55$ should be inserted into g. Since node g was changed, it had to be written out onto disk. The node h had also to be written out onto disk. Assuming that node c is still in internal memory, another disk access is needed to write out the new node c. The total number of accesses is therefore six. The tree obtained is that of Figure 11.14(b). Insertion of $x = 37$, 5, and 18 results in the trees of Figure 11.14(c), (d), and (e). Into this final tree let us insert $x = 12$. The appropriate node for insertion is node k. In determining this, the nodes a, b, and k were accessed from the disk. We shall assume that there is enough internal memory available to hold these three nodes in memory. Insertion into node k requires that it be split into two nodes k and l. The tuple $(15, l)$ is to be inserted into the parent node b. The new nodes k and l are written out onto the disk. Insertion into b results in this node splitting into two nodes b and m. These two nodes are written onto the disk. The tuple $(15, m)$ is to be inserted into the parent node a which also splits. The new nodes a and n are written out, leaving us to insert the tuple $(30, n)$ into the parent of a. Node a is the root node and thus has no parent. At this point, a new root node, p, with subtrees a and n is created. The height of the B-tree increases by 1. The total number of accesses needed for this insertion is ten.

One may readily verify that the insertion transformations described above preserve the index as a B-tree and take care of all possibilities. The resulting algorithm for insertion assumes all nodes on the path from the root to the insertion point are stacked. If enough memory is unavailable, then only the addresses need be stacked and *parent* $[p]$ can be used.

Analysis of *insertb*

In evaluating algorithm *insertb*, we shall use as our performance measure the number of disk accesses that are made. If the B-tree t originally has l levels, then the search of line 8 requires l accesses, since x is not in t. Each time a node splits (line 18), two disk accesses are made (line 19). After the final splitting, an additional access is made either from line 16 or from line 24. If the number of nodes that split is k, then the total number of disk accesses is $l + 2k + 1$. This figure assumes that there is enough internal memory available to hold all nodes accessed during the call of *msearch* in line 8. Since at most one node can split at each of the l levels, k is always $\leq l$. The maximum number of accesses needed is therefore $3l + 1$. Since in most practical situations l will be at most 4, this means about thirteen accesses are needed to make an insertion in the

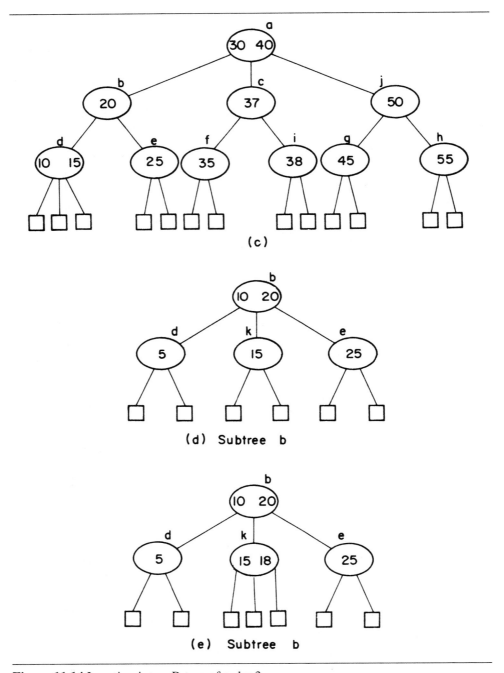

Figure 11.14 Insertion into a B-tree of order 3

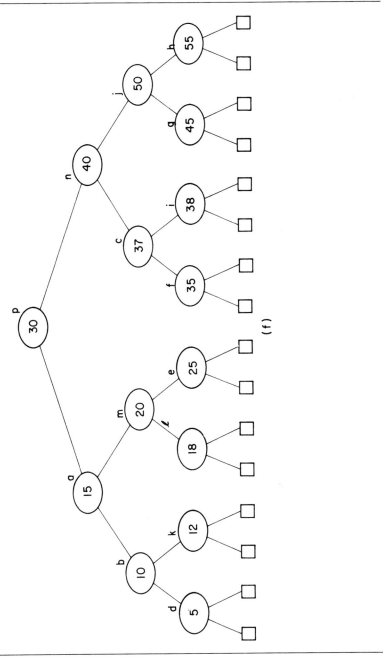

(f)

Figure 11.14 Insertion into a B-tree of order 3

```
1  procedure insertb(var t : mtree ; x :  integer);
2  {Key value x is inserted into the B-tree, t, of order m. t
3    resides on a disk}
4  label 99;
5  var  A, p, q, t :mtree; i, j, K: integer;
6  begin
7    A := nil; K := x; {(K,A) is tuple to be inserted}
8    msearch (t,x,p,i,j); {p is location of node for insertion}
9    if j < > 0 then goto 99; {x is already in t}
10   while P < > 0 do
11     begin
12       insert (K,A) into appropriate position in node at location p;
13       Let the resulting node have the form: n,A_0,(K_1,A_1), . . ., (K_n,A_n);
14       if n <= m − 1 then begin
15         {resulting node is not too big}
16         output node located at p onto disk; goto 99; end;
17       {node located at p has to be split}
18       Let node p and node q be defined as in equation 10.4;
19       output(p,q) onto the disk;
20       K := K_{⌈m/2⌉}; A := q; p := parent [p ];
21     end;
22     {a new root is to be created}
23     Create a new node r with format 1,t, (K,A);
24     t :=r; output t onto disk;
25 99: end; {of insertb}
```

Program 11.2 Insertion into a B-tree

worst case.

In the case of algorithm *insertb*, this worst case figure of $3l + 1$ accesses doesn't tell the whole story. The average number of accesses is considerably less than this. Let us obtain an estimate of the average number of accesses needed to make an insertion. If we start with an empty tree and insert N values into it, then the total number of nodes split is at most $p - 2$ where p is the number of nonfailure nodes in the final B-tree with N entries. This upper bound of $p - 2$ follows from the observation that each time a node splits, at least one additional node is created. When the root node splits, two additional nodes are created. The first node created results from no splitting, and if a B-tree has more than one node then the root must have split at least once. Figure 11.15 shows that $p - 2$ is the best possible upper bound on the number of nodes split in the creation of a p node B-tree when $p > 2$ (note that there is no B-tree with $p = 2$). A B-tree of order m with p nodes has at least

$$1 + (\lceil m/2 \rceil - 1)(p - 1)$$

key values as the root has at least one key value and remaining nodes have at least $\lceil m/2 \rceil - 1$ key values. The average number of splittings, s, may now be determined

$$
\begin{aligned}
s &= \text{(total number of splittings)}/N \\
&\leq (p - 2)/\{1 + (\lceil m/2 \rceil - 1)(p - 1)\} \\
&< 1/(\lceil m/2 \rceil - 1)
\end{aligned}
$$

For $m = 200$ this means that the average number of splittings is less than $1/99$ per key inserted. The average number of disk accesses is therefore only $l + 2s + 1 < l + 101/99 \approx l + 1$.

Deletion

Key values may be deleted from the B-tree using an algorithm that is almost as simple as the one for insertion. To illustrate the transformations involved, let us consider the B-tree of order 3 in Figure 11.16(a). First, we shall consider the problem of deleting values from leaf nodes (i.e., nodes with no children). Deletion of the key value $x = 58$ from node f is easy, since the removal of this key value leaves the node with 1 key value which is the minimum every nonroot node must have. Once it has been determined that $x = 58$ is in node f, only one additional access is needed to rewrite the new node f onto disk. This deletion leaves us with the tree of Figure 11.16(b).

Deletion of the key value $x = 65$ from node g results in the number of keys left behind falling below the minimum requirement of $\lceil m/2 \rceil - 1$. An examination of g's nearest right sibling, h, indicates that it has $\geq \lceil m/2 \rceil$ keys, and the smallest key value in h, i.e., 75 is moved up to the parent node c. The value 70 is moved down to the child node g. As a result of this transformation, the number of key values in g and h is $\geq \lceil m/2 \rceil - 1$, the number in c is unchanged and the tree retains its B-tree properties. In the search for $x = 65$, the nodes a, c and g had to be accessed. If all three nodes are retained in memory, then from c the address of h, the nearest right sibling of g, is readily determined. Node h is then accessed. Since three nodes are altered (g,c, and h), three more accesses are to be made to rewrite these nodes onto disk. Thus, in addition to the accesses made to search for $x = 65$, four more accesses need to be made to effect the deletion of $x = 65$. In case g did not have a nearest right sibling or if its nearest right sibling had only the minimum number of key values, i.e., $\lceil m/2 \rceil - 1$, we could have done essentially the same thing on g's nearest left sibling.

In deleting $x = 55$ from the tree of Figure 11.16(c), we see that f's nearest right sibling, g, has only $\lceil m/2 \rceil - 1$ key values and that f does not have a nearest left sibling. Consequently, a different transformation is needed. If the parent node of f is of the form $n,A_0,(K_1,A_1), \ldots, (K_n,a_n)$ and $A_i = g$ then we can combine the remaining keys of f with the keys of g and the key K_i into one node, g. This node will have $(\lceil m/2 \rceil - 2) + (\lceil m/2 \rceil - 1) + 1 = 2\lceil m/2 \rceil - 2 \leq m - 1$ key values which will at most fill

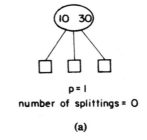

p = I
number of splittings = 0

(a)

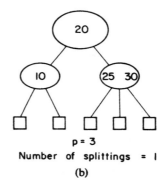

p = 3
Number of splittings = I

(b)

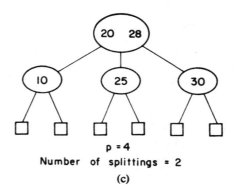

p = 4
Number of splittings = 2

(c)

Figure 11.15 B-trees of order 3

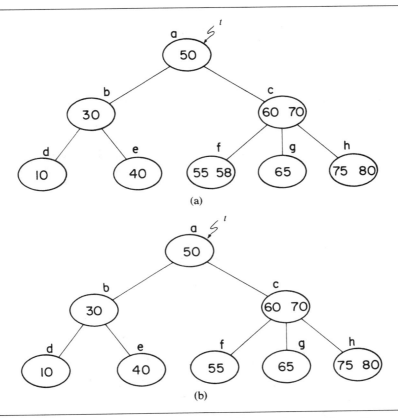

Figure 11.16 Deletion from a B-tree of order 3 (failure nodes have been dispensed with)

the node. Doing this with the nodes f, g and c results in the B-tree of Figure 11.16(d). Three additional accesses are needed (one to determine that g was too small, one to rewrite each of g and c). Finally, let us delete $x = 40$ from node e of Figure 11.16(d). Removal of this key value leaves e with $\lceil m/2 \rceil - 2$ key values. Its nearest left sibling d does not have any extra key values. The keys of d are combined with those remaining in e and the key value 30 from the parent node to obtain the full node d with values 10 and 20. This, however, leaves b with one value too few. Its right sibling c has no extra values and so the remaining keys of b are combined with the value 50 from a and the $\lceil m/2 \rceil - 1$ values of c to obtain a new node c. The root node a becomes empty and is discarded. This takes a total of four additional accesses (one to fetch each of d and c, one to rewrite each of the altered nodes c and d).

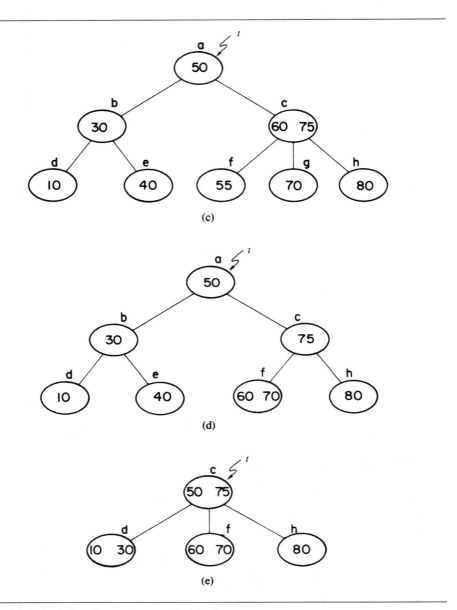

Figure 11.16 Deletion from a B-tree of order 3

When the key value x being deleted is not in a leaf node, a simple transformation reduces this deletion to the case of deletion from a leaf node. Suppose that $K_i = x$ in the node p and p is of the form n, A_0, (K_1, A_1), . . ., (K_n, A_n) with $1 \le i \le n$. Since p is not a leaf node, $A_i \ne 0$. We can determine y, the smallest key value in the subtree A_i. This will be in a leaf node q. Replace K_i in p by y and write out the new p. This leaves us with the problem of deleting y from q. Note that this retains the search properties of the tree. For example, the deletion of $x = 50$ from the tree of Figure 11.16(a) can be accomplished by replacing the 50 in node a by the 55 from node f and then proceeding to delete the 55 from node f (see Figure 11.17).

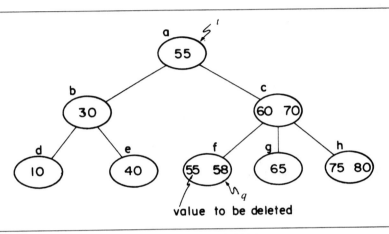

Figure 11.17 Deleting 50 from node n of Figure 11.16(a)

The details are provided in algorithm *deleteb* (Program 11.3). To reduce the worst case performance of the algorithm, only either the nearest left or right sibling of a node is examined.

```
 1 procedure deleteb (var t : mtree; x : integer);
      {delete x from B-tree t of order m. t resides on a disk}
 2 label 99;
 3 var i,j : integer; t,p,q,y,z : mtree;
 4 begin
 5    msearch (t,x,p,i,j);
 6    if j< > 1 then goto 99; {x is not in t}
 7    Let p be of the form: n,A₀(K₁,A₁), . . ., (Kₙ,Aₙ) and Kᵢ = x
 8    if A₀ < > 0 then
 9    {deletion from a nonleaf, find key to move up}
10       begin
```

11            $q := A_i$; {move to right subtree}

12   **while** q is not a leaf node **do**

13   **begin**

14   let q be of the form: $n_q, A_0^q, (K_1^q, A_1^q), \ldots, (K_n^q, A_n^q)$;

15                 $q := A_0^q$;

16   **end**;

17   Let q be of the form $n_q, A_0^q, (K_1^q, A_1^q), \ldots, (K_n^q, A_n^q)$;

18   replace K_i in node p by K_1^q and write the altered node p onto disk

19              $p := q$; $i := 1$;

20   let $n, A_0(K_1, A_1), \ldots, (K_n, A_n)$ be as defined by the new node p

21   **end** {of if $A_0 <> 0$}

22   {delete K_i from node p, a leaf}

23   from node $p: n, A_0(K_1, A_1), \ldots, (K_n, A_n)$ delete (K_i, A_i) and replace n by $n - 1$;

24   **while** $(n < \lceil m/2 \rceil - 1)$ **and** $p <> t$ **do**

25   **if** p has a nearest right sibling y **then**

26   **begin**

27   let $y: n_y, A_0^y, (K_1^y, A_1^y), \ldots, (K_n^y, A_n^y)$ and

28   let $z: n_z, A_0^z, (K_1^z, A_1^z), \ldots, (K_n^z, A_n^z)$ be the

29   parent of p and y;

30   let $A_j^z = y$ **and** $A_{j-1}^z = p$;

31   **if** $n_y >= \lceil m/2 \rceil$ **then**

32   {redistribute key values}

33   **begin**

34   {update node p}

35                 $(K_{n+1}, A_{n+1}) := (K_j^z, A_0^y)$;

36                 $n := n + 1$;

37   {update node z}

38                 $K_j^z := K_1^y$;

39   {update node y}

40                 $(n_y, A_0^y, (K_1^y, A_1^y), \ldots) :=$

41                              $(n_y - 1, A_1^y, (K_2^y, A_2^y), \ldots)$;

42   **output** nodes p, y, z onto disk

43   **goto** 99;

44   **end**; {of **if** $n_y >= \lceil m/2 \rceil$}

45   {combine nodes p, K_j^z and y}

46              $r := 2* \lceil m/2 \rceil - 2$;

47   **output** $r, A_0, (K_1, A_1), \ldots, (K_n, A_n), (K_j^z, A_0^y)$,

48             $(K_1^y, A_1^y), \ldots, (K_n^y, A_n^y)$ onto disk at location p

49   {update}

50              $(n, A_0 \ldots) := (n_z - 1, A_0^z, \ldots, (K_{j-1}^z, A_{j-1}^z), (K_{j+1}^z, A_{j+1}^z) \ldots)$

51              $P := z$;

52   **end** {of **if** p has a nearest right sibling}

53   **else** {node p must have a left sibling}

54   **begin**

```
55                    {this is symmetric to lines 28-52 and
56                        is left as an exercise}
57                    end; {of if and while}
58                if n < > 0 then
59                    output p: (n, A₀, . . ., (Kₙ,Aₙ))
60                else {change root}
61                    t := A₀;
62  99: end; {of deleteb}
```

Program 11.3 Deletion from a B-tree

Analysis of *deleteb*

The search for x in line 5, together with the search for the leaf q in lines 11-17, requires l accesses if l is the number of levels in t. In case p is not a leaf node at line 7, then it is modified and written out in line 18. Thus, the maximum number of accesses made in lines 5-20 is $l + 1$. Starting from a leaf, each iteration of the **while** loop of lines 24-59 moves p one level up the tree. So, at most $l + 1$ iterations of this loop may be made. Assuming that all nodes from the root t to the leaf p are in internal memory, the only additional accesses needed are for sibling nodes and for rewriting nodes that have been changed. The worst case happens when $l - 1$ iterations are made and the last one results in termination at line 44 or the corresponding point in line 56. The maximum number of accesses for this loop is therefore $(l - 1)$ for siblings, plus $(l - 2)$ updates at line 47 and the corresponding point in line 55, plus 3 updates at line 42 or the corresponding point in line 55 for termination. This figure is $2l$. The maximum number of accesses required for a deletion is therefore $3l + 1$.

The deletion time can be reduced at the expense of disk space and a slight increase in node size by including a delete bit, F_i, for each key value k_i in a node. Then we can set $F_i = 1$ if K_i has not been deleted and $F_i = 0$ if it has. No physical deletion takes place. In this case a delete requires a maximum of $l + 1$ accesses (l to locate the node containing x and 1 to write out this node with the appropriate delete bit set to 0). With this strategy, the number of nodes in the tree never decreases. However, the space used by deleted entries can be reused during further insertions (see exercises). As a result, this strategy would have little effect on search and insert times (the number of levels increase very slowly with increasing n when m is large). Insert times may even decrease slightly due to the ability to reuse deleted entry space. Such reuses would not require us to split any nodes.

For a variation of B-trees see Exercises 9 through 16.

Variable Size Key Values

With a node format of the form $n, A_0, (K_1,A_1), \ldots, (K_n,A_n)$, the first problem created by the use of variable size key values, K_i, is that a binary search can no longer be carried out since, given the location of the first tuple (K_1,A_1) and n, we cannot easily determine K_n or even the location of $K_{(1 + n)/2}$. When the range of key value size is small, it is best to allocate enough space for the largest size key value. When the range in sizes is large, storage may be wasted and another node format may become better, i.e., the format $n, A_0, \alpha_1, \alpha_2, \ldots, \alpha_n, (K_1, A_1), \ldots, (K_n, A_n)$ where α_i is the address of K_i in internal memory, i.e., $K_i = $ memory (α_i). In this case, a binary search of the node can still be made. The use of variable size nodes is not recommended since this would require a more complex storage management system. More importantly, the use of variable size nodes would result in degraded performance during insertion. For example, insertion of $x = 85$ into the 2-3 tree of Figure 11.16(e) would require us to request a larger node, j, to accomodate the new value being added to the node h. As a result, node c would also be changed since it contains a pointer to h. This pointer must be changed to j. Consequently, nodes of a fixed size should be used. The size should be such as to allow for at least $m - 1$ key values of the largest size. During insertions, however, we can relax the requirement that each node have $\leq m - 1$ key values. Instead, a node will be allowed to hold as many values as can fit into it and will contain at least $\lceil m/2 \rceil - 1$ values. The resulting performance will be at least as good as that of a B-tree of order m. Another possibility is to use some kind of key sampling scheme to reduce the key value size so as not to exceed some predetermined size d. Some possibilities are prefix and suffix truncation, removing vowels, etc. Whatever the scheme used, some provision will have to be made for handling synonyms (i.e., distinct key values that have the same sampled value). Key sampling is discussed further in Section 11.2.4.

11.2.4 Trie Indexing

An index structure that is particulary useful when key values are of varying size is the trie. A *trie* is a tree of degree $m \geq 2$ in which the branching at any level is determined not by the entire key value but by only a portion of it. As an example, consider the trie of Figure 11.18. The trie contains two types of nodes. The first type we shall call a *branch node* and the second contains 27 link fields. All characters in the key values are assumed to be one of the 26 letters of the alphabet. A blank is used to terminate a key value. At level 1 all key values are partitioned into 27 disjoint classes depending on their first character. Thus, $t\uparrow.link[i]$ points to a subtrie containing all key values beginning with the i'th letter (t is the root of the trie). On the j'th level the branching is determined by the j'th character. When a subtrie contains only one key value, it is replaced by a node of type information. This node contains the key value, together with other relevant information such as the address of the record with this key value, etc. In the figure, branch nodes are represented by rectangles while ovals are used for information nodes. Observe that a trie is a natural generalization of the binary tries of Chapter 10. Figure 11.19 shows the need to terminate each key with a blank.

Searching a trie for a key value x requires breaking up x into its constituent characters and following the branching patterns determined by these characters. The algorithm *trie*, Program 11.4, assumes that $p = $ **nil** is not a branch node, and that $p\uparrow.key$ is the key value represented in p if p is an information node.

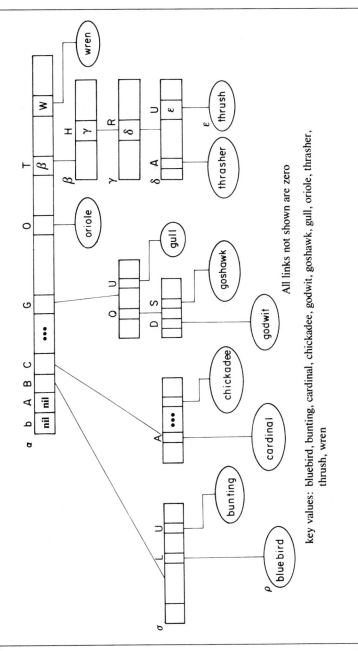

key values: bluebird, bunting, cardinal, chickadee, godwit, goshawk, gull, oriole, thrasher, thrush, wren

All links not shown are zero

Figure 11.18 Trie created using characters of key value left to right, one at a time

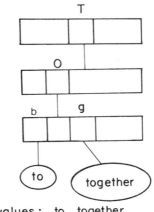

key values: to, together

Figure 11.19 Trie showing need for a terminal character (in this case a blank)

Analysis of Algorithm *trie*

The search algorithm for tries is very straightforward and one may readily verify that the worst case search time is O(l), where l is the number of levels in the trie (including both branch and information nodes). In the case of an index, all these nodes will reside on disk and so at most l accesses will have to be made to effect the search. (Also, note that in this case the pointer type cannot be used as Pascal does not allow input/output of pointers. The link field will now be implemented as an integer.) Given a set of key values to be represented in an index, the number of levels in the trie will clearly depend on the strategy or key sampling technique used to determine the branching at each level. This can be defined by a sampling function *sample* (x,i), which appropriately samples x for branching at the i'th level. In the example trie of Figure 11.18 and in the search algorithm *trie* this function is

(1) *sample* (x,i) = i'th character of x

Some other possible choices for this function are $(x = x_1 x_2 \ldots x_n)$

(2) *sample* $(x,i) = x_{n-i+1}$

(3) *sample* $(x,i) = x_{r(x,i)}$ for $r(x,i)$ a randomization function

```
 1 function trie(var t,p : TriePointer ; x integer): TriePointer;
 2 {Search a trie t for key value x. It is assumed that branching on
 3   the i'th level is determined by the i'th character of the key value}
 4 var c : char; i,k : integer;
 5 begin
 6 {assume we can always concatenate at least 1 trailing blank to x}
 7 k := x; concatenate (k,' ');
 8 i := 1; p := t;
 9 while p is a branch node do
10    begin
11      c := i'th character of k;
12      p := p↑. link [c ];
13      i := i + 1;
14    end;
15 if p =  nil or p↑. key < > x then trie := nil
16                                else trie := p
17 end; {of trie}
```

Program 11.4 Searching a trie

$$(4) \quad sample\,(x,i) = \begin{cases} x_{i/2} \text{ if } i \text{ is even} \\ x_{n-(i-1)/2} \text{ if } i \text{ is odd} \end{cases}$$

For each of these functions, one may easily construct key value sets for which that particular function is best, i.e., it results in a trie with the fewest number of levels. The trie of Figure 11.18 has five levels. Using the function (2) on the same key values yields the trie of Figure 11.20, which has only three levels. An optimal sampling function for this data set will yield a trie that has only two levels (Figure 11.21). Choosing the optimal sampling function for any particular set of values is very difficult. In a dynamic situation, with insertion and deletion, we wish to optimize average performance. In the absence of any further information on key values, probably the best choice would be (3). Even though all our examples of sampling have involved single character sampling we need not restrict ourselves to this. The key value may be interpreted as consisting of digits using any radix we desire. Using a radix of 27^2 would result in 2 character sampling. Other radixes would give different samplings. The maximum number of levels in a trie can be kept low by adopting a different strategy for information nodes. These nodes can be designed to hold more than one key value. If the maximum number of levels allowed is l, then all key values that are synonyms up to level $l - 1$ are entered into the same information node. If the sampling function is chosen correctly, there will be only a few synonyms in each information node. The information node will therefore be small and can be processed in internal memory. Figure 11.22 shows the use of this strategy on the trie of Figure 11.18 with $l = 3$. In further discussion we shall, for simplicity, assume that the sampling function in use is (1) and that no restriction is placed on the number of levels in the trie.

Insertion

Insertion into a trie is straightforward. We shall indicate the procedure by means of two examples and leave the formal writing of the algorithm as an exercise. Let us consider the trie of Figure 11.18 and insert into it the two entires: bobwhite and bluejay. First, we have x = bobwhite and we attempt to search for 'bobwhite' in t. This leads us to node σ, where we discover that $\sigma.link['O'] = $ **nil**. Hence, x is not in t and may be inserted here (see Figure 11.23). Next, x = bluejay and a search of t leads us to the information node p. A comparison indicates that $p.key < >x$. Both $p.key$ and x will form a subtrie of σ. The two values $p.key$ and x are sampled until the sampling results in two different values. The happens when the 5th letter of $p.key$ and x are compared. The resulting trie after insertion is in Figure 11.23.

Deletion

Once again, we shall not present the deletion algorithm formally but we will look at two examples to illustrate some of the ideas involved in deleting entries from a trie. From the trie of Figure 11.23 let us first delete 'bobwhite.' To do this we just set $\sigma.link['O'] := $ **nil**. No other changes need be made. Next, let us delete 'bluejay.' This deletion leaves us with only one key value in the subtrie, δ_3. This means that the node δ_3 may be deleted and p moved up one level. The same can be done for nodes δ_1 and δ_2. Finally, the node σ is reached. The subtrie with root σ has more than one key value. Therefore p cannot be moved up any more levels and we set $\sigma.link['L'] := p$. In order to facilitate deletions from tries, it is useful to add a *count* field in each branch node. This count field will at all times give us the number of information nodes in the subtree for which it is the root. See Exercise 25 for more on tries.

11.3 FILE ORGANIZATIONS

11.3.1 Sequential Organizations

The problems associated with sequential organizations were discussed eariler. The most popular sequential organization scheme is ISAM, in which a cylinder-surface index is maintained for the primary key. In order to efficiently retrieve records based on other keys, it is necessary to maintain additional indexes on the remaining keys (i.e., secondary keys). The structure of these indexes may correspond to any of the alternative index techniques discussed in the previous section. The use of secondary key indexes will be discussed in greater detail in connection with inverted files.

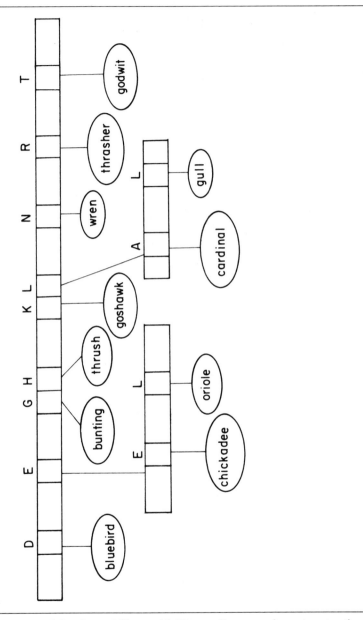

Figure 11.20 Trie constructed for data of Figure 11.18 sampling one character at a time, right to left

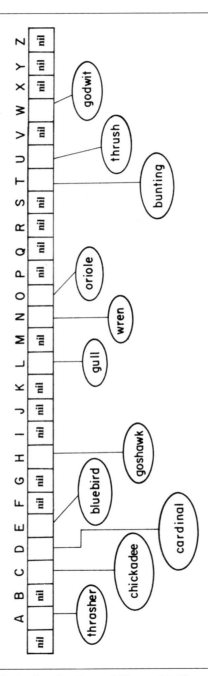

Figure 11.21 An optimal trie for the data of Figure 11.18; sampling on the first level done by using the fourth character of the key values

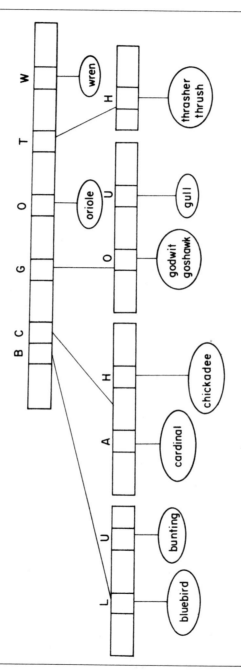

Figure 11.22 Trie obtained for data of Figure 11.18 when number of levels is limited to 3; keys have been sampled left to right one character at a time

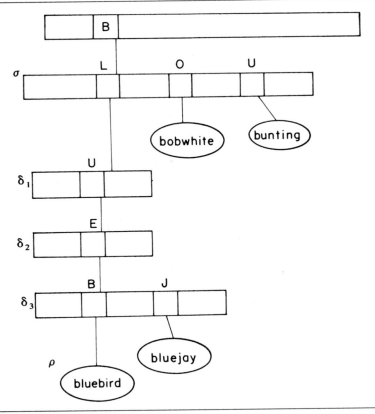

Figure 11.23 Section of trie of Figure 11.18 showing changes resulting from inserting bobwhite and bluejay

11.3.2 Random Organizations

In this organization, records are stored at random locations on disk. This randomization could be achieved by any one of several techniques. Some of these techniques are direct addressing, directory lookup and hashing.

Direct Addressing

In direct addressing with equal size records, the available disk space is divided out into nodes large enough to hold a record. The numeric value of the primary key is used to determine the node into which a particular record is to be stored. No index on this key is needed. With primary key = Employee #, the record for Employee # = 259 will be stored in node 259. With this organization, searching and deleting a record given its primary key value, requires only one disk access. Updating a record requires two (one to read and another to write back the modified record). When variable size records are being used an index can be set up with pointers to actual records on disk (see Figure 11.24). The number of accesses needed using this scheme is one more than for the case when memory was divided into fixed size nodes. The storage management scheme becomes more complex (Section 11.4). The space efficiency of direct accessing depends on the identifier density n/T (n = number of distinct primary key values in the file, T = total number of possible primary key values). In the case of internal tables, this density is usually very low and direct addressing was very space inefficient.

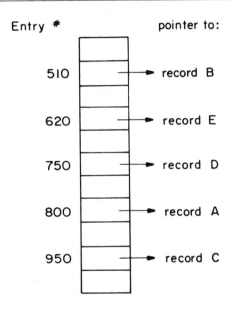

Figure 11.24 Direct access index for data of Figure 11.1

Directory LookUp

This is very similar to the scheme of Figure 11.24 for the case of direct addressing with variable size records. Now, however, the index is not of direct access type but is a dense index maintained using a structure suitable for index operations. Retrieving a record involves searching the index for the record address and then accessing the record itself. The storage management scheme will depend on whether fixed size or variable size nodes are being used. Except when the identifier density is almost 1, this scheme makes a more efficient utilization of space than does direct addressing. However, it requires more accesses for retrieval and update, since index searching will generally require more than one access. In both direct addressing and directory lookup, some provision must be made for collisions (i.e., when two or more records have the same primary key value). In many applications the possibility of collisions is ruled out, since the primary key value uniquely identifies a record. When this is not the case, some of the schemes to be discussed in Sections 11.3.3 and 11.3.4 may be used.

Hashing

The principles of hashed file organization are essentially the same as those for a hashed index. The available file space is divided into buckets and slots. Some space may have to be set aside for an overflow area in case chaining is being used to handle overflows. When variable size records are present, the number of slots per bucket will be only a rough indicator of the number of records a bucket can hold. The actual number will vary dynamically with the size of records in a particular bucket.

Random organization on the primary key using any of the above three techniques overcomes the difficulties of sequential organizations. Insertions and deletions become relatively trivial operations. At the same time, random organizations lose the advantages of sequential ordered organization. Batch processing of queries becomes inefficient as the records are not maintained in order of the primary key. In addition, handling of range queries becomes exceedingly inefficient except in the case of directory lookup with a suitable index structure. For example, consider these two queries: (1) retrieve the records with Employee Number > 800 and (2) retrieve all records with $301 \leq$ employee number ≤ 800. To do (1) we will need to know the maximum employee number in the file or else examine every node. If the maximum employee number is known then (1) becomes similar to (2), so let's look at (2). With direct addressing and hashing, we would have to search for records with employee number = 301, 302, . . ., 800, a total of 500 independent searches. The number of records satisfying the query may be much smaller (even 0). In the case of ISAM, we could in three accesses locate the record (if one exists) having the smallest employee number satisfying the query and retrieve the remaining records one at a time. The same is possible when a search tree type directory (index) is maintained.

11.3.3 Linked Organizations

Linked organizations differ from sequential organizations essentially in that the logical sequence of records is generally different from the physical sequence. In a sequential organization, if the i'th record of the file is at location l_i, then the $(i+1)$'th record is in the next physical position $l_i + c$ where c may be the length of the i'th record or some constant that determines the inter-record spacing. In a linked organization the next logical record is obtained by following a link value from the present record. Linking records together in order of increasing primary key value facilitates easy insertion and deletion once the place at which the insertion or deletion to be made is known. Searching for a record with a given primary key value is difficult when no index is available, since the only search possible is a sequential search. To facilitate searching on the primary key as well as on secondary keys it is customary to maintain several indexes, one for each key. An employee number index, for instance, may contain entries corresponding to ranges of employee numbers. One possibility for the example of Figure 11.1 would be to have an entry for each of the ranges 501-700, 701-900, and 901-1100. All records having $E\#$ in the same range will be linked together as in Figure 11.25. Using an index in this way reduces the length of the lists and thus the search time. This idea is very easily generalized to allow for easy secondary key retrieval. We just set up indexes for each key and allow records to be in more than one list. This leads to the *multilist* structure for file representation. Figure 11.26 shows the indexes and lists corresponding to a multilist representation of the data of Figure 11.1. It is assumed that the only fields designated as keys are: $E\#$, Occupation, Sex and Salary. Each record in the file, in addition to all the relevant information fields, has one link field for each key field.

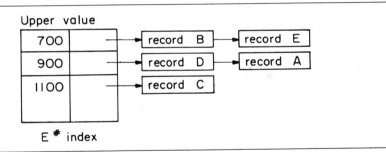

Figure 11.25 Records with E# in the same range are linked together

The logical order of records in any particular list may or may not be important depending upon the application. In the example file, lists corresponding to $E\#$, Occupation and Sex have been set up in order of increasing $E\#$. The salary lists have been set up in order of increasing salary within each range (record A precedes D and C even though $E\#(C)$ and $E\#(D)$ are less than $E\#(A)$).

Notice that in addition to key values and pointers to lists, each index entry also contains the length of the corresponding list. This information is useful when retrieval on boolean queries is required. In order to meet a query of the type, retrieve all records with Sex = female and Occupation = analyst, we search the Sex and Occupation indexes for female and analyst, respectively. This gives us the pointers B and B. The length of the list of analysts is less than that of the list of females, so the analyst list starting at B is searched. The records in this list are retrieved and the Sex key examined to determine if the record truly satisfies the query. Retaining list lengths enables us to reduce search time by allowing us to search the smaller list. Multilist structures provide a seemingly

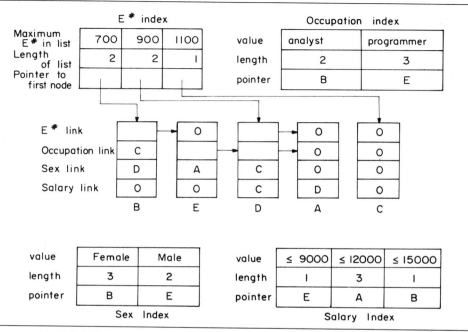

Figure 11.26 Multilist representation for Figure 11.1

satisfactory solution for simple and range queries. When boolean queries are involved, the search time may bear no relation to the number of records satisfying the query. The query $K1 = XX$ and $K2 = XY$ may lead to a $K1$ list of length n and a $K2$ list of length m. Then, $\min\{n, m\}$ records will be retrieved and tested against the query. It is quite possible that none or only a very small number of these $\min\{n, m\}$ records have both $K1 = XX$ and $K2 = XY$. This situation can be remedied to some extent by the use of *compound keys*. A compound key is obtained by combining two or more keys together. We could combine the Sex and Occupation keys to get a new key Sex-Occupation. The values for this key would be: female analyst, female programmer, male analyst and male programmer. With this compound key replacing the two keys Sex and Occupation, we can satisfy queries of the type, all male programmers or all programmers, by retrieving only as many records as actually satisfy the query. The index size, however, grows rapidly with key compounding. If we have ten keys $K_1, \ldots, K_{10}$, the index for K_i having n_i entries, then the index for the compound key $K_1\text{-}K_2\text{-}\ldots\text{-}K_{10}$ will have

$$\prod_{i=1}^{10} n_i$$

entries, while the original indexes had a total of

$$\sum_{i=1}^{10} n_i$$

entries. Also, handling simple queries becomes more complex if the individual key indexes are no longer retained (see the exercises).

Inserting a new record into a multilist structure is easy so long as the individual lists do not have to be maintained in some order. In this case the record may be inserted at the front of the appropriate lists (see Exercise 26). Deletion of a record is difficult since there are no back pointers. Deletion may be simplified at the expense of doubling the number of link fields and maintaining each list as a doubly linked list (see Exercises 27 and 29). When space is at a premium, this expense may not be acceptable. An alternative is the coral ring structure described below.

Coral Rings

The coral ring structure is an adaptation of the doubly linked multilist structure discussed above. Each list is structured as a circular list with a headnode. The headnode for the list for key value $K_i = x$ will have an information field with value x. The field for key K_i is replaced by a link field. Thus, associated with each record, y, and key, K_i, in a coral ring there are two link fields: $y \uparrow . alink\,[i]$ and $y \uparrow . blink\,[i]$. The *alink* field is used to link together all records with same value for key K_i. The *alinks* form a circular list with a headnode whose information field retains the value of K_i for the records in this ring. The *blink* field for some records is a back pointer and for others it is a pointer to the head node. To distinguish between these two cases, another field $y \uparrow . flag[i]$ is used. $y \uparrow . flag[i] = 1$ if $y \uparrow . blink\,[i]$ is a back pointer and $y \uparrow . flag[i] = 0$ otherwise. In practice, the *flag* and *blink* fields may be combined with $y \uparrow . blink\,[i] > 0$ when it is a back pointer and < 0 when it is a pointer to the head node. When the *blink* field of a record $y \uparrow . blink\,[i]$ is used as a back pointer, it points to the nearest record z, preceding it in its circular list for K_i having $z \uparrow . blink\,[i]$ also a back pointer. In any given circular list, all records with back pointers form another circular list in the reverse direction (see Figure 11.27). The presence of these back pointers makes it possible to carry out a deletion without having to start at the front of each list containing the record being deleted in order to determine the preceding records in these lists (see Exercise 31). Since these *blink* fields will usually be smaller than the original key fields they replace, an overall saving in space will ensure. This is, however, obtained at the expense of increased retrieval time (Exercise 30). Indexes are maintained as for multilists. Index entries now point to head nodes. As in the case of multilists, an individual node may be a member of several rings on different keys.

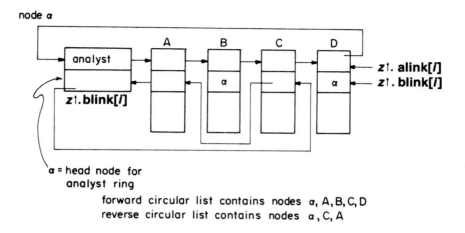

node α

α = head node for
analyst ring

forward circular list contains nodes α, A, B, C, D
reverse circular list contains nodes α, C, A

Figure 11.27 Coral ring for analysts in a hypothetical file

11.3.4 Inverted Files

Conceptually, inverted files are similar to multilists. The difference is that while in multilists, records with the same key value are linked together with link information being kept in individual records; in the case of inverted files this link information is kept in the index itself. Figure 11.28 shows the indexes for the file of Figure 11.1. A slightly different strategy has been used in the E# and salary indexes than was used in Figure 11.26, though the same strategy could have been used here too. To simplify further discussion, we shall assume that the index for every key is dense and contains a value entry for each distinct value in the file. Since the index entries are variable length (the number of records with the same key value is variable), index maintenance becomes more complex than for multilists. However, several benefits accrue from this scheme. Boolean queries require only one access per record satisfying the query (plus some accesses to process the indexes). Queries of the type $K1 = XX$ or $K2 = XY$ can be processed by first accessing the indexes and obtaining the address lists for all records with $K1 = XX$ and $K2 = XY$. These two lists are then merged to obtain a list of all records satisfying the query. $K1 = XX$ and $K2 = XY$ can be handled similarly by intersecting the two lists. $K1 = .not. XX$ can be handled by maintaining a universal list, U, with the addresses of all records. Then, $K1 = .not.XX$ is just the difference between U and the list for $K1 = XX$. Any complex boolean query may be handled in this way. The retrieval works in two steps. In the first step, the indexes are processed to obtain a list of records satisfying the query and in the second, these records are retrieved using this list. The number of disk accesses needed is equal to the number of records being retrieved plus the number to process the indexes. Exercise 33 explores the time savings that can result using this structure rather than multilists.

E# index	
510	B
620	E
750	D
800	C
950	A

Occupation index	
analyst	B,C
programmer	A,D,E

Sex index	
female	B,C,D
male	A,E

Salary index	
9,000	E
10,000	A
12,000	C,D
15,000	B

A,B,C,D,E indicate addresses of the records in the file.

Figure 11.28 Indexes for fully inverted file

Inverted files represent one extreme of file organization in which only the index structures are important. The records themselves may be stored in any way (sequentially ordered by primary key, random, linked ordered by primary key, etc.). Inverted files may also result in space saving compared with other file structures when record retrieval does not require retrieval of key fields. In this case, the key fields may be deleted from the records. In the case of multilist structures, this deletion of key fields is possible only with significant loss in system retrieval performance (why?). Insertion and deletion of records requires only the ability to insert and delete within indexes.

11.3.5 Cellular Partitions

In order to reduce file search times, the storage media may be divided into cells. A cell may be an entire disk pack or it may simply be a cylinder. Lists are localized to lie within a cell. Thus, if we had a multilist organization in which the list for *key*1 = *prog* included records on several different cylinders, then we could break this list into several smaller lists where each *prog* will now contain several entries of the type (*addr,length*), where *addr* is a pointer to the start of a list of records with *key*1 = *prog* and *length* is the number of records on this list. By doing this, all records in the same cell (i.e., cylinder) may be accessed without moving the read/write heads. In case a cell is a disk pack, then by using cellular partitions, it is possible to search different cells in parallel (provided the system hardware permits simultaneous reading/writing from several disk drives).

It should be noted that in any real situation a judicious combination of the techniques of this section would be called for, i.e., the file may be inverted on certain keys, ringed on others, and a simple multilist on yet other keys.

11.4 STORAGE MANAGEMENT

The functions of a storage management system for an external storage device (such as a disk) are the same as those for a similar system for internal memory. The storage management system should be able to allocate and free a contiguous block of memory of a given size. In Chapter 4 we studied several memory management schemes. For fixed size nodes we used a linked stack together with the routines *ret* and *GetNode* of Section 4.3. For variable size nodes the boundary tag method of Section 4.7 was good. We also studied a general purpose management scheme involving garbage collection and compaction in Section 4.9. When the storage to be managed is on an external device, the management scheme used should be such as to minimize the time needed to allocate and free storage. This time will, to a large extent, depend on the number of external storage accesses needed to effect allocation or freeing. In this section, we shall review and reevaluate the storage management schemes of Chapter 4 with emphasis on the number of device accesses required.

Fixed Size Nodes

All nodes that are free may be linked together into an available space list as in Sections 4.3 and 4.7. Assuming that the value of *av* is always in memory, the allocate and free algorithms take the form given in Programs 11.5 and 11.6.

```
 1 procedure GetNode (var i : integer);
 2 {Get a free node on disk. i is the address of this node
 3 Assume that av is global}
 4 begin
 5   if av = 0 then begin
 6                   writeln ('no more nodes');
 7                   goto 999; {999 is program end}
 8               end;
 9   i := av;
10   {get (x) reads the link field in a node n on disk}
11   av := get (av);
12 end; {of GetNode}
```

Program 11.5 Procedure to allocate a node

Each algorithm requires one access to carry out its function. In case the total number of free nodes at all times is small, this access can be eliminated altogether by maintaining the available space list in the form of a stack which contains the addresses of all free nodes. This stack would not be maintained in place as in the case of Section 4.3, where the free space itself made up the stack. Instead, the stack could reside permanently in

```
1  procedure ret (i : integer);
2  {free the disk node at address i}
3  begin
4     {out (n,y) sets the link field of node n on disk to y}
5     out (i, av);
6     av := i;
7  end; {of ret}
```

Program 11.6 Procedure to free a node

memory and no accesses would be needed to free or allocate nodes.

Variable Size Nodes

In the boundary tag method, the use of boundary tags made it possible to free a block while coalescing adjacent blocks in a constant amount of time. In order to do this it is essential that the free space be maintained in place as we need to test the tags at $p - 1$ and $p + n$ (see Section 4.7). Such a scheme would therefore require several accesses (Exercise 34) in order to free and allocate nodes. These accesses can again be eliminated by maintaining in memory a list of all blocks of storage that are free. Allocation can be made using first fit, and nodes can be freed in time $O(n)$ if n is the number of blocks in free space (Exercise 35). Since the cost of a disk access is several orders of magnitude more than the cost of internal processing, this scheme will be quicker than the boundary tag method even when free space consists of several thousand blocks. When free space contains many nodes, it may not be possible to keep the list of free nodes in memory at all times. In this case, the list will have to be read in from disk whenever needed and written back onto disk when modified. Still, the number of accesses will be fewer than when an in place free list is maintained (as is required by the boundary tag method).

Garbage Collection and Compaction

The principles for this technique stay essentially the same. The process was seen to be rather slow for the case of internal memory management. It is even slower for external storage because of the increased access times. In file systems that have a heavy activity rate (i.e., frequent real time update, etc.), it is not possible to allocate a continuous chunk of time large enough to permit garbage collection and compaction. It is necessary, therefore, to devise these algorithms so that they can work with frequent interruptions, leaving the file in a usable state whenever interrupted.

11.5 DIFFERENTIAL FILES

Consider an application where we are maintaining an indexed file. For simplicity, assume that there is only one index and hence just a single key. Further assume that this is a dense index (i.e., one which has an entry for each record in the file) and that updates to the file (inserts, deletes, and changes to an existing record) are permitted. It is necessary to keep a back up copy of the index and file so that we can recover from an accidental loss or failure of the working copy. This loss or failure may occur for a variety of reasons which include corruption of the working copy due to a malfunction of the hardware or software. We shall refer to the working copies of the index and file as the *master index* and *master file*, respectively.

Since updates to the file and index are permitted, the back up copies of these will generally differ from the working copies at the time of failure. So, it is possible to recover from the failure only if, in addition to the back up copies, we have a log of all updates made since the back up copies were created. We shall call this log the *transaction log*. To recover from the failure it is necessary to process the back up copies and the transaction log to reproduce an index and file that correspond to the working copies at the time of failure. The time needed to recover is therefore a function of the sizes of the back up index and file and the size of the transaction log. The recovery time can be reduced by making more frequent back ups. This results in a smaller transaction log. Making sufficiently frequent back ups of the master index and file is not practical when these are very large and when the update rate is very high.

When only the file (but not the index) is very large a reduction in the recovery time may be obtained by keeping updated records in a separate file called the *differential file*. The master file, is unchanged. The master index is, however, changed to reflect the position of the most current version of the record with a given key. We assume that the addresses for differential file records and master file records are different. As a result, by examining the address obtained from a search of the master index we can tell whether the most current version of the record we are seeking is in the master or the differential file. The steps to follow when accessing a record with a given key are given in Program 11.7(b). Program 11.7(a) gives the steps used when a differential file is not used.

Notice that when a differential file is used, the back up file is an exact replica of the master file. Hence, it is necessary only to back up the master index and differential file frequently. Since these are relatively small it is feasible to do this. To recover from a failure of the master index or differential file, the transactions in the transaction log need to be processed using the back up copies of the master file, index, and differential file. The transaction log can be expected to be relatively small as back ups are done more frequently. To recover from a failure of the master file, we need merely make a new copy of its back up. When the differential file becomes too large, it is necessary to create a new version of the master file by merging together the old master file and the differential file. This also results in a new index and an empty differential file.

Step 1: Search master index for record address.

Step 2: Access record from this master file address.

Step 3: If this is an update, then update master index, master file, and transaction log.

(a) No differential file

Step 1: Search master index for record address.

Step 2: Access record from either the master or differential file depending on the address obtained in Step 1.

Step 3: If this is an update, then update master index, differential file, and transaction log.

(b) Differential file in use

Step 1: Search differential index for record address. If the search is unsuccessful, then search the master index.

Step 2: Access record from either the master or differential file depending on the address obtained in Step 1.

Step 3: If this is an update, then update differential index, differential file, and transaction log.

(c) Differential index and file in use

Step 1: Query the Bloom filter.
If the answer is ''maybe'', then search differential index for record address.
If the Bloom filter answer is ''no'' or if the differential index search is unsuccessful, then search the master index.

Step 2: Access record from either the master or differential file depending on the address obtained in Step 1.

Step 3: If this is an update, then update Bloom filter, differential index, differential file, and transaction log.

(d) Differential index and file and Bloom filter in use

Program 11.7 Access steps

It is interesting to note that using a differential file as suggested does not affect the number of disk accesses need to perform a file operation (see Program 11.7).

Suppose that the index as well as the file are very large. In this case the differential file scheme discussed above doesn't work as well as it isn't feasible to back up the master index as frequently as necessary to keep the transaction log sufficiently small. We can get around this difficulty by using not just a differential file, but also a differential index. The master index and file remain unchanged as updates are performed. The differential file contains all newly inserted records and the current version of all changed records. The differential index is an index to the differential file. This also has null address entries for deleted records. The steps needed to perform a file operation when both a differential index and file are used are given in Program 11.7(c). Comparing with Program 11.7(a), we see that additional disk accesses are frequently needed as we will often first query the differential index and then the master index (Observe that the differential file is much smaller than the master file. So most requests are satisfied from the master file.)

When both a differential index and file are used, it is necessary to back up only these with high frequency. This is possible as both are relatively small. To recover from a loss of the differential index or file, we need to process the transactions in the transaction log using the available back up copies. To recover from a loss of the master index or master file, only a copy of the appropriate back up needs to be made. When the differential index and/or file becomes too large, the master index and/or file can be reorganized so that the differential index and/or file become empty.

The performance degradation that results from the use of a differential index can be considerably ameliorated by the use of a *Bloom filter*. This is a device which resides in internal memory and accepts queries of the type: "Is key k in the differential index?". If queries of this type can be answered accurately, then there will never be a need to search both the differential and master indexes for a record address. Clearly, the only way to answer queries of this type accurately is by having a list of all keys in the differential index. This isn't possible for differential indexes of reasonable size.

A Bloom filter does not answer queries of the above type accurately. Instead of returning one of "yes" and "no" as its answer, it returns one of "maybe" and "no". When the answer is "no", then we are assured that the key k is not in the differential index. In this case, only the master index is to be searched and the number of disk accesses is the same as when a differential index is not used. If the answer is "maybe", then the differential index is searched. The master index needs to be searched only if k is not found in the differential index. Program 11.7(d) gives the steps to follow when a Bloom filter is used in conjunction with a differential index.

A *filter error* occurs whenever the answer to the Bloom filter query is "maybe" and the key is not in the differential index. Both the differential and master indexes are searched only when a filter error occurs. The key to obtaining a performance close to that when a differential index is not used is to ensure that the probability of a filter error is close to zero.

Let us take a look at a Bloom filter. Typically this consists of m bits of memory and h uniform and independent hash functions $f_1, \ldots, f_h$. Initially all m filter bits are zero and the differential index and file are empty. When key k is added to the differential index, bits $f_1(k), \ldots, f_h(k)$ of the filter are set to 1. When a query of the type: "Is key k in the differential index?" is made, bits $f_1(k), \ldots, f_h(k)$ are examined. The query answer is "maybe" if all these bits are 1. Otherwise, the answer is "no". One may verify that whenever the answer is "no", the key cannot be in the differential index and that when the answer is "maybe", the key may or may not be in the differential index.

We can compute the probability of a filter error in the following way. Assume that there are initially n records and that u updates are made. Assume that none of these is an insert or a delete. Hence, the number of records remains unchanged. Further, assume that the record keys are uniformly distributed over the key (or identifier) space and that the probability that an update request is for record i is $1/n$, $1 \le i \le n$. From these assumptions, it follows that the probability that a particular update does not modify record i is $1 - 1/n$. So, the probability that none of the u updates modifies record i is $(1 - 1/n)^u$. Hence, the expected number of unmodified records is $n(1 - 1/n)^u$ and the probability that the $(u+1)$'st update is for an unmodified record is $(1 - 1/n)^u$.

Next, consider bit i of the Bloom filter and the hash function f_j, $1 \le j \le h$. Let k be the key corresponding to one of the u updates. Since f_j is a uniform hash function, the probability that $f_j(k) \ne i$ is $1 - 1/m$. As the h hash functions are independent, the probability that $f_j(k) \ne i$ for all h hash functions is $(1 - 1/m)^h$. If this is the only update, the probability that bit i of the filter is zero is $(1 - 1/m)^h$. From the assumption on update requests, it follows that the probabilty that bit i is zero following the u updates is $(1 - 1/m)^{uh}$. From this, we can conclude that if the $(u+1)$'st update is for an unmodified record, the probability of a filter error is $(1 - (1 - 1/m)^{uh})^h$. The probability, $P(u)$, that the $(u+1)$'st update results in a filter error is this quantity times the probabilty that the $(u+1)$'st update is for an unmodified record. Hence,

$$P(u) = (1 - 1/n)^u (1 - (1 - 1/m)^{uh})^h$$

Using the approximation

$$(1 - 1/x)^q \sim e^{-q/x}$$

for large x, we obtain

$$P(u) \sim e^{-u/n}(1 - e^{-uh/m})^h$$

when n and m are large.

Suppose we wish to design a Bloom filter that minimizes the probability of a filter error. This probability is highest just before the master index is reorganized and the differential index becomes empty. Let u denote the number of updates done up to this time. In most applications, m is determined by the amount of memory available and n is fixed. So the only variable in design is h. Differentiating $P(u)$ with respect to h and setting the result to zero yields

$$h = (\log_e 2)m/u \sim 0.693m/u$$

One may verify that this h yields a minimum for $P(u)$. Actually since h has to be an integer, the number of hash functions to use is either $\lceil 0.693m/u \rceil$ or $\lfloor 0.693m/u \rfloor$ depending on which results in a smaller $P(u)$.

11.6 REFERENCES AND SELECTED READINGS

For additional material on file structures and database management systems see: *File structures for on line systems*, by D. Lefkovitz, Hayden Book Co., New Jersey, 1969, *Data Management for on line systems*, by D. Lefkovitz, Hayden Book Co., New Jersey, 1974, *Computer data base organization*, by J. Martin, Prentice-Hall, Englewood Cliffs, 1975, and *An introduction to data base management systems*, by C. Date, Addison-Wesley, Reading, Massachusetts, 1975.

Additonal material on indexes can be found in: *The Art of Comptuer Programming: Sorting and Searching*, by D. Knuth, Addison-Wesley, Reading, Massachusetts, 1973, and "Binary search trees and file organization," by J. Nievergelt, *ACM Computing Surveys*, 6, 3, September 1974, pp. 195-207.

Our development of differential files parallels that of Severence and Lohman in the paper: "Differential files: Their application to the maintenance of large databases," by D. Severence and G. Lohman, *ACM Trans. on Database Systems*, 1, 3, 1976, pp 256-267. This paper also provides several advantages of using differential files. The assumptions of uniformity made in the filter error analysis are unrealistic as, in practice, future accesses are more likely to be for records previously accessed. Several authors have attempted to take this into account. Two referenees are: "A practical guide to the design of differential file architectures," by H. Aghili and D. Severance, *ACM Trans. on Database Systems*, 7, 2, 1982, pp 540-565, and "A regression approach to performance analysis for the differential file architecture," by T. Hill and A. Srinivasan, *Proceedings Third IEEE International Conference On Data Engineering*, 1987, pp 157-164.

11.7 EXERCISES

1. A file of employee records is being created. Each record has the following format:

E#	NAME	Occupation	Location

All four fields have been designated as keys. The file is to consist of the following 5 records:

A	10	JAMES	PROG	MPLS
B	27	SHERRY	ANAL	NY
C	39	JEAN	PROG	NY
D	50	RODNEY	KEYP	MPLS
E	75	SUSAN	ANAL	MPLS

Draw the file and index representations for the following organizations. Assume that an entry in an index is a tuple (value, pointer 1, pointer 2, . . ., pointer k) and that these tuples are kept sequentially.

(a) Multilist File

(b) Fully Inverted File

(c) Ring File

(d) Sequential ordered by name, inverted on E# and location, ringed on occupation

2. Write an algorithm to process a tape file in the batched mode. Assume the master file is ordered by increasing primary key value and that all such values are distinct. The transaction file contains transactions labeled update, delete and insert. Each such transaction also contains the primary key value of the record to be updated, deleted or inserted. A new updated master file is to be created. What is the complexity of your algorithm?

3. Show that all B-trees of order 2 are full binary trees.

4. (a) Into the 2–3 tree of Figure 11.29 insert the key 62 using algorithm *insertb*.

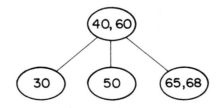

Figure 11.29 2–3 tree

Assuming that the tree is kept on a disk and one node may be fetched at a time, how many disk acceses are needed to make this insertion? State any assumptions you make.

(b) From the order three B-tree of Figure 11.30 delete the key 30 (use algorithm *deleteb*). Under the same asumptions as in (a), how many disk accesses are needed?

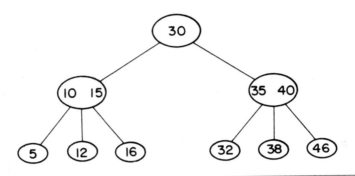

Figure 11.30 Order three B-tree

5. Complete line 55 of algorithm *deleteb*.

6. Write insertion and deletion algorithms for B-trees assuming that with each key value is associated an additional field f such that $f = 1$ iff the coresponding key value has not been deleted. Deletions should be accomplished by simply setting the corresponding $f = 0$ and insertions should make use of deleted space whenever possible without restructuring the tree.

7. Write algorithms to search and delete keys from a B-tree by position; i.e., *search* (k) finds the k'th smallest key and *delete* (k) deletes the k'th smallest key in the tree. (Hint: In order to do this efficiently additional information must be kept in each node. With each pair (K_i, A_i) keep $N_i = \Sigma_{j=0}^{i-1}$ (number of key values in the subtree $A_j + 1$).) What are the worst case computing times of your algorithms?

8. Modify algorithm *insertb* so that in case $n = m$ in line 16, then we first check to see if either the nearest left sibling or the nearest right sibling of p has fewer than $m - 1$ key values. If so, then no additional nodes are created. Instead, a rotation is performed moving either the smallest or largest key in p to its parent. The corresponding key in the parent together with a subtree is moved to the sibling of p which has space for another key value.

9. [Bayer and McCreight] The idea of Exercise 8 can be extended to obtain improved B-tree performance. In case the nearest sibling, Q, of P already has $m - 1$ key values, then we can spilt both P and Q to obtain three nodes P, Q, and R with each node containing $\lfloor (2m - 2)/3 \rfloor, \lfloor (2m - 1)/3 \rfloor$ and $\lfloor 2m/3 \rfloor$ key values. Figure 11.31 below describes this splitting procedure when Q is P's nearest right sibling.

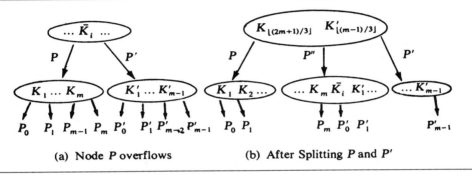

(a) **Node P overflows**   (b) **After Splitting P and P'**

Figure 11.31 Splitting P and its nearest right sibling P'

Rewrite algorithm *insertb* so that node splittings occur only as described above.

10. A B*-tree, t, of order m is a search tree that is either empty or is of height ≥ 1. When t is not empty, then the extended tree (i.e., t with failure nodes added) satisfies the following conditions:

(a) The root node has at least 2 and at most $2\lfloor (2m - 2)/3 \rfloor + 1$ children.

(b) The remaining nonfailure nodes have at most m and at least $\lceil (2m - 1)/3 \rceil$ children each.

(c) All failure nodes are on the same level.

For a B*-tree of order m and containing N key values, show that if $x = \lceil (2m - 1)/3 \rceil$ then

(a) The depth, d, of t satisfies:

$$d \leq 1 + \log_x \{(N + 1)/2\}$$

(b) the number of nodes p in t satisifies:

$$p \leq 1 + (N - 1)/(x - 1)$$

What is the average number of splitting if t is built up starting from an empty B*-tree?

11. Using the splitting technique of Exercise 9 write an algorithm to insert a new key value x into a B*-tree, t, of order m. How many disk accesses are made in the worst case and on the average? Assume that t was initially of depth l and that t is maintained on a disk. Each access retrieves or writes one node.

12. Write an algorithm to delete the identifier x from the B*-tree, t, or order m. What is the maximum number of accesses needed to delete x from a B*-tree of depth l? Make the same assumptions as in Exercise 11.

13. The basic idea of a B-tree may be modified differently to obtain a B'-tree. A B'-tree of order m differs from a B-tree of order m only in that in a B'-tree identifiers may be placed only in leaf nodes. If P is a nonleaf node in a B'-tree and is of degree j, then the node format for P is: $J, L(1), L(2), \ldots, L(j-1)$ where $L(i), 1 \le i < j$, is the value of the largest key in the i'th subtree of P. Figure 11.32 shows two B'-trees of order 3. Notice that in a B'-tree, the key values in the leaf nodes will be increasing left to right. Only the leaf nodes contains such information as the address of records having that key value. If there are n key values in the tree then there are n leaf nodes. Write an algorithm to search for x in a B'-tree t of order 3. Show that the time for this is O(log n).

14. For a B'-tree of order 3 write an algorithm to insert x. Recall that all non-leaf nodes in a B'-tree of order 3 are of degree 2 or 3. Show that the time for this is O(log n).

15. Write an algorithm to delete x from a B'-tree, t, of order 3. Since all key values are in leaf nodes, this always corresponds to a deletion from a leaf. Show that if t has n leaf nodes, then this requires only O(log n) time.

16. Let T and U be two B'-trees of order 3. Let V be a B'-tree of order 3 containing all key values in T and U. Show how to construct V from T and U in O(log$n$) time.

17. Write computer programs to insert key values into AVL trees, B-trees of order 3, B*trees of order 3 and B'-trees of order 3. Evaluate the relative performance of these four representations of internal tables.

18. Do Exercise 17 when the required operation are search for x, insert x and delete x.

19. Obtain search, insert, and delete algorithms for B'-trees of order m. If the tree resides on disk, how many disk accesses are needed in the worst case for each of the three operations? Assume the tree has n leaf nodes.

20. Draw the trie obtained for the following data: Sample the keys left to right one character at a time. Using single character sampling, obtain an optimal trie for the above data (an optimal trie is one with the fewest number of levels).

AMIOT, AVENGER, AVRO, HEINKEL, HELLDIVER, MACCHI,
MARAUDER, MUSTANG, SPITFIRE, SYKHOI

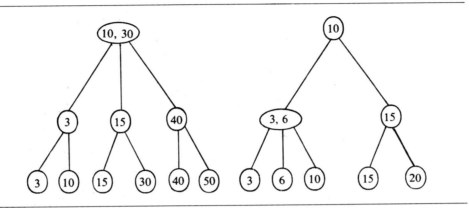

Figure 11.32 Two B'-trees of order 3

21. Write an algorithm to insert a key value x into a trie in which the keys are sampled left to right, one character at a time.

22. Do Exercise 21 with the added assumption that the trie is to have no more than six levels. Synonyms are to be packed into the same information node.

23. Write an algorithm to delete x from a trie t under the assumptions of Exercise 21. Assume that each branch node has a count field equal to the number of information nodes in the subtrie for which it is the root.

24. Do Exercise 23 for the trie of Exercise 22.

25. In the trie of Figure 11.23 the nodes δ_1 and δ_2 each have only one child. Branch nodes with only one child may be eliminated from tries by maintaining a *skip* field with each node. The value of this field equals the number of characters to be skipped before obtaining the next character to be sampled. Thus, we can have *skip* $[\delta_3] = 2$ and delete the nodes δ_1 and δ_2. Write algorithms to search, insert and delete from tries in which each branch node has a skip field.

In Exercises 26-33 records have n keys. The i'th key value for record x is $z\uparrow.key\,[i]$. The link field for the i'th key is $z.link\,[i]$. The number of accesses required by an algorithm should be given as a function of list lengths.

26. Write an algorithm to insert a record, z, into a multilist file with n keys. Assume that the order of records in individual lists is irrelevant. Use the primitives *search* (x) and *update* (x,a) to search and update an index. *update* (x,a) changes the address pointer for x to a. How many disk accesses (in addition to those needed to update the index) are needed?

27. Write an algorithm to delete an arbitrary record z from a multilist file (see Exercise 26). How many disk accesses are needed?

28. Write an algorithm to insert record z into a multilist file assuming that individual lists are ordered by the primary key $x\uparrow.key\,[1]$. How many accesses are needed for this (exclude index accesses)?

29. Assuming that each list in a multilist file is a doubly linked list, write an algorithm to delete an arbitrary record z. The forward link for key i is $z\uparrow.alink\,[i\,]$, while the corresponding backward link is $z\uparrow.blink\,[i\,]$.

30. Write an algorithm to output all key values for record z in a ring structure. How many accesses are needed for this? How many accesses are needed to do the same in a multilist file?

31. Write an algorithm to delete an arbitrary record z from a ring file.

32. Describe briefly how to do the following:

    (a) In a multilist organization: (1) output all records with $key1$ = PROG and $key2$= NY. How many accesses are needed to carry this out? (2) Output all records with $key1$ = PROG or $key2$ = NY. How many accesses are needed for this? Assume that each access retrieves only one record.

    (b) If a ring organization is used instead, what complications are introduced into (1) and (2) above ?

    (c) How could the following be carried out using an inverted organization:

    - output all records with $key1$ = PROG and $key2$ = NY
    - output all records with $key1$ = PROG or $key2$ = NY
    - inutput all records with $key1$ = PROG or $key2 \neq$ NY

    How many accesses are needed in each case (exclude accesses to get indexes)?

33. A 10^5 record file is maintained as an inverted file on a disk with track capacity 5000 characters. This disk has 200 tracks on each of its 10 surfaces. Each record in the file is 50 characters long and has five key fields. Each key is binary (i.e., has only two distinct values) and so the index for each key can be maintained as a binary bit string of length 10^5 bits. If one character is six bits long, then each index takes about four tracks. How should the five indexes be stored on disk so as to minimize total seek time while processing the indexes in order to determine which records satisfy a given boolean query Q? This processing involves reading in one track of each index and testing the query against records represented by this track. Then the next set of index tracks is input and so on. How much time does it take to process all the indexes in order to determine which records are to be retrieved? Assume a seek time of 1/10 sec and a latency time of 1/40 sec. Also assume that only the input time is significant. If k rcords satisfy this query, how much more time is needed to retrieve these k records? Using other file structures it may be necessary to read in the whole file. What is the minimum time needed to

read in the entire file of 10^5 records? How does this compare with the time needed to retrieve k records using an inverted file structure?

34. Determine how many disk accesses are needed to allocate and free storage using algorithms *allocate* and *free* of Section 4.7 for the boundary tag method when the storage being managed is disk storage.

35. Write storage management algorithms for disk storage maintaining a list of free blocks in internal memory. Use first fit for allocation. Adjacent free blocks should be coalesced when a block is freed. Show that both these tasks can be accomplished in time $O(n)$ where n is the number of free blocks.

36. By differentiating $P(u)$ (see Bloom filters) with respect to h, show that $P(u)$ is minimized when $h = (\log_e 2)m/u$.

37. Suppose that you are to design a Bloom filter with minimum $P(u)$ and that $n = 100,000$, $m = 5000$, and $u = 1000$.

    (a) Using any of the results obtained in the text, compute the number, h, of hash functions to use. Show your computations.

    (b) What is the probability, $P(u)$, of a filter error when h has this value?

INDEX